POLITICS AND THE CHURCHES
IN GREAT BRITAIN
1832 to 1868

Politics and the Churches
in Great Britain
1832 to 1868

G. I. T. MACHIN

'Part of the special work of this age ought to be to
clear the relations between Church and State.'

Gladstone to Bishop Wilberforce, 2 Oct. 1862

CLARENDON PRESS · OXFORD
1977

Oxford University Press, Walton Street, Oxford OX2 6DP

OXFORD LONDON GLASGOW NEW YORK
TORONTO MELBOURNE WELLINGTON CAPE TOWN
IBADAN NAIROBI DAR ES SALAAM LUSAKA ADDIS ABABA
KUALA LUMPUR SINGAPORE JAKARTA HONG KONG TOKYO
DELHI BOMBAY CALCUTTA MADRAS KARACHI

© *Oxford University Press 1977*

British Library Cataloguing in Publication Data

Machin, G I T
    Politics and the churches in Great Britain, 1832
    to 1868.
    1. Church and state in Great Britain   2. Great
    Britain – Church history – 19th century
    I. Title
    322′.1′0941   BR759   77–30296

ISBN 0–19–826436–4

*Printed in Great Britain by
Cox & Wyman Ltd,
London, Fakenham and Reading*

Acknowledgements

I WISH to acknowledge the generous assistance of the University Court of Dundee and (formerly) of St. Andrews towards the cost of numerous journeys for research purposes. My colleagues and students have given much help over many years, and I would particularly like to thank Professor D. F. Macdonald, Dr. D. G. Southgate, Dr. D. B. Swinfen, Dr. W. M. Walker, Dr. L. A. Williams, and Dr. D. A. Gowland. Dr. Southgate manfully read much of the typescript and, in consequence, improved the book. Professor Geoffrey Best, Professor Michael Brock, and Dr. John Walsh have always been ready to advise. Mrs. J. Young, Miss E. Aitken, and Mrs. M. Greatorex were very helpful with the typing. The staff of the Clarendon Press gave valuable assistance.

The owners of manuscripts and the authors or custodians of theses, as listed in the Bibliography, have been generous in permitting me to make use of their holdings and works. Lord Blake enabled me to see the Derby Papers while they were in his keeping, and the Earl of Derby permitted me to quote from them. The Earl of Clarendon and Sir Fergus Graham, Bt., allowed me to quote from the Clarendon and Graham Papers respectively, and Lord Hatherton permitted me to refer to his. The Earl of Dalhousie and Sir John Clerk of Penicuik, Bt., permitted me to make use of their papers in the Scottish Record Office.

I am most grateful to the staffs of many libraries and repositories, especially Dundee University Library, British Library, Public Record Office, Bodleian Library, National Library of Scotland, Scottish Record Office, County Hall (London), New College (Edinburgh), Pusey House (Oxford), National Trust (Hughenden Manor), Cambridge University Library, National Library of Wales, Lambeth Palace Library, Archbishop's House (Westminster), Methodist Church Archives, Keble College (Oxford), Liverpool Local History Library, Manchester Central Library (Archives Dept.), Dundee City Library, and Hull Local History Library.

Finally, I owe my wife and family a great deal for their understanding during the period of research and writing.

G. I. T. MACHIN

Dundee, *spring 1976*

Contents

Abbreviations

DNB	*Dictionary of National Biography*
EHR	*English Historical Review*
Hansard	Hansard's *Parliamentary Debates*, 3rd Ser.
Hist. Jl.	*Historical Journal*
JEH	*Journal of Ecclesiastical History*
P.P.	Parliamentary Papers
Scottish HR	*Scottish Historical Review*
Trans. Royal Hist. Soc.	*Transactions of the Royal Historical Society*
Welsh HR	*Welsh History Review*

CHAPTER I

Introduction: Church, State, and Society before 1832

THE CIRCUMSTANCES attending the establishment of the Church of England in the sixteenth century had lasting effects on the Church's future. As a middle way, a combined political and religious defence against Roman Catholics and extreme Protestants, the Church was subject to opposition from both sides; and the strong element of politics in its foundation and maintenance served as an argument against it. Reasons of State were prominent in the Henrician foundation of the Church and in its defence under Elizabeth I, in whose reign deviation from it was regarded as political treachery and Catholics and Protestant Dissenters were treated as dangerous threats to national security. There was, of course, support for the Church on genuine theological grounds as well as on merely Erastian ones. Transubstantiation was rejected for conscientious religious reasons. But a different theological opinion emphasizes a political aspect of this rejection by claiming that 'the idea of dominion founded on grace played straight into the hands of Papists and Puritans alike ... The new covenant between Church and State had, then, to be based on law and not on grace.'[1] To the Erastian nature of the Establishment there emerged clearly by the mid-nineteenth century both 'Catholic' or high church and Protestant Nonconformist objections. The former kind, while not opposing religious establishments in principle, sought to replace the latitudinarian theological basis of the Anglican Establishment by greater conformity to primitive 'Catholic' religious beliefs, and to introduce ecclesiastical self-government in place of unreliable Erastian forms of control which shifted according to political circumstance. Protestant Dissent went further in desiring the abolition of established Churches altogether on the ground that it was unscriptural to maintain religion by political means—though different Scriptural texts were used, with equal conviction, by the defenders of Establishments. These were the major challenges which established religion had to face in mid-nineteenth-century Britain, and with which this book is largely concerned.

Changes of monarch and Government modified the original nature of the Establishment. Political developments did not wait on men's ideals, and left behind them disappointed but strongly held opinions about the

[1] B. R. Marshall, 'The Theology of Church and State in relation to the Concern for Popular Education in England, 1800–1870' (unpubl. Univ. of Oxford D.Phil. thesis, 1956), 69.

degree of religious exclusiveness which a Government, having to deal not with one Church but several Churches, should maintain. Under the Stuarts in the early seventeenth century the concept of Divine Right, which claimed a special God-given role for the monarch as a religious governor, reinforced the royal supremacy. There followed the reaction of the interregnum, a brief period of satisfaction for Dissenters which provided historical inspiration for nineteenth-century Nonconformists in urging their claims. After 1660 the episcopalian Establishment was revived, and its ascendancy secured by the passage of restrictive laws against dissidents. Of these the most contentious were the Corporation Act of 1661 which prevented those who would not receive the sacrament according to Anglican rites from taking municipal office, and the Test Act of 1673 which barred them from civil and military office in the service of the Crown. Catholics, though not Protestant Dissenters, were also excluded from Parliament by an Act of 1678 following the rumoured 'Popish Plot'. The Catholic enthusiasm of James II prompted a Whig *rapprochement* between the Establishment and Dissent at the expense of Catholicism and some high churchmen. The ensuing revolution, a celebrated Protestant landmark, brought a new regime which abandoned Divine Right, established Presbyterianism as the religion of the Church of Scotland in 1690, and granted concessions to Protestant Dissenters in the Toleration Act of 1689. This measure gave trinitarian Dissenters freedom of worship, provided their ministers and chapels were licensed and their services held behind unlocked doors. But it was only the penalties of restrictive laws which were removed, not the laws themselves, and in the case of the Test and Corporation Acts the penalties were retained as well. Dissenters were thus kept firmly in an inferior legal capacity. In order to have their births registered Dissenters had still to be baptized by an Anglican clergyman; they had also to be buried by one. But they received favoured treatment in comparison with Catholics, who were not only excluded from the Toleration Act but—as citizens who were considered a particular danger to the State—subjected to the further severities of the Penal Code.

There was no doubt that Establishment ascendancy was being maintained. The concessions to Dissenters were precarious, as was shown during the Tory and high-church reaction under Queen Anne. State control of the Presbyterian Church of Scotland was stressed by an Act of 1712 reviving lay patronage (previously abolished in 1690) in the appointment of ministers to parishes, many of which were in the gift of the Crown. This measure was passed only five years after the Union between the kingdoms, and was regarded by opponents of patronage as a betrayal of that compact. But for most of the eighteenth century Erastian Moderatism held sway in the Kirk, upholding lay patronage, and dissident groups were driven to secede. In regard to Dissenters from the Church of England, an Act of 1711 re-emphasized the Test and Corporation Acts by forbidding 'occasional conformity', a disingenuous practice whereby Nonconformists might fulfil the regulations for gaining municipal or Crown office; and the Schism Act of 1714 prevented any Nonconformist from keeping a school. It required a further change of ruling dynasty and party to sway the ecclesiastical balance again. While the reasons for maintaining anti-Catholic legislation seemed to be reinforced by the rebellions of 1715 and 1745, the Hanoverian Whig Government made concessions to Protestant Dissent by repealing the Occasional Conformity and Schism Acts in 1719, and in the same year lightened the Corporation Act by conceding municipal office to Dissenters against whom no proceedings were started within six months of their appointment. Indemnity Acts, aimed to suspend the working of the Test and Corporation Acts, commenced in 1727, though from a Dissenter's point of view they were inadequate. By these means concession now slightly exceeded the level of 1689.

Beyond this, however, there was no relaxation. Whig concessions were limited to judicious toleration, and the ascendancy of an established Church was upheld under the decided control of the State. This control was demonstrated in 1717 by the prorogation of Convocation, the 'parliament' of the Church of England—the beginning of a suspension which was to last until 1855. With this action, 'Parliament was accepted as the proper legislature for the spiritual as well as the temporal estate'.[2] Only amidst the ecclesiastical controversies of the mid-nineteenth century did a strong movement arise for the revival of Convocation. Another example of secular domination was the Mortmain Act of 1736, preventing death-bed bequests to the Church. At the same time, however, the Church was being protected from ecclesiastical rivalry. Dissenting attempts to repeal the Test and Corporation Acts were rejected in 1736 and 1739, and no further effort was made for fifty years to remove these irritating legal relics. Lord Hardwicke's Marriage Act of 1753 tightened the restrictions on Dissenters by requiring that they should have an Anglican ceremony of marriage. It was not surprising that there was a movement of aristocratic and socially ambitious Dissenters into the Establishment. The last of the old Dissenting peers, Lord Willoughby of Parham, died in 1779. His demise, however, was not accompanied by a further decline in the legal standing of Dissent, for the ineffective retention of lineage was soon to be replaced by the more potent attribute of numbers. This was a factor to which current ecclesiastical theory of a utilitarian nature paid considerable attention.

The existing balance between Erastian control and restricted toleration was rationalized in William Warburton's treatise of 1736, *The Alliance between Church and State, or the necessity and equity of an Established Religion and a Test Law*. Warburton saw Church and State as two sovereign and independent powers which allied 'for mutual support and defence'. But he

[2] G. F. A. Best, *Temporal Pillars* (Cambridge, 1964), 60.

believed that the Church must surrender to the discretion of the State, as the physically stronger partner, all right to independent government such as Convocation. This surrender was in return for State protection, which included a test law to restrict the civil powers (though not the freedom of worship) of other denominations. A Church was not chosen to be established or maintained on account of its doctrinal truth, which the civil magistrate was not competent to judge, but on account of its numerical strength. Warburton wrote:

If there be more than one [Church] . . . the alliance is made by the state with the largest of the religious societies . . . because the larger the religious society is . . . the more enabled it will be to answer the ends of the alliance as having the greatest number under its influence . . . Hence we may see the reason and equity of the episcopal church being the established church in England, the presbyterian the established church in Scotland . . . [The alliance] subsists so long as the church thereby established maintains its superiority of extent; which when it loses to any considerable degree, the union is dissolved.[3]

Warburton believed, as did Thomas Arnold later, that the established Church should accommodate many religious viewpoints.[4] Whigs agreed with this emphasis on numbers and desire for comprehensiveness. Fox held that 'the truth of religion was not a subject for the discussion of Parliament; their duty only was to sanction that which was most universally approved, and to allow it the emoluments of the state'.[5]

Warburton may be said to have abandoned the imposition of truth in favour of the twin eighteenth-century tenets of latitude and utility, though it was left to Archdeacon Paley to state plainly that 'the authority of a church establishment is founded in its utility'.[6] In a non-autocratic society which accepted freedom of worship it was difficult to ignore the influence of denominational numbers on deciding the direction of ecclesiastical policy, as even high churchmen were later to find. Only the sterner methods of government in Ireland and the prevailing anti-Catholic climate can have prevented Warburton from advocating a Roman Catholic Establishment on the ground of numbers in that country, just as he approved of a Presbyterian Establishment in Scotland. In Britain also the potential challenge of a growing Dissenting population to the position of the Establishment was becoming obvious by the close of the eighteenth century.

It may be stated with fair certainty that for most of the eighteenth century Dissent was no numerical threat to the Establishment. The Compton Census

[3] Quoted N. Sykes, *Church and State in England in the Eighteenth Century* (Cambridge, 1934), 322.

[4] Ibid. 323.

[5] G. F. A. Best, 'The Whigs and the Church Establishment in the Age of Grey and Holland', *History*, XIV (1960), 104, 113.

[6] Sykes, op. cit. 326.

of 1676 displayed Dissenting weakness. Dissenters in general were shown as comprising perhaps 6 or 7 per cent of the population in the parts of England covered by this census;[7] and for the four Welsh dioceses a figure of only 4,193 Protestant Dissenters was returned (and 1,072 Catholics) compared with 153,046 Anglicans.[8] These returns, however, were made at an unfavourable juncture for Nonconformity, and the Toleration Act of 1689 appears to have had some effect in increasing Dissenting congregations. Of the Congregational churches in England and Wales surviving in 1950, 54 were added between 1689 and 1702 to the 309 which already existed.[9] But Dissenters, and especially Presbyterians, were affected by doctrinal dispute and uncertainty. First Arminian, then Arian and Socinian views, spread among Presbyterians and drove out the orthodox. The Presbyterian congregation at Nantwich, influenced by anti-trinitarian views, dropped from 300 members in 1719 to 30 in 1778.[10] Orthodox Dissent benefited from this secession, but did not show much sign of growth until the evangelical revival made its impact. It was said that in 1736 there were only 6 Dissenting chapels in the whole of North Wales, an area which a hundred years later was particularly rich in them.[11] As late as 1783 Dissent does not seem to have been much of a threat to the established Church, at least in some parts of the country. Returns from Wiltshire clergy to queries by the bishop of Salisbury in that year stated that only 75 parishes out of 233 had any Protestant Dissenters at all, and that only 20 had any Catholics;[12] in the remainder the refrain 'Thank God, not a dissenter in my parish'[13] was repeated, though usually in more muted terms. In several of the parishes Dissent was said to be declining.[14]

Since the Establishment shared the apathy of old Dissent it did not take advantage of relative freedom from competition to strengthen its hold on the country. After brief enthusiasm in Queen Anne's reign little was done to extend the Anglican Church. Only 10 churches were built in London during the entire eighteenth century.[15] In any case, the existing edifices were far from being filled. Even in rural areas, where church attendance was probably

---

[7] A. Everitt, *The Pattern of Rural Dissent : the Nineteenth Century* (Leicester, 1972), 17–18.

[8] W. T. Morgan, 'The Consistory Courts of the Diocese of St. David's, 1660–1858' (unpubl. Univ. of Wales M.A. thesis, 1962), 189.

[9] From information in *Congregational Year Book*, 1951 (London, 1951), 111 ff. Only churches, not mission stations, are included in these figures.

[10] R. B. Walker, 'Religious Changes in Cheshire, 1750–1850', *JEH* xvii (1966), 84.

[11] A. J. Johnes, *An Essay on the Causes which have produced Dissent from the Established Church in the Principality of Wales* (London, 1831; reprinted 1870), 10.

[12] M. Ransome (ed.), *Wiltshire Returns to the Bishop's Visitation Queries, 1783*, Wilts. Record Soc. xvii (Devizes, 1972), 7.

[13] Ibid. 137.

[14] Ibid. 45, 83, 124, 202, 213. Cf. M. B. Whittaker, 'The Revival of Dissent, 1800–1835' (unpubl. Univ. of Cambridge M.Litt. thesis, 1959), 56.

[15] É. Halévy, *A History of the English People in the Nineteenth Century*, i (2nd. ed., London, 1949), 399.

more accepted as a social custom than in the towns, habitual absence was common in the eighteenth century, and was of more concern to the Wiltshire clergy in 1783 than the existence of Dissent.[16] One of these clergy stated that 'the number of [absentees] is beyond any calculation', and the incumbent of Wootton Bassett complained that 'the body corporate seldom come to church unless to *qualify* themselves for their respective offices in the corporation', though admittedly the mayor himself was 'not ashamed to be seen at church'.[17] Obviously non-attendance was not a problem which arrived with industrialization, though this magnified it. William Cobbett, an Anglican who wished to see his Church disestablished, claimed from his own rural experience, probably with exaggeration, that 'not a twentieth part of [the people] go to church'.[18] Anxious nineteenth-century Church reformers tended to ascribe this legacy from an unregenerate past, no doubt with a degree of justice, to those eighteenth-century clerics who 'spent six days out of seven in tippling in ale houses, or in the rude sports of the demoralized squirearchy of their day'.[19]

It required the stimulus of evangelical movements to renew the vital popular appeal of religion. Evangelicalism developed within the Establishment as well as in Dissent, but the latter spread more markedly as a result of its influence. Wesleyanism, and in Wales Calvinistic Methodism, eventually became separate denominations, and stimulated older Dissenting denominations into fresh life. In the 1780s and 1790s the deliberately unorganized Congregationalists and Baptists, increasing in numbers, were coming to form county associations, perhaps partly as a means of competing with organized Wesleyanism.[20] Later they formed national unions.[21] The new or revitalized Dissenting denominations were doubtless successful in attracting many who gave little allegiance to the Establishment. They advanced in the country as well as in towns. The Religious Census of 1851 revealed that Wesleyans, Congregationalists, and Baptists all provided more accommodation, in proportion to the population, in rural districts than in large towns.[22] Cobbett claimed that he had found the parish church in the Hampshire parish of Botley virtually empty, '. . . while the Methodist meeting house was crammed three times a day, so full as for many of the people to be standing outside of the doors'.[23] Wales was swept by Nonconformity before parts of that country became industrialized: Welsh Dissenters had (allegedly) 110 congregations in 1742 and 954 chapels in 1810.[24]

---

[16] Ransome, op. cit. 7, 78, 83, 178, 238. Cf. R. A. Soloway, *Prelates and People: Ecclesiastical Social Thought in England, 1783–1852* (London, 1969), 233.

[17] Ransome, 42, 244.

[18] W. Cobbett, *Legacy to Parsons* (London, 1947; original edn. 1835), 70.

[19] Johnes, op. cit. 135–6.   [20] Halévy, op. cit. i. 422–3.   [21] Ibid.

[22] P.P. 1852–3 (1969), lxxxix, p. cxlv.   [23] Op. cit. 70.

[24] H. Richard, *Letters on the Social and Political Condition of the Principality of Wales* (London, 1866), 20; Hansard, lxxix. 64.

The phenomenal desertion which resulted in over 75 per cent of the churchgoers being outside the Establishment by 1851 was attributed (by a concerned Anglican) to the national and linguistic alienation of the Church from the Welsh people.[25] Dissent was also well entrenched in various parts of the English countryside by the mid-nineteenth century. It has been shown that some forms of rural economy were more conducive to Dissent than others. Dissent seemed to prosper more on subdivided land, in boundary settlements between parishes, in decayed market towns with some local industry, in very large parishes with dispersed hamlets which were difficult for the established Church to supervise, and in areas of intensive farming which required a large labour force.[26]

This is not of course to deny that the urban population explosion presented religion with an immense challenge, which for many years was met more successfully by Nonconformity than the Establishment, and which in consequence made the first half of the nineteenth century a unique period of Dissenting growth. The Churches of England and Scotland were hampered not only by lethargy but by a hidebound rural-based parochial system which required drastic extension and modification. In England a multitude of compact and well-endowed parishes in the south contrasted with few, poor, and straggling ones in the north—a situation which was scarcely well adapted to the distribution of population in the early eighteenth century and was much less relevant to that in the early nineteenth.[27] Southey said in 1829: 'They who suppose that the ecclesiastical Establishment in its present state, is competent to the duties expected from it, must have overlooked the new increase in population [he might have said, the new concentration of population], for which no provision has been made.'[28] The tenuous bonds which tied many agricultural labourers to the Establishment often weakened or snapped completely when the workers migrated to the badly churched towns. The Church was not quick to follow them thither in order to retain or reclaim them. The division of parishes and their reinforcement by chapels of ease were only belatedly carried out, largely in the 1830s and 1840s by the efforts of such men as W. F. Hook at Leeds and Thomas Chalmers in Scotland. It was then that churchmen lamented the omissions of their predecessors: 'Would to God', said Earl Fitzwilliam in 1837, 'that the hierarchy of this country had been wiser half a century ago, and had undertaken those measures of change and improvement in the ecclesiastical arrangements of this country which were, at that time, obviously necessary.'[29]

---

[25] Johnes, 50 ff.

[26] Everitt, op. cit. 20 ff.; cf. H. Pelling, *Social Geography of British Elections, 1885–1910* (London, 1967), 62, 108, 127.

[27] J. D. Gay, *The Geography of Religion in England* (London, 1971), 70 ff.

[28] Quoted A. M. Allchin, *The Silent Revolution: Anglican Religious Communities, 1845–1900* (London, 1958), 40.

[29] Hansard, xxxvi. 759 (21 Feb. 1837).

It was mainly the advance of Dissent which produced such sentiments, for Nonconformity, and especially Methodism, aided by greater zeal and more flexible organization, had rushed in where the Establishment had failed to tread. As the industrial population grew so did Dissent, if at a slower rate. Methodist groups may have made their particular contribution in industrial areas because older denominations were already reasonably well established in the countryside. Wesleyanism, the mother sect of the Methodist bodies and by far the largest of them, increased in membership from 26,283 in 1770 to 137,997 in 1810 and 358,277 in 1850. This represented an increase, in proportion to the rapidly growing population, from 1·22 per cent in 1811 to 1·77 per cent in 1841—the latter being the highest ratio which was reached in a decennial year of population census; it was followed by a steady proportional decline after 1850.[30] Methodism in general (excluding Calvinistic Methodism) reached its greatest strength in the counties of Cornwall, Yorkshire, Derbyshire, Lincolnshire, Durham, and Nottinghamshire, several of which were largely industrial.[31] The older Dissenting denominations could scarcely match these Promethean efforts, but none the less made strong progress themselves. This is shown, for example, by the increase of Independent (Congregational) churches in England and Wales from 849 in 1799 to 3,244 in 1851, and by that of Baptist churches (of all sects) from 592 to 2,793 in the same years (Wesleyan churches increased in the same period from 644 to 6,529).[32] Independent churches (of those surviving in 1950) grew in an increasingly industrial Lancashire from 32 in 1799 to 119 in 1849, and in Glamorgan from 20 to 90 in the same years.[33] Baptist churches in Lancashire increased from 14 in 1799 to 56 in 1849, and in Yorkshire from 29 to 79 in the same period.[34] Nevertheless, Independents and Baptists were still at their strongest in largely rural surroundings at the time of the 1851 Religious Census— Independents in South and North Wales, Essex, Dorset, Monmouthshire, and Suffolk; Baptists in Monmouthshire, South Wales, Huntingdonshire, Bedfordshire, Northamptonshire, Leicestershire, and Buckinghamshire.[35] It was shown that 'nonconformity owed what hold it had in large manufacturing towns above all to the efforts of the Methodists'.[36] An even clearer and more portentous revelation was that the urban drive of Dissent was only partially successful. The majority of the town workers lay outside the

---

[30] R. Currie, *Methodism Divided* (London, 1968), 90. But Methodism as a whole attained its greatest numerical successes in the 1850s and 1860s; Gay, op. cit. 156.

[31] Report on Religious Census of 1851, P.P. 1852–3 (1969), lxxxix, p. cxliv. Cf. the summary tables giving attendance by counties, ibid. clxxvii ff.

[32] Ibid. lvii f. The amount of accommodation (i.e. number of sittings) compares only roughly with the number of churches, but shows these three denominations in the same order (ibid. cxliv ff.). On the increase of Dissenting churches cf. Whittaker, op. cit., 41 ff., esp. 62 ff.

[33] From *Congregational Year Book*, 1951.   [34] From *Baptist Hand-Book*, 1871.

[35] P.P. 1852–3 (1969), lxxxix, p. cxliv.

[36] K. S. Inglis, 'Patterns of Religious Worship in 1851', *JEH* xi (1960), 85–6. Cf. Gay, 59–60.

ministrations of any Church. Of this fact Horace Mann, the author of the Census report, was acutely conscious.[37] London above all remained comparatively impervious to religion, with the largest provincial cities close behind: in Liverpool, Manchester, and Birmingham it was calculated that 'fewer than one person in ten . . . attended either Church of England or Nonconformist worship on Census day'.[38]

The consciousness of mass absence became an important challenge to the absorption of Victorian religion in political and theological disputes. But apart from the question of absence which affected most denominations, it was clear from the 1851 Census that Anglicanism was beginning to catch up with Dissent in industrial areas. Since the early 1830s an Anglican resurgence had begun. The Census report noted that, while the number of sittings in Anglican churches had continued to drop steadily in proportion to the rapidly expanding population (from 48·2 per cent in 1801 to 29·7 per cent in 1851), the decline had, thanks to a spurt in church-building, slowed down greatly in the last twenty years.[39] Much more attention was being given to the large towns, where Anglican sittings increased even faster than the population between 1841 and 1851;[40] though how to fill the churches when built was another problem. In 1830 the Church of England had been much closer to Halévy's comparison with the unreformed Parliament:

Formerly but half the province of York had been inhabited; now great centres of industry were being rapidly multiplied. But it still contained only six bishops as against twenty in the province of Canterbury, and 2,000 parishes for 10,000 in the Southern province. Bath, Chichester, Ely and Hereford possessed their bishops; Manchester, Leeds, Birmingham and Liverpool had none.[41]

Attitudes and prospects had indeed changed by 1851, but belated progress in challenging Dissent was slow. The Census showed that in 15 out of 29 large industrial towns attendances at Dissenting churches were over half the total attendances. Rochdale was top of this league with Dissenting attendances being 74·4 per cent of the total, and was, not surprisingly, a town particularly noted for its Church versus chapel contentions. In only 3 of the 29 towns were Anglican attendances more than half the total. Roman Catholic attendances were sufficiently high in the remaining 11 towns (especially in Preston, Liverpool, Wigan, and Manchester) to prevent either Anglican or Dissenting attendances from reaching half the total.[42] Towns having similar population figures but a different social and economic character were liable to display contrasting patterns of religious attendance. Such was the case, for example, with Bath (population 54,240) and Stockport

[37] P.P. 1852–3 (1969), lxxxix, pp. clviii ff.   [38] Inglis, op. cit. 85.

[39] P.P. 1852–3 (1969), lxxxix, pp. xxxix–xl. There was a drop of 2·3 per cent between 1831 and 1841, and one of 0·3 per cent between 1841 and 1851.

[40] Ibid. cxli.   [41] Halévy, i. 399.   [42] Inglis, 82–3.

(population 53,835): church attendance in general was much higher in Bath, and proportionately more Nonconformist in Stockport.[43]

The force which Dissent gained from rapid growth was hampered in its political effects by the restrictions of the parliamentary representative system. Despite this, Dissent had greater potency than mere numbers would indicate, owing to the fact that its urban leaders, whether of old mercantile or new manufacturing stock, attained great wealth and a high social station. Dissenters came to form a good proportion of the urban élite and often competed with the landowners on political and commercial as well as on religious grounds. In the towns, therefore, Nonconformity obtained political and social strength from the possession of an upper crust and a concentrated following. In the country, where Dissent might be flourishing but was none the less scattered and subordinate to the Anglican élite, Nonconformity found it much harder to acquire this political strength.

The rapid growth of Dissent posed problems for the State. Religious toleration was accepted within the circles of Establishment; foreign threats encouraging a revival of intolerance were absent; and it was widely believed, as Thomas Arnold said in 1833, that the destruction of Dissent by persecution was 'both wicked and impossible'.[44] Church extension and reform might prove effective long-term rivals to Dissenting advance, but were no immediate answer to the Dissenting population which already existed. Governments therefore had to come to terms with Dissent, if necessary by adopting new policies of concession. The matter was complicated by other threats to the Establishment in the later eighteenth century and afterwards. In particular there was the threat of democratic radicalism. This impinged on the issue of Dissenting claims, and did much to emphasize the conflict between established and non-established Churches.

A reasonably sympathetic association was natural between democratic theorists and politicians and the Nonconformists who were seeking similar liberties. Indeed, the revival of the civil demands of Dissent was a prominent feature of later eighteenth-century radicalism. The concurrent demand for parliamentary reform encouraged the desire of Dissenters and Catholics for civil redress, since the particular obstructions which hindered them were seen as part of the general restrictions of the established constitution. Dissenting and Catholic aspirations became associated with the aims of the Whigs and radicals, and the opposition to them relied on the Tories and the Crown. George III and the ultra-Tories held off some important civil concessions for many years; but the development of liberal Toryism within

[43] P.P. 1852–3 (1969), lxxxix, p. cclii. See table in Appendix, pp. 385-6 below.
[44] T. Arnold, *Principles of Church Reform* (1833), ed. M. J. Jackson and J. Rogan (London, 1962), 87.

the Government eventually led to crucial concessions being made by Tories themselves.

The dissenting aspect of radical upsurge in the later eighteenth century can be seen in the sometimes strident demands for religious equality advanced in the works of Joseph Priestley, Richard Price, and Robert Robinson. Whereas Robinson challenged the concept of an Establishment with exuberant zeal, more moderate apologists for toleration were careful to accept the established position of the Church and merely to advocate full civil equality. Neither of these different approaches was to lack followers in the coming century.

There were some partial approaches towards civil equality in the later eighteenth century. In 1767 Lord Mansfield's verdict in the Sheriff's Cause abolished a practice by the City of London Corporation, whereby Dissenters were elected to high municipal office and then fined heavily for being unable by law to assume the post. After campaigns to abolish compulsory sub-scription to the Thirty-Nine Articles of the Church of England, an Act of 1779 relieved Dissenting ministers and teachers of the necessity to subscribe. The demand for military recruits in wartime led to a Relief Act in 1778, removing oaths which had technically debarred Catholics from the forces. Despite the Gordon riots of 1780, Catholics received further concessions during the remainder of the eighteenth century, whereas Protestant Dis-senters were disappointed. Revived efforts to repeal the Test and Corporation Acts, concentrating on three parliamentary campaigns between 1787 and 1790, met with defeats in the House of Commons. On the last of these occasions, Fox's motion of 2 March 1790 was lost by the overwhelming majority of 294 votes to 105. The defeat was too early to be affected by extreme tendencies in the French Revolution. But it was unfortunate for Dissenters that success was not gained at that point, for the developments in France thenceforth so affected British opinion and politics that the hope of substantial reform was postponed for many years.

The effects of the French Revolution in Britain were ultimately severe for radicals in general, but not for all aspirants to religious equality. Catholics benefited from French developments for two reasons. Patriotic feeling against France meant that the exiled non-juring priests were welcomed to our shores, in respectable circles if not among the *populus*, with a hospitality which must have made the penal laws seem like a figment of the imagination. British anti-Catholicism was restrained by French anti-Catholic persecution, at a time when no such restraint was being shown towards Protestant Dissenters. Scarcely any opposition was voiced in 1791 when the Toleration Act was extended to Catholics, granting them freedom of worship. In addition, the desire for political security dictated the need to keep the Irish Catholics, who in spite of French rationalist republicanism might be more anti-British than anti-French, out of the Society of United Irishmen which hoped for French aid against the British Government. As an inducement to remain loyal, Irish Catholics received wide parliamentary enfranchisement with the forty-shilling freehold vote in counties under the Franchise Act of 1793. But only full 'Catholic emancipation', the right to sit in Parliament, would satisfy the Catholics, and the failure to grant this resulted in Catholic support for the unsuccessful rebellion of 1798. After this the obvious need for more security led to the Union. This event, if Pitt had had his way, would have been swiftly followed by Catholic emancipation—a major breach in the privileges of the Establishment at a time when the Government and much of society were zealously defending them. It was left to the Protestant resolution of George III and the resignation of Pitt in 1801 to preserve the general consistency of national policy.

The strength of pressure from Ireland which led Pitt to desire Catholic emancipation becomes more striking when one notes that he was contemplating, at about the same time, the introduction of tighter restrictions on Protestant Dissenting preachers and teachers by altering the Toleration Act.[45] The civil aspirations of Protestant Dissent were certainly less successful than those of Catholics in the 1790s. Dissenters were not separated geographically from Great Britain as were the Irish Catholics, nor were they a majority in Britain as were the Catholics in Ireland. Thus they lacked two powerful advantages which the Catholics possessed at a time of national insecurity. Dissenters were a minority and an increasingly numerous and vocal one, two features which are important in explaining the discouraging (though not persecuting) attitude taken by the Government towards them and the violence perpetrated against them by mobs. Their political leadership, being largely Unitarian, was associated with the rationalist ideas which lay behind French democracy. If 'Atheism was supposed to have produced Revolution by parthenogenesis',[46] it may well have been anticipated that Nonconformity would perform the same peculiar feat in this country: 'it seemed that infidelity, democracy and dissent were met together in an unholy alliance to wreck the constitution in Church and State'.[47] Indeed, some extreme attacks on the established Church were being made in association with advanced radical views. David Williams, the 'English Rousseau' (actually Welsh) who together with Paine, Priestley, Bentham, Sir James Mackintosh, and Wilberforce, was given honorary French citizenship, wanted annual parliaments, votes for women, and the abolition of established Churches.[48] Even the Chartists fifty years later fell short of this far-reaching catalogue.

[45] R. W. Davis, *Dissent and Politics, 1780–1830: the Political Life of William Smith, M.P.* (London, 1971), 87. The project failed through the intervention of Wilberforce; had it been successful it might also have affected evangelicals in the Church of England.

[46] V. Kiernan, 'Evangelicalism and the French Revolution', *Past and Present*, 1 (Feb. 1952), 45.

[47] Marshall, op. cit. 157.

[48] T. Evans, *The Background of Modern Welsh Politics, 1789–1846* (Cardiff, 1936), 35–6.

Dissenting radicalism greatly heightened the conflict between Church and Nonconformity which had been already looming on account of the growth of Dissent. Even before 1789 the turmoil of social change, population increase, political radicalism, and religious upheaval had led the supporters of authority in Church and State to seek new ways of extending social control, for example by spreading popular education.[49] The more obvious challenges of the 1790s hardened attitudes on the right and made it all the more necessary to underline the connection between Church and State. Edmund Burke undertook this task in his celebrated refutation of the French Revolution. In Burke's view a more closely integrated association was needed than the alliance which Warburton had set forth. Instead of being independent bodies, Church and State were parts of the same constitutional whole:

They [the majority of the English people] do not consider their Church establishment as convenient, but as essential to their state ... They consider it as the foundation of their whole constitution, with which, and with every part of which, it holds an indissoluble union. Church and state are ideas inseparable in their minds, and scarcely is the one ever mentioned without mentioning the other.[50]

Not only the Burkean defence of institutions aided conservatism, but also to some extent the deeper and subtler evangelical concepts of 'vital religion', the concentration on personal piety and salvation and the apparent discouragement of political agitation for short-term gains in the present world. But the attitude of Wilberforce and his associates did not completely fulfil the clear-cut requirements of governmental authority. Anglican evangelicals sympathized theologically with Dissenters. Enthusiasm for abolishing slavery led to the determined organization of public protest, which radicals admired and emulated and conservatives feared. The social schemes and assumptions of evangelicals made things uncomfortable for established attitudes and interests, Wilberforce believing that all ranks were 'vicious in the same degree'.[51] Wilberforce, who associated with Dissenters and supported Catholic emancipation, was not the complete Tory. He held the liberal Tory view of limited concession. Nevertheless, a more extreme Toryism, which rigidly defended the Protestantism of the constitution, did develop amongst Anglican evangelicals, and was to be particularly prominent in the mid-nineteenth century when the evangelical movement had perceptibly hardened and narrowed. In the 1790s Anglican evangelical conservatism opposed the political radicalism of Dissenters, while sympathizing with the religious objects of evangelical Dissent.

How far was Dissent a threat to the maintenance of constitutional order?

---

[49] G. F. A. Best, *Temporal Pillars*, 137 ff.; Marshall, 142 ff.

[50] E. Burke, *Works and Correspondence* (8 vols., London, 1852), iv. 232.

[51] Quoted Kiernan, op. cit. 48. See D. Spring, 'The Clapham Sect: some Social and Political Aspects', *Victorian Studies*, v (1961–2), 35 ff., esp. 43 ff.

Radical Unitarians such as Priestley were the most prominent Dissenting politicians, and this overshadowed the fact that the Dissenting revival was inspired by men of very different views. Wesley was conservative in politics, approved of the established position of the Church of England, and advocated political quiescence by his followers. These attitudes were impressed on the Wesleyan movement, and they overlaid for many years the large degree of potential democracy which existed within it, represented by its Arminian theology, its large lower-class following, and its development of lay participation in preaching and organization.[52] The conservative influence of the revival's leadership doubtless assisted the Government in maintaining order. But Congregationalists, Baptists, and seceding Methodists, who were inspired by evangelicalism, did not share the conservatism of the leading Wesleyans; hence it is difficult to establish a direct link between evangelicalism as such and political conservatism. As has been observed, personal study of the Bible was unlikely in itself to produce conservatism, and 'the strength of the Revival's appeal lay precisely in its omission to identify itself too obviously with sublunary dispensations'.[53] Whether or not an evangelical belonged to, or sympathized with, the established Church would have been of greater importance than his theology in deciding his political allegiance. In abandoning radical activity, many Dissenters submitted not to religious sanctions but to political reality. The temper of 'Church and King' opinion and a long period of Tory government were quite enough to produce the diplomatic moderation in urging their claims, also the official disapproval of radical social movements, which Dissenters showed from the 1790s to the 1820s. There was nothing evangelical about the religion of William Smith, the Unitarian M.P. and chairman of the Dissenting Deputies from 1805 to 1832, but he combined the firm championship of civil equality with the cautious political methods of sweet reasonableness.[54]

Thus evangelicalism is an inadequate explanation for the fact that 'during the first fifteen years of the nineteenth century only isolated and eccentric individuals among the Nonconformists demanded ... disestablishment and equal rights for all denominations'.[55] A judicious resignation to adverse political circumstance was more important. It proved fruitful in turning the flank of repression and winning further small concessions for Dissent after some years of conservative reaction; though patient patriotic submissiveness had also some unwelcome results—Lord Sidmouth apparently expected Dissenters to resign themselves uncomplainingly to his proposed new restrictions on them in 1811.[56] However, evangelical stress on self-discipline was no doubt an aid to maintaining quiescence. Order was as important as

---

[52] M. Edwards, *After Wesley* (London, 1935), 20 ff.; B. Semmel, *The Methodist Revolution* (London, 1974), 5, 8, 113 ff., 170–98.

[53] Kiernan, 53.   [54] Davis, op. cit. 88, 194–5.

[55] Halévy, i. 423, also 425–7.   [56] Best, *Temporal Pillars*, 173, n. 2.

liberty to Nonconformists—a fact which helps to explain the social and political influence they attained in the nineteenth century.

After 1800 Governments continued to be uneasy about the growth of Nonconformity and later of Catholicism, and they encouraged Church reform in order to increase the Establishment's influence. But the political quietness of Dissent also induced reward and encouragement by the extension of toleration; and there appeared a balanced policy of maintaining and extending the Establishment yet at the same time taking steps to meet the wishes of Dissenters and Roman Catholics. Different views of concession towards non-established denominations were shown on the one hand by reforming politicians—the Whigs holding concession as a positive principle, the liberal Tories regarding it more empirically—and on the other hand by ultra-Tories with their scarcely movable view of the constitution.[57]

During the opening decade of the new century both Catholic and Protestant Dissenters made some quiet advances in toleration. Some of these were directly due to the exigencies of war. In 1802 freedom of worship was allowed in the army with its large number of Catholic soldiers; though in 1807 the Whigs failed through royal resistance to open armed service commissions in Britain to Catholics. In 1809 Dissenters were allowed the right of burial in churchyards (though not with the performance of their own ceremonies there) and received equal exemption with Anglicans from having to pay road-tolls when travelling to and from Sunday worship. But a Tory Government anxious to defend established institutions could take little comfort from the great increase in Dissenting preachers among the lower classes, many of them lacking even the semblance of status gained from education or from having a 'settled congregation'. Attempts to curb their increase were made by the ultra Home Secretary, Lord Sidmouth. In 1809 he raised the matter in connection with the exemption of Nonconformist ministers from military service. Only ministers of settled congregations were legally exempt, and Sidmouth claimed that many were misusing the law by becoming licensed as ministers in order to avoid service. Parliament asked for lists of licences under the Toleration Act since 1760. The numbers of ministers receiving licences were seen to have risen from 80 in the period 1760–6, to 610 in 1788–94, and to 1,068 in 1802–8.[58] The evangelical earl of Harrowby expressed prevalent fears in 1810 by saying in the House of Lords that a majority of the nation would one day be Nonconformist.[59] When Sidmouth announced his intention to bring in legislation he showed concern not only with the numbers but the social class of the preachers. Could ministers who were 'cobblers, tailors,

[57] Best, 'The Whigs and the Church Establishment', 109, 111, 117–18.
[58] B. L. Manning, *The Protestant Dissenting Deputies* (Cambridge, 1952), 130. Between 1795 and 1801 the licences had amounted to 1,318, a higher total than in the subsequent period.
[59] Halévy, i. 428.

pig-drovers, and chimney-sweepers'[60] be anything but a menace to established society? Perhaps Sidmouth's fears were strengthened by the rise of ranting in some Wesleyan circles.

Sidmouth's bill, introduced in May 1811, aimed to restrict the opportunities for becoming a Dissenting minister. The bill required all would-be preachers to present testimonials, obtained from six 'substantial and reputable householders', to the magistrates before they could be registered. What constituted a sufficiently substantial and reputable householder only the magistrates could decide; therefore the latter, who were often clergymen, were given an undefined control over preachers which Dissenters contemplated with alarm. Seceding Methodists, Calvinistic Methodists, and older Dissenters joined in an association, which soon afterwards became the Protestant Society for the Protection of Religious Liberty and lasted until 1843 or later as a pressure group. Many Wesleyans, in an uncharacteristic spate of political activity explained by their own vulnerability to Sidmouth's proposals, assisted this body in a petitioning campaign. William Wilberforce supported these Dissenting evangelicals. The strength of the opposition persuaded Spencer Perceval, the evangelical Prime Minister, to withdraw Government approval from the bill, and it was rejected in the Lords.[61]

The defeat was an important turning-point. A Tory attempt at religious restriction had failed, not least because Tory ministers were unwilling to court opposition. This was a sign that Anglican exclusiveness could expect little effective sympathy even from ultra-Tories when they had to meet the pressures of office in a plural society.

After the defeat of Sidmouth's bill came measures to improve the security of Dissenters. The Relief Act of 1812 made concessions regarding the registration of places of worship and the interpretation of the Toleration Act, and repealed the Five Mile Act of 1665 and the Conventicle Act of 1670. But the 1812 Act kept a restriction on the number of persons meeting for worship in unregistered premises, and Sidmouth's original worries were reflected in a provision that ministers who pursued any occupation other than that of schoolmaster could not be exempted from military service.[62] An Act of 1813 gave to Unitarians the privileges of the Toleration Act. The adoption of the 'open system' of Government neutrality on the Catholic question may be regarded as another sign of liberal relaxation at this time.

But it remained important to the Government to strengthen the Establishment, for only in this way was it now envisaged that the advance of other denominations could be contained. Despite hindrances and timidity, significant new policies of Church reform were adopted. Some reforms were

---

[60] Davis, 151.
[61] Ibid. 151 ff.; Manning, op. cit. 130 ff.; Whittaker, op. cit. 96 ff. and 132 ff.
[62] Davis, 182–3.

weak and uncertain, for example Sir William Scott's Act of 1803 regarding non-residence—it was alleged that eight years after its passage, 5,024 out of the 10,421 Anglican benefices had no resident incumbent.[63] But other innovations had more effect, for example eleven grants of £100,000 made annually by Parliament from 1809 to supplement the funds of Queen Anne's Bounty for augmenting the income of poor livings.[64] A leading aim of Church reform was the division of unwieldy parishes and the building of new parish churches in industrial districts where Dissent and indifference were strong challenges. Before 1818 a special Act was needed to alter a parish boundary; but in that year the process was simplified and encouraged by a Church Building Act, which was perhaps hastened by fears resulting from the post-war social agitation. This Act, the first of a long series, provided £1,000,000 of Government money to build new churches and set up Church Building Commissioners to manage the fund. A number of other Acts in the 1820s had the same purposes, and a further grant of £500,000 was made in 1824. Also—and this was a fact for which churchmen were to be grateful, since Government aid might ebb and flow according to political circumstance—voluntary subscriptions were a great assistance. Between 1818 and 1832 voluntary means provided £1,500,000 for Anglican church extension.[65] The effects were soon obvious. While 55 Anglican churches were built between 1801 and 1811, and 97 between 1811 and 1821, 276 appeared in the years 1821–31.[66] After 1831, thanks to voluntary contributions—Government aid being no longer given—the numbers were much higher still. The Church was beginning to rival the growth of Dissent.

Such activities could hardly proceed without arousing the apprehensions of non-churchmen who objected to their taxes being spent on Anglican churches. The Church became deeply unpopular at the time of Peterloo. Two of the magistrates who ordered the military charge on that occasion were clergymen. Liberals reacted against Government approval of the action, and at Durham became embroiled in conflict with Tory clergy whose loyalism was championed by Henry Phillpotts—a rising cleric who gained practice in controversy which was later put to full use when he became bishop of Exeter. In December 1820 the dispute at Durham revived over the case of Queen Caroline, and in the following year anti-clerical attacks by a local radical newspaper led to a wider journalistic contest between Phillpotts and the *Edinburgh Review*, in which such questions as the gross inequality of clerical incomes became matters of debate.[67]

Against the background of church-building, urban growth, and radical protest an aspect of Anglican–Dissenting relations began to develop which

[63] Cobbett, *Legacy to Parsons*, 87.
[64] Best, *Temporal Pillars*, 205–6, 213 ff.
[65] Soloway, *Prelates and People*, 290.
[66] P.P. 1852–3 (1969), lxxxix, p. xl.
[67] Best, *Temporal Pillars*, 245–51. Cf. W. R. Ward, *Religion and Society in England, 1790–1850* (London, 1972), 125.

proved particularly abrasive because it united the calls of both conscience and pocket—forces which in combination must surely be of unrivalled potency. This was the long-lived debate on church-rates, a levy made at least since the time of Edward I and perhaps since Canute—when, as was pointed out, 'there were no Dissenters'[68]—on all occupants of property in a parish, except occupants of Crown property and those who could prove themselves destitute. The proceeds were used to maintain the fabric of the parish church and repair its fences, gates, and stiles, pay the clerk's salary, and provide sacramental bread and wine, cope, church bell, prayer-books, and other materials for services.[69] Rates might also be raised to provide heating, lighting, and an organ. In a widespread and mundane fashion, the matter symbolized the whole question of maintaining a Church establishment and its privileges. To churchmen (though some liberal ones demurred), maintenance of an Establishment such as they believed justified, indeed commanded, by religion, included the right to impose the rate on all occupants regardless of their denomination. A refusal to pay on conscientious grounds could not be allowed, for the result would be that 'the authority of the law would be superseded by the supremacy of private judgement'.[70] To the principled Dissenter, on the other hand, the rate was more than an irritating neo-feudal financial burden; it was an unjustified imposition by a Church and an Establishment with which he disagreed. In the Dissenting view church-rates joined tithes as a major grievance, and they were more provocative than tithes in embittering relations because, unlike tithes, they existed in the towns as well as the countryside.

An Act of 1813 altered the proceedings for wresting church-rates and tithes from recalcitrant payers. A provision, which had existed since 1695 for the benefit of Quakers alone, was now extended to all dissidents. According to this, church-rate or tithe of below £10 could be recovered by summary process before magistrates, who, in cases of continuing refusal to pay, could distrain and sell the defendant's goods.[71] This measure was something of an alleviation for Dissenters, for except in the case of sums over £10 (£50 for Quakers) they could now avoid long and costly suits in the ecclesiastical courts, whose foibles awaited lampooning in Dickens's depiction of Doctors' Commons. An Act of 1818, 'for the regulation of parish vestries', made another minor concession by requiring that before a church-rate could be levied by the parish vestry, churchwardens had to give at least three days' notice of a vestry meeting by placing posters on the doors of Anglican churches

---

[68] Bishop Maltby of Durham to Lord Holland, 17 Mar. 1837 (?) (Holland House Papers, British Library Add. MS. 51597 (the MS. nos. of this collection are provisional)).

[69] Report of Select Committee of House of Commons on Church Rates, P.P. 1851 (541), ix. 81–4, 176.

[70] C. G. Prideaux, *A Practical Guide to the Duties of Churchwardens* (3rd edn., London, 1845), 198.

[71] Ibid. 135 f.

in the parish.[72] Dissenting ratepayers could attend the meeting and attempt to stop the levy of a rate.

The church-building movement heightened Dissenters' concern over financial demands. Church-rates were sometimes raised to assist the building of new churches in large towns, and before 1830 it was their application to this purpose, rather than the principle of levying them at all, which was the matter in dispute. At Sheffield church-rates were refused in 1818 and 1819, and objections were made to a rate being used to support new churches in 1828. At Leeds the issue was part of a struggle between Tories and Liberals to control the parish vestry, in which Edward Baines, the influential Dissenting proprietor of the *Leeds Mercury*, led the Liberal attack.[73] The *Mercury* made the claim, which was repeated in similar disputes elsewhere, that more new churches were being erected than were required. In large towns the rate began to be abandoned.

In spite of these ominous quarrels church-rates had not yet become the pivotal conflict over ecclesiastical principle and policy which they were to be ten years later. Had they already become so prominent, the issue would have been embarrassing to the cautious metropolitan Dissenting committeemen who since 1817 had begun again to seek the long-desired repeal of the Test and Corporation Acts.

The new campaign for this repeal was not immediately successful, nor was the political situation propitious. The Government clearly wanted to assist the Establishment in the disturbed post-war years; and parliamentary reform, which would have helped to release the potential political strength of Dissent, had scarcely any success in the 1820s. A more promising development was the increasing pressure of the Catholic question. The marshalling of the Irish Catholics under O'Connell's leadership in the Catholic Association from 1823 posed a greater political challenge than British Nonconformists could have raised. The absorption of politicians in Catholic emancipation enabled the less controversial claims advanced by Protestant Dissent to achieve prior success.

This success is partly explained by the ambivalent relationship of Protestant Dissent to Catholic relief. The opposition of some (though not all) of the ultra-Tories to repeal of the Test and Corporation Acts may have been softened by the possibility of gaining Dissenters as allies against Catholic emancipation when their own claims had been met. It was possible to hope that repeal 'would stiffen the residual Protestantism of the Protestant constitution'.[74] In this respect the hope of some ultra-Tories was the fear of some liberal Tories: in 1828 Huskisson, Ellenborough, and others were

---

[72] P.P. 1851 (541), ix. 231; Prideaux, op. cit. 59 ff.

[73] R. W. Ram, 'The Political Activities of Dissenters in the East and West Ridings of Yorkshire, 1815–1850' (unpubl. Univ. of Hull M.A. thesis, 1964), 195 ff.

[74] Ward, op. cit. 115.

apprehensive that the relief of Dissenters would cause many of them to oppose Catholic emancipation thereafter.[75] Many Dissenters, indeed, were not anxious for Catholic relief. Nonconformist anti-Catholic petitioning occurred in 1825, while the Protestant Society, representing many evangelical Dissenters, held anti-Catholic views.[76] It is probable that evangelicalism strengthened anti-Catholic attitudes on religious grounds, for in deeply important ways the evangelical approach to faith differed from the Catholic, and, on the whole, nineteenth-century evangelicals lacked positive belief in universal toleration. To take one instance of religious difference, Bible-loving evangelicals of whatever denomination cannot have relished a news-paper report of a Catholic meeting at Liverpool in 1824 where a speaker said that the duke of York (a noted opponent of the Catholic claims) had 'lately evinced some approximation to Catholic principles by forbidding the promiscuous distribution of bibles among the soldiery'.[77] On the other hand, such factors as social position, education, political attitude, and other personal attributes undoubtedly modified anti-Catholic feeling among evangelicals. Besides the support for Catholic relief given by such prominent evangelicals as Wilberforce, Thomas Chalmers, and Jabez Bunting (the last-named being almost the only pro-Catholic among leading Wesleyans), the solidly pro-Catholic committee of the Dissenting Deputies contained evangelicals—though it should be remembered that Protestants sometimes saw Catholic relief as a channel to Protestant expansion rather than Catholic, envisaging with equanimity the free competition of both faiths when the double-edged barrier of artificial privilege had been removed.[78] On account of such factors, religious objections to Catholicism often stopped short of opposition to the political relief of Catholics.[79]

Whig politicians, taking an opposite view from the ultra-Tories, wished to bring about the repeal of the Test and Corporation Acts in order to form a breach in the constitution so that Catholics might more fully enter in. They might have felt confident, after receiving assurances, that Dissenters would forgo opposition to Catholic emancipation after their own relief. Whig initiative, helped by the acquiescence of other politicians, gained a significant concession for Dissent. In February 1828 Lord John Russell's motion for a Committee to consider the repeal of the Test and Corporation Acts was passed in the House of Commons by a majority of 44, which

[75] N. Gash, *Mr. Secretary Peel* (London, 1961), 461; Earl of Ellenborough, *Political Diary, 1828–30*, ed. Lord Colchester (2 vols., London, 1881), i. 36–43; *The Times*, 28 Feb. 1828. Huskisson's fear seems to have been partly justified: see J. H. Andrews, 'Political Issues in the County of Kent, 1820–1846' (unpubl. Univ. of London M.Phil. thesis, 1967), 134, 159.

[76] Davis, *Dissent and Politics*, 226–9.   [77] *Liverpool Mercury*, 8 Oct. 1824.

[78] e.g. Chalmers's view: W. Hanna, *Memoirs of the Life and Writings of Thomas Chalmers* (4 vols., Edinburgh, 1850–2), iii. 235 ff.

[79] To the above extent the writer agrees with Professor Davis, while maintaining his view that evangelicalism, as it developed in nineteenth-century Britain, had a natural tendency to be anti-Catholic; see Davis, 229 ff.

included 15 ultra-Tories.[80] There was little inclination to continue opposing repeal, either in the Cabinet or among the bishops. Peel and the bishops agreed on a form of declaration against injuring the established Church; persons selected for office were to subscribe to this instead of taking the sacramental test. The declaration was inserted in a repeal bill. In the Lords 18 bishops voted with the Government to accept the declaration, after adding the phrase 'upon the true faith of a Christian'. The phrase had the effect (though this may not have been its primary intention) of continuing the exclusion of Jews.[81] Thus there passed in May a measure which still officially safeguarded the established position of the Church of England but was nevertheless an inroad on its legal defences and an important symbolic victory for Dissent. The union between State and Church had been loosened.

Contemporaries, not foreseeing the future, on the whole took the measure quietly. Apart from the political gains which opposing parties hoped to obtain from the reform, there was no great desire among Anglicans to resist it on ecclesiastical grounds. Liberal churchmen supported the removal of civil restraints, and Anglican evangelicals had little distrust of evangelical Dissent. High churchmen were more exclusive than liberal churchmen and more doctrinally fastidious than evangelicals, but at that pre-Tractarian date they could still be regarded as Protestant, and were more concerned with the menace of the Catholic parliamentary claims than the lesser matter of giving Dissenters officially what they might possess in fact.[82] Parliamentary reform, which might give Dissenters political power to attack the Church, seemed a dead subject.

The relief of 1828 was an important if hypothetical encouragement to the supporters of Catholic emancipation and a heartening sign of the flexibility of Wellington's Government. But ultra-Tories could take comfort from the absence of any immediate reason for supposing that Catholic emancipation would follow. Wellington was not generally suspected of entertaining schemes for the latter. The County Clare election, to which emancipation is largely attributable, took place in July, two months after the repeal of the Test and Corporation Acts.[83] It was only in retrospect, after Catholic emancipation had passed and a Whig ministry presented a further threat to the bonds linking Church and State, that the repeal of 1828 was regarded as an originating triumph or disaster, the first of a series of constitutional infringements. The Rev. W. F. Hook, a high churchman, wrote in 1831: 'I refer our calamities to the repeal of the Test Act; for then the State *virtually*

[80] J. Prest, *Lord John Russell* (London, 1972), 34; Diary of E. J. Littleton, p. 32 (26 Feb. 1828; Hatherton Papers).

[81] U. Henriques, *Religious Toleration in England, 1787–1833* (London, 1961), 183–4. Quakers were exempted from the oath.

[82] Cf. G. F. A. Best 'The Protestant Constitution and its Supporters, 1800–1829', *Trans. Royal Hist. Soc.* 5th Ser. viii (1958), 110.

[83] G. I. T. Machin, *The Catholic Question in English Politics, 1820 to 1830* (Oxford, 1964), 122 ff.

renounced any connection with religion'.[84] Much later, Archdeacon Denison was to say that 'English dis-establishment began [in] 1828'.[85]

The passage of Catholic emancipation was a much greater constitutional shock. Many evangelicals as well as high churchmen were more dismayed by concessions to Roman Catholics than by concessions to Protestant Dissent. If evangelicals were more Protestant than high churchmen, the veneration of the latter for the early Christian Church did not extend to sympathy with modern Roman Catholicism, which they regarded as corrupt. The fact that the Protestant constitution had been breached by a Tory Government added to the concern, for it meant that many churchmen could have but an uncertain confidence in politicians of either party in the future. Least of all could they trust the Whigs, whose accession to office in November 1830 was ironically assisted by the opposition of ultra-Tories to Wellington and Peel over Catholic emancipation.

Catholic relief assisted the progress of parliamentary reform in diverse ways, lending colour to both the one and the other face of Reform. The ultra-Tories who helped to defeat Wellington's Government believed that parliamentary reform, particularly by abolishing rotten boroughs controlled by Liberals or ministerialists, would prevent further undesirable ecclesiastical or economic reforms. But such an idea conflicted with the very different Liberal view of reform, which regarded Catholic emancipation as a welcome opening in the constitution and an auspicious beginning to an era of change in ecclesiastical and other spheres. The ultra hopes did not long survive, for it seemed clear that the Whig proposals for enfranchisement and distribution would by no means fulfil the ultras' needs. The Whig reform did indeed provide for the maintenance of the rural landowning interest by increasing the number of county seats and accepting the Chandos clause enfranchising £50 tenants-at-will.[86] But the reform also contained the £10 householder franchise in boroughs and the creation of industrial urban constituencies. In these ways it proposed to enhance the political power of middle-class town-dwellers. Many of these were Dissenters whose political and ecclesiastical aspirations were strongly at variance with those of aristocratic Tory high churchmen. When parliamentary reform assumed this prospect the ultras retreated into opposition under Wellington and Peel and the issue tended to solidify into a conflict of Tory and churchman against Whig, radical, and Dissenter.

The promise of further changes held out by parliamentary reform encouraged radicals to strike blows at different parts of the Establishment.

[84] Rev. W. F. Hook to Hon. and Rev. A. P. Perceval, 25 May 1831 (W. R. W. Stephens, *The Life and Letters of the Very Rev. W. F. Hook* (2 vols., London, 1878), i. 222).

[85] G. A. Denison, *Notes of My Life* (2nd edn., Oxford, 1878), 66.

[86] M. Brock, *The Great Reform Act* (London, 1973), 222–9.

Among these targets the established Churches were prominent. Dissenters, having gained the repeal of some disabilities in 1828, were more confident and perhaps readier to ally with secular radicalism. The wealth and laxity of the Church of England were assailed as never before. In December 1830 radicals at Merthyr Tydfil assembled on the consecrated territory of the Establishment, in the parish church itself, to demand an extreme reform of the parliamentary system, and a Unitarian minister 'burst into a fiery denunciation of bishops who starved their clergy, proclaimed that the poor were living on carrion, and indulged in revolutionary exhortation, to loud cheers and the stamping of feet'.[87] This was not the style of William Smith, the Unitarian doyen who had worked so patiently for Dissenters' relief. The unsettled political climate encouraged resistance to church-rates.[88] New editions of John Wade's *Extraordinary Black Book* in 1831 and 1832 gave the Church of England a place of honour among established institutions in dire need of reform. This volume launched an increasingly familiar attack on non-residence, pluralities, and the poverty which curates had to bear.[89] The author indicted the Church of England as 'a monstrous, overgrown Croesus in the State', the amount of whose revenues was 'incredible, unbearable, and out of proportion with every other service and class in society'.[90] As for some of its clergy, 'these reverend gentlemen . . . pretend sickness in order to obtain a license for non-residence, that they may bawl at the card-table, frequent the playhouse, tally-ho, shoot, play at cricket, brandish the coachman's whip and bully at fashionable watering-places'.[91] Many Anglicans were conscious of the Church's shortcomings, but were anxious to forestall the radicals by pressing their own suggestions for reform. Bishop Kaye of Lincoln had said in his Primary Visitation Charge in 1828: 'If we shrink from the task [of reform] . . . it will be taken up and executed with unsparing severity by others, who entertain no friendly feeling towards us . . .'[92]

Parliamentary reform was deprecated by most Anglican clergy as a sure triumph for their radical enemies, and the Church appeared solidly Tory. A list of Whig clergy in the Holland House Papers—which since it is undated cannot be applied exactly to this time—contains only 128 names, to which were ascribed varying degrees of partisanship.[93] One Whig clergyman later claimed that 'I was almost thrown out of society by the Reform Bill. All looked on me with an evil eye, and some absolutely broke off all

---

[87] G. A. Williams, 'The Making of Radical Merthyr, 1800–1836', *Welsh HR* i. 2 (1961), 175–6.

[88] G. I. T. Machin, 'A Welsh Church Rate Fracas, Aberystwyth 1832–1833', *Welsh HR* vi. 2 (1973), 462–8; Report of Select Committee of House of Commons on Church Rates, P.P. 1851 (541), ix. 466.

[89] *Extraordinary Black Book* (1832 edn.), 6, 30 ff.

[90] Ibid. 5, 53.   [91] Ibid. 35.

[92] Canon R. Foskett, 'John Kaye and the Diocese of Lincoln' (unpubl. Univ. of Nottingham Ph.D. thesis, 1957), 107.

[93] Holland House Papers, Add. MS. 51922.

intercourse with me.'[94] Poll-books for the general elections of 1830–2 show a preponderance of Tory voting by Anglican clergy, in clear contrast to the Liberal proclivities of Dissenting ministers.[95]

The attitude of the bishops, nearly all of whom had been created by Tory Governments, particularly invited radical opposition. In October 1831 the bishops divided 21 to 2 against the second Reform Bill in the Lords. In this division the bill was rejected by a majority of 41; the bishops therefore appeared in the unfortunate light of a crucial bloc which, if it had voted the other way, would have just carried the bill. The Church seemed to be thoroughly entwined with the old order. Popular hostility was shown in a variety of incidents, some of which predictably occurred, by a transposition of denominational targets, on 5 November.[96] The Church was indeed on the run: Bishop Copleston of Llandaff's response to the Bristol riots was 'to have a round hat and a brown great coat in readiness, should it be expedient to escape at the back of the house over the fields'.[97]

Amidst the upheaval the Whig ministers were an interposing factor in the struggle between Church and Dissent, a position which presaged their moderate ecclesiastical conduct in the future. The bishops were to be encouraged to change their votes on Reform in return for Government protection of the Church from popular wrath. Holland wrote to Grey regarding Blomfield, bishop of London: '. . . if he will support what you deem right in the state he may reasonably expect you to co-operate in allaying the publick cry against the Church and to confine reforms and regulations . . . in the Church to such objects as will leave the establishment untouched.'[98] Blomfield was impressed with this reasoning,[99] and although he abstained from voting, the second reading of the third and final Reform Bill was passed in the Lords with the aid of 12 episcopal votes. But a partial change of this nature, coming after numerous popular demonstrations, appeared like yielding to pressure, and made little difference to the original impression of ecclesiastical intransigence.

Many Dissenters became thoroughly involved in the cry for reform in Church and State, but in differing degrees and at different levels, largely depending on their social status and denominational adherence. The middle-class Committee of the Dissenting Deputies was unwilling to intervene as a separate body in the parliamentary reform issue, and made the cautious statement that 'Dissenters will be almost universally found in their Individual and Parochial capacities amongst the foremost to support the laudable

[94] Rev. M. Marsh to Holland, 13 May 1834 (ibid., Add. MS. 51712).
[95] J. R. Vincent, *Pollbooks: How Victorians Voted* (Cambridge, 1967), 67–8 ff.
[96] O. Chadwick, *The Victorian Church* (2 pts., London, 1966–70), i. 28.
[97] Ibid. i. 27; W. J. Copleston, *Memoir of Edward Copleston* (London, 1851), 148–9.
[98] 26 Oct. 1831 (Grey Papers); cf. Holland to Grey, 1 Nov. 1831 (ibid.).
[99] Blomfield to J. H. Monk, bishop of Gloucester, 24 Nov. 1831: A. Blomfield, *A Memoir of C. J. Blomfield* (2 vols., London, 1863), i. 171; Chadwick, op. cit. i. 30 f.

endeavours of the Whig party'.[100] In Leeds and Hull middle-class Dissenters supported the moderate Reform Associations, leaving the more extreme Political Unions in radical and less markedly Dissenting hands, and Edward Baines and the *Leeds Mercury* opposed universal suffrage.[101] Wesleyans did not usually regard themselves as Dissenters. The conservative or non-political attitude of their leading ministers penetrated the denomination and inhibited active radicalism by members, except the rebellious spirits who were censured or encouraged to leave the denomination. But the Methodist sects which had seceded from Wesleyanism were democratic in organization and political attitude, and probably of a lower average social status than the Wesleyans. Members of the Methodist New Connexion were prominent in radical Political Unions.[102] The bonds of electoral influence sometimes intervened between Dissenting voters and their presumed Liberal interests. In the Pembrokeshire election of May 1831 it appears that some Dissenters, including a Baptist minister, voted for the Tory candidate whose family owned the estate on which they lived.[103] Examples of this influence were to be found many years after 1832—though of course there were also less visible reasons why a Dissenter should decide to vote Tory.

Social differences and political influence and expediency may also have diversified the Dissenting opposition to the Church of England during the Reform crisis. If the language was sometimes extreme, it was employed against definite grievances such as church-rates rather than directly in favour of the ultimate and connected principle of disestablishment or Voluntaryism—the demand that all Churches should be supported by voluntary means alone without State aid. Not all radicals wanted dis-establishment: even John Wade thought, at that juncture, that 'a Worship patronized by the state is best, provided it be *cheap*'.[104] Voluntaryism was, however, currently being discussed. It was vindicated in an important sermon preached on 9 April 1829 by the Rev. Andrew Marshall, a minister of the Scottish United Secession Church which since its formation in 1820 had taken an overt Voluntary position. The sermon, which was published as *Ecclesiastical Establishments Considered*, had been stimulated by fear that Catholic emancipation might lead to Catholicism becoming the established religion in Ireland.[105] But its arguments were as much a challenge to existing establishments as to hypothetical ones. A prolific pamphlet warfare began, and for several years Voluntaryism was more pronounced among Scottish Dissenters than English. The Church of Scotland, as its opponents

[100] I. G. Jones, 'The Liberation Society and Welsh Politics, 1844–1868', *Welsh HR* i. 2 (1961), 199.

[101] Ram, op. cit. 110 ff.   [102] Ibid. 110, 113, 117.

[103] D. Williams, 'The Pembrokeshire Elections of 1831', *Welsh HR* i. 1 (1960), 47.

[104] *Extraordinary Black Book* (1832 edn.), 93.

[105] A. B. Montgomery, 'The Voluntary Controversy in the Church of Scotland, 1829–1843' (unpubl. Univ. of Edinburgh Ph.D. thesis, 1953), 3–4.

recognized, was far less vulnerable on the grounds of wealth and abuses than its English counterpart.[106] Although Scottish Dissenters, like the English, had to pay to support their established Church, they had no liturgical differences from it or grievances regarding baptism, marriage, burial, and university degrees (they were officially excluded, however, from teaching posts in universities and parish schools). This comparative absence of tangible objects to attack probably explains the early concentration of Scottish Dissenters on the theoretical basis of Voluntaryism. Organization followed the original stimulus. A Voluntary Church Association was launched in Edinburgh in September 1832 and one in Glasgow in November. Others followed in town and county, and a central organization, the Scottish Central Board for extending the Voluntary principle (generally known as the Central Board of Scottish Dissenters), was formed in December 1834, several years before a similar body in England with the same definite objects.[107] Even in Scotland, however, Voluntary organization blossomed only after parliamentary reform had safely succeeded.

The Reform Act was a crucial stage in the development of relations between Government and Churches. Wellington wrote to Croker in March 1833: 'The revolution is made, that is to say that power is transferred from one class of society, the gentlemen of England, to another class of society, the shopkeepers, being dissenters from the Church, many of them Socinian, others atheists ...'[108] The observation was wildly exaggerated—indeed Wellington immediately qualified it—and the extended suffrage made no immediate change to the composition of the House of Commons.[109] But the potential strength was there and could be used in the future. Representation or a larger franchise had been given to towns where Dissenters were concentrated, and if political organization were developed their voice might be increasingly heard in Parliament. More important than immediate political rearrangements was the symbolic power of the victory of Commons over Lords and the challenge of Dissent to the Church which was implied in the victory. Irish Catholics, though greatly disappointed in the Reform as it affected their country, could still share to some extent the sense of victory and anticipation. To high churchmen the change was worse than that of 1688. They had only to await the Whig reform of the Church of Ireland in the first session of the reformed Parliament to see the ecclesiastical first fruits

---

[106] The *Dissenter*, No. 9 (Sept. 1833), 170 (a Voluntary journal published at Perth); Ward, *Religion and Society*, 130–1.

[107] Montgomery, op. cit. 93; J. McKerrow, *History of the Secession Church* (2 vols., Glasgow 1841), ii. 482–92.

[108] L. J. Jennings (ed.), *The Correspondence and Diaries of the late Rt. Hon. John Wilson Croker* (3 vols., 2nd edn., London, 1885), ii. 205–6.

[109] S. F. Woolley, 'The Personnel of the Parliament of 1833', *EHR* liii (1938), 246 ff. Cf. *Eclectic Review*, 3rd Ser. viii (1832), 270.

of the constitutional revolution. R. H. Froude believed that 'in 1832 . . . the great power accidentally given to dissenters by the Reform Act, gave a concluding blow to the ancient [ecclesiastical] system'.[110] A remonstrance to Gladstone from Oxford University in 1863 expressed the same view: 'The changes in the Legislative Assemblies of Parliament [in 1832] gave far more effect to the change [of 1828] . . . than was probably anticipated in 1828.'[111] If the liberal Tories had made concessions to growing religious forces, the Whigs gave these forces greater scope for political expression, and hence greater power to achieve their desires, than the Tories had anticipated. Amidst the social and political reactions to the Act of 1832 and the shifts and compromises which attended their working-out, the problems of Church and State were to be continually to the fore.

[110] *Remains*, ed. J. Keble and J. H. Newman (4 vols., London and Derby, 1838–9), iii. 207.
[111] Gladstone Papers, Add. MS. 44400, fos. 133–4.

CHAPTER II

Whigs, Conservatives, and Ecclesiastical Reform, 1832–1841

I. WHIGS AND THE ESTABLISHMENT

THE DEMAND for reform in the 1830s was enhanced by anticipation arising from, or disappointment with, the 1832 Reform Act. The demand was expressed in a variety of ways—the Irish desire for ecclesiastical, agrarian, and national justice, the commercial hope for the relaxation of trade, the Chartist cry for further political enfranchisement. The demand for ecclesiastical reform was as loud as any of these, and its more extreme manifestations bore the same marks of disappointed expectation. In this as in other spheres, radicals gained less than they hoped from the Whig Government.

But when the Whigs were returned with a huge majority in December 1832 it was feared that they might undermine or even destroy the Church Establishment. Were the Whig leaders even Christians? Some doubted it. Lord Dudley thought that Charles Grant, ex-Tory and evangelical, was the only member of the Government who believed in a soul. Charles Lloyd, bishop of Oxford, had fearfully imagined these men in office: 'Lord Holland, his wife an atheist, and himself not far from it. Lord Landsdowne, a confessed Unitarian, Brougham a Deist, and others whom I could easily enumerate, of the same principles.'[1] But the passage of Catholic emancipation had blurred the ecclesiastical distinctions between the Whigs and their political opponents. The political contortions of 1829–30 produced a ministry which contained not only members suspected of atheism and utilitarianism but the former ultra-Tory duke of Richmond. Earl Grey was a sure defender of the Church. He rejected Archbishop Howley's suggestion that a national day of humiliation should be observed in December 1831 as a protection against cholera: while privately approving of it, he thought it would encourage many to scoff at religion.[2] A high churchman stated in January 1831 that 'the present Ministry are doing better for us than the last'; and three years later a correspondent informed Newman that clergymen of his acquaintance, 'although they look on the ministers as little better than incarnate fiends, wish to let them have their way for two or three years,

[1] Best, 'The Whigs and the Church Establishment', 103.
[2] Grey to Howley, 21 Nov. 1831 (Grey Papers).

because they think they will do some good in a rough way which our Bishops would never do'.[3]

But high churchmen least of all could take comfort from Whig latitudinarian views. In the opinion of many Whigs an established Church was not sacred but the creature of the State, which could alter or even remove it. Lord Howick, Grey's heir, argued that Roman Catholicism should be made the established religion in Ireland; this could only strengthen the Church Establishment in England, 'since the Establishments in each of the three divisions of the United Kingdom could then be supported on the irresistible grounds of their practical utility to the great bulk of the population'.[4] Earl Fitzwilliam said in the Lords in 1837: 'I should rejoice to see that day come in which the members of the Church of England and the Dissenters ... should agree together to worship their God within the same walls.'[5] On general religious and moral grounds, however, the Whigs believed in some kind of Establishment, and thought that the existing one needed only reforms to make it satisfactory. Their expressions of impatience with the Church came from basic goodwill rather than destructiveness.

There is no need, therefore, to take too seriously such comments as that of Lord Holland, that the unpopularity of bishops made 'the tenure of their seats in [Parliament] ... very precarious indeed. We have but to hold up our finger and the flock of "magpies to right of Woolsack" (as Erskine used to designate them) are scared from the ground for ever.'[6] But the Whigs did intend to carry further the concessions already made to Catholics and Dissenters; and despite some indulgence towards the clerical ambitions of his Tory brother Edward, Grey promoted liberal churchmen who agreed with Government views. For example, he raised Edward Maltby, who was accused of heterodoxy by high churchmen, to the bishopric of Chichester in 1831. Grey also expressed dislike of the fact that Dissenters would be unable to take degrees at the new university founded by the dean and chapter at Durham; though when it was explained that the Cambridge system would be adopted, requiring subscription to the Anglican Articles not on admission but only when members took degrees, he accepted the plan.[7] The readiness

---

[3] F. C. Massingberd to Edward Churton, 14 Jan. 1831 (quoted Best, op. cit. 118); letter to Newman, 4 Jan. 1834 (A. Mozley (ed.), *Letters and Correspondence of John Henry Newman during his Life in the English Church* (2 vols., London, 1891), ii. 17).

[4] Howick to Sir James Graham, 16 (?) Mar. 1835, enc. (Graham Papers, microfilms, 110).

[5] Hansard, xxxvi. 761; cf. Arnold, *Principles of Church Reform* (1833), 134 ff. What, replied the horrified Bishop Blomfield, would happen to true religion if 'the same half-educated people were called upon to hear a Trinitarian preach in the morning, and a Unitarian preach in the evening, or a clergyman of the Church of England in the morning, and an Antipaedo Baptist in the evening?' (Hansard, xxxvi. 766).

[6] Holland to Hon. Henry Fox, 28 June 1833 (Holland House Papers, Add. MS. 51753). Probably Thomas Erskine, the defender of Thomas Hardy in 1794 and Whig Lord Chancellor in 1807, was meant.

[7] E. Hughes, 'The Bishops and Reform, 1831-3: some fresh Correspondence', *EHR* lvi (1941), 470, 489-90; Hansard, xii. 1216-17.

to make concessions was by no means incompatible with a desire to maintain the established Church and to render it more secure by means of salutary reforms. A reformed Establishment would be sheltered from the onslaught of Dissenters, who, having received concessions, would be less ready to attack. Preferably the reforms should be undertaken by churchmen themselves; just as churchmen should provide the money for church extension which, if financed by the State, might provoke radicals and Dissenters. Between 1832 and 1852 the State contributed only £511,385 to church-building, about a third of the amount spent by the Tory Government before 1830.[8]

Before 1835 the Whig Government's direct contributions to Church reform were unobtrusive and inconclusive. An Ecclesiastical Revenues Commission was appointed in June 1832, but, after two renewals, had not reported when the Whigs went out of office in 1834. By the time the report appeared a year later, Peel's Ecclesiastical Commission had been established to deal with the problems revealed. A Royal Commission on church courts made extensive proposals, but only one change was made. This was the abolition in 1832 of the High Court of Delegates established by Henry VIII and the transfer of its appellate jurisdiction to the Privy Council. In the following year a Judicial Committee was formed from legally qualified privy councillors to hear all appeals to the King in Council; and the Church Discipline Act of 1840 provided that bishops who were privy councillors would be added to this committee when ecclesiastical cases were heard. Although doubts were expressed whether the Privy Council would be sufficiently ecclesiastical, the inefficiency of the Court of Delegates seems to have been generally accepted, and Brougham's bill of 1832 passed Lords and Commons with little debate.[9] The new judicial procedure became a mighty cause of controversy between Church and State in the storm over the Gorham Judgement in 1850, when the Committee's right to judge in doctrinal questions was fiercely attacked. But this matter was not raised when the new court was created, and the change in 1832 was not an obvious cause of the later disputes, which arose out of growing doctrinal controversy. The old court was technically no more of an ecclesiastical court than the new one. The reform did, however, transfer final appeals to judges who were less familiar with ecclesiastical law.[10]

Because of his desire for voluntary reform by the Church, Grey advised Archbishop Howley that the bishops themselves should evolve, and quickly, a scheme of reform to protect the Church of England.[11] Any encouragement of disestablishment he firmly resisted, despite the risk of hostility from

[8] Soloway, *Prelates and People*, 298.
[9] Hansard, xiv. 78–82, 259–60; *Mirror of Parliament*, 1831–2 session, iv. 2989–90, 3117–18.
[10] Chadwick, *Victorian Church*, pt. i, 256–8.
[11] Grey to Howley, 19 Oct. 1832 (Grey Papers).

extreme radicals and Dissenters. Grey's views found acceptance even among the more restless and radical spirits in his ministry. Brougham in August 1831 was disposed to do all he could to help the Church, believing that a religious Establishment was desirable for moral purposes and that the Church of England was 'the best and most tolerant and most learned' of Establishments.[12] Lord Durham, while rejecting the abuses of the established Church and stressing the need for full civil and religious liberty, thought that 'in the first instance, the State was bound to tender religious instruction to its inhabitants'.[13]

The Whig ministers were practically unanimous in their desire to maintain the Church Establishment and to encourage constructive reforms. But ecclesiastical differences emerged between them, particularly in connection with reform of the Church of Ireland. They found that an attempt to do religious justice to Ireland involved them in dispute and fragmentation similar to those experienced by their immediate predecessors, the Wellington ministry, over the same broad issue. If the Whigs had gained from the division of 1829, the Conservatives (as they were coming to be called) gained from that of 1834.

II. IRISH CHURCH REFORM

Catholic emancipation had not quietened the Irish but groomed them for further assault. On taking office the Whigs faced a growing O'Connellite movement to repeal the Union and an incipient revolt against tithes. The Whigs, being reformers, were prepared to concede, but being also Unionists they limited their concessions. They were determined to maintain Government authority, if necessary by coercion, and they acted strongly against rebelliousness. The Whigs did, however, tackle an outstanding grievance by vigorously pruning the Church Establishment. The maintenance of the Church of Ireland in its existing extent was difficult to justify on realistic political or economic grounds, for it was undoubtedly the Church of only a small minority. Estimates of its membership and revenues differed according to the political complexion of the assessors. The radical H. G. Ward said in March 1835 that members were only 600,000, or 1 in 14 of the population, while Lord John Russell would have accepted 750,000. More official sources put the membership at 800,000.[14] In the same debate Russell stated that annual revenues were £791,721, but Ward claimed they were £937,456. Two days later Lord Stanley said, not without justice, that 'minute and fair enquiry' would show them to be only £450,000, and Peel supported him.[15] The official reckoning for 1835 was £815,331, but much of this was not

[12] Brougham to James Losh, Aug. 1831 (Hughes, op. cit. 463–4).
[13] Speech in Lords, 6 Mar. 1834 (Hansard, xxi. 1192).
[14] Hansard, xxvii. 370, 402; A. Macintyre, *The Liberator: Daniel O'Connell and the Irish Party, 1830–47* (London, 1965), 36–7.
[15] Hansard, xxvii. 367, 402, 627, 736.

received on account of refusals to pay tithes.[16] If the official amount had been received it would have provided a generous cash ratio of over £1 per member —a clear invitation to better cost-effectiveness in a utilitarian age. Both the official wealth of the Church and the fact that innumerable tithe-refusers were withholding it were arguments for reforming the Establishment; as were the facts that some parishes contained no Protestants or very few, that incumbents were non-resident in a third of the benefices and that church cess (the Irish equivalent of church-rates) was levied on Catholics and Presbyterians as well as churchmen.

In proposing reforms the Whigs encountered the perpetual dilemma of combining concession with maintenance of the Union. Irish problems were urgent enough for Ireland to be treated differently from the rest of the United Kingdom, but if this were done repeatedly it might only encourage the demand to repeal the Union as a standing illogicality. Moreover, among the proposed changes might be the reform of institutions which were integral parts of British ones. If the Irish extremities were surgically truncated, might not the British torso next fall victim to the knife? The Union might indeed provide reasons for common reform as much as common retention. A natural cause of such concern was reform of the Church of Ireland, for the Act of Union had made that Church a part of the constitution and of the Church of England. Some churchmen apparently believed that what had been joined by politicians had been joined by God, and that for later politicians to tamper with one section of the united Church was a sacrilegious act which would inevitably be repeated in the other section. In the inflamed ecclesiastical atmosphere of the 1830s this prospect became obsessive, the dream of radicals and Dissenters and the nightmare of many churchmen. Not for the first or last time the more pressing problems of Ireland magnified British controversies. It was a constant theme of opponents of Irish Church reform that, if allowed to succeed, the example would be applied to the English Church.[17] During 1833 English as well as Irish clergy petitioned against the Government's Irish Church Bill, and indeed this measure provoked the Oxford movement.

The Government's Irish Church Temporalities Bill was introduced by Lord Althorp in the Commons on 12 February 1833. The bill proposed to abolish (that is, to merge with others on the next vacancy) 10 sees out of 22; to reduce two archbishoprics to bishoprics; to suspend appointments to parishes where no services had been held for three years; to abolish church cess; to replace the first-fruits on benefices by a graduated tax on clerical incomes over £200 (raised to £300 in the final bill); to cut the revenues of

---

[16] Macintyre, op. cit. 182.

[17] Hansard, xxvii. 500 (Sir Robert Inglis, 31 Mar. 1835), 784–5 (Sir Richard Vyvyan, 3 Apr. 1835), 904 (Sir George Sinclair, 7 Apr. 1835); Sir James Graham to Lord Howick, 13 Mar. 1835 (Graham Papers, microfilms, 110); cf. G. F. A. Best, 'Church and State in English Politics, 1800–33' (unpubl. Univ. of Cambridge Ph.D. thesis, 1955), 90 ff.

Armagh and Derry, the two wealthiest sees; to abolish deans and chapters where they had no cure of souls; and to enable the tenants of Church lands to convert their leases into permanent tenancies. An Ecclesiastical Commission was to be created to dispose of the money saved, which was expected to amount to £150,000. The crux of the bill was the fate of surplus money after the Commission had provided for repairing churches and augmenting low stipends. The celebrated Clause 147 merely stated, with studied vagueness, that any such surplus would be used as Parliament should later decide. The question [of appropriation]', Althorp said, 'will be perfectly open.'[18]

Ultra-conservative churchmen were appalled. Sir Robert Inglis, member for Oxford University, said immediately after Althorp's speech that to destroy half of an Establishment was to destroy the whole.[19] Van Mildert, bishop of Durham, said the bill was 'an atrocious measure and bodes great evil to ourselves at no distant period'.[20] But among the great majority of M.P.s the bill was a success, obtaining support not only from Whigs, radicals, Dissenters, and Irish Repealers but also to a considerable extent from Peel.[21] O'Connell was most enthusiastic; and if the Government had been able to retain all this support it would have removed much of the odium incurred by its Coercion Bill, whose foreshadowing in the King's Speech had been bitterly denounced by O'Connell in the Commons only a week before.[22] But ministers were unable to sustain their initial success.

Behind the bold and apparently confident bill lay a serious Whig division. The difference had arisen over the use of surplus Church revenues. Edward Stanley, the Chief Secretary for Ireland who was ill equipped for the task of pacifying Irish Catholics, opposed in principle the appropriation of these revenues for secular purposes, and wished to use them only to augment existing livings and provide new ones. He had expressed such opinions since 1824.[23] In March 1831 he had told Grey that, while Parliament might redistribute a Church's property among members of that Church, he denied 'the right of the legislature, under any pretext, to appropriate [Church] property to the exigencies of the State'.[24] With this proviso he was 'not only ready, but anxious' to remove bishoprics and sinecures, abolish church cess, and suspend appointments to preferments having no cure of souls.[25] Indeed he even favoured, 'as a measure of police', State payment of the Catholic clergy, which was to become a feature of Whig policy.[26] In spite of his willingness to advance so wide a reform, Stanley's reservation was large

---

[18] Hansard, xv. 561–77. On the bill see D. H. Akenson, The Church of Ireland: Reform and Revolution, 1800–85 (New Haven, 1971), 171 ff.

[19] Hansard, xv. 581.   [20] Hughes, 480.

[21] N. Gash, Sir Robert Peel (London, 1972), 48–50; Macintyre, 40; M. D. Condon, 'The Irish Church and the Reform Ministries', Journal of British Studies, iii (1964), 128–9.

[22] Macintyre, 46–7.   [23] Hansard, xxvii. 618 (1 Apr. 1835).

[24] Stanley to Grey, Mar. 1831 (Grey Papers).

[25] Stanley to Grey, 4 Aug. 1832 (ibid.).

[26] L. C. Sanders (ed.), Lord Melbourne's Papers (2nd edn., London, 1890), 173 n.

enough to split the Government. Lord John Russell, Althorp, and Durham, his opponents in the Cabinet on the issue, saw appropriation as essential for religious equity and social improvement: reservation of all its revenues to the Church would be excessive expenditure on a body which had the allegiance of only a small minority of the people, and an extravagant symbol of continued Protestant ascendancy.

Much radical and Irish support would be found for appropriation, but in the Cabinet its votaries were in a minority. The difference was aired in Cabinet in July 1832.[27] Grey appreciated Stanley's usefulness in reconciling Protestant and episcopal opinion to the proposed reforms, and especially his having won the confidence of the Protestant Primate of Ireland, the archbishop of Armagh.[28] The Premier did not want to lose this advantage, nor to excite the fears of those English churchmen who would naturally see in any Irish Church reform a precedent for treatment of the Church in England.[29] He told Lord Holland: '. . . if we attempt to carry our measures further which I am afraid Johnny [Russell] is inclined to push unreasonably we shall infallibly [?] break up and throw the whole weight of the Church and all the Protestant feeling of the country into the arms of our enemies'. The hope of conciliating the Irish Repealers and Catholic clergy was, he added, unattainable in any case.[30] Russell, who did hope to conciliate Repealers and radicals, was so annoyed that he offered to resign, but he was persuaded to remain.[31] Durham, Grey's son-in-law, was equally opposed to a plan which 'only stuffed the saddle more equally, [and] did not take off the weight'.[32] They obtained an unsatisfactory compromise, for Stanley and the duke of Richmond were prevented in Cabinet from including in the bill a positive declaration that Church revenues would be used only for Church purposes.[33] The question of whether or not to appropriate was left unconcluded; hence the vagueness of Clause 147. Appropriation was not specifically adopted, and the Government as a whole would resist its introduction into the bill. But the general principle of appropriation lived on.[34]

There the matter might have rested, with the ministers agreeing to differ. But the disputants took to pressing their opposing principles in a manner which could only strain tempers and lessen the possibility of reconciliation.

[27] Holland's Political Journals, 9 July 1832 (Holland House Papers, 51869, p. 543).
[28] Grey to Stanley, 27 Sept. and 2 Nov. 1832 (Derby Papers, 117/5); cf. Richard Whately, archbishop of Dublin, to Stanley, Jan. 1831 (Derby Papers, 124/1). For the negotiations between Stanley and the Primate see also Akenson, op. cit. 167-71.
[29] Grey to Althorp, 21 Oct. 1832 (Grey Papers).
[30] Grey to Holland, 29 Oct. 1832 (Holland House Papers, 51556).
[31] Prest, Lord John Russell, 57-8.
[32] Durham to Edward Ellice, 28 Oct. 1832 (Ellice Papers, E 29, fo. 71).
[33] Grey to Holland, 29 Oct. 1832, (loc. cit.); Holland's Pol. Jls., autumn 1832 (loc. cit., pp. 569-70).
[34] Ibid. 570.

Durham began in mid-November by sending a paper to members of the Cabinet reasserting his view of appropriation. Stanley, naturally riled, complained to Grey that the matter had been decided so far as the Government was concerned. Grey agreed: the bill had omitted appropriation without insisting on the 'abstract principle' of non-appropriation, and anyone who still disputed this arrangement could resign.[35] But the high-mettled Chief Secretary, unsatisfied by this, wanted a fresh declaration of the Cabinet's position and a clear decision 'between Durham and myself'.[36] Grey now thought that Stanley was being unreasonable. He had already been reassured by Grey; the first post-Reform election campaign was no time for a Government split; and Durham's child was 'lying on her death-bed (the third [child] within less than 14 months)', which made it inappropriate to force immediate resignation upon the father.[37] Stanley thereupon relaxed his pressure, and Durham remained in the Government until his own ill-health, and probably the ministry's Irish policy, led him to resign in March 1833.[38] Very soon after Stanley desisted, Russell resumed the controversy by questioning the accuracy of Stanley's notes on Durham's paper, and reaffirming his own attachment to appropriation as a principle. But Stanley was able to provide him with a form of words which he could accept.[39] The ministry's triumphant electoral majority, obtained at this very time, concealed bitter and fateful contentions.

Barely a month later, in a still ragged state but with superficial unity, the ministers brought in their Irish Church Bill. A radical amendment introducing secular appropriation into Clause 147 was resisted by ministers, including those who defended the appropriation principle. In June it was decided to drop the clause altogether, against strong radical and Repealer opposition, rather than invite rejection of the whole bill by the Lords.[40] Ministers could not engage the peers in full-scale constitutional combat for the sake of a principle on which they themselves were divided. Thus their disagreement had robbed them of a clear opportunity not only to conciliate the Irish but to discipline the House of Lords, for any such constitutional contest they could—with their large majority and great popular support in the year after the Reform Act—most probably have won. But the discreet abandonment of their controversial clause at least enabled them to forget their disunity for a time in the aim of getting the body of the bill through the Upper House against ultra-Tory and episcopal resistance. To do this there was no

[35] Stanley to Grey, 15 Nov. 1832 (Grey Papers); Grey to Stanley, 17 Nov. 1832 (Derby Papers, 117/5; copy in Grey Papers).

[36] Stanley to Grey, 18 and 29 Nov. 1832 (Grey Papers).

[37] Grey to Stanley, 2 Dec. 1832 (Derby Papers, 117/5); Stanley to Grey, 5 Dec. 1832 (Grey Papers).

[38] Durham to Ellice, 22, 23, and 27 June 1833 (Ellice Papers, E 29, fos. 118–23); C. W. New, Lord Durham (Oxford, 1929), 225–32.

[39] Prest, 58–9; Durham to Ellice, 1 Jan. 1833 (Ellice Papers, E 29. fos. 85–6).

[40] See Chadwick, i. 58–9.

need to create new peers, as Russell had advised.[41] The dropping of Clause 147 did not seem to mollify the ultras, but ministers were aided by circumspect Conservatives. Peel, in a letter whose acumen was rewarded by future advantage to his party, urged the duke of Wellington to advise concession in the Lords so that Ireland would not be outraged, the ministry would not resign, and the Conservative party would not be placed in a damaging predicament. He thought it unlikely that a lasting Conservative Government could be formed at that point, and considered that, on account of Dissenting votes, a Church question would be a bad one on which to fight electoral contests.[42] The duke, as had been seen in 1829, was not one to raise an Irish storm by maintaining an ultra position, and he well understood this reasoning.[43] The King had previously, on his own initiative, acted in the better interests of Conservatism by advising restraint in a letter to the archbishop of Canterbury.[44] These moderate counsels prevailed, and the bill passed the Lords on 30 July after amendment.[45]

The measure had divided both Whigs and Conservatives. The latter, however, had avoided a debilitating conflict with the country, to their own advantage and that of the Church of England. They were now to benefit from the failure of their opponents to unite; for the appropriation question remained strongly alive, and Whig division flourished with it.

An Irish tour by Lord John Russell in the autumn convinced him that, among other remedies, tithe should be replaced by a land tax to be used for 'concurrent endowment'—the payment of Catholic, Presbyterian, and Church of Ireland clergy by the State.[46] He also believed, though he kept this to himself for the time, that appropriation was desirable to provide additional funds for concurrent endowment.[47] In the 1834 session Russell demanded that a commission be appointed with power to recommend the appropriation of surplus tithe revenues for educational purposes. Stanley said he would resign if such a commission were appointed. Russell was at first inclined to let him, but then yielded to Holland's advice on the matter of the commission and Stanley remained in the Government.[48] But breakdown was near, and Grey was not allowed to realize his ambition of 'keeping everything smooth to ye end of ye session when he means to resign'.[49] Sir

---

[41] Prest, 60; Holland's Pol. Jls., 16 June 1833 (Holland House Papers, 51869, p. 616).

[42] Gash, *Sir Robert Peel*, 51–3.

[43] Wellington to Peel, 23 July 1833 (C. S. Parker (ed.), *Sir Robert Peel, from his Private Correspondence* (3 vols., London, 1899), ii. 218).

[44] N. Gash, *Reaction and Reconstruction in English Politics, 1832–52* (Oxford, 1965), 33; Holland's Pol. Jls., 5 June 1833 (loc. cit., p. 602 ff.).

[45] By a majority of 54 on the third reading, following one of 59 on the second (Hansard, xix. 1016, xx. 126).

[46] Russell to Grey, 2 Oct. 1833 (Grey Papers).

[47] Russell's journal of his visit, 7 Sept. 1833 (quoted Prest, 61).

[48] Ibid. 64.

[49] Lord Howick's journal, 2 May 1834 (Grey Papers, C3/1B).

James Graham had offered to resign in February over a minor Irish dispute, but withdrew his offer when he was satisfied.[50] On 2 May Russell tendered his resignation again, but as before he was apparently 'talked out of this whim'.[51] It seems that Russell could no longer contain his feelings in the Commons, though he may also have realized the advantage to himself of overcoming Stanley and insisting on a policy which appealed to Irish, radicals, and Dissenters. In a Tithe Bill debate on 6 May, on the strength of his interpretation of a remark of Stanley which cannot be found in Hansard, he declared to Irish and radical applause that when tithes had been settled he would assert his opinion on appropriation.[52] He had reacted not to the words but to the person. In doing so, John Russell had upset the coach.

Grey and Althorp were furious with Russell, and Holland thought he had spoken 'unnecessarily warmly and prematurely'.[53] Stanley and Graham immediately said they would resign. They were dissuaded. But any possibility that they and like-minded ministers would remain for long was destroyed by radical determination to obtain a clear opinion from the Commons on appropriation. They were clearly out of place in a ministry which was under such pressure from most of its supporters. Henry George Ward, a radical M.P., was ready to move an appropriation resolution. At first it was hoped among ministers to avoid debate on this delicate issue by moving the previous question. But some ministers thought this would not succeed and that Ward's resolution would be carried even against the Government. It was believed that the ministry's position would be strengthened if the seceders were to resign before the motion was debated on 27 May, so that ministers could support it without the embarrassment of opposition from colleagues.[54] Stanley himself suggested this course, and the timing of the resignations pleased the ministers who kept their places.[55] The resignations of Stanley and Graham, both traditional constitutional Whigs, Richmond the ex-ultra, and Ripon the ex-Canningite were all accepted on 27 May. But victory for appropriation did not follow. The Government remained cautious, not wishing to commit itself to appropriation without careful inquiry into Irish Church revenues. When Ward introduced his resolution to reduce the temporalities of the Church of Ireland, Althorp first obtained an adjournment on account of the ministerial split;[56] then on 2 June he stated that a lay commission had been appointed to inquire into all aspects of Irish Church property, and asked Ward to withdraw his motion. Ward refused, and

[50] Graham to Grey, 13 Feb. 1834 (C. S. Parker, (ed.), *Life and Letters of Sir James Graham, Bt.* (2 vols., London, 1907), i. 184–5).

[51] Howick's journal, 2 May 1834 (loc. cit.).

[52] Hansard, xxiii. 659–66; *Mirror of Parliament*, 1834 session, ii. 1549–52; D. Southgate, *The Passing of the Whigs, 1832–86* (London, 1962), 46–8.

[53] Holland's Pol. Jls., 1834 (Holland House Papers, Add. MS. 51870, p. 716).

[54] Howick's journal, 22 and 26 May 1834 (loc. cit.); Holland to Grey, 24 May 1834 (Grey Papers).

[55] Holland to Grey, 25 May 1834 (ibid.).   [56] Hansard, xxiii. 1368–1400.

Althorp moved the previous question. Althorp's motion was carried by 396 votes to 120: the Government's tactic had succeeded.[57]

During this debate Stanley, supported by Peel, had replied to Ward's contention that 'civil utility alone, [was] the basis of the connexion between the Church and the State', by saying that such a principle could ultimately lead to placing all religion on a voluntary basis.[58] The difference over the Irish Church which had divorced the Stanleyites from utilitarian radicals was thus based on principles which concerned British religion as a whole. This was so despite the fact that seceding ministers justified their action on constitutional rather than theological grounds—an attitude which must have seemed somewhat shallow to the ardent high churchmen of the recently launched Oxford movement. The seceders' reason for taking a stand on appropriation was defence of the Anglo-Irish Union and of the Protestant Establishment which had been affirmed by the glorious revolution of 1688.[59] They shared these historical sentiments with Whigs in general, including even Russell as was later shown in the Ecclesiastical Titles controversy of 1850. But they held them more intensely, to the extent that they placed them above the policy which most Liberals entertained for the sake of civil and religious equity in Ireland. Reform, as Graham said, was one thing, confiscation quite another.[60] These views led the disaffected ministers to separation and to precarious independence as a 'Derby Dilly' between the two large parties before they found a resting-place (still only temporary, as far as Stanley and Richmond were concerned) in the moderate Conservatism of Peel.[61]

The secession of 1834 was an early stage in the Whig decline, the Conservative revival, and the gradual return of confidence in the established Church. The departed ministers were replaced by more liberal ones and Russell was free to enlarge on the need for wide reform in Ireland. This made the Government increasingly uncongenital to King William, who on 28 May had assured a worried deputation of Irish Protestant bishops that he was determined to defend the Protestant Church to which his family owed its throne.[62] The ministry was still in disagreement over Irish coercion, Grey resisting pressure to abolish the ban on public meetings in the 1833 Coercion Act. It was revealed that ministers more liberal than Grey had been in unauthorized communication with O'Connell, giving him the mistaken impression that the Cabinet had agreed to remove the ban. This

[57] Ibid. xxiv. 10 ff.

[58] Ibid. xxiii. 1395.

[59] Ibid., xxiv. 265–6, 268–70 (speeches of Ripon and Richmond in the Lords, 6 June 1834). See also C. S. Parker (ed.), i. 195–6; W. D. Jones, *Lord Derby and Victorian Conservatism* (Oxford, 1956), 45.

[60] A. B. Erickson, *The Public Career of Sir James Graham* (Oxford, 1952), 118–19.

[61] D. W. Johnson, 'Sir James Graham and the "Derby Dilly"', *University of Birmingham Historical Journal*, iv (1953–4), 66 ff.

[62] *Annual Register*, lxxvi (1834), 43–4.

caused Grey's resignation in mid-July. The new Prime Minister, Lord Melbourne, did not remove the King's fears about growing Government capitulation to radicals and Repealers. He refused William's request that he should form a Whig–Conservative coalition. The King assented to Melbourne's view that the Church Establishment in both England and Ireland required 'reconsideration and remodelling';[63] but he must have assented reluctantly, and he cannot have welcomed the passage of a diluted Coercion Bill, omitting the public meetings ban, straight after the new ministry took office. As Melbourne ill-advisedly informed the King, there was still a serious division in the Cabinet on the extent of Irish Church reform. Hopes of the Government's disintegration encouraged William to hasten the process, and he seized the chance provided in November by the removal of Althorp to the Upper House on his father's death. Melbourne recommended that Russell should succeed Althorp as Leader of the Commons, but William was repelled by the thought of one who personified appropriation, and informed Melbourne that his ministry was dismissed. The King had thus reversed his conciliatory attitude of the previous year when he had advised the bishops not to resist the Irish Church Bill. He had taken a more anachronistic course, based on a rigid conception of Church defence. Encouraged by the partly justified but exaggerated belief that 'the Church and Conservative Party is of great and growing strength in the Country',[64] he had thrown himself on the royal prerogative and the House of Lords against a ministry which had the clear support of the elected Chamber. The Whigs could only wait for the deeper currents of political development to swell once more and carry them back into office.

III. THE DEMANDS OF DISSENT

The stages in the disintegration and dismissal of the Whigs had been largely decided by the Irish Church question. But this question was part of a broader ecclesiastical issue, not only on account of its implications for the Church of England but also on account of the role of Protestant Dissent. The demands of Dissenters deepened Establishment fears that State reduction and Voluntaryism threatened the Church of England or Scotland as well as that of Ireland. The fear was by no means lessened by the fact that the increased political opportunities obtained by Dissenters in 1832 were not as yet reflected in the number of Dissenters returned to the Commons. The evangelical Dissenting bodies had only two M.P.s (John Wilks and Joseph Pease) in the 1833 Parliament, with a third (Edward Baines) being returned at a by-election in February 1834. The much less numerous but more educated and socially elevated Unitarians had considerably more

---

[63] Melbourne to the King, 15 July 1834 (Sanders (ed.), *Melbourne's Papers*, 205–8); Holland's Pol. Jls., 1834 (loc. cit., p. 737).
[64] Melbourne to Grey, 14 Nov. 1834 (Grey Papers).

representatives. But the lack of direct representation made Dissenters more dependent on the alliance of numerous radicals, who were liberal Anglican or free-thinking, and of Roman Catholic Irish Repealers. This alliance did nothing to make Dissenters less impatient for reform or more satisfied with the Whig Government. The strength of Dissenting attachment to the Whigs began to be questioned.

Members of the older Dissenting denominations were traditionally connected with the Whigs as the defenders of their political interests, and the enlarged Dissenting borough electorate after 1832 generally voted Liberal rather than Conservative. Membership of a closely knit and defensive religious denomination probably encouraged political homogeneity. In the general election at Leicester in 1832, 1,024 Dissenters were said to have voted Liberal and only 83 Conservative; a by-election at Devizes in 1835 showed a similar ratio of 110 to 13, and a by-election at Christchurch (Hampshire) in 1837 a ratio of 61 to 8.[65] The Liberal:Conservative ratios for the voting of churchmen in the same three elections were respectively 125 to 811, 35 to 144, and 44 to 108.[66] These were narrower ratios, indicating a good deal of Liberal voting among Anglicans. Thirty of the infants baptized at Fish Street Independent chapel, Hull, from 1803 to 1832, may be indentified as having voted Liberal in the Hull election of 1857, and 11 Conservative. A membership list of this chapel, when compared with poll-books, shows 49 members voting Liberal in 1841, and 6 voting Conservative.[67] A sample of voters in the Manchester election of 1832 shows a similar Liberal bias among electors who were baptized at Grosvenor Street Independent chapel and its predecessor.[68] But important factors must have disturbed the voting pattern of Dissenters, such as the competing claims of secular interests and causes, the policies and personalities of individual candidates, and the exercise of political influence by social superiors.[69] If in the industrial boroughs the influence of Nonconformist or Liberal Anglican employers stiffened the Liberal voting of Dissenters, Conservative landlords in the

[65] D. H. Close, 'The General Elections of 1835 and 1837 in England and Wales' (unpubl. Univ. of Oxford D.Phil. thesis, 1966), 141; Halévy, *History of the English People*, iii. 62 n.

[66] D. H. Close, op. cit., 141; Halévy, iii. 62 n.

[67] The identifications, which are tentative, have been obtained from a comparison of the Fish Street chapel baptismal register in the Public Record Office (R.G.4, 3388) and the Poll-Book of the Kingston-upon-Hull election of 1857 (Local History Library, Hull); also of the List of Members, Fish Street Congregational church (Local History Library, Hull, No. 14), and the Poll-Book for the borough of Kingston-upon-Hull, 30 June 1841 (Hull, 1841; Local History Library, Hull). There is scope for selective and local studies of denominational voting from the poll-books, the numerous baptismal registers in the Public Record Office, and the lists (perhaps rare) of church members in local libraries or in the custody of churches.

[68] From baptismal register of Grosvenor Street chapel, Manchester (P.R.O., R.G.4, 2693) and Poll-Book of Manchester election of 1832 ('The Electors' Guide'; Archives Dept., Central Library, Manchester).

[69] Cf. T. J. Nossiter, 'Elections and Political Behaviour in Co. Durham and Newcastle, 1832–74' (unpubl. Univ. of Oxford D.Phil. thesis, 1968), 523–7; R. W. Davis, *Political Change and Continuity, 1760–1885: a Buckinghamshire study* (Newton Abbot, 1972), 100.

counties and country towns continued to sway their Dissenting tenants and tradesmen in the opposite direction. This is implied in a letter to Lord Holland: '. . . the Dissenters . . . are very strong in the populous district of Bradford and Trowbridge [Wiltshire] and there being at present no Lord Bath might be favourable to the Reformers'.[70]

The voting of Wesleyans was less predictable than that of older Dissenters. They lacked the harmony between the influence of ministers and employers and their own personal interests which combined, in the case of other Dissenters, to favour the same party. The influential Wesleyan ministers—notably Jabez Bunting, the authoritarian successor of Wesley as the dominant force in the denomination—showed decided political conservatism; this also, or at least a sedulous non-involvement in politics, probably characterized the ministerial body as a whole. Ministers discouraged opposition to church-rates; and the Rev. Joseph Rayner Stephens, the future Chartist and agitator for the ten-hour day, was driven to resign from the Connection in 1834 for playing an open and official part in a disestablishment body, the Ashton-under-Lyne Church Separation Society.[71] Wesleyan leaders showed a reverence for the Church Establishment which was the more remarkable in that Anglican clergy who strongly upheld the Apostolical Succession refused to acknowledge the titles of Nonconformist ministers. Similarly, the attachment of Wesleyans to the Conservative party received verbal tribute but little tangible reward. They were not usually of the right social class to obtain parliamentary seats or magistracies, or even to reach the dizzy heights of local Tory society which, in Rochdale for example, revolved round the parish church, the Flying Horse Inn, the grammar school, and the local military.[72]

If there was sometimes contradictory tension in the Tory attitudes of Wesleyan leaders, the discrepancy was much clearer between the conservative assumptions of ministers and some powerful laymen and the radical interests of many of the tradesmen and skilled workers who composed the mass of Wesleyan laity. An expelled Wesleyan claimed that 'fifteen out of every twenty Methodists are favourable to a liberal government'.[73] In 1832 political differences were submerged in a tide of Wesleyan thankfulness for suffrage extension, but they reappeared in the later 1830s.[74] These differences, together with the example of Congregationalists and Baptists flourishing under a more democratic ecclesiastical system, strengthened the forces

---

[70] Rev. M. Marsh to Holland, 1 July 1837 (Holland House Papers, 51712).

[71] Jabez Bunting to Rev. James Kendall, 24 Apr. 1834, and to Rev. Isaac Keeling (Bunting Letters, Methodist Church Archives); Ward, *Religion and Society in England*, 156–8; D. M. Thompson (ed.), *Nonconformity in the Nineteenth Century* (London, 1972), 94–5.

[72] J. Vincent, *The Formation of the Liberal Party, 1857–68* (London, 1966), 112.

[73] Currie, *Methodism Divided*, 49. Cf. Ward, op. cit. 253; Close, op. cit. 143–4.

[74] D. A. Gowland, 'Methodist Secessions and Social Conflict in South Lancashire, 1830–57' (unpubl. Univ. of Manchester Ph.D. thesis, 1966), 175 ff.

for liberal change in Wesleyan organization—the demands for representation of laity as well as ministers in the ruling Conference, and the increase of local circuit independence from that body. Repeated secessions from the denomination over these questions demonstrated the external political as well as the internal constitutional tension. The seceding sects were decidedly more radical in political attitude, and perhaps of a lower social status on average, than the original Connection. These sects were the Wesleyan Methodist Association (formed in 1835), the Wesleyan Reformers, who seceded in 1849, and the New Connection and Primitive Methodists who had seceded earlier.[75] The New Connection Methodists, once called 'Tom Paine Methodists', were as much to the fore as Congregationalists and Baptists in petitioning Parliament against Dissenting grievances in 1833. The seceders were similar to older Dissent in their attachment to liberal politics, and their departure from Wesleyanism was potentially beneficial to the Liberal party.

How long the Liberal Dissenters would remain loyal to the Whigs depended, as far as their denominational interests were concerned, on how far the latter would satisfy their demand for civil equality. Extreme political Dissenters were already inclined to raise the cry of Voluntaryism. The Whigs would not entertain this policy. But most Dissenters might have been pacified by lesser concessions, and might have been deterred both from Voluntaryism and from rejecting the Whigs. The latter, however, torn between the desire to maintain the Establishment and the wish to satisfy Dissent, did not concede enough to prevent the growth of Dissenting militancy.

Early in 1833 there were signs that Dissenters, emboldened by the Reform Act and the growth of Voluntaryism in Scotland, were becoming more insistent. In January the *Leeds Mercury* demanded exemption for Dissenters from church-rates.[76] The United Committee, formed in March with the same title as previous Dissenting organizations, was dominated by well-established and moderate bodies, including the Committee of the Dissenting Deputies, 12 delegates from the Body of Ministers in London, and 3 delegates from the Protestant Society. But potential militancy might have been discerned in the inclusion of 3 delegates from the Scottish United Secession Church, which had espoused Voluntaryism.[77] In resolutions adopted on 11 May the United Committee called for relief from six grievances, as if in a Dissenters' version of the later People's Charter. These were marriage according to Anglican rites; church-rates; the alleged liability of

[75] Ibid. 182 ff., 281–2, 541–2.

[76] R. W. Ram, 'The Political Activities of Dissenters in the East and West Ridings of Yorkshire', 203.

[77] *Eclectic Review*, new Ser., v (Jan.–June 1839), 16; Halévy, iii. 134–5; Gash, *Reaction and Reconstruction*, 66. Wesleyans and Quakers, who might have given the body a more conservative and peaceful tone, declined to participate.

places of worship to the poor rate; the lack of civil registration of births and deaths; the inability of Dissenters to receive burial by their own rites in the parish churchyards; the religious tests at Oxford and Cambridge, and the need of a charter for a university at London which would not have such tests. The Government had no specific measures to offer, but Grey informed a deputation from the United Committee on 25 May that Government would not resist John Wilks's bill exempting Dissenting chapels from the poor rate. With the passage of this bill in July one contentious question was settled.[78]

The five remaining problems proved more intractable. Dissenters were left to marshal their case for the next parliamentary session, and some were tempted to become more extreme. *The Case of the Dissenters*, an anonymous letter to the Lord Chancellor published in December 1833, ended with a lengthy argument against established Churches which implied that they would be better abolished.[79] But the United Committee remained moderate in its approaches to ministers, and was informed that its claims were being considered in Cabinet. Lord Holland optimistically wrote to Grey in January 1834: 'There is among [Dissenting] leaders a great and earnest desire to be satisfied with a little but there is also among them a great alarm lest a cry for more than is practicable or reasonable should be provoked by a denial or postponement of what is reasonable.'[80] The Government's measures proved too little and had too much regard for the Establishment to prevent the more extreme Dissenting cry which Holland mentioned. The Marriage Bill, introduced in March by Lord John Russell, disappointed Dissenters by retaining the calling of banns in the parish churches and registration by the diocesan authorities, and by restricting marriages to certain chapels.[81] The Dissenting *Leeds Mercury* said the Government was 'quailing before the Church'.[82] High churchmen, for their part, objected to calling banns of marriages which were to be solemnized in Dissenting chapels; like the Dissenters, they preferred complete separation of Anglican and Dissenting marriages. But Newman was right in thinking that 'the Dissenters themselves will do our business for us by their clamouring against the Bill'.[83] On account of Dissenting opposition the measure was dropped in April. An irritated Russell grumbled that Dissenters could not reasonably complain of a violated conscience 'if you subject them to no other hardship than having their names called three times in church'.[84]

[78] *Journals of House of Commons*, vol. lxxxviii (1833), 260, 262, 488, 507, 518, 543; Gash, op. cit. 66. For this grievance see Whittaker, 'The Revival of Dissent', 170–4.

[79] Cf. Gash, 67 n. The letter was by Rev. A. Reed.

[80] Grey Papers. Cf. Holland to Grey, 15 Dec. 1833, 14 Jan. 1834 (ibid.).

[81] Hansard, xxi. 776–9.   [82] 8 Mar. 1834 (quoted Ram, op. cit., 155).

[83] Hon. Edward Grey, bishop of Hereford, to Earl Grey, 18 Feb. 1834 (Grey Papers); Russell to Grey, 28 Jan. 1834 (ibid.); Newman to Keble, 3 and 18 Mar. 1834 (Mozley, *Newman Correspondence*, ii. 30); Rev. Samuel Wilberforce to Gladstone, 1 May 1834 (copy, Wilberforce Papers, e. 2).

[84] Russell to Grey, April, n.d., 1834 (Grey Papers).

A similar fate befell Lord Althorp's church-rate scheme, introduced in April. This proposed to abolish the rates, which were said to amount to £560,000 a year, and to raise the much lower sum of £250,000 through an annual charge on the land tax.[85] It was again shown that Dissenters were not easily satisfied. Public meetings were held in protest. Joseph Hume said in the Commons that 'it was merely paying the money out of one pocket instead of out of the other', and that by substituting a general for a local tax the plan would make payment more obligatory.[86] Another speaker said that the new general charge would be imposed on Scotland and Ireland, in opposition to the Government's own concessionary policy.[87] A bill was brought in but was dropped before it reached a second reading.

The Commons had already been discussing a petition from Cambridge calling for the admission of Dissenters to university degrees. Since 1775 undergraduates at Cambridge had not been required to subscribe to the Thirty-Nine Articles, but still had to subscribe in order to graduate. At the more Tory and Anglican Oxford the test was imposed on undergraduates as well as graduates. In the 1834 debate John Wilks, one of the Dissenting M.P.s, said it was shameful that Nonconformists of the eminence of Isaac Watts and Philip Doddridge had had to obtain degrees from Scotland or America.[88] Stanley and O'Connell found themselves supporting the Cambridge petition in incongruous union.[89] Stanley objected to compulsory attendance at college chapel, and found sybaritic support from Palmerston: 'Was it either essential or expedient, that young men should be compelled to rush from their beds every morning to prayers, unwashed, unshaved, and half dressed; or, in the evening, from their wine to chapel, and from chapel back again to their wine?'[90] But Peel tried to restore sobriety to the debate by claiming that Dissenters' admission to university degrees was 'without exception, the most extravagant demand which has been advanced in modern times. If we have not the right to exclude Dissenters from the benefits of university education, we have not the right to maintain the connexion between the Church and the State.'[91] On 17 April leave was given to the Unitarian George Wood to introduce a bill giving equal rights to university admission and equal eligibility to degrees (except degrees in divinity). The bill passed the Commons but was thrown out by the Lords on 1 August, in accordance with their new intransigent mood which was also responsible for the rejection of the Irish Tithe Bill ten days later.[92]

In June the Lords had also rejected, as in 1833, a Jewish Relief Bill which had passed the Commons by a large majority. Jews suffered from several peculiar disadvantages which prevented their achieving, until 1858, rights

---

[85] Hansard, xxii. 1012 ff. [86] Ibid. 1019–21.
[87] Ibid. 1051–2; *Eclectic Review*, N. S. v (Jan.–June 1839), 18 f.
[88] Hansard, xxii. 631. [89] Ibid. 632–7, 690–8.
[90] Ibid. 701. [91] Ibid. 703–4.
[92] Gash, *Sir Robert Peel*, 74–5. Cf. Chadwick, i. 89 ff.

which Dissenters and Catholics had already obtained. Defensive opinion which had developed as a reaction from the events of 1828–32 was determined to uphold Christianity as an official condition of entry to the Legislature. If a Jew were admitted, who could keep out an atheist, a Parsee, or a Mahometan? Jews could be accused, however unjustly, of having no patriotic loyalty to their country of residence.[93] Perhaps most important, in an age when the demand for toleration needed political force to be effective, British Jews numbered only about 27,000 in 1830, and showed little inclination to combine for their own emancipation.[94] The contrast with the Catholic Association of the 1820s was obvious:

Where was the Jewish association, acting in defiance of law, assuming a power beyond the reach of control, and coercing the Legislature into a compliance with its sovereign decrees? Where was the Hebrew agitator? Where were the combined millions of exasperated Israelites thundering for admission at their doors?[95]

Jews obtained minor concessions during the 1830s.[96] But the refusal of the Lords to grant the major claim of entry to Parliament must have contributed to the frustration of Dissenters in general with the powerlessness of a Whig Government when confronted by a determined Upper House.

The disappointments of 1834 drove the more impatient Dissenters into extreme and independent courses. There were fears that Dissenting resentment was having an adverse effect on Whig candidates at by-elections; in seven of these, Conservatives were successful during 1834.[97] Church-rate contestants were far from being pacified by the events of 1834. At Manchester, against the loyal defence of Anglicans and Wesleyans, fierce opposition to the rate developed under the outspoken leadership of George Hadfield, a Congregational solicitor who later became M.P. for Sheffield. There were narrow victories for the rate in 1833 and 1834. On the latter occasion, it was claimed, '. . . the stir was greater than at any Election for Members of Parliament. Mills were stopt that the men might vote, bands of music preceded long lines of voters, and waggons and carts full of voters poured in from the out townships amidst loud cheers from the people.'[98] In the following year the rate was decisively rejected, and was never again compulsorily levied in Manchester.[99] Guinness Rogers, later a noted Congregational minister, attended with other boys from a Congregational boarding

---

[93] e.g. Hansard, xxiii. 1158–66; xxiv. 722–3 (speeches of Major Cumming Bruce and the earl of Malmesbury). Jews were accused of other 'alien' faults as well; e.g. 'they were never seen wielding the flail, or mounting the ladder with the hod' (ibid. xxiv. 722).

[94] U. Henriques, 'The Jewish Emancipation Controversy in Nineteenth Century Britain', *Past and Present*, 40 (Aug. 1968), 126 ff.

[95] Hansard, xxiii. 1172 (Sir Daniel Sandford, M.P. for Paisley). Similar arguments were used by peers and prelates (e.g. ibid. xxiv. 726).   [96] Henriques, op. cit. 129.

[97] D. H. Close, 28–9; *Eclectic Review*, N.S. v (Jan.–June 1839), 18.

[98] MS. 'Personal Narrative' of George Hadfield (1860), 69–73 (Archives Dept., Central Library, Manchester).   [99] Ward, *Religion and Society in England*, 179–82.

school 'a great meeting about Church rates' which was held about this time in Yorkshire.[100] There were also the fairly innocuous beginnings of the Braintree disturbances, leading to a classic legal contest which lasted until 1853. Samuel Courtauld, a Unitarian textile manufacturer whose firm became famous, began in 1834 to agitate against the rate, though at first he found it difficult to persuade Dissenters to join him.[101]

Opposition to the rate, itself stiffened by the growth of Voluntary propaganda, served in turn to strengthen the call for disestablishment. During 1834 Voluntaryism in England began to respond more positively to the Scottish example, emerging from the shadows of formal denominational resolutions[102] into the revealing light of parliamentary petitions, public meetings, Voluntary associations, and (in the case of J. R. Stephens) resignation from a denomination. The Nonconformist *Eclectic Review* approvingly commented in April on the 'revolution towards Voluntaryism' which had taken place in the public mind 'within the last few months'.[103] Voluntary petitions from Scotland were prominent—one from Glasgow aroused scepticism because the number of signatures was equal to the whole adult male population of the city[104]—but they were joined by one from Manchester signed by about 33,000 persons.[105]

Daniel O'Connell, seeing the Dissenting agitation as lending support to the appropriation principle, told Nonconformists from his own experience of Catholic agitation that 'if they would only make "a long pull, a strong pull, and a pull together", they would obtain more than ever they could expect from their courtesy towards the present Government'.[106] Union, as was noted by the Rev. John Angell James of Birmingham (a politically moderate Congregationalist), was clearly lacking among Dissenters: some petitioned for disestablishment but most of them only petitioned for the relief of grievances.[107] An overt demand for disestablishment was seen by some as an obstruction to the settlement of tangible grievances. Lord Holland was informed by a Dissenting minister on 6 March: 'The theory of a separation of the State and the Church need alarm no one . . . Wild, unreflecting, and comparatively few (I trust) are the men of intelligence

[100] J. Guinness Rogers, *An Autobiography* (London, 1903), 41–2.

[101] Report of Select Committee of House of Commons on Church Rates, P.P. 1851 (541), ix. 67, 71. For church-rate disputes in Lincolnshire at this time see R. J. Olney, *Lincolnshire Politics, 1832–85* (London, 1973), 99.

[102] Article IX of the Congregational Union of England and Wales, adopted at its third general meeting in 1833, stated: 'the power of a Christian Church should in no way be corrupted by union with temporal or civil power' (Jones, 'The Liberation Society and Welsh Politics', 203).

[103] 3rd Ser. xi. 320, 325.   [104] Hansard, xxiii. 856–7.   [105] Hansard, xxiii. 513–14.

[106] Ibid. xxii. 397–8.

[107] James to Rev. Dr. Patton (U.S.A.), 14 Mar. (?) 1834 (R. W. Dale (ed.), *The Life and Letters of John Angell James* (London, 1861), 338–9). For Dissenting disunion see H. R. Martin, 'The Politics of the Congregationalists, 1833–56' (unpubl. Univ. of Durham Ph. D. thesis, 1971), 35 ff.

who wish Government to effect such a result.'[108] The Whig Government could therefore take comfort from the belief that Dissenting militancy would not inflict further damage on their party at a time when it was suffering from the appropriation split. A London conference of Dissenters on 8 May, reluctantly summoned by the United Committee to oppose Althorp's Church Rate Bill, decided (after disagreement) to include disestablishment in the demands which they made to the Government.[109] But the account which Holland received of the meeting was encouraging; it noted that 'they will not knowingly lend a hand to bring in the Tories'.[110] When Spring Rice stood for re-election at Cambridge on being appointed to Stanley's old office, Holland said that '. . . every dissenter to a man . . . voted for him'.[111]

The preservation of the Whigs' ecclesiastical policy, and perhaps even their parliamentary majority, depended on Voluntaryism not becoming too strong or insistent. For the Whigs desired, as they constantly stated, to keep Dissenting support without deserting the Establishment.[112] They held to the policy of relieving the civil grievances of Dissent without entertaining Voluntaryism, and prepared such a policy for the next parliamentary session in 1835: '. . . our object is, if possible, to conciliate the Dissenters, and having framed our measures with that end, strenuously to resist the separation of Church and State . . .'[113] The question as to whether or not this policy would satisfy Nonconformists was postponed by the appointment of a Conservative ministry, an event which repaired for a time the alliance of Whigs and Dissent.

IV. PEEL, THE CHURCH, AND DISSENT

When Peel accepted the premiership on 9 December 1834 Conservative revival did not run deep enough for a lengthy stay in office, and the King was soon compelled to eat his hastily concocted policy. Yet if a Conservative ministry run on liberal Peelite lines had succeeded in maintaining power it might have done more to pacify disparate elements than the Whigs. Not least was this possible in the relations of Church and Dissent. Peel, despite the suspicions which remained from 1829, commanded as a Conservative more confidence among churchmen than did the Whigs;[114] and the Church

[108] Rev. Dr. J. Pye Smith to Holland, 6 Mar. 1834 (Holland House Papers, Add. MS. 51838).

[109] E. Baines, jun., *Life of Edward Baines* (2nd edn., London, 1859), 165; Close, 27; Gash, *Reaction*, 68; H. R. Martin, op. cit. 115-20.

[110] Holland to Grey, 19 May 1834 (Grey Papers).

[111] Holland to Hon. H. E. Fox, 13 June 1834 (Holland House Papers, 51753).

[112] Hansard, xxi. 992-3 (Durham and Grey, 3 Mar. 1834), xxii. 1048-51, xxiii. 507-8 (Russell, 21 Apr. and 5 May 1834).

[113] Russell to Holland, 24 Aug. 1834 (Holland House Papers, 51677).

[114] Cf. O. Brose, *Church and Parliament . . . 1828-60* (London, 1959), 43-4; Gash, *Sir Robert Peel*, 100.

was therefore readier to accept reforms at his hands. Dissenters, realizing the hopelessness of asking for extreme reforms from a Conservative Government, might have accepted less from Peel than from his predecessors in office. Since the new Government was in a minority, seeking to increase its strength in an immediate general election, it was all the more important to win support rapidly from a variety of sources. While Conservative unity should be preserved by retaining the support of the ultras—an object which was partially attained[115]—more liberal opinions had also to be conciliated.

In an age of intense religious commitment Peel's devotion to the interests of the Church of England was not at first sight obvious. His congenital reserve gave a misleading impression of irreligious nonchalance, which had led the passionate evangelical Lord Ashley to write: 'Humanly speaking, I can see nothing worse than that Peel should be called to the helm of affairs.'[116] Peel, personally a sound churchman, had as much zeal for the Church as more open enthusiasts, and was determined to undertake constructive action. Correspondents were encouraged to send him their views on the necessity for Church reform. Letters and addresses sent to him by Anglicans stressed the need for Church extension as a means of improving morality and reducing Dissent; they advised that pluralism be prohibited and that a substitute be found for church-rates. Such opinions worked to confirm Peel's sentiments, for his own ideas on the subject were well rooted and perhaps owed a good deal to the trenchant and popular scheme produced in 1832 by his evangelical brother-in-law, Lord Henley.[117] Like the Whigs, Peel wished the Church to carry out its own reform, seeing this as being far more appropriate and effective than Government direction. Therefore he earnestly sought the co-operation of Church leaders. 'I do earnestly ask', he wrote to the bishop of Durham, 'whether it be fit that the great manufacturing towns and districts of the country should be left, as to the means of spiritual instruction, in their present state?'[118] To Henry Phillpotts, bishop of Exeter, he wrote: 'all mere political considerations . . . are as nothing in my mind, compared with the great objects of giving real stability to the Church in its spiritual character'.[119] In Peel's broad view, the stability of the established Church was coterminous with the greater contentment of Dissenters. He was not blind to the advantage which his Government might gain even from Dissenters if it resolved their grievances where the Whigs had failed.[120] While wishing to leave the universities in the hands of the Church, he was anxious to settle the questions

---

[115] B. T. Bradfield, 'Sir Richard Vyvyan and the Country Gentlemen, 1830-4', *EHR* lxxxiii (1968), 741-3.

[116] Ashley's diary, 12 July 1834 (E. Hodder, *The Life and Work of the Seventh Earl of Shaftesbury* (3 vols., London, 1880-2), i. 197). On Peel's religious views see Gash, *Sir Robert Peel*, 182-6.

[117] *A Plan of Church Reform* (6th edn., London, 1832); Best, *Temporal Pillars*, 283-90.

[118] Lord Mahon and E. Cardwell (eds.), *Memoirs by the Rt. Hon. Sir Robert Peel* (2 vols., London, 1856-7), ii. 81.

[119] Peel to Phillpotts, 22 Dec. 1834 (Peel Papers, Add. MS. 40407, fo. 109).

[120] William Borrodaile, jun., to Peel, 16 Dec. 1834 (ibid. 40405, fos. 276-7).

of Dissenters' marriages and church-rates, and obtained the co-operation of his colleagues and of Church leaders.[121] The Tamworth Manifesto, issued on 18 December in preparation for the general election, not only described the Reform Act as 'a final and irrevocable settlement' but embraced the general spirit of moderate reform, seeing this as 'a careful review of institutions, civil and ecclesiastical, undertaken in a friendly temper'. In Opposition, ran the Manifesto, Peel had supported Althorp's church-rate scheme and accepted Russell's Marriage Bill: he was not 'actuated by any illiberal or intolerant spirit towards the Dissenting body'. Similarly, he advocated the solution of the tithe dispute by means of commutation, and accepted the need to redistribute the revenues of the Church of Ireland in order to extend its influence, but was opposed to the appropriation of Church property in Ireland or Britain.[122]

All that Peel needed to carry out his programme was sufficient electoral and parliamentary support. Stanley's refusal to join him at the outset of his ministry, on the ground that he agreed with Peel only on ecclesiastical questions, was a great disappointment. The need to convince the voters in a general election became all the greater. The election of January 1835 hinged on the harnessed issues of Church and constitution. The conciliatory message of the Tamworth Manifesto proved attractive to moderate electors of both parties who wished to keep out a radical,[123] but against the barrier between Church and Dissent its electoral value was limited. Conservatism, with its ultra ingredients, was still branded as defending the existing order in Church and State; the Manifesto could modify this impression but not remove it.

Most Anglican clergy had reconciled themselves to Church reform undertaken by Conservatives, and intervened decisively on the Conservative side.[124] The Grand Orange Lodge of Great Britain expelled two members at Rochdale, and suspended a third, for voting for the Liberal candidate.[125] Dissenters, on their side, were decidedly anti-Tory, and this was the first general election in which independent Nonconformist activity was conspicuous. A Dissenters' Parliamentary Committee was formed, and corresponded with many local committees consisting of Congregationalists, Baptists, and Methodist seceders. The Committee declared its grievances and sent its demands to candidates in an effort to ensure parliamentary support.[126] In four constituencies—including Bradford, where George

---

[121] Speeches of Peel, Hansard, xxiv. 354–5; xxvii. 289 ff.; Peel to Phillpotts, 22 Dec. 1834 and 21 Jan. 1835 (Peel Papers, 40407, fos. 107–8; 40411, fo. 33). But see Gash, *Sir Robert Peel*, 100–1.
[122] *Memoirs*, ed. Mahon and Cardwell, ii. 61–6.
[123] Close, 'General Elections of 1835 and 1837', 63–4.
[124] Ibid. 157–9; Andrews, 'Political Issues in the County of Kent', 55–6.
[125] Report and Evidence of Select Committee of House of Commons on the Orange Institutions of Great Britain, P.P. 1835 (605), xvii. 158–9.
[126] Close, 149–50.

Hadfield stood—candidates who were especially favoured by Dissent stood unsuccessfully.[127] Whatever may have been the case had the election been called by a Whig instead of a Conservative Government, this Dissenting action was subsidiary to the Liberal cause rather than competing with it.[128] Despite previous dissatisfaction with the Whigs and the notable vagueness of the Whig electoral programme on the subject of their grievances, Dissenters plumped for familiarity. Except perhaps for Wesleyans, they bent much of their effort to ousting Peel's Government. Contributing to this end was the expectation of Dissenting benefit from the Whigs' proclaimed policy of elective municipal corporations. The Irish Repealers were linked even more closely to the Whig cause by O'Connell's formation of an anti-Tory association.

In the election it appears that the Conservatives came near to doubling their numbers, and now formed the largest single party in the Commons, while their opponents were a motley collection of Whigs, radicals, Stanleyites, and Repealers.[129] But the Opposition, if united, could muster a majority of at least 78 against the Government.[130] Peel counted on their disunity and the attraction of his own measures to keep him in office. But his opponents were to prove more united than he hoped and he was not given time to introduce many measures.

The one memorable act of his Government was non-parliamentary, the issue of a Royal Commission to carry out reforms in the Church of England. The decision was made at a conference on 8 January between Peel, the archbishop of Canterbury, and the bishop of London. It was then agreed that the Commission should concern itself primarily with episcopal and diocesan reorganization, also with the ending of sinecures and pluralities, the augmentation of poor livings, and the reform of patronage. These objects were close to Henley's *Plan*, which had anticipated some of the recommendations that the Commission eventually made.[131] The Commission was issued on 4 February, being known at first as the Ecclesiastical Duties and Revenues Commission and becoming the Ecclesiastical Commission in the following year. It was composed of 5 prelates (including the 2 archbishops) and 7 Anglican and Conservative laymen, including the Lord Chancellor and Peel. The scheme was to encourage the Church to reform itself, though Peel

---

[127] Ibid. 150; 'Personal Narrative' of George Hadfield, 126–7; D. G. Wright, 'Politics and Opinion in Nineteenth Century Bradford' (unpubl. Univ. of Leeds Ph.D. thesis, 1966), 119–39.

[128] In only one constituency, Finsbury, did a Dissenting candidate stand against another Liberal candidate (Close, 150).

[129] Gash, *Sir Robert Peel*, 101; but see Close, 213 ff.

[130] Gash, 101; Macintyre, *The Liberator* 137.

[131] Henley had proposed that all bishops should receive £5,000 p.a., with the following exceptions: Canterbury £15,000, York £12,000, London £10,000, Durham £8,000, Winchester £7,000 (*Plan*, 80). The Commission's first report (1835) suggested general episcopal incomes of £4,500 to £5,500, with the same prelates to receive more.

seemed prepared to use firm methods if necessary.[132] Like other instruments of reform in the 1830s the Commission was dedicated to the current concept of greater usefulness. Peel wrote that its entire object was 'to extend the sphere of [the Church's] usefulness, and to confirm its just claims upon the Respect and affection of the People'.[133] But it is important to distinguish this from any idea that the Commission was a capitulation to utilitarian ideas of Church reform, which were more drastic and iconoclastic than Peel ever envisaged. The Commission was rather intended to defeat extreme radical proposals such as disestablishment and disendowment. Indeed, the method of reform by Royal Commission fulfilled Peel's wish to keep Church reform away from the House of Commons with its unfriendly radical members.[134] As he wrote to a doubting Phillpotts, it was plain that clerical sinecures had to go, and it was better that they should go by friendly rather than unfriendly hands.[135] The objects of the Commission were not so much Benthamite as Coleridgean. They sought to effect Coleridge's idea of a ubiquitous and respected 'clerisy', to be distributed 'so as not to leave the smallest integral part or division without a resident guide, guardian or instructor'.[136]

Peel also prepared plans for pacifying Dissent and Catholicism, but these became entangled in the opposition he had to face in Parliament. Only a Dissenters' Marriage Bill and an Irish Tithe Bill were introduced. The former proposed a civil ceremony (as well as encouraging a religious one in Dissenting chapels) for Dissenters who declared themselves such on oath before a magistrate. The register was still to be kept by the parish clergyman. There were Dissenting objections both to the degradation of taking the oath and to registration by Anglican clergy.[137] The Irish Tithe Bill provided an opportunity to dislodge the administration. The Lichfield House Compact had cemented the alliance of Whigs, radicals, and Irish Repealers. The support of the Repealers, whose numbers had greatly increased in the elections, was necessary to the Whigs in their depleted state. An active policy of Irish reform was therefore desirable, and the Tithe Bill provided the chance of reviewing the appropriation question. Henry Ward had offered to resign this issue into Russell's hands, on condition that he would bring forward resolutions early in the session asserting the State's right to

[132] *Memoirs*, ed. Mahon and Cardwell, ii. 69–71; Gash, *Sir Robert Peel*, 103–4; Brose, *Church and Parliament*, 126–7; Best, *Temporal Pillars*, 297 f.

[133] Peel to Rev. J. C. Franks of Huddersfield, 9 Mar. 1835 (Peel Papers, 40416, fo. 141). Cf. Brose, 120.

[134] Peel to van Mildert, bishop of Durham, 23 Feb. 1835 (*Memoirs*, ii. 78–9).

[135] Peel to Phillpotts, 21 Jan. 1835 (Peel Papers, 40411, fo. 34).

[136] S. T. Coleridge, *On the Constitution of Church and State according to the Idea of Each*, ed. J. Barrell (London, 1972), xix, 41–2 (original edn. 1830).

[137] Resolutions of the committee of the United Dissenters of Manchester, sent to Peel 21 Mar. 1835 (Peel Papers, 40417, fos. 320–2). There were also Anglican objections; Gash, *Sir Robert Peel*, 105.

appropriation.[138] On 27 March Russell announced that he intended to move for a Committee of the whole House to consider applying surplus revenues of the Irish Church to 'the religious and moral instruction of all classes of the community'.

On 30 March Russell moved his resolution. The debate lasted four days, allowing a wide range of opinions to be expressed. Stanley claimed that appropriation, if adopted, would not benefit Ireland until the year 1886 or even the year 2500, and preferred the Government's tithe proposals.[139] Graham saw the chief danger in the extinction of the Protestant Establishment in Ireland and the weakening of the Protestant Establishment in England. He argued that 'so long as the Union continues, the Protestant religion is the religion of the majority'. But Howick claimed that such an idea was astonishing from someone who lived near the Scottish border: why did not Graham emulate Charles I and attempt to force episcopacy on the Presbyterians?[140] Ward's long speech asserted the general principle that Church property, unlike private property, was not immune from State interference and appropriation. He also maintained that numbers, not truth, were the justification for a Church Establishment: how otherwise could it be that 'truth' was different north and south of the Tweed?[141] But the young Gladstone, who was to carry a more radical reform of the Church of Ireland thirty-four years later, now insisted that Church property was as sacred as private property and that the Irish Church needed every penny it possessed.[142]

Russell's motion was carried by a majority of 33 on 2 April. The next day Russell moved in the Committee of the whole House that any surplus should be 'applied locally to the general education of all classes of Christians'. The Government opposed adjourning for further debate and was defeated by 38 votes. When the debate was resumed Russell's motion was carried by 25 votes. On 7 April Lord John further moved that the foregoing resolution be embodied in the Government Tithe Bill, and said that if necessary he would move an address to the Crown to this effect. The motion was carried by 27 votes. These slender majorities may have slightly disappointed the Liberals but were quite enough to confirm Peel's inclination to resign. On 8 April he announced his resignation in the Commons.[143]

The ministry withdrew at the right time. Continuance in office might only have undermined Peel's growing reputation as a political leader, and the Conservative revival in the country, by a damaging clash with Liberal forces. As it was, the Conservative party had been encouraged in policy, seats, and organization. A new definition of liberal Conservatism had been made and

[138] H. G. Ward to Russell, 18 Feb. 1835 (Russell Papers, 1E, fos. 33-4).
[139] Hansard, xxvii. 631.   [140] Ibid. 426-30, 444.
[141] Ibid. 397 ff., 415-16.   [142] Ibid. 507 ff.
[143] Ibid. 770-7, 859-64, 963-74 (division lists), 980-5; Gash, Sir Robert Peel, 116-18.

new heart had been put in the Church of England. It was no loss to Peel that a Government consisting of his opponents was left with diminished and diverse forces. It was only surprising that he did not return to power until 1841.

V. WHIGS AND THE CHURCHES, 1835-1837

The Whigs under Melbourne resumed their conduct of the Government in an unenviable condition. A substantial majority could be mustered only when unity of viewpoint existed among the Government's heterogeneous supporters. The Conservative revival was rendered none the less menacing by Peel's cautious determination to eschew impetuous opposition and bide his time. Popular reaction against the Government, particularly over the new Poor Law of 1834, worked to the advantage of the Conservatives. The House of Lords with its Conservative majority was ready to reject measures which would have pleased the Government's radical and Irish supporters, and it was little comfort to ministers that the Lords were sometimes restrained only by the leader of the Opposition. The ministry had the general if embarrassing support of the Irish Repealers, on account of Lord John Russell's manifest enthusiasm for Irish reform and the mutual desire to exclude a Tory Government. But the adoption of Irish wishes, especially appropriation, caused Stanley and Graham to move into closer association with Peel. The Whigs, assisted first by the Irish alliance and then by the favour of Queen Victoria, remained shakily in office for six years in spite of a steady decline in the number of their parliamentary supporters and the growth of restless extra-parliamentary pressure groups. On ecclesiastical issues the weakness of the Government made it desirous of retaining Dissenting support yet unable to carry sufficient reform to prevent Dissenting alienation. At the same time the Government's commitment to maintaining the Establishment was rendered suspect by its radical, Dissenting, and Irish connections. Its link with Irish Catholicism made it the butt of a no-Popery campaign run mainly by Anglican evangelicals. The Church reforms which the Government carried out on the recommendation of the Ecclesiastical Commission attracted to the Whigs an unpopularity in both radical and high church circles which might otherwise have been bestowed on Peel, the Commission's founder; and Peel, in Opposition, obtained a loyalty from Tories which he might in other circumstances have forfeited.

Russell announced in the Commons on 20 May 1835 that the Government would confine itself in that session to English municipal and Irish Church reform. The new Government had been formed on the understanding that it would introduce an Irish Church Bill combining appropriation with commutation of tithe, in accordance with the resolution of 7 April. Melbourne had overcome the King's objection that such a measure might violate his Coronation Oath.[144] The report of the commission of inquiry appointed in May 1834 was presented, and the bill was drawn up. Tithe was to be replaced by a rent charge. Not only was there to be appropriation of surplus Church revenues for educational purposes, but the Government was to try and make sure that a sizeable surplus would exist by suspending presentations to hundreds of livings where the Establishment had fewer than 50 members. The bill passed the Commons, the appropriation clauses being strongly opposed by Peel, Stanley, and Graham, who wanted the bill to be divided. This was done by the Lords in August: they accepted the rent charge but rejected appropriation. The entire bill was consequently abandoned.

English Dissenters obtained greater satisfaction in 1835 than Irish Catholics. The passage of the Municipal Reform Bill rewarded their aspirations for a larger share in local government and gave greater representation to their electoral strength than had the 1832 Reform Act. In towns such as Leeds and Sheffield Dissenters had long joined in the attack on the old councils, and actively supported the bill.[145] The reform, introduced by Russell on 5 June, proposed a suffrage for ratepayers of three years' standing, in order to elect councillors for three years. Both Peel and Stanley generally approved of the bill, as did Dissenting M.P.s; but the Tory peers did not. Four days after the Lords had defeated the Irish Church Bill they returned the Corporations Bill to the Commons with swingeing amendments. One of these, which had been advanced by Lord Lyndhurst on 25 August, proposed that Church patronage belonging to corporations should only be exercised by the Anglican members. This amendment was blocked by the insertion of Russell's counter-amendment that all corporation livings should be sold. But other amendments were accepted or altered in the general compromise over the bill produced by the conciliatory attitudes of Peel and Russell and their mutual desire to avoid a constitutional struggle.[146] The bill passed on 10 September.

Liberal expectations of resounding success were gratified in the first elections under the Act in December 1835. So too were those of Dissent. Unitarians, Congregationalists, and Baptists were especially numerous among the returns. At Hull, only 1 of the 56 councillors and aldermen returned in the first elections was a Conservative, and 23 were Dissenters. Half the mayors of Hull between 1835 and 1850 were Dissenters, and 13 of the Dissenting councillors in the same period were members of the Fish Street Independent chapel. In Leeds, all 10 mayors between 1835 and 1845

[144] Gash, *Peel*, 127-8; Holland's Pol. Jls., 15 Apr. 1835 (Holland House Papers, Add. MS. 51870, pp. 801-3, 809).

[145] Ram, 'The Political Activities of Dissenters', 43 ff., 176-7.

[146] Gash, *Peel*, 131-40; Prest, *Russell*, 95-7; G. Kitson Clark, *Peel and the Conservative Party, 1832-41* (2nd edn., London, 1964), 261-95; G. B. A. M. Finlayson, 'The Politics of Municipal Reform, 1835', *EHR* lxxxi (1966), 683-8.

were Dissenters, including 5 Unitarians and one Roman Catholic.[147] At Leicester the religious allegiance of the 42 councillors and 14 aldermen elected in 1835 (only 4 of whom were Conservatives) was as follows: 16 churchmen, 12 Unitarians, 12 Baptists, 10 Independents, 3 Quakers, 2 Wesleyans, and 1 member of the Countess of Huntingdon's Connection.[148] At Liverpool also the election of the new council was a Liberal triumph (though the Conservatives were to reverse it in 1841), and the presence of 3 Roman Catholics was a slight reflection of the large Catholic element in the city's population.[149] Nonconformist prominence in the new councils consolidated the urban strength of Dissent and stimulated their demands and organization. The *Eclectic Review* of January 1839 did not exaggerate in seeing municipal reform as the most effective political advance which Dissent had yet made. Before this reform, the repeal of the Test and Corporation Acts had been only 'a nominal and formal concession', granting shadow without substance.[150] Dissent was grateful to the Whigs for the Act, but the Whigs were not grateful for the more extreme Dissenting demands which the Act helped to encourage.

Municipal reform, for all its importance to Dissenters, was an incidental benefit which had not formed part of the canon of grievances put forward by the United Committee. Five of these grievances remained, and Dissenters, having aided the Whigs in the general election, had hoped that action would be taken on them in the new Parliament's first session. Church-rates were discussed in the Commons in connection with the case of a stubborn East Anglian worthy, John Childs of Bungay, a substantial printer who had been imprisoned for refusing to pay 17s. 6d.[151] But in order to give full rein to its Irish and municipal measures the Government decided to postpone this issue together with those of marriage and civil registration. Peel said he thought ministers should do something before next session about church-rates, but Spring Rice and other Liberals warned Dissenters not to be 'dazzled by this new-born zeal of the tories'.[152] John Wilks and Joseph Pease said that Dissenters were satisfied to wait, and the former reiterated the confidence of Dissenters in the Government.[153] Holland noted that London Dissenters were friendly, but were 'apprehensive that their brethren in the Country will be less so', regarding the postponement.[154] In July another University Tests Bill was defeated in the Lords.[155]

[147] Ram, 182-90.
[148] A. T. Patterson, *Radical Leicester, 1780-1850* (Leicester, 1954), 214-15; R. W. Greaves, *The Corporation of Leicester, 1689-1836* (Oxford, 1939), 133-6.
[149] J. A. Picton, *Memorials of Liverpool* (2 vols., Liverpool, 1903), i. 469; T. Burke, *A Catholic History of Liverpool* (Liverpool, 1910), 48.
[150] *Eclectic Review*, N.S. v (Jan.-June 1839), 23-4.
[151] Hansard, xxviii. 51 ff. (25 May 1835).　　　　　　[152] Hansard, xxviii. 66-9, 73, 77, 82.
[153] Ibid. 76-8; xxix. 13.
[154] Holland's Pol. Jls., 27 May 1835 (Holland House Papers, Add. MS. 51871, p. 843).
[155] Hansard, xxix. 496-546.

The Government began the 1836 session in fresh heart following the Liberal successes in the municipal elections which, Holland delightedly exclaimed, had 'surprized and appalled the Tories'.[156] Ministers prepared an Irish Municipal Corporations Bill and an Irish Church Bill, but both were abandoned after opposition in the Lords. Dissenters, however, were gratified by the passage of a Civil Registration Bill for births, marriages, and deaths—a measure which had become desirable for such purposes as the verification of ages under the 1833 Factory Act as well as for meeting the needs of Dissent.[157] There was also a Marriage Act which finally did away with Hardwicke's Act of 1753. These linked reforms were received by Dissenters with a fair measure of satisfaction. But there were complaints about the high cost of marriage licences, the required publication of marriages by licence before the Poor Law Guardians, and the presence of a registrar at marriages in Dissenting chapels and not in Anglican churches. An unsuccessful attempt to defeat the Marriage Bill because it legalized civil contracts was made by the earl of Lincoln, supported by Ashley, Gladstone, Inglis, and Peel. The provision that marriage might be exclusively civil, if the parties so desired, tended to be forgotten amidst the Church and chapel rivalry but was to be important as this rivalry diminished.[158]

This session had previously seen the passage of a bill for the compulsory commutation of English tithes. The bill was to be operated by three commissioners, two of whom were appointed by the Crown and one by the archbishop of Canterbury. Holland said that this Act was 'a great and an useful measure', but that it was 'too favorable to the Church' and was allowed 'probably for that bad reason, to pass the house of Lords'.[159] The question of University Tests was avoided this session, but a charter was given to the undenominational London University to grant degrees.

Although Dissent obtained considerable satisfaction in 1836, an attempt to settle church-rates was again put off, though Russell expressed constructive intentions on this and on the burial and university questions.[160] So Dissenting uneasiness continued. Dissenters in Suffolk passed a resolution against the Government's delay over church-rates, and after the session ended plans were prepared for a Church Rate Abolition Society, founded on 19 October. The Dissenting Deputies did not look very kindly on this society, which represented something of a new and harder tone in English Dissenting organization.[161] In the previous March the Unitarians had

---

[156] Holland to H. E. Fox, 1 Jan. 1836 (Holland House Papers, 51755).

[157] Edwin Chadwick, *Report on the Sanitary Condition of the Labouring Population of Great Britain*, 1842, ed. M. W. Flinn (Edinburgh, 1965), 27 n.

[158] See, however, O. Anderson, 'The Incidence of Civil Marriage in Victorian England and Wales', *Past and Present*, 69 (1975), 50–87.

[159] Holland's Pol. Jls., 1836 session (Holland House Papers, 51871, p. 948).

[160] Hansard, xxxi. 378–9 (12 Feb. 1836).

[161] *Eclectic Review*, N.S. v (Jan.–June 1839), 28; Manning, *The Protestant Dissenting Deputies*, 187. Cf. H. R. Martin, 'The Politics of the Congregationalists', 150–3.

seceded from the Deputies on account of a dispute between Unitarians and evangelical Dissenters over rights to an endowment fund, known as Lady Hewley's Case. In the same month they had seceded from the General Body of London ministers. This was a temporary reverse to Dissenting political efforts, for Unitarians had led the cause for half a century, and possessed beliefs, education, and social eligibility of a kind to commend them to the inner circles of Whiggery. The *Eclectic Review* remarked, 'they had the ear of Ministers; they were the only class of Dissenters known to the political coteries or clubs'.[162] The same journal could find solace in the statement that 'the value of their co-operation had long been equivocal'.[163] Indeed, the resignation of William Smith, the intimate of Grey and Holland, from his long chairmanship of the Deputies in 1832 might almost have been timed to coincide with the onset of a new, more strident era of Dissenting agitation in which radicalism replaced caution, evangelicalism rejected rationalism, and the provinces jostled the metropolis. Smith, it was noted, had 'never manifested any strong repugnance to the principle of an Establishment', and Thomas Belsham, 'the patriarch of Unitarianism', had strenuously advocated established Churches.[164] The Unitarian secession was a stage in the loosening of traditions and associations which, in the next few years, was to lead political Dissent away from the Whigs and into more independent forms of organization.

Dissenting concern over church-rates in 1836 was occasioned not simply by Government postponement of the question but by reforms in the Church of England which, it was believed, might increase economic pressure on the Church and therefore encourage continuance of the rate. The Whigs thankfully accepted the example which Peel had set, and treated English Church reform much more gently than Irish. Their Church reform bills were directly founded on reports of the Ecclesiastical Commission, which Peel had initiated. Melbourne had continued the Commission with its 5 prelatical members and 3 of the laymen who had previously sat; the only change was that 5 Whig ministers replaced the 4 Conservatives. Archbishop Howley had agreed to continue his membership, on condition that Government recognized its duty to maintain the churches of the Establishment and that Church property would not be used for purposes now supposed to be covered by church-rates.[165] Two years later the question of this assurance was to cause conflict between Government and bishops.

But in the meantime there was comparative harmony. The Established Church Bill, introduced into the Commons in July 1836, was the first of

[162] *Eclectic Review*, op. cit. 26. See K. R. M. Short, 'London's General Body of Protestant Ministers: its disruption in 1836', *JEH* xxiv (1973), 388 ff.

[163] *Eclectic Review*, op. cit. 26.

[164] Ibid. 10. Belsham had died in 1829 and Smith in 1835.

[165] Correspondence of Melbourne and Howley, May 1835 (copies, Russell Papers, 1E, fos. 97–100, 102, 113–15, 143, 147–8).

three important statutes. The bill embodied the proposals of the Ecclesiastical Commission reports.[166] There was to be greater equality in episcopal incomes: all bishops were to receive £4,000 a year, except Canterbury, York, London, Durham, and Winchester, who were to receive more. It was intended to unite the bishopric of Bristol with Gloucester and St. Asaph with Bangor, and to transfer the two redundant prelacies to Ripon and Manchester, where they would more usefully serve large and benighted populations.[167] The junction of St. Asaph and Bangor never materialized, but this did not prevent the creation of a new see at Manchester in 1847. The see of Sodor and Man was also to unite with Carlisle on the next vacancy. The Ecclesiastical Commission was to be permanent and to have executive powers. Its recommendations could be carried out by Orders in Council, of which Parliament would be informed in an annual report.

Opposition to the bill was voiced from two contrasting quarters—a few (though by no means all) Conservative churchmen who thought that the powers and recommendations of the Commission were excessive, and many radicals who thought the Commission had not gone far enough in its proposals. The former opinion was voiced in the Commons by Sir Robert Inglis and in the Lords by the duke of Cumberland and Edward Grey, bishop of Hereford. Inglis, who had previously said that 'no such Commission ought ever to have been appointed', now stated that the bill 'subjugated the Church in its property and in its regulations to the control of the State' and that it 'changed the character of the Prelates of England from great proprietors to stipendiaries'. He would not admit that some bishoprics were richer than they should be, or that the archbishop of Canterbury had more than his duties, rank, or position required.[168] The opposition of radicals and Dissenters came in an endless stream. They said that the Commission was usurping the rightful authority of Parliament over the Church, that the bill should have abolished episcopal translations, non-residence and pluralities, lowered episcopal incomes further, raised low clerical incomes to a higher level, and removed the bishops from the House of Lords.[169] Joseph Hume and Joseph Brotherton said that the bill should have abolished church-rates, and Daniel Whittle Harvey wanted to see surplus Church of England revenues appropriated.[170] Edward Baines said that the archbishop of York's income would still be 217 times as great as that of most of his clergy,[171] and George Grote, the historian of ancient Greece and champion of the secret ballot, took a low view of archiepiscopal functions: '... was it possible to conceive any set of duties which could

[166] See Best, *Temporal Pillars*, 302-7.

[167] It was objected that Bristol had a dense population also; B. T. Bradfield, 'Sir Richard Vyvyan and Tory Politics, 1825-46' (unpubl. Univ. of London Ph.D. thesis, 1965), 186-7.

[168] Hansard, xxxii. 162; xxxv. 347; cf. Brose, *Church and Parliament*, 140.

[169] Hansard, xxxv. 27-35, 42-4, 349-50; Brose, 139.

[170] Hansard, xxxv. 36-7, 541, 543.   [171] Ibid. 538-9.

be more easily or tranquilly performed, or which were more exempt from all those difficulties that required labour, assiduity, and talent to surmount them, than those allotted to the Archbishop of Canterbury ?'[172]

But the opposition could only muster small minorities of 44 (mostly radicals) on two occasions against the bill. Russell did something to allay hostility by saying that Government intended to bring in a church-rate abolition bill next session,[173] and one or two radicals said that in spite of their feelings they did not wish to embarrass the Government. In the Lords the bill encountered little opposition. Archbishop Howley successfully moved an amendment to omit the requirement that the bishops of Welsh sees should have a knowledge of Welsh. This, he said, was an unnecessary restriction on the choice of bishops as all the Welsh clergy understood English.[174] The amendment doubtless sprang from a reasonable desire to appoint prelates from as wide a field as possible. But it was arguable that in view of the prevalence of Nonconformity in Wales, and its close association with the Welsh language as a defence against an anglicized Establishment, the deletion meant the loss of both a real and a symbolic means of making the Church more attractive in the Principality. A recent essay, written by an Anglican, had given the lack of Welsh-speaking bishops as one reason for the Church's unpopularity in Wales.[175] The amendment having been accepted on 4 August, the bill was passed the following day. It was the most important parliamentary victory for gradual Church reform, and it might already have been said that 'the Whigs had saved the church from the Radicals'.[176] The passage of this measure and of the Registration, Marriage, and English Tithe Bills in one parliamentary session was a notable success for the Whig (and Peelite) policy of reasonable concessions to those outside the Church, as well as for internal reform of the Church itself.

The 1837 session was less successful for the Government. The familiar counterpoint of Irish and Dissenting reform was resumed. But whereas in 1836 Dissenting reform had succeeded and Irish had not, both failed in 1837. In accordance with Russell's assurances the ministry tried again to settle church-rates. A committee of Cabinet recommended that the rate should be abolished. The churches should be maintained by pew rents and by higher returns from the leases of Church property, whose management should be in the hands of a special commission with 11 members. It was thought that this method would raise £250,000, the same amount which Althorp's ill-fated plan of 1834 had sought to obtain. Russell believed that such a measure was essential to defeat the Voluntary principle. Melbourne agreed, though he thought it would mean 'another desperate battle with the Church'.[177] Dissenting demands for a settlement were running strongly. A

[172] Ibid. 536.   [173] Ibid. 545.   [174] Ibid. 901–2.
[175] Johnes, *An Essay on the Causes which have produced Dissent* . . ., 51–2.
[176] Prest, *Russell*, 108.   [177] Ibid. 112–13.

meeting on 1 February, organized by the Church Rate Abolition Society, was attended by 419 delegates from Dissenting congregations. A deputation from the United Committee had seen Russell.[178] During the session petitions containing 674,719 signatures were presented in favour of abolition, including many from the new town councils. But Church defence was gaining in confidence, thanks to the progress of church-building and reform. Petitions against abolition, organized on the Church's behalf by a London committee, contained 330,123 signatures.[179] The Church reaction was to be the more effective in this episode.

Melbourne did his best to persuade the King that the Government plan was necessary for the prosperity of the established Church.[180] When the scheme was introduced on 3 March it was seen that, if Dissenters generally welcomed it, churchmen were against its whole conception.[181] The spectre of disestablishment was used by the bill's opponents to support their arguments, in Parliament and elsewhere. At a Church meeting in Liverpool on 9 March (in opposition to a Dissenting meeting), it was said that if the bill passed it would 'practically dissever the union between the Church and the State'.[182] The archbishop of Canterbury was particularly disturbed by the proposals, since in 1835 he and the other episcopal members had consented to remain on the Ecclesiastical Commission on the understanding that the State would continue to keep Anglican churches in repair. This condition seemed to have been violated by the new proposals. At a meeting at Lambeth Palace on 9 March, 15 prelates declared against the plan, and on the same evening there was an angry interchange between Howley, Blomfield, and Melbourne in the Lords.[183] A letter to Melbourne from most of the members of the Ecclesiastical Commission on 10 March objected to any general reorganization of the tenure of ecclesiastical property, especially for the purpose of relieving lay property from church-rates. It was also objected that the transfer of Church estate management to a commission would transgress 'the Principle . . . of leaving to the several Bishops the Property and the Management of their Estates, and to the several Chapters the Property and Management of the Estates belonging to them in their corporate capacity'. The letter concluded with a refusal to join in any further recommendations for Church reform while the church-rate measure was pending.[184]

---

[178] *Eclectic Review*, N.S. v (Jan.–June 1839), 28.

[179] Ibid. 29; Close, 'The General Elections of 1835 and 1837', 298.

[180] Melbourne to the King, 13 and 20 Feb. 1837 (Sanders (ed.), *Melbourne's Papers*, 327, 329–30).

[181] Hansard, xxxvi. 1207 ff.

[182] Picton, op. cit. i. 477–8. However, moderate counsels among churchmen discouraged inflammatory language and looked for means of compromise: Edward Copleston, bishop of Llandaff, to Sir Thomas Phillips, 14 Mar. 1837 (Copleston, *Memoir of Edward Copleston*, 162–4).

[183] *Annual Register*, lxxix (1837), 85–6; Gash, *Reaction*, 72–3; Holland's Pol. Jls., 2 Apr. 1837 (Holland House Papers, Add. MS. 51871, p. 1004).

[184] Ecclesiastical Commissioners to Melbourne (copy, Russell Papers, 2E, fos. 124–6).

With the Ecclesiastical Commission on strike, Church defence at a higher pitch in the country than for some years, and Nonconformists simultaneously clamouring for redress, the Government's difficulties in trying to pacify both Church and Dissent were graphically displayed. Well might Melbourne complain: 'On one side we have been accused of acting with the recklessness of a Wat Tyler or a Jack Straw; while, on the other side we have been accused of acting with a timidity and a hesitation that is perfectly contemptible.'[185] But the crisis was soon resolved. While Melbourne regained the archbishop's co-operation,[186] the church-rate scheme was undermined by its reception in the Commons. Even some Whig M.P.s who belonged to the established Church (either of England or Scotland) opposed, or abstained from voting on, a measure which seemed to threaten the Church of England as a State-supported Establishment. H. D. Goring, Whig M.P. for Shoreham, said that he was reluctantly compelled to oppose 'those Gentlemen I generally find myself able to support'.[187] After the House had discussed the scheme in Committee, the Government obtained a majority of only 23 on 15 March. A bill was pessimistically prepared and obtained a majority of only 5 (287 votes to 282) on its second reading in the early morning of 24 May.[188] On this occasion 'the shouts of the tories', noted Edward Baines, 'were overwhelming'.[189] The measure was then officially postponed until a Select Committee had inquired into the tenure of Church lands. But in fact the scheme was abandoned. It was a notable victory for the militant supporters of the established Church. Not until 1866 did a Government again support a church-rate abolition bill. Opposition to the rate continued, but militant Dissenting organization faded in the next few years.

Meanwhile the Irish reform programme had broken down. Given the composition and attitude of the Lords, ministers could only hope to get their Irish measures through on sufferance, and their projects floundered amidst inter-party bargaining. The brightest gleam for ministers in 1837 was the change of monarch and the young Queen's predilection for Lord Melbourne and his party. The Whigs now benefited from royal favour, the same archaic source which had helped their opponents in 1834–5. But royal favour only kept the Whigs in an increasingly false position, for it was not reflected by growing favour in the country.

The general election of 1837, held by constitutional provision on the death of a monarch, left the Whigs weaker than before. Even more than in 1835 religious issues dominated the election, and they sharply divided the two parties. Samuel Wilberforce regretfully determined to oppose the likeable Whig candidate for the Isle of Wight, as he thought 'the question is Church

---

[185] 21 Feb. 1837 in the Lords (Hansard, xxxvi. 767–9).
[186] Prest, 115.
[187] Hansard, xxxvi. 1261; *Annual Register*, lxxix (1837), 96, 98.
[188] Hansard, xxxviii. 1073–7 (division lists).　　　　　　　[189] Baines, op. cit. 194.

or no Church now'.[190] Conservative candidates seized the anti-Catholic opportunities offered by the Government's Irish Church Bills, and the pro-Church opportunities provided by the Government's church-rate measure.[191] The annual Maynooth grant was attacked. The Protestant Association, formed in 1835, issued an election address against 'baleful Popish ascendancy' over the Government;[192] and it is said that 'church rates clearly aroused stronger feelings among the electorate, in England and Wales generally, than any other issue of the election'.[193] There was little mention of disestablishment in this election, though 'Onesimus' of Chatham advocated it.[194] Dissenters, thankful for the Acts of 1836 and the Government's willingness to abolish church-rates, were generally enthusiastic in support of the Whigs. But they disparaged some radical candidates. The defeat of J. A. Roebuck at Bath was probably explained in part by his contempt for the Sabbatarianism of some of his Dissenting followers.[195] In Scotland the declared opposition of many Liberal candidates to Government grants for the Church of Scotland was believed to have won them Dissenting support and contributed to their success.[196] The elections brought Conservative gains and radical losses, but gains for Irish Whigs and Repealers. The Government had a depleted majority of about 22, which was wholly dependent on the continued support of the Irish Repealers.[197] Ministers saw Church issues as the main reason for their reverses. Melbourne asserted that 'the Church has been more active and more uniformly against us at the last than at any former general election'. He had been told of 'many Clergymen who were formerly with us but who now have gone against us'.[198] He thought that church-rates were primarily responsible. But Russell thought this question had not turned any Whigs out and had actually helped one Whig in, and it was believed that opposition to the new Poor Law had had more effect.[199]

VI. WHIGS AND THE CHURCHES, 1837–1841

The Whigs' difficulties were not eased by their losses in 1837, apart from the fact that the removal of some radicals was not an unmixed sorrow to them. Lord Ripon wondered how long they could go on 'with no other majority than the riff raff of the Irish Tail'.[200] Instead of adopting a bold policy which might have brought them eventual gains in the country

[190] Wilberforce to Sir Charles Anderson, 30 May and 10 Aug. 1837 (Wilberforce Papers, d. 25).
[191] Close, op. cit. 342–6.   [192] Ibid. 404.   [193] Ibid. 402–3.
[194] Andrews, 'Political Issues in the County of Kent', 168.
[195] Close, 371, 398–9.
[196] Montgomery, 'The Voluntary Controversy in the Church of Scotland', 198 f.
[197] Prest, Russell, 118; Close, 467; Gash, Sir Robert Peel, 195; Macintyre, The Liberator, 63.
[198] Melbourne to Holland, 22 Sept. 1837 (Holland House Papers, Add. MS. 51558).
[199] Prest, 118.
[200] Ripon to Graham, 11 Aug. 1837 (Graham Papers, microfilms, 111).

ministers looked instead to the dangers of their parliamentary weakness and became, for a time, extremely cautious. When a new Parliament met in November, 'Finality Jack' doused radical desires for franchise extension, shorter Parliaments, and the ballot. It was finality for Dissent and Irish appropriation too. On church-rates, he noted, 'we have proposed two Bills, one objected to by the Dissenters, the other by the Church. I do not think we are bound to revive the Bills, or propose another, till a better temper prevails.'[201] A church rate settlement was indefinitely postponed, and appropriation was given up. In 1838 a protracted parliamentary wrangle over the ministers' suggested Irish reforms resulted in the commutation of tithe to a rent charge and no appropriation.[202] It seemed that the tempestuous appropriation affair was dying unresolved. Henry Ward in the Commons, and Brougham in the Lords, were left to lament that 'appropriation should be given to the winds, as if the thing had never been talked of; as if it had never been the means of seating one ministry, and unseating another'.[203] But the last had not been heard of appropriation.

Limited reform of the Church of England, carefully purged of any collateral attempt to remove church-rates, progressed further. The Pluralities Bill, based on proposals of the Ecclesiastical Commissioners, passed after amendment in 1838.[204] The Act provided that two benefices could not be held concurrently if they were more than 10 miles apart, or if the population of one of them exceeded 3,000, or if their joint annual value exceeded £1,000. An exception was made for hard-working pluralists, if one of their benefices had a population of over 2,000 and an annual value of under £150, but a dispensation had to be obtained in such cases from the archbishop of Canterbury. No one holding two benefices could hold a third, or any cathedral preferment; and (with certain exceptions for archdeacons) preferments could not be held in more than one cathedral. In exceptional cases bishops might issue licences for non-residence. Clergy could not engage directly in trade, though they were allowed to have a financial interest in it, and could not farm more than 80 acres of land without the consent of their bishop.[205]

Before this bill was introduced, strong resistance had been made to the execution of one of the provisions of the Established Church Act of 1836— the suppression of the see of Sodor and Man upon the next vacancy and its amalgamation with Carlisle. Petitions against suppression came from Manxmen (with over three-quarters of their clergy), from the clergy of

---

[201] Russell to Melbourne, 13 Sept. 1837 (Russell Papers, 2F, fos. 113–15).
[202] Prest, 124–8.
[203] *Annual Register*, lxxx (1838), 138, 144.
[204] Hansard, xl. 722–4; xlii. 906 ff., 1161 ff.; xliii. 597 ff.; xliv. 380, 1015.
[205] *Annual Register*, lxxx (1838), 224 f. Non-resident incumbents diminished rapidly after the Act; curates serving non-residents dropped from 3,078 in 1838 to 955 in 1864; A. T. Hart, *The Curate's Lot* (London, 1970), 135.

several other dioceses, and from 'certain inhabitants of Birmingham'.[206] But in November 1837 leave had been refused to introduce a bill cancelling the scheme, and in December the archbishop of Canterbury and the bishop of London had defended the amalgamation in the Lords. Archbishop Howley said it would have been inconsistent with the Commissioners' duty to allow a see with only 45,000 people to continue, when the most populous see had two million.[207] But the Commissioners changed their minds, and in February 1838 a bill was before the Lords to reprieve the diocese. The archbishop now said that the continued existence of Sodor and Man was not a damaging infringement on the principles of the 1836 Act, and that he agreed with the bill.[208] On 16 June the third reading of the bill passed the Commons by a majority of 64, only 5 voting against and even Dissenters voting in favour.[209] In July a bill to abolish diocesan courts and to concentrate their jurisdiction in the Court of Arches was shelved by the Lords after a strong speech by Bishop Phillpotts.[210] Conservative churchmen were clearly gaining in confidence.

In 1839 the Government's education scheme caused severe conflict with the Church. In that year Ireland and Dissent were comparatively quiet, but the Government was embarrassed instead by the Chartist and anti-Corn Law movements and by colonial troubles. In May Melbourne resigned after the Government had obtained a majority of only 6 on its proposal to suspend the Jamaican constitution. At this point it would seem that the Whig Government, with semi-democratic logic, should have finished. The Conservatives had been continuing to make by-election gains since 1837, and, had they established themselves in office and dissolved Parliament, would most probably have won an election. But the fortuitous intervention of royal favour through the Bedchamber Crisis—a benefit which the aggressive Whigs of 1832 would neither have welcomed nor expected—bestowed on them a further two years in office. On returning they proceeded with their educational proposals, and encountered a Church reaction on the scale of 1837.

Educational extension absorbed much reforming attention, and was closely entwined with the Churches. Since 1833 the Government had contributed £20,000 a year to the two major educational societies, in proportion to the voluntary contributions which they raised. These two societies represented conflicting educational viewpoints. The British and Foreign Schools Society, supported by Dissenters and liberal Anglicans, provided a general and undenominational religious education, in keeping with the

---

[206] Samuel F. Wood to Newman, Apr. 1836; Mozley (ed.), *Letters of Newman*, ii. 189–90.
[207] Hansard, xxxix. 355–9, 1070 ff.
[208] Ibid. xli. 4–6.
[209] Ibid. xliii. 783–4. On this matter see E. C. Wilson, *An Island Bishop, 1762–1838: Memorials of William Ward, D.D., Bishop of Sodor and Mann, 1828–38* (London, 1931), 157–209.
[210] Hansard, xliv. 603–31.

religious pluralism which had developed in society.[211] The National Society, on the other hand, was strictly Anglican, and built schools where the liturgy and catechism of the Church of England were taught; its aims were supported by high churchmen like Joshua Watson and by conservative evangelical churchmen like the Rev. Hugh Stowell. The rival societies therefore reflected, in the matter of education, the battles being fought in other spheres between Church and Dissent, and between strict churchmen and latitudinarians. As Brougham was to say: 'The Church wished for education; but they wished to keep down the sects a little more. The Dissenters wished for education; but they wished to pull down the Church a little more.'[212] A third opinion, wanting compulsory unsectarian education in schools financed and controlled by the State, was seen in the Central Society of Education, formed in 1836. This was the view of Roebuck, Cobden, and the utilitarian radicals, but it had as yet made little progress.[213]

On 12 February 1839 Lord John Russell outlined in the Commons a plan to increase the Government contribution to £30,000 a year. To this proposal formidable appendages were added. State grants were to be paid according to local need rather than the size of voluntary contributions raised by the societies. They were also to be paid to 'reputable' schools outside the National and British societies: a strictly Nonconformist or even a Roman Catholic school might now receive Government money. But grants would be paid only if State inspection were accepted; and the inspectors would themselves be supervised by a new Government body, a Committee of the Privy Council (or 'Board of Education'). Clerics were deliberately excluded from the Committee, which was to consist of lay Privy Councillors who might be of any denomination. In addition, it was intended to establish a 'normal' school for teacher training and two model or 'demonstration' schools, one a boarding house for 450 children and the other a day school. In these schools a distinction would be made between 'general' unsectarian religious education, and 'special' denominational instruction received either from the permanent Anglican chaplain or from visiting Dissenting ministers.[214]

People of widely differing opinions were unhappy with the plan. To Voluntaries it was a step towards centralized control; to evangelical Anglicans and Wesleyans it was a dangerous encouragement to Roman Catholicism; to conservative churchmen a further move away from education under Church auspices; to high churchmen an unpalatable extension of undenominational education. Dissenters, although they disliked the move

---

[211] G. F. A. Best, 'The Religious Difficulties of National Education in England, 1800–70', *Cambridge Hist. Jl.* xii (1956), 161 ff.

[212] Hansard, l. 594 (26 Aug. 1839).

[213] S. E. Maltby, *Manchester and the Movement for National Elementary Education, 1800–70* (Manchester, 1918), 49–54.

[214] Hansard, xlv. 273 ff.; *Annual Register*, xl (1839), 140 ff.; F. Smith, *The Life and Work of Sir James Kay-Shuttleworth* (London, 1923), 79 ff.

towards State supervision and the apparent preference given to Anglican education in the projected normal school, found that in other respects their interests were encouraged, and (apart from Wesleyans) they gave the scheme guarded support. There was far more in the plan to worry supporters of the National Society. Fierce resistance came from conservative churchmen of differing religious views—from the evangelical Lord Ashley as well as Blomfield and Phillpotts. Lord Winchilsea, the veteran ultra, thought the plan was the most dangerous attack on Protestantism since the 1829 Relief Act.[215]

Church resistance was the greater because Anglican educational efforts had recently been advancing, providing a notable contribution to Church revival. The National Society had made greater headway than the British and Foreign Society. The latter obtained support from wealthy Nonconformist industrialists in large towns, but over the country as a whole the support of Anglican squires for the National Society was more decisive.[216] Of the £100,000 granted by the Government in the five years from 1833 the National Society obtained about £70,000.[217] In Lancashire in the same period the British Society obtained only £2,314 against the National Society's £17,000, though admittedly the British Society was weaker and the National Society stronger in Lancashire than elsewhere.[218] In 1838 and 1839 the formation of 24 diocesan and sub-diocesan Boards of Education, largely through the efforts of laymen such as Gladstone and Ashley, was a further testimony to Anglican zeal.[219] Such progress was not welcome to members of other denominations whom the Government wished to placate; and ministers told James Kay (later Kay-Shuttleworth), the first secretary of the new board, that they wished 'to prevent the growth of inordinate ecclesiastical pretensions'.[220] But churchmen were in no mood to see their efforts weakened and frustrated by State encouragement to other denominations. They had rebutted the church-rate scheme two years before, and hoped to dispatch this one in the same way. A large public meeting of the National Society on 28 May resolved that religious education was essential and should conform with Anglican doctrines. At a meeting in Leeds chaired by the bishop of Ripon, W. F. Hook, declared: 'we may . . . fairly assert that we have the education of the people in our hands; and why should it be taken away from us?'[221]

On 4 June Russell announced that, in response to many petitions against the scheme, the proposed normal and model schools would be abandoned.[222]

[215] Hansard, xlviii. 694.

[216] M. Sanderson, 'The National and British School Societies in Lancashire, 1803–39', in T. G. Cook (ed.), Local Studies and the History of Education (London, 1972), 15–16.

[217] Chadwick, i. 338.   [218] Sanderson, op. cit. 15.   [219] Gash, Reaction, 77–8.

[220] Quoted Chadwick, i. 340.   [221] Stephens, Hook, i. 453.

[222] Hansard, xlvii. 1378–81. A figure of 3,000 hostile petitions is given by Soloway, Prelates and People, 400. See list of hostile petitions in Journals of the House of Commons, xciv (1839 session), index.

But the matter of supervision by a secular Board remained. The prospect of unlimited powers over curricula being wielded by this Committee was extremely alarming, even if only imaginary. On the question of going into a Committee of Supply to obtain the grant on 14 June, Lord Stanley moved an amendment that the Queen be asked to rescind the Order in Council establishing the committee, and waxed theological in his theme. Since an essential part of education was spiritual, it should not be removed from clerical control and handed over to a committee of laymen. Education could not be considered apart from questions of faith and doctrine:

For instance, the great scheme of redemption, the doctrine of justification by faith, the efficacy of infant baptism, the solemn mystery of the holy eucharist; . . . one and all of these they must consent to concede at once, and to put aside, as matters not to be treated of in public education, if they insisted on adopting the Government scheme of instruction.[223]

Lord Ashley, supporting the high church Stanley, could not tolerate the prospect of all decisions on education, including its doctrinal content, being taken by a lay committee. The plan, he believed, was 'hostile to revealed religion itself'. He asked how it was possible to divide religion into 'general' and 'special'—a separation which he apparently thought was still threatened by the scheme. Such a division he had never heard of; it rested with 'the crude and . . . presumptuous analogies of the committee of the privy council'.[224] Sir James Graham invoked the disestablishment spectre by saying that the equal endowment of all religious creeds, starting with education and possibly leading to other fields, would destroy 'a paramount State religion'.[225] Peel said that the Church of England was 'properly intrusted with the religious education of the community'.[226] Supporters of the scheme countered these arguments with those of latitudinarian religion and social necessity. Russell denied that religious instruction 'was confined to the distinctions between different bodies and sects of Christians'.[227] The lack of elementary education, as Thomas Wyse put it, produced irreligion, crime, and expensive ignorance:

. . . it was stated in the most able agricultural reports, that by the injudicious use of lime many thousand acres in many parts of the kingdom have been reduced to a state of almost total infertility. Again, with respect to manure, [it was complained that there had not been found] anything like system in the mechanical arrangement of the component parts of farm-yard mixings, which [were] generally found put together, without any regard to rule.[228]

[223] Hansard, xlviii. 240–1; *Annual Register*, xl (1839), 143.
[224] *Annual Register*, op. cit. 146–7; a similar view was expressed by Gladstone (ibid. 155–6). The debate is printed at greater length in Hansard, xlviii. 229 ff.
[225] *Annual Register*, xl (1839), 157.   [226] Ibid. 160.
[227] Ibid. 158.   [228] Ibid. 149–50.

As had happened over church-rates in 1837, some Anglican supporters of the Government were unable to agree with the scheme.[229] The majorities obtained by Government were even narrower than on that occasion. There was a majority of only 5 for going into a Committee of Supply on 19 June, and of only 2 for the increased education grant on 24 June. But Peel announced that the Opposition would not divide the Commons again, as all except 24 members had voted in one or other of these divisions.[230] The amount of money concerned did not require the consent of the Lords, so there was no question of rejection by them. But the peers showed their opinion by carrying on 5 July (by a majority of 229 to 118) an address to the Crown containing a set of resolutions against the plan, moved by Archbishop Howley and supported by Blomfield and Phillpotts and the duke of Wellington. Phillpotts said that 'the broader question of establishment lay at the root of the argument', and only 3 bishops—Maltby of Durham, Otter of Chichester, and Stanley of Norwich, all recent Whig appointments—supported the Government.[231] The Queen replied that while she could not accede to the protest, she trusted that the funds would be distributed 'with a faithful attention to the security of the Established Church'.[232] But on conscientious grounds most Anglican clergy refused to apply for State money which now brought compulsory inspection with it. Further negotiation was needed before conservative churchmen could be brought to entertain the scheme. On 15 July 1840 it was agreed that inspectors of National Society schools were to send reports to the bishop of the diocese and the archbishop of the province as well as to the Education Committee of the Council; and that the archbishop would have power to veto the appointment of these inspectors, and to remove them from office. The old method was revived of allocating grants in proportion to private contributions, a system which favoured the Church.[233] Roman Catholic schools made no applications for grants, so their admission to the scheme was purely academic. After the 'concordat' the National Society renewed its applications for State grants, but not all its members had been brought to agree with the modified system. Joshua Watson resigned as treasurer of the Society.

While the result was not complete victory for conservative churchmen, it was far from defeat. So much had been conceded to the Church that Nonconformists were dissatisfied, and believed that inspectors who were partially under the Church's control might destroy the independence of British and Foreign Society schools. The British Society demanded equal rights with the Church in the appointment of inspectors, and this they were to obtain in 1843.[234] Meanwhile the outcome of the education dispute had

[229] Ibid. (Sir George Staunton, M.P. for Portsmouth).
[230] Ibid. 162.
[231] Debate summarized in Soloway, op. cit. 401 ff.
[232] *Annual Register*, xl (1839), 163–71. [233] Smith, *Kay-Shuttleworth*, 95–6, 98–100.
[234] Ibid. 101.

joined the retention of church-rates and the abandonment of appropriation in demonstrating the increasing strength of both Conservatism and the Church.

The Opposition cast around for further religious issues to embarrass the Government. In December 1839 Graham suggested reasons for a motion of no confidence as soon as Parliament reassembled. Such a reason might be the ministers' omission to state, in the Speech from the Throne, that the Queen's fiancé was a Protestant. This assurance had already been omitted from the announcement of the betrothal to the Privy Council. It was 'highly criminal', Graham declared; it had 'raised unfounded suspicions in the public mind with regard to the Creed of the Prince, and an undue prejudice against him'; it was 'an act of time-serving Party subserviency to O'Connell and the Papists . . . in defiance of the Protestant feelings of Great Britain'.[235] When Parliament met, the Conservatives—perhaps seeking revenge for their own snub at royal hands in the Bedchamber Crisis—duly scored some victories with radical help at the expense of the unfortunate prince, who was more Protestant than some of the carping politicians. But the Government proved unexpectedly resilient: it won 6 by-elections early in the session, and the no-confidence motion on 31 January was lost by 21 votes, a surprisingly large majority for ministers.

In the remainder of the 1840 session there was a comparative lull in parliamentary ecclesiastical controversy. The ministers pleased many churchmen by extending the Ecclesiastical Commission to include all the bishops (besides 3 deans, 6 judges, and 6 other laymen), and by providing that members would no longer be removable at the will of the Government. The complaint thenceforth was not that the Commission was too restricted but that it was too vast.[236] The extension was part of the Ecclesiastical Duties and Revenues Act, the third major measure of Church reform. The main object of this measure was to effect the most radical proposals of the Ecclesiastical Commission by abolishing all non-resident prebends and all sinecure rectories attached to cathedrals, and resident canonries above the number of 4 to each cathedral. Exceptions were allowed for Westminster Abbey, Christ Church at Oxford, Durham, Ely, and Canterbury cathedrals, each of which might have 6 resident canons, and for Winchester and Exeter cathedrals which might each have 5. The money saved was to augment poor livings and create new parishes. The bill passed with little debate; it was supported by Peel but resisted by Inglis in the Commons and Phillpotts in the Lords.[237] The defence of existing cathedral offices by Conservatives (and Sydney Smith) on the grounds that such posts rewarded gentle birth, superior learning, or pastoral merit was thus defeated. But the defenders could take comfort in the fact that, since the Commissioners respected the life interests

---

[235] Graham to Peel, Dec. 1839 (Peel Papers, 40318, fos. 164–5).
[236] Chadwick, i. 138–9.   [237] Hansard, liii. 590–619.

of existing cathedral clergy and adopted other delaying methods, the actual reduction of preferments was a gradual process.

On 30 June 1840 Church confidence was somewhat encouraged by Inglis's failure by only 19 votes to carry a motion for a parliamentary grant to build churches. The motion, which challenged the Government's policy of financial neutrality, was opposed by Dissenters. A public meeting in support of a petition against the scheme had been held by Dissenters in the Freemasons' Hall the previous March, and had been chaired by the duke of Sussex, a long-standing royal sympathizer with religious equality. In the parliamentary debate Edward Baines argued, somewhat irrelevantly in the eyes of conservative Anglicans, that the statistics of church accommodation quoted by Inglis did not include the vast amount provided by Dissenting denominations.[238] The question of church-rate relief, revived by celebrated cases of imprisonment and by numerous petitions, was raised twice in the session by private members but without success. In February Thomas Slingsby Duncombe was refused leave, by a majority of 55, to bring in a bill permitting the exemption of Dissenters from the rate. The Government opposed the motion, though Russell made an offer, duly spurned as an inadequate side-issue, to transfer cases of non-payment of the rate from the ecclesiastical to the civil courts.[239] In July Sir John Easthope also moved for leave to introduce a bill to exempt Dissenters from payment; but his motion had to be dropped on the technical ground that a similar one had already been negatived in the same session.[240] Altogether it was a successful session for Church defence, though ultra-conservative churchmen disliked cathedral reform and the allocation of the proceeds of the Canadian clergy reserves to the use of Catholics as well as Protestants.[241]

In May 1841 Easthope was again unfortunate in his design. Moving now for leave to introduce a bill abolishing the rate, he withdrew the motion after objections that he was interrupting the marathon debate of eighteen nights' length on the sugar duties. He was defeated a fortnight later, seeking to substitute adequate yields from pew-rents for the rate, though he had Government support.[242] Economic issues predominated in the Melbourne Government's final session. A string of budget deficits had caused ministers to seek greater revenue from increased consumption, and for this reason to lower protective duties on imported sugar, timber, and corn. The Government was defeated on the sugar duties on 18 May, and on 4 June Peel won a motion of no confidence, in a very full division, by 312 votes to 311. On 7 June the dissolution of Parliament was announced, to take place as soon as necessary business was completed. Three days before, the House of Lords

[238] Hansard, lv. 342 ff.
[239] Hansard, lii. 88–117. For the anti-church-rate agitation in the country, see below, p. 102 ff.
[240] Hansard, lv. 545–53 (7 July 1840).   [241] See Prest, *Russell*, 161.
[242] Hansard, lviii. 185–8, 765–99 (11 and 25 May 1841).

had rounded off a decade of resistance by rejecting a bill allowing Jews to take office in municipal corporations—a measure which had easily passed the Commons against the strong opposition of Inglis and Gladstone.[243] If ultras regretted the Repeal Act of 1828, they were doing their best to maintain its declaration 'on the true faith of a Christian'.

VII. THE 1841 ELECTION

The Free Trade issues which had recently absorbed parliamentary attention, and the persistent Poor Law dispute, dominated the general election of June and July 1841. But ecclesiastical disputes could scarcely fail to find a place in propaganda during the 1841 election. The addresses of Conservative candidates made brief references to the necessity for maintaining the union of Church and State. Sir Edmund Filmer, who was returned unopposed for West Kent, said at his nomination on Penenden Heath that this union must continue, since no Government could exist without the blessing of God; his colleague thought it necessary to uphold 'every right and privilege which [the Church] has by the law of the land'.[244] The Conservative candidates for Lambeth linked Church defence with the desire 'to preserve and cherish the institutions which have given to Britain a station in wealth, in arms, in liberty, and in moral character, the highest that has ever been occupied by any people upon earth'.[245] Among specific matters of dispute the extension of education was approved by the Conservative committee in the City of London provided it was on Church principles alone; and Lord Alford, who was returned unopposed for Bedfordshire, said he was sure that Peel would encourage Church extension and Church education.[246]

Rivals of the Establishment were the objects of attack, especially Catholics. Colonel Scarlett, Conservative candidate for Guildford, was applauded for saying that 'he could not but look upon the union of the Protestant Dissenters with the Roman Catholics to attack the Protestant Church as most unholy'.[247] Sir Francis Burdett, a new recruit to Conservatism who had fought long and valiantly for Catholic emancipation as a renowned radical, now denounced the threat of Papists to the constitution and said it must be met by 'a direct and determined opposition'.[248] At Liverpool the radical candidate, Sir Joshua Walmsley, was blamed for presiding at a society meeting for the protection of Papists; and at Westminster the proposer of a Conservative candidate said that, unless a great Protestant party was formed, 'in a few short years it would be too late to roll back the tide of Romanism and Popery'.[249] A letter to *The Times* said that candidates should be questioned particularly on their attitude to Catholicism. They should be asked whether

[243] Ibid. lvi. 504–7; lvii. 84–100, 754–68; lviii. 1048–9, 1448–57.
[244] *The Times*, 7 July 1841, p. 2; 12 June 1841, p. 10.
[245] Ibid. 28 June 1841, p. 3.   [246] Ibid. 16 June 1841, p. 1; 8 July 1841, p. 2.
[247] Ibid. 30 June 1841, p. 4.   [248] Ibid. 10 July 1841, p. 3 (North Wiltshire).
[249] Ibid. 14 June 1841, p. 4; 30 June 1841, p. 3.

they were prepared 'to lop off the legs and arms of the modern "Dragon",
by opposing the money grants to Maynooth College, as well as every bill
friendly to Popery and inimical to the national church . . . and to vote for
the entire repeal or effectual amendment of the Romish Relief Act'.[250]
The first annual meeting of the Protestant Operative Association, which
had been formed 18 months before, was held in Exeter Hall on 16 June with
Lord Kenyon in the chair. One speaker hoped that No Popery would be
'rung in the ears of every candidate at the ensuing election'; and the Rev.
Hugh McNeile, a ubiquitous attender at such meetings, said that Protestant
voters must unite in order to turn out the Whigs, who had defiled themselves
by allying with O'Connell, had endangered the Protestant religion of the
country, and were now seeking to delude the populace with the cry of 'cheap
bread'.[251] This society's parent body, the Protestant Association, issued a
handbill addressed to the electors which posed the voter's choice between
the 'sound Protestant principles of our forefathers' and 'the new system of
modern Liberalism, under which truth and error are to be alike sanctioned
and alike disregarded'. Because of the Government's slim majority, the 41
Catholics returned to Parliament in 1837 had been able to decide nearly
every division in the Commons. Papists, moreover, had used their power to
gain several offices. Four had become Privy Councillors, three had become
judges in Ireland, and others had become Treasurer of the Household, a
Lord of the Treasury, Irish Solicitor-General, Vice-President of the Board
of Trade, and Secretary to the Admiralty. Electors were not asked to vote
for a particular party, but were urged to scrutinize individual candidates
and not to support any one who 'directly or indirectly favours Popery or
Infidelity'.[252] Such exhortation may have been assisted by the dislike of
Irish immigrants which showed itself during the election period. Disputes
between English and Irish labourers were reported at Stalybridge in north
Cheshire.[253] At Liverpool anti-Catholic feeling was gratified by electoral
success. Conservative candidates won the two parliamentary seats, and at
the municipal elections in the following November the Liberals were
ousted: 13 out of 16 wards returned Conservatives. The Conservatives
controlled the city council for the next fifty years.[254]

The natural reply of most English Catholics was to maintain their Liberal
allegiance. But they were not unanimous. Though most of the Catholic
landowners were Whig, the *Tablet* (founded in 1840) was very annoyed that
a Catholic Liberal candidate in south Lancashire was not supported by a
certain Catholic landowner, who asked his tenants to vote against him.
Frederick Lucas, the impassioned editor of this paper, a former Quaker and
a cousin of John Bright, declared the offending gentleman to be 'a man of

[250] Ibid. 12 June 1841, p. 8.
[252] Copy of handbill in British Library.
[254] Picton, *Memorials of Liverpool*, i. 494–5.

[251] Ibid. 17 June 1841, p. 5.
[253] *The Times*, 26 June 1841, p. 3.

large property, of Heaven knows how much religion, endowed, his friends say, with a plentiful lack of understanding, and whose principal ambition it is, we believe, to purchase by any amount of servility the patronage and notice of his Protestant neighbours'.[255]

In this election Dissenting ministers generally voted Liberal, in contrast to the Conservative voting of most Anglican clergy.[256] But there was evidence of growing Dissenting dissatisfaction with the Whigs, stirred by the intensity of the church-rate dispute and the Government's failure, on account of the intractability of the problem, to propose any further solution after 1837.[257] The militant tone of the *Eclectic Review* had swelled since that year, when Dr. Thomas Price, a Baptist minister, had become editor. This periodical now openly and vehemently demanded disestablishment. In January 1839 it had urged that the apathy and restrictions of existing Dissenting associations called for the formation of an effective new body, and had supported a proposed 'general union for the promotion of religious equality'.[258] The Religious Freedom Society had indeed been formed in that year, and advocated disestablishment. In 1841, therefore, the alliance of Whigs and Dissent was less secure than it had been in the 1837 election. A member of a committee set up by the West Riding Association of Baptist Churches complained of the injury inflicted by 'the neglect and . . . the occasional contempt, which [the Whig administration] have lately deemed themselves justified in showing towards the claims of the Dissenters', and warned that 'Baptists throughout the West Riding would only vote at the coming election for candidates sympathetic to Dissenting claims'.[259] Resolutions carried at the annual meeting of this association, held at Sheffield a month before the elections, recommended that candidates should be closely questioned whether they would vote to abolish church-rates, support bills to prevent the imprisonment of Dissenters by ecclesiastical courts for non-payment of the rate, and oppose 'all measures for Church Extension in England, in Scotland, in Ireland, or in the colonies'.[260] The *Patriot* declared that Dissenters should strive to return their own members.[261]

But in the absence of lengthy preparation and widespread organization these sentiments bore little fruit. Little was heard of Dissenting grievances in the elections, although a Whig minister (F. T. Baring, Chancellor of the

[255] B. Ward, *The Sequel to Catholic Emancipation, 1830-50* (2 vols., London, 1915), ii. 34-7.
[256] For examples of these different voting tendencies see Vincent, *Pollbooks*, 84, 128, 134, 142, 148, 162, 164, 172, 192.
[257] *Eclectic Review*, N.S. ix (Jan.-June 1841), 101-14 (article on 'Nonconformist Prisoners and Nonconformist Duties').
[258] Ibid. v (Jan.-June 1839), 34-7.
[259] Rev. J. E. Giles to Lord Morpeth, Whig M.P. for the constituency (Ram, 'The Political Activities of Dissenters in the East and West Ridings of Yorkshire', 164-5).
[260] 4 June 1841 (Fitzwilliam Papers (Sheffield City Library), G 11).
[261] B. J. Mason, 'The Rise of Combative Dissent, 1832-59' (unpubl. Univ. of Southampton M.A. thesis 1958), 102.

Exchequer, standing for Portsmouth) as well as some other Liberal candidates declared for the abolition of church-rates.[262] In a general election, especially one in which a Liberal ministry was clearly at stake, other interests of Dissenting voters were engaged as well as purely ecclesiastical ones; and it was doubtful whether even the latter could be served by withholding support from the Whigs and thereby assisting a Conservative victory. Peel's references on the Tamworth hustings to his previous support for religious liberty contained no promises for the future.[263] The Conservative majority of 78[264] undoubtedly owed something to defence of the established Church. But this was not mentioned by the *Eclectic Review* among its reasons for the Whig defeat. These were loss of confidence in a ministry which had failed to abolish church-rates; the effectiveness of Tory registration efforts and Tory corruption, which was unchecked by needful electoral reforms such as the ballot; opposition to Free Trade by the aristocracy and the delusion of the workers that cheap bread would mean low wages; and Chartist support for the Conservatives in opposing the Poor Law.[265] The Whigs, said this periodical, had only themselves to blame for their losses, and their defeat might persuade them to be firmer in the future.[266] Thus a leading organ of militant Dissent still looked nostalgically to union with the Whigs. The threatened independent line had not as yet materialized. The powerful Voluntary organization of 1844 was caused by reaction to the policies of a Conservative Government.

When Parliament reassembled the Whigs were defeated on amendments to the address. On 30 August the resignation of the ministry was announced. Peel took office at the head of a new Government. The most intriguing question of the time was how long he would succeed in maintaining the unity which had shored up his party in Opposition. Among the elements in this question ecclesiastical problems, now complicated by strong and varied reactions to the policies and tendencies of the thirties, were not the least disturbing.

[262] *The Times*, 29 June 1841, pp. 2, 4; 10 June, p. 6.
[263] Ibid. 29 June 1841, p. 2.
[264] *Eclectic Review*, N.S. x (July–Dec. 1841), 226; B. Kemp, 'The General Election of 1841', *History*, xxxvii (1952), 150.
[265] N.S. x (July–Dec. 1841), 222–6; cf. Kemp, 151–2, 155–6.
[266] *Eclectic Review*, N.S. x (July–Dec. 1841), 223, 484.

CHAPTER III

Reactions to Reform: Tractarians, Ultra-Protestants, and Voluntaries

THE GOVERNMENTS of the 1830s had adopted liberal but Erastian policies in response to conflicting ecclesiastical pressures. In pursuing this course of compromise, whether from conviction or through the demands of quotidian supervision, they pleased latitudinarians but collided with ideals based on different spiritual conceptions. Traditional high churchmen and Tractarians objected to the erosion of their ideal of an Establishment, caused by the concessions made by an apostate Parliament and Government, and by the control over the Church exercised by these increasingly alien bodies. Evangelicals in the Establishment particularly disliked the concessions made to Catholicism, and in their increasingly Erastian outlook opposed also the claims of Protestant Dissenters with whom they sympathized theologically. The Voluntaries, in contrast, believed that the removal of ecclesiastical privileges should go further and extend to the complete abolition of established Churches. These forms of reaction gathered strength in the 1830s in opposition either to the excess of reform or its inadequacy, depending on differing ecclesiastical viewpoints.

I. THE OXFORD MOVEMENT AND THE STATE

The Tractarians helped to breathe life into dry bones. They added spiritual depth, evangelical ardour, and poetic romanticism to the old high church tradition. Old high churchmen opposed the reforms of the 1830s with a firm defence of the Establishment, expressing opinions which the Tractarians were at first to develop and intensify and later to question. The arguments of politicians against religious concessions were constitutional, Erastian, and, in appropriate cases, Protestant affirmations of the necessity to maintain the ascendancy of the Establishment.[1] The theological content was superficial or absent altogether. To a religious enthusiast, whether high churchman or evangelical, such arguments might appear to take a religious view of Government

---

[1] e.g. Speech of Sir Richard Vyvyan defending the Church of Ireland, 3 Apr. 1835 (Hansard, xxvii. 784–5); speeches of Henry Goulburn, Sir Robert Inglis, the earl of Winchilsea, and the archbishop of Canterbury defending University Tests (ibid. xxii. 590–2, 683–90; xxiii, 360–7; xxix. 514–20); 4th duke of Newcastle, *Thoughts in Times Past tested by subsequent Events* (London, 1837).

and society without justifying such an outlook. They might seem to affirm the end-product of religious conviction without displaying its formation and sustenance by means of an intermediate divine connection, whether attained through faith alone or through sacramental works. They seemed, for example, to vindicate the ascendancy of the Church of England without mentioning the apostolical succession. Tractarianism ensured that the high-church conception of these matters was sustained and deepened, and made the question of Church defence subordinate to theological conviction. As it was a clerical and university movement, however, Tractarianism had little influence in politics, except through a small number of outstanding politicians of Tractarian views.

The Oxford movement began in 1833 but owed much to earlier influences. Relics of seventeenth-century high churchmanship still existed, especially in the episcopal Church in the north of Scotland.[2] The Hackney Phalanx had initiated a notable high-church revival, though ardent Tractarians regarded it as somewhat desiccated and in need of divine afflatus. Non-juring traditions were strong in the families of Keble and Froude and were thus directly linked with the Oxford movement. Evangelicalism gave an example of intense piety and enthusiasm, even of puritanism, which was to influence the Tractarians and distinguish them from their high-church predecessors. Sacramentalism was not necessarily rejected by early evangelicals. The concept of the Real Presence in communion had imbued the hymns of Charles Wesley, who was himself of a high-church family and influenced by seventeenth-century sacramentalism. Amongst later evangelicals, however, such beliefs were not sustained. Several prominent Tractarians, including Newman and Manning, came from an evangelical background, and the original imprint was by no means erased by their later proclivities. Romantic influences can be discerned in Tractarianism, as also in evangelicalism. Both movements were in revolt against the eighteenth century. Both rejected utilitarianism and German rational speculation, and sought spiritual depth and other worldly experience.[3] Keble may be described as a more religious Wordsworth. His celebrated collection of poems *The Christian Year*, a progenitor of Tractarian spirituality, was published in 1827 and was avidly read for many years by high churchmen (and evangelicals). Keble showed a Wordsworthian appreciation of nature but explicitly found in all its manifestations the expression of divine love.[4]

But literary efforts were not so effective as acts of Government in driving high churchmen to re-examine their theological beliefs and ecclesiastical standpoints. High churchmen were troubled by the gathering clouds of

[2] W. Perry, *The Oxford Movement in Scotland* (Cambridge, 1933), 37–8.

[3] O. Chadwick, *The Mind of the Oxford Movement* (London, 1960), 26 ff.; Y. Brilioth, *Three Lectures on Evangelicalism and the Oxford Movement . . .* (London, 1934), 56–76.

[4] J. Keble, *The Christian Year: Thoughts in Verse for the Sundays and Holydays throughout the Year* (2 vols. in one, Oxford, 1827); Chadwick, *Victorian Church*, i. 67–8.

reform and indifference before their great outpouring in 1829. Keble wrote in January 1827: 'To myself the present situation of the country is quite a mystery, and the conduct of the King in particular, past explanation . . . Nor has there been any time in my memory when the Church of England, as an establishment, seemed in so much jeopardy.'[5] High churchmen still retained their allegiance to Protestantism, and the repeal of the Test and Corporation Acts in 1828 alarmed them far less than the relief of Catholics in 1829. The former might be viewed as a means of dividing the liberals and defending Protestantism by helping to unite its votaries. Keble, Newman, and Froude were opposed to Peel on Catholic emancipation at the Oxford University by-election in February 1829. 'Two years back', wrote Newman in March 1831, 'the State deserted [the Church].'[6] The deluge was thus firmly dated in 1829. The State's indifference had then been revealed. Future enthusiastic converts to Rome began by rejecting Catholic emancipation. But Catholic relief, once carried, helped high churchmen to loosen their Protestantism. Keble, as early as March 1829, before the Relief Bill had passed, saw Catholics as potential allies against liberalism: 'they must perceive that not their church, but no church, would take the place of ours in the case of a revolution'.[7] Conditions after 1829 thus became more propitious for the expression of high churchmanship, and seemed also more pressing. The change of Government and the development of liberal policy hardened the tendencies of a few minds into a movement.

To high churchmen, Whigs were even less trustworthy than Tories. The Whig Reform Bill promised to establish a Parliament still more alienated from the Church. In 1833 R. H. Froude penned some 'Remarks on State interference in matters spiritual', in which he noted that in the newly assembled Parliament there was little trace of a Lay Synod of the Church of England—the character which, according to Hooker, Parliament should bear. He now saw the constitutional changes of the last five years as an ecclesiastical revolution. The combined effect of the measures of 1828, 1829, and 1832 had been 'to cancel the conditions on which [the House of Commons] has been allowed to interfere in matters spiritual'. He saw the Anglican situation as comparable to that of French Catholics, equally oppressed by a secular State; the actions of Lamennais and the Ultramontanes in defence of their Church should be emulated.[8] Newman too had been affected by recent French developments. The Revolution of 1830 had shocked him, for he 'held that it was unchristian for nations to cast off

[5] Keble to A. P. Perceval, 29 Jan. 1827 (quoted Marshall, 'The Theology of Church and State', 375).

[6] Newman to J. W. Bowden, 13 Mar. 1831 (Mozley (ed.), *Letters of Newman*, i. 237).

[7] Quoted R. H. Greenfield, 'The Attitude of the Tractarians to the Roman Catholic Church, 1833–50' (unpubl. Univ. of Oxford D.Phil. thesis 1956), 45.

[8] *Remains*, iii. 185, 193–4, 198–200, 207. See W. G. Roe, *Lamennais and England* (London, 1966), 93 ff.

their governors, and, much more, sovereigns who had the divine right of inheritance'.[9] When engaged on his work on the Arians of the fourth century (published in 1833), he sadly compared the apathy and heterodoxy of the moment with the single-mindedness of the early Church. He later described his feelings in a passage which illuminates the movement's impetus:

With the Establishment thus divided and threatened, thus ignorant of its true strength, I compared that fresh vigorous Power of which I was reading in the first centuries . . . her triumphant zeal on behalf of that Primeval Mystery . . . The self-conquest of her Ascetics, the patience of her Martyrs, the irresistible determination of her Bishops, the joyous swing of her advance, both exalted and abashed me. I said to myself, 'Look on this picture and on that'; I felt affection for my own Church, but not tenderness; I felt dismay at her prospects, anger and scorn at her do-nothing perplexity. I thought that if Liberalism once got a footing within her, it was sure of the victory in the event. I saw that Reformation principles were powerless to rescue her. As to leaving her, the thought never crossed my imagination . . .[10]

Soon came the Irish Church Temporalities Act to deepen his gloom. Zealous Church defenders could not ignore a measure which dealt with episcopal sees 'as if they were so many nine-pins to be knocked prostrate for amusement'.[11] The bill's impact reached out to Newman on his Mediterranean journey. This proof of ministerial policy enraged him: 'Well done! my blind premier, confiscate and rob, till, like Samson, you pull down the political structure on your own head!'[12] On his return home things seemed no better, for amongst the vast pile of pamphlets awaiting him was Arnold's *Principles of Church Reform*.[13] Phillpotts's Primary Visitation Charge at Exeter in August 1833 lamented, in language resembling Newman's own, 'the gloom and darkness which hang over every institution which we have been wont to regard with pride, with affection, or with reverence'.[14] Keble, to whom Phillpotts had already unsuccessfully offered a living and whom Newman hoped would prove a second St. Ambrose,[15] preached an assize sermon on 'national apostasy' on 14 July, the anniversary of the taking of the Bastille. The sermon was against the Irish Church Bill and the wider dangers which it represented. The discourse was not original or constructive enough to be a Tractarian manifesto, but it announced concern and invited

[9] *Apologia pro Vita sua*, ed. M. J. Svaglic (Oxford, 1967), 39.
[10] Ibid. 40.
[11] W. P. Palmer, *A Narrative of Events connected with the Publication of Tracts for the Times* (London, 1883), 44–5.
[12] Newman to his mother, 28 Feb. 1833 (Mozley (ed.), 353).
[13] T. Mozley, *Reminiscences chiefly of Oriel College and the Oxford Movement* (2nd edn., 2 vols., London, 1882), ii. 51.
[14] G. C. B. Davies, *Henry Phillpotts, Bishop of Exeter* (London, 1954), 147.
[15] Phillpotts to Keble, offering the living of Paignton, 1 Aug. 1832 (Keble Papers, D 118; see also DNB); Newman to his sister, 20 Mar. 1833 (Mozley (ed.), i. 377).

action. The concern was with the general religious indifference of the age: 'Under the guise of charity and toleration we are come almost to this pass; that no difference, in matters of faith, is to disqualify for our approbation and confidence, whether in public or domestic life.'[16] Before the sermon was published the offending bill had passed. An introduction to the publication stated that the worst fears anticipated in the sermon had been realized, that it now appeared that 'the Apostolical Church in this realm is henceforth only to stand, in the eye of the State, as one sect among many'.[17]

Action soon followed in the path of concern. H. J. Rose, R. H. Froude, William Patrick Palmer, and A. P. Perceval met at Hadleigh from 25 to 29 July to discuss policy. Their great object was 'to *familiarize* men with sound and strong principles'.[18] Keble and Newman strongly supported the initiative. The bishops being considered too Erastian and indecisive, lesser clergy felt themselves justified in acting independently. Newman lamented that Archbishop Howley, though a man of the highest principle who would willingly die a martyr, had not 'the little finger of Athanasius', and lacked 'the boldness of the old Catholic prelates'.[19] It was intended to form societies to defend the Church liturgy and primitive doctrines such as apostolical succession, and to issue tracts with the same objects.[20] The founding of societies seems to have begun hopefully—Newman said at the end of August that they were already beginning in six southern counties.[21] Little, however, was done to realize the avowed but lukewarm desire of Newman, Froude, and Keble to make a wide popular appeal, calling on lower social strata to fight middle-class liberals and Dissenters. Newman wrote that just as the people had in former ages been the fulcrum of the Church's power, so they might be again: 'Therefore, expect ... to see us all cautious, long-headed, unfeeling, unflinching Radicals.'[22] But these terms show that the prospect was hardly serious. The Tractarians did not become Socialists or campaigners for universal suffrage—though some of their later followers did—and their movement, as it developed, became the reverse of popular in the face of popular Protestantism.

There were, however, organized efforts to obtain avowals by clergy and laity of their support for Church principles. In February 1834 one address

[16] J. Keble, *National Apostasy considered* (Oxford, 1833), 15.

[17] Ibid. iii.

[18] Rose to Keble, 19 Aug. 1833 (Keble Papers, E 125).

[19] Newman to J. W. Bowden, 31 Aug. 1833 (Mozley (ed.), i. 448). Cf. D. Bowen, *The Idea of the Victorian Church* (Montreal, 1968), 41 f.

[20] Mozley (ed.), i. 448; J. T. Coleridge, *A Memoir of the Rev. John Keble* (3rd edn., 2 vols., London, 1870), i. 219–20.

[21] Newman to Frederic Rogers, 31 Aug. 1833 (Mozley (ed.), i. 450).

[22] Newman to R. F. Wilson, 8 Sept. 1833 (ibid. 454). Cf. Froude, *Remains*, i. 312; Keble to Newman, Feb. 1834 (Keble–Newman letters, copy). Froude wrote characteristically to his father: 'the notion that a priest must be a gentleman is a stupid Protestant fancy, and ought to be exploded'; W. G. Peck, *The Social Implications of the Oxford Movement* (London, 1933), 71.

to the archbishop of Canterbury was signed by 7,000 clergy and another by 230,000 lay heads of families.[23] Sixty-six short and pithy *Tracts for the Times* were issued in the first two years of the movement until, after Pusey's intervention with an elaborate three-part tract in the autumn of 1835 defending baptismal regeneration, the series slowed down into periodic, lengthy, and fundamental treatises on doctrine. As yet the Tractarians were not clearly separated from traditional, Protestant high churchmanship. The original anti-Catholic leaning of the movement was shown by the direction to booksellers for the sale of the tracts: they were to be advertised as 'tracts . . . on the privileges of the Church and against Popery and Dissent'.[24] Similarly, the Tractarians as a body did not advocate separation of Church and State. This was an individual matter. Some favoured the idea on account of recent State policy and the hostility of the House of Commons, but still adhered to the ideal of an established Church under improved conditions.[25] It was the subsequent evolution of Tractarian views on doctrine and especially on the Church of Rome which clearly distinguished radical from conservative high churchmen, and then ultra-radicals from moderate radicals.

The Tractarian contribution to Church defence, later weakened by the departure of some Tractarians from the Church, was an affirmation of catholic doctrine within the capacious limits of Anglicanism. In their emphasis on doctrine the Tractarians were unique in their time. The religious similarity of Anglican evangelicals to Nonconformity prevented them from evolving a distinct doctrinal attitude to correspond with their firm views on the need for a State Church. Latitudinarians such as Arnold minimized the importance of doctrinal distinctions in a search for broad Erastian comprehension. Newman could only ridicule Arnold's *Principles of Church Reform*:

If I understand it right, all sects (the Church inclusive) are to hold their meetings in the parish churches, though not at the same hour of course . . . surely there will be too many sects in some places for one day . . . I should say pass an Act to oblige some persuasions to *change* the Sunday. If you have two Sundays in the week you could accommodate any probable number of sects . . . Luckily the Mahomedan holiday is already on a Friday, so there will be no difficulty in that quarter.[26]

In the first tract of the series Newman indicated a theological route which led far away from both evangelicals and broad churchmen: 'They [the Government] have been deluded into a notion that present palpable useful-

[23] Newman to William Palmer of Worcester College, Oxford, 24 Oct. 1833 (Mozley (ed.), i. 467).
[24] S. L. Ollard, *A Short History of the Oxford Movement*, ed. A. M. Allchin (London, 1963), 25.
[25] Mozley (ed.), i. 449; Greenfield, op. cit. 102–3.
[26] Newman to R. F. Wilson, 18 Mar. 1833 (Mozley (ed.), i. 374–5).

ness, producible results, acceptableness to your flocks, that these and such like are the tests of your divine commission. Enlighten them in this matter. Exalt our Holy Fathers, the bishops, as the representatives of the Apostles, the Angels of the Churches . . .'[27] High churchmen in general set out along the route, but the stages they reached were widely separated. Slight disagreements in 1833 had become wide divisions by 1840. By then Froude had mortally faded from the race, but his frenetic drive had touched Newman and Keble, who had streaked far ahead, the steady wind of Dr. Pusey in their rear. The swift catholic pace had left William Palmer·far behind with the conservative high churchmen.[28] As for H. J. Rose, the exorbitant drive of the front-runners was said to have aggravated the physical disorder which carried him to an early death in 1838.[29] W. F. Hook, another conservative high churchman, had preferred to depict an uncomfortable ride on a conveyance: 'my Oxford friends . . . are certainly the most injudicious of mortal men . . . I am afraid they will upset the coach, they are such very Jehus.'[30]

By 1838 the more radical Tractarians had won control of the movement from the conservatives. Palmer had failed to stop the tracts and Newman had become editor of the *British Critic*, taking it out of the hands of the Hackney Phalanx.[31] Samuel Wilberforce complained in 1838 that 'Newman has just . . . declined receiving any more articles from me in the British Critic because my sentiments do not "sufficiently accord with those of Dr. Pusey and himself"'.[32] With rapid strides Newman was justifying the charge of Romanization which he had been so anxious to reject. In his *Lectures on the Prophetical Office of the Church*, published in 1837, he stigmatized Rome, with excessive self-defence, as 'a Church beside herself, abounding in noble gifts and rightful titles, but unable to use them religiously; crafty, obstinate, wilful, malicious, cruel, unnatural, as madmen are'.[33] But in the following year he and Keble reverently produced the first half of Froude's *Remains*, in which appeared the following startling comments: 'odious Protestantism sticks in people's gizzard' (1833); 'as to the reformers, I think worse and worse of them' (October 1834); 'really I hate the Reformation and the Reformers more and more' (26 December 1834).[34] It was small comfort that Popery was also condemned: 'How Whiggery has by degrees taken up all the filth that has been secreted in the fermentation of human thought! Puritanism, Latitudinarianism, Popery, Infidelity; they have it all now, and

---

[27] R. W. Church, *The Oxford Movement, 1833–45*, ed. G. Best (Chicago and London, 1970), 84 (tract reprinted).

[28] Greenfield, 17 ff., 99 ff., 177–80.

[29] J. W. Burgon, *Lives of Twelve Good Men* (2 vols., London, 1889), i. 264.

[30] Hook to W. P. Wood, 13 Nov. 1837 (Stephens, *Hook*, i. 412).

[31] Greenfield, 121–2; Marshall, op. cit. 480–520.

[32] Wilberforce to Sir Charles Anderson, 31 Aug. 1838 (Wilberforce Papers, d. 25).

[33] Quoted Greenfield, 156.   [34] *Remains*, i. 322, 379, 389.

good luck to them' (25 January 1834).[35] Protestants, of whatever hue, were duly shocked. Lord Morpeth read extracts from the *Remains* in the House of Commons, using them to condemn Tractarian views.[36] The reaction to Tract 90 was ascribed partly to anger at the *Remains*.[37] Conservative high churchmen were clearly losing sympathy with the movement by 1839. Edward Churton wrote: 'In my early days I used to be a kind of marked man among my acquaintances for High Church bigotry and extravagance . . . Now I find myself so fairly outdone, that I am unable to follow the flights of many who are advocating the same views.'[38]

Rejection of the Reformation did not amount to acceptance of the contemporary Church of Rome. This Church could still be seen as having been perverted by the decrees of the Council of Trent from the purity of the primitive Church. But the daring advance continued. Newman's Tract 85 challenged the Bible as the primary source of doctrine.[39] After the summer of 1839 he had 'a great and growing dislike . . . to speak against the Roman Church herself or her formal doctrines', though he still had 'an unspeakable aversion to the policy and acts of Mr. O'Connell, because as I thought, he associated himself with men of all religions and no religion against the Anglican Church . . .'[40] O'Connell for his part later gave a guarded welcome to 'Puseyism' as being 'in the direction of the true Church, and [tending] to the triumph of the true religion'.[41]

Newman's Tract 90 indirectly began the parting of the ways between himself and Keble, initiating an ultra-radical (and more Roman) development. The tract, published on 27 February 1841, sought to show that the Thirty-Nine Articles of the Church of England were not irreconcilable with pure Catholic teaching but only with Catholic 'corruptions'. James Mozley commented: 'This is no more than what we know as a matter of history, for the Articles were expressly worded to bring in Roman Catholics. But people are astonished and confused at the idea now, as if it were quite new.'[42] The tract also held the Articles to be imperfect, and provocatively characterized the Church of England as '. . . teaching with the stammering lips of ambiguous formularies . . .'[43] Too much had gone to produce suspicions of Romanization for the tract to be treated as a matter of entirely rational debate. Conservative high churchmen reacted strongly. Edward Churton said that William Palmer, Joshua Watson, '& all good men of my acquaintance' condemned the tract,[44] Gladstone thought the tract was one of the shocks that

---

[35] Ibid. i. 340.   [36] *Annual Register*, lxxx (1838), 144.

[37] Coleridge, *Keble*, i. 253–4.

[38] Churton, Archdeacon of Cleveland, to Rev. W. Gresley, 20 Sept. 1839 (second letter) (Churton Papers). Cf. Churton to Pusey, 17 May and 9 Dec. 1841 (ibid.).

[39] Greenfield, 227–35.   [40] *Apologia*, 117.

[41] 2 Mar. 1841 (Hansard, lvi. 1255).   [42] Quoted Church, op. cit. 196.

[43] Quoted Chadwick, *Victorian Church*, i. 184.

[44] Churton to A. P. Perceval, 20 Mar. 1841; Churton to William Gresley, 19 Mar. 1841 (Churton Papers).

sadly strain the vessel.[45] But high churchmen thought that the heads of Oxford colleges had exceeded their powers in censuring the tract; this, as an ecclesiastical matter, was rather the province of Convocation.[46] The uproar only drove Newman further into his own thoughts. His influence in the English Church was at an end. 'It was an impossibility that I could say anything henceforth to good effect,' he wrote, when 'I had been posted up by the marshal on the buttery hatch of every College of my University, after the manner of discommoned pastry-cooks, and when in every part of the country ... I was denounced as a traitor who had laid his train and was detected in the very act of firing it against the time-honoured Establishment.'[47] While the rumbustious quarrels continued at Oxford, Newman retired physically to Littlemore and spiritually near to Rome, being incited by the bold views of younger out-runners like W. G. Ward and Frederick Oakeley. He was finally received into the Roman Church by Father Dominic, the leader of the Passionist mission, on 9 October 1845. Numerous other conversions took place in the next few years, but many Tractarians remained in the Church of England under Pusey's lead, adding their distinctive opinions and controversies to a confused ecclesiastical situation.

The theological development of Tractarians had unexpected and tortuous effects on their attitude to the liberal policies of the Government. In this respect their cloistered, donnish character helped to distinguish them from statesmen who lived amidst the competing clamour of mundane reality. With Dissent, Tactarians had no doctrinal sympathy. Tract 36 divided opponents of the Church of England into three classes: 'those who reject the Truth' (Socinians, Jews, Deists, and atheists); 'those who teach more than the Truth' (Roman Catholics and Irvingites);[48] and 'those who receive and teach only part of the Truth', who included Presbyterians, Independents, Methodists, Baptists, Quakers, also 'especially in Wales, Jumpers and Shakers' ...[49] These three classes, said the tract, had united their forces, the 'Unbeliever, Papist, and Protestant Dissenter, obeying Satan's bidding', to 'overthrow and destroy our branch of the Catholic and Apostolic Church'.[50] The *British Critic* in 1835 asserted, against Thomas Binney's pamphlet *Dissent not Schism*, that Dissent was indeed evil schism: it placed weapons in the hands of the sceptic.[51] Tract 57 castigated Congregationalists for 'their systematical disparagement of the holy Sacraments, their horror (for it is more than disregard) of authority and antiquity, and the tendency

---

[45] Gladstone to J. R. Hope, 25 Nov. 1841, 'private', copy (Gladstone Papers, 44214, f. 196 ff).

[46] William Palmer to W. Gresley, 16 Mar. 1841 (Gresley Papers); Churton to A. P. Perceval, 20 Mar. 1841 (loc. cit.).

[47] *Apologia*, 88.

[48] Irvingites (the Holy Catholic Apostolic Church) believed in Christ's imminent coming and in the divine gift of tongues.

[49] Tract entitled *An Account of Religious Sects at present existing in England* (London, 1834; no pagination).

[50] Ibid.　　　　　　　　　　[51] *British Critic*, xvii (1835), 409-10.

of their instructions and devotions to make Faith a matter of *feeling* rather than a strict relative duty towards the persons of the Holy Trinity'.[52]

The ecclesiastical ideas of Tractarians led them, with theological consistency, to oppose some Dissenting claims but not others. Their criterion was always the best means of serving pure Church principles. Accordingly, the relaxation of University Tests had to be resisted. Pusey wrote: 'With lax notions about ye Church, vague and low and inadequate notions about ye Sacraments, and sometimes very poor instruction in ye great truths of Xty, our [Anglican] pupils . . . could not be with any regard to their safety mixed up with Baptists, Socinians, or Roman Catholics . . .'[53] It was therefore desirable that Dissenters should be educated elsewhere than at Oxford and Cambridge. In regard to Dissenting marriages, however, Tractarians believed that Church principles were more obviously weakened by continuing to perform such marriages in parish churches than by allowing them to be performed in separate Dissenting services. Keble wrote: '. . . only let such persons as we decline to marry, or such as decline to be married by us, get their names stuck on some Meeting House door, and duly register their intentions before a magistrate'.[54] Dissenting demands regarding marriage therefore obtained more favour from Tractarians than did their university claims. Similarly, on the demand for burial by Dissenting rites in parish churchyards, instead of by Anglican rites, Keble wrote: '. . . the heretics will not be satisfied without the consecrated ground; but, on the whole, I am inclined to think the profanation less that way than as it is at present, for now we profane the ground and the service too'.[55]

Thus greater insistence on Church purity led to greater emphasis on religious exclusiveness, which could in some matters be achieved better by liberality than by compulsion. Hence came, at a later date, the partial compatibility of Gladstone's Tractarian beliefs with his liberal championship of Nonconformist claims.[56] There is rather less inconsistency than is often thought between Gladstone's *State in its Relations with the Church*, first published in 1838 in defence of an Establishment based on the apostolic succession, and his later support for concessions to Roman Catholics, Jews, and Dissenters. Even in regard to recognizing different forms of Church Establishment the book was not illiberal. An Establishment, it was held, could be justified not only on grounds of truth but also by spiritual worth. The Church of Scotland, though not teaching the whole truth, was of proved spiritual usefulness, and had moreover been established by solemn legal compact.[57]

[52] Tract No. 57 entitled *Sermons on Saints' Days*, 3 (London, 1835), 11–12.
[53] Pusey to Gladstone, 5 May 1835 (Gladstone Papers, 44281, fo. 8).
[54] Keble to Newman, Jan. 1835 (Mozley (ed.), ii. 88).
[55] Ibid. 88–9. Cf. Newman to Keble, 17 Nov. 1841 (ibid. 365–6).
[56] See below, p. 325.
[57] See also Gladstone to Manning, 23 Apr. 1837 (D. C. Lathbury (ed.), *Correspondence on*

But religious liberalism was by no means an immediate characteristic of the Oxford movement, and Dissenters could scarcely have perceived its potential benefit to themselves. The high-church revival seemed entirely inimical to them. Tract 29 on Christian liberty had, claimed Newman, 'raised quite a storm at Bocking [Essex], and (I think) caused refusal of a church rate'.[58] So far removed was, as yet, the abolition of church-rates thirty-four years later on the initiative of a Tractarian, Gladstone himself.

The desire to defend Church principles caused Tractarian opposition to State reform of the Church. One of the most powerful internal Church reform movements of the century was sadly at variance with well-meaning reforms by the State. To Tractarians both Government and Parliament seemed increasingly alien from true religion; and therefore increasingly disqualified to direct the Church, which they were increasingly doing. The Ecclesiastical Commission was seen as an organ of Erastianism. Pusey wrote of it: 'We shall live under the threat of the Commission, it will be our legislative, executive, the ultimate appeal of our bishops; it will absorb our Episcopate; the Prime Minister will be our Protestant Pope.'[59] Manning deprecated the Commission as 'an open assumption of the principle that all legislative authority, ecclesiastical as well as civil, is derived from the secular power'.[60] Opposition to State direction led high churchmen to condone pluralities and non-residence. But indolence and indifference were quite foreign to the personal practice of zealous Tractarian priests; and the *British Critic* was not opposed to certain reforms, provided they came from the Church itself rather than Parliament.[61] Among reforms which the Tractarians disliked was the proposed union of the see of Sodor and Man with Carlisle. 'The discipline of [the see] is most primitive', noted a correspondent of Newman, 'the Bishop sitting in open court with his Presbyters, adjudging, excommunicating, etc.'; the same correspondent also pointed out, consistently with anti-Erastian views, that 'the Bishop having no seat in the House of Lords is a valuable precedent'.[62] Keble sent to Newman a draft petition to the Lords against the union, deprecating diocesan alterations by the Legislature in disregard of 'the sacred prerogative . . . of the Church Universal'.[63]

Church and Religion of W. E. Gladstone (2 vols., London, 1910), i. 35 ff. Cf. W. F. Gray, 'Chalmers and Gladstone: an unrecorded Episode', *Records of the Scottish Church History Society*, x (1950), 8–17.

[58] Note by Newman (Mozley (ed.), i. 487).

[59] *British Critic*, xxiii (1838), 526; quoted Bowen, op. cit. 20. Cf. Brose, *Church and Parliament*, 144 ff.

[60] H. E. Manning, *The Principle of the Ecclesiastical Commission examined, in a letter to the . . . Bishop of Chichester* (London, 1838), 9–10. Gladstone, however, had a more lenient view (Gladstone to Manning, 27 Sept. 1837 (Lathbury, op. cit. i. 41)).

[61] *British Critic*, xvii (1835), 487.

[62] Samuel F. Wood to Newman, Apr. 1836 (Mozley (ed.), ii. 189–90).

[63] Keble to Newman, 4 Mar. 1837 (Keble–Newman letters (copies)).

As remedies for current thraldom, Tractarians and other high churchmen considered both disestablishment and clerical power to legislate for the Church. In August 1833 Keble believed that, sooner than become slaves of the State, 'we ought to be prepared to sacrifice any or all of our endowments ... "Take every pound, shilling and penny, and the curse of sacrilege along with it; only let us make our own Bishops, and be governed by our own laws." This is the length I am prepared to go; but of course if we could get our liberty at an easier price, so much the better.'[64] Gladstone was against the Voluntary principle: Government support, he held, was the surest means of achieving 'the greatest holiness of the greatest number'.[65] But in a criticism of Gladstone's *State in its Relations with the Church*, Keble said that State-enslaved Establishments were worse than no Establishments.[66]

The dilemma of Tractarians between the hope that a true Establishment might be restored and the suspicion that only a disestablished Church could realize the truth was to prevent them, as a party, from developing any clear view on the Voluntary question. But their consideration of the merits of Voluntaryism was another striking departure from the old, constitutional high churchmanship. It was another unexpected link, though not necessarily a sympathetic one, between Tractarianism and Dissent. Even more unexpected were Gladstone's partial advances towards Voluntaryism in later years.

Tractarians wished the clergy to have a greater share in ecclesiastical legislation. But they were reluctant, in their early years, to advocate the revival of Convocation, which they thought might be Erastian and theologically unhelpful to their cause. Several works in the early 1830s, including Lord Henley's *Plan*, urged that Convocation be restored; this was also advised by a few radicals such as Joseph Hume and Sir William Molesworth. In May 1837 Peter Borthwick, Conservative member for Evesham, moved in a thin House of Commons that the Crown should be asked to convene Convocation periodically in order to advise Parliament, and was defeated by 24 votes to 19.[67] But the subject was not mentioned in the Oxford tracts,[68] and conservative high churchmen shared this lack of enthusiasm. The demand to revive Convocation did not become strong or organized until the later 1840s.

Tractarians disliked the promotion of heterodoxy by the Government, and clerical appointments by the Crown were suspiciously watched. In 1836 an outcry was caused by the advancement to the Oxford Regius Chair of Divinity of Dr. Renn Dickson Hampden, friend of Arnold and Whately,

---

[64] Keble to Newman, 8 Aug. 1833 (Mozley (ed.), i. 442).

[65] *The State in its Relations with the Church* (London, 1838), 41–5, 92–7 (also revised and enlarged 4th edn., 2 vols., London 1841, i. 44 ff., 105 ff.; ii. 346 ff.).

[66] Quoted Lathbury, i. 17–18. Gladstone accepted the validity of Keble's view (ibid. 18).

[67] Hansard, xxxviii. 458–62.

[68] See J. B. Sweet, *A Memoir of the late Henry Hoare* (London, 1869), 17 ff.

author of some anti-dogmatic Bampton Lectures and of a liberal pamphlet entitled *Observations on Religious Dissent*. On receiving a copy of the second edition of this pamphlet from Hampden in 1834, Newman had replied that its principles tended 'altogether to make shipwreck of Christian faith';[69] while Arnold, on the other hand, told Hampden that '. . . your sentiments on so many points [are] . . . in agreement with my own'.[70] Hampden had an appropriate family connection with his seventeenth-century namesake.[71] The nine names recommended by the archbishop of Canterbury for the Regius Chair included Pusey, Newman, and Keble. But Melbourne, on broad Church advice, and in accordance with the general tendency of Whig appointments, decided on Hampden. He told Hampden in his letter of appointment on 7 February that among the reasons for selection was his 'liberal spirit of inquiry tempered by due caution'.[72] But Hampden's spirit was too liberal for high churchmen and for evangelicals such as Ashley. Pusey sent to Gladstone a list of Hampden's objectionable opinions. These included the following: 'The divine part of Christianity is its facts; the received statements of doctrines are only some out of infinite theories which may be raised on the texts of Scripture'.[73] High churchmen could not permit their doctrines to be described as mere human speculation. To Edward Churton, Hampden was a 'sophistical heretic', and to Samuel Wilberforce his opinions were 'very shocking in a divinity professor, who ought to be one to nail his colours to the mast and uphold orthodoxy to the very utmost'.[74]

Protest had time to gather strength, for the appointment was strongly rumoured in Oxford twelve days before it was publicly known. A petition to the Crown was promoted by Newman, Keble, and Richard Greswell of Corpus Christi College, and signed by seventy-three tutors; and the appointment was lashed by the Tory Press.[75] But opposition was fruitless. The appointment was gazetted on 17 February. On 5 May the Oxford protesters enjoyed some compensation by carrying a statute by a huge majority in the University Convocation; this statute prevented Hampden from taking part in the choice of select preachers and from being consulted over sermons which were called in question before the Vice-Chancellor.[76] There was satisfaction in having challenged the State, not without impact. The reputed

[69] *Apologia*, 61–2; H. Hampden (ed.), *Some Memorials of R. D. Hampden* (London, 1871), 37–8. For the controversy over Hampden's appointment see Chadwick, *Victorian Church*, i. 112 ff.; R. W. Church, 113–24.

[70] Arnold to Hampden, 17 May 1835 (Hampden, op. cit. 37).

[71] Ibid.   [72] Quoted Chadwick, i. 114.

[73] Pusey to Gladstone, 14 Mar. 1836, enc. (Gladstone Papers, 44281, fo. 16).

[74] Churton to A. P. Perceval, 7 Mar. 1836 (Churton Papers); Wilberforce to Sir Charles Anderson, 25 Feb. 1836 (Wilberforce Papers, d. 25).

[75] Henry Liddell to Roundell Palmer, 12 Feb. 1836 (Selborne Papers, vol. 1861, fos. 16–17); Chadwick, i. 116.

[76] Ibid. 119–20; Pusey to Gladstone, n.d. and 6, 17, and 20 Mar. 1836 (Gladstone Papers, 44281, fos. 12–13, 20–3).

dullness of Hampden's lectures may have stopped them having the feared effect amongst undergraduates, but he was to collide again with high churchmen.

There were even worse prospects for ecclesiastical appointments. A recurring Tractarian nightmare was that Arnold might be made a bishop.[77] His intervention in the Hampden dispute with an article in the *Edinburgh Review*, given the title of 'The Oxford Malignants' by the editor, had redoubled Tractarian aversion to him. But after the Hampden experience Melbourne would not go so far as this. 'What have Tory churchmen ever done for me' he asked, 'that I should make them a present of such a handle against my government?'[78] After Hampden he tried to appoint only safe though liberal men and avoided the heterodox, but the ensuing appointments did not pacify Tractarians.[79]

The *cause célèbre* of the Jerusalem bishopric was another clash between Tractarians and the Government. Coming soon after Tract 90, this affair erupted when both Tractarianism and the reaction to it were reaching extremes. The establishment of a bishopric at Jerusalem to serve both Anglicans and German Protestants in the Middle East was suggested to the British Government by Chevalier Bunsen, a noted liberal speculative thinker, on behalf of the King of Prussia in the summer of 1841. Prussia wished to promote her commercial and colonial interests as well as Protestant unity. The plan appealed to Whig ministers, and especially to Palmerston as Foreign Secretary, as a means of strengthening British interests in the Ottoman Empire and of counter-balancing the influences of the Orthodox and Roman Catholic Churches, which were already aiding the interests of Russia and France respectively. Peel and Aberdeen were far less enthusiastic, but on coming into office were confronted with a *fait accompli*. The scheme was supported by old high churchmen such as Howley, Blomfield, and Hook, who believed it might be a means of introducing the apostolical succession into the Prussian Lutheran Church; by Ashley, who hoped it would assist the expansion of evangelicalism; and by liberal churchmen as an encouragement to broad comprehension.[80] Arnold said that '. . . the idea of my [*Principles of Church Reform*] . . . which was so ridiculed and condemned, is now carried into practice by the Archbishop of Canterbury himself'.[81] Tractarians were divided in opinion. Gladstone, and initially

---

[77] Rev. J. F. Christie to Newman, 9 Feb. 1836 (Mozley (ed.), ii. 166); Edward Maltby, bishop of Durham, to Holland, n.d. (Holland House Papers, 51597).

[78] W. T. M. Torrens, *Memoirs of Lord Melbourne* (2 vols., London, 1878), ii. 181. Cf. Holland's Pol. Jls., 1836 (Holland House Papers, 51871, p. 962).

[79] Keble to Newman, 26 July 1840 (copy, Keble–Newman letters), complaining of the appointment of Connop Thirlwall as bishop of St. David's. See Chadwick, *Victorian Church*, i. 123–6.

[80] R. W. Greaves, 'The Jerusalem Bishopric, 1841', *EHR* lxiv (1949), 328–52; P. J. Welch, 'Anglican Churchmen and the establishment of the Jerusalem Bishopric', *JEH* viii (1957), 193–204; Hodder, *Life and Work of Shaftesbury*, i. 372 ff.

[81] Quoted Stephens, *Hook*, ii. 96.

Pusey, were optimistic about the religious benefits of the scheme, but Newman abhorred the threatened debasement of the apostolical succession through unity with a Church which did not hold such a doctrine: 'If any such event should take place I shall not be able to keep a single man from Rome.'[82]

The necessary Foreign Bishoprics Bill became law on 5 October, and the first bishop, Michael Solomon Alexander, was consecrated on 7 November; his polygot antecedents as a converted Prussian Jew, now an Anglican clergyman and Professor of Hebrew, seemed to make him an ideal choice. Newman sent a protest to the bishop of Oxford, saying that Lutheranism and Calvinism were heresies repugnant to Scripture, and that by consecrating a bishop of Jerusalem on co-operative terms Anglican prelates had formally recognized heretical doctrines.[83] Keble thought the protest disrespectful, but he himself protested in 1842 against the Queen's choice of a Lutheran prince as a godfather for the Prince of Wales.[84] As for Newman, if he had previously lost faith in the State he had now also lost faith in the Church. He at least could not be kept much longer from Rome.

If Government actions and their own theological development were taking some Tractarians Romewards, some Roman Catholics were more than ready to welcome them. Foremost among these was Ambrose Phillipps de Lisle, a Leicestershire squire who had become a Catholic at the age of 15 and had more than the usual fervour of the convert. His optimism for the conversion of England was strong even before the Oxford movement began. He showed outstanding zeal and little realism. He wrote in 1831 to the Hon. George Spencer, a more cautious convert, brother of Lord Althorp and later a Passionist priest under the name of Father Ignatius: '. . . I think in about 50 years England will be Catholick again . . . That something striking will very probably take place in England in favour of Catholicity before the end of the year '32 I believe and hope, but I cannot anticipate the total reconversion of the country, in *so short* a period.'[85] He saw the *Tracts for the Times* as beginning a movement which would end in Anglican return to the Catholic Church. In 1835 he presented land in Charnwood Forest which was used for building the Trappist monastery of Mount St. Bernard; and chapels were built through his aid in the Leicestershire villages. At times, however, he had doubts: on one occasion he sadly thought it would be many years before even the single Leicestershire parish of Whitwick was converted.[86]

---

[82] Newman to J. W. Bowden, 10 Oct. 1841 (Mozley (ed.), ii. 353); cf. Greenfield, 355-60.

[83] Mozley (ed.), ii. 362-3; *Apologia*, 134-6 (protest printed). Cf. R. Ornsby, *Memoir of James Robert Hope-Scott* (2 vols., London, 1884), i. 283-328.

[84] Mozley, *Reminiscences*, i. 221.

[85] De Lisle to Spencer, 3 July 1831 (E. S. Purcell, *Life and Letters of Ambrose Phillipps de Lisle* (2 vols., London, 1900), i. 50-1 and *passim*).

[86] Ibid. i. 105. The Vicar of Whitwick was Francis Merewether, a prolific writer in defence of Protestantism and the established Church.

Also sanguine was Nicholas Wiseman, rector of the English College at Rome; from 1833, when he was visited by Newman and Froude, he '. . . never for an instant [wavered] in my conviction that a new era had commenced in England . . . to this grand object [of conversion] I devoted myself'.[87] Wiseman's own London lectures in 1835 led to the foundation of the *Dublin Review* and the Catholic Institute for the propagation of doctrines and the defence of Catholic interests. After becoming, in 1840, Coadjutor to the Vicar-Apostolic of the Central District in England and President of Oscott College, Wiseman set about drawing the Tractarians towards Rome, though his efforts were disliked by conservative English Catholics and by the *Tablet*.[88] His *Letter to the Earl of Shrewsbury* of 1841 showed his great expectations from the Oxford movement: the English populace, he wrote, was ready to hear and appreciate 'men of mortified looks and placid demeanour, girt with the cord of a St. Francis, or bearing on their breasts the seal of Christ's passion'.[89] He had already, in January 1840, petitioned Pope Gregory XVI to establish an institute of missionary priests in England. No immediate action had been taken.[90] But the Passionists came to England later in 1840 with Wiseman's encouragement—to find their task much harder than he or Phillipps de Lisle would have led them to believe. The Passionist Father Dominic Barberi landed on, of all dates, 5 November, 'to inhale fog and . . . [see] effigies of the Pope and venerable ecclesiastics of our Church consigned to the flames'.[91] But he later took charge of a new foundation at Aston Hall near Birmingham, and Passionist parish missions commenced in 1844. Rosminians (Fathers of Charity) had been working in England since 1835, led by Father Luigi Gentili, and the Redemptorists arrived in 1843.[92] Father Dominic received Newman into his Church: thus Newman's theological development had not only led him to Rome, but had helped to explain the presence of an Italian priest in England to receive him.

Protestant opinion did not fail to notice and magnify these connections. Tractarians had lost any credibility as defenders of the Church Establishment. They were seen as internal instruments of perversion, destroyers of the Establishment to which they professed to belong, and even more pernicious than the Church for which they were believed to yearn. In March 1841 Lord Morpeth in the Commons made one of his attacks on the Romanizing tendencies of the Oxford movement, though his argument was somewhat weakened when it received O'Connell's support.[93] Latitudinarians,

---

[87] W. Ward, *The Life and Times of Cardinal Wiseman* (2 vols., London, 1897), i. 118–19.

[88] Ibid. 233 ff., 289 ff., 377 ff.; B. Ward, *The Sequel to Catholic Emancipation*, ii. 84 ff.

[89] Quoted B. Ward, op. cit. ii. 100–1.

[90] C. Charles, 'The Origins of the Parish Mission in England and the early Passionist Apostolate, 1840–50', *JEH* xv (1964), 60–2.

[91] Quoted U. Young, *The Life and Letters of the Ven. Dominic Barberi* (London, 1926), 174.

[92] For details see Charles, op. cit. 64–73.

[93] Hansard, lvi. 1239.

themselves by no means lacking in vigour and confidence through the inspiration of biblical criticism, saw their entire religious tradition threatened by the Oxford movement, and reacted against it. Macaulay, in a biting attack on Gladstone's *State in its Relations with the Church*, described it as 'the strenuous effort of a very vigorous mind to keep as far in the rear of the general progress as possible', and derided an apostolic succession through lack of historical proof.[94] But broad churchmen upheld liberty of theological interpretation, and could scarcely withhold from Tractarians the toleration they gave to Catholics and Protestant Dissenters. Evangelicals in the Church of England were generally less tolerant of Catholicism and they defended the Protestant Establishment in a straightforward and uncomplicated way. The fiercest opposition to Tractarianism came from them.

II. ULTRA-PROTESTANT ORGANIZATION

As Tractarian views obtained more influence they helped to banish the old Protestant image of high churchmanship, and the defence of Protestantism as an essential feature of the Church of England was left more and more to the evangelical movement. Though it could still be a great stimulus to religious revival, evangelicalism often appeared in the mid-nineteenth century in a negative and defensive light on account of the anti-Catholic and anti-Tractarian attitudes of many of its votaries. The generous expansiveness of the evangelical movement was endangered by a vehemently hostile and punitive attitude to Catholicism; a social parallel might be found in the ultra-censoriousness of some Victorian evangelicals. The Government's policy towards the Church of Ireland, which had sparked off the Tractarian movement, produced also a contrasting ultra-Protestant reaction. The Catholic theology of the Tractarians found no sympathy and little rivalry among Anglican evangelicals, whose own dislike of liberalism was expressed somewhat negatively in anti-Catholicism and defence of the Protestant Establishment. If evangelicals regarded much high-church theology as superfluous, high churchmen regarded evangelical theology as incomplete. The Tractarian G. A. Denison said that the evangelical movement had succeeded in recalling men 'from a dry, cold and powerless morality, to the prime source of all that is most excellent in the regenerated nature, the love of Christ'; but that it had failed 'in respect of care for the means ordained of Christ for the perpetual administration of His kingdom upon earth, and for the regeneration and renewal of the individual soul'. What was needed was a system 'resting neither in faith without works, nor in works without faith'.[95]

The anti-Catholic bias in the Erastianism of Anglican evangelicals was

---

[94] *Works* (London, 1907): *Essays and Biographies*, iii. 148, 160.
[95] Denison, *Notes of My Life*, 54 ff.

emphasized by their religious sympathy with Protestant Nonconformists, whose views on a State Church were contrary to their own. Tractarians, on the other hand, were regarded as a Romanizing group within the Church, and were if possible more disliked than Rome itself.[96] Evangelicals stressed their Protestant view of the Establishment and this made Tractarians all the more discontented with such an Establishment. For the rest of the nineteenth century the Tractarian and evangelical movements pulled the Church of England in opposite directions, the broad churchmen pulling it in a third.

The political attitude of many Anglican evangelicals reflected the reaction of the 1830s in favour of Church defence. In opposing the Irish Church Bill of 1833 the evangelical *Christian Observer* said that the Government was treating the Protestant Establishment as 'an evil to be borne with and mitigated rather than as a blessing of which we should wish the extension and perpetuity'.[97] For the expression of such views there existed Orange institutions in both Ireland and Britain. Declared illegal in 1825 along with the Catholic Association, they had openly revived in 1828 in opposition to Catholic emancipation. By 1835 there was again a lively demand for their suppression, encouraged by the findings and reports of parliamentary committees.[98] A Select Committee of the Commons to inquire into Orange lodges in Great Britain and the colonies was appointed in August 1835 on the motion of Joseph Hume.[99] The committee had 23 members, representing different opinions on the question.[100] Its report, submitted to the Commons on 7 September, dramatically declared 'the existence of an organized institution, pervading Great Britain and her Colonies to an extent never contemplated as possible'; this institution was 'highly injurious to the discipline of His Majesty's Army, and dangerous to the peace of His Majesty's subjects'.[101] The report stated that the rules, signs, and passwords of the British lodges came from the Irish lodges, and a warm feeling of solidarity existed between Orangemen in the two islands. The supreme head of the association was the duke of Cumberland, entitled Grand Master of the Empire, and Lord Kenyon was Deputy Grand Master.

The Orangeman's main object was to uphold Protestant Ascendancy. In some places he helped to raise funds to assist poor fellow members. The Orangeman was expected to have strict standards of 'temperance and

[96] Cf. G. F. A. Best, 'The Evangelicals and the Established Church in the early Nineteenth Century', *Journal of Theological Studies*, N.S. ix (1958), 63–78; Bowen, *The Idea of the Victorian Church*, 146 ff., 380; G. F. A. Best, *Shaftesbury* (London, 1964), 62.

[97] Quoted W. L. Mathieson, *English Church Reform, 1815–40* (London, 1923), 78.

[98] e.g. resolutions moved by Joseph Hume and adopted by the Commons, 4 and 11 Aug. 1835 (Hansard, xxx. 58–109, 266–312). See H. Senior, *Orangeism in Ireland and Britain, 1795–1836* (London, 1966), 254 ff.

[99] Hansard, xxx. 236 ff.

[100] Report of Select Committee, P.P. 1835 (605), xvii. 1.

[101] Ibid. iv.

sobriety, honesty and integrity', and to direct his exertions to 'the honour and glory of his King and country . . .' He should be humane and law-abiding, and should eschew violence. About 300 lodges were said to exist in Great Britain, grouped in 47 districts; there were 93 lodges unattached to districts, including those in the army and the colonies. Enrolment was, according to the Committee's evidence, low in the South and Midlands of England and comparatively high in south Lancashire, Ayrshire, and the Glasgow region. The areas of high Orange membership were also, not surprisingly, areas of high Catholic population. Some of the antagonism was imported from Ireland by rival groups, many Orangemen being Irish Protestant immigrants. The members represented a wide social range. Members of the Wigan lodge were said to be 'all miners . . . as black as my coat with dust and dirt, but very loyal men . . .' Several Anglican clergymen were prominent in the lodges. No Dissenting ministers in England, and only two clergymen of any persuasion in Scotland, appeared to have joined the institution; but many lay Dissenters (of unspecified denomination, perhaps Wesleyans) were said to be members.

An Orange address to the Carlton Club and the Conservatives of England in 1834 had extolled the political potentiality of an institution which 'includes persons of every rank and grade, from the first male subject in the realm [Cumberland] down to the humblest individual'. The Select Committee stated that almost all Orange proceedings had some political end in view; and that the effect of the institution, as of the Catholic Ribbonmen, was to produce conflict between Catholic and Protestant. Riots had occurred at Girvan (Ayrshire) in July 1831 when an Orange procession took place, preceded by 'a cart containing whisky, which was distributed to [the Orange-men] in large quantities'. At Airdrie on 13 July 1834 (12 July was a Sunday that year) an Orange procession had caused a body of Catholics (said to be led by Ribbonmen) to come from Glasgow and commit violence in the town before they dispersed through fear of the military. On the night of 19 July the rumour of another Catholic onslaught had caused a large crowd at Airdrie ('It is a mining population; all Protestants') to attack Catholic houses and a chapel.[102]

The reports of the Select Committees did not immediately persuade the Government to suppress Orange societies.[103] But radicals and Irish Repeal-ers, on whom the Whigs depended for support, were determined to see Orangeism banned. Hume and Sir William Molesworth spread rumours of an Orange *coup d'état* to gain the Crown for Cumberland over the head of Princess Victoria. The facts were against the existence of a serious

---

[102] Ibid. iv–v, viii, x–xi, xvi–xviii, xxvii, 24, 33, 43–4, 141–4; appendix, 85–7; R. L. Hill, *Toryism and the People, 1832–46* (London, 1929), 60; J. E. Handley, *The Irish in Scotland* (one-vol. edn., Glasgow, 1964), 142–6.

[103] Cf. Russell to Grey, 27 Oct. 1835 (Grey Papers).

conspiracy of this kind. Despite greatly inflated membership figures which were accepted, for opposite political reasons, by both Orangemen and their enemies, there were probably only 6,000 Orangemen in Britain; in the army there were only about 500 members to lend military assistance to a *coup*.[104]

Hume moved in the Commons in February 1836 an address to the King asking that all Orangemen be dismissed from judicial and police offices.[105] Molesworth, supporting him, claimed that Orange societies were illegal under various statutes and said that members of such societies, including Cumberland himself, should be transported: 'A few years residence on the shores of the Southern Ocean would teach him and other titled criminals that the laws of their country are not to be violated with impunity.'[106] Russell agreed that the societies should be suppressed, since there was a danger of their party feeling transcending the law. But he disapproved of Hume's motion for the removal of Orange judicial officials, and proposed instead an address asking the King to take measures 'for the effectual discouragement of Orange lodges, and generally of all political societies, excluding persons of different religions, and using secret signs and symbols, and acting by means of associated branches'.[107] Orangemen in the Commons defended their organization. Henry Maxwell, M.P. for Cavan, maintained that in Ireland, where Protestant institutions were subject to imminent danger, Orange societies were absolutely necessary. Colonels Perceval and Verner, members for Sligo and Co. Armagh respectively, wanted the stigma of a specific reference to Orange societies to be omitted from the motion, and were supported by Stanley and Peel. Both colonels, however, said that as loyal subjects they would conform with any royal commands on the future of the societies.[108] Russell's motion was adopted. The King's reply, of which Russell informed the Commons on 25 February, agreed that Orange lodges and similar political societies should be discouraged. On the following day Russell announced that he had received a letter from the duke of Cumberland, saying that he and other Orange officials had recommended immediate dissolution in conformity with the loyal principles of that institution.[109] In the Lords Cumberland said that, though the societies were dissolved, 'their principles could not and would not die'.[110]

Before the dissolution of the Orange lodges occurred, a society had been formed in Britain which upheld the same Protestant principles of Orangeism without its military aspect or secrecy. This was the Protestant Association, whose resounding anti-Catholic ring came not least from its bearing the same title as Lord George Gordon's supporters in 1780. The body was officially founded at a meeting in Exeter Hall, London, in June 1835, but

[104] Senior, op. cit. 269–73.   [105] Hansard, xxi. 779 ff.   [106] Ibid. 819.
[107] Ibid. 830.   [108] Ibid. 837, 849, 850–61.   [109] Ibid. 870, 946–7.
[110] Ibid. 934, 1281.

action awaited further meetings in the summer of 1836. Like the Tractarians, the Protestant Association opposed the heterogeneous religious attitude of the State; it also condemned the pressure of Catholics and the 'infidel party'. The determined if incongruous object of the Roman Catholic was destruction of the established Church: 'he readily lays aside, for the moment, all the high pretensions of his Church to infallibility and sole dominion over the consciences of men, and joins with the professor of liberality . . . in contending that the State, in maintaining a certain form of Christianity, and giving preference to a certain mode of belief, does violence to the rights of conscience . . .' To this end the Catholic allied with the unbeliever and 'the mistaken and deluded nonconformist'.[111]

Thus the Association implicitly declared a more lenient view of Protestant Dissenters, despite the fact that the Association existed primarily to defend the Establishment while Dissenters were attacking it more strongly than Catholics. This comparative lenience came from evangelical religious affinity which transcended the bounds of Anglicanism. As the Tractarians became more Catholic in theology, and the evangelicals in the Association affirmed their Protestant position, different interpretations of truth were increasingly emphasized within the same Anglican Church. The Association sought to complement and not to duplicate the functions of the Reformation Society (British Society for Promoting the Religious Principles of the Reformation) which had existed since 1827. The latter, as its title showed, defended the religious principles of the Reformation. The Protestant Association defended the political result and 'natural offspring' of these beliefs, the Protestant constitution established by the Revolution of 1688.[112]

Nevertheless, the propagation of anti-Catholic religious views was a conspicuous part of the Protestant Association's activities. The Rev. Hugh McNeile of St. Jude's, Liverpool, one of the Irish clergy in England who were staunch supporters of the Association, delivered numerous inflammatory speeches against Popery and priestly celibacy.[113] McNeile wrote *Anti-Slavery and Anti-Popery*, whose subject was 'the inconsistency, on either side, of opposing one of these systems, without opposing the other . . . Both of these systems invest man with arbitrary irresponsible authority over his fellow-man.'[114] He attempted to gain the alliance of Protestant Dissenters: '. . . although they may see abuses in the details of the Established Church, yet, when they see on the other side the black legion of the beast, the harlequin troops of Rome, they will again make their choice between

---

[111] Protestant Association, *Publications*, vol. i (London, 1839): *Statement of Views and Objects*, 2–3. Cf. the five fundamental resolutions of the Association; Sixteenth Annual Report, 12 May 1852 (London, 1852).

[112] *Statement of Views and Objects*, 4.

[113] One of his speeches is printed in *Report of Second Annual Meeting of Hereford Protestant Association* (Cheltenham, 1837).

[114] 2nd edn. (London, 1838), 7.

Popery and the truth'.[115] Although many Wesleyans were susceptible to
such appeals, Baptists, Congregationalists, and other Dissenters who
opposed the Establishment were not swayed by their own dislike of Catholicism to abandon their radicalism or to join the Association. Dissenters,
claimed the *Eclectic Review*, did not support Protestant associations. Instead,
Dissenters 'endeavor [sic] to promote Protestantism by preaching Protestant
sermons, circulating Protestant tracts, and seeking the destruction of an
Establishment which has been popish once and may be popish again . . .
We do not join Protestant associations because we do not join the Church
which . . . is their great embodiment of Protestantism, and we do not join
that Church because it is too popish for us.'[116]

The increase in the number of Roman Catholics, of Catholic seminaries
and nunneries, and the spread of Catholic education and political influence,
were of great concern to the Association. It was stated that whereas there
had been only 30 Catholic chapels in Great Britain in 1796, there were 560
in 1839. In the same period seminaries had increased from about 3 to 80.[117]
It was noted that the Catholic Institute had been founded in 1838 to raise
building funds, circulate publications, and organize local committees, and
that several branches had been established.[118] In one year alone (1838-9)
three Catholics—Thomas Wyse, Richard Sheil, and R. M. O'Ferrall—held
office in the Government.[119] This was a result of the 1829 Relief Act, whose
repeal was a major object of the Association. It was held that Catholic
M.P.s had violated their oath that they would not subvert the Protestant
constitution.[120] They had disregarded the oath when voting for the suppression of Irish bishoprics and for appropriation, and in the 1837 session
had formed the exact majority of 23 in favour of the English Church Rate
Bill. Irish Catholic prelates had ignored the requirement of the Relief Act
that they should not take territorial titles which duplicated those of Protestant sees.[121] Since 1829, it was believed, 'England has lost alike her pre-
eminence abroad, and her confidence at home'.[122] It was therefore the duty

[115] Speech of McNeile at Second Annual Meeting of Protestant Association, Exeter Hall, 10 May
1837 (Protestant Association Publications, No. 10; 3rd edn., London, 1839), 13-14.

[116] N.S. ix (Jan.-June 1841), 613-14.

[117] G. H. Woodward, *Claims of the Protestant Association on public support* (Protestant Association Publications, No. 1; London, 1839), 5-6. Cf. *A Few Facts to awaken Protestants* (Publications
No. 11; London, 1839), 1. The rate of increase of Roman Catholics far outstripped the population
growth, mainly on account of Irish immigration.

[118] *A Few Facts to awaken Protestants*, 2-3. For details on the Catholic Institute see J. Kitching,
'Roman Catholic Education from 1700 to 1870' (unpubl. Univ. of Leeds Ph.D. thesis 1967),
169 ff.

[119] *A Few Facts*, 2-3.

[120] Speech of J. E. Gordon at second annual meeting of Protestant Association, 10 May 1837
(Publications, No. 9; 3rd edn., London, 1839), 4-8.

[121] Hansard, xxxix. 339 (speech of duke of Newcastle); *Annual Register*, lxxx (1838), 106.

[122] Rev. G. Croly, *England the Fortress of Christianity* (Protestant Association Publications, No.
8; London, 1839), 6.

of Protestants to '. . . demand without delay, the repeal of the Act of 1829'.[123]
A petition of the Association for this repeal in 1837 obtained 3,000 signatures
and was presented in both Houses; a similar petition from Liverpool was
said to have obtained more signatures.[124]

The annual Government grant to Maynooth College was a further outrage
to ultra-Protestants, and its termination was an object of the Protestant
Association. Thirty-nine petitions against the grant, containing 11,000
signatures, were presented to the Commons in 1838.[125] 'It is the Maynooth
priest', Sir Robert Inglis said, 'who is the agitating priest.'[126] Irish reforms
which would have benefited Catholics, such as the introduction of elective
municipal corporations, were opposed by the Association, and Stanley's
bill of 1840 to stiffen the Irish franchise qualifications was supported.[127] In
1839 the Association's fourth annual meeting deprecated the attempt to
withdraw education from the established Church as 'a part of the system
of hostility now in operation against our Protestant institutions'.[128] But
reforms in the Establishment, particularly the enforcement of a resident
clergy, were urged as a means of increasing the Church's influence.[129]

The secretary and later president of the Association was James Lord, a
barrister and anti-Catholic speaker and writer. Among the vice-presidents
were the fourth duke of Newcastle, the earl of Winchilsea, Earl Brownlow,
the earl of Dalhousie, Lord Farnham, Lord Redesdale, and M.P.s such as
J. P. Plumptre—names which revived memories of the Brunswick Clubs of
1828-9. But the Association was no mere constitutionalist, petitioning
coterie of gentry, Anglican clergy, M.P.s, and military officers. Evangelical
zeal and sense of mission were seen in its assiduous propaganda and attempts
to attract people of different social classes and denominations. Anglicans,
Wesleyans, and (from 1843) Scottish Free Churchmen served the Association in an official capacity.[130] Tracts and handbills were widely distributed,
and stimulated popular anti-Catholicism. The Association claimed to have
issued 70,000 copies of its publications in 1837-8; 45,000 in 1838-9; 287,280
in 1839-40; and 269,206 in 1840-1.[131] In 1838 the committee began to

[123] Speech of J. E. Gordon (loc. cit. 10).

[124] Second Annual Report of Protestant Association, presented 9 May 1838 (2nd edn., London,
1839); Hansard, xxxix. 339-54; xl. 941-7; xli. 284-320; xlviii. 692-701.

[125] Third Annual Report (London, 1839), 13-14.

[126] Quoted in speech of J. C. Colquhoun at Exeter Hall, 11 Mar. 1836; Publications, No. 2
(London, 1836), 6.

[127] Fifth Annual Report, 12 May 1841 (London, 1841), 10.

[128] Third Annual Report, vi.

[129] J. C. Colquhoun, The Uses of the Established Church to the Protestantism and Civilization
of Ireland (Protestant Association Publications, No. 3; 2nd edn., London, 1839), 6.

[130] Sixteenth Annual Report (London, 1852): list of names including the Free Churchmen Robert
Buchanan (Glasgow) and James Begg (Liberton, Edinburgh). On Wesleyan participation see
Gowland, 'Methodist Secessions and Social Conflict in South Lancashire', 193, 467; W. R. Ward,
Religion and Society in England, 212-13.

[131] Second Annual Report, 13-14; Fifth Annual Report (1841), 11.

direct the monthly *Protestant Magazine*, which was given to all who subscribed 10s. and above annually; nearly 20,000 copies were issued in
1838–9.[132] Protestant Association libraries were formed.[133] Public meetings
were held, both at Exeter Hall and elsewhere in the country. An eloquent
sermon was delivered annually to the society by Hugh McNeile. The
formation of local associations was encouraged, and a travelling agent (a
Mr. Eccleston of Trinity College, Dublin) was appointed to help this purpose.[134] During 1838–9 associations were reported to have been founded in
Manchester, Bath, Bristol, and Sheffield, and county associations to be in
the course of formation in Hertfordshire, Derbyshire, and Norfolk. In 1841
69 local associations were listed, most of them in England (with a high
proportion in the North), 7 in Scotland, and none in Wales.[135] But by 1852
only 54 local associations were listed—perhaps a sign of the society's
decline.[136]

Protestant Operative associations were encouraged: 21 of these existed
in 1841, mostly in London, Lancashire, and Yorkshire, but only 22 in
1852.[137] In April 1840 the first monthly issue of the *Penny Protestant
Operative*, under the Protestant Association's direction, summoned the
operatives of England to resist 'the insidious approaches of Popish influences,
the subtle sophistries and specious reasoning of Romish emissaries ...',
and indicated its historical basis by printing an article on the martyrdom of
Cranmer. The Manchester Operative Association was said by the Rev.
Hugh Stowell to comprise between 700 and 800 working men.[138] The social
tensions created by Irish Catholic immigration, which was already considerable before the famine of 1845, may well have been responsible for such
figures. Protestant Operative associations were scarcely distinguishable from
Operative Conservative societies, the first of which was founded at Leeds
early in 1835, followed by societies in ten other northern towns by March
1836. An operative, it was urged, should join such a society if he appreciated
'all those great blessings and advantages which, as an Englishman, he
enjoys, and which have accrued to him from living under that invaluable
constitution which is the pride of his country and the glory of all lands'.[139]

Members of Protestant associations, evangelical in conviction though they
may have been, held constitutionally conservative opinions which were

---

[132] *Third Annual Report*, 12.
[133] One such was opened in the vestry of St. Paul's, Nottingham, in 1844; R. A. Church, *Economic
and Social Change in a Midland Town* (London, 1966), 315.
[134] *Third Annual Report*, 15–16.   [135] Ibid. 12; *Fifth Annual Report*, vii–viii.
[136] *Sixteenth Annual Report*, vii–viii.
[137] *Fifth Annual Report*, viii; *Sixteenth Annual Report*, viii. Cf. G. Cahill, 'The Protestant Association and the Anti-Maynooth Agitation of 1845', *Catholic Historical Review*, xliii (1957), 283.
[138] Quoted W. R. Ward, op. cit. 212.
[139] W. Paul, *A History of the Origin and Progress of Operative Conservative Societies* (3rd edn.,
Durham, n.d. [1838]; 'printed by the author, of whom it may be had, also at the *Leeds Intelligencer*
office'), 7–13.

typical of old high churchmen. Lord Ashley and Sir Robert Inglis represented this duality of viewpoint, as did Hugh McNeile in his *Lectures on the Church of England*. Protestant associations naturally looked to a Conservative electoral victory for the success of their demands. But, as ultra-Protestants well realized, the Conservative leader had been prominent in the 'great betrayal' of 1829; and when Peel came to office in 1841 his policies proved no more satisfactory to ultra-Protestants than did those of the Whigs. Ashley lamented that true Protestant, Anglican Conservatism was being neglected: '. . . the few, compared with the numbers of "the great", in this realm, who have brought oil in their lamps, will hardly form the proportion of the ten to the population of Gomorrah'.[140] Not the least sign of this was the fact that a great many Protestants dissented in religion from the established Church and in politics from Conservatism, and dissipated the potential anti-Catholic strength of British Protestantism by finding common political ground, with some Catholics, in radical Voluntaryism.

III. VOLUNTARYISM

Whereas evangelicals and initially Tractarians sought to resist on conservative grounds the liberal policy of Parliament and Government, Voluntaries were dissatisfied with this policy for the opposite reason that it was not radical enough. The partial nature of Whig concessions produced growing Dissenting detachment from the Whigs and an increasing tendency towards Voluntaryism. The Conservative revival in politics and the development of Tractarianism strengthened the unpalatable aspect of the Establishment and encouraged militancy among Dissenters. These were not unimpressed by the spiritual intensity of Tractarianism; and they must have been aware of the encouragement which Tractarian views gave to some of their own demands for liberty. But they did not on this account neglect the opportunity for an attack on the Establishment provided by the growth of Catholic theology within it.

Professor Robert Vaughan, although at that time a moderate Dissenter who did not advocate disestablishment, was alarmed both by Tractarianism and the tendency of evangelicalism in the Church of England. He praised the expansion of evangelicalism within the Church but said that 'the Evangelical clergy of the present day . . . are characterized by a singular absence of sympathy [with Dissenters] in their objections to many things in the discipline and worship of the Established Church, and in their ardent attachment to the principles of free government'. Illiberality was a recent and unwelcome development amongst evangelicals.[141] The Wesleyans, being conservative and evangelical, were much more perturbed by Tractarianism,

---

[140] Hodder, *Shaftesbury*, i. 288–9.

[141] R. Vaughan, *Religious Parties in England: their Principles, History, and Present Duty* (2nd edn., London, 1838), xlvi, 106–7, 109–11.

which led them to re-emphasize their evangelical view of faith and draw closer to Dissent. Bishop Phillpotts, in one of his more conciliatory moods, had said of the Wesleyans in his Primary Visitation Charge of 1833: 'they agree with us . . . in all which the most rigidly orthodox among us would deem essential parts of the Christian covenant . . . Would to God that the narrow partition which divides them from us could be broken down!'[142] But with the spread of Tractarian views the partition became thicker. In the Walsall by-election of February 1841 an appeal was made to Wesleyans not to vote Conservative on the ground that beneath the Conservative banners were found many 'Puseyitish Churchmen'.[143] In 1842 a series of *Wesleyan Tracts for the Times* was challenging the doctrines of the Oxford movement. Liberal Dissenters saw this as an example of the essential but unrecognized Nonconformity of the Wesleyans.[144] Such hopes of the Wesleyans were premature, as they were of the Calvinistic Methodists. But among Nonconformists of older denominations and Methodist secession groups, moderates were doubtless driven by religious developments in the Church of England to have more sympathy with their militant brethren. An increase in Voluntary strength resulted.

Voluntaryism issued partly from specific, irritating grievances—examples of Establishment privilege which hit hard at conscience and pocket. These grievances were especially concerned with church-rates after 1836. It was tempting for supporters of established Churches to accuse Voluntaryism of being exclusively material. This view was strengthened by the tendency of Voluntaries to describe their movement as one for 'free trade in religion' as though it were an extension of currently fashionable theories of political economy. Voluntaries, however, increasingly adopted religious arguments, and the attitude of some of them was undoubtedly shaped by spiritual conviction. This added a further dimension to the radical and utilitarian view of Voluntaryism as a branch of civil liberty.

A religious and theoretical side of the case was first stated by Scottish Voluntaries, who were less concerned than their English brethren with practical grievances. Five of the ten reasons for disestablishment given by Andrew Marshall, the United Secession minister who awakened Voluntaryism in Scotland, were of a religious nature. They included the insistence that the Church and not the State had been Scripturally enjoined to preach the gospel; that the early Christians had spread without the aid of a Church Establishment; that religious Establishment was but a human device, not a spiritual guarantee of the establishment of God in the hearts of men; that civil authority had but a secular influence on the Church, and conferred no spiritual authority or benefit; and that maintenance or extension by State grants contravened Christ's ordinance that churches should be supported by

---

[142] Quoted Davies, *Phillpotts*, 148–9.   [143] J. B. Smith Papers, S. 336.
[144] *Eclectic Review*, 4th Ser. xiii (1843), 74–7.

the free-will offerings of members. Other arguments were advanced by Marshall, including the need of Churches, like commerce, for rivalry and competition, and the tendency of Establishments to create social distinctions.[145]

Dr. Ralph Wardlaw, a Glasgow Congregationalist and celebrated Voluntary lecturer, emphasized 'the *religious* aspect [of Voluntaryism], with its bearing on the interests of the true kingdom of Christ, and of pure, vital, saving Christianity'.[146] A resolution of the Perthshire Voluntary Church Association held that religious Establishments might counteract the spread of vital Christianity.[147] In a speech of the Rev. David Young, a United Secession minister, at the formation of this association, all established Churches were held culpable although the Church of Scotland was 'less exceptionable' than that of England, Wales, and Ireland. The British established Churches were particularly guilty because, although religiously distinct, they submitted to be maintained by the same Government: 'It is not scriptural for one and the same civil government to establish Episcopacy as the true religion in England and Presbytery as the true religion in Scotland . . .'[148] Establishments, said Mr. Young, might be satisfactorily condemned purely as a secular grievance, but '. . . I prefer a graver charge: I stand . . . on the high ground that my Master disowns, although not the Churches, yet the Establishments of the Churches of Scotland and England and Ireland . . .'[149] Scottish Voluntaries, like English high churchmen, objected to decisions on doctrine by a secular Parliament in an Erastian system: '. . . the mere idea of the present parliament sitting in judgement on a confession of faith, "article by article", would fill the whole country with sounds of derision'.[150] These Scottish Voluntary views affected English Dissenting opinion by means of publications and the influence of Scottish ministers who visited England or resided there.[151]

Although rejecting the maintenance of a specific form of religion by the State, Voluntaries did not wish to eliminate entirely the religious duties of civil Government. A broad protection for religion, not limited to one denomination, was desirable. The civil magistrate should protect religion without patronizing or directing it.[152] The State should not be Church of England or Church of Scotland but still decidedly Christian.

Voluntaryism was an extreme reaction to the constitutional, conservative opinion that an established Church should be preserved as a traditional

[145] Montgomery, 'The Voluntary Controversy in the Church of Scotland', 9–23.

[146] W. L. Alexander, *Memoirs of the Life and Writings of Ralph Wardlaw, D.D.* (Edinburgh 1856), 317.

[147] *Report of the Speeches delivered in the North United Secession Church, Perth, at the formation of the Perthshire Voluntary Church Association* (Dundee, 1833), 1 ff.

[148] Ibid. 13–14.   [149] Ibid. 16.

[150] The *Dissenter* (published monthly at Perth), No. 9 (Sept. 1833), 174.

[151] Cf. W. R. Ward, op. cit. 129–32.

[152] *Eclectic Review*, 3rd Ser. xi (Jan.–June 1834), 65.

institution which possessed exclusive privileges. In defence of the Establishment, religious arguments were used against those of the Voluntaries. Others beside Gladstone justified the establishment of the Church of England on the ground of its being in the line of apostolic succession. 'It is established,' wrote the Rev. Charles Girdlestone, 'not only by the law of the land, but by the Gospel of Jesus Christ. Its ministers have that appointment which at the first came from Him.'[153] It was believed that the established Church, if it were reformed and made more comprehensive, offered the most promising means of Christian reunion.[154] It was urged, on the lines of Coleridge's ideal of a national 'clerisy', that an Establishment whose territorial structure covered the entire country provided a stable, nationwide pastoral superintendence unequalled by Dissent. John Kaye, bishop of Lincoln, said in a sermon of April 1834 that a State Church guaranteed a regular parochial ministry for poor congregations who could not afford to support a minister from voluntary contributions.[155] (This argument would have less weight, however, as Dissenting denominations became more stable and extensive.) In contradiction to the Voluntary claim that Erastianism caused indifference and infidelity, it was said that these were more likely to be encouraged by the separation of Church and State.[156]

Some liberal Anglicans doubted whether State maintenance provided any satisfactory support for their religion, and adopted the Voluntary position.[157] These included such political advocates of disestablishment as Charles Lushington, Lord Nugent, Sir Culling Eardley Smith, and William Williams. A few Anglicans even became Dissenters because they disapproved of an Erastian Church.

In spite of emphasis by Voluntaries on religious reasons, the latter were linked to material ones, at least so long as church-rates continued to provide a direct, painful, and everyday barrier between Church and Dissent. However, church-rates assisted spiritual opposition to the Establishment as well as financial enmity, for it was believed that Churches should be maintained only by those who were convinced of their truth. The abolition of church-rates was also desired for the sake of civil equality and the general progress of civilization. George Offor, a Dissenting bookseller in Hackney, drew a connection between church-rate abolition and national glory: 'Happy, prosperous, magnificent, will be Great Britain, when all compulsive [*sic*] payments for services, called religious, shall cease; and every inhabitant shall be honoured, esteemed, and patronized, by the government, according to his talents and virtue, without the slightest sectarian preference!'[158]

[153] C. Girdlestone, *Church Rates lawful, but not always expedient* (sermon preached 6 Oct. 1833; London, 1833), 11.

[154] Ibid. 12–13.   [155] Soloway, *Prelates and People*, 270–1.

[156] Rev. J. Esdaile, *The Spirit, Principle and Reasoning of Voluntaryism exposed* (Perth, 1834), 50.

[157] *Legacy to Parsons*, 104–5.

[158] G. Offor, *The triumph of Henry VIII over the Usurpations of the Church* (London, 1846), 77.

Church-rate disputes were an important contribution to the growth of Voluntary feeling which marked the new decade of the 1840s. It was later stated before a Commons committee that these disputes were occurring at the end of the 1830s in many places where Dissent was strong, from Llanelly to Rochdale, from Polperro (Cornwall) to Whitechapel. In Whitechapel the opposition of Jews and Protestant Dissenters prevented a rate of more than a penny in the pound being proposed after 1839.[159] George Offor testified that feeling ran so high on this point that once 'when the church party beat the other party, they absolutely had a hurrah in the middle of the church'.[160] In West Hackney parish, where Offor resided, a rate had not been levied since the uproar at the time when 'Mr. Clarke's music stool was taken from his house'.[161] In the parish of St. John's, Hackney, in 1840 a carpenter named Nunn refused to pay a rate of 3s. 4d., for which he was cited before the ecclesiastical court and ordered to pay this amount plus costs of £250. Nunn became insane and died in a madhouse. Varty and Mopsey, the churchwardens in the case, died soon afterwards. Although none of them was young, a connection between their deaths and the case was strongly hinted at.[162]

Against this background of protest the more celebrated cases took place. The first Braintree Case, in the county of Essex with its strong Dissenting traditions, reached a height of controversy in 1840 and 1841. This case concerned the right of churchwardens to levy a rate after it had been refused by a vestry meeting. The Consistory Court of London upheld this right on the precedent of *Gauden* v. *Selby* (1799). Mr. Burder, the recalcitrant Dissenter in the case, then moved for a prohibition against the rate in the Court of Queen's Bench; the prohibition was granted on 1 May 1840, Lord Chief Justice Denman declaring a rate invalid which was levied after a defeat in vestry. This judgement was affirmed in the Exchequer Court in February 1841, but it was suggested by the judge that if the rate had been made at the meeting where a majority opposed it, and not apart from this meeting, the rate might have been valid. Therefore Veley, the persistent churchwarden solicitor, began the second and more tortuous Braintree Case. At a vestry meeting in July 1841 a rate was proposed, and Samuel Courtauld carried an amendment that all compulsory payments for the support of religion were unscriptural and against the 'pure and spiritual character of the religion of Christ'. Despite this the churchwardens levied the rate, and its validity was debated in a variety of courts before a final judgement was given against it in the House of Lords in 1853.[163]

Another Essex case concerned John Thorogood, a Chelmsford shoemaker.

---

[159] Report of Select Committee of House of Commons on Church Rates, P.P. 1851 (541), ix. 568.
[160] Ibid. 3.   [161] Ibid. 10 f.   [162] Ibid. 14 ff.
[163] Ibid. 40 ff. See Chadwick, *Victorian Church*, i. 154–8.

Thorogood not only refused to pay a rate of 5*s*. 6*d*. but questioned the validity of the rate, thereby removing from the magistrates their power of summary jurisdiction and consigning his case to the Consistory Court of London. He showed his contempt for this court by failing to appear before it. On this ground of contempt he was imprisoned in January 1839. He stayed in prison for eighteen months, for he refused to purge his contempt by pleading. During this period he provided an example of martyrdom for the sake of conscience which was highly significant at a time of growing Dissenting unrest. Allowed to see his wife in a separate room on a Sunday, he used the occasion to harangue a crowd from a window.[164] His case was discussed several times in Parliament, and petitions were presented for his release. Edward Baines linked the incident with a general demand for the abolition of church-rates; Hume, supporting him, mentioned as an example of the strength of opposition 'the treatment of Church Rate victims at Truro the other day, when a splendid procession, and an elegant dinner awaited them on their liberation from prison . . .'[165] At length in July 1840 an Act of Parliament was passed which allowed Thorogood to be released.

Hume had said that the agitation against the rates had spread through Devonshire, Wiltshire, Essex, and the whole of Wales.[166] Wales had recently contributed the famous cases of Llanon and Llanelly, concerning Dissenting churchwardens, and a dispute at Llanfihangel Lledrod among others.[167] At Llanon, Carmarthenshire, a church-rate was refused at a vestry meeting; a poor Unitarian churchwarden, David Jones, was summoned before the Consistory Court of St. David's for not supplying bread and wine and for allegedly blaspheming in an alehouse on the Lord's Day. A verdict was given against Jones in April 1838; he was ordered to pay £38. 14*s*., refused to do so, and was imprisoned in December. The case was discussed in Parliament in connection with a motion of Benjamin Hawes (M.P. for Lambeth) to abolish the jurisdiction of inferior ecclesiastical courts.[168] Released on a technicality after seven months, Jones was prosecuted again but died before reincarceration. Imprisoned in the same month and in the same gaol as Jones was John James, a Congregational churchwarden in the parish of Llanelly, which was held by the formidable Rev. Ebenezer Morris in plurality with Llanon. James was a member of the congregation of the Rev. David Rees, editor of the monthly periodical *Y Diwgiwr*, an advanced radical organ which was especially hostile to church-rates.[169] Cited before the Con-

[164] Ibid. 150.

[165] Hansard, xlvii. 697. For the Truro matter see Chadwick, i. 147–8.

[166] Hansard, xlvii. 688.

[167] For Llanfihangel Lledrod, Whitchurch (Pembs.), and other cases, see Morgan, 'The Consistory Courts of the Diocese of St. David's', 85ff. For disputes at Merthyr Tydfil see G. A. Williams, 'The Making of Radical Merthyr', 185 f.

[168] Hansard, xlvii. 522–49.

[169] For the Llanon and Llanelly cases, see W. T. Morgan, op. cit. 123 ff., also *idem*, 'Disciplinary

sistory Court for refusing to discipline loiterers in the churchyard during divine service, James pleaded guilty but refused to pay costs. He was imprisoned, but released a few days later on paying a much higher sum.

Leicester and Rochdale provided examples of disputes in strongly Dissenting English urban centres where the attempts to levy rate had not yet, as in some similar places, been completely abandoned. In 3 out of 5 parishes in Leicester the rate had ceased to be levied by 1836; therefore the attempt to abolish it was all the greater in the two remaining ones. The more militant Dissenters of Leicester formed a powerful opposition, marshalled by some of the leading ministers in England holding Voluntary views—the Rev. J. P. Mursell (Baptist), the Rev. Edward Miall (Congregational), and the Rev. Dr. George Legge (another Congregationalist, who came from Scotland). Their views were expressed by the *Leicestershire Mercury*, founded in 1836, and by the Voluntary Church Society, established in the town in October of the same year, which had an influence far beyond Leicester.

A campaign against church-rates in Leicester was closely linked with disestablishment; and the Leicester Voluntaries were scornful of metropolitan Dissenting ministers who were 'so satisfied with mere toleration that they hardly dreamt of religious equality'.[170] In St. Margaret's parish Miall and twenty others were summoned before the magistrates in 1836 for non-payment of a rate. When they refused to appear, some of their goods were seized and put up for auction, but the feeling of the crowd prevented a bid being made and the goods had to be disposed of privately. In 1837 an anti-rate majority was elected to the select vestry of St. Margaret's parish, and future efforts to obtain a rate there failed. But in St. Martin's parish the rate continued to be voted, and bitterness persisted in spite of the mollifying efforts of the vicar, the Hon. and Rev. H. D. Erskine, Whig son of the former Whig Lord Chancellor. In 1838 William Baines, a parishioner of St. Martin's but a member of Miall's congregation, was cited before the Court of Arches for non-payment. Regarding the court's authority as unscriptural, he declined to appear. After a legal battle the Court of Queen's Bench finally judged against him for contempt in the summer of 1840, whereupon some staunch churchmen rang the bells of St. Martin's. Baines was lodged in the county gaol, where he was comfortably treated and allowed to play cricket in the yard. Like Thorogood he attracted wide sympathy. During his imprisonment he was elected a councillor by the largest ward in the town. A petition for his release came from 6,000 inhabitants of Leicester 'without reference to religious persuasion', and an address to the throne on his behalf was signed by '7,000 of the females of Leicester'—also presumably without reference to religious persuasion. A meeting was arranged by the Voluntary

Cases against Churchwardens in the Consistory Courts of St. David's', *Journal of the Historical Society of the Church in Wales*, x (1960), 17 ff.

[170] Quoted D. M. Thompson (ed.), *Nonconformity in the Nineteenth Century*, 101.

Church Society, and chaired by the recently liberated Thorogood. In May 1841 Baines was released under Thorogood's Act when the sum required of him was paid anonymously. But the legal contests in St. Martin's parish persisted until the annual proposal of a rate was defeated in 1849. The church-rate controversies in Leicester also had important effects on the growth of the national Voluntary movement.[171]

In Rochdale fierce church-rate disputes were natural at that time. The town had an exceptionally high proportion of Dissenters: 74·4 per cent of its church attendances were Nonconformist at the 1851 Census. The Wesleyan Methodist Association, which had seceded from Wesleyanism in 1835, was a numerous force centred on the powerful Baillie Street chapel and had 24·9 per cent of the 1851 attendances. The Methodist Associationists allied with other radical Dissenters in a local Religious Freedom Society and in opposition to church-rate.[172] Resistance to the rate was well rooted in the town. The Quaker Jacob Bright, father of John, had his goods distrained twenty-one times between 1811 and 1833, and the Rev. William Whittle Barton, a Baptist minister, unsuccessfully contested a rate in the Consistory Court.[173] Conflict was intensified by the appointment of a redoubtable Tory vicar, the Rev. J. E. N. Molesworth, in 1839.

At a vestry meeting in July 1840 a rate of $\frac{1}{2}d.$ in the pound was proposed. Molesworth rejected a suggestion that payment should be voluntary. A poll followed between 13 and 17 July: 'The chief pressure of the voting was on the last day, and a wall was thrown down by the crowd, and a man injured, and many people rolled down the hill into Mr. Samuel Taylor's field ... The scale was turned by the Todmorden men, who were sent by the Messieurs Fielden in waggons and by train.'[174] A majority, stated as 84, was obtained against the rate.[175] But another meeting was immediately summoned to renew demand for a rate, and held on 29 July. The gathering of 5,000 parishioners overflowed into St. Chad's graveyard. John Bright took a notable step to fame by making his 'tombstone' speech: 'My friends, the time is coming when a State Church will be unknown in England, and it rests with you to accelerate or retard that happy consummation.'[176] The view proved even more visionary than his prophecy in the 1880s of a Channel tunnel, though few would have regarded it in this light amidst the growing agitation and real grievances of the time. Another poll took place; Molesworth claimed a majority of 113 for the rate, his opponents a majority of 7

---

[171] Patterson, *Radical Leicester*, 247–55, 259; Hansard, lvi. 256–9; lvii. 305–15, 360–91; A. Miall, *The Life of Edward Miall* (London, 1884), 26 ff.

[172] Gowland, 'Methodist Secessions and Social Conflict in South Lancashire', 281, 290–1.

[173] Ibid. 284.

[174] F. R. Raines, *The Vicars of Rochdale* (Chetham Society Publications, new Ser., ii, pt. 2, Manchester, 1883), 336.

[175] Gowland, op. cit. 285 f. Raines gives a majority of 66 against the rate (op. cit. 336).

[176] Raines, 340.

against it.[177] Both parties celebrated victory. The anti-rate people had 'music and dancing all night',[178] and decided to refuse payment. In January 1841 nine men (four of whom were Methodist Associationists) appeared before the magistrates for non-payment; but they were dismissed on a technicality, and no further attempt was made to levy a compulsory rate in Rochdale.[179] Even if John Bright's rather lukewarm attitude to Voluntaryism in later years was a disappointment to some Dissenters, his early championship had contributed to the growth of Voluntary feeling.

The prevalence of church-rate disputes demonstrates that the Voluntary message had more than stony ground to fall on. Recently formed societies existed to propagate the message. The Religious Freedom Society had been established in May 1839 on the initiative of Josiah Conder.[180] Aiming to include liberal Anglicans as well as Nonconformists, its principles included freedom of worship, no compulsory support of religious rites, and opposition to State Churches. Possessing a central committee and local branches, it aimed to return suitable members to Parliament and to obtain desirable parliamentary measures.[181] The Evangelical Voluntary Church Association also attempted to unite Dissenters and Anglicans in support of disestablishment, but concentrated on religious persuasion rather than political action.[182] Elected as chairman and treasurer of this body in December 1839 was Sir Culling Eardley Smith, an Anglican aristocrat. He was described by Samuel Wilberforce as 'certainly an extraordinary goose',[183] but despite this he was to achieve a considerable amount for religious toleration in foreign lands.

Neither the Religious Freedom Society nor the Evangelical Voluntary Church Association lasted many years. The former was in decline by 1843, the latter dissolved in 1844. But out of the church-rate disputes of the period emerged a more notable leader and, eventually, a more persistent organization. The Leicester church-rate agitation, the influence of Scottish Voluntaries, and particularly the imprisonment of his friend William Baines persuaded Edward Miall to leave his pastorate and devote himself fully to the Voluntary cause.[184] The first-fruit of his new departure was the *Nonconformist*, which became the journalistic mainstay of Victorian militant Dissent. Miall's

---

[177] Ibid. 343; Gowland, 287.

[178] W. R. Ward, *Religion and Society in England*, 188.

[179] Gowland, 287–8. For the Rochdale case see also W. Robertson, *The Life and Times of the Rt. Hon. John Bright* (3 vols., London, 1883), i. 98–110; Sir G. L. Molesworth, *The Life of J. E. N. Molesworth* (London, 1915), 51–61.

[180] W. H. Mackintosh, *Disestablishment and Liberation* (London, 1972), 8.

[181] *Report presented at the First Annual Meeting of the Religious Freedom Society* (London, 1840); E. R. Conder, *Josiah Conder: A Memoir* (London, 1857), 284–6.

[182] Mackintosh, op. cit. 8; principles of Society published in a pamphlet of Rev. J. Burnet, *The Church of England and the Church of Christ* (London, 1840).

[183] Wilberforce to Sir Charles Anderson, 4 Apr. 1838 (Wilberforce Papers, d. 25). Sir Culling dropped the 'Smith' from his name in 1847 (see DNB).

[184] Miall, op. cit. 37.

relentless vehemence in print smacked of literary compensation in one who was privately shy and courteous. The first number, appearing on 14 April 1841, dinned as the first trump in the ears of dozing Dissenters. The West Riding Association of Baptist Churches passed a resolution welcoming its appearance.[185] The paper called on Dissenters to recover the unity and sense of purpose which had marked their campaigns for the repeal of the Test and Corporation Acts. A bolder face and absolute commitment were needed: 'they must begin again the struggle with intolerance ... THE ENTIRE SEPARATION OF CHURCH AND STATE is really their object.'[186] Implied in such statements was the growing impatience of Dissent with the Whigs. But it was the Conservative ministry formed in 1841 which was to experience the first onslaughts of the new pugnacity.

Voluntaryism was linked with other radical movements. With the Free Trade movement it had clear connections. Many manufacturers were Nonconformist, and the two movements sought support from many of the same people. Dissenting ministers, perhaps for ideological as well as practical financial reasons, supported economic liberalism. Voluntaryism could be seen as springing from the same liberal, individualist root as Free Trade. The direct financial interests of Dissenters were expected to advance through Free Trade: the reduction in corn prices which was expected to follow the repeal of the Corn Laws would cause a reduction, in the same proportion, of the cash payments for which tithes had been commuted.

It was not surprising, therefore, that many Dissenting ministers, whether militant Voluntaries or not, wholeheartedly supported the Anti-Corn Law League. A conference of 645 ministers (mostly Congregationalists and Baptists), organized by the League at Manchester in August 1841, denounced Protection on religious and humanitarian grounds.[187] The political distinction, not only between Nonconformity and the Establishment, but between liberal and conservative Dissenters, was revealed by attendance at this gathering. A correspondent wrote to Dr. Thomas Chalmers: 'The Church of England ministers stand wholly aloof from the movement, with the exception of one curate. The Methodists [i.e. Wesleyans] hitherto have also stood entirely aloof ... None of our Presbytery [Church of Scotland] have taken [sic] anything to do with it, although invited, of course.' This correspondent added that many ministers, including himself, privately desired an extensive alteration of the Corn Laws, but thought that a public demonstration was inappropriate to their sacred office.[188] If Church of Scotland

---

[185] Ram, 'The Political Activities of Dissenters in the East and West Ridings of Yorkshire', 207.
[186] D. M. Thompson (ed.), op. cit. 106–7.
[187] N. McCord, *The Anti-Corn Law League, 1838–46* (London, 1958), 104–7. For a denominational analysis of the ministers attending, see K. R. M. Short, 'English Baptists and the Corn Laws', *Baptist Quarterly*, N.S. xxi (1965–6), 309–20. Cf. H. R. Martin, 'The Politics of the Congregationalists', 218–24.   [188] Rev. Alexander Munro of Manchester to Chalmers, 11 Aug. 1841 (Chalmers Papers, bound vol. for 1841).

ministers living in Manchester itself were not present, 30 ministers of the United Secession Church and 12 of the Relief Church travelled from Scotland especially for the occasion.[189] Members of the Wesleyan Methodist Association also actively supported anti-Corn Law politics.[190]

The Manchester conference was emulated elsewhere. In December 1841 a meeting of North Wales ministers was held at Caernarvon in support of the League.[191] In Scotland there was a similar conjunction of interests. Duncan McLaren, a prominent Voluntary and Leaguer, instigated an inquiry into Dissenting views. A questionnaire was sent to all Scottish Dissenting ministers—the great majority of whom belonged to the Secession, Relief, Congregational, or Baptist Churches—asking their opinions and those of their congregations on the Corn Laws. Most of the replies condemned the Laws.[192] This led to an anti-Corn Law conference at Edinburgh from 11 to 13 January 1842, attended by many Dissenting ministers.[193] Church of Scotland ministers were not invited, as it was supposed they would not attend, allegedly on the ground that '. . . their annual stipends were, with comparatively few exceptions, payable according to the price of certain fixed quantities of corn'.[194] Ministers of the Scottish Episcopal Church had shown themselves unfavourable to the aims of the League; out of 90 of these ministers to whom the questionnaire was sent, only 21 replied, indicating the view that ministers should not meddle with politics. The replies of Wesleyan ministers were similar.[195] Free Trade and Voluntaryism lent each other mutual assistance. The League was not an unmixed blessing to the Voluntaries for it absorbed much of the political exertion of Dissenters until repeal came in 1846. But the League's organization and methods were an inspiration to the Anti-State Church Association formed in 1844.

The Voluntary leaders, since they usually belonged to well-established denominations whose composition may have been getting more middle class, were socially attuned to the Anti-Corn Law League rather than to the rival Chartist cause. The Christian strand in Chartism was a reaction not only against the Establishment but against 'respectable' Nonconformity, and Chartists sometimes formed their own churches. Miall, however, held wide radical views—he advocated, amongst other advanced causes, the abolition of capital punishment—and he lent moderate support to the

[189] K. J. Cameron, 'Anti-Corn Law Agitations in Scotland, with particular reference to the Anti-Corn-Law League' (unpubl. Univ. of Edinburgh Ph.D. thesis 1971), 209.

[190] W. R. Ward, op. cit. 200; Gowland, op. cit. 338. For support of repeal among some lay Wesleyans, see letter on Walsall by-election, 29 Jan. 1841 (J. B. Smith Papers, S. 336).

[191] Cameron, op. cit. 210.

[192] D. McLaren, *The Corn Laws condemned . . . by upwards of five hundred Ministers of different Denominations resident in Scotland* (Edinburgh, 1842), i ff.

[193] J. B. Mackie, *The Life and Work of Duncan McLaren* (2 vols., London, 1888), i. 232–5; Cameron, 208–12.

[194] McLaren, op. cit. vii.

[195] Ibid. 52–6.

People's Charter. A wider franchise was expected to help the aims of Dissent. The Chartists, for their part, were avowed Voluntaries. The *Nonconformist* attempted in a series of articles to unite middle and working classes in support of suffrage extension, and hence advocated the Complete Suffrage Union. At the first National Complete Suffrage Conference at Birmingham in April 1842, Miall, Bright, and Mursell shared the platform with William Lovett, James Bronterre O'Brien, and Henry Vincent, and the *Nonconformist* became the official organ of the Union.[196] The experiment in co-operation did not last, but Chartists and Voluntaries still occasionally coalesced in politics until the clear decline of Chartism itself. After this Miall continued to demand a democratic suffrage.

About Voluntaryism there was always something of Chartism, and perhaps of millenialism. Concentration on Voluntaryism probably helped to obstruct the removal of the remaining more tangible grievances of Dissent —church-rates, burials, and university degrees. This was feared by those who, though Voluntary by conviction, doubted the wisdom of extreme demands. Angell James, the well-known Birmingham Congregational minister, desired disestablishment but said in 1834 that 'any immediate and urgent attempt at the severance of the Church and the State ... would delight and strengthen the Tories ... and would prevent the Dissenters from progressively procuring [the] redress of practical evils ...'[197] Many Anglicans recoiled from a vehement, single-minded Voluntary movement. To the Liberal party Voluntaryism was, in great measure, a liability. The desires of the electorate could only partially be served by such a movement. Liberals had to entertain many more aims than Voluntaryism, and this applied to radicals as well as Whigs. Not only the Anglican Cobden but the Quaker Bright showed impatience with Voluntaryism. It was an embarrassment to the Liberals unless it could be restricted to lesser ends which non-Dissenting (also non-militant Dissenting) Liberals could support. Thus the growth of Voluntaryism increased the fragmentation of the Liberal party.

By the early 1840s the centuries-old ecclesiastical tensions of England had been intensified by the growth of competing movements. Tractarianism, ultra-Protestantism, latitudinarianism, Voluntaryism all intersected and, while attempting to hinder one another, stimulated each other's growth. The mid-century period of intense religious activity and expansion was also, therefore, one of intense disputation and competition. This helped to keep religious topics to the forefront, even if not always in an edifying form. On account of these controversial developments, Governments found it difficult

---

[196] Miall, op. cit. 85–7. See R. G. Cowherd, *The Politics of English Dissent, 1815–48* (London, 1959), 111–15; H. U. Faulkner, *Chartism and the Churches* (New York, 1916), 96 ff.; Martin, 233–63.   [197] Dale (ed.), *James*, 167.

to tread a delicate, well-meaning path between Erastianism and concession. Peel, in seeking to follow this path after 1841 as the Whigs had done previously, found himself buffeted by the turbulent winds of sharply conflicting opinions. On entering office he met the gusts of a flourishing ecclesiastical quarrel north of the border.

CHAPTER IV

Crisis in the Church of Scotland, 1834–1843

I. SCOTTISH VOLUNTARYISM AND THE ORIGINS OF NON-INTRUSION

IN FACING the troubles in the Church of Scotland, British Governments had to deal with a very different Establishment from the one which most of their members knew. The ecclesiastical development of Scotland since the Reformation had produced a Church not only doctrinally or liturgically dissimilar and administratively distinct from that of England but much more independent of the State. Presbyterianism had been officially recognized as the religion of the Kirk in 1690. Royal supremacy was not acknowledged by the northern Establishment. A General Assembly met annually to legislate for the Church, in stark contrast to indefinitely suspended Anglican Convocations. Lay patronage in the appointment of clergy, exercised by the Crown or others, was questioned only by a few in the Church of England but was a matter of deep and continuous dispute in the Kirk. Abolished in the Presbyterian settlement of 1690, with the patrons receiving compensation, patronage had been restored in 1712 at a time of high-church and Erastian revival under Queen Anne. But the Act of 1712 came after the Union of 1707, which confirmed the settlement of 1690. Could not therefore the restoration of patronage be considered a betrayal of the conditions of Union? Moreover, the surveillance, since the Union, of two distinct Establishments by the same Government raised the question of whether one Government could do justice to two Churches.

In the 1830s and early 1840s Governments were unreceptive to the claims being made in the Church of Scotland for a popular veto in the appointment of ministers, leading to the broader desire for spiritual independence of the civil Government. Even though these claims sought to strengthen rather than subvert the Establishment, they still demanded great sacrifices from the State—no less than the virtual abandonment of civil authority over spiritual government, yet maintenance of the temporal privileges and protection traditionally accorded to the Church as a religious Establishment. Erastians found this combination very hard to accept, particularly at a time when the Tractarians were arousing resistance by their own desire for spiritual independence. There was a tendency to oppose such claims, whether centred as in England on the apostolical succession or as in Scotland on a popular choice of ministers. On the particular issue of ministers' appointments, moreover, Whigs and Conservatives naturally disliked the idea of a democratic veto—some on religious grounds, some on political grounds, and some on both. These opinions counteracted the sympathy of Anglicans, as members of a fellow Establishment beset by similar problems of Dissent and indifference, with the efforts of the Church of Scotland to expand its influence.

Of more direct importance in Government reactions were the views of the Moderate party in the Church of Scotland, which upheld lay patronage and civil authority. The Moderates were in a position to reinforce the Erastian predilections of Governments sitting remotely at Westminster. But the other side of Government policy, concession to Dissent, held no comfort for the reformers in the Church of Scotland. These reformers wished to revive the Establishment and prevent the spread of Dissent. The Whig Government, wishing to conciliate Dissent, thus had an additional reason for rebutting reforming claims in the Kirk.

State discouragement was augmented by ignorance of Scottish Church questions in a largely non-Scottish Parliament. Another significant factor was the lack of political force behind the reforming claims. While having the support of a majority in the General Assembly of the Church, the claims were not strongly expressed through the medium of parliamentary elections or popular organization. Hence the Government was strengthened in its hopeful belief that the demands were merely those of a paranoid clerical faction, which would drastically contract before the chill prospect of quitting the material securities of the Establishment. Growing extremism and alienation was to produce the Disruption of 1843, a greater and more far-reaching cataclysm than the Government had expected.

The Disruption fractured the Church of Scotland and stimulated Dissenting and radical opponents of Church Establishments. But the movement which terminated in schism had, ironically, commenced as an effort to defend the Kirk against Dissent, especially in its vehement Voluntary manifestation. The United Secession Church formed in 1820 signalized the unity and confidence of the 'New Lights', whose Voluntary views had prevailed among many of the eighteenth-century seceders from the Church of Scotland. The Relief Church, also consisting of seceders, had become Voluntary after 1770. In the 1820s there came from the United Secession Church statements of Voluntary principle, first in 1824 the Rev. John Ballantyne of Stonehaven's *Comparison of Established and Dissenting Churches*, then Andrew Marshall's more effective proclamation of 1829.[1] There had followed local Voluntary societies, a central organization, and petitions to

---

[1] Montgomery, 'The Voluntary Controversy in the Church of Scotland', 27–32; J. H. S. Burleigh, *A Church History of Scotland* (Edinburgh, 1960), 323–4.

Parliament.[2] The 1832 enfranchisement—so much more radical in Scotland than in England—and the return of a large Liberal majority stimulated Dissenting demands.

Apart from its considerable influence in England, the Scottish Voluntary movement displayed potential strength in the size of the United Secession and other Dissenting Churches. In 1839 the United Secession Church had 361 congregations, 357 ministers, and a total following of 261,345;[3] the population of Scotland in 1841 was 2,620,184. The Secession Church and the smaller Relief Church united in 1847, and the returns of the 1851 Religious Census (confessedly less reliable for Scotland than for England and Wales) gave this United Presbyterian Church total attendances, including duplicates and triplicates, of 336,412 out of 1,752,688 in all Scottish churches.[4] In the 1835 election Voluntary societies apparently attempted to influence the voting of their members.[5] At this time, however, only one Scottish M.P. was a non-episcopalian Dissenter—W. D. Gillon, the Unitarian member for the Falkirk burghs.

Scottish Dissenters did not share the English Dissenters' grievances over baptisms, marriages, burials, and university degrees. But they complained about the exclusion of Dissenters from teaching posts in parish schools and their official exclusion from such posts in universities.[6] Moreover, the annuity tax in Edinburgh—a compulsory levy of 6 per cent on the occupants of houses and shops (with certain exceptions) for providing the stipends of Church of Scotland ministers—was a local grievance comparable to church-rates amongst the large Dissenting population of the Scottish capital. First authorized in 1634, this tax had been extended to the new parts of Edinburgh in 1809; a similar tax had been levied in Montrose since 1690.[7] Objections were heard from the beginning of the century, and the growth of Voluntaryism and general reforming ardour brought them to a head in 1833.[8] As well as Dissenters, some churchmen opposed the tax, both for pacificatory reasons and because they objected to the exemption of certain classes from the tax—the well-to-do members of the College of Justice, and suburb-dwellers outside the Edinburgh city boundaries who attended city churches.[9]

In June 1833 the Lord Advocate introduced a bill to reduce the tax and remove the exemption of the members of the College of Justice, but the bill

[2] See above, p. 26.

[3] M'Kerrow, History of the Secession Church, ii. 541–3.

[4] J. H. Dawson (ed.), Abridged Statistical History of Scotland (2nd edn., Edinburgh, 1857), 1106 ff.

[5] Alexander, Memoirs of Ralph Wardlaw, 349.

[6] Hansard, xl. 822–3 (speech of Gillon).

[7] Report of Select Committee of House of Commons on the Annuity Tax, P.P. 1851 (617), vii. 1, 25 ff., 524 ff.

[8] Ibid. 4 ff.

[9] Ibid. 5–6, 236–7.

was dropped.[10] In 1833, 846 inhabitants of Edinburgh were prosecuted for refusing to pay; and in the first elections to the reformed town council in that year the poll in Ward I was headed by William Tait, editor of *Tait's Magazine*, who had been imprisoned in Calton gaol for four days until he paid the tax.[11] It was suggested by the new council that the tax might be abolished, that the number of city ministers should be reduced from 18 to 13, and that they should be paid from pew-rents, supplemented if necessary by a tax on heritable property. But this solution was rejected by the Presbytery of Edinburgh: with a growing population they could not accept a reduction of ministers, and the plan would mean raising the pew-rents which already helped to keep the poor away from the churches.[12] In December 1834 Peel showed concessionary temper by suggesting that, in compensation for replacing church-rates by a land tax which would include Scotland, the annuity tax might be removed. But the Lord Advocate, Sir William Rae, told him that this proposal would not be considered as a relief by Scotland in general, since only Edinburgh (and Montrose) would benefit from it.[13] So the dispute continued. In January 1836 the Rev. John Brown, a United Secession minister, refused to pay the tax on conscientious grounds, and in April Thomas Russell and Thomas Chapman (both non-payers) anticipated Thorogood and Baines by receiving visits in Calton gaol from 200 local Voluntaries.[14] Gillon, presenting a petition from Chapman in the House of Commons, said that the House must either repeal the tax or build more gaols in Edinburgh.[15] A fruitless recommendation to commute the tax was made by a Commons Select Committee in 1836.[16]

Until a compromise was reached in 1860, and even after this, the tax supported the arguments in favour of Voluntaryism. As in England, however, the Establishment had defensive resources. Though hindered by divisions, these resources were less dispersed by theological disunity than in England. Indeed, most Scottish Protestant Dissenters, being themselves Presbyterians, were similar in theology to the Establishment men. The differences which had driven them from the Church in the eighteenth century came from patronage rather than more fundamental theological questions, although there was also a doctrinal disharmony in the retreat of strict Calvinism in face of the liberalism of the Moderate party. Within the Kirk the Moderates were being increasingly challenged in the early nineteenth century by evangelicals, of whom Dr. Thomas Chalmers became the leader. The Calvinist doctrinal standards of the Westminster Confession of

[10] *Journals of the House of Commons*, lxxxviii (1833), 446, 544.

[11] P.P. 1851 (617), vii. l, 40; Montgomery, op. cit. 180 ff.

[12] Hanna, *Memoirs of Thomas Chalmers*, iii. 428-33; Montgomery, 194-5; Burleigh, op. cit. 327.

[13] Peel to Sir William Rae, 31 Dec. 1834, 'most private' (Peel Papers, Add. MS. 40339, fos. 337-8); Rae to Peel, 3 Jan. 1835 (ibid. fos. 339-40).

[14] Montgomery, 184-6.   [15] Hansard, xxxiii. 329.   [16] P.P. 1851 (617), vii. i, 70 ff..

1644 were officially recognized by both Moderates and evangelicals. But neither felt comfortable with them. Questioned by Moderates on rational, enlightened grounds, they were also dubious in the eyes of many evangelicals, to whose missionary zeal universal atonement was more appropriate than predestination. Thus the spiritual attitudes of the two sides differed in emphasis rather than specific points of doctrine. Evangelicals were dissatisfied with the rationalism of the Enlightenment and of the Moderates. They sought to awaken souls and consciences with the methods of a Knox, a Wesley, or a Wilberforce, shaming the 'blether of cold morality' supposedly characteristic of Moderate ministers.

Among the leading objects of evangelicals in the Church was the defeat of the Dissenting threat. Societies were formed for this purpose, and periodicals and pamphlets were published. An Association for Promoting the Interests of the Church of Scotland was founded at Glasgow in 1833.[17] The Edinburgh Young Men's Church Association, formed in 1834, arranged anti-Voluntary lectures by leading evangelicals who were themselves to be later accused of weakening the connection between Church and State, including the Rev. Robert Candlish, the Rev. William Cunningham, and Alexander Murray Dunlop.[18]

Evangelicals also had important practical methods of revival, including the building of churches and the adoption of policies to widen the Kirk's popularity. At the General Assembly of 1834, a gathering famed for its measures to encourage Church expansion, Chalmers was elected convener of the Church Accommodation Committee. He enthusiastically promoted the cause of Church extension.[19] In July 1834 a deputation went to London to request government endowment for the chapels of ease which were being constructed to relieve large and populous parishes. Melbourne and other ministers responded favourably.[20] But the possibility of State support caused a Dissenting uproar, which the Central Board of Scottish Dissenters helped to organize. The quarrel, which lasted for four years at its height, concerned partly the principle of religious endowment by the State, and partly the extent of Nonconformist church accommodation which, in the Dissenting view, largely made up the deficiency which was deplored by the Church of Scotland.[21] Dissenters, as Peel was told by Sir William Rae, a former Tory Lord Advocate, 'see that affording church accommodation at a cheap rate will cut up their congregations most materially. This however is one of the very objects we have in view.'[22] The Whigs were hampered in their response

[17] *Speeches at a Glasgow Public Meeting*, 31 Jan. and 1 Feb. 1833 (Glasgow, 1833).
[18] Montgomery, 55–6, 64–5. Cf. Esdaile, *The Spirit, Principles and Reasoning of Voluntaryism exposed*, and *idem, The Voluntary Church Scheme without foundation in Scripture, Reason, or Common Sense* (Perth, 1834).
[19] See Hanna, op. cit. iii. 449 ff.   [20] Ibid. iii. 461–2; iv. 19–20.
[21] Montgomery, 151 f.; Mackie, *McLaren*, i. 172; M'Kerrow, op. cit. ii. 504 ff.
[22] Rae to Peel, 13 (?) July 1836 (Peel Papers, 40339, fo. 366).

to the Church by their connection with Dissent, whose political support they did not wish to lose.

The attitude of the Conservatives, on coming into office in November 1834, was more encouraging. The King's Speech in February 1835 made a favourable reference to the required endowment. Numerous petitions against a grant were presented, some of them urging disestablishment.[23] English Dissenters took part in this opposition: one petition came from the Committee of Dissenting Deputies, and others later from the Dissenters of Barnsley and Dewsbury.[24] Petitions were also presented in favour of endowment, and disparaging allegations were made as usual by each side about the worth of their opponents' petitions. Major Cumming Bruce, Conservative M.P. for Inverness, who supported endowment, said that '. . . in Nairn and Forres . . . petitions against the Church, purporting to come from those towns, had been hawked about through all the surrounding parishes in the country, and lads dragged in on market days from the streets, . . . in a state of half intoxication, to sign them'.[25]

A change of Government occurred before anything came of Conservative intentions. In July 1835 Lord John Russell carried a proposal that a Commission be appointed to inquire into church accommodation in Scotland.[26] The Commission's first report was not presented until February 1837, and was confined to the situation in Edinburgh. The total accommodation was enough for 48·2 per cent of the city's population.[27] Following this report Sir William Rae (an Episcopalian) moved on 5 May that the Government should provide new endowments for the Church of Scotland. But Russell said that further reports of the Commission should be awaited; and Rae's resolutions were defeated, Scottish Conservative members voting for them and most Scottish Liberal members against.[28]

Church endowment was an issue in the 1837 election in Scotland.[29] Further reports of the Commission on church accommodation appeared at the end of the year, one showing that Glasgow had sittings for 39·5 per cent of the population. A Government plan was at last announced. An ancient fund known as the bishops' estates or bishops' teinds (i.e. tithes) would be used to assist religious deficiency in certain Highland and other rural parishes. Nothing was proposed for the needs of the large towns. The scheme satisfied neither side in the dispute. To extensionists it bore the marks of a precarious Government unwilling to annoy its Dissenting supporters;[30] to Voluntaries it went too far in granting any State endowment at all. Dissenting feeling threatened to lead, as in England a little later, 'not

[23] Hansard, xxvii. 777-9, 782-4, 828-31, 1255-66.
[24] Ibid. xxviii. 654-5; xliii. 966-8.   [25] Ibid. xxviii. 216.
[26] Ibid. xxix. 136-53.   [27] Hanna, iv. 21.
[28] Hansard, xxxviii. 605, 617, 652-5.
[29] M'Kerrow, ii. 521; Sir James Graham to Peel, 15 Nov. 1837 (Peel Papers, 40318, fo. 103).
[30] See Fox Maule to Andrew Rutherfurd, undated (Rutherfurd Papers, 9697, fos. 294-5).

indeed to the Dissenters supporting the Tories, but to a very lukewarm and partial support, if not abandonment of the Whigs'.[31] Rival deputations saw Melbourne. Faced with such conflicting claims the Whig Government took no action. The church endowment issue which Aberdeen stated (though surely with exaggeration) had agitated Scotland more than any domestic question since the Union, subsided amidst frustration and acrimony.[32] Yet striking advances in Church extension were achieved through private liberality, as in the case of the Church of England. Chalmers informed the 1838 General Assembly that nearly 200 churches had been built in four years, thanks to private subscriptions of over £200,000.[33]

Church extension was a campaign in which evangelicals and Moderates could combine. But they differed over patronage and the rights of the ministers of chapels of ease (technically called *quoad sacra* churches). Evangelicals wished to give these ministers the same right as parish ministers to be members of Church courts—Presbyteries, Synods, and the General Assembly—and to govern by means of Kirk Sessions. In 1834 the Chapels Act granting these rights was passed by the General Assembly[34]—the evangelicals having gained a majority in the Assembly which they kept until the Disruption in 1843. Moderates opposed the measure, fearing that it would be a means of introducing more evangelicals into the General Assemblies. Thus a tripartite ecclesiastical division was developing, with the conflict between Moderates and evangelicals absorbing more attention, until 1843, than that between Voluntaries and the Establishment.

Evangelicals wished to reform aspects of the Kirk which seemed to hinder its advance, and concentrated their purging zeal on patronage. They saw patronage as a civil obstruction to the spiritual freedom and progress of the Church. Chalmers had already proclaimed his dislike of 'artificial' civil sanctions. In 1828 he had welcomed the repeal of the Test and Corporation Acts as removing artificial securities from an Establishment.[35] In supporting Catholic emancipation in the following year he said: '. . . What other instruments do we read of in the New Testament for the defence and propagation of the faith, but the Word of God and the Spirit of God?'[36] Lay patronage was criticized on similar grounds of civil spuriousness. The reform of patronage, like Church extension, was intended to blunt the edge of Voluntaryism, indifference, and infidelity. Indeed it might be a means of reclaiming Dissenters for the Kirk, for objection to patronage had been a major reason for important secessions.[37] The seceders of 1733 and 1752 had opposed the

---

[31] Andrew Rutherfurd to Fox Maule, 20 Nov. 1837 (Dalhousie Papers, 642 (1)).
[32] Hansard, xlii. 112; Hanna, iv. 23-4.   [33] Hanna, iv. 32.
[34] *Acts of the General Assembly of the Church of Scotland, 1638–1842* (Edinburgh, 1843), 1035-6; R. Buchanan, *The Ten Years' Conflict* (2 vols., Glasgow, 1849), i. 317 ff.
[35] Hanna, iii. 218.   [36] Ibid. 237-8.
[37] A. L. Drummond and J. Bulloch, *The Scottish Church, 1688–1843* (Edinburgh, 1973), 39 ff., 58-62.

enforcement of the Act of 1712, according to which a candidate presented to a parish by a lay patron had to be accepted, provided that the Presbytery (i.e. the district court of ministers and elders) was satisfied with regard to his 'life, literature and manners' (i.e. morals). Under Moderate sway, unpopular 'intrusions' of ministers were made in accordance with the letter of this Act and against congregational wishes; hence the name 'Non-Intrusionists' which described the would-be reformers of patronage more precisely than the wider term 'evangelicals'.

A Society for Improving the System of Patronage had been founded in December 1824, and accounts of its annual meetings were published; it developed about forty auxiliary branches and issued the *Church Patronage Reporter*, afterwards named the *Anti-Patronage Reporter*. A leading aim of the Glasgow Association for Promoting the Interests of the Church of Scotland was 'a thorough remedy of the grievous evil of Patronage'.[38] At the 1832 General Assembly a demand for the restoration of the congregational 'call' to new ministers was defeated. At the 1833 Assembly Chalmers moved that a veto of male heads of families be established over appointments, but his motion failed by 12 votes. On this occasion it was said that Voluntaries well realized that such a reform '. . . will endear [Presbyterian Dissenters] . . . to their Mother Church—that it will bring back many of those who, upon principle, have become seceders'.[39] Fox Maule, a Whig who became a leading Non-Intrusionist, later wrote to his close friend Andrew Rutherfurd, the Whig Solicitor-General for Scotland who held similar views: 'We wish to abolish patronage in order to render the church more acceptable to *all* the people and obtain their support for continuing its connection with the state . . .'[40]

Although many Non-Intrusionists later wanted the complete abolition of patronage, many would originally have been satisfied with a veto of the male heads of families over presentees. This was the object of the Society for Improving the System of Patronage.[41] It was also the provision of the crucial Veto Act (or 'Act anent Calls') passed by the 1834 General Assembly, following Chalmers's narrow defeat in the previous year. This Act declared that 'the dissent of a majority of the male heads of families being members of the congregation and in full communion with the church, ought to be of conclusive effect in setting aside the presentee', *without reasons being given for the dissent*.[42] The Moderates took strong exception to the veto; they understandably believed that such a provision, without even requiring

---

[38] *Speeches at a Glasgow Public Meeting*, 1, 6 ff. Cf. Montgomery, 127 ff.; *Regulations of the Church Defence and Anti-Patronage Electoral Association* (Edinburgh, 1840).

[39] Quoted Montgomery, 132.

[40] 14 May 1838 (Rutherfurd Papers, 9697, fos. 138–9).

[41] 'John Knox the Younger', *First Blast of the Trumpet against the Monstrous Usurpations of Church Patrons in Scotland* (Edinburgh, 1833), 33 ff.

[42] *Acts of the General Assembly*, 1044–5; Buchanan, op. cit. i. 289 ff.

reasons to be stated, might lead to biased, uninformed, and irresponsible decisions on ministerial appointments.[43] Against the pretensions of the General Assembly, the supreme ecclesiastical court which supported the veto, the Moderates obtained the decisions they wanted from the civil courts. Thereby, in the view of Non-Intrusionists, the spiritual independence of the Church was being hindered. The dispute became a conflict between civil and ecclesiastical jurisdictions, between the authority of the Church and that of the State. The quarrel proved irreconcilable and led to schism ten years after the passage of the Veto Act.

The Scottish Non-Intrusionist movement occupied a distinctive position among current religious controversies. The desire of Non-Intrusionists to maintain a Church Establishment, albeit one reformed according to their views, clearly separated them from Voluntaryism, and they resisted Voluntary appeals to seek complete disengagement from the State. Their wish for spiritual independence within a Church Establishment resembled that of the Oxford movement, and they made a popular appeal which Tractarians sometimes seemed to desire. Tractarians were similarly anxious to vindicate the independence of ecclesiastical law from civil law. Advocates of the revival of Convocation envied the existence and powers of the General Assembly, and urged that a similar freedom should be allowed to the Church of England.[44] But the theology of Non-Intrusionists was very different from that of Tractarians, and the issues over which the broad principle of spiritual independence was contested were clearly distinct. Congregational choice of ministers was directly opposed to the Tractarian conception of the clergy. Tract No. 1, written in 1833, implicitly condemned the Non-Intrusionist aim in this respect: 'They [the Government] have been deluded into a notion that present palpable usefulness, producible results, *acceptableness to your flocks*, that these and such like are the tests of your divine commission. Enlighten them in this matter.'[45] Bishop Phillpotts, although once approvingly quoted by Chalmers in the General Assembly for a declaration of independence from the Legislature, later lamented to Keble that holy communion was held only once a year, as he claimed, in most Scottish Presbyterian churches.[46] More sympathetic to the aims of Non-Intrusion was Thomas Arnold's advocacy of greater lay participation in the government of the Church of England, and his suggestion that the election of ministers might in some circumstances be adopted in that Church; though he did not believe in weakening the State connection.[47] Wesleyans also had some sympathy with the Non-Intrusionist position. Chalmers obtained warm support from

[43] J. Bryce, *Ten Years of the Church of Scotland* (2 vols., Edinburgh, 1850), i. 21-42.
[44] Sweet, *A Memoir of the late Henry Hoare*, 25.
[45] R. W. Church, *The Oxford Movement*, 84 [my italics], also 81 ff.
[46] Hanna, iv. 112; Phillpotts to Keble, 29 Mar. 1852 (Keble Papers, E118).
[47] T. Arnold, *Principles of Church Reform*, 120, 125 f.

Jabez Bunting for his general principle of a purified and spiritually free Establishment;[48] though Wesleyans did not agree with the popular appointment of ministers. The Calvinistic Methodists in Wales also resembled Non-Intrusionists in their attitude to an Establishment.[49] Thus, although *sui generis*, Chalmers's standpoint had resemblances elsewhere and found support therein.

II. THE DEVELOPMENT OF CONFLICT, 1834-1841

After the 1832 Reform Act, Scottish Church patronage was discussed in Parliament as well as in the General Assembly. In 1833, 153 petitions for the alteration of patronage were presented in the Commons, and 172 in 1834.[50] In July 1833 George Sinclair, member for Caithness, sought leave to introduce a bill repealing the Act of 1712. Peel and Sir Robert Inglis spoke against the motion, which was withdrawn when it was observed that the necessary consent of the Crown, patron of about a third of the livings in the Church of Scotland, had not been obtained.[51] In February 1834 Sinclair moved that a Select Committee be appointed to inquire into the right of patronage.[52] In the ensuing debate Major Cumming Bruce said that the matter should be left to the Church. The General Assembly made the effort three months later by passing the Veto Act. Sinclair's motion was also opposed by Peel. The real object of the motion, he said, was to introduce popular elections into the Church of Scotland: this would lead to canvassing and associated evils.[53] Peel remained consistent in his opposition to any element of popular election in clerical appointments, and hence in his opposition to the Non-Intrusionist cause. But the motion, strongly supported by Gillon, was carried. The Committee was duly appointed, and reported the following year. The report was indecisive, but vaguely favoured an alteration in the law of patronage.[54] Following its appearance Andrew Johnston (Liberal member for the St. Andrews burghs) moved in June 1835 an address to the Crown for the abolition of patronage, but attendance was thin and the House was counted out.[55] Johnston tried again on 10 July, saying 'he was aware that Scotch questions in general were not received with much cordiality by that House'.[56] He wished to repeal the 1712 Act: 'The House

[48] Bunting to Chalmers, 23 Jan. 1841 (Chalmers Papers); T. P. Bunting and G. Stringer Rowe, *The Life of Rev. Dr. Jabez Bunting* (2 vols., London, 1859-87), ii. 318 ff.

[49] Alec G. Fraser to Thomas Gee, 2 Apr. 1842 (Thomas Gee Papers (National Library of Wales), 8310D, fo. 448).

[50] *Journals of the House of Commons*, lxxxviii (1833), index; lxxxix (1834), index. There were few petitions on patronage from 1835 to 1839, but in 1840 the number of petitions to the Commons for the alteration of patronage shot up to about 1,000 (ibid. xcv, index).

[51] Hansard, xix. 704-18.   [52] Hansard, xxi. 926 ff., also 206-10.

[53] Ibid. 935. But see Peel to Sir William Rae, 24 Jan. 1835 (Peel Papers, 40339, fos. 349-51) for a more conciliatory view on the patronage of newly built churches.

[54] P.P. 1834 (512), v. iii-iv.   [55] Hansard, xxviii. 882-6.   [56] Ibid. xxix. 412.

had granted the political franchise to the people of Scotland; why should they not also have the right of choosing their ministers ?'[57] But the motion was withdrawn after Fox Maule, who agreed with Johnston's views, had pointed out that it had been irregularly introduced.

Thus far the political reception of the desire to modify patronage was cool but indeterminate. But a series of disputed presentations to parishes, in which the Veto Act was put to the test, hardened the different opinions and caused political decisions to be made. The first of these disputes, the classic Auchterarder Case, commenced in 1834 and lasted five years and more. Robert Young was presented to the parish of Auchterarder by the patron, the earl of Kinnoul. Under the operation of the new Veto Act a majority of the male heads of families dissented from the appointment, and Young was rejected by the Presbytery. Young then appealed against his rejection to the Court of Session, the highest court in Scotland. Thereby he sought to overcome ecclesiastical legality by appealing to civil, encouraging the conflict of jurisdictions which became the core of the quarrel. In March 1838 the court declared in his favour and against the Veto Act by a majority of 8 judges to 5.[58] The General Assembly of 1838 rejected this civil intrusion; declared that 'in all matters touching the doctrine, government and discipline of the Church, her judicatories possess an exclusive jurisdiction, founded on the Word of God';[59] and appealed against the judgement to the House of Lords. But the Lords' judgement, given on 4 May 1839, upheld that of the Court of Session. The battle between jurisdictions was clearly joined.

The poor political prospect for Non-Intrusion seemed to be confirmed when the judgement was supported by prominent Whigs and prominent Conservatives alike. Brougham said later that 'he had never seen such a clear case. It seemed to be all one way.'[60] Aberdeen told John Hope—Dean of the Faculty of Advocates, counsel for Robert Young in the case, and constant adviser on the Moderate side—that 'if . . . the Assembly should resist the decision of the House of Lords, they must bid adieu to additional endowment, and in fact they would go far to sever the connection with the State'.[61] In the 1839 Assembly the Non-Intrusionist majority did resist the implied intrusion of the decision, voting for a motion of Chalmers by 204 against 155.[62] In support of this motion Chalmers reaffirmed the principle of the veto, though he did not finally adhere to it until a later stage, thus inviting allegations of inconsistency. In this speech he repeated opinions already

---

[57] Ibid. 414.
[58] G. W. T. Omond, *The Lord Advocates of Scotland*, 2nd Ser., 1834–80 (London, 1914), 54 ff. For the Auchterarder Case in detail see also H. Watt, *Thomas Chalmers and the Disruption* (Edinburgh, 1943), 157 ff.; Buchanan, i. 398–491; ii. 1–15; Bryce, i. 42–72.
[59] Buchanan, i. 478–9.
[60] Hanna, iv. 96 ff.; Hansard, l. 374.
[61] Aberdeen to Hope, 13 June 1838 (Lady Frances Balfour, *Life of George, fourth Earl of Aberdeen* (2 vols., London, 1922), ii. 50–2).
[62] Hanna, iv. 103 ff.; Watt, op. cit. 181–2.

explained in his London lectures of 1838,[63] by rejecting the unwanted intrusion of the recent civil decision into the Church's government: 'we are never, in any instance, to depart from the obligations which lie upon us as a Christian Church, for the sake either of obtaining or perpetuating the privileges which belong to us as an Established Church'.[64] If there was no clear threat of secession in this, Chalmers pointed at such an outcome plainly enough in a letter to Sir James Graham in June:

... rather than be placed at the feet of an absolute and uncontrolled patronage, there are ... very many of our Clergy, and these the most devoted and influential in Scotland who are resolved to quit the Establishment and who, if they do so, will by stripping it of all moral weight, leave it an easy prey for the Radicals and Voluntaries and Demi-infidels both in and out of Parliament who are bent upon destroying it.[65]

The Non-Intrusionist cause was sustained by further legal cases and by newspaper and pamphlet controversy. John Hope produced a rambling 290-page defence of the Moderate cause in September 1839.[66] Non-Intrusionists avidly seized on this dissertation: 'Monster of indolence! and wife of idleness!!', thundered Fox Maule to Rutherfurd, 'John Hope has written a book on the Veto and thou hast not sent it to me.'[67] When Non-Intrusionists read it they were relieved by its prosy disorganization. Chalmers said, not without justice, that Hope was 'almost safe and beyond the reach of attack, because entrenched, as it were, in the mazes of his own confusion'.[68] A printed reply by a Non-Intrusionist lawyer and politician, Alexander Murray Dunlop, apparently sought to defeat Hope in length as well as in argument.[69]

Patrick Stewart, M.P. for Renfrewshire, was soon writing that 'the Church question is growing like a tropical turnip'.[70] Further legal disputes were widening the conflict. A particularly long and tortuous dispute was at Marnoch in Banffshire. In this parish the great majority of male heads of families dissented in 1837 from the appointment of a ministerial candidate who was nominated by a firm of lawyers representing the trustees of the earl of Fife. The candidate, John Edwards, received his only positive assent from a village inn-keeper.[71] The Presbytery of Strathbogie inclined to a Moderate

[63] T. Chalmers, *Lectures on the Establishment and Extension of National Churches* (Glasgow, 1838), 12.

[64] Hanna, iv. 109.

[65] 6 June 1839 (Graham Papers, microfilms, 128). Cf. Parker (ed.), *Graham*, i. 373-4.

[66] J. Hope, *A Letter to the Lord Chancellor on the Claims of the Church of Scotland* (London, 1839).

[67] 25 Sept. 1839 (Rutherfurd Papers, 9697, fo. 260).

[68] Quoted W. L. Mathieson, *Church and Reform in Scotland, 1797-1843* (Glasgow, 1916), 331.

[69] *An Answer to the Dean of Faculty's Letter to the Lord Chancellor* (Edinburgh, 1839).

[70] Stewart to Maule, 9 Jan. 1840 (Dalhousie Papers, 646).

[71] It was said that the village had five public houses, 'three too many'; *The New Statistical Account of Scotland* (15 vols., Edinburgh, 1845), xiii. 386.

course. Seven ministers against four initially decided not to impose the procedure of the Veto Act against Edwards; but when the General Assembly of 1838 ordered that the Act be enforced, the Presbytery obeyed. Edwards, however, appealed to the Court of Session, which upheld his appointment and thus lent confidence to the Presbytery, which now somersaulted and decided to take the presentee 'on trials' for ordination according to the usual procedure. The issue of conflicting jurisdictions was emphasized by the question whether a Presbytery might decide to follow the ruling of the Court of Session rather than the General Assembly. Confirmed Erastians maintained that civil jurisdiction must have the ascendancy; Non-Intrusionists insisted that the General Assembly had supreme power to legislate for the Church.

Ecclesiastical authority was asserted. A Commission of the Assembly decided in December 1839 that the seven offending ministers of the Strathbogie Presbytery should be suspended from office, and the 1840 Assembly decided to continue the suspension. Prominent Non-Intrusionist ministers, supported by the Commission of Assembly, preached in the open air (respecting civil authority over church buildings, as belonging to the temporal sphere) to members of the congregations whose pastors were suspended. But the Court of Session held the suspension invalid, and the seven ministers then resumed their pastoral functions. Furthermore, when Mr. Edwards successfully brought a fresh action requesting the Court of Session to authorize his ordination, the seven ministers proceeded to ordain and induct him in January 1841. Almost the entire congregation left the church in protest and departed through the snow.[72]

The Moderates maintained that the ministers had rightly obeyed the 'supreme tribunals' of the country.[73] Non-Intrusionists, they believed, were making arrogant claims of superiority to the State.[74] But to Non-Intrusionists, bent on vindicating spiritual independence, an ordination performed by suspended ministers was an intolerable instance of civil tyranny.[75] Marnoch provided an early example of disruption: the seceding congregation built a commodious new church and manse and received the ministrations of the Rev. D. Henry.[76]

As these cases produced deadlock between the courts, the pressure grew for a parliamentary adjudication. 'It is absolutely necessary that there should be legislative interference,' Lord Advocate Rutherfurd wrote in December 1839.[77] There was little political sympathy for Non-Intrusion among either

---

[72] T. Brown, *Annals of the Disruption* (Edinburgh, 1893), 23–4; Hanna, iv. 214–19.

[73] See Dr. George Cook to Brougham, 6 June 1840 (Brougham Papers, 33509).

[74] e.g. Rev. David Aitken to earl of Minto, 14 Dec. 1839 (Minto Papers, 118A/2).

[75] e.g. Dundee Presbytery Minutes, CH2/103/18, 206 ff. For the Marnoch Case in detail see Watt, 206–21; Buchanan, ii. *passim*; Bryce, i. 101–59, 195–217; ii. 53–172.

[76] *New Statistical Account*, xiii. 387.

[77] Rutherfurd to Maule, 31 Dec. 1839 (Dalhousie Papers, 642/1).

Whigs or Conservatives, but more perhaps could be expected from the latter than from the Whig Government. Although Rutherfurd and Fox Maule held Government office, they obtained no support for the Non-Intrusionist cause from their Whig leaders. While Scottish Conservative politicians were usually Moderates, among the party leaders Lord Aberdeen was more conciliatory to Non-Intrusion than the Whigs. Although most of the leading Non-Intrusionist ministers were Liberals,[78] Chalmers was Conservative in politics and thus had little influence with Liberal politicians. Certainly he made a strong adverse impression on Melbourne, who showed little of his habitual rational impassivity in the remark that 'I particularly dislike Chalmers; I think him a madman and all madmen are also rogues'.[79] There were other reasons for Government resistance. The Government had to remember its political connection with Dissenters and radicals who did not want a solution which might strengthen the Kirk.[80] The Whig leaders, moreover, were both aristocratic and Erastian: they were unlikely to submit to the vehement pressure of Presbyterian clergy (or of any clergy), especially in the cause of a semi-democratic veto. Melbourne, while admitting that he was 'practically utterly ignorant' of the question,[81] was quite clear in his discouragement:

First, I do not know how I could reconcile it to my conscience to take the part of any Church or of anything ecclesiastical anywhere, in opposition to the law ... Secondly, I do not know how I could ... agree to anything which was to place the election of ministers more in the hands of the congregation than it is at present. And thirdly, even if the Church were right in their desires, the manner in which they have been asserted and enforced cannot be justified or even excused.[82]

Despite this, the Whigs were in a weak political position and did not wish to alienate their Non-Intrusionist supporters. Hence there was considerable prevarication in their public attitude. A Non-Intrusionist deputation, presenting its claims to Ministers after the Lords' judgement in the Auchterarder Case, was assured that the Veto Act would be applied in the case of the extensive Crown patronage. This promise was consistently fulfilled;[83] and it assisted the Whigs in keeping the support of many Non-Intrusionists. But Melbourne refused to go further and attempt a general settlement on Non-Intrusionist lines. Instead he hedged on the question. In February and March 1840 he stated in the Lords that the Government was considering the matter, but was undecided; and finally on 30 March, in reply to accusations of disingenuous delay from Lord Aberdeen, he said that he was 'not prepared

---

[78] Hope to Aberdeen, 19 June 1841 (Aberdeen Papers, 43205, fos. 89–90).

[79] Melbourne to Maule, 28 Oct. 1840 (Dalhousie Papers, 640).

[80] Cf. Aberdeen to Hope, 14 Dec. 1839 (Aberdeen Papers, 43202, fo. 253); Omond, *Lord Advocates*, 73.

[81] Melbourne to Lord Dunfermline, 20 Apr. 1841 (Sanders (ed.), *Lord Melbourne's Papers*, 416).

[82] Ibid.

[83] *Witness*, 9 June 1841; A. Turner, *The Scottish Secession of 1843* (Edinburgh, 1859), 174–5.

at present to pledge the Government to introduce any measure on this subject'.[84] Meanwhile Conservatives had been impressed with the result of a Perthshire by-election in February: a Conservative candidate who was something of a Non-Intrusionist had defeated a Liberal who was more of one. This encouraged Conservatives to propose their own solution.[85] On 31 March 1840, therefore, Aberdeen announced that he would introduce a measure himself;[86] this intention may well have explained his pressure on Melbourne the previous day.

Aberdeen's bill was the main attempt to settle the dispute by compromise. As a member of the Church of Scotland who had strongly supported Government aid for its extension, Aberdeen was anxious to prevent the Kirk's revival from being weakened by internecine quarrels. Although urged by Dr. Robert Buchanan, a prominent Non-Intrusionist minister, to propose the congregational veto,[87] he paid more attention to the Moderate arguments of John Hope, who (now and throughout the crisis) sent him very abundant and ample letters. Aberdeen did nothing to stem the flow of Hope's epistolary importunity. It would seem, indeed, that he had respected Hope's views for some time. He had told Hope in October 1839 that his *Letter to the Lord Chancellor*, though it was so long that not even the Lord Chancellor would read it, had convinced Aberdeen himself.[88] Aberdeen wished to modify the veto. His bill stated that when a presentation was opposed by members of a congregation, the reasons for objection should be stated and should be judged by the Presbytery, which should decide whether to accept or reject the presentee.[89] The veto of male heads of families was to be replaced by a veto of the Presbytery.

Aberdeen's proposal might have succeeded at an earlier stage in the conflict. But the Auchterarder judgement and the Marnoch Case (usually called the Strathbogie Case) had hardened the attitude of Non-Intrusionists and made them less likely to adopt a compromise solution. The proposed settlement might place decisions in the hands of Presbyteries containing a majority of Moderates, who would be prepared as in the Marnoch Case to accept presentees unwanted by the congregations. Furthermore, Sir George Clerk (another Scottish Conservative, then M.P. for Stamford and once chief Whip) made a more attractive suggestion than Aberdeen—that Presbyteries should, even if not accepting the reasons for objection to a presentee, take account of the numbers making the objections. Non-Intrusionists

[84] Hansard, liii. 225–7.

[85] Buchanan, ii. 155–9; Alexander Currie to Maule, 24 Feb. 1840 (Dalhousie Papers, 626); Aberdeen to Hope, 11 and 25 Mar. 1840 (Aberdeen Papers, 43202, fos. 297, 330).

[86] Hansard, liii. 260.

[87] Buchanan to Aberdeen, 25 Mar., 7 Apr., and 1 May 1840 (Aberdeen Papers, 43237, fos. 132–5, 141–2).

[88] Aberdeen to Hope, 1 Oct. 1839 (ibid. 43202, fos. 248–9).

[89] Bryce, i. 168–84.

regretted that Aberdeen's plan would only allow Presbyteries to reject presentees if Presbyteries believed that the reasons were sufficient. In the ensuing months efforts were made in meetings and letters between Aberdeen and Non-Intrusionist leaders to narrow the gap between his views and those of Clerk, and Non-Intrusionists apparently believed that they were succeeding in this aim.[90] They were disillusioned. Chalmers may have exaggerated his own influence in persuading Aberdeen to modify his opinions; or, as Aberdeen's biographers have suggested, a late intervention by Hope in the flesh may have overborne Aberdeen's conciliatory intentions, deciding him to stand by his original terms for the presbyterial veto.[91] Whatever the reasons for the misunderstanding, Non-Intrusionists were bitterly disappointed when they saw Aberdeen's draft bill, proposing a veto by Presbyteries based on their judgement of stated reasons. The draft was rejected by Non-Intrusionists, and the chances of success plummeted before the measure was even introduced.

Bringing the bill into the Lords on 5 May, Aberdeen widened his distance from Non-Intrusionists by describing a popular veto as 'the exercise of an arbitrary, capricious, and groundless will of a congregation without any assigned reason'.[92] The Non-Intrusionists were up in arms. In the Synod of Lothian, which condemned the measure by 60 votes to 20, it was said that the bill 'deposed the Lord Jesus Christ from his Throne'.[93] The General Assembly voted against the bill by 221 to 134; an observer of their proceedings said that they seemed 'ready to go the whole hog'.[94] The *Witness*, a new Non-Intrusionist paper, and the *Caledonian Mercury* stimulated opposition.[95] Aberdeen was swayed by the outcry, and wrote that he did not wish 'to cram this measure down their throats, if they dislike it'.[96] But he decided none the less to move a second reading of the bill. Hope insisted, in a thirteen-page letter, that in moving the second reading Aberdeen should hold firm to an anti-vetoist line.[97] The earl followed this advice in his speech of 16 June. He condemned the Veto Act and the 'monstrous and extravagant pretensions' of the General Assembly and said that Melbourne should declare himself on the issue: 'the noble viscount could not continue to sit chuckling inwardly at the confusion and distraction which pervaded Scotland'.[98]

[90] *The Earl of Aberdeen's Correspondence with the Rev. Dr. Chalmers, etc.* (Edinburgh, 1840), 22-4, 49-50; Buchanan, ii. 164-72; Turner, op. cit. 224-32. But cf. A. Murray Dunlop to Rutherfurd, 8 Apr. 1840 (Rutherfurd Papers, 9689, fos. 224-6).

[91] Sir A. Gordon, *The Earl of Aberdeen* (London, 1893), 129-30; Lady Frances Balfour, op. cit. ii. 72-3. Cf. Hope to Aberdeen, 14 Apr. 1840 (Aberdeen Papers, 43203, fos. 9-24).

[92] Hansard, liii. 1216 ff.

[93] Rev. Dr. William Muir to John Hope, 13 May 1840 (Aberdeen Papers, 43203, fo. 161).

[94] Sir A. Pringle to Hope, 2 June 1840 (ibid., fo. 244); Buchanan, ii. 195-214.

[95] Lord Dunfermline to Lord Minto, 15 May 1840 (Minto Papers, 118A/2).

[96] Aberdeen to Hope, 21 May 1840 (Aberdeen Papers, 43203, fo. 214).

[97] Hope to Aberdeen, 13 June 1840 (ibid., fos. 308-21).

[98] Hansard, liv. 1205-7.

Melbourne said the bill should be dropped on account of inadequate support in Scotland.[99] This opposition from the Government was crucial. Although the Lords with their majority of Conservatives passed the second reading by 74 votes to 27, the bill faced defeat in the Commons with its majority of Liberals.[100] Aberdeen therefore decided to withdraw his measure: on 10 July he announced that it would be abandoned for the current session.[101] That the measure had considerable support, however, was shown by a declaration in its favour signed by 244 ministers and 454 elders.[102] The advocates of compromise were many, but the opposition was strong and the circumstances inclement.

During the remainder of 1840 the conflict worsened. The Marnoch Case continued to irritate feelings, municipal elections were affected by the quarrel, and the Non-Intrusionist marquess of Breadalbane was elected Rector of Glasgow University.[103] Any attempt at a parliamentary solution lay once more with the Government. But Melbourne's attitude was unaltered, as was his need to retain as much electoral support as possible. Not the least of the Whigs' worries was the discontent of Scottish Dissenters. They were already accusing the Government of unfair treatment, saying that they were excluded from a committee for printing the Bible and from chaplaincies of gaols.[104] They continued to oppose Non-Intrusion, which, as a popular method of upholding the Establishment principle, seemed to threaten their own position. In reply to Chalmers's London lectures of 1838, a series of London lectures was given the following year by Dr. Ralph Wardlaw, a leading Scottish Voluntary, at the invitation of the Dissenting Deputies.[105] Voluntaries obstructed the return of Non-Intrusionist elders to the General Assembly,[106] and fought Non-Intrusionists in municipal elections, notably in a contest for the Provostship of Edinburgh in November 1840. Adam Black, a Congregationalist, was defeated in this election by Sir James Forrest, who was supported by Non-Intrusionists.[107] Dissenters planned revenge in future parliamentary contests. Sir James Gibson-Craig, a veteran Edinburgh Whig, wrote in agitation to Fox Maule:

The Non Intrusionists here and in Glasgow have acted on the principle, that no Dissenter shall be elected. This the Dissenters have taken up as the greatest

[99] Ibid. 1233-7.

[100] Ibid. 1241-2; Aberdeen to Hope, 17 June 1840 (Aberdeen Papers, 43204, fo. 7).

[101] Aberdeen-Hope letters (ibid., fos. 17-48, 126-7); Hansard, lv. 593-5.

[102] Aberdeen Papers, 43204, fos. 134-5; Aberdeen to Peel, 24 Nov. 1840 (Peel Papers, Add. MS. 40312, fo. 335).

[103] Aberdeen to Hope, 6 Dec. 1840 (Aberdeen Papers, 43204, fo. 211).

[104] Sir James Gibson-Craig to Fox Maule, 8 Oct. 1840 (Dalhousie Papers, 628); Macaulay to Duncan McLaren, 5 and 11 Dec. 1840 (Mackie, McLaren, i. 216, 219-20, also 173).

[105] National Church Establishments examined (London, 1839).

[106] A. Murray Dunlop to Rutherfurd, 13 Apr. 1840 (Rutherfurd Papers, 9689, fos. 248-9).

[107] See A. Nicolson (ed.), Memoirs of Adam Black (2nd edn., Edinburgh, 1885), 106-7; Mackie, i. 214 ff.; Rutherfurd to Maule, 6 and 29 Oct., 3 and 10 Nov. 1840 (Dalhousie Papers, 642/2).

possible insult, and have called a meeting . . . for the purpose of adopting Resolutions, to oppose every Non Intrusionist, who may be a candidate for Parliament. They will do to the Non Intrusionists, what they have done to the Dissenters, and if they cannot otherways exclude them, they will join the Tories, rather than not do so . . . The consequence of this must be the utter destruction of the Liberal party, as well as of the Non Intrusionists.[108]

Maule complained in reply:

I have found them [Dissenters] . . . always stickling upon some isolated principle, to the injury of the general [Liberal] cause, to which they profess to be friendly. I have always regarded the genuine dissenter as an impracticable Politician. No boon you can confer on him entails any gratitude. The moment it is granted, a new hare is started and if parties are nearly balanced on [sic] an election of consequence, the past is forgotten and a bullying coercion established for the future.[109]

Some Conservatives believed that political gain was to be had from this Liberal division. But Peel said it was impossible for Conservatives to ally with the aims of Scottish Dissenters.[110] Soon after the unfortunate Edinburgh contest, Non-Intrusionists began to exchange *Friendly Addresses* with Dissenters in an effort to find agreement.[111] In the first address, Non-Intrusionists asked Dissenters: 'If we can succeed in retaining our independence along with our endowments, why should we relinquish either? Why rather, should not you join with us in the full enjoyment of both?'[112] But Dissenters firmly replied: 'Where there is State pay, there must be State dependence.'[113]

With this persistent distrust of Non-Intrusion among Dissenters, and with his Government in jeopardy, Melbourne could do nothing to satisfy the Non-Intrusionists. He stated on 3 May 1841 in the Lords: 'neither on the one side nor on the other am I prepared to alter the constitution of the Church of Scotland'.[114] But the 7th duke of Argyll, a Conservative, attempted a legislative solution in this parliamentary session. His measure was more conciliatory to Non-Intrusionists than Aberdeen's bill, and in an important way went even beyond the Veto Act. He proposed to give the right of veto to all male communicants over the age of 21; though he also provided that

[108] 5 Nov. 1840 (Dalhousie Papers, 628).

[109] Maule to Gibson-Craig, 7 Nov. 1840 (ibid.). Cf. Maule to Rutherfurd, 26 Nov. 1840, describing Duncan McLaren, the Edinburgh Voluntary, as 'a vile brute' (Rutherfurd Papers, 9698, fo. 86).

[110] Aberdeen to Peel, 11 Dec. 1840 and 14 Jan. 1841, with enclosures (Peel Papers, 40312, fos. 343–5, 350–61); Aberdeen to Hope, 10 Feb. 1841 (Aberdeen Papers, 43204, fo. 235).

[111] Anon., *Friendly Address to the Dissenters of Scotland*, dated 24 Dec. 1840, written by Robert Candlish (Edinburgh, 1840); Anon., *Friendly Reply to the Friendly Address . . .*, 7 Jan. 1841, written by Hugh Heugh (Edinburgh, 1841); Anon., *Second Friendly Address to the Dissenters of Scotland*, Candlish (?) (Edinburgh, 1841); Anon., *Friendly Reply to a second Friendly Address*, Heugh (Edinburgh, 1841). Cf. H. M. MacGill, *Life of Hugh Heugh* (2nd edn., Edinburgh, 1852), 346 ff.

[112] *Friendly Address*, 6.

[113] *Friendly Reply to a second Friendly Address*, 4. Cf. *Eclectic Review*, N.S., vi (July–Dec. 1839), 232.

[114] Hansard, lvii. 1385.

if the veto were proved to have resulted from irrational prejudice or dis-ruptive motives it should be set aside.[115] Conservative party leaders would go no further than Aberdeen's bill, and could not support Argyll's plan. Its parliamentary reception was most disheartening. When the first reading was debated in the Lords on 6 May, many peers left the chamber as they had no interest in the matter; only twenty-three, 'almost all Scotch, or connected with Scotland', were left at the end of the debate.[116]

The bill could scarcely hope to reach its second reading. But if Parliament was hostile or indifferent, the General Assembly with its majority of increasingly ardent Non-Intrusionists gave a warmer welcome to the bill. The debates in this Assembly were extremely heated. Hope, who tended to suspect his opponents of insanity,[117] stated that 'one poor creature . . . went raving mad on the spot, and the Assembly had to adjourn till he could be put under restraint and removed'.[118] The Assembly declared, against the Lords' judgement, that the Auchterarder charge was vacant and was to be filled by a congregational call. The ordination of Edwards at Marnoch was declared void, the seven ministers who had conducted the ordination were deposed and the rival candidate, who was supported by the congregation, was declared rightfully appointed. In other cases the Veto Act was upheld.[119] A demand for the complete abolition of patronage had recently been gaining support, and was put forward by a large party at the Assembly. But this group decided to support Argyll's bill—either as a basis on which to erect their demand for abolition later, as Hope alleged, or as an indication that they were not fixed on this demand.[120] The Moderates were outraged by the Assembly's proceedings, and were determined to maintain Erastian authority. 'The presumption manifested by the General Assembly', said Aberdeen, '. . . was never equalled by the Church of Rome.'[121] As contrasting opinions strengthened, the likelihood of a satisfactory legislative solution weakened. Melbourne again deprecated a parliamentary enactment on the question; he preferred that the dispute should 'work itself out by the efforts of con-flicting parties'.[122] The Whigs, however, were relieved of an embarrassing problem by defeat in Parliament, followed by their decision to dissolve. This led Argyll to postpone his bill. The ensuing general election provided an opportunity for the rival parties in the conflict to demonstrate their political strength.

[115] Hanna, iv. 229; Eighth duke of Argyll, *Autobiography and Memoirs*, ed. Dowager duchess of Argyll (2 vols., London, 1906), i. 169, 176–81.

[116] Hansard, lvii. 1478–88; Sir George Sinclair to Chalmers, 7 May 1841 (Chalmers Papers).

[117] e.g. he had said that Robert Candlish had 'a strong touch of craze in his mind at present'; Balfour, *Aberdeen*, ii. 67.

[118] Hope to Aberdeen, 1 June 1841 (Aberdeen Papers, 43205, fo. 40).

[119] Buchanan, ii. 367 ff.; Hanna, iv. 219 ff.; Hope to Aberdeen, 30 May 1841 (Aberdeen Papers, 43205, fos. 29 ff.).

[120] Hope to Aberdeen, 30 May 1841 (Aberdeen Papers, 43205, fos. 29 ff.); Buchanan, ii. 340 ff.

[121] Hansard, lviii. 1505.   [122] Ibid. 1506–7.

III. THE 1841 ELECTION

It was anticipated that Scottish Church issues would play a part in the 1841 election;[123] but Moderates denied that Non-Intrusion had much political strength. Possibly Non-Intrusionists had, in proportion to their numbers, fewer parliamentary votes than Moderates. There was, moreover, no campaigning organization for the electoral expression of Non-Intrusion. This lack was regretted by zealous Non-Intrusionists, one of whom said: 'at present the extent of our strength is scarcely known to ourselves'.[124] The absence of political organization may be partly attributed to the essentially clerical leadership of the Non-Intrusionist movement. The views of ministers were probably of considerable importance in deciding lay attitudes to the question, except in parishes which were intrinsically disturbed by congregational antipathy to a presentee. Even in the Highlands, where tenants who resented the clearances by landlords turned against the landlords' church patronage, and where a strong socio-economic tendency may have appeared to dwarf individual efforts, the influence of individual ministers or of evangelical laymen was of crucial importance. In the parsh of Kilmonivaig in Lochaber, where clearances for sheep-farming had taken place, the minister kept most of his congregation with him in the established Kirk in 1843; while in the neighbouring parish of Kilmallie, where the same economic grievances existed, most of the congregation followed their Non-Intrusionist minister into the Free Church.[125] The importance of ministerial leadership in the Non-Intrusionist cause may well have contributed to its political weakness, for ministers were unwilling or unready to direct a lay political movement. Non-Intrusionist ministers were divided in their party politics and in their precise ecclesiastical aims. Even ministers who asserted their views and influenced parties in the General Assembly were not accustomed to positive and sustained action in the field of secular politics. There was little sign of such action before the 1841 election. Non-Intrusionists asked Chalmers for whom they should vote in the election, and one of them sought his verbal influence in aid of Patrick Stewart, the Non-Intrusionist Liberal standing for Renfrewshire.[126] Robert Candlish wrote rather diffidently to Jabez Bunting: 'We are somewhat anxious to have our cause advanced, or, at least, to have

[123] Letter from Joseph Parkes, 7 May 1841 (Russell Papers, 4A, fo. 281).

[124] Speech of John Brodie at a Non-Intrusionist meeting (*Caledonian Mercury*, 1 July 1841).

[125] J. R. Cameron, 'The Disruption in Lochaber' (unpubl. Univ. of Dundee M.A. Hons. thesis 1970), 23-4. Cf. the interesting details of the influence of evangelical ministers and lairds on the size of the secession in north-eastern rural parishes, in G. B. Robertson, 'Spiritual Awakening of the North-East of Scotland and the Disruption of the Church in 1843' (unpubl. Univ. of Aberdeen Ph.D. thesis 1971), 448-56. See also Rev. David Aitken, minister of Minto (Roxburghshire) to earl of Minto, 2 Mar. 1840 (Minto Papers, 118A/2).

[126] Duncan Darroch to Chalmers, 22 June 1841 (Chalmers Papers, bound vol. 1841). Cf. Rev. J. J. Bonar (of Greenock) to Chalmers, 9 June 1841 (ibid.).

our cause fairly stated, in the approaching general election; and especially where your body [Wesleyans] have influence, we think that something might be done.'[127] There was no positive ministerial campaigning until Chalmers launched an attempt to gain popular support in August, when the elections were over. The effort had considerable success.[128]

Another hindrance to electoral demonstration of Non-Intrusionist strength was the discouragement of Non-Intrusion by both political parties, and the danger posed by Non-Intrusionist demands to party interests. The Whigs generally favoured Moderatism, and were beset by Dissenting discontent; a positive attempt to satisfy Non-Intrusionists would lose them both Moderate and Dissenting support. Scottish Whigs who were Moderates appreciated the value of Dissent as a weapon against Non-Intrusion. Sir James Gibson-Craig had said in October 1840 that the Dissenters might 'hold back' at the next election, 'leaving the Whigs to be overwhelmed everywhere by the Tories';[129] and he warned Fox Maule, as a Non-Intrusionist, not to stand for Edinburgh with its particular Dissenting problems, 'for the Dissenters would to a man vote against you'.[130] Non-Intrusionist Whigs who were disappointed with the Government would, it was hinted, '... support such as declare themselves for [the] ... cause, whether Whig or Tory'.[131] But the Conservatives, as a party, were no readier to adopt Non-Intrusion. Most Conservatives would advance no further than Aberdeen's bill as a proffered solution. With discouragement to Non-Intrusion on both sides, the dispute had little obvious effect in the election. Many election addresses said much about import duties and nothing of the Church question.[132] Only 23 Scottish seats out of 53 were fought—the smallest number in an election since the Reform Act;[133] and the balance of parties was scarcely altered. But the Non-Intrusion question may have had more subtle and concealed effects.

Even in England the Scottish Church dispute received some mention in the election. Referring to questions on Non-Intrusion at the City of London election, Hope said: 'The answers of the Conservatives are admirable. Who could have framed them[?], for the men probably never heard of the subject previously.'[134] In Scotland the matter seemed threatening enough to arouse fears for party unity. Zealous Non-Intrusionist electors might well prefer a Non-Intrusionist candidate of the other party to a Moderate candidate of their own party. Cross-voting of this kind was encouraged by the *Witness*,

[127] June 1841 (Bunting and Stringer Rowe, *Jabez Bunting*, ii. 321).
[128] Watt, *Chalmers*, 230–2. Cf. G. B. Robertson, op. cit. 422 ff.
[129] Gibson-Craig to Fox Maule, 8 Oct. 1840 (Dalhousie Papers, 628).
[130] Gibson-Craig to Maule, 17 May 1841 (ibid.).
[131] A. Murray Dunlop to Maule, 15 May 1841 (ibid. 658).
[132] See *Caledonian Mercury*, 14 June 1841.
[133] N. Gash, *Politics in the Age of Peel* (London, 1953), 441; T. Wilkie, *The Representation of Scotland* (Paisley, 1895).
[134] Hope to Aberdeen, 5 July 1841 (Aberdeen Papers, 43205, fos. 106–7).

which urged Non-Intrusionist voters to put religion before party.[135] This prospect was worrying to party politicians such as Aberdeen, for a coalition of Non-Intrusionists in disregard of party divisions was not likely to be emulated by a similar union of Moderates, and the two political parties were unlikely to produce equal numbers of Non-Intrusionist candidates in the right places.[136] *The Times* urged Conservative Non-Intrusionists to work for party unity: 'Most earnestly do we counsel them to wave [*sic*] that dispute for the present … While friends are quarrelling, their common enemy is stepping in to destroy the church *in toto*.'[137]

To some extent the Church question had the feared effect on party solidarity. At Aberdeen it was believed that some seventy-five Conservative Non-Intrusionists voted for the Liberal Non-Intrusionist candidate, Alexander Bannerman.[138] A candidate at Glasgow, James Campbell, made known his Non-Intrusionist views and thereby alienated many Conservatives, who threatened not to support him.[139] A Mr. Speir declined to stand as a Conservative for Paisley because he was a Moderate and many of his expected supporters were Non-Intrusionists.[140] On the Liberal side there was also the possibility of division over the question, and the *Caledonian Mercury* recommended that differing views should not be pressed.[141] But independent electoral action was threatened by the Dissenters, and this may have kept Moderate and Non-Intrusionist Liberals together, for such action was unwelcome to both. At Edinburgh Dissenters had begun to threaten separate action after their municipal defeat in the previous year. On 21 May 1841 a committee of Edinburgh Dissenters met to consider choosing a promising candidate of Voluntary views. Joseph Hume and Sir Culling Eardley Smith were suggested, but the proposal of Smith was withdrawn in favour of Hume, who was considered by Duncan McLaren to have a wider radical appeal.[142] Hume did not stand for Edinburgh, and was defeated at Leeds; in the following April, however, he was returned at a by-election for Montrose, which like Edinburgh had the problem of an annuity tax. William Ewart, another well-known radical, also declined a Dissenting request to stand for Edinburgh,[143] and was returned for the Dumfries burghs. No Voluntary candidate was persuaded to stand for the city, and Macaulay and William Gibson-Craig were returned unopposed as Liberal members.

Liberals probably gained the advantage over Conservatives in winning Non-Intrusionist support. Among the few uncompromising election speeches

[135] 19 June 1841. Cf. ibid. 9 June 1841, leading article.
[136] Cf. Aberdeen to Hope, 13 July 1841 (Aberdeen Papers, 43205, fo. 123).
[137] 29 June 1841, p. 6.
[138] Aberdeen to Hope, 4 and 11 July 1841 (Aberdeen Papers, 43205, fos. 102, 121).
[139] Hope to Aberdeen, 5 July 1841 (ibid., fo. 106).
[140] *The Times*, 22 June 1841, p. 6.   [141] 28 June 1841, leading article.
[142] *The Times*, 1 June 1841. Cf. Mackie, *McLaren*, i. 175–6.
[143] *The Times*, 28 June 1841; *Caledonian Mercury*, 24 and 28 June 1841.

in favour of Non-Intrusion were those of Fox Maule and Patrick Stewart, both of whom were Liberals and both of whom were returned in contested elections.[144] The Government's record of respecting congregational feelings in Crown presentations of ministers worked to the Liberal advantage among Non-Intrusionists. Moreover, alleged statements by Peel to a Non-Intrusionist deputation in June, consisting of A. Murray Dunlop and Dr. Robert Buchanan, were far from encouraging. Peel apparently said that he could not accept Argyll's bill for a popular veto, that in any settlement the Church must submit to the civil courts, and that in particular the deposed Strathbogie ministers must be restored.[145] Liberal Non-Intrusionists were quick to appreciate the political value of this incident, and a report of the interview by Murray Dunlop was published in the form of a letter to the Non-Intrusionist electors of Renfrewshire.[146] A Church of Scotland minister in Liverpool urged Peel to issue a corrected version saying that he had not committed himself to any specific course.[147] But on account of Dunlop's report of the interview, Non-Intrusionist support for the Liberals was probably strengthened. Peel was now said to be 'evidently much more hostile than Melbourne';[148] and the *Witness* advised Non-Intrusionist electors that, in any constituencies where both a Conservative and a Liberal Non-Intrusionist were standing, the Liberal should be preferred.[149]

An electoral result of the Non-Intrusionist movement may have been to uphold the Liberal vote. Although this was not shown in an increase of Liberal seats it was perhaps indicated by the smallness of the Conservative gain in Scotland, compared with the large over-all Conservative gain. If the Non-Intrusionist movement had not developed, Church of Scotland electors might have tended to vote Conservative, on account of Conservative support for Church extension grants and Liberal refusal to make them. But in Scotland the net Conservative gain was only 2 seats, and the Liberals had a majority of 9. The balance of seats was nearly the same as before the election, and Non-Intrusion may have helped to explain this.

The results did not clearly display this possible effect, though in several constituencies the Non-Intrusionist issue had to be reckoned with. Aberdeen thought that the result in Renfrewshire was the only one that had turned on the question.[150] Here the Liberal Patrick Stewart gained the seat, scraping home by 14 votes after Dunlop's account of Peel's statements had been addressed to the electors of the county. It was supposed that Conservative

---

[144] For Stewart's address see *The Times*, 10 July 1841, p. 4.
[145] *Caledonian Mercury*, 24 June 1841; Hope to Aberdeen, 17 June 1841 (Aberdeen Papers, 43205, fos. 83-4).
[146] Sir William Rae to Peel, 25 June 1841 (newspaper cutting enclosed, containing Dunlop's letter; Peel Papers, 40339, fos. 373-5); Buchanan, *Ten Years' Conflict*, ii. 420-1.
[147] Rev. Dr. Hugh Ralph to Peel, 1 July 1841 (Peel Papers, 40485, fos. 12-13).
[148] Rev. Thomas Duncan to Chalmers, 26 June 1841 (Chalmers Papers).
[149] 19 June 1841.
[150] Aberdeen to Peel, 19 July 1841 (Peel Papers, 40312, fo. 377).

Non-Intrusionists had voted for Stewart.[151] It was also said that if the Liberals had contested Lanarkshire on Non-Intrusionist principles they would have gained this seat, which had been lost to the Conservatives in 1837 by 1 vote.[152] In Roxburghshire, home county of the Elliots of Minto, it was hoped that the support of 'the Non-Intrusion party' would give the Liberal candidate, Hon. J. E. Elliot, 40 votes and enable him to keep the seat;[153] but in the event the seat was won by the Conservative. At Edinburgh Macaulay was questioned on his opinion and refused to pledge his support to parliamentary enactment of the veto. Non-Intrusionists then threatened to ally with the Conservatives. But Macaulay was able to mollify them by saying that he would support a bill to resist the intrusion of unacceptable ministers, and the reported statements of Peel helped to save him by discouraging a Non-Intrusionist alliance with the Conservatives.[154]

In Bute there was Conservative division over the question, and perhaps this was the only constituency where Non-Intrusion produced rival candidates of the same party. Sir William Rae, the former Tory Lord Advocate who had been three times returned unopposed for this constituency, was unexpectedly challenged by a Conservative Non-Intrusionist, Henry Dunlop. This interference was most disgraceful, a Glasgow Conservative told Peel: 'It was the doing of a few men perfectly mad on the Church question and incapable of being reasoned with.'[155] Rae, an Episcopalian, won the contest, but had been moved by the Non-Intrusionist challenge to issue an address making some attempt to satisfy Non-Intrusionist opinion.[156] Though the address was non-committal enough, Moderate Conservatives were annoyed with Rae's conduct, for as a former Conservative Minister who was expected to return to office, he might have seemed to be foisting a concessionary policy on the next Government. Rae's explanation can scarcely have mollified his party associates: 'I was obliged to sail as near the wind as possible', he wrote, 'and am happy to think that I have got out of the scrape without committing myself in any way'.[157]

The impact of Non-Intrusion on the election results was variously interpreted by Non-Intrusionists and their opponents. *Blackwood's Magazine*, Tory and Moderate, accused Non-Intrusionists of seeking votes by prayers and preaching, 'combined with the more usual appliances of wheedling and whisky'; and claimed that 'nowhere ... have these presumptuous men secured one representative who is likely to serve the purpose to which they

[151] Robert Lamond to Peel, 9 July 1841 (ibid 40485, fo. 122).
[152] Ibid.
[153] Jon. J. E. Elliot to earl of Minto, 15 and 17 June 1841 (Minto Papers, 120/1).
[154] *Caledonian Mercury*, 28 June and 1 July 1841; *Witness*, 30 June and 3 July 1841; Sir G. O. Trevelyan, *The Life and Letters of Lord Macaulay* (London, 1908), 404.
[155] Robert Lamond to Peel, 9 July 1841 (Peel Papers, 40485, fo. 122).
[156] Printed address dated 3 July 1841 (ibid., fo. 119).
[157] Rae to Hope, 11 July 1841 (Aberdeen Papers, 43205, fo. 135). See also Aberdeen–Hope letters (ibid., fos. 104–5, 116–17, 120–1, 144–5, 214–19).

truly look'.[158] The return of Fox Maule, Rutherfurd, Stewart, Alexander
Bannerman, Campbell of Monzie, and other Non-Intrusionists did not bear
out this claim. The Non-Intrusionist Alexander Thomson of Banchory,
however, exaggerated in the opposite direction in saying that 'of the members
returned by Scotland 34, much more than a half [i.e. of 53], are pledged to
non-intrusion principles'; though he qualified this by saying that 'it remains
to be seen how far the opinions professed on the Hustings will be followed
up in the House'.[159] Voting on the question in the Commons was to show that
fewer than 34 Scottish M.P.s supported Non-Intrusion even in the most
general way. But it was also shown that many Scottish members, even if not
committed to Non-Intrusion, were prepared to consider methods of settling
the question.

IV. THE CONSERVATIVES AND NON-INTRUSION, 1841-1842

The electoral effects of Non-Intrusion were certainly not obvious enough to
persuade the new Government to make concessions. Peel's commitment to
Erastianism would not, or would only with great reluctance, be relaxed in
order to accommodate Non-Intrusionist claims. He had made dampening
statements on the issue since 1834, and most recently during the elections.
The open and impassioned demands of Non-Intrusionist leaders did not
appeal to his restrained temperament. His private reaction was one of revulsion from 'the Popish-Presbyterian party' and from 'the use made by some
of these zealots of the name of the "Lord Jesus" and their efforts to get
power for themselves or to injure their neighbours under the pretended
sanction of that sacred authority'.[160] Similar views were held by those
ministerial colleagues who were closely concerned with the question. Sir
James Graham, a member of a Cumberland landed family of Scottish
descent, wished to maintain civil ascendancy. As Home Secretary, however,
he followed the example of his Liberal predecessor in dispensing Crown
patronage in accordance with congregational wishes.[161] Aberdeen, now
absorbed in the duties of Foreign Secretary, had been affronted by the
General Assembly's rejection of his bill, and would not entertain any solution which went beyond this measure.[162] He was still constantly receiving
Hope's views about the unlikelihood of a substantial secession from the
Church. In one letter Hope went so far as to say that 'there are not six or
ten [ministers] who would secede'.[163]

But further attempts at settlement were suggested. Sir George Sinclair,
former Conservative M.P. for Caithness, proposed the alteration of a clause

---

[158] *Blackwood's Edinburgh Magazine*, l (July–Dec. 1841), 131, 139.
[159] Thomson to Aberdeen, 14 Aug. 1841 (Aberdeen Papers, 43237, fos. 270–1).
[160] Peel to Aberdeen, 16 Dec. 1840 (ibid. 43061, fos. 257–8). Cf. Gash, *Sir Robert Peel*, 379.
[161] J. T. Ward, *Sir James Graham* (London, 1967), 200; Parker, *Sir James Graham*, i. 383–6.
[162] Aberdeen to Hope, 4 May 1841 (Aberdeen Papers, 43204, fo. 274).
[163] Memorandum by Hope, 6 Dec. 1841 (ibid. 43205, fo. 241).

in Aberdeen's bill in order to give more weight to congregational objections to a presentee. Even if the objections were not thought conclusive by the Presbytery they might, if coming from numerous worthy people, suffice to cause the presentee's rejection; though the Presbytery would be equally entitled not to sustain the objections.[164] This proposal was initially discouraged by Aberdeen and Hope on the grounds that it went too far towards a popular veto. But Sinclair succeeded in arranging meetings between Hope and Candlish, and both Hope and Aberdeen agreed with the proposal.[165]

Thus it seemed that 'Sinclair's clause' might prove to be the necessary bridge between the opposing banks of opinion. But the move failed. Peel had said that, before legislation could be passed, the seven ministers of Strathbogie would have to be restored to office. Sinclair and Hope tried to achieve this by pressing the ministers to submit to the General Assembly's ruling in their case. But this the ministers refused to do, and the Government's incentive to attempt the settlement was removed. Moreover, Non-Intrusionists were unhappy with the proposal to leave the ultimate decision on presentations in the hands of the Presbytery and not in those of the congregation.[166] On 31 December 1841 the plan was rejected by the Non-Intrusion Committee of Assembly. A speech by Sir William Rae (when standing for reelection in Bute on being appointed Lord Advocate) was believed to have swayed Non-Intrusionists against the clause by hinting that ministers were considering a scheme more favourable than that of the duke of Argyll.[167] A suggestion by Lord Cottenham, the former Whig Lord Chancellor, was more in keeping with Non-Intrusionist views than was Sinclair's clause. Cottenham had proposed that Presbyteries should be compelled to reject a presentee if objections were made, together with stated reasons, by a clear majority (perhaps two-thirds) of the communicants.[168] But this held no appeal for Moderates.

The failure of Sinclair's clause temporarily ended communication between Government and Non-Intrusionists. The restoration of the Strathbogie ministers was, in Peel's view, an essential opening to renewed discussions.[169] Non-Intrusionists would not accede to Government wishes on this point, and indeed displayed their own unrelenting temper by forming Church

---

[164] Sir George Sinclair to Peel, 29 Nov. 1841 (Graham Papers, microfilms, 128); Watt, *Chalmers*, 232–3.

[165] Aberdeen to Hope, 27 Sept. 1841 (Aberdeen Papers, 43205, fos. 196–7); Hope to Aberdeen, 29 Sept. 1841 (ibid., fos. 199–205).

[166] Sir G. Sinclair (ed.), *Selections from the Correspondence carried on during certain negotiations for the adjustment of the Scottish Church question* (Edinburgh, 1842), esp. 73–9, 119–21; Turner, *Scottish Secession*, 254–66.

[167] Gordon, *Aberdeen*, 147–9; Hope to Aberdeen, 30 Sept. 1841, 2 letters (Aberdeen Papers, 43205, fos. 206–11).

[168] Sinclair, op. cit. 162–78.

[169] Peel to Graham, 3 Jan. 1842 (Peel Papers, 40446), fo. 288.

defence associations.[170] Consequently, there was no Government offer of a settlement during the session of 1842. Peel announced at the beginning of the session that ministers had no plan to introduce.[171] When on 15 March Sir Andrew Leith Hay, Liberal M.P. for the Elgin burghs, called for an immediate solution and moved that the Queen be addressed on the subject, Graham said that the Government would not propose legislation, and Hay's motion was negatived.[172] Very soon after this, on the same day, Alexander Campbell of Monzie, a Conservative Non-Intrusionist who sat for Argyll, moved for a Select Committee to examine the dispute, and his motion had the general approval of Liberal Non-Intrusionists.[173] But he was defeated by 139 votes to 62; only half of the Scottish members voted, and of these only 12 out of 26 supported the motion.[174] This scarcely bore out the more optimistic forecasts of Non-Intrusionist parliamentary strength made after the election. Peel had discouraged the proposal, but had suggested that Campbell might introduce a definite bill later.[175] This was done when Campbell revived the duke of Argyll's measure for a popular veto, and the bill had its first reading on 14 April. Graham said that the Government would not oppose the reading but would not support legislation on the question.[176]

Thus it seemed unlikely that the Government would accept Campbell's bill. This was made still less likely by the appearance of a crack in Non-Intrusionist ranks. A 'middle party', consisting of some forty ministers in the synod of Glasgow and Ayr, was formed in March and led by the Rev. Drs. Matthew Leishman and Alexander Simpson. They were ready to accept a compromise in the shape of Sinclair's clause.[177] Leishman promised considerable support for a Government bill seeking this solution, and Simpson believed that, given a satisfactory response from the Government, the disposition to compromise would 'proceed triumphantly throughout the Church'.[178] Accordingly, ministers began to consider a conciliatory approach. Campbell of Monzie was asked by Graham to postpone the second reading of his bill, and this course was decided on by the Commons, a motion by Fox Maule to the contrary being defeated by 131 votes to 48.[179]

This development gratified the middle party, but it was confounded by the adverse reaction of the militant majority in the General Assembly which

---

[170] Rev. David Aitken to earl of Minto, 12 Feb. 1842 (Minto Papers, 121/1); Dundee Presbytery Minutes, 2 Feb. 1842 (CH2/103/18, p. 227).

[171] Hanna, iv. 279.   [172] Hansard, lxi. 618-26 and ff.

[173] Ibid. 646-7; Rutherfurd to Fox Maule, 12 and 13 Mar. 1842 (Dalhousie Papers, 642/2); A. M. Dunlop to Maule, 10 Mar. 1842 (ibid. 658).

[174] Hansard, lxi. 654-5.   [175] Ibid. 650-3.   [176] Ibid. lxii. 496-7.

[177] J. F. Leishman, *Matthew Leishman of Govan and the Middle Party of 1843* (Paisley, 1924), 120 ff.; Watt, op. cit. 239 ff.; A. Turner, op. cit. 266 ff. Leishman to Graham, 15 Apr. 1842 (Graham Papers, microfilms, 128).

[178] Leishman to Graham, 15 Apr. 1842 (Graham Papers, microfilms, 128); Alexander Simpson to Sir George Clerk, 16 Apr. 1842 (Clerk of Penicuik Papers, 3515).

[179] Hansard, lxiii. 97-110.

opened on 19 May. No *via media* would tempt this body into giving up the struggle. Indeed, the Assembly seemed to raise its demands further by adopting a motion to abolish patronage, disregarding pleas from the middle party not to antagonize the Government; and then by adopting a crucial Claim of Right setting out the historical and legal justifications for freedom from the 'illegal coercion' of the civil courts.[180] The Claim of Right ended with a threat to secede from the Kirk unless an adequate settlement were made—an intention which was being increasingly heard. Some members of the middle party could not resist joining the large majority in support of the Claim,[181] and the party was thus being destroyed amidst the countervailing temptations of militancy. Moderates were dismayed by the actions of Assembly. Hope said that the pretensions to power in the Claim of Right were 'equalled only by the declarations of *some* of the Popes', and that the anti-patronage declaration 'puts an end for the present to all hope of satisfactory adjustment'.[182] Hope's opinions coincided with the reaction of an Erastian Government when confronted by clamorous cries for spiritual independence. Graham announced in the Commons that since the General Assembly the hope of a settlement had perished, and that Campbell's bill would be opposed.[183] On 15 June this bill's second reading was shelved on the grounds that consent of the Crown—whose extensive rights of patronage would be affected by the bill—had not been obtained.[184]

Sinclair's clause had failed to produce a settlement. After this the Government suggested no solution; it was left to the Opposition to propose one. Fox Maule said that if no ministerial scheme were forthcoming early in the next session, he would take the matter in hand himself, and Peel raised no objection.[185] A determined and conciliatory parliamentary intervention might still have resolved the conflict. Chalmers himself wrote on 22 August that secession from the Church was too serious a step to take after a mere legal judgement by a civil court. Parliament alone had the power to create and destroy established Churches: the final step, therefore, should not be taken until it was seen what the next parliamentary session would bring.[186] But Parliament was most unlikely to find agreement on a scheme which would satisfy the Non-Intrusionists. The House of Lords declared its judgement in the second Auchterarder Case in August. This stated that

---

[180] Ibid. 250–9; Buchanan, ii. 499–523. The Claim is printed in full in Buchanan, ii. 633–47, also in *Acts of the General Assembly*, 1130–41.

[181] Marquess of Bute to Graham, 25 May 1842 (Graham Papers, microfilms, 129).

[182] Hope to Brougham, 30 May 1842 (Brougham Papers, 34774); Hope to Aberdeen, 24 May 1842 (Aberdeen Papers, 43205, fos. 253–4).

[183] Hansard, lxiii. 1428–9. Cf. Graham to Rev. Dr. William Muir, 14 June 1842 (Graham Papers, microfilms, 129).

[184] Hansard, lxiii. 1584–5; Buchanan, ii. 527–8. Fox Maule asked Peel to use his prerogative to set aside this objection, and Monzie protested that the objection had not been raised on the first reading, nor against Argyll's bill the previous year. But Peel supported the objection.

[185] Hansard, lxiv. 90–2.   [186] Hanna, iv. 305.

the Church was liable to civil penalty for having disobeyed the Court of Session in the first Auchterarder Case, and helped to confirm extreme Non-Intrusionist opinions.[187] In November a 'Convocation' of Non-Intrusionist ministers adopted resolutions in favour of the Claim of Right. It was then agreed by 354 ministers that unless a satisfactory proposal were made by the State they would 'tender the resignation of their civil advantages which they can no longer hold in consistency with the full and free exercise of their spiritual functions'.[188] The threat to secede was now made in earnest. Chalmers presented to the Convocation a complete scheme of financial support for the anticipated Free Church, and in December he told an American correspondent that unless Parliament granted redress the decision of the next General Assembly would confirm that of the Convocation.[189]

V. DISRUPTION AND ITS IMPACT

By the beginning of 1843 the Non-Intrusionists were preparing to form a new Church, but still hoped that the Government would intervene to prevent the necessity for such a step. However, legal decisions and the Government's attitude remained adverse. In January the Court of Session decided, in the Stewarton Case, that ministers of *quoad sacra* churches could not be members of Church courts, and thus held invalid the Chapels Act of 1834.[190] This decision was said by a Non-Intrusionist minister to be a greater intrusion than rejection of the Veto Act, for the latter concerned only the civil rights of patrons while the former concerned the composition of the Church's organs of government and jurisdiction.[191]

The Claim of Right required a reply from the Crown. Hope advised that this reply should be sent before the General Assembly met; a secession, he said, would be less effective if it occurred before the Assembly than if it took place during the Assembly. The reply, showing the Government's attachment to the existing law, should even be sent before the meeting of Parliament, for the Government's stand might then sway many Conservatives who might otherwise be inclined to support a Non-Intrusionist motion.[192] Hope clung to his view that secession would not be vast, claiming that a recent decline in church attendance in Glasgow, especially in the churches of Non-Intrusionist ministers, was 'an alarming proof to the leaders, of the consequences of secession, and never were they more anxious *not* to go out'. Legislation, he thought, need not be attempted until the effects of secession were seen.[193]

---

[187] Watt, 264-5; Bryce, ii. 293 ff.
[188] Watt, 272-3; Buchanan, ii. 534 ff.; Turner, 309-27; detailed record of the Convocation in W. Wilson, *Memorials of R. S. Candlish* (Edinburgh, 1880), 219-59.
[189] Hanna, iv. 319.   [190] For the case see Watt, 280-5.
[191] Rev. Henry Duncan to Brougham, 17 Feb. 1843 (Brougham Papers, 13508).
[192] Hope to Aberdeen, 27 Nov. 1842 (Aberdeen Papers, 43205, fos. 269, 271-2).
[193] Ibid., fos. 272-4.

Hope's opinions still carried weight with ministers. His letter containing this advice was sent to Peel by Aberdeen. Graham as Home Secretary very shortly drafted a 'Queen's Letter' which broadly followed the lines suggested by Hope, with the exception that legislation was to remain a possibility.[194] The letter, he informed Peel, would show that 'we remain disposed to legislate and to grant honourable terms'; most ministers would be ready 'to seize any excuse for retaining possession of their Manses and Glebes'.[195] A draft of the Queen's Letter was sent to the Lord Advocate (Duncan McNeill) and the duke of Buccleuch, a Cabinet Minister, and some additions and corrections were made at their suggestion.[196] The final letter, dated 4 January, was sent to the Moderator of the General Assembly. It said that Government could not accept the Claim of Right, since the Claim stated that the General Assembly had the right to decide the boundaries between civil and ecclesiastical jurisdiction.[197] This was denied by the Non-Intrusionists, who insisted that their claims were within the historic limitations of the Church's jurisdiction and that they did not presume to decide legal boundaries. Employing terms which Moderates used against them, Non-Intrusionists denied any attempt to identify the Claim of Right with 'the arrogant pretensions of the Church of Rome'.[198]

There was no attempt at Government legislation. Asked in Parliament on 23 February whether they intended to introduce a bill, ministers replied in the negative; Graham reaffirmed the opinions in the Queen's Letter as a final standpoint.[199] There were efforts, however, from the Opposition benches. Fox Maule moved on 7 March that a Committee of the whole House should consider a petition of the General Assembly for Non-Intrusion. There was a two-day debate on the motion—the lengthiest parliamentary attention given to the question—but it had little hope of success. Ministers repeated their opposition to Non-Intrusionist claims. Graham said that the time had come when all suspense on the question must be removed: the House of Lords had given a clear and final interpretation of the law.[200] Peel rebutted the motion in Moderate and Erastian terms. First he rejected popular choice of ministers:

The duty of a minister is to teach, to admonish, and frequently to perform unpopular functions, and to establish that relation between a minister and his flock which would be established if you make him dependent upon the popular voice, would be to degrade the office of the minister, and to deprive him of all chance of being useful in his sacred calling.[201]

[194] Graham to Peel, 10 Dec. 1842 (Peel Papers, 40448, fos. 59–60).
[195] Graham to Peel, 30 Dec. 1842 (ibid., fos. 164–6).
[196] Graham to the Lord Advocate, 4 Jan. 1843; Graham to the duke of Buccleuch, 4 Jan, 1843 (Graham Papers, microfilms, 129).
[197] Turner, 331–2; Buchanan, ii. 564.   [198] Buchanan, ii. 564.
[199] Hansard, lxvi. 1151–8.   [200] Ibid. lxvii. 378–94.
[201] Ibid. 497–8.

Secondly, he denied the right of an established Church to spiritual self-government:

It is a perfect anomaly and absurdity that a church should have all the privileges of an establishment . . . and yet claim an exemption from those obligations which . . . must exist on its side with reference to the supreme tribunals of the country.[202]

Finally, he pointed to the wider implications of accepting the Non-Intrusionist claims, perhaps with the Tractarians in mind:

. . . these claims, if admitted on the part of the Church of Scotland, cannot be limited to their present extent, or confined to that Church. Principles are involved in the question which, if relinquished by the House of Commons on the present occasion, they must be prepared to carry further.[203]

Although Peel said that the Government would not refuse to legislate 'if they observed a prospect of a satisfactory settlement',[204] his firm statements invited secession by those who still maintained their opinions. Maule's motion was defeated by 211 votes to 76. But the Scottish M.P.s voted 25 to 12 in its favour;[205] 10 Scottish members who had formerly voted against Non-Intrusion abstained on this occasion. Although the motion was only a general one, and its supporters were not necessarily committing themselves to a Non-Intrusionist solution, it was not unjust to complain that 'the voice of Scotland . . . was overborne'.[206] The Government's discouraging stand had a clear effect on the division. Only one Scottish Conservative, Campbell of Monzie, voted for the motion, while of the 12 Scottish M.P.s voting against it 10 were Conservatives. The general opposition to the motion came mainly from Conservatives, and the support came from Liberals, including such noted radicals as Dr. Bowring, Joseph Brotherton, Charles Buller, Richard Cobden, W. Smith O'Brien, and C. P. Villiers.[207] The negation amounted to a parliamentary refusal to avert the approaching schism.

Before disruption occurred, the House of Lords discussed the issue three times.[208] But nothing was done to change the Commons' decision; indeed, the Government's stand was reaffirmed. Aberdeen said in the last of these debates, on 9 May, that Non-Intrusionists were determined to assert unheard-of claims and that ministers would oppose them by every means in their power.[209] On 18 May, when the General Assembly met, the long-heralded secession occurred: 451 ministers, over a third of the clerical strength of the Kirk, signed a deed of demission, leaving the material embrace of Establishment to face a future whose bleakness was, however, alleviated by the conviction of spiritual rectitude and the financial promises of lay supporters. But 752 ministers remained in the Kirk.[210] The size of the

---

[202] Ibid. 503.   [203] Ibid.   [204] Ibid. 505.
[205] Ibid. 510–12.   [206] Buchanan, ii. 581–2; Hanna, iv. 631.
[207] Hansard, lxvii. 510–12; Aberdeen to Hope, 10 Mar. 1843 (Aberdeen Papers, 43205, fo. 279).
[208] Hansard, lxviii. 37–8, 218–73, 1137–40; lxix. 12–17; Bryce, ii. 340–52.
[209] Hansard, lxix. 1720.
[210] Turner, 459.

defection may have disappointed some Non-Intrusionists, who had hoped to secure a majority of ministers, but the belittling anticipations of Moderates were dashed. On the brink of disruption, John Hope had foretold a secession of only two to three hundred ministers.[211] While the period after the Disruption was marked by instances of hardship and heroism, the most protracted material struggles concerned the effort to obtain building sites from unwilling landowners, in order to build churches for which the money was readily forthcoming.[212] A year after the Disruption a host of solid stone churches mocked Hope's prediction that 'people will wonder at the anxiety they at first felt and will laugh at the secession and its wooden churches'.[213] Free Church membership soared (especially in the larger towns and Highland counties), and, later, rival schools as well as rival churches testified to immense sacrifices which could have been of great service to the Establishment. The loss of personnel, including many of the ministerial giants of the Church, was very marked. It was not surprising that some politicians later regretted that they had not done more to preserve the Church's unity. In 1854 Graham wrote of the Disruption: '. . . when I look at its consequences I take great blame to myself and have a painful misgiving, that more might have been done by me to avert so great a calamity'.[214]

The Government may indeed have seemed indifferent to the magnitude of the problem. The absence of political and popular expression on the subject, particularly in the general election; Hope's role as the principal Moderate channel of information and advice; the Erastian predilections of politicians and their dislike of a democratic veto—all these factors distorted the true situation. Compromise, in the shape of Aberdeen's bill, might have seemed in Government eyes to be all that was needed. Had they believed that outright concession was imperative they might have yielded the veto without creating great disturbance. Adamant opposition to this course would probably not have come from the great majority of non-Scottish M.P.s, who were more indifferent than hostile to Non-Intrusion; few Conservatives would have helped to bring down the Government on a Scottish Church question, and their opponents were divided on the subject. The pressure of events, of argument, and of their own ecclesiastical thought persuaded ministers that it was unnecessary to yield to the veto. Hence they treated the ecclesiastical demands of Scotland in a different way from the much more politically forceful demands of Catholic Ireland.

·   ·   ·   ·   ·

[211] Memo of Hope to Aberdeen, May 1843 (Aberdeen Papers, 43206, fo. 22).

[212] On this subject see Hansard, lxxxii. 307 ff., 1090–8; lxxxvii. 207–28, 1036–7; lxxxix. 679 ff.; xcviii. 1150–67; xcix. 476 ff.

[213] Memo of Hope to Aberdeen, May 1843 (Aberdeen Papers, 43206, fo. 23); Burleigh, *Church History of Scotland*, 355.

[214] Graham to Sir George Clerk, May 1854 (Clerk of Penicuik Papers). Cf. Graham's speech in Commons, 7 June 1848 (Hansard, xcix. 493), and the view in Parker, *Graham*, i. 395–6.

Although the main effects of the Disruption naturally took place in Scotland, the event was not without impact south of the border. English Dissenters had been watching the dispute with great interest, and were dissatisfied with the failure of Non-Intrusionists to take a Voluntary position. The *Eclectic Review* urged them to demand complete independence from the State: 'Go farther, we beseech you—shew that you are as independent of the state for pay, as you ought to be for patronage.'[215] When disruption took place, its severe effects on a Church Establishment gratified the Voluntaries. But their pleasure was hindered by the declared adherence of the Free Church to the principle of a State connection. At the new Church's first General Assembly, the opening speech by Chalmers stated firmly: '... though we quit the Establishment, we go out on the Establishment principle; we quit a vitiated Establishment, but would rejoice in returning to a pure one ... we are the advocates for a national recognition and national support of religion—and we are not Voluntaries.'[216]

Voluntaries could only hope that, since the Free Church was in effect a Dissenting Church supported by voluntary contributions, the logic of its situation would undermine its Establishment principle, and that it would become more Voluntary as time went on.[217] Meanwhile the Wesleyans had more in common with Free Churchmen over the principle of a State connection—though in the matter of the congregational appointment of ministers, Wesleyans had less in common with Free Churchmen than had Congregationalists, many of whom were Voluntaries. Welsh Calvinistic Methodists, whose older ministers and members tended to be as respectful as Wesleyans towards the State, were generous with goodwill and, no less important, monetary contributions. 'We intend', Lewis Edwards of Bala wrote to Chalmers, 'to collect from eight to nine hundred pounds without putting the Free Church to any expense in sending deputations to Wales. Her cause has been explained in all our pulpits, and I have no doubt that every congregation belonging to the Welsh Methodists has contributed something, or will do so very soon. I understand they have already sent £105 from Liverpool.'[218]

Anglican reactions to the formation of the Scottish Free Church were diverse. One Anglican correspondent was baffled and distressed by Chalmers's part in the disruption of the Scottish Establishment, after he had so vigorously defended it.[219] But another said: 'What is proved good for Scotland may in time be found good for England—a Free Church.'[220]

---

[215] *Eclectic Review*, 4th Ser. xiii (Jan.–June 1843), 144.
[216] Hanna, iv. 348.
[217] *Eclectic Review*, 4th Ser., xiv (July–Dec. 1843), 108. Cf. speech at a great meeting of Scottish Dissenters, Edinburgh, 2 July 1845 (*Report of the Speeches* . . . (Edinburgh, 1845), 12, 16).
[218] 7 Oct. 1843 (Chalmers Papers, bound vol. for 1843).
[219] Rev. Henry Thompson to Chalmers, 19 (?) Oct. 1843 (ibid.).
[220] Rev. Thomas J. Knowlys to Chalmers, 3 July 1843 (ibid.).

Gladstone (personally much involved in the revival of high-church Episcopalianism in Scotland) praised the Disruption as an effective blow at Erastianism.[221] The Hon. and Rev. Baptist Noel, who was to leave the Church of England on Voluntary grounds and join the Baptists in 1848, wrote a book supporting the Free Church principle of spiritual liberty from the State.[222]

In Scotland the effect of disruption was to place a new body of Presbyterians in separation from the others. The union of the Secession and Relief Churches to form the United Presbyterian Church on 13 May 1847 established the division of the 'three Kirks'—Established, Free, and United Presbyterian—which lasted for the rest of the nineteenth century. In the Religious Census of 1851 *total* attendances of the Free Church were assessed at 555,702 against 566,409 of the Church of Scotland and 336,412 of the United Presbyterians.[223] The three Churches—although they had but little to distinguish them in doctrine—were sometimes at issue with each other in parliamentary and local elections as well as in attitude towards the State.[224] But the main political effect of the Disruption was to strengthen the forces opposed to the privileges of the Establishment. Free Churchmen strengthened the opposition to the annuity tax (though they were not, like Voluntaries, against the tax in principle), and wanted to abolish the religious tests which were reimposed, after the Disruption, on appointments to lay university chairs. The latter aim was eventually realized in Parliament in 1853, and compromise was reached on the annuity tax seven years later.[225]

Antagonism between Free Church and Establishment became all the greater on account of the acts of the Church of Scotland immediately after the Disruption. Whereas the Free Church General Assembly extended the congregational veto to all members (including women), the General Assembly of the Church of Scotland moved the other way, ignoring the Veto Act and the Chapels Act. A somewhat more popular measure was the passage of Aberdeen's presbyterial veto on the appointment of ministers (taking account of congregational objections), in the form of the Benefices Act of 1843.[226] But this increased the hostility of Free Churchmen, who had spent much energy on opposing the plan and did not wish to see the established Church become more popular. Nor did they take kindly to the passage, in the same year, of Graham's bill facilitating the building of *quoad sacra* churches in the

[221] J. R. Fleming, *A History of the Church in Scotland, 1843–74* (Edinburgh, 1927), 31.

[222] *The Case of the Free Church of Scotland* (London, 1844); D. W. Bebbington, 'The Life of Baptist Noel: its Setting and Significance', *Baptist Quarterly*, N.S. xxiv (1971–2), 394.

[223] Dawson, *Abridged Statistical History of Scotland*, 1106. For county and burgh breakdowns of the attendance figures see ibid. 1106 ff.

[224] For examples of the effects on electoral divisions, see A. Murray Dunlop to Fox Maule, 10 Feb. and 27 May 1844 (Dalhousie Papers, 658); Mackie, *McLaren*, i. 294–6.

[225] For debates on the Tests question see Hansard, lxxiv. 465–502 (1844); lxxxii. 226 ff. (1845); cvi. 1314 (1849).

[226] Aberdeen–Hope correspondence, 14 June–24 Aug. 1843 (Aberdeen Papers, 43206, fos. 41–71).

Establishment. They could take comfort, however, from their own rapid expansion, built on the wealth of their many middle-class supporters—which compensated for the comparative absence of the aristocracy[227]—and from the spread of their influence in education. No less than 513 Free Church schools existed by 1847.[228] A dispute over whether to seek a national system of education or to insist on sectarian education was resolved in favour of the latter course, which was championed by Robert Candlish against James Begg. At the Free Church General Assembly in 1850 Candlish obtained the crushing majority of 254 votes to 16.[229] But Free Churchmen became more receptive to a national system, and the Scottish Education Act of 1872 took both Church of Scotland and Free Church schools into Government hands. Thus the educational conflict between the two Churches was removed, and the role of the State was strengthened while denominational assertiveness weakened.

The solid confrontation between the Establishment and the seceders of 1843 could not suddenly dissolve. Even the decline of Moderatism in the established Church and the growing influence within it of evangelicals such as Norman McLeod (a former member of the 'middle party') led to increased defensiveness among Free Churchmen. A move to abolish patronage in the Church of Scotland, which succeeded when a parliamentary Act was passed in 1874, met with fierce Free Church opposition.[230] But in fact Free Churchmen, caught in their delicate position between the embattled ranks of Establishment and Voluntaryism, could contemplate future union with either side. Whereas some Free Churchmen upheld the Establishment principle, others were inclined to join the United Presbyterians in accepting Voluntaryism. In May 1853 Dr. James Begg spoke of the desirability of 'cultivating a good understanding with the Dissenting denominations throughout the country',[231] but he later showed that he was determined not to accept Voluntaryism as the price of such an understanding. Through the initiative of Sir George Sinclair, the former mediator in the Non-Intrusion conflict who had finally joined the Free Church in 1851, some Free Churchmen publicly began in 1857 to advocate joining the United Presbyterians, and the desire was reciprocated among the latter.[232] In 1863 both Churches

[227] Burleigh, op. cit. 373. Cf. Lord Panmure (formerly Fox Maule) to Edward Ellice, 18 Dec. 1854 (Ellice Papers, E45, fos. 71–2).

[228] A. Todd, 'The Effect of the Disruption on the Educational Schemes of the Church of Scotland and the Free Church, 1843–50' (unpubl. Univ. of Dundee M.A. Hons. thesis 1972), 17.

[229] D. J. Withrington, 'The Free Church Educational Scheme, 1843–50', Records of the Scottish Church History Society, xv (1963–5), 103–15.

[230] Burleigh, 375–6. Cf. comments of the Free Church politician Charles Cowan in his Reminiscences (privately printed, 1878), 296–7.

[231] T. Smith, Memoirs of James Begg, D.D. (2 vols., Edinburgh, 1885–8), ii. 197 f.

[232] Fleming, op. cit. 130 ff.; Sir G. Sinclair, A Letter addressed to the non-established Presbyterian Communions of Scotland (Edinburgh, 1854), 6 ff. Cf. United Presbyterian Magazine, N.S., 1 (1857), 237–8, 282–4.

appointed committees to confer on the matter, and strenuous efforts were made to narrow the difference over Voluntaryism. But union was strongly opposed within the Free Church by a substantial minority on Establishment grounds, and in 1873 negotiations were fruitlessly terminated.[233]

Eventually Free Churchmen resolved their dilemma by forming successive unions with both sides. First, in 1900, there was union with the majority of the United Presbyterian Church to form the United Free Church; then in 1929, following a statute of 1921 which abandoned any parliamentary competence to interfere with the spiritual freedom of the Kirk, most of the United Free Church joined the Church of Scotland. Although small minorities stayed out on each occasion, the cataclysmic divisions of the nineteenth century were thrust firmly into the historical background. The unions in Scotland were extreme manifestations of the tendency to interdenominational understanding throughout Great Britain, and were eased by the comparative absence of doctrinal division.

[233] Burleigh, 363 ff.; Fleming, 176 ff.; A. R. MacEwen, *The Life and Letters of John Cairns* (London, 1895), 498 ff.; T. Smith, op. cit. ii. 494–513.

CHAPTER V

Sir Robert Peel, Dissent, and Catholicism, 1841-1846

I. PEEL AND THE CHURCH OF ENGLAND

PEEL HAD been returned to office partly as a defender of the Church Established, but his return was not entirely reassuring to enthusiasts for Church defence. He was inseparable from his dubious past, and previous actions were perhaps a better guide to his policies than were the hopes and interests of his followers. Attitudes taken up in opposition to the Whigs would not necessarily be maintained in office. As the author of the Ecclesiastical Commission, he had shown a decided though not uncriticized regard for the Church's interests. But he had also fathered the liberal Tamworth Manifesto and had assisted in the greater apostasy of 1829. The reforms of 1828-32 had made it impossible to return to the Establishment ascendancy of a former age; those who believed otherwise were doomed, almost inevitably, to sink helplessly in an ultra-Tory political backwater. That this was true in the commercial as well as in the ecclesiastical sphere only emphasized the poignant anachronism of the ultra-Tories. Peel's role, in contrast, was not that of a martyr to lost causes. His Tamworth Manifesto had accepted not only the reformed constitution but some of its ecclesiastical implications, and had been friendly in tone towards the demands of Dissent. Only his failure to stay in office had prevented this document from damaging Conservative unity.

The long spell in Opposition from 1835 to 1841 had strengthened Peel's party. But on returning to office he pursued a moderately liberal and potentially dangerous policy in religious matters. This policy was practically inescapable for a Prime Minister, of whatever political complexion, in the plural society—and, as far as Ireland was concerned, the politically insecure society—of the United Kingdom in the nineteenth century. Peel's policy was generally similar to the Whig compromise in the 1830s—a moderate desire to maintain and strengthen the Establishment together with a moderate readiness to bow to the pressure of Catholics and Dissenters. But his similarity to the Whigs was by no means complete. Peel after all was a Conservative; consequently, his support for the Church Establishment was more positive than that of the Whigs, his attitude to Dissent more negative, his concessions to Catholicism more obviously bestowed as pragmatic solaces for Irish discontent. There was more of inspired empiricism than of basic liberal principle in his policy. Many of his followers were unfavourable to his reforms. There was much disgruntled opposition, culminating in the disastrous party split of 1846.

Peel's personal religion contributed to his empiricism. His sincere churchmanship was broad and undogmatic, neither high church nor evangelical and more than a little contemptuous of both. Enthusiasts on either side could only view his Premiership with apprehension. Ashley, who was to clash with Peel over the 'ten hours' factory campaign, privately noted with typical emotional intensity his belief in Peel's 'love of expediency, his perpetual egoistry, his dread of an immovable principle, his delight in the praise of men . . . a well-turned phrase of compliment, and eulogy from John Russell or Macaulay, will attract him more than "Hast thou considered my servant Job?"'[1] On the same day that this was written, Ashley warned him against the Romanizing menace of the Tractarians; they must, he urged, be kept out of high ecclesiastical office.[2] Peel did not need to be warned against Tractarians, for they had already said in the *British Critic* that his name was 'a nullity in any question in the least connected with religion' and that his whole career had been 'one continual defalcation', while conceding that he had 'great weight in questions of malt, registration and sugar'.[3]

But to those churchmen who did not expect too much from a Prime Minister hard pressed by competing religious claims, Peel's ministry had its comforting side. It was preferable to that of the Whigs, if not on very definable grounds. Peel sought the counsel of bishops, particularly that of Blomfield, and wanted reforms in the Church in order to scout nepotism and plurality and to improve parochial provision. His ecclesiastical appointments avoided controversy, and were less concerned with theology than with hard work. Some of them were made on Blomfield's advice, and sometimes the Premier appealed to Ashley in support of them.[4] Though rarely anti-Tractarian they were never Tractarian, and an applicant for a living took care to state '. . . I am no Puseyite'.[5] Peel's New Parishes Act of 1843 allowed the Ecclesiastical Commission to form, on the authority of an Order in Council, new parochial districts in heavily populated areas. There was no direct Government aid for the purpose and the commissioners had to borrow the necessary funds themselves.[6] But the Premier made a private

---

[1] Diary, 24 July 1841 (Hodder, *Shaftesbury*, i. 342).

[2] Ashley to Peel, 24 July 1841 (ibid. 343–5).

[3] *British Critic*, xxx (July 1841), 47; quoted P. J. Welch, 'Blomfield and Peel: a Study in Co-operation between Church and State, 1841–6', *JEH* xii (1961), 71.

[4] P. J. Welch, op. cit. 75–6; Chadwick, *Victorian Church*, i. 226–9; Peel to Ashley, 22 Jan. 1842 (Peel Papers, Add. MS. 40493, fo. 46).

[5] Rev. John S. Baron to Peel, 11 July 1844 (ibid. 40549, fos. 165–6).

[6] Gash, *Reaction*, 90–1; Best, *Temporal Pillars*, 357–9.

contribution of £4,000 to further the object of this bill, and made other donations to help the Church.[7] Some liberal acts of his ministry, however, drew strong disapproval from Blomfield;[8] and of Government money for the Church there was, disappointingly, none. The *Eclectic Review* had rightly prophesied that 'there will be no money forthcoming; not a sixpence towards church extension . . .'[9] Although Peel had supported Inglis's motion of 1840 for a parliamentary grant, he believed on coming into office that this policy would, by arousing a storm of opposition, only endanger the true interests of the Church.[10] Dissenters were too numerous, and too powerful under the reformed constitution, to miss such a chance for attacking both Church and State.

Peel's attitude to this question was probably for the good of the Church, but his opposition to the increase of bishoprics was perhaps unduly rigid and nervous. He opposed the earl of Powis's bill to keep the dioceses of St. Asaph and Bangor separate. This anticipated union had been included in the Established Church Bill in 1836, and an Order in Council containing the plan of union had been published in 1839. The junction was intended to provide, financially and constitutionally, for the creation of a new see at Manchester. The new see could thus be formed without increasing the number of bishops (and the number of mitred heads in the House of Lords) and therefore without unduly antagonizing radicals and Dissenters. Many churchmen, however, wished to prevent the union. They dwelt on the availability of other sources of revenue for Manchester, and on the geographical objections to creating an extensive diocese in a mountainous area. Defenders of the union, on the other hand, pointed out that the sees, even when united, would contain only 258 benefices, whereas the diocese of Lincoln had 1,072.[11] In 1843 Powis introduced his first bill into the Lords to stop the union, suggesting in compensation that, when the see of Manchester had been formed, the junior bishop (initially the occupant of the new diocese) should not sit in the Lords; thus, though the number of bishops would increase, the number in the House of Lords would not. Somewhat surprisingly, the main obstacle to this solution was not radicalism and Dissent but the Conservative Government.

The bill of 1843 was withdrawn in May after Government opposition had been expressed by Wellington.[12] Peel stood firmly by the settlement of 1836. He may have been unwilling to increase the number of bishops lest this should cause radical reaction. At the same time he may not have wanted to set a precedent of excluding a bishop from the Lords, lest this should

---

[7] Gash, op. cit. 91; Gash, *Sir Robert Peel*, 383-4.
[8] See below, pp. 166, 172. [9] 4th Ser. x (July–Dec. 1841), 481.
[10] Welch, op. cit. 78-9; Gash, *Reaction*, 89-90, and *Sir Robert Peel*, 382-3; Graham to Peel, 17 Sept. 1842 (Peel Papers, 40447, fos. 164-5).
[11] Hansard, lxix. 769 f., 800-2; lxxx. 80-1 (speech of Stanley, 2 May 1845).
[12] Ibid. lxix. 756-804.

encourage radical demands for a more general exclusion.[13] Though he may have had pro-Church reasons, he received little clerical support, particularly in the sees threatened with enforced union.[14]

Powis introduced his bill again in June 1844, and cited the continued separate existence of Sodor and Man as a precedent.[15] The bishops of Bangor, St. David's, Lincoln, Exeter, and Salisbury spoke in favour of the bill, though Howley and Blomfield spoke against.[16] The bishop of Bangor, Christopher Bethell, defending his diocese from merger, expressed the quaint view that the creation of the Manchester see might be regarded as an exchange for the abolition of the diocese of Westminster in 1550—in such a case the Welsh sees need not be disturbed.[17] Advocates of the union, he said, were too inclined to regard dioceses as equal units of area or population, as '... mere matters of arithmetic, or of pounds, shillings, and pence'.[18] Despite the passage of the bill, Powis announced that it would be withdrawn because of Government opposition and the likelihood of defeat in the House of Commons.[19] By 1845 some episcopal opponents of the measure were weakening, but the bill was defeated in the Lords by 129 votes to 97.[20] In 1846 the bill was finally passed; Blomfield now spoke for it, though some bishops were still against it and the new Whig Government was adverse.[21] The Church was pleased, but the question of additional bishops in the Lords was still unsettled. By the passage of the Manchester Bishopric Bill in 1847 a flexible solution was reached which gave something to the Church and to radicals. The new see was created but the number of bishops in the Lords was not increased. New bishops would only take their seats in that House as episcopal vacancies arose.

II. THE FAILURE OF EDUCATIONAL REFORM, 1843

Peel's refusal to support State grants to the Church and to increase the number of bishops in the upper House gratified Dissenters and disappointed many churchmen. None the less, the events of the ministry as a whole were probably more irritating to Dissenters than to churchmen. The defeat of Nonconformity over church-rates in 1837, powerful Anglican opposition to the education scheme of 1839, and the recent electoral victory with Church support had made an impression on Conservatives which had not yet been counteracted by the growing militancy of Dissent under the prodding of Edward Miall. Concessions to Dissent would not be readily forthcoming from a Premier who had many ardent defenders of the Establishment among his followers. Sir John Easthope, M.P. for the strongly Dissenting borough

---

[13] P. S. Morrish, 'The Manchester Clause', *Church Quarterly*, i. 4 (Apr. 1969), 322.
[14] Rev. M. Williams to Peel, 16 July 1844 (Peel Papers, 40548, fos. 266–7).
[15] Hansard, lxxv. 486–7.   [16] Ibid. 496–520.   [17] Ibid. 499.
[18] Ibid.   [19] Ibid. lxxvi. 591–3.   [20] Ibid. lxxx. 95–7.
[21] Ibid. lxxxvii. 1269 ff.

of Leicester, on making another unsuccessful parliamentary assault on church-rates in June 1842, reminded Peel of his conciliatory tone on this topic in the Tamworth Manifesto and summoned him to act.[22] But a Government initiative to resolve this question cannot have been seriously expected; and when questioned again by Easthope in August, Peel said he had no plans for introducing a church-rate measure in the session of 1843.[23]

Instead of concession, Dissenters were faced in 1843 with dismaying educational proposals which revealed the gulf between the Government and newly confident Dissent. Educational provisions (for England and Wales) were to form part of a measure for reducing the labour of children in cotton, woollen, flax, and silk factories to $6\frac{1}{2}$ hours per day. The child-workers (whose minimum age was lowered from 9 to 8) were to spend 3 hours a day receiving education in new factory schools, which would be supported from the rates and inspected by the Government. The bill, supervised by Graham as Home Secretary, was under discussion from the autumn of 1841. Nothing materialized for many months, but the riots in depressed industrial areas in 1842 raised the expected value of increased educational provision. The bill was introduced in the following year.

Not surprisingly, after the educational uproar of 1839, the religious nature of the schools was a vital problem. Nor was it surprising that ministers should have been more careful of Church interests than of Dissenting interests. In October 1841 Graham told Brougham: 'amidst the conflict of contending sects the State, if it make a choice, must prefer the established creed . . .'[24] Brougham, despite his zeal for undenominational education, reluctantly recognized that the Church would be given a large part in the scheme.[25] But at first Graham tried to achieve neutrality and acceptability to both sides. He originally suggested that mixed school boards, consisting of Anglicans and Dissenters, should appoint the schoolmasters without requiring that they should be Anglicans. Dissenting mill-owners on the school boards might thus influence the appointment of Dissenting school-masters.[26]

By the end of 1842, however, the proposals had shifted in a pro-Church direction, while a neutral front was still ostensibly maintained. Graham told Peel on 28 December that educational clauses had been prepared in consultation with two factory inspectors, '. . . Mr. Horner, who has influence with the Dissenters, and . . . Mr. Saunders, who has the confidence of the Bishop of London . . .'[27] But Mr. Saunders, the inspector for the north of

---

[22] Ibid. lxiii. 1613 ff.   [23] Ibid. lxv. 963-4.

[24] Graham to Brougham, 24 Oct. 1841 (J. T. Ward and J. H. Treble, 'Religion and Education in 1843: Reaction to the Factory Education Bill', *JEH* xx (1969), 80).

[25] Brougham to Graham, 21 Oct. 1841 (Parker, *Graham*, i. 337).

[26] Gash, *Reaction*, 86 n. 3.

[27] Graham to Peel, 28 Dec. 1842, 'private' (Peel Papers, 40448, fo. 150); J. T. Ward, *Sir James Graham*, 195 and ff.

England, apparently made a firm Anglican impression on the bill. For he seems to have made the suggestion, accepted by Graham, that the school-masters would have to be approved by the bishop as being competent to give Anglican instruction—that is, that the schoolmasters would virtually have to be Anglicans.[28] The clauses, including this new provision, were shown to the archbishop of Canterbury and Blomfield, bishop of London, also to the bishops of Chester and Ripon in whose dioceses lay most of the factories concerned.[29] The clauses which emerged from episcopal examina-tion and Cabinet discussion contained, as well as the requirement regarding the appointment of schoolmasters, provision of a board of trustees for each school. The chairman of each board would be the officiating Anglican clergy-man of the school district, or (if the district contained more than one clergy-man) a minister appointed by the bishop. It was also provided that, while religious instruction for all pupils would be from the Bible alone and would be non-doctrinal, in certain periods daily instruction in the Anglican cate-chism and liturgy was to be given. Dissenting parents could keep their children away from such Anglican instruction.[30] 'All attempts at proselytism are prevented by the strongest guards', Graham declared when introducing the bill in the Commons on 28 February 1843.[31]

It was shown that, whatever the Government had done to conciliate the powerful Anglican opinion which had hampered Whig educational reform, their optimistic venture would have an even rougher passage than that of 1839. A new category of schools was being proposed in England and Wales, apart from those run by the two societies. The new schools would be built with Government loans and maintained through the poor rate. It was natural that dogmatic and conflicting educational opinions should exercise them-selves afresh on this scheme, that they should find it an unsatisfactory compromise and should strive to mould it to their own views or reject it altogether. To the party of secular, centralized, and compulsory education the plan was too restricted, being limited to children working in factories, and the instruction too denominational. Cobden said that the bill was not compre-hensive enough and, though an Anglican himself, blamed the Church for obstruction.[32] Criticism came also from champions of Church-controlled education; buoyed up by the success of National Society schools and by their partial victory in 1839, they continued to oppose educational control by a secular Government department. In spite of the weight given to the Church, the scheme aimed at providing combined education for children of different denominations. This was the reason why Kay-Shuttleworth, a *bête noire* of

---

[28] Gash, *Reaction*, 87.

[29] Ibid.; Graham to Blomfield, 27 Dec. 1842 (Parker, op. cit., i. 342–3); Graham to Peel, 28 Dec. 1842 (Peel Papers, 40448, fo. 150).

[30] Hansard, lxvii. 75 ff.   [31] Ibid. 90.

[32] Ibid. lxvii. 1469–71 (24 Mar. 1843). Cf. J. A. Roebuck's view: D. M. Thompson, *Non-conformity in the Nineteenth Century*, 112; Hansard, lxix. 537–8 (18 May 1843).

Church educationists, gave his support to the scheme.[33] Gladstone, a member of the Government, raised one of the difficulties of combined education—which Dissenters felt more than churchmen in this episode—when he questioned whether it would always be possible for a schoolmaster to give Scriptural instruction without doctrinal bias.[34]

Sir Robert Inglis, a champion of Church authority, at first yielded a grudging support to the scheme, but later was glad to see it abandoned. On 28 February in the Commons he took exception to Graham's statement that proselytism would be 'strictly guarded against': 'he could not support any system of national and extended education . . . which, in the very first instance, would guard against the promotion of truth . . .'[35] On 24 March Inglis claimed for the established Church 'the maintenance of her office as the supreme instructress of the people of this country', and held that a national education could be firmly based only on a national Church.[36] As it was, he continued, the Church's educational functions were being transferred to the State's organ, the Committee of the Privy Council—none of whose members need be Anglican.[37] Dissenters claimed that the Church was being favoured; but, Inglis said, they exaggerated the pro-Church bias in the composition of the boards of trustees of the proposed schools. For example, each board was to contain two churchwardens, but far from necessarily being Anglicans these might be Dissenters and among 'the bitterest enemies of the Church'. Similarly, two mill-owners were to be on each board, and '. . . twenty-seven out of sixty, or nearly one-half of the owners of mills, were dissenters'.[38]

But other prominent churchmen were positively in favour of the bill. Ashley was initially enthusiastic about its expected benefits.[39] W. F. Hook, mistakenly attacked by Dissenters during this very crisis as the 'Puseyite' vicar of Leeds,[40] thought that the Church could only vindicate her right to educate the entire poeple if she raised the money herself: '. . . why may not the Bishops with the Clergy of England tax themselves fifty per cent, aye if need should be, a hundred per cent and become beggars rather than permit the Education of the People to pass out of their hands [?]'[41] But instead of this self-sacrifice '. . . there is a monstrous notion that our B[ishops] and Clergy are to demand all the money they require whether for education or church extension [from] the state . . . I call this a monstrous notion in a free state where there is full toleration and where the taxes are paid by Dissenters as well as by Churchmen.' If the State supplied the funds, he proceeded, 'the State is in duty bound to regard the just claims of Dissent-

[33] F. Smith, *Kay-Shuttleworth*, 147 ff.
[34] Gladstone to Graham, 25 Mar. 1843 (Gladstone Papers, Add. MS. 44163, fos. 17–18).
[35] Hansard, lxvii. 104–5.   [36] Ibid. 1444–5.
[37] Ibid. 1445. Cf. Ward and Treble, op. cit. 83–4.   [38] Hansard, lxvii. 1446.
[39] Ashley to Graham, 1 Mar. 1843 (Parker, i. 340–1).   [40] Ward and Treble, 90.
[41] Hook to Gladstone, 28 Mar. 1843 (Gladstone Papers, 44163, fo. 42).

ers'. In general, he believed that the bill satisfied this criterion, and, while suggesting certain modifications, approved of the scheme. The Government, he thought, had done everything in its power to give precedence to the Church.[42] Hook gained little support for his ideal of unlimited clerical donation: Samuel Wilberforce, for one, thought that '. . . to strip a class, to impoverish our Bishops and to sell their Palaces, would only be the hopeless career of Revolution'.[43]

Although many churchmen disliked the bill, they were generally resigned to acquiescence. Much fiercer opposition came from Dissent. This attack was not limited to the older Nonconformist denominations and Methodist seceders, since Wesleyans played an unusual participatory role; nor was the opposition even limited to Protestant Dissenters, for Catholics also protested. Wesleyans, being numerous in the factory areas, would be strongly affected by the measure. But their opposition was rather different from that of Congregationalists and Baptists. Wesleyans objected not to the weight given to the established Church as a State institution, but primarily to the dangers of giving control over religious instruction to a Church influenced by Tractarian theology. It was natural at that time to exaggerate the effect of Tractarianism in the Church, but it was ironical that Peel's Government should be accused of furthering it. This fear was displayed in an address by the Wesleyan Conference later in the year:

Opinions concerning the insufficiency of Scripture, as the sole authoritative and universal rule of faith and practice, the exclusive validity of Episcopal Ordination, and the necessarily saving efficacy of the Sacraments . . . which in their necessary consequences lead directly to Popery, have been revived when they were almost extinct . . .[44]

But the fact that Wesleyans objected did not mean that they allied completely with Dissent. In Rochdale, for example, Dissenters and Wesleyans appointed separate deputations to complain to their member of Parliament.[45] Wesleyan political protest was only temporary, unlike the sustained campaigning of radical Dissent. The next Government educational proposals, in 1846, were accepted by Wesleyans after alterations had been made, and they refused to take part in Dissenting opposition.[46]

Congregationalists and Baptists, who were prominent in organizing extraparliamentary opposition to Graham's bill, also dwelt on the Tractarian threat. But as Voluntaries they were primarily opposed to the use of Government authority and public funds to extend the influence of an established

[42] Ibid., fos. 43-4. Cf. Hook to Samuel Wilberforce, 5 July 1843 (Wilberforce Papers, d. 38).
[43] Wilberforce to Hook, 29 July 1843 (ibid.).
[44] D. M. Thompson, op. cit. 116-17. Cf. *On the Educational Clauses of Sir James Graham's Factory Bill: a letter to the Hon. J. Stuart Wortley*, by the Leeds Wesleyan Deputation (Leeds, 1843), 5.
[45] Gowland, 'Methodist Secessions and Social Conflict in South Lancashire', 296.
[46] See below, p. 183.

Church. The authors of the bill, said the *Eclectic Review*, were not concerned so much with education as with the desire 'to buttress their tottering church'; the plan was really 'a church extension scheme'.[47] This presumption was linked to a general condemnation of Government control, a *laissez-faire* attitude which was applied by many middle-class Nonconformists to religion, commerce, labour, and education. A Government, said the *Eclectic* with Lockian fidelity, should concern itself only with protecting the persons and property of its subjects: 'The centralizing tendencies of this age will soon vest in the minister of the day all real and substantial power.' Government-controlled education 'could scarcely fail to produce an emasculated and servile generation, possessed, it may be, of the simpler elements of knowledge, but destitute of the free spirit and brave thoughts which constitute the noblest heritage of man'.[48] This attitude led to a prolonged movement for voluntary denominational education, led by Edward Baines the younger, editor of the *Leeds Mercury*, who played a prominent part against the plan of 1843.

The more specific objections of Dissenters to the bill included the role of the established clergy and other Anglicans in the control of the schools, episcopal approval for the appointment of schoolmasters, and insufficient provision for the exemption of children of Dissenters from Anglican instruction. On the requirement that Dissenting parents wishing exemption should formally express their conscientious objections, it was suggested that social pressure might deter them from doing this: '. . . what candid man can fail . . . to perceive that in the circumstances of our operatives, very few of them can be expected to hazard the consequences of such a step [?]'.[49] Since mill-owners, many of whom were Nonconformists, would sit on the school boards, these fears seem exaggerated; but it was understandable, especially in the climate of growing Dissenting militancy, that such opposition should be expressed.

Roman Catholics were also numerous in the factory area of south Lancashire, and they also showed alarm at the bill. They differed from Protestant Dissenters (except Wesleyans) in not linking their opposition to a general principle of religious Voluntaryism. Catholics leaned more exclusively on specific religious objections. To the Government their opposition was less significant politically than that of Protestant Dissenters, since they were far less numerous and few of them had the vote: perhaps only in Liverpool and Preston were there enough Catholic voters to exert a marked influence in elections.[50] The poverty of most Catholics laid them open to the danger of proselytism through the scheme, or to ignorance if they avoided the scheme. Although officially exempted from attendance at the proposed schools,[51] it

[47] 4th Ser. xiii (Jan.–June 1843), 582, 593–4. [48] Ibid. 580–2.
[49] Ibid. 588–9; Hansard, lxvii. 1423 (speech of William Ewart), 1429–33 (Benjamin Hawes); *On the Educational Clauses . . .*, op. cit. 6–7.
[50] For an example of effective Catholic electoral action in Liverpool, see below, pp. 188–9.
[51] Hansard, lxvii. 90.

was believed that the children of Catholics would be sent to them because lack of finance had drastically retarded the spread of Catholic schools. Over half the Catholic children in England, the *Tablet* stated, were unable to obtain a Catholic education;[52] many of these children inhabited areas where the factory schools would be established. The prospect of unpalatable religious influence in the schools was as alarming to Catholics as to other Dissenters—more so, indeed, for the Authorized Version of the Bible, which was not recognized by the Catholic Church, was to be used for Scriptural instruction. On the other hand, the nature of the scheme could also be blamed for continued educational neglect of those Catholic children who were kept away from the new schools for reasons of conscience.

Frederick Lucas, the convert who edited the *Tablet*, demanded outright rejection of the scheme, but had little hope that the English or even the Irish Catholic M.P.s would resist sufficiently to prevent Catholic children from being 'perverted through its active malignity, or allowed to grow in vice through its positive neglect ...'[53] The gulf was revealed between politically assertive Catholicism of this kind and the more cautious, conservative variety. The earl of Arundel and Surrey, heir to the duke of Norfolk, the leading English Catholic layman, sought amendments to the bill in the House of Commons, but recognized that the established Church should predominate in the management of a Government educational system.[54] Lucas was infuriated, describing the earl as either a bungler or a traitor to his religion. The attack was scarcely just, for Surrey had consulted the Catholic bishops (i.e. 'vicars-apostolic') and had accepted most of their suggestions before making his amendments.[55] Lucas also upbraided Nicholas Wiseman, coadjutor to the vicar-apostolic of the Central District, for having visited Graham to discuss the scheme, but in fact Wiseman disapproved of the bill and his purpose had been to present the objections of his fellow bishops.[56] The Catholic Institute, one of whose purposes was the support of Catholic education, was accused by Lucas of 'high treason to Catholic interests'.[57] The *Tablet*'s demand for resistance was successful, for even when the Government bill had been amended it was opposed by the Catholic Institute and by Catholic vicars-apostolic and clergy.[58] The *Tablet* also encouraged coalition between Catholics and Dissenters. One demonstration of such unity was a combined meeting of the bill's opponents held at Newton-le-Willows (midway between Liverpool and Manchester) on 12 June 1843: a petition to the Queen was adopted, and M.P.s who did not vote against the measure were threatened with the loss of Nonconformist and Catholic support.[59] This was not the first or last instance of such an

[52] Quoted Ward and Treble, 94.   [53] Quoted ibid. 96.
[54] Hansard, lxvii. 1425-6; B. Ward, *The Sequel to Catholic Emancipation*, ii. 50-1.
[55] Ward and Treble, 100.   [56] Ibid.   [57] Ibid. 99.
[58] Ibid. 102.   [59] Ibid. 106.

alliance, but its rationale may have seemed particularly complex at a time when one of the reasons for Dissenting protest was Romanization in the established Church.

The opposition to the Government scheme had impressive numbers. By the end of April 2,068,059 signatures had been placed on 13,369 petitions against the bill. The hostility of older Dissent, Wesleyanism, and Catholicism, indirectly supported by the indifference of many churchmen, was well nigh irresistible, as the Government soon appreciated. The second reading was carried on 24 March, but immediately afterwards Graham bitterly informed Stanley and Gladstone that the Dissenters would overcome the bill, or at least destroy its purpose as a 'measure of peace'.[60] But he attempted compromise in order to save the bill. On 10 April Russell tabled several amendments to meet Dissenting and Catholic objections,[61] and Graham set about preparing substantial modifications with the aid of Blomfield and J. B. Sumner, bishop of Chester.

Graham announced his alterations in the Commons on 1 May. The structure of the school boards was changed in order to diminish the appearance of Anglican bias and to increase the elective element. There would still be 7 trustees, but the clerical trustee would now select only one other trustee instead of 2. One trustee would be elected by the leading subscribers of funds to the school, and the 4 remaining trustees would be elected by those rate-payers who were assessed at £10 for the period of twelve months before the election. In an effort to prevent all 4 trustees elected by rate-payers from representing only churchmen or only Dissenters, no rate-payer would be allowed to vote for more than 2 trustees.[62] The power of bishops over the appointment of schoolmasters was reduced. Only the appointment of the headmaster would require the approval of the bishop, and assistants were to be appointed by the trustees. Any trustee might appeal to the Committee of Council against a decision made by the other trustees.[63] Other important religious concessions were made. No child attending the new schools would be compelled to attend the Sunday schools which the bill also intended to establish. Additional safeguards were provided against the reception of Anglican instruction by the children of unwilling parents. This instruction would be given to Anglican children in a separate room, at a time when non-Anglican children would not have to attend it. A time would also be provided for the children of Dissenters to receive religious instruction from Dissenting ministers.[64] Graham hoped that these concessions would satisfy Protestant Dissent. Additional attention was paid to Catholic scruples: Catholic children would not have to attend prayers, or Scripture readings from the Authorized Version.[65]

[60] Ibid. 107.   [61] Russell's amendments listed ibid. 107-8.
[62] Hansard, lxviii. 1113-15.   [63] Ibid. 1115-16.   [64] Ibid. 1110-11.
[65] Ibid. 1112-13.

The changes in the bill, Graham concluded, were intended as an olive branch; they had been framed with due respect both to the established Church and to the established principles of religious freedom.[66] No statement could have better illustrated the religious aims of many Whig and Conservative politicians. But the continued hostility to the measure showed that a great many people—whether Dissenting or pro-Establishment—regarded these aims as contradictory. The amendments, while weakening Church support still further, did not remove the opposition of non-Anglicans. Dissenters disliked the modified extent of Anglican control scarcely less than the previous proposals. In the debate on the amendments, Russell said it was evident that headmasters would always have to be Anglicans. He also said that by allowing a substantial minority of rate-payers—which, in many heavily Dissenting manufacturing districts, would consist of churchmen—to elect 2 trustees, the Government was giving 4 trustees (a majority out of the 7) to the Church of England.[67] Inglis and Dr. Bowring queried (from opposite viewpoints) whether Anglican schoolmasters could realistically be required, as a condition of employment, not to impart their own conscientious beliefs.[68] Catholics were still concerned that the withdrawal of children from the prayers and Scripture readings would depend on the initiative of parents.[69] Churchmen who had supported the original bill were even less enthusiastic about the revised version. Ashley was able to continue his support, but only with great difficulty. 'A hair's breadth in addition would render my acceptance of it impossible'; and yet, he added, 'I will take the Bill, because the whole Word of God is put into the hands of the scholar and is read by him.'[70]

The amended bill brought in new loads of adverse petitions—11,839 of them, containing 1,920,574 signatures. Many of the subscribers might have petitioned against the original bill; certainly many of the later petitions came from the same places as earlier ones.[71] The 'olive branch', however, had been spurned. Ministers wisely decided to avoid intense national and local feuding, which would doubtless have resulted from the bill's enactment, by withdrawing the measure. On 15 June Graham announced this retreat, ascribing it to Church indifference and Nonconformist revulsion.[72] The venture had alienated bodies of opinion which were more powerful and confident than the Government appreciated. The encouragement given to Church influence in education was incompatible with growing demands for religious equality. The ecclesiastical balance had been overweighted, and a

---

[66] Ibid. 1117: D. M. Thompson, 111.   [67] Hansard, lxviii. 120 f.

[68] Ibid. 1122-4 (Bowring wanted unsectarian education).

[69] Ward and Treble, 104.

[70] Diary, 11 May 1843 (Hodder, op. cit. i. 457-8).

[71] *Journals of the House of Commons*, xcviii (1843), index. For the number of petitions see Ward and Treble, 108.

[72] Hansard, lxix. 1567-8.

well-intentioned attempt to advance education had been destroyed. 'A few thoughts and regrets', wrote Ashley, 'may be given . . . to those miserable thousands, who might have been brought within the pale of physical and moral regeneration! God be their helper!'[73]

To Ashley's pleasure the clauses reducing the hours of factory labour were salvaged and passed in 1844. But the effect of the educational crisis was to check State attempts at 'combined education' and throw progress back on voluntary and denominational efforts. Tractarians might later have regretted the abandonment of the 1843 clauses as a capitulation 'to the assertion of the right of private judgement in the interpretation of Scripture'.[74] But to Ashley it seemed that 'the perilous pranks of Dr. Pusey and his disciples' had played a large part in the failure; henceforth, he said, combined education should never again be attempted.[75] To fill the void, the National Society set about raising voluntary contributions in order to extend its own schools in poor industrial areas. Peel gave £1,000, and in 1844 alone £160,000 was raised for the purpose.[76] Extended activity by the Society led to the increase of its Government grant. Many Dissenters and Catholics also strove for voluntary denominational education. Through Baines's initiative, a Congregational Board of Education was founded at a meeting of the Congregational Union in October 1843;[77] the results, however, were not very encouraging.

Nonconformists were the object of Government odium for their obstruction in 1843. 'It is', wrote Peel, 'but a sorry and lamentable triumph that Dissent has achieved.'[78] But the triumph was a real one to Dissenters and Catholics, and they were in no mood to slip back into old-time quietism, or to allow any further unpalatable policies to pass by default. 'The Dissenters', said Monckton Milnes, '. . . are so cocky at having beat the Government on the education measures that they think they have everything in their own hands.'[79] Their victory stimulated the Voluntary principle, in whose progress an important step was soon to be taken.

III. MILITANT VOLUNTARY ORGANIZATION, 1844

When the factory education clauses were abandoned, Dissenters were also taking heart from the Scottish Disruption in May. Although the Free Church

---

[73] Diary, 16 June 1843 (Hodder, i. 460).   [74] Denison, *Notes of My Life*, 168 f.

[75] Ashley to Peel, 17 June 1843 (Peel Papers, 40483, fo. 114).

[76] Soloway, *Prelates and People*, 418.

[77] J. R. Lowerson, 'The Political Career of Sir Edward Baines, 1800-90' (unpubl. Univ. of Leeds M.A. thesis 1965), 141-2. See Baines's *Education best promoted by Perfect Freedom* (Leeds, 1854), 28 ff. (quoted J. Briggs and I. Sellers (eds.), *Victorian Nonconformity* (London, 1974), 131-4). For Catholic voluntary educational efforts, see Kitching, 'Roman Catholic Education from 1700 to 1870', 228 ff.

[78] Peel to Ashley, 16 June 1843 (Parker, *Peel*, ii. 560).

[79] R. Monckton Milnes to C. J. MacCarthy, 30 June 1843 (T. W. Reid, *The Life, Letters and Friendships of Richard Monckton Milnes, first Lord Houghton* (2 vols., London, 1891), i. 300-1).

was against the Voluntary principle, an established Church had suffered schism, and Dissenters could take vicarious if somewhat mystified pleasure in the event. English, Welsh, and Irish Dissenters gave support to the new Church. At the same time, contests over church-rates were by no means exhausted. A dispute in St. Mary's parish, Nottingham, was proceeding in the early months of 1843;[80] and a contest involving the Rev. William Brock, later an eminent Baptist minister, occurred at Norwich in 1844.[81] The Braintree Case continued on its chequered course. Consciousness that the Church of England was expanding, and belief that the Conservative Government would do even less for Nonconformist claims than the Whigs, contributed to a growing demand for independent action. Alliance with the Whigs had muzzled Dissent, said the *Eclectic Review*, but 'the advent of toryism has left us politically free . . .'[82] Miall was determined to oppose the whole Church–State nexus which had produced the factory education clauses.[83] Existing societies were not strong or determined enough for the militants. The Religious Freedom Society upheld the Voluntary principle, but dissolved in 1843. By the autumn of that year the Dissenting ministers of the Midland counties and particularly of Leicester (the sanctuary of Miall, Mursell, Legge, and William Baines) were challenging their more conservative metropolitan brethren to take action. 'Leicester was in the van, and impatient of delay.'[84]

An address from Leicester, supported by seventy-six ministers of the Midland counties, appealed to London ministers to take part in a convention for the promotion of Voluntaryism.[85] The appeal had little success, but a meeting at Leicester on 7 December resolved to hold a national conference in London.[86] An executive committee, elected to prepare for the conference, comprised 11 Congregationalists and 6 others, including a churchman, Dr. John Lee.[87] The conference, held at the Crown and Anchor tavern on 30 April 1844, consisted of 728 delegates. Most of these were Congregationalists and Baptists from the Midlands and North of England, but there were also some prominent Scottish Dissenters, the Rev. Robert Eckett, former President of the Wesleyan Methodist Association (which had seceded from Wesleyanism), the Quaker Joseph Sturge, and 22 delegates from Wales.[88] The conference founded the British Anti-State Church Association, which became known as the Liberation Society in 1853 (its full title then was

---

[80] Ven. George Wilkins, archdeacon of Nottingham, to the earl of Lincoln, 3 Mar. 1843 (Peel Papers, 40481, fos. 103–5); Foskett, 'John Kaye and the Diocese of Lincoln', 151–61.

[81] C. M. Birrell, *The Life of William Brock, D.D.* (London, 1878), 136–9.

[82] 4th Ser. xvi. (July–Dec. 1844), 345.

[83] *Nonconformist*, 21 June 1843; Mackintosh, *Disestablishment and Liberation*, 24.

[84] Miall, *Edward Miall*, 92.   [85]Ibid.; Patterson, *Radical Leicester*, 256–7.

[86] Patterson, 256–7; *Eclectic Review*, 4th Ser. xv (Jan.–June 1844), 345 ff.

[87] Mackintosh, op. cit. 27.

[88] Mason, 'The Rise of Combative Dissent', 68 ff.; Miall, op. cit. 256–7; I. G. Jones, 'The Liberation Society and Welsh Politics', 203–4.

the Society for the Liberation of Religion from State Patronage and Control). The principle of the Association, adopted by the conference as part of its constitution, stated:

That in matters of religion man is responsible to God alone; that all legislation by secular governments in affairs of religion is an encroachment upon the rights of man, and an invasion of the prerogatives of God; and that the application by law of the resources of the state to the maintenance of any form or forms of religious worship is contrary to reason, hostile to human liberty, and directly opposed to the Word of God.[89]

The officers of the society consisted of a treasurer, 3 secretaries, 3 auditors, a council of 500 members and an executive committee of 50.[90] The composition of these bodies, which included both ministers and laymen, reflected the denominational composition of the national conference. Members had to pay at least a shilling annually, and a grand conference of the Association was held every three years. Propaganda methods owed a great deal to the powerful and sympathetic Anti-Corn Law League, and Association spokesmen sometimes encountered hostility from Tory crowds resembling the opposition which Leaguers had met from Chartists. The Association's methods included the printing and distribution, by a literary sub-committee, of books, tracts, original essays, and parts of public documents; lecture tours of all parts of Britian by prominent Voluntaries such as Miall and Mursell, and by less well-known but promising recruits; the formation of local committees, whose members had to be approved by the executive committee, and later the division of England into districts, each under the supervision of an agent who collected subscriptions.[91] A printed circular dated 7 March 1850 stated that 'it is absolutely essential that an effective agency of some kind should be actively employed in every part of the country'.[92] Great emphasis was placed on political progress and defence. Attention was given to every measure discussed in Parliament which involved the society's principles and objects, and to 'the return to parliament, wherever practicable, of men of known integrity and ability, conversant with the principles of this Society ... and ready to promote its object ...'[93]

The Association resembled other Victorian pressure groups, and, since it survived well into the twentieth century, was much longer lasting than its early contemporaries. Indeed, it was so prominent for the rest of the

---

[89] D. M. Thompson, op. cit. 124-5.

[90] Ibid. 125; *Eclectic Review*, 4th Ser. xvi (July–Dec. 1844), 348–50, 363–5; D. M. Thompson, 'The Liberation Society, 1844–68', in P. Hollis (ed.), *Pressure from Without* (London, 1974), 216–18.

[91] Minutes of executive committee of Anti-State Church Association, vol. II (Jan. 1850–Oct. 1853), *passim*; Thompson, 'Liberation Society', 218, 229–30. See also Vincent, *The Formation of the Liberal Party*, 68 ff.

[92] Circular kept with minutes of executive committee of Anti-State Church Association.

[93] Thompson, *Nonconformity in the Nineteenth Century*, 125–6.

nineteenth century that it became something of a national institution, a semi-established rival of the Establishment. Its ultimate object, the disestablishment of all State Churches in the United Kingdom, was not realized. It saw the achievement of Irish disestablishment in 1869 and Welsh in 1920, though it seems that in both Ireland and Wales the political pressure of a large non-conforming population bulked large enough to render the Association's role of minor importance. In Parliament the Association never attained the strength or influence for which it hoped.

As well as the wider aim of disestablishment, the Association worked hard to correct the more direct and material grievances of Dissenters—church-rates, university degrees, and burials—which were fairly satisfactorily dealt with by 1880. Such, however, was the hostility aroused by aggressive Voluntaryism that the society's aid might have seemed a retardatory rather than a succouring factor in these struggles. Whereas some liberal churchmen joined the Association, these were a small minority, and, on the other hand, by no means all Dissenters agreed with the Association. The acerbity of Miall's views, as expressed both within and without the Association's channels, added considerably to the conflict of Church and chapel which was so ubiquitous until the early twentieth century that it must have often seemed a monolithic divide.[94] But under the deceptively comprehensive term of 'Dissent' (excluding Wesleyans) there was a diversity of opinions on Voluntaryism, a complexity of reaction which ran through denominations and congregations. This difference was seen before the Anti-State Church Association was formed, in the distinct attitudes of cautious, grave metropolitan ministers and more impetuous provincial ministers within the same denomination. But the difference was not simply one of capital city against provinces, since of course no such neat division existed. Nor was it simply one of wealth against relative poverty, or of respectability against vulgarity. The distinction was intrinsically personal, or the result of personal influence.

The *Eclectic Review*, which supported the Anti-State Church Association, complained in 1846 that this society was opposed by 'very many of the leading members of the dissenting body in England'.[95] John Benjamin Smith, a Unitarian and former President of the Anti-Corn Law League, wrote in 1847 to Duncan McLaren: 'The Manchester dissenters are not agreed on the church question. The aristocratic portion do not appear to see the distinction between religious *liberty* and religious *equality* and are perfectly satisfied with the former.'[96] The only general denominational body which sent official delegates to the inaugural conference of the Anti-State Church Association was the Baptist Union, representing the Particular

[94] For the division see Augustine Birrell's comments (reprinted ibid. 169); B. Harrison, *Drink and the Victorians, 1815-72* (London, 1971), 29-30, 258-9; and, in general, V. Cunningham, *Everywhere Spoken Against—Dissent in the Victorian Novel* (Oxford, 1975).
[95] 4th Ser. xix (Jan.–June 1846), 234-5.
[96] 6 Sept. 1847 (J. B. Smith Papers, S. 335). Cf. Davis, *Political Change and Continuity*, 188.

Baptists.[97] Congregationalists, for all their prominence in the formation of the Association, were deeply divided on the Voluntary question. Against Miall and Edward Baines the younger stood the Rev. John Blackburn, editor of the *Congregational Magazine*, who indicted the Voluntary conference of April 1844 as follows:

... we object to this Conference as a means for the promotion of political ends ... because we think that in such an object Christian ministers have no special concern, and Christian Churches and congregations, as such, no proper concern at all. We think that our ministers have nobler and better objects to pursue—that few are qualified for successful political agitation, and that all may be more usefully employed. Our Christian societies are formed for mutual improvement in piety, and for the extension of Christian truth and privileges to all. If they are ever made political associations, so far their Christian character must be obscured, and their Christian usefulness lessened ...[98]

Blackburn was soon involved in a fierce collision with Miall over the political objects and actions of Voluntaries.[99]

In spite of the urgency of ecclesiastical and electoral issues for Dissenters, appeals for concentration on spiritual aims found, among many Nonconformists, welcoming ground: '... the political response is only a small part of the Church's total response to the changes of the period. The political involvement of the Churches needs to be kept in its proper perspective.'[100]

The Anti-State Church Association provided a more effective theatre for militant Voluntaryism than any previous organization. But its political impact and success depended partly on the reaction of politicians. Voluntaryism did not find sympathy among Whigs, Conservatives, or some of the radicals. Conservatives generally wished to maintain the established Churches; so too did the Whigs. Many radicals, especially those of utilitarian views, supported disestablishment. But their reforming interests were too wide for them to commit themselves to the sectarian limitations of disestablishment and voluntary education. Political advance, for the Anti-State Church Association, depended largely on its success in concentrating the attention of an expanding Nonconformist electorate on Voluntaryism as a primary interest, and in using this strength to change the attitude of Liberal politicians. For many years this aim seemed within reach. But, in the long term, the extension of the franchise was to prove no great help to the full realization of Voluntaryism.

[97] Mason, op. cit. 20.

[98] *Congregational Magazine*, N.S. viii (1844), 393–4 (quoted Thompson, *Nonconformity in the Nineteenth Century*, 127–8); Mason, 75–6.

[99] See below, p. 176.

[100] D. M. Thompson, 'The Churches and Society in Leicestershire, 1851–81' (unpubl. Univ. of Cambridge Ph.D. thesis, 1969), 343. Cf. J. H. Lea, 'Baptists in Lancashire, 1837–85' (unpubl. Univ. of Liverpool Ph.D. thesis 1970), 380 ff.

IV. UNITARIAN RELIEF AND IRISH CONCESSION, 1844

Soon after the formation of the Anti-State Church Association, Dissenters were at odds with Peel's Government. In July 1844 the Dissenters' Chapels Bill was passed, allowing Unitarians to remain in possession of chapels which they had held continuously for the last twenty-five years and for which no particular doctrinal affiliation or mode of worship was laid down in the original trust deed.[101] The growth of Unitarianism had meant that many chapels had undergone a change in the doctrine and form of worship observed in them. By the Act of 1813, extending the Toleration Act of 1689 to Unitarians, they were allowed legal possession of their chapels. But controversy had begun over Unitarian retention of chapels which had been founded by orthodox Christians but for which no definite doctrine had been specified. Orthodox Dissenters hoped to regain these chapels. They had also challenged the employment, for Unitarian benefit, of endowment funds established by orthodox Christians. George Hadfield, a Congregational solicitor and later an ardent Voluntary politician and M. P., had commenced an attack on the management of Lady Hewley's Trust. A chancery decision had been given against Unitarians on this matter in 1836, in which year they seceded from the Dissenting Deputies and the General Body of Ministers. On appeal, a similar judgement was given by the House of Lords in 1842. Unitarians—who were said to form about 2 per cent of the Dissenting body[102]—then sought Government aid for the protection of their rights to chapels. A committee to urge this cause was chaired successively by two Unitarian M.P.s, G. W. Wood and Mark Philips, and valuable legal advice was given by the Unitarian solicitor Edwin Wilkins Field. The result was the introduction of the Dissenters' Chapels Bill by the Government in the Lords, with the agreement of the Opposition.

In their reaction to this measure Dissenters were caught between the claims of evangelical orthodoxy and the claims to property which might lead them to oppose the bill, and the demands of religious toleration which might persuade them to support it. There was considerable Dissenting (including Wesleyan) opposition to the bill in the country, and about 2,600 petitions were presented against it in the Commons, though not all of these would have come from Dissenters.[103] There was resentment at the support given to the measure by Liberal M.P.s, including Dissenting ones such as John Bright and Joseph Brotherton.[104] The elder Edward Baines supported

[101] R. M. Montgomery, 'The Significance of the Dissenters' Chapels Act of 1844', *Transactions of the Unitarian Historical Society*, viii (1943–6), 45–51; F. Hankinson, 'Dissenters' Chapels Act, 1844', ibid. 52–7. Cf. Chadwick, *Victorian Church*, i. 392–5.

[102] Hansard, lxxiv. 592.

[103] *Journals of the House of Commons*, xcix (1844), index; Minutes of Protestant Dissenting Deputies, xi. 2, 6–15.

[104] Hansard, lxxv. 391.

the bill, it was said, 'against the pretty general opinion of the evangelical Dissenters, as well as of the evangelical Church and the Wesleyans'.[105] Many Catholic M.P.s voted for the bill.[106] R. L. Sheil recalled the 'breaches of trust' over Catholic property at the Reformation: 'To the defrauded spirit of William of Wykeham (worth a hundred Lady Hewleys), let restitution be made . . .'[107]

The main parliamentary opposition came from churchmen who were aggrieved that a Conservative Government had sponsored such a bill. Blomfield resisted the measure on strictly orthodox grounds, and failed to persuade Peel to withdraw it.[108] In the Lords Blomfield said that founders of chapels had had no need specifically to proscribe Unitarian doctrines, since the law had at that time forbidden their teaching. Sooner than assist the spread of erroneous doctrines, '. . . the pious men who founded the Chapels in question, would . . . have had their right hands cut off . . .'[109] The bill was also strongly opposed by Bishop Phillpotts and Lords Winchilsea and Kenyon, but the opposition in the Lords could only muster 9 votes against the third reading.[110] In the Commons opposition was voiced by Sir Robert Inglis and by Fox Maule, a member of the new and strongly evangelical Scottish Free Church.[111] Gladstone, however, showed his tendencies towards religious liberalism by supporting the bill. This was sufficiently striking for Sheil to declare that Gladstone, 'the champion of free trade, will ere long become the advocate of the most unrestricted liberty of thought'.[112] The bill easily passed the Commons after amendments, which were accepted by the Lords. Through the passage of the measure, it is said, nearly 200 chapels were retained in Unitarian hands.[113] The thanks of Unitarians were bestowed on Peel, Gladstone, and other ministers.[114] The Government had passed a judicious measure of equity and a measure of toleration for a small body with little political strength (that is, in terms of numbers, though not of prominence and ability), but in doing so they had increased their unpopularity with ultra-Tories and many orthodox Dissenters.

The next major issue of ecclesiastical moment, the Maynooth grant, confirmed the reactions of ultra-Protestants to the Government, and produced more open political divisions—between Government and ultra-Tories on the one hand and Whigs and Voluntaries on the other. Since the beginning of Peel's ministry the demands of Ireland, no longer softened by

[105] Baines, *Edward Baines*, 318-19.
[106] Hansard, lxxv. 391.
[107] Ibid. 381-2.
[108] Welch, 'Blomfield and Peel', 81.
[109] Hansard, lxxiv. 591.
[110] Ibid. 598-601, 605-8, 821-32.
[111] Ibid. lxxv. 332-7, 359-64.
[112] Ibid. 364-77 (Gladstone), 377 f. (Sheil); Stafford Northcote to Gladstone, 4 June 1847 (Gladstone Papers, Add. MS. 44216, fos. 67-8).
[113] Montgomery, op. cit. 50.
[114] Peel Papers, 40549, fos. 59 ff., 82-3, 90, 92-3, 130-1.

the Whig alliance, had loomed large among the problems of Government. After losing many parliamentary seats in the 1841 election, the Repeal movement had been revitalized by O'Connell's mass meetings. The Government's response had at first been one of legal coercion. A bill to control firearms was passed in 1843. O'Connell was arrested in October 1843, tried by a Protestant and Conservative jury, and sentenced in May 1844 to a year's imprisonment (which actually lasted four months). Conciliation was the next ministerial approach: '. . . mere force,' said Peel, 'however necessary the application of it, will do nothing as a permanent remedy for the social evils of that country'.[115]

Radical reformers hoped for more sweeping Irish measures than were considered by ministers. But it did not seem that the public mood in Great Britain, whether motivated by anti-Catholicism, constitutional Unionism, or vigorous Voluntaryism, was in sympathy with the radical reforms proposed. H. G. Ward, radical M.P. for Sheffield, had no success when he revived the contentious appropriation question, in the form of a motion of 1 August 1843 to redistribute the property of the Church of Ireland. This proposed to hand over to the Roman Catholics the bulk of the annual funds enjoyed by the Establishment.[116] The old irreconcilable arguments of the 1830s were brought out again. Inglis defended the Church of Ireland with its existing endowments as being, like its inseparable partner the Church of England, 'the truth established'.[117] Ward, on the other hand, maintained that 'the State is no judge of the truth of religions, and that it never ought to undertake that duty'.[118] But it was late in the session and there was so little interest in his motion that the House was counted out, fewer than forty members being present.[119] Another prospect, State payment of the Catholic priests, was said by Macaulay to be unattainable in the current climate of public opinion: 'Against such a measure there are all the zealots of the High Church, and all the zealots of the Low Church; the Bishop of Exeter, and Hugh Macneile; Oxford, and Exeter Hall; all the champions of the voluntary system; all the English Dissenters; all Scotland; all Ireland, both Orangemen and Papists.'[120]

Ministers also believed, while not against it in principle, that State payment of the priesthood was then impracticable. Their practical aims were more modest, though to their ultra-Protestant supporters they seemed little better. These aims included efforts to conciliate the Catholic Church and detach it from the Repeal movement. The Government would have liked to secure the good offices of the Pope in dampening nationalist sympathies among the Irish Catholic bishops. But the Papacy was delphic on the subject. Enough papal intervention occurred to annoy the nationalist leaders

[115] Quoted Gash, *Sir Robert Peel*, 411. [116] Hansard, lxxi. 118–61.
[117] Ibid. 190–1. [118] Ibid. 155. [119] Ibid. 219.
[120] Trevelyan, *Macaulay*, 444.

but a public rebuke to the firebrands among the clergy was not forthcoming.[121] Ministers placed more hope in policies of concession to Irish Catholics.

On 11 February 1844 Peel circulated a memorandum to the Cabinet suggesting two important but, as it turned out, controversial moves. He proposed that the parliamentary grant to Maynooth College should be increased and that, in order to lessen the dependence of Irish priests on the financial support of seditious flocks, the law should be altered so that landed proprietors could make endowments to the priests. In a second memorandum on 17 February he gave special importance to Catholic higher education, both lay and clerical, and underlined his points in a third document at the end of the month.[122] On Maynooth he said in the last document:

The College ... as at present governed and scantily provided for, is a public nuisance ... We educate Priests, more than half the number required for the yearly supply of all Ireland, and the wit of man could not devise a more effectual method for converting them into sour, malignant demagogues, hostile to the law ... living by agitation, inclined to it and fitted for it by our ... penurious system of education.[123]

The question of Maynooth was shelved for a year. In the 1844 parliamentary session a bill to lower the Irish county franchise qualification was dropped, but the Charitable Trusts Bill succeeded. The bill sought to change the wholly Protestant composition of the Board of Charitable Bequests in order to include Catholic members, and to allow the gift of landed property to Catholic priests. The only objections in Parliament came from those who wished to see greater representation of Catholics on the Board, and, after certain amendments had been proposed by Graham for the satisfaction of Catholics, the bill passed in August.[124] Phillpotts believed that certain words in the original bill implied recognition of papal authority, but was later satisfied by alterations in the wording.[125] After its passage the Act was severely tested. Archbishop MacHale bitterly denounced it, and O'Connell, seeing it as challenging his own movement among the Catholics, campaigned against its acceptance. Representations were made at Rome for and against the Act, but the papal attitude was generally neutral and neither side was satisfied. By December sufficient co-operation had been obtained with difficulty from Catholic prelates for the composition of the Board to

---

[121] J. F. Broderick, *The Holy See and the Irish Movement for the Repeal of the Union with England, 1829–47* (Rome, 1951), 166–88; William Petre, special envoy at Rome, to Aberdeen, 15 and 21 Jan. 1845 (Aberdeen Papers, Add. MS. 43151, fos. 208–11).

[122] Gash, *Sir Robert Peel*, 416–20.   [123] Quoted ibid. 420.

[124] Hansard, lxxvi, 1516–41, 1658–69, 1780–1.

[125] Phillpotts to Peel, 24 and 28 July 1844; Peel to Phillpotts, 25 July and 6 Aug. 1844 (Peel Papers, 40549, fos. 1–18).

be announced, including its complement of Catholic members.[126] By March 1845 the agitation had greatly subsided.[127]

Protestants were more opposed to a bill to repeal various ancient penal enactments against Roman Catholics, which was also passed in 1844. The object of this measure, introduced in the Lords in July, was to relieve 'unqualified' Catholics—i.e. those, said to be 99 per cent of Catholics, who had not actually taken the oaths prescribed by the various Relief Acts[128]— from the possibility of punishment under the Acts. Among the penalties repealed were those of the first Uniformity Act of Edward VI and of the Elizabethan Act of Supremacy. Lord Beaumont, a Catholic peer, presented the bill, and it was adopted by the Government. Blomfield spoke against the measure. After the bill had been amended in committee, however, the Lords accepted it without a division—Blomfield said 'not content', but the Lord Chancellor declared that the 'contents' had it.[129] The bill was further amended in the Commons, and passed in August. Peel, who had moved the second reading, told Beaumont that he was very pleased to have directly assisted a measure which 'is indicative of the kindly and liberal spirit of the legislature, and calculated to be satisfactory to the feelings of my Roman Catholic fellow subjects'.[130] This attitude, when exhibited in more concrete terms the following year, dismayed many of his supporters.

V. MAYNOOTH, 1845

In 1845 the Government resumed its interested wooing of Irish Catholicism with two educational measures, an enlarged and permanent grant to Maynooth and the formation of unsectarian university colleges. In Ireland the outcry against the Maynooth grant was less important than in Britain,[131] where, it has been claimed, 'not since the great reform struggle [of 1830–2] had a measure so excited the public and parliament . . .'[132] If the Government had been lulled by the absence of Protestant opposition to its concessions of 1844, it must have expected more resistance to the Maynooth Bill, for many Conservative M.P.s had already voted against the grant at its annual renewals, and the Protestant Association had long opposed the grant. Maynooth significantly widened the rent in the Conservative party along the lines which had already been torn apart by commercial policy and the factory hours' question. The passage of the bill leant on Liberal support,

---

[126] Gash, *Sir Robert Peel*, 421–4; K. B. Nowlan, *The Politics of Repeal: a Study in the Relations between Great Britain and Ireland, 1841–50* (London, 1965), 67–9.

[127] William Walsh to Bishop Griffiths, Vicar-Apostolic of the London District, 9 Mar. 1845 (Wiseman Papers, W.1/2, 734).

[128] Hansard, lxxvi. 1165 (speech of Lord Beaumont).

[129] Ibid. 1552–3.

[130] Peel to Beaumont, 5 Aug. 1844 (Peel Papers, 40549, fo. 227).

[131] Nowlan, op. cit. 82.

[132] R. Stewart, *The Politics of Protection, 1841–52* (Cambridge, 1971), 23.

though even this was weakened by the opposition of Voluntaries to State endowment of religion. The great political crisis of 1846 was foreshadowed by the lesser but more complex one of 1845.

The final Cabinet draft of the Maynooth Endowment Bill was written in March, after satisfactory discussions with Irish Catholics. The new bill had the support of O'Connell, who had previously opposed the grant. Protectionists had already been alarmed by the commercial liberalism of the budget of that year,[133] and the ultra-Protestants among them were all the readier to join the anti-Catholic cry which was gathering volume outside Parliament well before the bill was brought in. A Government grant to Catholics was all the more outrageous after grants to the Churches of England and Scotland had been refused. Ultra peers such as Newcastle, Winchilsea, and Kenyon, who had marshalled traditional anti-Catholic sentiment in 1828-9, repeated their exhortatory role in 1845. More efficient and organized methods had been employed by the Protestant Association since 1835. This Association found a new means of demonstrating its vitality by taking the lead against the Maynooth Bill. Through its initiative there was formed on 18 March a Central Anti-Maynooth Committee, chaired by Sir Culling Eardley Smith, with a largely clerical membership of evangelical Anglicans, Wesleyans, Congregationalists, and other Nonconformists.[134] In Liverpool the Protestant Operative Society was 'roused from nearly absolute dissolution' by the bill, and held a large and spirited meeting of protest.[135] Amid such enthusiasm, repeated throughout the country, the few Catholic meetings in favour of the bill were swamped.[136]

Transferring its venue from Exeter Hall to the London Coffee House in Ludgate Street, the Anti-Maynooth Committee dispatched printed forms of petition to be signed in different localities and returned for submission to Parliament.[137] This activity was no doubt largely responsible for the presentation to the House of Commons, between 4 February and 30 May, of 10,204 petitions against the bill, containing 1,284,296 signatures.[138] This number of signatures, though considerably smaller than that recorded against the Factory Education Bill, was enough to show the extent of public feeling. The Anti-Maynooth Committee tried to increase its supporters in the

---

[133] Gash, *Sir Robert Peel*, 459-72.

[134] There were 39 Anglicans, 19 Congregationalists, 4 Presbyterians, and 9 Wesleyans on the Committee; Rev. J. Blackburn, *The Three Conferences held by the Opponents of the Maynooth Endowment Bill* (London, 1845), 21-4 (cf. E. R. Norman, *Anti-Catholicism in Victorian England* (London, 1968), 29 ff.). For Wesleyan views against the bill see the *Watchman* (1845), pp. 103, 127, 139, 151, 163.

[135] *The Times*, 16 Apr. 1845.

[136] Such a meeting of Catholics in favour of the grant was reported in *The Times*, 16 Apr. 1845.

[137] The Committee's methods are described by one of its Anglican members, Rev. A. S. Thelwall in *Proceedings of the Anti-Maynooth Committee* (London, 1845).

[138] G. I. T. Machin, 'The Maynooth Grant, the Dissenters and Disestablishment, 1845-7', *EHR* lxxxii (1967), 64 n. 4.

Commons by threatening electoral reprisals against those who favoured the bill.[139] Some timely by-elections, indeed, illustrated the political possibilities. In West Kent a pro-Maynooth candidate deemed it advisable to withdraw, and an anti-Maynooth candidate was returned unopposed.[140] The marquess of Blandford resigned his seat at Woodstock, allegedly on account of disagreement with the anti-Maynooth views of his father the duke of Marlborough, who owned the borough. He was replaced by an anti-Maynooth representative.[141] At Greenock Alexander Murray Dunlop, a leading Free Churchman, failed by only 6 votes to win the seat after entering the contest late as a declared opponent of the bill.[142]

Anglican opposition to the bill probably owed something to disappointment that Peel's Government had not done more for the Establishment.[143] The Maynooth Bill was more serious than the Government's previous shortcomings in this respect. The measure could be seen as weakening the constitutional position of the Establishment through the incipient extension of 'concurrent endowment' to another Church—though of course any such weakening was far from being intended. More specifically, and more dangerously, the grant appeared to undermine the Protestant nature of the Establishment. In the year when the Oxford movement reached its most ominous stage, the bill was seen as encouraging not only Roman Catholicism but, even more sinister, the supposed Romanizing designs of the Tractarians. Evangelicals, said Lord Monteagle, were 'alarmed at the doctrines not of Maynooth but of Oxford . . .'[144] Oxford's catalytic role apart, it was feared that the bill might be only one episode in a horrifying catalogue of infringements on the Protestant constitution—leading, perhaps, to State payment of the priests ('concurrent endowment'), a full Catholic establishment, possibly even the disestablishment of the Church of Ireland.[145] Were these steps beyond the polluted vision of one who had already, in 1829, helped to execute a monumental betrayal of Protestant ascendancy? 'What a strange ignorance, or haughty contempt of the deep, solemn Protestant feeling in the hearts of the British people!', was Ashley's comment after the introduction of the bill.[146]

That the question could produce such deep fears and heartfelt sentiments displays the profundity of the issues raised, in almost ludicrous contrast with the prosaic, practical details of the measure itself. As explained by Peel in the Commons on 3 April, the bill proposed a permanent annual grant of

[139] Thelwall, op. cit. xvii; *The Times*, 2 May 1845.
[140] *The Times*, 14, 16, and 18 Apr. 1845; Andrews, 'Political Issues in the County of Kent', 185–7.
[141] *The Times*, 28 Apr., 2 May 1845; *Nonconformist*, 30 Apr. 1845, p. 274.
[142] *The Times*, 19 Apr. 1845; Dunlop to Fox Maule, 11 and 15 Apr. 1845 (Dalhousie Papers, 658).
[143] As is suggested by R. Stewart, op. cit. 25.
[144] Hansard, lxxxi. 79 (4 June 1845).
[145] Ashley looked to some of these possibilities in his diary, 8 Apr. 1845 (Hodder, ii. 101).
[146] Diary, 7 Apr. 1845 (ibid.).

£26,000 (with detailed provision for the professorial salaries and student maintenance on which it should be spent) and an extra single payment of £30,000 to provide much-needed buildings; charged the Board of Works with payment for repairs and maintenance; and proposed annual visitations of the College.[147] The first division in the Commons granted leave to introduce the bill by a comfortable majority of 113, but the number of Conservative opponents was ominous, and this aspect was increasingly disturbing to ministers as the bill proceeded. On the second reading, which passed by a majority of 147 on 19 April, the Government had a majority of only 12 Conservatives on its side (66 Conservatives not voting), and depended on the support of 165 Liberals.[148] Some of these Liberals (such as Lord Howick and, less strongly, Lord John Russell) wanted State payment of the Catholic clergy or even an Irish Catholic establishment,[149] and their support was embarrassing. On the third reading, passed by 133 on 21 May, Peel was in a bare majority among Conservative voters, 148 against 149, and depended even more heavily on 169 Liberal votes.[150] Peel had staked his ministry on the passing of the bill; but even though the ministry survived, the damage to the Conservative party was 'incalculable'.[151] The Maynooth crisis reinforced the ecclesiastical and constitutional distrust underlying the divisions over economic and social policy. Most of the Conservative anti-Maynooth opponents of Peel voted against the repeal of the Corn Laws in 1846.[152]

The Maynooth crisis emphasized some current political divisions, though one was temporarily obscured—Scottish Free Churchmen and members of the Church of Scotland were generally at one in their anti-Maynooth opinions. Anglican evangelicals and conservative high churchmen such as Blomfield and Phillpotts who denounced the bill were opposed by liberal churchmen, many of whom wrote to Peel expressing their approval of the measure as 'calculated to tranquillize Ireland for the present, and to be the means of its emancipation from the corruptions of Popery in the end'.[153] The Rev. J. W. Brameld, curate of Louth, said that 'the thinking and reasoning part of the population are with the government . . . I am looked upon as little better than a Jesuit because I will not go with the mob.'[154] Disraeli, the former radical turned Conservative, underlined his division

[147] Hansard, lxxix. 18–38.

[148] Figures in *The Times*, 21 Apr. 1845, and Gash, *Reaction*, 151 n.

[149] Howick's Journal, 3 Apr. 1845 (Grey Papers, C3/11).

[150] Gash, *Reaction*, 151 n.; S. H. Walpole, *The Life of Lord John Russell* (2 vols., London, 1889), i. 400 n. But see J. B. Conacher, *The Peelites and the Party System, 1846–52* (Newton Abbot, 1972), 12.

[151] Gash, *Sir Robert Peel*, 477.

[152] Stewart, 54–5; Conacher, op. cit. 12; A. Briggs, *The Age of Improvement* (London, 1959), 342.

[153] Rev. Richard Garvey to Peel, 4 Apr. 1845 (Peel Papers, 40564, fo. 75); Hansard, lxxx. 1198–1209, 1345–59 (Blomfield and Phillpotts).

[154] Brameld to Peel, 13 May 1845 (Peel Papers, 40566, fo. 359). For many other pro-Maynooth letters from Anglican clergy see ibid. 40564–7, also some from Unitarian ministers, e.g. Rev. R. Brook Aspland to Peel, 22 Apr. 1845 (40565, fos. 72–3).

from Peel by attacking the bill (and more especially the Premier),[155] and thereby separated himself from his 'Young England' Tractarian friends, Lord John Manners and George Smythe, though he was soon to be reconciled with Manners.[156] Disraeli's argument was 'essentially *ad hominem*', a chance seized for denouncing Peel as 'a great Parliamentary middleman . . . who bamboozles one party and plunders the other . . .'[157]

Gladstone, the former ultra-Tory turned Peelite, took a further liberal step by supporting the bill, though he believed his action was sufficiently serious to warrant resignation from the Government.[158] His pro-Maynooth attitude can have been no surprise to those who had observed his growing ecclesiastical liberalism, for example his support for the Dissenters' Chapels Bill and his abstention from voting on the annual renewals of the Maynooth grant since 1840. He had written in October 1841: 'Unable to bring myself to resist the grant when it was proposed by a Government which I did not support, I could not . . . with consistency have accepted office under the present administration, which to my knowledge or full persuasion intended to renew the proposal, if I had meant on a future occasion to alter my course . . .'[159] His support for the bill in 1845 was a clear public avowal of his liberal course in ecclesiastical matters, a renunciation of the claim made in his book (though even then significantly modified) that a Government should endow only the truth. Though still believing that this was an ideal to be observed in the right circumstances, he recognized that it was impossible to do so in face of 'the law of representation and equality of claims according to number and will . . .'[160] As a Tractarian, moreover, he believed that the Church was distinct from the Establishment and did not depend on legal exclusiveness.[161] His decision on the Maynooth Bill weakened his desire to maintain the Church of Ireland as an Establishment. Ultra-Protestant peers disliked the defection of their once promising protégé;[162] but as a Tractarian he had been

---

[155] Hansard, lxxix. 565 ff.

[156] C. Whibley, *Lord John Manners and his Friends* (2 vols., Edinburgh and London, 1925), i. 179 ff.

[157] Stewart, 29–30; R. Blake, *Disraeli* (London, 1966), 188–9; Hansard, lxxix. 565 (Disraeli's speech, 11 Apr. 1845).

[158] For Gladstone's previous attitudes to Maynooth see Gladstone to Manning, 2 and 23 Apr. 1837 (Lathbury, *Correspondence of Gladstone*, i. 30–2, 39); also *The State in its Relations with the Church*, 4th. ed., ii. 300–5.

[159] Gladstone to James Lord, 8 Oct. 1841 (Lathbury, i. 52).

[160] Gladstone to Newman, 19 Apr. 1845 (ibid. i. 73). Cf. J. Morley, *The Life of William Ewart Gladstone* (3 vols., London, 1903), i. 278–9.

[161] Gladstone to Rev. Dr. Christopher Wordsworth, 15 Mar. 1844, 3 Dec. 1845 (Lathbury, i. 60–1, 74–5); cf. Rev. W. F. Hook to Gladstone, 15 Apr. 1845 (Gladstone Papers, Add. MS. 44213, fos. 71–2). Pusey also favoured the Maynooth Bill (E. B. Pusey to Philip Pusey, 13 June 1846; copy, Pusey Papers).

[162] Gladstone to earl of Winchilsea, 4 June 1845 (Gladstone Papers, 44362, fos. 223–4); Winchilsea to Gladstone, 5 June 1845 (ibid., fos. 225–8). Cf. Duke of Newcastle to Gladstone, 3 Feb. 1845 (ibid. 44261, fos. 96–9); J. Martineau, *Life of Henry, fifth Duke of Newcastle* (London, 1908), 53–4.

suspect and as an ecclesiastical theorist he had meant little to them, for they had tended to regard his tortuous religious homily as a straightforward constitutional truism and therefore somewhat redundant. Gladstone's attitudes now bore little relation to Mark Philips's remark in 1841: 'What an insult to the Commercial interests and the friends of free trade to have a negro driver appointed a Vice President of the Board of Trade!'[163]

Palmerston conjectured that ultra-Protestants might prefer a Voluntary system in Ireland to Catholic endowment: 'If so we shall have Inglis and Howick and Daniel [O'Connell] all voting with Ward for the simple abolition of the Protestant Establishment.'[164] This of course proved inaccurate, but Voluntaryism was a strong element in the opposition to the Maynooth Bill. When H. G. Ward moved unsuccessfully on 23 April that the money for Maynooth should come from the surplus funds of the Church of Ireland, several Voluntary M.P.s supported him.[165] This showed the division between militant Voluntary and ultra-Protestant resistance to the Maynooth Bill. Evangelicals believed that Catholic endowment would weaken the Church of Ireland, while militant Voluntaries feared that State support of Catholics would indirectly reinforce the existing State Church. The *Nonconformist* described the Maynooth Bill as 'a masterpiece of Machiavellian policy' to preserve the Church of Ireland'.[166] The bill, moreover, extended State support of education, and the Voluntaries were enthusiastic in opposing this. It is debatable whether the difference between ultra-Protestant and Voluntary opposition to the bill was entirely clear to Catholics, especially when some Voluntary protests contained an anti-Catholic element. Adam Black, a leading Edinburgh Dissenter, urged that the Maynooth Bill should not be publicly opposed even on Voluntary grounds, since it would be difficult to appreciate that these grounds were distinct from anti-Catholicism.[167]

The Anti-State Church Association and the Dissenting Deputies stood strongly against the bill for Voluntary reasons. Dissenters were, however, hampered by their own receipt of a State grant—the embarrassing *regium donum* to needy Nonconformist ministers, whose rejection they were quite unable to secure in Parliament and which lasted until 1852. Militancy, moreover, did not please all Voluntaries. Moderate Voluntaries like Sir Culling Eardley Smith adopted tactics which were conciliatory towards Anglicans, and even preferred to join the Anglican and Wesleyan evangelicals of the Protestant Association than to unite with militant Voluntaries. The Rev. John Blackburn, a leading Congregationalist who disliked the Anti-

---

[163] Mark Philips to George Wilson, 4 Sept. 1841 (George Wilson Papers).

[164] Palmerston to Russell, 9 Jan. 1845 (G. P. Gooch (ed.), *The Later Correspondence of Lord John Russell, 1840-78* (2 vols., London, 1925), i. 79).

[165] Hansard, lxxix. 1313-14; Thelwall, lxxvii-lxxxv.

[166] 5 Apr. 1845, p. 77.

[167] Nicolson, 130. An example of the mixed views he perhaps had in mind was a memorial of the Scottish Relief Church addressed to Peel, 9 Apr. 1845 (Peel Papers, 40564, fos. 194-5).

State Church Association, took an anti-Catholic line. But militant Voluntaries claimed to support the true interests of the Irish Catholics—opposing the Maynooth Bill in order to prevent Catholic clergy becoming, in John Bright's words, 'as tame as those of Suffolk and Dorsetshire'.[168] Both moderates and militants hoped to advance the Voluntary principle. Blackburn wanted the Church of Ireland to become a Voluntary body, the more effectively to prevent a Catholic establishment being formed;[169] extreme Voluntaries wanted the Irish Catholics to reject the Government's offer and cleave to the Voluntary principle.[170]

At first the Anti-Maynooth Committee tried to accommodate the different views.[171] But the attempt foundered, for Anglicans and militant Voluntaries could not combine. Extreme Voluntaries believed that they were the only consistent enemies of the Maynooth measure. As the *Nonconformist* put it, '. . . the ministerial proposition to endow all [sects] can . . . only be repelled by those who are all prepared to contend for the endowment of none'.[172] The gulf appeared at an unpropitious time for the anti-Maynooth agitation. After the bill's second reading had passed in the Commons, the Anti-Maynooth Committee convened a vast conference of 1,200 delegates at the Crown and Anchor tavern on 30 April. The Committee attempted to maintain a show of unity for the sake of the public face and political success of the agitation. But the conference split on the Voluntary issue. A group of militant Voluntaries withdrew to a separate room in the tavern and drafted a declaration against the 'No Popery' character of the main assembly. On 2 May these seceders held a further meeting when they passed a resolution against all State endowments of religion; and on 21 and 22 May militant Voluntaries held a conference at Crosby Hall, Chelsea, where they adopted an address to the Irish Catholics saying that 'of all the grievances under which your country has laboured, the establishment of the Anglican Church in Ireland is the most unjustifiable and oppressive . . .' This rift in the agitation was gratifying to supporters of the bill. Any prospect that extra-parliamentary agitation would destroy Government policy, as in 1843, was rapidly disappearing.[173] The bill finally passed the Lords on 16 June, though the earl of Winchilsea and Bishops Blomfield, C. R. Sumner, J. B. Sumner, and others entered a protest.

The split within the opposition grew deeper while the bill continued on its successful parliamentary course. The Irish Anti-Maynooth Committee held a conference at the Dublin Rotunda on 4 and 5 June, in an effort to

[168] Machin, 'Maynooth Grant', 68-9 ff.

[169] *Congregational Magazine*, N.S., ix (1845), 258-9.

[170] Address to the Roman Catholics of Ireland adopted by a Voluntary meeting, 31 May 1845 (Blackburn, *Three Conferences . . .*, 21-4).

[171] Ibid. 3.   [172] 2 Apr. 1845, p. 206.

[173] Machin, 'Maynooth Grant', 70-1. Cf. Norman, op. cit. 44 ff.; Cowherd, *The Politics of English Dissent*, 160.

influence the House of Lords and the Crown against the bill. John Blackburn and Sir Culling Eardley Smith went as representatives of the London Committee; Blackburn praised the Church of Ireland and called for united Protestant defence against the establishment of Catholicism.[174] Thereupon Smith and Blackburn were attacked by the militant Voluntary Press, Blackburn being accused of betraying the true principles of Nonconformity. The *Patriot* described Blackburn as a convert from English Liberalism to Irish Orangeism, and Miall referred with characteristic intensity to 'men in whose hearts the life of Dissent has expired, leaving behind it the cold and putrefying remains of a nominal profession—ministers of the Gospel whose public conduct strangles without remorse the power of their pulpit instructions...'[175] Blackburn held to his opinions, and the journalistic feud between the two Congregationalists continued for many months.

The difference between the opponents of the Maynooth Bill continued to be displayed in their political behaviour. Both groups agreed, however, in distrust of their respective parties which had supported the bill. Members of the Anti-Maynooth Committee advised preparation for the next general election, in order to resist the endowment of the Irish Catholic Church and other unwelcome possible sequels to the Maynooth measure. On 17 June 1845, the day after the Maynooth Bill passed the Lords, many ultra-Protestant politicians seceded from the Carlton Club and formed the National Club, which served as the London headquarters of the Protestant Association.[176] Militant Dissenters took a distinctive line. They rejected the ultra-Protestant plea that 'sound Protestantism is far more important than Voluntaryism'.[177] They distrusted the anti-Catholic Evangelical Alliance, a body formed with Sir Culling Eardley Smith as chairman in 1846 following demands for such an organization from the Anti-Maynooth Committee, Scottish Free Churchmen, and moderate Voluntaries such as Angell James of Birmingham. Militant Voluntaries made electoral preparations based on their principles. While ultra-Protestant Tories concentrated their distrust on Peel, Voluntaries concentrated theirs on the Liberal politicians who had supported Peel's bill. The *Eclectic Review* announced that further Liberal disregard of Voluntary opinions could not be tolerated: 'The time of our separation has come.'[178] A measure introduced by a Conservative Government had brought out the ecclesiastical schisms of the Liberal party. The second reading of the bill in the Commons had been opposed by 31 Liberals as well as by ultra-Tories: apart from two Scottish Free Churchmen (Fox Maule and Patrick Stewart) these Liberals were

---

[174] Blackburn, op. cit. 29, 34–5, 39–40; Thelwall, cxxvii.

[175] *Nonconformist*, 11 June 1845, p. 412.

[176] Cahill, 'The Protestant Association and the Anti-Maynooth Agitation', 300.

[177] Thelwall, clxxxiv.

[178] *Eclectic Review*, 4th Ser. xvii (Jan.–June 1845), 613 ff.

Voluntaries.[179] Not only Whigs were in bad odour with Voluntaries, but also those radicals who preferred the Maynooth Bill to Voluntaryism. Joseph Hume, who had championed Dissenting causes, Richard Cobden (separated on this issue from Bright, and against Voluntaryism in his support of State education), J. A. Roebuck (noted for his support of a State educational system), and many other radicals had voted for the bill.

An increasing sense of alienation from Whigs and other radicals led Voluntaries to envisage a party organization for themselves.[180] Electoral bodies were formed in order to return Voluntary candidates to Parliament— for example, the Anti-State Church Electoral Association at Bristol.[181] Expectations were high, but the *Eclectic Review* showed a good deal of wishful thinking when it claimed that Voluntaries would be justified in standing in 350 constituencies.[182] Although Voluntaries hoped to widen their appeal through their support of Free Trade and universal suffrage, many supporters of these causes were not Voluntaries. In by-elections Voluntary candidates were disappointed. Miall, contesting Southwark in September 1845, obtained only a fifth of the votes gained by his radical rival, Sir William Molesworth, who approved of the Maynooth grant and refused to commit himself against the endowment of the Irish Catholic Church.[183] Sir Culling Eardley Smith, still a Voluntary though not single-minded enough for some Voluntaries, similarly failed when challenging Macaulay at Edinburgh in July 1846. The Corn Law struggle during 1846 mended Liberal division, and seemed to justify the *Nonconformist*'s fear that 'love of free trade [would] put out the eyes of dissenters'.[184] But fresh cause for Voluntary indignation soon arose, and a degree of electoral success lay ahead.

VI. FURTHER CATHOLIC CONCESSIONS, 1845–1846

Another important Irish measure, the Academical Institutions Bill, was introduced in May 1845. In Ireland this caused more controversy than the Maynooth Bill. The new bill established undenominational Queen's Colleges for secular university education at Belfast, Cork, and Galway; in 1850 the Queen's University in Ireland was created as an examining and degree-giving body for the three Colleges.[185] The undenominational and secular nature of the Colleges was a matter of fierce dispute. The Catholic hierarchy was at loggerheads on the question. John MacHale, archbishop of Tuam

[179] List of names in *The Times*, 21 Apr. 1845.
[180] *Eclectic Review*, 4th Ser. xvii (Jan.–June 1845), 620 ff.; *Nonconformist*, 23 Apr. 1845, 260, 28 May 1845, 381.
[181] *Nonconformist*, 20 Aug. 1845, 573.
[182] *Eclectic Review*, 4th Ser. xviii (July–Dec. 1845), 489.
[183] Ibid. 491; *Nonconformist*, 17 Sept. 1845, 645.
[184] 23 Apr. 1845, 260.
[185] T. W. Moody, 'The Irish University Question in the Nineteenth Century', *History*, xliii (1958), 95–9.

(supported by O'Connell), opposed the bill, while Archbishops Crolly and Murray and the Young Irelanders were prepared to accept it.[186] Both the Government and the protesters sought the backing of Rome for their attitude.[187] Pope Pius lent his ear to the protesters, and between 1847 and 1850 three papal rescripts were issued against the Colleges. In England the Colleges Bill caused much less stir than Maynooth. The interests of Voluntaries were not closely involved; but opposition came from ultra-Protestants such as Inglis, who coined the description (taken up by O'Connell) of 'godless education'.[188] The third reading in the Commons passed on 10 July by a majority of 151, with only 26 votes against—an incongruous lobby of ultras and Irish Repealers.[189]

The final session of Peel's ministry in 1846 was mainly concerned with Corn Law repeal, which the Protectionist A. J. Beresford Hope described as forming 'a just crowning point to that strange heterogeneous mass of legislation, the Maynooth Grant, the Irish Colleges, and those other measures which constituted the political life of the Parliament of 1841'.[190] But in this session there were also debates on Catholic relief. In February W. H. Watson, an Englishman who was M.P. for Kinsale, moved for leave to bring in a bill to relieve Catholics from penalites remaining on the statute-book. This bill had been defeated in 1845, in spite of the passage of the much more controversial Maynooth concession and of a bill admitting Jews to municipal corporations. Three restrictive clauses of the 1829 Relief Act were included in the proposed repeal—those forbidding Catholic clerics to take territorial titles held by Protestants and to wear sacerdotal robes outside their churches, and one which forbade any Jesuit or member of a monastic order to enter the country without a six-monthly licence from the Government.[191] The bill was opposed by Inglis, Colonel Sibthorp, J. C. Colquhoun, and other ultra-Protestants, and more liberal Conservatives were cool towards it.[192] Sibthorp, displaying the strong feeling shown towards Peel since the Maynooth crisis, said that he would describe Peel as a Roman Catholic rather than Protestant.[193] But the Liberals were in agreement on this measure, unlike the Maynooth Bill, and only Conservatives voted against it.[194] Despite this, the bill was defeated in Committee in June.[195]

A similar measure, the Religious Opinions Relief Bill, had been making its way in the House of Lords since April under the sponsorship of Lord Chancellor Lyndhurst. Wider than Watson's, this measure concerned over

[186] Nowlan, op. cit. 83 ff.

[187] Aberdeen to William Petre, British envoy at Rome, 25 Nov. 1845 (draft, Aberdeen Papers, Add. MS. 43151, fo. 218); memo of Petre to Aberdeen, 19 Dec. 1845, copy (ibid. 43169, p. 10).

[188] Hansard, lxxx. 377–80.   [189] Ibid. lxxxii. 379–81.

[190] Ibid. lxxxiii. 595.   [191] Ibid. 495 ff.

[192] Hansard, lxxxiii. 497–9; lxxxiv. 940–6, 957–8, 971; lxxxvi. 141–52; lxxxvii. 917–25.

[193] Ibid. lxxxvi. 162–3.

[194] Ibid. lxxix. 973; lxxxvi. 161–2; lxxxvii. 935–71.

[195] Ibid. lxxxvii. 917–37.

thirty Acts of Parliament which penalized Jews and Dissenters as well as Catholics, including an ancient statute of Henry III prohibiting Jews from holding land, and another of Edward I ordering Jews to wear distinctive badges.[196] Catholics were not to be relieved to the same extent as in Watson's bill, especially in regard to the prohibitory clauses of the 1829 Act,[197] though older penalties were to be removed. For the sake of those who thought it was unnecessary to repeal obsolete Acts, Lyndhurst reminded the House that in 1841 'fourteen or fifteen convictions had taken place under these statutes of recusancy'.[198] Brougham elaborated this point with graphic detail:

Three or four men had been prosecuted for poaching; but in consequence of a clumsy laying of the information the worthy magistrates who presided could not prosecute to a conviction. They, being guardians of the law and of the game, having failed to convict, the accused men would have departed. 'Oh, but,' said one of the magistrates, 'were you at church last Sunday?' 'No.' 'Or the Sunday before that?' 'No.' 'Or the Sunday before that again?' 'No.' 'Oh, you must pay Queen Elizabeth's shilling then.' Thus, as the men could not be convicted of poaching, the magistrates contrived to convict them of recusancy, and they were each sentenced to a penalty which, with costs, amounted to 28s. or 29s. They were poor men, common day labourers, and could not pay the money—they were sent to prison for three or four months, and the families of some of them came upon the parish.[199]

Against the strong opposition of Phillpotts, the bill passed the Lords at the end of July, then the Commons in August.[200] Russell, the new Prime Minister, moved the second reading in the Lower House.[201] The new relief measure still left Catholics to seek repeal of the restrictive clauses of the 1829 Relief Act, and this problem became contentious.

Peel's constructive ecclesiastical policy had branded him a 'renegade' in the eyes of some churchmen.[202] The policy had helped to split his party, and left embarrassing questions to his successors who were haunted by the divisions over Maynooth. Peel's general contribution had been to demonstrate once again the advisability of moderate religious concession while at the same time giving some encouragement to the Establishment. In carrying his concessions he had aroused opponents who were a serious threat to the established Church—namely, the Voluntaries, or even the ultra-Protestants, whose extremism was likely to stiffen demands for concession on the other side. Many of these opponents were in his own party and the passage of

[196] Ibid. lxxxv. 1252 ff.
[197] On this point see the dispute between Lord Camoys, a Catholic peer, and Bishop Phillpotts (ibid. 1273-84).
[198] Ibid. 1263-4.   [199] Ibid. 1264-5.
[200] Ibid. lxxxvi. 300-28, 581-612; lxxxviii. 360-6, 630-8; B. Ward, Sequel to Catholic Emancipation, ii. 80-1.
[201] Hansard, lxxxviii. 360-3.
[202] Rev. H. H. Norris to Hon. and Rev. A. P. Perceval, 23 Feb. 1847 (Churton Papers).

some concessions had rested on Liberal support. But his Liberal successors were in an even less happy state than Peel, for they did not begin with an over-all and united majority in the Commons. In this weak situation it was extremely doubtful whether they could satisfy the demands which Dissenters and Catholics would more readily make on a Liberal than on a Conservative Government.

CHAPTER VI

Whig Toleration in Dilemma:
Lord John Russell, 1846-1852

I. RUSSELL AND THE CHURCH

ON TAKING office in June 1846 Russell led a Whig Government even weaker than that of 1837–41. The Liberals were far short of having even a nominal majority in the House of Commons. In 1846–7, before the general election, Liberals and Protectionists numbered approximately 270 each, with 'liberal Conservatives' (i.e. Conservatives who agreed with Peel's commercial policy) not far short of 120.[1] In this position it was important for Russell to prevent a reunion of Protectionists and Peelites—an event which seemed quite likely in 1846 and which, in the case of back-bench Peelites if not the leaders, eventually occurred.[2] Russell sought Peelite support for his commercial measures, which were unacceptable to Protectionists. On ecclesiastical matters his policy was less clear cut. While on some religious questions Peelites were more liberal than Protectionists, they would not countenance a radical challenge to the Establishment; nor, indeed, would the Whigs. Russell therefore avoided sweeping ecclesiastical reform. He adopted policies which were generally acceptable to Peelites and, at times, to Protectionists. This attitude reflected the long-standing Whig desire to protect the Establishment from radical attack—a policy whose importance was increased in the later 1840s by the Government's weakness.

But this policy was far from pleasing everyone, and it exacerbated the divisions in Russell's own party. Radicals, Irish Repealers, and Dissenters were extremely restive and favoured policies which would have united the Conservatives and brought down the Government. The almost exclusively Whig and aristocratic composition of Russell's Government did nothing to lessen their discontent.[3] It was fortunate for Russell that these dissident groups did not have identical aims. Many radicals (and Whigs) favoured State endowment of the Irish Catholic Church ('concurrent endowment'), which was anathema to Voluntaries. Though urged by Russell and supported by many Peelites, this scheme did not reach the form of a parliamentary bill.

[1] F. A. Dreyer, 'The Administration of Lord John Russell, 1846–52' (unpubl. Univ. of St. Andrews Ph.D. thesis 1962), 80; Conacher, *The Peelites and the Party System*, 15–16.
[2] Conacher, op. cit. 14–15.
[3] See Southgate, *The Passing of the Whigs*, 197–200.

The Irish Catholic bishops, valuing their independence, were against it, and massive ultra-Protestant and Voluntary opposition would have been raised in a repetition of the Maynooth outcry. Such were Russell's difficulties on the ecclesiastical front alone, that it is not altogether surprising that in 1850 he sought help through opposition to the restored Catholic hierarchy.

While Russell, having already supported Peel's Maynooth Bill, continued to affront Voluntaries by favouring concurrent endowment, Dissenters in general gained no concessions from his shaky Government respecting church-rates, burials, or University Tests, and took issue with the ministry's education policy. The interests of the established Church, on the other hand, seemed to enjoy Government favour. In July 1847 a bill establishing the see of Manchester was passed with Government support, though it was provided that the number of bishops in the Lords would not be increased. The bill was opposed by Hume, Roebuck, Molesworth, Edward Horsman, and other radicals as a misuse of surplus Church funds which, they said, would be more usefully spent on poor clergy and special areas of religious destitution.[4] Sir James Graham incongruously added his opposition.[5] But only 15 M.P.s opposed the second reading of the bill, and 14 the third reading.[6] The Government wished to establish three more bishoprics. Southwell, Bodmin, Westminster, and St. Albans were discussed as possible centres;[7] but no further sees were founded until 1877, when St. Albans and Truro were established. It seemed extraordinary, said the radical Bernal Osborne in the Manchester bishopric debate, that Russell, 'who throughout the whole of his career had always been coquetting with dissenters ... should abandon them now that he was in office, and get up a flirtation with the Church'.[8]

While encouraging the Church, Russell was anxious to impress his own religious viewpoint upon it. He adhered, with a deep personal tenacity, to the Protestant and Erastian traditions of the Whigs. When supporting the Manchester Bishopric Bill he said that he 'sincerely wished to see the Church of England united in harmony and concord ... and he trusted that the Protestant character of that Church would be maintained by its bishops and its clergy for ever'.[9] He disliked and feared Tractarianism as a divisive and Romanizing force in the Church, and Tractarians found no favour in his

---

[4] Hansard, xciv. 243–61 (Horsman), 338–43 (Hume), 366–70, 534–9 (Molesworth), 468–76 (Roebuck).

[5] Ibid. 348–64; Graham to Peel, 'private', 16 July 1847 (Peel Papers, Add. MS. 40452, fos. 214–15); Gladstone to Graham, 21 July 1847 (Lathbury, *Correspondence of Gladstone*, i. 75–9).

[6] Hansard, xciv. 236–76, 337 ff., 630–4.

[7] Samuel Wilberforce to Robert Wilberforce, 9 Jan. 1847 (Wilberforce Papers).

[8] Hansard, xciv. 400–1. For Russell's religious views cf. Chadwick, *Victorian Church*, i. 232–4; Southgate, op. cit. 218 ff.; Prest, *Russell*, 79–80.

[9] Hansard, xciv. 651 (speech of 21 July 1847); quoted G. I. T. Machin, 'Lord John Russell and the Prelude to the Ecclesiastical Titles Bill, 1846–51', *JEH* xxv (1974), 279.

episcopal appointments. All ten of these appointments, with the possible exception of Thomas Vowler Short (elevated to St. Asaph in 1846), were of evangelicals or broad churchmen.[10] Bishop Wilberforce, a moderate high churchman, referred to Russell's 'miserable appointments', and to 'the weakening of all our [i.e. the bishops'] just influence by the introduction of such men as Lord John has put amongst us . . .'[11] High churchmen showed their dissatisfaction with Government policy and with State control in general. Thus Russell quarrelled with both Dissenters and high churchmen until 1850; thereafter he quarrelled with Roman Catholics as well. During his ministry conflicts between Government and the Churches were sharpened and extended.

II. THE 1847 ELECTION

Early in his ministry Russell incurred the anger of Voluntaries through his educational proposals. These enlightened plans were contained in the minutes of the Educational Committee of the Privy Council for August and December 1846. They proposed to give retirement pensions to worthy and long-serving teachers, to encourage the training of selected children as apprentice 'pupil teachers' in certain schools, and to arrange that the best of these apprentices should be sent as 'Queen's scholars' to training colleges, where they would join others in preparation for a professional career. Government grants would be made to teachers who trained pupil teachers, to the Queen's scholars, and the training colleges. Trained and certificated teachers would receive higher salaries than others.[12] Educational reforms seemed bound to arouse ecclesiastical controversy, and religious battle was joined over the proposals. The Church of England seemed generally satisfied with the scheme.[13] Ultra-Protestants disliked grants being offered to Catholic schools, but this part of the plan was abandoned for the moment. The exclusion of Catholics caused Wesleyans, encouraged by Ashley, to accept grants under the scheme.[14] Dissenters were disappointed at losing the Wesleyan support which they had enjoyed in their last educational campaign in 1843, and they and some radical politicians claimed that ministers had made a compact with the Wesleyans to exclude Catholics.[15] But there had been no such arrangement.[16] Russell said that he hoped to extend grants to Catholic schools in the following year. This was done, and

[10] Short was said to be sympathetic to the Tractarians: see DNB.

[11] Wilberforce to Gladstone, 26 Dec. 1851 (R. K. Pugh, ed., *The Letter-Books of Samuel Wilberforce, 1843–68*, Oxfordshire Record Society, xlvii (1969) (Oxford, 1970), 221).

[12] F. Smith, *Kay-Shuttleworth*, 172 ff.; Prest, op. cit. 156–7.

[13] Marshall, 'The Theology of Church and State', 577; Hansard, lxxxiv. 877–82 (speeches of Blomfield and Howley).

[14] Ashley's diary, 1, 7, 15 Apr. 1847 (Hodder, *Shaftesbury*, ii. 214–15).

[15] *Eclectic Review*, 4th Ser. xxi (Jan.–June 1847), 641 ff.; R. E. Leader, *The Life and Letters of J. A. Roebuck* (London, 1897), 174; Hansard, xci. 982–6.

[16] Hansard, xci. 950–2 (speech of Russell).

the Wesleyans, who were then receiving Government money themselves, made no further protest.[17]

The opposition to Government educational plans in 1847 was thus not so extensive as it had been in 1843. Protest was now left to the dedicated proponents of voluntary education, and the scheme was condemned mainly because it extended State intervention. This was the principal objection to the measure at a great meeting—said to consist of at least 15,000 people—at the Cloth Hall Yard, Leeds, on 17 March 1847; the elder Edward Baines was then opposed by W. F. Hook, vicar of Leeds, who in the previous summer had already won the Baineses' hostility by announcing a startling conversion to State education.[18] The Congregational Board of Education linked educational to religious Voluntaryism, saying that such a measure might 'prepare the way for the payment and pensioning of the ministers of all denominations'.[19] Complaints were also made about Anglican influences in the scheme, especially the fact that (on account of the 'concordat' of 1840) the inspectors who would examine pupil teachers in Church schools would be Anglican clergymen.[20]

In condemning the proposals, the Voluntaries showed the experience they had gained from their anti-Maynooth agitation. Crosby Hall was the scene of a conference of nearly 500 delegates, convened on 13 April, and petitions to Parliament against the scheme contained about half a million signatures.[21] But Dissenters were again divided. Not only did Unitarians support the measure,[22] but different opinions were held among members of the same denomination. The Congregationalist Robert Vaughan, who supported the scheme, was embroiled in pamphlet dispute with the younger Baines, though Vaughan's position was later said to have softened.[23] At Westminster the opposition was slight. When, on 22 April, the Commons divided on whether to increase the education estimates by £100,000 in order to finance the scheme, the Government enjoyed a victory of 372 votes to 47, though the 47 were something more than 'Bright and a few eccentric individuals', as Halévy described them.[24] The composition of the minority emphasized the parliamentary weakness of militant Dissent, for the minority consisted largely of radicals who were not Dissenters but who (like Roebuck)

[17] Prest, 256; S. Gilley, 'Protestant London, No-Popery and the Irish Poor, 1830–60', pt. I, *Recusant History*, x (1969–70), 216, 227 n. 66; Baines, *Edward Baines*, 286–7.

[18] Baines, op. cit., 284–6; Stephens, *Hook*, ii. 205–11; D. Fraser, 'Edward Baines', in Hollis (ed.), *Pressure from Without*, 197.

[19] *Eclectic Review*, 4th Ser. xxi (Jan.–June 1847), 516.

[20] Ibid. 365–7, 517–18; Hansard, cxi. 1090 (speech of Bright), 1161–2 (Sir W. Clay); Resolutions of the Dissenting Deputies against the scheme: Minutes, xi. 373.

[21] *Eclectic Review*, xxi (Jan.–June 1847), 635 ff.; Cowherd, *Politics of English Dissent*, 161.

[22] e.g. J. B. Smith to Duncan McLaren, 17 Apr. 1847 (J. B. Smith Papers, S. 343).

[23] E. Baines, jun., *Letters to the Rt. Hon. Lord John Russell . . . on State Education* (London, 1846); R. Vaughan, *Popular Education in England, with a reply to Mr. Baines* (London, 1846); *Eclectic Review*, xxi (Jan.–June 1847), 509.

[24] Halévy, *History of the English People*, iv. 176.

disliked the Government's exclusion of Catholics.[25] Radicals such as Cobden, who desired State education, were further divided from Voluntaries over this episode, and found the attitude of the younger Baines and his followers an irritating hindrance in radical politics for years afterwards.[26]

The Voluntaries had lost an educational battle with a Liberal Government, having succeeded in one with a Conservative Government four years before. Members of Russell's Government were well aware that their educational scheme had brought renewed discontent among former supporters. Voluntary opposition to the scheme had caused renewed determination to oppose the Government at the polls. The electoral impulse created by the Maynooth crisis had been revived by the educational crisis. A further reason for opposing the Russell Government was its enlargement of the Establishment through the creation of an additional bishopric.[27]

The electoral preparations promised after the Maynooth crisis began in earnest during the educational controversy. Representatives of many constituencies with a large proportion of Nonconformist electors ignored Dissenting wishes by voting money for the educational proposals,[28] and the approaching election gave Dissenting voters the chance of revenge. Russell, said the *Eclectic Review*, had assisted the 1843 educational measure, voted for the Maynooth Bill, advised State payment of the priests, and, finally, urged the new educational scheme.[29] The Crosby Hall conference resolved that M.P.s who supported the educational proposals should be regarded as disqualified from representing 'the friends of civil and religious liberty', and that no candidate should be supported unless he promised to oppose all further State grants for such purposes.[30] Dissenters, it was said, had lacked proper representation hitherto. The first triennial conference of the Anti-State Church Association, appropriately held in May while Voluntary tempers still burned over their defeat on the educational issue, called for nationwide organization.[31]

Words were followed by action. The Crosby Hall conference established a Dissenters' Parliamentary Committee to promote the return of Voluntary M.P.s. Samuel Morley, a Congregational businessman, was chairman, and a list of fifty-three possible candidates was drawn up.[32] The Dissenting Deputies drew up a list of suitable candidates for London boroughs; and in Scotland similar action was taken by a Committee for Maintaining the Civil

---

[25] Hansard, xci. 1236–9.

[26] Lowerson, 'The Political Career of Edward Baines', 147 ff.; Cobden to Bright, 28 Aug. 1848 (Cobden Papers, Add. MS. 43649, fos. 71–4); Cobden to George Combe, 15 May 1848, 9 Nov. 1850 (J. Morley, *The Life of Richard Cobden* (London, 1906), 486, 547–9).

[27] This was condemned in the *Nonconformist Elector*, 30 July 1847, p. 49.

[28] *Eclectic Review*, 4th Ser. xxi (Jan.–June 1847), 635.

[29] Ibid. 527.   [30] Ibid. 639.   [31] *Nonconformist*, 10 May 1847, 325–9.

[32] E. Hodder, *The Life of Samuel Morley* (2nd edn., London, 1887), 100–3 (list of names given). Cf. electoral activities of Protestant Dissenting Deputies: Minutes of the Deputies, xi. 360–6 (22 Jan. and 19 Feb. 1847).

Rights of Congregational Dissenters.[33] The *Nonconformist Elector* was issued as a guide to Dissenting voters twice a week from 9 July to 24 August, the period of campaigning and polling. Voluntaries 'blacked' all M.P.s who had voted for either or both of the two crucial issues, the Maynooth Bill and the education grant. Dissenters were urged either to support a Voluntary candidate or to abstain.[34] As early as February two candidates were being sought for Leicester who would support universal suffrage and Voluntaryism in religion and education.[35] Voluntary declarations by electors or candidates were reported from many places during the campaign. The Voluntary response, said the *Nonconformist*, had been wider than expected: 'more than one Liberal politician, disposed in times gone by to speak of Dissenters as "sanctimonious humbugs", are beginning to inquire for the best works elucidatory of Nonconformist principles'.[36]

The 1847 election showed an extraordinary complexity of different groups and interests, reflecting religious and commercial pressures and the disrupted party politics of the time. The 'railway interest', according to Halévy, was represented by 102 M.P.s in the new House, which contained an unprecedented number of businessmen.[37] Chartism and reform of the Poor Law and game laws were electoral issues. But religious questions dominated the polls. It was not only a noted Protestant election but also a noted Voluntary one.

Among Tories, ultra-Protestantism was more vital than Protection, on account of temporary agricultural prosperity: 'protection [was] dead for the present', Sir George Cornewall Lewis wrote, and 'the only question on which there was anything like a popular feeling was the dangerous state of Protestantism'.[38] The *Monmouthshire Beacon* gave a list of eleven questions which Conservative voters should put to candidates; the first three questions concerned the repeal of the Maynooth grant, opposition to the endowment of Catholic priests and to the further relief of Roman Catholics. Only in question five was Protection raised.[39] F. R. Bonham told Peel that the Maynooth question had destroyed several Peelites in the election, while 'Free Trade' had had little effect.[40]

Yet ultra-Protestantism created difficulties among the Protectionists and

---

[33] *Nonconformist*, 14 July 1847, 506; *Nonconformist Elector*, 16 July 1847; *Eclectic Review*, 4th Ser. xxii (July–Dec. 1847), 358.

[34] *Nonconformist*, 12 May 1847, 348–9.

[35] Letter from Leicester Electoral Committee to George Wilson, 18 Feb. 1847 (G. Wilson Papers); William Biggs to G. Wilson, 28 Feb. 1847, 'private & confidential' (ibid.).

[36] 26 May 1847, 396; also 9 June 1847, 428.

[37] Halévy, op. cit. iv. 181. Cf. Rev. W. J. Cookesley of Eton College to Disraeli, 25 May 1847 (Disraeli Papers, B/I/C/9).

[38] Sir G. C. Lewis to earl of Clarendon, 19 July 1847 (Clarendon Pagers, c. 530).

[39] I. W. R. David, 'Political and Electioneering Activity in South East Wales, 1820–52' (unpubl. Univ. of Wales M.A. thesis 1959), 160–1.

[40] Bonham to Peel, 2 Aug. 1847 (Peel Papers, Add. MS. 40599, fo. 122). For a modifying view see R. Stewart, *The Politics of Protection, 1841–52* (Cambridge, 1971), 110–11.

tended to divide some leaders from the rank and file. Neither Lord George Bentinck, the enigmatic ex-Canningite who had voted for the Maynooth Bill, nor Disraeli, the sinuous ex-radical, had ideological or personal ties with Protestant exclusiveness. Disraeli privately disliked Inglis, whom he thought a wretched speaker and whose eyes, he said, twinkled with voluptuous self-complacency. He gleefully committed to paper a hilarious verbal *gaffe* which Inglis made in the Commons.[41] Bentinck and Disraeli differed from most of their followers (and, at this point, from Stanley) in supporting Jewish Emancipation—a question which gained fresh prominence in this election, Lionel de Rothschild being returned for the City of London and four Jews standing for other constituencies. They were also ready to entertain State endowment of the Catholic priests. Bentinck spoke in favour of Catholic endowment as a candidate for King's Lynn.[42] It was seen that ultra-Protestantism was subject to questioning even in the Protectionist party.

Ultra efforts, however, were conspicuous in the elections, and the division between the Peelite leaders and Protectionists hardened. Peel himself, in voting for both Inglis and Gladstone in the Oxford University election,[43] gave an impressive display of Conservative unity which by no means generally prevailed. Ultra-Protestants were thoroughly opposed to the Catholic endowment which Peel and the Liberals had already carried and to the further endowment which they were believed to support. This belief was, according to Peel's own Tamworth address in this election, well justified.[44] The Protestant Association and the National Club had been campaigning through pamphlets, circulars, and local branches for the return of a Protestant Parliament.[45] At the annual meeting of the Protestant Association in May 1847 Hugh McNeile had urged support for any candidate who resisted Catholic endowment.[46] James Lord, the secretary of the Association, issued a pre-election address in which he indicated supernatural signs of calamity in recent Popish advances: 'A dark cloud seems to be lowering over our land. Society appears to be undergoing a process of disorganisation . . . The fountains of the great deep seem to be breaking up, and anarchy and despotism to be struggling for ascendancy.'[47] A National Protestant Society had been formed by the earl of Roden and the duke of Manchester in order to supply 'No Popery' candidates.[48] Altogether, ultra-Protestants in Great

---

[41] Disraeli Papers, A/X/28; printed in H. M. and M. Swartz (eds.), *Disraeli's Reminiscences* (London, 1975), 32–3.

[42] Charles Greville to Clarendon, 1 Aug. 1847 (Clarendon Papers, c. 521). Cf. Bentinck to Disraeli, 23 July 1847 (Disraeli Papers, B/XX/Bc/30).

[43] Peel to Goulburn, 5 Aug. 1847 (Goulburn Papers).

[44] *Letter to the Electors for the Borough of Tamworth* (2nd edn., London, 1847); copy in Peel Papers, 40599, fo. 24 ff. (esp. fos. 30–1).

[45] Cahill, 'The Protestant Association and the Anti-Maynooth Agitation', 301.

[46] Ibid. 302.

[47] *An Appeal to Protestants, on the subject of the approaching Election* (London, 1847), 3.

[48] *Liverpool Mercury*, 29 June 1847.

Britain did not need the advice given to them by the Grand Orange Lodge of Ireland, that only candidates avowing 'religious truth' were to be supported.[49]

But the ultra-Protestant efforts had disappointing results. Although some Peelites were said to have been defeated by anti-Catholic feeling, most of them survived to sit in the new Parliament. Gladstone, despite his Tractarianism, his support for the Maynooth and Dissenters' Chapels Bills, and his declared adherence to religious liberty, gained the second seat at Oxford University (though he had far fewer votes than Inglis) in an election almost wholly concerned with religious issues.[50] He was supported by Puseyites and by latitudinarians such as A. P. Stanley and Benjamin Jowett[51]—an indication of his own complicated religious development. Somewhat surprisingly, at Liverpool, where Tories dominated the corporation and heavy Irish Catholic immigration was contributing to the Orange–Catholic feuds of the city,[52] there was another victory for religious liberalism. The ultra-Protestants, stimulated by Hugh McNeile, wished to return two candidates representing their views. To one candidate, Sir Digby Mackworth, a Protectionist and anti-Catholic who wished to repeal the Act of 1829, Anglican and Wesleyan ultra-Protestants gave their support. But they were loath to extend this aid to Lord John Manners, who, though a Protectionist, was also a Tractarian and a supporter of the Maynooth Act. An alliance of these two candidates proved impossible—though over 1,700 votes were split between them—and the consequent Tory weakening enabled Sir Thomas Birch, a Liberal, and Edward Cardwell, a Peelite, to win the seats.[53] There was a large number of Catholic electors in Liverpool—said to be 1,200,[54] though still very low in relation to the total Catholic population of the city (110,160, or 29 per cent, in 1851); and their strategy was planned by the local Catholic association, formed in 1844. A resolution was passed that

. . . the Catholic electors be most earnestly urged not to vote until after one o'clock on the day of election; and should Sir Digby Mackworth be then first, second, or third on the poll, they are requested to vote for the two candidates that may be highest, excluding Sir Digby Mackworth. If he be last on the poll at one o'clock,

[49] Machin, 'The Maynooth Grant', 79.

[50] Morley, *Gladstone*, i. 327–36; Gladstone to Stafford Northcote, 23 Jan. 1847, draft (Gladstone Papers, Add. MS. 44216, fos. 53–5).

[51] Morley, op. cit. 335.

[52] It was estimated that, between 1 Nov. 1846 and 12 May 1847, immigration through the port of Liverpool was no less than 137,519 (excluding transients who sailed for America); Burke, *Catholic History of Liverpool*, 84 f.

[53] *Liverpool Mercury*, 25 June, 2, 30 July 1847; *Liverpool Courier*, 21, 28 July 1847; E. Cardwell to Peel, 22 June, 15 July 1847 (Peel Papers, 40598, fos. 360–1; 40599, fos. 18–21); B. E. Burrows, 'The Maynooth Agitation and its effect on Liverpool Politics, 1845–7' (unpubl. Univ. of Dundee M.A. Hons. thesis 1969); Whibley, *Lord John Manners and his Friends*, i. 238–42.

[54] Burke, op. cit. 92.

the electors will judge for themselves which of the three candidates they will support . . . it is confidently hoped that no Catholic will, under any circumstances, record his vote for Sir Digby Mackworth.[55]

At one o'clock on the day, Mackworth was high on the poll; but Manners, for whom many Catholics had been inclined to vote, was bottom. A notice was accordingly displayed, telling Catholics to split their votes between Birch and Cardwell, Mackworth's two closest rivals. This probably had a decisive effect on the final result: Cardwell 5,581; Birch 4,882; Mackworth 4,089; Manners 2,413.[56] Strong ultra-Protestant feeling doubtless lay behind the 1,485 'plumpers' for Mackworth. But split votes between Cardwell and Birch were as many as 4,119[57]—an indication of the Liberal–Peelite understanding in these elections, especially under the pressure of particular local circumstances.

Anti-Catholic efforts to secure satisfactory pledges from candidates were directed at Disraeli, who stood for Buckinghamshire. In this region the ultra influence of the duke of Buckingham contributed to the defeat at Aylesbury of R. R. Clayton, who had voted for the Maynooth Bill and the repeal of the Corn Laws.[58] Disraeli must have found it embarrassing to be billed as not only 'a friend of agriculture' but an 'opponent of Popery'.[59] His printed address said that his opposition to the Maynooth Bill was 'consistent with an earnest desire to secure to our Roman Catholic fellow subjects the civil and political equality to which they are entitled'.[60] This did not satisfy anti-Catholic freeholders, whose principles were as 'firm as in the days of the Brunswick Club'.[61] They wished to ensure that Disraeli would defend the Church Establishment and oppose Catholic endowment.[62] It is not known whether Disraeli wholly satisfied his worried questioners, but the matter did not affect his election, which was uncontested.

The Voluntaries made their first major effect in a general election. No less than forty-six candidates opposed to the Church–State connection are said to have stood.[63] Where Voluntaries refrained from voting for a Liberal whose views were unsatisfactory, they might have indirectly helped an anti-Catholic candidate and weakened Liberal unity in spite of appeals to maintain it.[64] But there was no more sign than in the Maynooth crisis of an alliance

---

[55] Ibid. 91–2; *Liverpool Mecury*, 23 July 1847.

[56] *McCalmont's Parliamentary Poll-Book, 1832–1918*, ed. J. Vincent and M. Stenton (Brighton, 1971), 181.

[57] *Liverpool Courier*, 28 July 1847.

[58] Davis, *Political Change and Continuity*, 159–61.

[59] J. Neale to Disraeli, 8 June 1847, encl. (Disraeli Papers, B/I/C/111, 111a).

[60] Ibid. C/192.

[61] R. Sutton to Disraeli, 3 June 1847 (ibid. C/95).

[62] W. Jenner to Disraeli, 1 June 1847; R. Deane to Disraeli, 14 June 1847; Rev. Francis Merewether to Disraeli, 1 July 1847 (ibid. C/91, 39/153).

[63] Mason, 'The Rise of Combative Dissent', 108.

[64] e.g. appeal by *Liverpool Mercury*, 16 July 1847.

between anti-Catholics and Voluntaries. The Dissenters' Parliamentary Committee heartily disclaimed such a union: 'We have no sympathy with ... the old "No Popery!" cry. We have suffered from its intolerance. We detest it from our very souls.'[65]

Dissenters conflicted with Wesleyans on the Voluntary issue, for example in the Stockport election, where James Heald, a Wesleyan and Peelite, narrowly squeezed the Voluntary James Kershaw into third place on the poll. Heald claimed at the Wesleyan Conference of 1847: 'The battle has been between the Church and Methodism on the one side, and political Dissent on the other.'[66] The main targets of Voluntary electors were Liberals and Peelites who had extended State endowment of religion and State control of education. Miall named three prominent Liberals who had been particularly negligent or contemptuous of Dissenting claims, and whose defeat should be especially sought—Russell, Macaulay, and J. A. Roebuck.[67] The defeat of Macaulay at Edinburgh gratified Voluntaries and others. At the head of the poll in that city was Charles Cowan, a Free Churchman who had managed to obtain Voluntary support and who was aided by Macaulay's personal unpopularity and by demands for reform of the whisky excise.[68] But Free Churchmen (and perhaps Voluntaries) fared less well at Greenock, where Lord Melgund (brother-in-law of the Prime Minister) defeated the Free Church champion A. M. Dunlop.[69] In the Falkirk burghs the Peelite Lord Lincoln succeeded against 'the Free Kirk and all the Dissenting ministers', despite 'the pains of hell', as he claimed, being preached against him.[70] At Glasgow the Liberals John MacGregor and Alexander Hastie defeated a Voluntary challenge; MacGregor had informed Russell that he only expected to win with Conservative aid.[71]

Russell himself emerged unscathed at the head of the poll in the City of London. Miall at Halifax and Joseph Sturge at Leeds, both prominent Voluntaries, were defeated by Liberals with the help of Conservatives.[72] But Roebuck's defeat at Bath was as heartening to Voluntaries as that of Macaulay. He had not only supported the Maynooth Bill but opposed immediate disestablishment and championed State education.[73] After his defeat he

[65] *Eclectic Review*, 4th Ser. xxii (July–Dec. 1847), 361.

[66] Machin, 'Maynooth Grant', 80–1; B. Gregory, *Sidelights on the Conflicts of Methodism, 1827–52* (London, 1899), 415–16.

[67] *Nonconformist*, 10 May 1847, 328.

[68] A. Craw, 'The Scottish Disruption and its effect on Politics, with special reference to Edinburgh' (unpubl. Univ. of Dundee M.A. Hons. thesis 1969), 19 ff.; Trevelyan, *Macaulay*, 467, 471 ff.; Cowan, *Reminiscences*, 212–13.

[69] Lord Melgund to Russell, 5 June 1847 (Russell Papers, 6D); Melgund to earl of Minto, 10, 19, and 26 June, 1, 9, 10, 16, and 20 July 1847 (Minto Papers, 128/30).

[70] Lincoln to Peel, 3 Aug. 1847 (Peel Papers, 40481, fos. 414–15).

[71] MacGregor to Russell, 17 July 1847 (Russell Papers, 6D).

[72] Sir Charles Wood to Russell, 1 Aug. 1847 (Russell Papers, 6E); *Leeds Mercury*, 26 June 1847 (supplement, p. 10), 31 July 1847 (p. 4).

[73] Roebuck to Rev. D. Wassell, 2 July 1847 (Leader, *Roebuck*, 183–5).

told Brougham that he was delighted to stop being 'the slave as I have for years been of a set of intriguing canting dissenters'.[74]

Voluntaries who were fighting a 'centre' alliance of Whigs and Peelites tended to form an understanding of the 'left' with Chartists, and thus further emphasized their separation from the Whigs. Chartists had opposed the Maynooth Bill on the Voluntary principle,[75] though some of them had favoured the Government educational scheme. In the election Chartists and Voluntaries adopted each other's causes, while giving primacy to their own.[76] At Halifax, Miall and Ernest Jones fought together.[77] 'The new bishops and churches,' said Fergus O'Connor's Northern Star, 'the new endowments and Education scheme, are so many brittle shields held up against the on-march of the Charter.'[78] But O'Connor's return for Nottingham, the only Chartist success in the elections, was not welcomed by the Voluntary Press, for it was gained over a purer Voluntary, Thomas Gisborne.[79] There was, however, cause for satisfaction that O'Connor had defeated J. C. Hobhouse, a Whig minister. Some Catholic voters also aided the Voluntary cause. A meeting of Catholic electors at Leeds urged that Joseph Sturge should be supported: they hoped that disestablishment, which he desired, would include the Church of Ireland.[80] But in general Catholic voters probably supported (as at Liverpool) Liberals and Peelites whom Voluntaries were advised to oppose.

The success of the Voluntary intervention in these elections has sometimes been underestimated.[81] Several candidates who subscribed to Voluntaryism triumphed in London boroughs. These included George Thompson (Tower Hamlets), Charles Pearson (Lambeth), Charles Lushington (Westminster), and T. S. Duncombe and Thomas Wakley (Finsbury). Thompson and Pearson defeated Liberal ministers, one of whom (Benjamin Hawes) held Voluntary opinions himself but nevertheless belonged to an unsatisfactory Government.[82] It was said that 14 out of the 15 candidates recommended by the Dissenting Deputies for the London area had been elected; this figure, however, included several candidates who were opposed to any future religious endowments by the Government but not to the existing Church–State connections.[83] In south Lancashire and the West Riding, areas where Dissenting voters were numerous, the Voluntaries had also striven hard and

---

[74] Roebuck to Brougham, 29 July 1847 (Brougham Papers, 21, 690); cf. Leader, op. cit. 186–8.
[75] Northern Star, 12 Apr. 1845.   [76] Ibid. 24 July 1847 (list of candidates, p. 1).
[77] Ibid. 17, 24 July 1847; Leeds Mercury, 5 June (supplement, p. 11), 19 June 1847 (p. 11); Nonconformist, 30 June (p. 480), 14 July 1847 (p. 512).
[78] Northern Star, 17 July 1847, p. 4.   [79] Leeds Mercury, 7 Aug. 1847.
[80] Ibid. 31 July 1847 (supplement, p. 10). Cf. J. O'Neill to Lord Melgund, 12 June 1847 (Minto Papers, 128/4).
[81] Halévy, iv. 183–4; Gash, Reaction, 103 ff.
[82] Cf. Southgate, Passing of the Whigs, 199.
[83] Cowherd, op. cit. 162. Lists of victorious candidates supporting these different propositions are in the Nonconformist, 1 Sept. 1847, 634–5.

gained a certain amount of success: John Bright, Dr. Bowring, Joseph Brotherton, Sharman Crawford, W. J. Fox, and Charles Hindley were returned, though Miall and Sturge were defeated. A fairly moderate estimate —though, considering the ephemeral nature of some of the 'pledges' given by candidates, probably an uncertain one—listed 26 successful candidates who were pledged to detach Church from State, and 60 more members who would resist new State endowments of religion.[84] Thus a hopeful foundation seemed to be laid for further action. 'The ice is broken,' announced the *Nonconformist*. 'The spell which sealed the eyes, and paralysed the will, of the Nonconformist body is dissipated. They have had a taste of independence, and they will never again forget it.'[85] The Voluntary Press looked forward to the opening of independent political channels—a central body like the Dissenters' Parliamentary Committee, an institution similar to the Reform Club and a scheme for electoral registration[86]—but these plans were only partially realized. The 1847 election was none the less a notable breakthrough for political Dissenters. Their electoral efforts remained strenuously alive for several decades, and saw a fluctuating but generally increasing number of M.P.s returned to Parliament.

The Voluntaries' electoral successes—particularly in contests with noted Whigs and radicals—accentuated their divisive presence within the loose federation of Liberals. Even if the total number of Liberals returned was as high as 337—an increased number, ostensibly giving a small over-all majority in the Commons—this figure concealed deep and worrying divisions. Although it was soon shown that there was no strong party division between Protectionists and Peelites—many Peelites being ready to vote frequently with the Protectionists—the number of firm Protectionists had been reduced, perhaps to only a little over 200, while the Peelites remained apparently stable at about 110. On the other hand, the fluidity among some Conservatives was such that Protectionists could be placed at 225, and Peelites at 90.[87] Conservative divisions compensated Russell for the divisions among his own following, and he was able to retain office precariously for four and a half years longer.

III. POLITICIANS, JEWS, AND DISSENTERS, 1847–1851

The elections had brought little strength to the Government. Russell still had to tread delicately, and avoid motions which would unite his opponents against him or antagonize his supporters. In April 1848 radicals revolted against income tax proposals and Government expenditure, and, numbering

---

[84] Miall, *Edward Miall*, 128.   [85] 4 Aug. 1847, 557.

[86] *Nonconformist Elector*, 6 Aug. 1847, 80. Cf. *Eclectic Review*, 4th Ser. xxii (July–Dec. 1847), 378–81.

[87] Charles Wood to Russell, 14 Aug. 1847 (Russell Papers, 6E); Conacher, *The Peelites and the Party System*, 30, 220–32; Stewart, *Politics of Protection*, 112; Prest, 262–3.

about fifty, declared themselves a separate party.[88] To the difficulties of parliamentary management were added intractable problems, Irish and European. The ministry, it was said, was marked by 'famine, commercial revulsion, and a state of political agitation both at home and abroad such as the world has scarcely ever witnessed'.[89] Onlookers, even Whig ones, were scarcely sympathetic to the Government: '. . . this Govt. has been continually falling in publick estimation', said Charles Greville in June 1848, '. . . and I regret to say that John Russell himself appears a great failure . . . his wife torments him to death. She is not in good health, & she worries him, & keeps him in a constant state of nervous excitement.'[90] Given these formidable obstacles, a legislative record which included the Public Health Act, the Irish Encumbered Estates Act of 1849, and the repeal of the Navigation Laws was quite an impressive one.

Ecclesiastical controversy, like other matters, demanded a delicate touch. Early in the first session of the new Parliament, on 16 December 1847, Russell enthusiastically reintroduced the question of Jewish disabilities, which had been revived by Rothschild's return as Russell's fellow representative for the City of London. Rothschild, like O'Connell in 1828, was prevented by law from taking his seat, and Russell was attempting to obtain a solution as swift and yielding as that of 1829. Moving for a Committee of the whole House to consider the question, he called on Parliament to relieve a small and politically weak people, and not to let it be thought that concessions were only made as political expedients to the powerful.[91] The motion succeeded. A Relief Bill was subsequently introduced which passed the Commons but was rejected on 25 May 1848 in the Lords.[92] This pattern was repeated in 1849.

On the Jewish question Russell was confident, as far as the Commons was concerned. He had full Liberal support, and both wings of his opponents were thrown into dissension. Bentinck and Disraeli spoke and voted for Russell's motion in December 1847.[93] But the opinion of most Protectionists on the subject was expressed by Inglis, who argued that if Jews were admitted to Parliament any non-Christians might be allowed in: '. . . the very gentleman whom he saw in his turban under the gallery three or four evenings ago, Rango Bapojee, the vakeel of the late Rajah of Sattara, might as fitly take his place amongst us as the Jew . . .'[94] He feared, as did 'an excellent petition from St. Jude's, Liverpool' (Hugh McNeile's parish), that Jewish relief would hasten the separation of Church and State.[95] Bentinck and Disraeli were unpopular with their followers over the question. Bentinck

[88] Dreyer, op. cit. 101–8; Prest, 281–2. [89] Quoted Prest, 300–1.
[90] Greville to Clarendon, 23 June 1848 (second letter) (Clarendon Papers, c. 521).
[91] Hansard, xcv. 1235–6. [92] *Annual Register*, xc (1848), 92.
[93] Hansard, xcv. 1321–30 (Disraeli), 1381–90 (Bentinck). For Disraeli's views see Blake, *Disraeli*, 258–61.
[94] Hansard, xcv. 1253. [95] Ibid. 1265.

was informed that Protectionists would not recognize his leadership, where-upon he resigned and took his place on the back benches. For the rest of the session the Protectionists were in confusion, though agricultural recession was shortly to revive them. 'The National Club have done it all', Bentinck protested, 'and the great Protectionist Party has degenerated into a "No Popery", "No Jew" League.'[96] Bentinck died in September 1848, but Disraeli was still suspected of wishing to pay the Catholic priesthood, until he reassured his followers on this point early in 1849.[97]

The Peelites were also divided on the Jewish question, most of the rank and file refusing to follow leaders such as Peel, Graham, Lincoln, Sidney Herbert, and Gladstone in support of the bill.[98] Gladstone (voting pro-Jew for the first time) declared notably that 'the Constitution . . . has altogether ceased to require of us the recognition of any fixed standard or body of Christian truths as an indispensable element of fitness for legislative duties...'[99] His attitude was unpopular among his Oxford constituents. The Rev. Richard Greswell, who assisted Gladstone's electoral interests, told him that Keble and others felt strongly against the concession.[100] Pusey's reaction verged on hysteria. In the course of a severe and emotional letter to Glad-stone he said that he had voted for him 'on the plain principle of personal confidence in you as a religious statesman'; and that he had not anticipated his support for 'an anti-Christian measure' such as the Jew bill, which he saw as preparing the 'final apostasy' of the State.[101] Gladstone sympathized, but said it was against the true interests of religion to try and maintain as a substance that which had already been negated by events:

For what I thought the true principle of national religion I stood, until no man stood by me. Nor would it then have been time to retire had a standard been ordained for national religion without relation to the elements of which the nation is composed. The State recedes from its ancient and high position: in England more slowly than elsewhere, yet still truly and sensibly.[102]

Pusey thought better of Gladstone for his opposition, on Scriptural grounds, to a bill allowing marriage with a deceased wife's sister in 1849;[103] though, in the future, other liberal compromises in political matters which Glad-stone felt compelled to make were to strain relations between the Tractarian don and the Tractarian statesman. Gladstone, however, had the support of some high churchmen (in addition to Lincoln, Sidney Herbert, and Roundell Palmer) on Jewish relief. J. R. Hope and W. F. Hook approved of Glad-

---

[96] Whibley, op. cit. i. 272 ff., esp. 291–3.   [97] Dreyer, 154–5.
[98] Peelite voting on the second reading is analysed by Conacher, op. cit. 222–5.
[99] Hansard, xcv. 1282, 1296.
[100] Greswell to Gladstone, 18 Jan. 1848 (Gladstone Papers, Add. MS. 44181, fo. 21). See also Greswell to Gladstone, 12, 30 June, 3 July 1848 (ibid. fos. 26–36).
[101] Pusey to Gladstone, 13 Dec. 1847 (Pusey Papers: part printed in H. P. Liddon, *The Life of E. B. Pusey*, ed. J. O. Johnston and R. J. Wilson (4 vols., London 1893–7), iii. 175–6).
[102] Gladstone to Pusey, 14 Dec. 1847, 'private' (Pusey Papers).
[103] Pusey to Gladstone, 24 Apr. 1849 (Gladstone Papers, 44281, fo. 54 ff.).

stone's position, thinking that such concessions would help to weaken the State connection with the Church and thereby assist the cause of spiritual independence. Hope wrote:

Better have the Legislature declared what it is—not professedly Christian, and then let the Church claim those rights and that independence which nothing but the pretence of Christianity can entitle the Legislature to withhold from it. In this view the emancipation of the Jews must tend to that of the Church, and at any rate a 'sham' will be discarded.[104]

On the question of Jewish relief Russell escaped danger from the opposition of Protectionist and most Peelite back-benchers because he had general Liberal support. On other religious questions, however, Liberal division showed itself when the Government re-encountered opposition from Dissent. Russell wished to carry out the highly controversial endowment of Catholic priests as one means of pacifying the Irish. A scheme of endowment was seriously discussed by ministers in the summer and autumn of 1848.[105] The alarm of Voluntaries at the prospect of concurrent endowment was shown at the West Riding by-election in November. The Liberal candidate, Charles Fitzwilliam, aroused opposition because he refused to condemn State endowment of the priests. Such payment, said the *Leeds Mercury*, would be 'a giant step towards the universal endowment of every form of religion—a policy which [is] . . . dishonouring to sacred truth, deadening to all religion, paralysing to the best energies and independent feelings of the people . . .'[106] Fitzwilliam withdrew, and Sir Culling Eardley (he had dropped the 'Smith' from his name) was adopted as a candidate by the Voluntaries. But he was defeated by a Conservative who was aided by the Fitzwilliam influence. Voluntary feeling on the endowment question was also shown at a meeting of the Stirling Anti-State Church Association held on 4 January 1849.[107]

The Government endowment plan had been dropped in December, on account of hostility from the Irish Catholic bishops who did not want to become dependent on the State.[108] But there was the possibility that the plan might be revived, and Dissenters had other reasons for dissatisfaction with the Government. The church-rate question was brought into Parliament for the first time since 1842. On 13 March 1849 John Trelawny, M.P. for Tavistock and an Anglican, moved for the abolition of church-rates; Russell flatly opposed the motion, which was defeated.[109] The abolition of the *regium donum* was announced in July 1851, which pleased Voluntary purists if not

---

[104] Hope to Gladstone, 9 Dec. 1847 (Ornsby, *Hope-Scott*, ii. 78). Cf. Hook's very similar views: Hook to Gladstone, 9 Feb. 1848 (Stephens, ii. 248).

[105] Prest, 290–2; Southgate, 189.

[106] 4 Nov. 1848, p. 4. See F. M. L. Thompson, 'Whigs and Liberals in the West Riding, 1830–60', *EHR* lxxiv (1959), 233 ff.

[107] *Stirling Observer*, 11 Jan. 1849; extract in J. B. Smith Papers, S. 335.

[108] Prest, 292; Nowlan, *Politics of Repeal*, 225–6.

[109] Hansard, ciii. 639–84 (Russell's speech, 672–5).

the indigent ministers who benefited from the grant. But Dissenters obtained no other concessions from Russell's beleaguered ministry. Meanwhile the ranks of radical Dissent and Voluntaryism were potentially increased when many Wesleyans began to secede from their denomination, objecting to autocratic Buntingite rule and demanding lay participation in denominational government.[110] Desire for democratic reform within Wesleyanism was accompanied by radicalism in general politics, and it was shown that many Wesleyans were less contentedly Tory or a-political than Lord Fitz-Booby had stated in Disraeli's *Coningsby*: 'I am told these Wesleyans are really a respectable body. I believe there is no material difference between their tenets and those of the Establishment . . . We have too long confounded them with the mass of Dissenters . . .'[111]

IV. RUSSELL AND HIGH CHURCHMEN, 1847–1850

It was with high churchmen that Russell had most religious friction in the later 1840s. High churchmen were as anxious as ever to protect the Church of England from heterogeneous parliamentary hands, and feared the designs of Erastian and latitudinarian Whigs. Russell, for his part, had no time for the 'mummeries of superstition', as he said in the Durham Letter of 1850,[112] or, as he was to repeat in 1875, for 'men . . . [who] put on all kinds of harlequin dresses, and perform all sorts of antics, to resemble . . . the great and memorable sacrifice of Christ's propitiation . . .'[113] His ministry was marked by acts of policy and legal judgements which greatly increased high-church discontent with State control. Russell's views, on the other hand, only stiffened when Erastianism was attacked. His Protestantism may well have been strengthened by reaction to the Tractarian ceremonies introduced into Russell's own church at Knightsbridge by the Rev. W. J. E. Bennett, and apparently observed by the Prime Minister Sunday after Sunday.

In education there was continued high-church resistance to the extension of State control over Church schools; though the resistance was weakening, perhaps on account of the Protestant *crise de conscience* among Tractarians following the conversion of Newman and others. An important change in the running of National Society schools, emanating from the Educational Committee of the Privy Council, was achieved with episcopal agreement, including that of Phillpotts. Management clauses, drafted by Kay-Shuttleworth and issued in June 1847, weakened clerical control over these schools. As a condition of receiving State grants, each National school was to be

---

[110] By 1856, 100,000 members had been lost (though many later returned), and only in that year was the increase of Wesleyans resumed (E. R. Taylor, *Methodism and Politics, 1791–1851* (Cambridge, 1935), 189). The radical Dissenting Press welcomed the schism (e.g. *Eclectic Review*, 5th Ser. iv (July–Dec. 1852), 385–6, 477–92), and the seceders supported the cause of disestablishment.

[111] B. Disraeli, *Coningsby, or the New Generation* (London, 1927), 90; original edn. 1844.

[112] See below, p. 210.

[113] Earl Russell, *Recollections and Suggestions, 1813–73* (London, 1875), 425 f., also 157–8, 171.

managed by a lay Anglican committee, chaired by the incumbent of the parish. The objects were to provide a more permanent and broadly based controlling body than the clergyman alone, and to lessen the possibility of Dissenters being excluded from the schools. Opinion in the National Society was divided. Though the majority view favoured acceptance of the clauses, G. A. Denison led a determined fight for exclusive clerical control in order to preserve high-church influence over as much education as possible. His alarm was increased by the growth of the secular education movement, seen in the formation of the National Public Schools Association, with radical and Dissenting support, at Manchester in October 1850.[114] But Denison was increasingly isolated. His attempt to resist compulsory operation of the management clauses was defeated in Church Unions and at the stormy annual meeting of the National Society in 1851.[115] The clergy, Denison said, had made a fatal mistake: they had 'transferred the charge of the school teaching of the children of the Church from themselves to a department of Government—a Government which has *no creed*'.[116]

High-church opposition to the Government was much more pronounced over the nomination of Professor R. D. Hampden to the see of Hereford in November 1847. The choice seemed almost a calculated Erastian challenge by Russell, in view of the uproar over Hampden in 1836. Anti-Hampden feeling had not disappeared. An attempt to remove the university restriction on him had failed in 1842, and he had sustained Tractarian revulsion by trying for two and a half years (unsuccessfully) to exclude the Tractarian R. G. Macmullen from the degree of B.D. 'It was hardly worth while to rekindle embers which had long ceased to burn,' said Charles Greville of Hampden's new appointment.[117] Burn the embers surely did, and, though they contained both evangelical and high-church elements, emitted more of a distinctively high-church glow than in 1836. Ashley, who had objected in 1836, now approved of the elevation of one who had, he said, recently written 'very beautiful and orthodox discourses'.[118] Similarly, the evangelical Bishop J. B. Sumner of Chester (who was elevated to Canterbury two months later) refused to sign an episcopal remonstrance against the appointment, organized by Phillpotts and sent to Russell; though his brother C. R. Sumner of Winchester, also having evangelical views, joined twelve other bishops in signing it.[119]

When the Government nominated a bishop, the dean and chapter of the

[114] For Denison's views see his letters to Gladstone, 19, 24 June, 28 Nov. 1847, 14 Feb. 1850 (Gladstone Papers, 44140, fos. 1–6, 14–15, 31–2); Denison to Russell, 12 July 1850 (L. Denison (ed.), *Fifty Years at East Brent* (London, 1902), 15–18). See also Chadwick, *Victorian Church*, i. 343–6.
[115] Marshall, op. cit. 580–624.
[116] Denison, *Notes of My Life*, 151 and ff.
[117] Greville to Clarendon, 16 Nov. 1847, 'private' (Clarendon Papers, c. 521).
[118] Diary, 13 Dec. 1847 (Hodder, *Shaftesbury*, ii. 232).
[119] J. B. Sumner to Samuel Wilberforce, 27 Nov. 1847 (Wilberforce Papers, d. 47, fos. 8–11).

diocese were legally required to elect him, officially on pain of *praemunire* —imprisonment for life and confiscation of their goods. The dean of Hereford, Dr. John Merewether, nevertheless voted against Hampden, and many electors stayed away. But a majority of the chapter voted in his favour. Thus was prevented a bitter legal confrontation between many churchmen and the Government in which the latter would have felt bound to enforce its authority.[120] The Court of Queen's Bench refused (by a legal hair's breadth) to compel the archbishop of Canterbury or his vice-general to hear the objections to Hampden; and the new bishop was consecrated (by the new archbishop, J. B. Sumner) in March 1848.[121]

Few high churchmen could regard the Hampden appointment with the cheerful equanimity of Edward Churton, archdeacon of Cleveland, a survivor of the Hackney Phalanx, who wrote: 'Even if Hampden is made a bishop, he will be better there [i.e. at Hereford] than at Oxford. The University will be delivered from a blockhead . . .'[122] Others saw the matter as a crucial Church–State issue. There was serious questioning of a system of episcopal appointments which produced such unacceptable ones as this. If the system were not reformed, wrote Archdeacon Robert Wilberforce, who later joined the Church of Rome, '. . . the sooner we cut the cord [i.e. leave the Church] the better'.[123] Gladstone deplored the fact that such appointments rested solely on the Prime Minister of the day, and wished that a 'substantial check' could be imposed on this power.[124] Russell, in reply to these opinions, was determined to uphold State authority. He refused to yield the supremacy which the Crown held by law. Moreover, he believed that Hampden's appointment would reinforce the Church's Protestant character, which was then so threatened by other tendencies.[125]

The opposition to Hampden was defeated, but the acrimony lived on. '. . . I have no doubt', wrote Clarendon, 'that [the Church's] ill-conditioned sons will enlarge their own error by implacable hostility to J[ohn] R[ussell]'.[126] There was still the occasional controversial appointment to stoke the boiler. In 1849 Henry Hart Milman, who twenty years before had published a scientific and secular *History of the Jews* which had caused his faith to be suspected, became dean of St. Paul's. In the same year another liberal cleric, Samuel Hinds, was appointed bishop of Norwich. 'The man

---

[120] Chadwick, *Victorian Church*, i. 241–3.

[121] Ibid. 245–8. For the changing attitudes of some of the bishops who had signed the remonstrance, especially Wilberforce, see A. R. Ashwell and R. G. Wilberforce, *Life of the Rt. Rev. Samuel Wilberforce* (3 vols., London, 1880–2), i. 442 ff.; D. Newsome, *The Parting of Friends: A Study of the Wilberforces and Henry Manning* (London, 1966), 337–40.

[122] Churton to A. P. Perceval, 18 Nov. 1847 (Churton Papers).

[123] Robert to Samuel Wilberforce, 31 Dec. 1847 (Wilberforce Papers, d. 11, fo. 107).

[124] Gladstone to Blomfield, 31 Jan. 1848 (Lathbury, i. 80–1).

[125] Russell's replies to opponents in the Hampden Case, printed in Anon., *What will the bishops do?* (London, 1847), 7–9. Cf. Hampden, *Memorials of Hampden*, 273–7.

[126] Clarendon to Sir G. C. Lewis (Clarendon Papers, c. 532).

I have heard most against . . . next to Hampden', said Russell, 'is Hinds. The Bishop of Oxford did all he could to raise a storm agst. him . . . This is the way in which bigots try to prevent liberal men from rising in the Church.'[127]

Thus Russell reaffirmed his desire to advance liberal churchmen. High churchmen, in parallel contrast, stressed their desire to bring greater independence to the Church. The demand grew for an active and legislating Convocation, which high churchmen saw as a possible means of expressing and enforcing their opinions. Since 1717 Convocation had only met with extreme brevity and bare formality. The Convocation of Canterbury met for worship at the opening of a new Parliament; a few days later it met again, for a maximum time of one day, when the upper house (consisting of bishops) drafted an address to the Crown, and the lower house (of clergy, some of whom were elected by other clergy) made slight amendments to the address as a vindication of independence. The recent demonstration of the much greater powers claimed by the General Assembly of the Church of Scotland had doubtless stimulated the demand for a more powerful Anglican assembly.

The outcry over Hampden's appointment coincided with the opening of a new Parliament and therefore with the meeting of Convocation. Anti-Hampden feeling initiated a serious campaign to give teeth to this assembly. The Church, it was hoped, would gain an official mouthpiece against unwelcome State appointments. On 24 November 1847 Convocation was attended by greater numbers than had been known for over a century. They debated the address for the entire period allowed (one day), and an amendment was carried requesting the Crown to revive convocational powers. It was proposed that the Queen should be petitioned to delay Hampden's *congé d'élire*, but this was defeated as being probably outside the purview of Convocation.[128] W. F. Hook said that if Jews were admitted to Parliament (which he favoured), objections to Parliament as a legislature for the Church would be increased, and the regulation of Church affairs by Convocation might be desirable.[129] Thus, further liberal concessions were desired by some, as a means to spurring the demand for Church independence.

The Convocation movement continued, and both Gladstone and the banker Henry Hoare were prominent in it. The two Houses of Parliament, said an address of 1848, were secular bodies which could not be regarded as substitutes for the deliberative assembly of the Church.[130] A *Plan for the Co-operation of Churchmen*, published early in 1848 by the conservative high churchman William Palmer, advocated, besides Church extension and a larger episcopate, the restoration of a Church legislature or a national

---

[127] Russell to Clarendon, 31 Mar. 1850 (ibid., Irish box 26).
[128] Chadwick, *Victorian Church*, i. 310–11.
[129] Hook to William Page Wood, 6 Dec. 1847 (Stephens, ii. 246–7); cf. Sweet, *Henry Hoare*, 50 f.
[130] Sweet, op. cit., 66–7.

synod.[131] At this time there also developed Church Unions, bodies of high
churchmen seeking defence against unpalatable State actions. The first
was the Bristol Church Union, founded on 9 January 1848 with G. A.
Denison as secretary. It was reported in August 1849 that similar Unions
had been formed 'at Gloucester, Liverpool, Plymouth, in Dorset, at Leam-
ington, Warwick, Kenilworth, Stockport, Huntingdon, Beverley, Chester,
Manchester, in Leicestershire and in London'.[132] In November 1850 a
Society for the revival of Convocation was formed. By no means only
Tractarians wanted the revival,[133] but Erastian evangelicals generally disliked the prospect, and the gradual progress of the Convocation movement
came about through the force of high-church objections to State control
and State policy.

As well as the demand for a revived Convocation well removed from
Parliament's control, there were also attempts to increase ecclesiastical
power within Parliament by building a Church defence party. The Rev.
Francis Merewether, a Leicestershire rector, brother of the anti-Hampden
dean of Hereford and a tireless pamphleteer in favour of Church interests
and privileges, wrote to a not wholly sympathetic Disraeli in September
1848. He had previously sent letters to eight M.P.s in his locality, suggesting
that a 'Church party' be formed in Parliament. These letters, dispatched in
the preceding May, had stated that the infringements made by legislation
of the preceding twenty years 'on the spiritual functions & legitimate constitution of the Church of England' had caused some staunch Anglicans to
entertain schism between Church and State. A party, Merewether urged,
was needed to work for greater harmony between legislation and Church
interests, and should comprise M.P.s who wished to alter the method of
episcopal appointments, to increase the episcopate and revive Church
synods.[134] He included, among current causes of friction between churchmen
and the Government, the 'management clauses' imposed on National
Society schools and the proposed Jewish relief.[135] Lord John Manners
warned Disraeli that Merewether was 'the greatest bore in Christendom'—
'if you don't see him he will weary you with letters; if you do, he will button
hole you, & spit in your face for a couple of hours'—but said that he was 'a
worthy, well meaning man' who could 'collect some forces together'. But,
said Manners, the division of ultra-Protestants from high churchmen would
prove an obstruction: 'The National Club calls itself the Church party, &
would insist on exclusive Protestantism being the basis of the party'.[136] By

---

[131] Ibid. 50 ff.   [132] Ibid. 62.

[133] Chadwick, *Victorian Church*, i. 313 and n.

[134] Merewether to Disraeli, 25 Sept. 1848 and encs. (Disraeli Papers, B/XXI/M 318 and 318 a,
b, c); also Merewether to Disraeli, 17 Oct., 2 Nov. 1848 (ibid. 319–20).

[135] F. Merewether, *A Letter to C. W. Packe, M.P., on the desirableness and necessity of a Church
Association in Parliament* (London, 1849), 37 ff.

[136] Manners to Disraeli, 24 Nov. 1848 (Disraeli Papers, B/XX/M/36).

December 1848, after 'a somewhat extensive correspondence', Merewether feared there was but slight prospect of a formal Church party, and later he wrote that Disraeli had convinced him that the construction of a formal party was impracticable and undesirable.[137]

Among the Church–State issues which concerned Merewether, Manners, and others was the case of the Madeira chaplaincy. The Rev. R. T. Lowe, Church of England chaplain in the Portuguese island of Madeira since 1833, annoyed his congregation of British residents by introducing practices of a suspiciously high-church tendency. After an unsuccessful request to Lowe in June 1845 that he abandon the practices, appeals were made by part of the congregation to the bishop of London (who customarily licensed foreign chaplains, and had licensed Lowe) that he would advise Lowe to conform with the complainants' liturgical wishes. It was said that many people had already begun to attend a Dissenting chapel in the island.[138] Blomfield sympathized with Lowe and refused to withdraw his licence. An appeal was then made to successive Foreign Secretaries, first to Aberdeen and then to Palmerston, who had appointed Lowe when previously holding the office. Neither Aberdeen nor Palmerston sympathized with Lowe, and Palmerston took issue with Blomfield. In June 1847 the Foreign Secretary said in Parliament that he had decided to withhold the Government portion of Lowe's stipend and to supersede him by another nominee.[139] In January 1848 Lowe was formally dismissed and another Government chaplain, the Rev. T. Kenworthy Brown, was sent out. The quarrel coincided with the Hampden upheaval and contributed to the conflict between high churchmen and Government control. Since Blomfield would not revoke Lowe's licence, Palmerston, with characteristic unilateral verve, informed the bishop that in future he would not trouble him 'to license Chaplains sent out to Foreign Stations'. In other words, proceeded Blomfield:

. . . he will withdraw from all Episcopal jurisdiction and controul [sic], all the Clergy of our Church who receive a part of their Salaries from the British Government. My license is certainly not required by Law in such cases, but it is contrary to the principles of Church government that Clergymen so circumstanced, should exercise their functions without license . . .[140]

A committee of Church defenders was formed in England to fight for Lowe.[141] 'You may safely conclude', wrote Manners to Disraeli, 'that the Church is disgusted with and opposed to the present Government. Now its influence and favour will in consequence be given to one section or other of

---

[137] Merewether to Disraeli, 17 Jan. 1850 (Disraeli Papers, B/XXI/M/322).

[138] *Correspondence between the Lord Bishop of London, the Chaplain and the Congregation of the British Church Establishment in Madeira* (London, 1846), 3 ff.

[139] Sweet, 10–11.

[140] Blomfield to Earl Nelson, 24 Jan. 1848 (Disraeli Papers, B/XX/M/23a).

[141] Sweet, 11.

the Tory party—make it your business to secure it for us.'[142] Manners held that Lowe was supported by most of the Anglican communicants in Madeira. Aided by a pamphlet written by Viscount Campden in Lowe's defence, Manners accused the Foreign Office of 'miserable tyranny' and of desiring 'to act as Bishop, or rather Pope, to all Chaplains abroad'.[143] 'It is quite clear', he wrote, 'that the most active and intellectual of the Clergy won't stand a Pope in Whitehall ... and if the Union of Church and State is to be maintained, there must be some guarantee against the despotism of the Minister.'[144] That Palmerston should be accused of papistical ambitions was highly ironical, in some ways at least; but Manners was thinking less of Palmerston's doctrinal views (or lack of them) than of the Erastian supremacy which he and his Government colleagues seemed to want. Manners desired Disraeli to obtain the political alliance of Gladstone and Roundell Palmer, and thus acquire some high-church Peelite intellect for his party. Manners greatly preferred such an alliance to one with firmly Protestant Peelites (such as Goulburn) which was 'so favoured by the Exeter Hall rump'.[145] But Gladstone and Palmer were generally anti-Protectionist, and the ultra-Protestant 'Exeter Hall rump' was, despite Manners's contempt, the mainstay of the Protectionist party. Disraeli's hands were therefore tied, and the threatened opposition to the Government on Church issues did not materialize. Soon Blomfield and Viscount Campden were advising that the Madeira matter should not be contested in Parliament, on the ground that Palmerston's behaviour, however reprehensible, was legally correct.[146] But proposals for anti-Government action continued to be made, and the affair troubled high churchmen for many months.[147] The matter was kept alive by Lowe's continuing his Madeira ministry in a hired chapel, supported by private subscribers.[148] An official and an unofficial Anglican chaplain thus competed in Madeira—an example of disruption in the Church of England, and one perhaps happily remote from English shores.

The chagrin of high churchmen culminated with the celebrated Gorham judgement. The importance of this case was swollen by the current tensions between high churchmen and the State; by the fact that a leading participant in the case was Bishop Phillpotts, doyen of many law-suits and surplice

---

[142] Manners to Disraeli, 19 Jan. 1848 (Disraeli Papers, B/XX/M/20).

[143] Manners to Disraeli, 19 Jan., 2, 3 Feb. 1848 (ibid. 20-2); Viscount Campden, *The British Chaplaincy in Madeira* (London, 1847). For an opposite view see Rev. T. Kenworthy Brown, *The Madeira Chaplaincy treated of . . . in a letter addressed to the Rev. R. T. Lowe* (London, 1848).

[144] Manners to Disraeli, 2 Feb. 1848 (Disraeli Papers, B/XX/M/22).

[145] Manners to Disraeli, 1 Feb. 1848 (ibid. 21).

[146] Manners to Disraeli, 7 Mar. 1848 (ibid. 26).

[147] Rev. R. Greswell to Gladstone, 17 July, 10 Aug. 1848 (Gladstone Papers, Add. MS. 44181, fos. 40-3); Stafford Northcote to Gladstone, 24 July 1848 (ibid. 44216, fos. 131-2).

[148] Manners to Disraeli, 7 Feb., 7 Mar. 1848 (Disraeli Papers, XX/M/24, 26). Cf. Rev. R. T. Lowe, *Protest against the ministrations in Madeira of the Rev. T. K. Brown, in opposition to episcopal authority and in violation of the laws and conditions of the Church of England* (Funchal, 1848).

riots and a relentless combatant for high-church opinions against liberalism and State encroachment; and by the anxiety of evangelicals and latitudinarians to vindicate their religious views against those of high churchmen. On 11 March 1848 Phillpotts declared, after a marathon examination of the Rev. G. C. Gorham, that he could not institute him to the parish of Brampford Speke, near Exeter—a living to which Gorham had been presented by the Whig Lord Chancellor in the preceding August.[149] Gorham held evangelical views on the efficacy of baptism. Evangelicals, with their stress on moral regeneration and conversion, argued that the description of the baptized infant in the Anglican prayer-book as 'regenerate' could mean only a conditional regeneration, a 'sign' which needed to be confirmed by the baptized individual's future acts and future faith. High churchmen, and more especially Tractarians, believed on the contrary that the sacrament as a divine instrument conferred unconditional regeneration (in the case of infants but not necessarily of adults).

The growth of theological controversy in the past fifteen years had hardened these different opinions. Pusey, for example, had presented in his monumental treatise the high-church view of baptism. This had made evangelicals all the more anxious to insist on the reverse view. The disagreement over whether Gorham was a heretic lay at the root of the case, but it was linked with other important problems. The question was posed, as it had been posed so momentously in Scotland, whether a patron might secure the institution of a presentee despite the objections made by ecclesiastical authority.[150] Moreover, could the linked questions of heresy and rightful institution be decided by a civil court, or even by a more ecclesiastical court which was none the less under the civil authority of the royal supremacy? Even a doctrinal judgement satisfactory to high churchmen might not reconcile them to civil authority over the Church if the judgement came from a civil court. Such a judgement might be considered valueless because not pronounced by an independent ecclesiastical court; and if this view were taken the royal supremacy would be fundamentally challenged. The doctrine and authority of the Church of England became matters of wide and searching debate. 'Were we together', wrote Gladstone to Manning, 'I should wish to converse with you from sunrise to sunset on the Gorham case. It is a stupendous issue . . .'[151]

In April 1848 Gorham issued a public letter complaining of Phillpotts's 'cruel exercise of episcopal power', and in June he requested the Court of Arches to compel Phillpotts to institute him. In August 1849 the Dean of Arches pronounced judgement against Gorham and in favour of regeneration in infant baptism. But Gorham appealed against the judgement to the

---

[149] For detailed accounts of the case see Chadwick, *Victorian Church*, i. 250 ff.; Davies, *Phillpotts*, 230 ff.; J. C. S. Nias, *Gorham and the Bishop of Exeter* (London, 1951).

[150] Chadwick, *Victorian Church*, i. 253–4.   [151] 30 Dec. 1849 (Lathbury, i. 96).

supreme court of appeal in ecclesiastical causes, the Judicial Committee of the Privy Council. This court consisted of laymen, and did not need to contain any lawyers trained in ecclesiastical law. Since the Church Discipline Act of 1840, however, bishops who were Privy Councillors had been invited to become members when an ecclesiastical case was heard. Though little questioned by churchmen when established in 1833, the court had, in the increasingly heated religious atmosphere since then, come under fire from high churchmen as a secular court judging cases which might concern doctrine. Phillpotts himself was among those who wished to reform the system.[152] In 1847 and 1848 Blomfield had introduced a bill to create a new court of appeal, but the bills had been suspended.[153] In February 1849 he had moved again to give a much stronger ecclesiastical content to the final court of appeal in cases of doctrine, blasphemy, or schism, but later he dropped this bill in favour of another.[154]

The Judicial Committee first met to consider Gorham's appeal on 11 December 1849. The members comprised two lay judges, the two archbishops, and Bishop Blomfield. The members' opinions were thought to weigh on Gorham's side, and high churchmen gloomily discussed the implications of the judgement before it was given.[155] After Blomfield had decided hesitantly for Phillpotts, Sir James Knight-Bruce (the Vice-Chancellor) strongly for Phillpotts, and all the others for Gorham, judgement was delivered on 9 March 1850. The court, it was stated, did not attempt to define doctrinal truth, but only whether a doctrine could be held consistently with the Articles and formularies of the Church of England. On the basis, it need not be held that baptism was invariably accompanied by regeneration, and Gorham's opinions were 'not contrary or repugnant to the declared doctrine of the Church of England ...' Therefore, to return to the muttons of the matter, he should be instituted to the parish of Brampford Speke.[156] After further attempted obstruction by Phillpotts, Gorham was at last inducted by commission on 10 August.

The judgement strengthened the faith of evangelicals and latitudinarians in the Church of England.[157] But to high churchmen the judgement was a painful crux, causing deep conscientious searching and momentous decisions. Some were uncertain whether they could remain in a Church which did not confine its teaching to the pure catholic faith and whose doctrinal decisions were made by a non-ecclesiastical court. There were diverse

---

[152] Phillpotts to Pusey, 20 Feb. 1850 (Pusey Papers).

[153] Blomfield, *Memoir of Blomfield*, ii. 127.

[154] Chadwick, *Victorian Church*, i. 258, 264–5.

[155] Liddon, op. cit. iii. 229; Lathbury, i. 86.

[156] Chadwick, *Victorian Church*, i. 259–61.

[157] *16th Annual Report*, Protestant Association, 12 May 1852 (London, 1852), 2: 'A decision of the Privy Council checked the progress of Tractarian Popery [and] re-asserted the principles of the Reformation ...'

high-church reactions, ranging from acquiescence and determined optimism to final decisions to embrace Roman Catholicism. Archdeacon Churton was 'quite content' with the judgement, for he believed that one in Phillpotts's favour would have caused popular clamour on Gorham's side, and 'the cause of Truth would have been in danger of being over-borne by the passions and prejudices of the multitude'.[158] Similarly, Samuel Wilberforce, though inclining to Phillpotts, thought that the court would have been unduly rigid to condemn Gorham's belief.[159] He supported Blomfield's attempt to give the bishops the power of finally judging appeals in doctrinal matters—an effort aimed at deterring schism and preventing the formation of a 'free episcopal Church'.[160] This scheme, introduced as a bill in the Lords and enthusiastically supported by Lord Stanley, was defeated on its second reading in June 1850 by 84 votes to 51.[161] Wilberforce, speaking in its favour, emphasized the concession which had been made to the Church of Scotland by Aberdeen's Benefices Act after the Disruption: 'If they would accord to the Church of England what they accorded to the Kirk of Scotland, she would be abundantly satisfied; but she did not ask so much.'[162] It is unlikely, however, in view of the differing theological views of the bishops, that such a measure would have been generally satisfactory to high churchmen. Given the prevailing divisions, a 'spiritual' appeal court would not have been enough; indeed the troubles might have worsened.

Blomfield's bill was certainly not enough for extreme and restless souls such as Manning and William Maskell (chaplain to Phillpotts).[163] There were demands for a public declaration, preferably by the bishops, on the doctrine of baptism. Such was the minimum demanded—failing the restoration of Convocation and a suitable Act of Parliament—by a series of resolutions signed on 19 March by fourteen persons, including Pusey, Keble, Manning, Robert Wilberforce, Henry Wilberforce, W. J. E. Bennett, and G. A. Denison.[164] But the bishops were far from taking any combined action which could satisfy high churchmen. Among them only Phillpotts and Richard Bagot, bishop of Bath and Wells—both of whom had been appointed bishops before the Whigs came into office in 1830—were at all extreme in their high churchmanship. Blomfield said that the two archbishops and probably sixteen bishops would not sign a declaration which was proposed, and that most of these objected to signing any declaration at all.[165] Bagot was the only bishop to attend vast high-church meetings

---

[158] Churton to Rev. W. Gresley, 26 Mar. 1850 (Churton Papers).
[159] Ashwell and Wilberforce, op. cit. ii. 40 ff.
[160] Blomfield, op. cit. ii. 125 ff.   [161] Hansard, cxi. 598–675.
[162] Ibid. 667.
[163] Chadwick, *Victorian Church*, i. 265; Liddon, iii. 256–7, 287.
[164] Liddon, iii. 240–1; Denison, *Notes of My Life*, 197–9.
[165] Blomfield to Bishop Wilberforce, 5 Apr. 1850, 'private' (Wilberforce Papers, d 34), also 15 May 1850 (ibid.).

in St. Martin's Hall and Freemasons' Hall, London, on 'The Day' (23 July), though Phillpotts wrote expressing warm approval. Bagot presented to these meetings a protest rejecting the Gorham judgement and asking for a spiritual appeal court and the right to synodical government of the Church.[166]

Apart from Bagot's example, Blomfield's judgement and bill, and Phillpotts's threat to withhold communion from Archbishop Sumner,[167] the more pointed protests came from outside the episcopate. From Pusey, Keble, and Gladstone rolled fulminations against the way in which the royal supremacy was being exercised. Pusey wrote *The Royal Supremacy not an arbitrary authority but limited by the laws of the Church . . .*; this claimed that 'twelve pious, unlettered communicants of our peasantry would have been more likely to give a sound judgement, than the members of the Privy Council.'[168] Such disasters as the Gorham decision must be prevented by returning to the principle that only the Church should decide ecclesiastical causes. This demand, Pusey held, was not incompatible with maintenance of the royal supremacy; it merely required the delegation of authority in such cases to the Church.[169]

Gladstone in his *Remarks on the Royal Supremacy* similarly indicted the existing law. He claimed that the royal supremacy was quite compatible with an appellate jurisdiction which would convey the sense of the Church in doctrinal questions, and saw the old Court of Delegates, with its ecclesiastical judges, as being far preferable to the Judicial Committee. In future years, however, Gladstone came to believe that a wholly civil court arriving studiously and impartially at ecclesiastical decisions (without the presence of disputatious clerics) would cause less doctrinal confusion and conflict than the existing tribunal.[170] Gladstone's dissatisfaction with the existing methods of State control over the Church made him more sensitive to the claims of others—Roman Catholics and Nonconformists—against the State. The Gorham judgement joined the series of milestones on his liberal progress.

Keble, in his *Trial of Doctrine* (written just before the judgement was pronounced) also preferred the Court of Delegates, as consisting of churchmen, to the Judicial Committee, most of whose members did not have to be churchmen or even Christians; he too held that submission to the royal supremacy was compatible with ecclesiastical judgement of doctrine.[171] He complained that Anglicans alone were denied the religious self-government of other Churches:

---

[166] Chadwick, *Victorian Church*, i. 267–8.   [167] Ibid. 263.

[168] E. B. Pusey, *The Royal Supremacy* . . . (Oxford, 1850), 172, 177–8, 195.

[169] Ibid. 196 ff.; Liddon, iii. 210–13, 257–8.

[170] W. E. Gladstone, *Remarks on the Royal Supremacy: a letter to the Bishop of London* (London, 1850), 6–7, 38 ff., 56, 67 ff.; M. D. Stephen, 'Gladstone and the composition of the Final Court in Ecclesiastical Causes, 1850–73', *Hist. Jl.* ix (1966), 191–200.

[171] Printed in J. Keble, *Church Matters in 1850* (Oxford, 1850), 2 ff., 12–13, 20–1.

... If it should appear that Establishment is, in our case, incompatible with [liberty], we earnestly implore that measures may be speedily taken for relieving us of such painful support ... we had rather be a Church in earnest separate from the State, than a counterfeit Church in professed union with the State.[172]

There was indeed talk of forming a 'Free Church of England', but no constructive purpose was shown.[173] Rome already offered an alternative to high-church Anglicans. Keble decided to remain in the Church of England and strive for internal reforms. But others, already more strongly drawn to Rome, were less inclined to patience. The restraint of some high churchmen helped to drive others from the Anglican communion. The Rev. William Dodsworth, in a published letter of 7 May 1850, called for a more complete denunciation of Gorham's baptismal doctrine than Pusey had given.[174] Pusey still looked ideally to conciliation, even with evangelicals, but Dodsworth and others were theologically beyond this, and only separated themselves far enough from the Gorham judgement by eventually joining the Roman Church. Several others—a minute but striking portion of the Church of England—acted likewise at different times, including William Maskell, Henry Wilberforce, T. W. Allies, and Viscount Feilding. The Romeward tendency of Manning and others (including Dodsworth and Viscount Campden) was completed when they were unable to agree with the opposition to a restored Roman Catholic hierarchy the following winter.[175]

Faced with these worrying secessions, G. A. Denison advised William Palmer to draft a declaration of fidelity to the Church of England, for loyal high churchmen to sign.[176] Palmer, who was more anti-Roman than Denison, produced a strong declaration of refusal to join the Roman Church until it had reformed itself. But Pusey believed this would only provoke further secession: 'Loose not one single band which, however tremblingly, holds one single heart; keep, if you can, every one who still clings to his mother ...'[177] He first won Keble to his view, then easily defeated Palmer's declaration at a Bristol Church Union meeting on 1 October 1850; at a meeting of the London Church Union on 15 October the 'anti-Roman declaration' was withdrawn without being put to a vote.[178]

The Gorham judgement spurred the demand for government of the Church by the Church. Most high churchmen who remained in the English Church wanted the revival of Convocation and diocesan synods. On the

---

[172] Ibid. 12–13.
[173] Duke of Buccleuch to Aberdeen, 5 Oct. (?) 1850 (Aberdeen Papers, Add. MS. 43201, fo. 51); G. A. Denison to Oswald Jackson, 8 Nov. 1850 (L. Denison, op. cit. 22); Marshall, 610.
[174] W. Dodsworth, *A Letter to the Rev. E. B. Pusey* ... (London, 1850), 6–18.
[175] Newsome, op. cit. 366.
[176] Denison to Palmer, 2 Sept., 26 Oct. 1850 (L. Denison, 19–21).
[177] Quoted Greenfield, 'The Attitude of the Tractarians to the Roman Catholic Church', 551.
[178] Liddon, iii. 274–85; Greenfield, op. cit. 539–52; *Guardian*, 9, 16 Oct. 1850, p. 714 ff.

other hand, Erastian evangelicals such as Hugh McNeile wished to keep ecclesiastical judgements in the hands of the temporal power, so as to avoid as far as possible the danger of high-church decisions.[179] Keble had suggested before the judgement that, assuming an unfavourable verdict, Phillpotts should summon a diocesan synod which should 'set forth the true doctrine'. In June 1851 an Exeter diocesan synod was held, and unanimously adopted a declaration on baptismal regeneration which Phillpotts had circulated.[180] By this time, State rebuttal of 'papal aggression' had supplemented the effect of the Gorham judgement by stimulating the movement for an active Convocation and other Church assemblies. Phillpotts disliked the 'Papal Aggression' but probably disliked State interference with religion even more.

The Gorham judgement had joined previous alarms to produce a struggle between high churchmen and Erastians for the direction of the Church of England. If high churchmen had reacted particularly strongly to the Government because it was Whig and therefore inherently suspect, the ministers themselves reacted to high churchmen because they themselves were Whigs, Erastians, and latitudinarians. Russell held particularly fervently to such opinions. But the anti-Gorham reaction initially found him moderate. He was anxious to preserve Church unity, but also believed that high-church reforms were to be avoided since they might cause more conflict than they would resolve. On being informed by Archbishop Sumner of Blomfield's plan for an episcopal court to judge doctrinal cases, he said that such a court would be 'more intent on theology than on law and liberty';[181] and Blomfield's bill was opposed in the Upper House by Lord Lansdowne, Lord President of the Council, who represented the Government. The bill, said Lansdowne, would rob the Privy Council of some of its judicial power, and challenged the Crown's ancient prerogative to govern the Church. He did suggest that bishops who were Privy Councillors should sit de jure when the Judicial Committee was considering doctrinal cases, and not merely by invitation; also that non-Anglican members of the Council should not sit to consider such cases. But Lord Redesdale said that Gorham might be the next bishop—a lightning objection not only to Lansdowne's speech but also, in fact, to Blomfield's bill.[182]

Although Russell was patient at first, the continuance of high-church agitation irritated him. In July came the great London protest meetings, and objections by Manning and others to the royal supremacy; in October the anti-Roman declaration was rejected by Church Unions. Could Russell remain unperturbed and concessionary when the underlying Erastian conditions of Whig toleration were being sorely tried? The question was

---

[179] *The Royal Supremacy discussed in a correspondence between Archdeacon [Robert] Wilberforce and the Rev. Hugh McNeile* (London, 1850), 6–44.

[180] Keble to Pusey, 24 Feb. 1850 (Liddon, iii. 226); Davies, op. cit. 278–86.

[181] Quoted Walpole, *Russell*, ii. 117. See also Prest, 321.

[182] Hansard, cxi. 620–8, 642.

similar to Scottish Non-Intrusion, and had even less political force behind it. The Premier made it clear that there would be no yielding. On 30 September he wrote to Clarendon that 'some good work separating Tractarianism from Protestantism & treating Tractarianism as the Romish Church in disguise, is much wanted'.[183] On 13 October he suggested that a committee of 25 clergymen might be set up in order to maintain Reformation principles in the Church.[184] In reply to a suggestion from Brougham that legal concessions should be made to the Tractarians in order to avert secession to Rome, Russell bluntly wrote on 9 October: 'if [the Church] can only remain Protestant at the cost of their secession, I shall be ready for one to pay the price. Like Arnold I prefer the Roman Catholic foe to the Tractarian spy.'[185]

On the day after the last of these letters, 14 October, *The Times* drew attention to a papal brief establishing a Catholic archbishop in England. On 29 October the new Cardinal-Archbishop Wiseman's rash and inflammatory pastoral 'from the Flaminian gate' appeared in the Press. The 'Papal Aggression' was on England, and many anti-Catholics happily linked it to the chain of high-church agitation since the Gorham judgement. Hugh McNeile thus concluded a literary argument with Robert Wilberforce over the royal supremacy: 'The country, disgusted by masked Romanising, starts into simultaneous activity against unmasked Romanism'.[186] Russell, however, was at first restrained, perhaps unusually so. He did not rush out a public denunciation of the Pope's deed, for his protesting Durham Letter —so called because it was dispatched to the receptive Whig Bishop Maltby of Durham—was not written until 4 November, three weeks after the brief was publicized.[187] The Durham Letter was only published on 7 November, so clearly had not been held back in order to stimulate the Guy Fawkes celebrations. But these were ardent enough without any such encouragement. Pope Pius, Archbishop Wiseman, and some of the other new bishops were treated as guys for burning—though this and other demonstrations occasionally showed hilarity as well as hostility, a sign perhaps that this was not the sixteenth century after all.[188] This was the peak of public hostility which had been roaring for three weeks, stoked by *The Times*, Bishop Blomfield, and the impetuous words of Wiseman and Newman.[189] Tractarians were attacked as well as Papists. The Rev. W. J. E. Bennett, whose uses of ritual had long been impugned (and had perhaps helped to make Lord John Russell, a member of his congregation, more anti-Tractarian), attracted

---

[183] Clarendon Papers, Irish box 26.

[184] Russell to Clarendon, 13 Oct. 1850 (ibid.); Prest, 321.

[185] Brougham to Russell, 30 Sept. 1850 (Russell Papers, 8E); Russell to Brougham, 9 Oct. 1850 (quoted Prest, 321).

[186] *The Royal Supremacy discussed* . . ., op. cit. 44.

[187] On 2 November Russell had written to Palmerston that the Government should not proceed in a hurry but should seek an explanation from the Pope (Prest, 321). Cf. Conacher, 76–7.

[188] Chadwick, *Victorian Church*, i. 294–5.

[189] Ibid. 292–4.

hostile crowds to services in his new church, St. Barnabas, Pimlico, during November.[190]

Russell's Durham Letter—a pondered missive from the leader of a Liberal Government and not the hasty screed of a compulsive anti-Papist—was intended to exploit this feeling for the sake of much-needed popularity and political support. It was saved, however, from being purely an act of political calculation by the sincerity of Russell's anti-Tractarian and anti-Catholic religious views.

Given Russell's dislike of Tractarians, their prominence in the letter was not surprising. The Tractarian tendency to produce secessions to Rome was condemned in the reference to 'clergymen of our own Church, who have subscribed the Thirty-Nine Articles and acknowledged ... the Queen's supremacy, [and] have been most forward in leading their flocks [quoting Blomfield] "step by step to the very verge of the precipice"'. Russell seemed more alarmed by this than by the immediate cause of the letter, the formation of the Roman hierarchy: 'What then is to be apprehended from a foreign prince of no great power compared to the danger within the gates from the unworthy sons of the Church of England herself?'[191] By stressing the role of Tractarians as instruments of Romanization, whose possible effects were displayed in the establishment of Catholic bishops with territorial titles, Russell hoped to gain wide support for his anti-Tractarian schemes. The new hierarchy was, to him, a godsend; it enabled him to appear as the country's saviour from Tractarian danger.[192]

Yet the Durham Letter indicated that, if legislative proceedings followed, they would be directed against the Roman Catholic titles and not against Tractarians. The Prime Minister would not have threatened the Catholic Church (including its Irish members) merely to discourage Tractarians—a desire which could have been more easily realized. He was moved to punish not only Tractarians but Roman Catholics, and his new attitude to Catholics was a strong paradoxical element in the curious policy he espoused.

V. RUSSELL AND THE POPE, 1846–1850

Thus far in his life Russell had helped to make concessions to Catholics in accordance with his liberal political creed. He had supported Catholic emancipation and the Maynooth Bill. He had moved the second reading of the Religious Opinions Relief Bill in 1846, saying that it would 'get rid of ... much absurd legislation'.[193] In even sharper contrast to his later policy, he had said of the clause in the 1829 Relief Act which prohibited Catholic bishops and deans from taking titles held by bishops of the established

---

[190] F. Bennett, *The Story of W. J. E. Bennett* (London, 1909), 97 ff.

[191] Durham Letter printed in Norman, *Anti-Catholicism in Victorian England*, 159–61, and in Prest, 429–30.

[192] Cf. Russell to Clarendon, 27 Nov. 1850 (Clarendon Papers, Irish box 26).

[193] Hansard, lxxxviii. 363.

Church, that 'he could not conceive any good ground for the continuance of this restriction'.[194] These statements were made before he became Premier and had to steer a precarious Government away from dangerous topics. He had not supported Catholic Relief Bills after 1846, and these bills had failed.[195] On the other hand, Government grants were made to Catholic schools in 1848 and an extra grant to Maynooth in June 1850; Irish Catholic bishops were allowed to use the titles of their sees, and Catholic bishops in the colonies were addressed in their titular form.[196] The Premier had clearly been far less sensitive to Catholic titles than he suddenly became in the autumn of 1850. His opponents—Conservative, Catholic, or Tractarian— accused him of having encouraged the introduction of the hierarchy by his previous liberality.[197] Extracts from Russell's earlier speeches were circulated among Catholic clergy in November 1850 as a means of defending the new hierarchy.[198] Moreover, Russell was not simply enforcing an old restriction but initiating a new one. The restrictive clause on titles in the 1829 Act had applied only to the assumption of titles held by Protestants. The new titles carefully avoided this hazard, for they were restricted to places where there were no Protestant bishops. New preventive legislation was therefore required.

The change in Russell's attitude is largely explained by his failure to achieve satisfactory relations with the papacy. The change was partly a disappointed reaction, partly a tougher attempt (unsuccessful, as it turned out) to persuade the Pope to accede to Government wishes in the appointment of bishops and in other matters.[199] Ministers had believed that a compact with the Pope would strengthen their hold on Ireland. In 1846 the accession of a liberal Pope coincided with that of a Liberal British Government, and Russell had high hopes of an understanding. After some promising early contacts, the earl of Minto, Russell's father-in-law and Lord Privy Seal, was sent to Italy in September 1847 at the suggestion of Wiseman,[200] and was hopefully armed with *quid pro quos*. In return for helping Pius IX by restraining radicalism and promoting a 'concert of Sovereigns & people' in Italy,[201] the Government wanted papal co-operation in quietening Ireland. This became more necessary when Pius, in October 1847, issued a

[194] 9 July 1845 (ibid. lxxxii. 290).

[195] For the unsuccessful attempts to remove penalties after 1846, see ibid. xc. 451 ff.; xci. 753–810; xcv. 800–45; xcvi. 701–57; xcvii. 314–31; xcix. 134–70, 1291–1305; cii. 370–3.

[196] Ibid. cxiv. 233; xcv. 816; *Quarterly Review*, lxxxviii (1850–1), 254 ff.

[197] e.g. J. M. Gresley, *The Real Occasion of the 'Papal Aggression'* (London, 1850).

[198] Rev. Edgar Estcourt to W. B. Ullathorne, R.C. bishop of Birmingham, 12 Nov. 1850 (Wiseman Papers, W3/28 (1850), 69).

[199] See Prest, 330; J. B. Conacher, 'The Politics of the "Papal Aggression" Crisis, 1850–1', *Canadian Catholic Historical Association Report* (1959), 17, 19–20.

[200] Palmerston to Russell, 21 Aug. 1847 (Gooch, *Russell*, i. 308); W. Ward, *Cardinal Wiseman*, i. 479 ff., 571–7.

[201] MS. 'Notes on Italy and Sicily', n.d. (Minto Papers, 130/2).

rescript against the undenominational Queen's Colleges, which the Russell ministry had inherited as an act of policy from Peel. The rescript, complained Palmerston, 'was little to be expected at the hands of the Pope at the very moment that we were stepping out of our way to be of use to him'.[202] Minto's task was to induce the Pope to withdraw his condemnation of the Colleges and to discourage the involvement of Irish clergy in political movements.[203]

Minto apparently enjoyed good personal relations with Pius,[204] but received little satisfaction in his mission. The Pope was relinquishing his alliance with the Italian liberals, and the presence of the outspokenly liberal British minister was an embarrassment.[205] On the Irish question the Pope was more liberal, the British Government less. On this question Pius could perceive little need to meet the British Government's wishes, for it seemed that a traditionally liberal Government could scarcely persecute the Irish Catholics. Minto, in fact, had insufficient bargaining material.[206] The Pope's impression was heightened by the counter-propaganda of militant Irishmen such as Archbishop MacHale.[207] In consequence, only the mildest of papal warnings was given to the Irish priests not to meddle in worldly politics, and the Pope repeated his condemnation of the colleges instead of withdrawing it. Minto left Italy in April 1848 practically empty-handed, and the Government had to answer a series of embarrassing parliamentary questions about the mission.[208] Minto's task of quietening the Italian nationalists was also unsuccessful, which was not surprising in one who had attended the opera with liberals and allegedly called out from a balcony 'viva l' IndepBndenza dell Italia' in a North British accent.[209]

Russell's Government would have had greater bargaining power in negotiating with the Pope if it had been fully aware that plans for a Catholic hierarchy in Engand and Wales had been drawn up. The subject of a hierarchy had been under discussion for many years both in England and at Rome. Support for a hierarchy had been growing in England, fed by the confidence and administrative needs springing from a rapidly expanding Catholic population, the result especially of Irish immigration. Catholics in England and Wales have been estimated at about 80,000 in 1770.[210]

---

[202] Palmerston to Minto, 29 Oct. 1847 (E. Ashley, *The Life of H. J. Temple, Viscount Palmerston, 1846–65* (2 vols., London, 1876), i. 39–40).

[203] 'Notes on our Relations with the Pope', in Russell's hand, n.d. (Minto Papers, 127); Palmerston to Clarendon, 13, 18 Nov. 1847 (Clarendon Papers, c. 524).

[204] Machin, 'Lord John Russell . . .', 286.   [205] W. Ward, op. cit. i. 485–6.

[206] Southgate, *The Passing of the Whigs*, 190.

[207] Nowlan, *The Politics of Repeal*, 177–8; B. O'Reilly, *John MacHale, Archbishop of Tuam—his Life, Times and Correspondence* (2 vols., New York, 1890), ii. 116 ff.

[208] Hansard, xcv. 1052 ff.; xcvi. 728–41; xcvii. 1143–4.

[209] Palmerston to Minto, 15 Aug. 1848 (Minto Papers, 130/1); Hansard, xcv. 1056, 1061. Cf. Minto to Ralph Abercromby, 10 Nov. 1847 (Minto Papers, 127).

[210] J. Bossy, *The English Catholic Community, 1570–1850* (London, 1975), 185. Cf. T. G. Holt, 'A Note on some Eighteenth Century Statistics', *Recusant History*, x (1969–70), 4–5.

There were over 400,000 in 1837,[211] and the number of vicars-apostolic (Catholic bishops, having regional supervision but not territorial titles) was doubled to eight in 1840. An estimate of 679,067 has been given for 1851.[212] The Catholic increase was even greater in Scotland, on account of higher proportional Irish immigration.[213] But Scottish anti-Catholicism was currently even more militant than English, and no Scottish hierarchy was as yet attempted. Both vicars-apostolic and priests saw benefits in the establishment of a regular canonical organization. The vicars-apostolic wanted more independence from the Roman Propaganda, the priests wanted more independence from the vicars-apostolic—security of tenure for themselves, and the institution of chapters to advise on episcopal appointments.[214] Tractarian converts, with typical enthusiasm for their new faith, were anxious for a hierarchy, being ready to initiate and expand where cautious hereditary Catholics hung back. Wiseman mirrored the zeal of the converts and pressed the need for a hierarchy on the Papal Curia.

The Pope had sanctioned a plan for a hierarchy (an archbishop at Westminster and seven bishops) in October 1847; and this scheme, later to be altered, was printed on 1 November, a few days before the Pope saw Minto. Pius was said (though perhaps not reliably) to have told Wiseman later that he 'spoke of [the plan] at the time to Lord Minto, and I understood that the English Government would not oppose the execution of my design'.[215] Minto denied that he had read a document on this subject or that he had suspected any design beyond the single nomination of an archbishop of Westminster. He admitted, it seems, that a paper was pointed out to him (in the Pope's presence), but that he had not thought it worthy of attention.[216] During the outcry over 'Papal Aggression' in 1850–1 it was important to the Government to uphold this denial, in order to emphasize that the announcement of the hierarchy was not expected. Supporters of the hierarchy, on the other hand, said not only that the plan had been shown to Minto but that he had passed on the details to Russell.[217] Ironically, the interests of the

[211] P. Hughes, 'The English Catholics in 1850', in G. A. Beck (ed.), *The English Catholics, 1850–1950* (London, 1950), 45.

[212] Ibid.

[213] Handley, *The Irish in Scotland*, 43 ff., 197–8, and J. E. Handley, 'Scotland', in P. J. Corish (ed.), *A History of Irish Catholicism*, vi (Dublin, 1968), 7–12.

[214] W. B. Ullathorne, *History of the Restoration of the Catholic Hierarchy in England* (London, 1871), 2–5, 20; R. J. Schiefen, 'The Organization and Administration of Roman Catholic Dioceses in England and Wales in the Mid-Nineteenth Century' (unpubl. Univ. of London Ph.D. thesis 1970), 15–17, 47 ff.; Hansard, cxv. 432–3 (speech of W. Fagan).

[215] B. Ward, *The Sequel to Catholic Emancipation*, ii. 207–8.

[216] Minto to Russell, 21 Nov. 1850 (Gooch, *Correspondence of Russell*, ii. 53–4); Lady Anna Maria Donkin to Minto, 2 Dec. 1850 (Minto Papers, 133); Minto to Abbé Hamilton, 14 Dec. 1850, copy (Russell Papers, 8G, fo. 60). Cf. Hansard, cxiv. 155–6 (speech of Minto).

[217] Wiseman to Russell, 4 Nov. 1850 (Gooch, ii. 49–50). Cf. K. O'Meara, *Thomas Grant, first Bishop of Southwark* (2nd edn., London, 1886), 75; B. Fothergill, *Nicholas Wiseman* (London, 1963), 146, 166–7; G. Albion, 'The Restoration of the Hierarchy, 1850', in G. A. Beck, op. cit. 89.

British Government might have been better served if Minto had paid more attention to the plan and informed Russell of its contents. The advisability of obtaining their agreement to a scheme of which they had been notified would have strengthened ministers in their negotiations with the Pope over Ireland. As it was, Russell cannot have been ignorant of the unpublished plan's existence, for word of it reached the columns of the *Tablet* and was frequently mentioned and criticized in Parliament.[218] But he seems to have had no official information, and in any case the implementation of the scheme was prevented by Catholic uncertainty.[219] Discussion of the plan was resumed when Bishop Ullathorne, vicar-apostolic of the Western District, went to Rome in May 1848. In July it was decided to establish 12 sees instead of 8. But political events intervened to change the whole situation.

In 1848 both Catholic and ministerial aims might have been realized on the basis of Government acceptance of a Catholic hierarchy and papal assistance in Russell's Irish policy. This possibility might have been stronger if the Government had succeeded in its design to open official diplomatic relations with Rome, which had been forbidden since the sixteenth century. A bill for this purpose was introduced by Lansdowne in the Lords in February 1848. The bill passed its second reading, but the Protectionist earl of Eglintoun moved an amendment in Committee that no ambassador from Rome should be an ecclesiastic, in order to ensure that a papal embassy in London would not be 'a nucleus for the Jesuits'.[220] He was supported by Aberdeen and Stanley, the Peelite and Protectionist leaders in the House, and the amendment was carried by a majority of 3.[221] The bill then passed the Lords, but Minto's departure from Rome robbed the measure of its urgency, and there was a long delay before it was presented in the Commons. Palmerston introduced the second reading there in August, characteristically remarking that, if we enjoyed diplomatic relations with Rome, our communications with India could pass through the Papal States when railways were built.[222] Both ultra-Protestants and Catholics opposed the bill, the *Tablet* saying that it would enable ministers to subordinate the Catholic Church in Ireland.

The bill passed easily, but failed nevertheless, for the Pope would not send an ambassador on the terms of the Eglintoun clause. Had the attempt succeeded it might have smoothed the restoration of the hierarchy which many Catholics wanted and perhaps have assisted the Irish policy which many Catholics disliked. In the event, however, relations had deteriorated. Russell must have been losing his hopes in the Pope, and the postponement

---

[218] B. Ward, op. cit. ii. 207–9; Hansard, xcvi. 707, 719; ci. 212, 229, 512.
[219] On the reasons for delay see Chadwick, *Victorian Church*, i. 286–7.
[220] Hansard, xcvi. 285. Cf. Grenville to Clarendon, 10, 19 and 24 Feb. 1848 (Clarendon Papers, c. 521); Palmerston to Clarendon, 9, 18 Mar. 1848 (ibid. c. 524).
[221] Hansard, xcvi. 878 ff., 891.   [222] Ibid. ci. 203–4.

of further developments by political upheaval did nothing to restore his optimism.

Revolution in Rome caused the Pope to flee in November 1848. A republic was later proclaimed, but was overcome by French forces in July 1849. When Pius eventually returned to Rome in April 1850 he had lost his former liberalism and rested on the support of France, whose foreign policies were strongly suspected by Britain. The appointment of a firm Ultramontane, Paul Cullen, as archbishop of Armagh and Primate of Ireland, seemed to indicate a more rigid papal attitude: '... we have a Devil incarnate here', wrote Clarendon, the Lord Lieutenant, 'in the shape of a new R. C. Primate sent over by the Pope in revenge for the Eglintoun Clause & the Palmerstonian policy in Italy . . .'[223] In fact Cullen later antagonized extreme nationalists by his moderation, but his policy in 1850, in conjunction with the issue of another rescript from Rome against the Queen's Colleges, seemed to display papal intransigence. The Synod of Thurles, summoned by Cullen in August, annoyed the Government by opposing its educational policy. The Synod concluded with the issue of an address on 9 September by the archbishops and bishops (adopted, however, by only a very narrow majority and encountering considerable opposition among Irish Catholics), condemning 'the propagation of error through godless systems of education'.[224] The Whigs disliked this Ultramontane recrudescence. Palmerston had written a year previously that 'the Pope is a Donkey & his drivers are mules', and that 'it would be hard to say who or what will mend him, or rather the Cardinals who govern him, but at present he is reestablishing the Inquisition of the middle ages'.[225] Russell condemned the episcopal address at the Synod of Thurles as clerical interference with State policy[226]—a criticism which he developed when opposing the Catholic hierarchy.

Worsening relations between ministers and the Catholic Church formed an unpromising background for a restored hierarchy. The Pope, as reported in a conversation with Wiseman, apparently thought that the British Government was as friendly in 1850 as in 1847.[227] If he did believe this, he showed scant appreciation of recent circumstances and indeed of the whole complex nature of Whig attitudes to religious questions. He now essayed a forward policy while offering ministers no inducement to acquiesce in it. The continuous liberal policies of British Governments may have concealed from Roman eyes the fact that Erastian control was still a firm underlying principle of both Whig and Tory Ministers. Under the pressure of clerical demands and assertions, the Whigs were caught between liberal and Erastian tendencies. If the pressure were great enough, Erastianism would gain the edge.

[223] Clarendon to Sir G. C. Lewis, 18 June 1850 (Clarendon Papers, c. 532).
[224] P. MacSuibhne, *Paul Cullen and his Contemporaries* (3 vols., Naas, 1961–5), ii. 57.
[225] Palmerston to Clarendon, 25 Aug., 2 Sept. 1849 (Clarendon Papers, c. 524).
[226] Hansard, cxiv. 189–92.   [227] B. Ward, ii. 284–5.

This dilemma was forcefully posed in 1850 when the restoration of the hierarchy was announced. Whig sensitivity to encroachment on civil authority, aggravated by the attitudes of high churchmen in England and Catholics in Ireland, was compounded by Russell's fierce personal Protestantism.[228] On the other hand, it is doubtful whether the Government reaction would have been so strong if increased public support had not been sorely needed.

During the late summer of 1850 Russell was still hoping to re-establish good relations with the papacy. Wiseman, when leaving England in August to receive a cardinal's hat, was asked unofficially to present the Government's view to the Pope, and allegedly gathered from his interview with Russell that ministers would not oppose a hierarchy.[229] On 20 September Russell wrote that he hoped to send another special envoy to Rome in the person of R. L. Sheil, a former Irish Repealer who had since been Master of the Mint. The Premier remained inclined to conciliation until 14 October, the day on which the papal brief restoring the hierarchy was mentioned in the English Press. On 13 October he expressed disagreement with Minto's view that, if the Pope interfered in British affairs, he should be regarded as hostile to our interests: 'I [Russell] am quite against going this length, even in conversation'.[230] It was in this letter that he suggested forming a committee of clergymen to uphold Protestant principles in the Church of England, thus showing that hostility to the Tractarians rather than the Pope was still uppermost in his mind.[231]

After the brief was published, however, he must have been as annoyed with the Pope as with Tractarians. The restored hierarchy proclaimed a Roman confidence which Tractarianism had helped to build up. The restoration, which the papacy had hoped to slip quietly into a supposedly unhindered stream of liberal concession, was met not only by popular opposition but by that of the Government. Russell was probably alarmed that the new hierarchy was led by Wiseman, who had preached a celebrated sermon against the Gorham judgement and seemed to embody the connection between Tractarians and Rome which the Premier so much feared.[232] Moreover, the hierarchy was announced without any supplication for the Crown's agreement, and even without prior notification. This omission, which Russell described in Parliament as an intolerable insult,[233] was naturally wounding to Erastian Whigs—more so than the actual provisions of the scheme. The State's authority was being ignored by a Church which owed

---

[228] Cf. Southgate, op. cit. 191.

[229] W. Ward, *Life and Times of Wiseman*, i. 524–5; ii. 31.

[230] Russell to Clarendon, 13 Oct. 1850 (Clarendon Papers, Irish box 26).

[231] See above, p. 209.

[232] W. Ward, op. cit. i. 519–20; Thomas Grant to Wiseman, 20 May, 2 July 1850 (Wiseman Papers, 137/15).

[233] 7 Feb. 1851 (Hansard, cxiv. 192–3).

toleration and concession to State magnanimity. British toleration had come to a crisis: it would either go forward in spite of the provocation of the hierarchy or it would recede on account of it. The issue was potentially a wide one involving other Churches beside the Roman Catholic, and affected the whole question of State treatment of religious groups.

The Durham Letter announced that toleration was not unlimited. It said that 'the present state of the law shall be carefully examined, and the propriety of adopting any proceedings with reference to the recent assumption of power, deliberately considered'.[234] The danger from Tractarians, said the letter, was greater than 'any aggression of a foreign sovereign', but it was against Roman Catholics and not Tractarians that legislation was to be 'deliberately considered'. The Pope and the Irish prelates were to be punished for their recalcitrance, and their future co-operation perhaps obtained through severity. This intention had been strengthened by Wiseman's unnecessarily grandiloquent pastoral, containing the assertion that, as archbishop of Westminster, '... we govern and shall continue to govern the counties of Middlesex, Hertford and Essex as ordinary thereof, and those of Surrey, Sussex, Kent, Berkshire, and Hampshire, with the islands annexed, as administrator with ordinary jurisdiction'.[235] The Durham Letter seized on the literal sense of these words and used them for its own purpose, in protesting against 'a pretension of supremacy over the realm of England, and a claim to sole and undivided sway, which is inconsistent with the Queen's supremacy ... and with the spiritual independence of the nation'.[236] Wiseman's *Appeal to the Reason and Good Feeling of the English People*, issued on 11 November immediately after his return to England, was an attempt to moderate the impression produced by his pastoral. But it was too equivocal to calm matters, and came too late to have much influence, except among those who were already disposed to accept the hierarchy.

Tractarians and the Pope had affronted the political and ecclesiastical assumptions of Whiggery. But it is doubtful whether Russell would have interrupted a lifetime of liberalism for this reason alone. More positive and immediate political reasons were involved. The Premier seized on anti-papal legislation in an attempt to gain strength and popularity for a Government which had neither. The support of Conservatives in Parliament, and of anti-Catholic opinion outside it, was to be sought in order to strengthen the Government. Indeed, it was important for the Government to act before the Conservatives announced any intention to do so. But the search for immediate gains on this basis was at odds with the liberal tradition, and such gains might be only temporary and illusory. The Cabinet was clearly conscious of this prospect. Some of its members were unwilling to be led by

[234] Norman, *Anti-Catholicism in Victorian England*, 160.

[235] G. M. Young and W. D. Handcock (eds.), *English Historical Documents*, xii. 1, 1833–74 (London, 1956), 365–6.

[236] Norman, op. cit. 159–60.

Russell, especially as he had not consulted them before sending the Durham Letter. The decision to bring in new legislation was reached only narrowly on 13 December,[237] and thus there was a lack of confidence in the policy from the start.

The bill proposed to extend the fine of £100—imposed in 1829 on the assumption of titles duplicating those of the United Church of England and Ireland—to the assumption of any territorial title in the United Kingdom by clerics outside the established Churches. Clergy of the Scottish Episcopal Church were declared exempt by a clause inserted later, to the displeasure of Prince Albert among others. The second clause declared that the professional acts and writings of any cleric taking an illegal title were to be null and void. The third clause was more penal than the first, for it ordered that endowments bestowed on persons taking forbidden titles should be forfeited to the Crown. But the bill was considerably modified before it passed.

VI. REACTIONS TO 'PAPAL AGGRESSION'; PASSAGE OF THE ECCLESIASTICAL TITLES BILL, 1851

Russell, who had already observed public reaction before writing his Durham Letter, could justifiably claim public support for his bill. There were of course many Protestants who rejected the anti-Catholic onslaught.[238] But no-Popery feeling was no weaker than in 1829 or 1845, and (on account of the coincidence of 5 November, and the effects of Irish immigration) was more dramatically and riotously expressed. The difference between 1850 and previous anti-Catholic upheavals was that the Government now joined the crowd.

Warnings which had been long delivered by the Protestant Association were taken up in popular protest under the pointed impact of the hierarchy. Many county meetings were held (and gatherings in countless towns and villages) to proclaim outrage at the Pope's deed.[239] At the Devon county meeting in December an anti-Tractarian address 'was moved amidst loud applause by Parson Gorham, [and] carried by acclamation',[240] and the meeting broke up with 'three Groans for the Bishop of Exeter'.[241] No doubt the blind, automatic no-Popery of the ages contributed much to this hostility. But deeper and more religious objections were also in evidence. Bishop Hampden wrote: 'What a glorious letter that is of Lord John Russell's! Tractarianism has never had such a blow yet;'[242] and Ashley said the letter

---

[237] Prest, *Russell*, 322–3.
[238] Norman, 71; *Scotsman*, 16 Nov. 1850 (quoted Handley, op. cit. 251–2); J. Templer to Wiseman, 14 Nov. 1850 (Wiseman Papers, W3/28 (1850), 109).
[239] See *The Times*, Nov. and Dec. 1850, *passim*. But cf. speech of Philip Howard, a Catholic M.P., 15 May 1851 (Hansard, cxvi. 1005).
[240] Earl Fortescue to Russell, 21 Dec. 1850 (Russell Papers, 8G, fo. 71).
[241] Ibid. fo. 72.   [242] Hampden, *Memorials of Hampden*, 192.

was 'bold, manly, Protestant and true'.[243] An Oxford diocesan protest was signed by 393 out of 547 incumbents, and some did not sign because it was not Protestant enough.[244] New societies were founded during the crisis, such as the Protestant Alliance (commenced on 25 June 1851) and the Scottish Reformation Society (started in December 1850). A London meeting of the Protestant Association on 25 November carried resolutions against 'papal usurpation', and branch meetings of the Association were given lectures on 'Papal Aggression'.[245] If 'aggression' implied the need to defend Protestant doctrine, 'usurpation' called forth the associated defence of civil supremacy. The National Club wanted Protestant committees to be formed, preferably in every parish and at least in every town and division of a county. These committees were to urge the need for a parliamentary statute strong enough 'to vindicate the supremacy of our Crown, the majesty of our laws, and the independence of our nation'.[246]

Such language reflected the inflated terms of Wiseman's pastoral rather than the true dimensions of the Pope's action and the limitations of his power. But the protests were not restricted to ultra-Protestants, or to latitudinarians whose anti-Catholic views got the better of their liberalism. Catholics themselves were divided on the issue. The *Tablet* (now published in Dublin) championed the hierarchy. Phillipps de Lisle, A. W. Pugin, and other Catholics wrote pamphlets in its favour,[247] and Catholics upheld it either at Protestant meetings or at their own meetings.[248] But some aristocratic liberal Catholics could not reconcile the 'Papal Aggression' with long-standing Cisalpine views—opinions which were increasingly challenged within English Catholicism by the Ultramontanism of converts and Irish immigrants. The duke of Norfolk held that 'ultramontane opinions are totally incompatible with allegiance to our Sovereign and with our Constitution',[249] and became an Anglican communicant, though his heir, the earl of Arundel and Surrey, did not follow him. T. Chisholm Anstey, Catholic M.P. for the Irish borough of Youghal, said that Catholic members

---

[243] Hodder, *Shaftesbury*, ii. 327.

[244] Open letter of Bishop Wilberforce to his fellow bishops, 25 Jan. 1851 (Wilberforce Papers, c. 20); Wilberforce to dissentient clergy of Oxford diocese, 21 Jan. 1851 (Pugh (ed.), *The Letter-Books of Samuel Wilberforce*, 206–7).

[245] *Protestant Magazine*, xii (Dec. 1850), 183–9; xiii (Feb. 1851), 64.

[246] *Address to the Protestants of the Empire*, issued by National Club, 12 Mar. 1851 (London, 1851), 7.

[247] Lisle Phillipps, *A Letter to the Earl of Shrewsbury on the re-establishment of the Hierarchy* (London, 1850); *Protestant Aggression: remarks on the Bishop of Durham's letter to the Archdeacon of Lindisfarne*, by a Catholic clergyman (London, 1850).

[248] Burke, *Catholic History of Liverpool*, 97; D. F. Guirron, 'The Ecclesiastical Titles Crisis: its effect on Liverpool, including the election of 1852' (unpubl. Univ. of St. Andrews M.A. Hons. thesis 1969), 6–8; T. Macher to Rev. Francis Serle, 14 Dec. 1850 (Wiseman Papers, W3/28, 1850, 96); Minute of meeting of Catholic clergy of Dublin diocese, 18 Nov. 1850 (ibid. 77).

[249] W. Ward, *Wiseman*, ii. 15.

who opposed the bill were guided too much by their faith and too little by civil loyalty.[250]

Some Catholics thought that the restored hierarchy prejudiced the spiritual independence of English Catholicism.[251] Lord Beaumont gave in the House of Lords a lengthy vindication of his Cisalpine, liberal Catholic viewpoint. He denied that 'the spiritual power of the Pope ought to extend to the limits which he, the Pope in his infallibility, thought proper to assign it. Such doctrine is Roman, and not Catholic, it is local and not universal, suited to the interests of the Vatican, and hostile to the welfare of distant churches.' Forgetting that Cisalpine vicars-apostolic had long wanted a hierarchy, he claimed that the latter was merely a concession to illiberal converts. Finally, the hierarchy was nothing less than an attempt 'to enslave the mind of Europe', and he was only sorry that the Ecclesiastical Titles Bill was not stronger.[252] These views were not representative of English Catholicism as it stood in 1850, but their expression strengthened Russell's claim to be acting against an illiberal, unconstitutional intrusion.

High churchmen were also concerned about spiritual independence, but this led some of them to oppose the bill. Gladstone, whose long condemnation of the bill on 25 March 1851 was one of his most notable oratorial performances,[253] believed that opposition to the hierarchy would strengthen the royal supremacy and therefore discourage high-church teaching. He feared that the Church of England, by calling in the secular arm for defence, would lose more of its independence: '. . . new liberties for ourselves and new restraints upon others cannot stand together . . .'[254] To avoid this danger he defended the liberty of the Church of Rome to organize itself without Government interference, and linked his stand with the broad question of religious liberty: 'Are you going to spend the latter half of the nineteenth century in undoing the great work which with so much pain & difficulty your greatest men have been achieving during the former ?'[255]

Similarly, Pusey commented ruefully on the difficulty of getting people to protest against the royal supremacy when there was the spectre of papal supremacy to distract them.[256] Archdeacon Denison, though he opposed the hierarchy, deplored 'the putting aside, in the excitement of our present alarm, the fact of the extreme peril to which the Church of England is exposed from the aggressions of the civil power'.[257] Phillpotts, while regret-

---

[250] Hansard, cxvi. 1372–3.
[251] Hansard, cxiv. 35 f.
[252] Ibid. cxviii. 1101, 1110, 1112.
[253] Ibid. cxv. 565–97.
[254] Memo of Gladstone to Bishop Wilberforce, 22 Jan. 1852 (Lathbury, i. 89).
[255] Hansard, cxv 594–5.
[256] Pusey to Keble, Nov. 1850 (Pusey Papers). For Keble's view cf. F. Awdry, *A Country Gentleman of the Nineteenth Century—a short memoir of Sir William Heathcote, Bt.* (Winchester, 1906), 97–8.
[257] Denison to E. A. Sanford, 2 Dec. 1850 (Denison, *Notes of My Life*, 211).

ting the papal rescript, defended the Tractarians against Russell's censure.[258] But W. F. Hook, whose anti-Tractarian tendency had been sharpened by disputes with the clergy of St. Saviour's, Leeds, was simply 'boiling over with indignation at the attack which has been made upon the Institutions of my Country, my Church and my Religion . . .'[259] Russell probably hoped that this feeling would prevail among many high churchmen, reconciling them to their own Church and even to State control for the sake of resisting outside attack, and that those troublesome Tractarians who vociferously challenged the State would join Rome. The 'Aggression' seemed to have given him the means of obtaining the Protestant affirmation which he desired. Sir George Cornewall Lewis, a Whig minister, wrote that the crisis would 'bring the Puseyites to their bearings; it will be an instantia crucis to them which will compel them to choose one road or the other. The extreme left will become Roman, the middle and the extreme right will . . . relapse into old-fashioned High Church opinions . . .'[260]

But this prophecy was not borne out. Though the Government's response to the hierarchy gave Manning a final Romeward push, other Tractarians remained in the Establishment without relaxing their beliefs, and continued to dispute the control of the State and to demand active Convocations. After the storm, the broad ecclesiastical pattern of England remained unaltered.

This is also shown by the reaction of Dissenters. They were divided by the crisis, as in 1845, some being predominantly anti-Papist and some predominantly Voluntary. But their disagreement was temporary, and they were not reconciled to Russell and the Whigs. Russell may have hoped that his policy would conciliate Dissenters, but this was another of his disappointments. The *Nonconformist* warned Dissenters not to join in the agitation: 'So long as Roman Catholics support by voluntary contributions their own orders of priesthood, let the Pope confer upon them what ecclesiastical titles and powers he may please.'[261] The territorial claims of Anglican bishops, said this paper, were as much to be condemned as Wiseman's, and the Establishment harboured the Tractarianism which had encouraged the Pope.[262] Recent Methodist seceders held similar views. The Rev. William Griffith, a secession leader, moved at a Derby meeting 'that a resort to the secular arm, for the purpose either of repressing supposed error, or of promoting received views of truth, is at once a persecution of our fellow-men for their conscientious dissent, and a libel on our Divine religion . . .'[263] At Edinburgh, Birmingham, Bristol, and Worcester disputes took place

[258] H. Phillpotts, *Reply to the Addresses of the Clergy of the Archdeaconry of Exeter on the recent Romish Aggression* (London, 1850), 4 ff.

[259] Hook to Gladstone, 23 June 1851 (Stephens, *Hook*, ii. 294–5).

[260] Lewis to Sir Edmund Head, 23 Dec. 1850 (Rev. Sir G. F. Lewis (ed.), *Letters of Sir George C. Lewis to various friends* (London, 1870), 232–3).

[261] *Nonconformist*, 16 Oct. 1850, 838.   [262] Ibid. 6 Nov. 1850, 889.

[263] Ibid. 20 Nov. 1850, 935.

between Voluntaries and defenders of the royal supremacy.[264] Bright, Baines, Sturge, and Miall opposed Government action. Miall seized the opportunity to attack the Establishment in speech as well as in the *Nonconformist*, and was roughly ejected from the platform by two outraged clergymen at an Islington meeting.[265] This showed that 'Papal Aggression' had not united Protestants. At Hull a promising Congregational minister named Christopher Newman Hall denied that the hierarchy posed any political or religious threat.[266]

Different views were expressed by other Nonconformists. Wesleyans, undistracted by Voluntaryism, joined in the straightforward anti-papal denunciations of Anglican evangelicals.[267] Some Dissenting M.P.s, including Samuel Morton Peto and Joseph Brotherton, supported the Titles Bill although it was opposed by other Dissenting M.P.s.[268] Some Voluntaries, including the Rev. J. P. Mursell, the Rev. Thomas Binney, and the Rev. James Guinness Rogers, a young Congregational minister at Newcastle, strongly disagreed with the *Nonconformist* and joined forces with churchmen and Wesleyans on the issue.[269] Mursell championed the prerogative of 'our beloved Queen'.[270] Wide differences of opinion may have lain behind the tight-lipped statement in the minutes of the Anti-State Church Association— the only reference to the crisis in these full records—that the Catholic hierarchy was the subject of 'extended conversation, but [that] no proceeding thereon was adopted'.[271] The Dissenting Deputies also had their differences, but at two of their meetings resolutions were carried against the hierarchy, amendments in favour of religious liberty being defeated.[272] Ashley was able to praise 'the great majority of the Nonconformists' (as he alleged) for making 'common cause against the common enemy'.[273] Russell's stand against the hierarchy was well calculated to encourage Nonconformist anti-papal attitudes and to interrupt the Voluntary attack on the Government. But this hiatus proved as transient as the anti-Titles campaign itself.

Gratifying as public support undoubtedly was, parliamentary approval of his bill was of more direct importance to Russell's needs, and this he gained

---

[264] Ibid. 935–6; S. Hobhouse, *Joseph Sturge, his Life and Work* (London, 1919), 87.

[265] Miall, *Life of Miall*, 164–5. On the varied opinions of Dissent see Norman, *Anti-Catholicism*, 65–7, 75–6.

[266] C. Newman Hall, *Dissent and the Papal Bull—No Intolerance: a response to the cry of 'No Popery'* (London, 1850), 2 ff. Cf. C. Newman Hall, *Autobiography* (London, 1898), 93–4.

[267] Leading articles in the *Watchman*, 16, 23, 30 Oct.; 6, 13, 20, 27 Nov. 1850, etc. Cf. Hansard, cxv. 548–9 (speech of Joseph Hume).

[268] Hansard, cxiv. 65 f., 698–9; cxvii. 1022–3.

[269] Mursell's letters to *Nonconformist*, 27 Nov., 24 Dec. 1850; T. Binney, *The Dissenters and the Papacy* (London, 1850); Rogers, *An Autobiography*, 93–6.

[270] Letter in *Nonconformist*, 24 Dec. 1850.

[271] Minutes, ii. 140 (14 Nov. 1850).

[272] Manning, *The Protestant Dissenting Deputies*, 206–10.

[273] Hansard, cxiv. 301.

in abundance. Although the bill was brief, and parliamentary support for it was great, the Irish Catholic M.P.s were very obstructive and the measure took up a great deal of parliamentary time. In the months of debate which commenced on 7 February 1851 there was also opposition from the radicals, though even these were divided. Roebuck was disgusted to find a Liberal Administration going backwards, as were Bright, Cobden, Hume, W. J. Fox, and Milner Gibson.[274] Bernal Osborne said the bill, though it did not provide for 'disembowelling priests, and hanging and beheading laymen', was none the less a penal measure.[275] But Colonel T. Perronet Thompson dismayed fellow radicals by strongly supporting the bill and saying it did not go far enough.[276]

About 40 Irish and English Catholic members, some 17 Liberal Irish Protestant members, some radicals, and a small minority of about 20 Peelites were an ineffective opposition to the bill, and sometimes not all of these troubled to vote against it. The three main majorities obtained for the bill in the Commons were 322, 343, and 217, and the minorities on these occasions were only 63, 95, and 46.[277] Added to the support of most Liberals and Peelites for the bill was that of the Protectionists, and it might be thought that Russell had found the ideal measure for disarming his multifarious opponents. But low agricultural prices had been reviving Protectionist fortunes since the end of 1848,[278] and the Protectionist leaders did not forget their party interest. They, and Disraeli in particular, were primarily interested in the political advantage to be gained from no-Popery. They asserted that the Government's previous policy of concessions to Catholics had encouraged the announcement of the hierarchy, and demanded a stronger bill.[279] They did nothing to save the Government from defeat on the radical Locke King's motion to equalize the county and borough franchises on 20 February. In the ensuing political crisis they were quite unable to form a Government, and this (though disappointing to some of them) relieved them of having to shoulder the burden of no-Popery legislation. Indeed, when Stanley was trying to form a Government he had told the Queen he hoped to avoid such legislation.[280]

When Russell resumed office, he softened the bill by removing the second and third clauses, which had proposed to annul the deeds and writings and confiscate the endowments of clerics who took the forbidden titles. Protectionists, however, now resumed their wooing of no-Popery opinion,

[274] Ibid. 68 ff., 211 ff., 242 ff., 489, 370 ff., 675 ff.; cxvi. 1130–2.
[275] Ibid. cxv. 346–7.   [276] Ibid. cxiv. 487–9.
[277] Ibid. cxiv. 699–703; cxv. 618–21; cxviii. 240–2.
[278] Stewart, *The Politics of Protection*, 142 ff.
[279] Speeches of Stanley, 4 Feb. 1851 (Hansard, cxiv. 25–30) and Disraeli, 7 Feb., 25 Mar. 1851 (ibid. 256–62; cxv. 601–2); Stanley to Disraeli, 15 Nov. 1850 (Disraeli Papers, B/XX/S/19); Disraeli to Stanley, 7 Dec. 1850 (W. F. Monypenny and G. E. Buckle, *The Life of Benjamin Disraeli, Earl of Beaconsfield* (6 vols., London, 1910–20), iii. 271–3).
[280] Stewart, op. cit. 183–4.

condemning the excisions and demanding that the bill be strengthened again.[281] Amendments moved on 27 June by Sir Frederick Thesiger were adopted against the Government. These made the declaratory clause apply to all rescripts and not only that establishing the hierarchy; gave the prosecuting power to any individual with the sanction of the Crown officers; and imposed penalties on the introduction of bulls.[282] Moreover, Disraeli and Stanley (soon to become Derby) had helped to devise David Urquhart's motion of 9 May, which declared that the Government was responsible for the Pope's policy. They hoped to carry a vote of censure against Russell by this means, but the twist was too much for some ultra-Protestants such as Inglis, J. P. Plumptre, and other members of the National Club who believed that the motion might destroy the bill. They supported the Government, others abstained, and the motion—on which, if all Protectionists had voted for it, the Government would have been defeated—was lost by 280 votes to 201.[283]

Protectionist support for the bill was thus very qualified, but at least it gave Russell larger majorities and helped him to eke out the life of his ministry. But he also antagonized the Irish Catholics and offended the Peelite leaders. During the parliamentary recess most of the leading Peelites (Goulburn being excepted)[284] had decided independently of each other that penal legislation must be opposed. Graham thought there was 'no more danger to be apprehended from Rome than from the Emperor of China. The Bull [sic] is an impertinence, but harmless; the missive from Downing St. is a more serious matter . . .'[285] Peelites did not have uniform reasons for opposing Russell's bill. Aberdeen and Graham were concerned with religious liberty on broad, political grounds. The attitude of Gladstone, Lincoln (who became fifth duke of Newcastle in January), and Sidney Herbert was coloured by Tractarianism and opposition to the Gorham judgement, and they were provoked by Russell's special condemnation of the Tractarians. There was little religious sympathy between the two groups. Graham wrote: 'I . . . dislike both Puseyism and Gladstonism as much as Ld. John does . . .'[286] But they could agree, for rather different reasons, on opposition to the bill. Graham, Gladstone, Herbert, and Roundell Palmer in the Commons, and Aberdeen and Newcastle in the Lords, made notable speeches against the Government.[287] Not many back-bench Peelites joined them, and

---

[281] Hansard, cxiv. 1141–6, 1152–4, 1159, 1161–2, 1370–1 (speeches of Inglis, G. Bankes, C. N. Newdegate, J. P. Plumptre, and Col. Sibthorp). Cf. speech of Disraeli (ibid. cxv. 601–2).

[282] *Annual Register*, xciii (1851), 61–4; Hansard, cxvii. 365–9, 1328 ff.

[283] Hansard, cxvi. 780–834; Dreyer, 'The Administration of Lord John Russell,' 240–1; Stewart, 184–5.

[284] Goulburn to Graham, 'private', 14 Nov. 1850 (Graham Papers, microfilms, 123).

[285] Graham to Edward Ellice, 'private', 14 Nov. 1850 (Ellice Papers, E16A, fo. 68).

[286] Graham to Ellice, 14 Nov. 1850 (ibid. E16A, fo. 69); Sidney Herbert to Graham, 4 Dec. 1850 (Lord Stanmore, *Sidney Herbert, A Memoir* (2 vols., London, 1906), i. 135).

[287] Hansard, cxiv. 1347–64 (Palmer); cxv. 164–82 (Herbert), 280–309 (Graham), 565–97 (Gladstone); cxviii. 1072–93 (Aberdeen), 1240–63 (Newcastle).

the Peelites divided 71 to 20 in favour of the bill's second reading in the Commons.[288] But the opinion of the leaders was politically important, in view of Russell's need to form a coalition with them. He attempted such a junction after his defeat on Locke King's motion and subsequent resignation; but the penal legislation gave Peelites a weighty reason for refusing to coalesce.[289] The same reason prevented Aberdeen and Graham from trying to form a Government, and (in addition to the obstacle of commercial policy) from forming a joint ministry with the Protectionists.[290] As the Whig Fox Maule put it, country and Commons had to submit again to the '*vile* whigs' governing by themselves.[291] It was not until December 1852, after the first Derby Government had held office, that a Whig–Peelite coalition was achieved.

The bill antagonized Irish as well as Peelites. Apart from Russell's annoyance with Catholic opposition to his Irish educational policy, it was held that Ireland could not be excluded from the bill without foreshadowing legal independence. This would encourage Irish nationalism, threaten the Union, and weaken the position of the Church of Ireland.[292] Not only Protectionists, but concessionary Peelite leaders also, said that constitutional and Church interests required the inclusion of Ireland.[293] The Government—to the dismay of Clarendon, the unfortunate Lord Lieutenant—duly included Ireland in the bill, and thereby helped to stimulate Irish nationalism in a different way. Russell, however, recognized the distinction between England and Ireland so far as to say that the law should be 'separately administered' in Ireland; that it would be difficult to prosecute Irish prelates who had long assumed a territorial title; and that (in regard to England), 'the novelty [of taking territorial titles] constitutes much of the offensiveness . . .'[294] He proceeded to explain to Clarendon:

Suppose a case to occur in England of violation of the provisions of our Bill. We should ask our law officers who might advise prosecution . . . Suppose a similar case to occur in Ireland. Your [i.e. the Irish] law officers might say 'You have no chance of a verdict, it is of no use to prosecute' . . . the result might be some difference in the mode of administering the law. It might be MacHale's object to be prosecuted, sure of a triumphant acquittal. . . . My impression is that we must

[288] Analysis in Conacher, *The Peelites and the Party System*, 226–9.

[289] Prest, *Russell*, 327–8; speeches of Aberdeen, Russell, and Graham, 28 Feb. 1851 (Hansard, cxiv. 999–1003, 1029–40, 1043–51).

[290] Conacher, op. cit. 81–2; memo of Disraeli, written in 1860s (Monypenny and Buckle, op. cit. iii. 288–96).

[291] Fox Maule to Andrew Rutherfurd, 25 Feb. 1851 (Rutherfurd Papers, 9699, fo. 55).

[292] Speech of Sir George Grey, 7 Mar. 1851 (Hansard, cxiv. 1127–8); Aubrey de Vere to Gladstone, 2 Mar. 1851 (Gladstone Papers 44370, fo. 20). For a different view see Sir G. C. Lewis to Russell, 4 Mar. 1851 (Gooch, *Correspondence of Russell*, ii. 61 f.).

[293] Speech of Aberdeen, 21 July 1851 (Hansard, cxviii. 1091–2). Cf. Marquess of Londonderry to Disraeli, 12, 20 Jan. 1851 (Disraeli Papers, B/XX/V/52–3); Manners to Disraeli, 7 Jan. 1851 (ibid. B/XX/M/72); Hansard, cxvii. 1061 (speech to Inglis).

[294] Russell to Clarendon, 23, 29 Jan. 1851 (Clarendon Papers, Irish box 44).

propose our Bill & profess to act upon it both in England & Ireland. That action will be not to allow any one to be recognized in England or Ireland as Bishop of any place or diocese & to prosecute him only when necessary. But not to go further, & if any thing more penal is put into the Bill & reaches its final stage to throw up the bill & the Govt. along with it.[295]

The final sentences of this passage, written on 31 January, illustrate Russell's confusion and uncertainty even before he sought leave to introduce the bill. His vacillation over Ireland did not save the political support of Irish Catholics (or Irish Liberal Protestants) who attacked the bill relentlessly in Parliament against impossible odds. Their anger was shown by John Reynolds, M.P. for Dublin City, who said that until 4 November 1850 (the date of the Durham Letter) Stanley had been the most unpopular peer in Ireland, but that Russell had superseded him.[296] Reynolds plainly admitted that Irish Catholic M.P.s were now voting against the Government on any motion, regardless of its merits, simply to demonstrate their lack of confidence. Twenty of them supported a motion of Disraeli on 13 February to relieve agricultural distress, and the Government majority against the motion was only fourteen.[297] They also refused to support Russell against Locke King's motion, thereby helping to cause the Government's resignation.[298] Not content with this, after Russell had diluted the bill they even assisted Tory efforts to strengthen it, walking out of the Commons when Thesiger's amendments were introduced and leaving the Government to be defeated.[299] It had become more important to them to embarrass the ministry than to weaken the bill—a sign perhaps that they expected the bill to be ineffective, or that they thought they could make it so. The bill certainly helped to revive independent Irish political action. From the demands of the Irish Tenant League, formed in August 1850 and concerned with land grievances, and, more obviously, from the opposition to the Titles Bill, emerged the independent 'Irish Brigade'—a separate parliamentary party which returned a large number of M.P.s at the 1852 election, but then declined.[300]

Rather than support Russell, Irish Catholic M.P.s had indirectly supported Derby, and for many years afterwards some Catholics were inclined to vote Conservative.[301] Disraeli welcomed this tendency, but a firm alliance could scarcely develop when many Conservatives were ultra-Protestant. Over the question of maintaining the Church of Ireland as an Establishment, Irish

[295] Russell to Clarendon, 31 Jan. 1851 (ibid.).

[296] Speech of 14 Mar. 1851 (Hansard, cxiv. 1338–9).

[297] J. H. Whyte, *The Independent Irish Party, 1850–9* (Oxford, 1958), 22.

[298] Sir G. C. Lewis to Sir Edmund Head, 6 Mar. 1851 (Lewis (ed.), *Letters of Lewis*, 238).

[299] Whyte, op. cit. 22–3; *Annual Register*, xciii (1851), 63.

[300] Whyte, 28 ff.

[301] J. L. Altholz, 'The Political Behavior of the English Catholics, 1850–67', *Journal of British Studies*, iii (1964), 89 ff.; K. T. Hoppen, 'Tories, Catholics and the General Election of 1859', *Hist. Jl.* xiii (1970), 48 ff.

Catholics were even more at cross purposes with Tories than with Whigs. Russell had lost Irish Catholic support, but others were to regain it for the Liberals in the 1860s.

Opinions for and against the Ecclesiastical Titles Bill continued to be expressed in Parliament—sometimes with astonishing provocation and bitterness[302]—until the Lords passed the measure at the end of July. The bill was almost the only measure introduced by Government in 1851, and occupied Parliament for six months. Despite his own embarrassment and the attacks of Irish Catholics, Russell must have temporarily gained in confidence from his huge majorities. But the session passed and he was left with his problem of Government instability, now increased by the formation of the Irish Brigade. Debates on the Titles Bill had been ironically interspersed with debates on a Jewish Relief Bill, lost in the House of Lords but supported by the Government.[303] This may have served to show that ministers were still attached to religious toleration, provided it did not become too demanding. It was argued by supporters of the Titles Bill that true toleration required resistance to 'Papal Aggression'. But toleration as it had developed in Britain was hindered by the measure. Such obstruction was clearly in tune with great sections of public opinion, and anti-Catholic feeling was demonstrated long after the crisis. There were anti-Catholic riots at Greenock in July 1851 and throughout 1852 and more celebrated ones at Stockport in June 1852—though the connection of these with the Titles crisis may have been tenuous.[304] The agitation of 1850–1, however, was the last nationwide exhibition of no-Popery feeling, and the Titles Act was the last measure of discrimination between religious denominations passed by a British Government. The Act was disregarded by some of the new bishops, who used their titles from the first, and no one was prosecuted under the measure, which lasted until it was quietly repealed by Gladstone in 1871. A fresh penal statute was out of tune with the age, a jarring note in the development of tolerance and concession in the relations of State and Church. The note had been struck by a Government which did not really believe in what it was doing, and after 1851 ministers wanted to forget about their action. Russell made only a minimal reference to it in his *Recollections* in 1875.[305]

The Government's difficulties, created or exacerbated by the bill, continued after the measure had passed, and were compounded in the autumn by the quarrels between Palmerston and the rest of the Cabinet over the conduct of foreign affairs. After the dismissal of Palmerston on 19 December there were new efforts to strengthen the Government by making

[302] Speech of Henry Drummond, M.P. for West Surrey, 20 Mar. 1851 (Hansard, cxv. 261–80, also 533–5), with outraged interruptions.

[303] Ibid. 1006–17; cxvi. 367 ff.; cxviii. 143–6, 859–909.

[304] For the Greenock riots see Handley, *The Irish in Scotland*, 234–6; for Stockport see below, pp. 238–9.

[305] Russell, *Recollections*, 256–7.

offers to Peelites. Russell offered the Irish Lord Lieutenancy to the duke of Newcastle, but Newcastle refused to administer the Titles Act in Ireland and objected to the anti-Tractarian Church appointments during Russell's Government.[306] In mid-January negotiations with Newcastle were abruptly closed. The Government met the new session with a Parliamentary Reform Bill over which there was considerable dissension among ministers, but this bill had scarcely been introduced when Palmerston carried by 11 votes an amendment to the Government's Militia Bill and the ministry immediately announced its resignation, on 20 February. The alienation of Irish supporters and the failure to obtain Peelite co-operation—still largely owing to the Ecclesiastical Titles Act—contributed to this end. Ten Peelites had voted for Palmerston's amendment, though 7 against it. More pointedly, 15 Irish Liberals voted with Palmerston, enough to turn the vote against Russell.[307] The Titles legislation had dogged Russell to the end of his term.

Derby accepted the Queen's commission to form a Government on 22 February. He was now in a stronger position to do so than he had been a year previously, for the Whigs had been more decisively defeated, they were more divided, and were no nearer forming a coalition with Peelites. But the new ministry had only minority support in the Commons, despite the drift of Peelites to its ranks. The ardent Protectionist G. F. Young said there were 280 ministerialist M.P.s;[308] probably he included former Peelites who now voted frequently with the Protectionists. It was essential for the Government to win support at a general election. Whether policies which had been upheld in Opposition could serve the new ministry's interests, or whether ways would be found to abandon them, was a foremost question of the day. This led to the further question whether the abandonment of Protection and ultra-Protestantism could now unite and strengthen a party which had been rent by these very issues.

[306] Russell's memo of interview with Newcastle, 31 Dec. 1851 (Martineau, *Life of Newcastle*, 108–10); Conacher, 94–6.
[307] Conacher, 97; Gash, *Reaction*, 103 ff.
[308] Stewart, 199.

CHAPTER VII

The First Derby Ministry
and the Election of 1852

i. DERBY'S ECCLESIASTICAL BALANCE

THE NEW Government needed to increase its following. Protection and ultra-Protestantism, which had been upheld in Opposition, were still supported by many of the ministry's followers, both in Parliament and in the country; but they were not policies likely to win new support, especially from the Peelites and the Irish Catholics whom the Whig Government had antagonized.

Revival of the Corn Laws was scarcely realistic at that point, for it would not have assisted the Government's parliamentary position and would not have impressed electors who were enjoying commercial prosperity. Derby, despite his professions of loyalty to Protection, appointed to his two major financial and commercial posts 'the two most outspoken free traders in the party' (Disraeli and Henley).[1] He did not match this by appointing any Roman Catholics to the Cabinet, but this by no means guaranteed an ultra-Protestant policy. Derby had hinted in February 1851 that he was not unalterably attached to the Ecclesiastical Titles Bill. In office, the maintenance of no-popery might drive the independent Irish party towards the Whigs, and would certainly fail to win leading Peelites for the Government. On the other hand, Derby could not afford to alienate his anti-Catholic supporters, as he pointed out when rejecting a proposal that he co-operate with the Irish party against the Whigs.[2] Russell, when he resigned in February 1851, had said that Stanley would not treat the Catholics more leniently than the Whigs had done.[3] Clearly, the new Prime Minister would find it difficult to tread the ecclesiastical tightrope between liberality to Catholics and satisfaction to ultra-Protestants, much as he would have liked to carry off this feat. While intending to pursue a moderately liberal line in ecclesiastical matters, such as would not antagonize Catholics and Peelites, Derby appeared, partly through misunderstanding and despite more delicate intentions, to come down on the anti-Catholic side.

Ultra-Protestants were hoping that a Conservative Government would pursue a positive anti-Catholic policy. The Rev. Francis Merewether had written to Disraeli in April 1851 about the need to 'reverse the timid policy

[1] Stewart, *The Politics of Protection*, 192.   [2] Ibid. 204.
[3] Russell to Clarendon, 21 Feb. 1851 (Clarendon Papers, Irish box 44).

that has influenced public measures, on Popish affairs, since 1829'.[4] Ultras did not seriously hope to repeal the 1829 Act, though they sometimes raised in Parliament their desire to do this. But they had more hope of repealing the Maynooth Act of 1845, a scar on their memories which they bore with increasing impatience as a result of the anti-Catholic feeling demonstrated in 1850–1. After the Ecclesiastical Titles Bill had been carried, the Maynooth grant (feared to be supporting an increasingly Ultramontane college) became the next point of attack, and provided ultra-Protestants with a major means of political expression for many years. At the second annual meeting of the Scottish Reformation Society on 9 December 1851 a speech was delivered on 'Maynooth endowment, a sin and a blunder'.[5] The Protestant Alliance agitated on the matter, and its first tract was a condemnation of the 1845 Act.[6] Ultra-Protestant M.P.s wished to raise the subject in the 1852 parliamentary session, and Derby and Disraeli were not at all anxious to support them. Derby, though not Disraeli, had supported the bill of 1845. The Premier had heard from C. N. Newdegate that ultras wanted to bring the question forward. 'This makes it necessary', he told Disraeli, 'that we should be prepared with our line, and especially that we should decide whether I shall or shall not move in the House of Lords for a Committee on the whole R. Catholic question, which may, I think, be a useful safety valve.'[7]

A safety-valve was more necessary to Derby when he became Prime Minister. His first ministerial statement in the Lords on 27 February was non-committal on religion, just as it threw the question of restoring Protection on the decision of the electorate. While determined to uphold the rights of the established Church, he desired religious liberty for all so long as they did not injure the Establishment.[8] On the same day Richard Spooner, Newdegate's twin representative for North Warwickshire and a relative of the Wilberforce family, struck a discordant note by giving notice in the Commons that he would move to inquire into the Maynooth grant. The motion did not specifically mention abolition, but Spooner—'such a Socrates', according to Disraeli, and having in his companion Newdegate 'the Alcibiades of Warwickshire'[9]—plainly said that the grant should cease. He stated that those who had supported it in 1845 could vote to abolish it with a clear conscience, since 'Papal Aggression' had annulled the conciliation on which the grant had been based.[10]

Spooner's motion was delayed for two and a half months. In the meantime

---

[4] 10 Apr. 1851 (Disraeli Papers, B/XXI/M/329).

[5] *Witness*, 29 May 1852.

[6] *The Maynooth Endowment Act*, Protestant Alliance Tract, No. 1 (London, 1852); cf. *Eclecic Review*, 5th Ser. iii (Jan.–June 1852), 519 ff.

[7] Derby to Disraeli, 5 Feb. 1852 (Disraeli Papers, B/XX/S/44). Cf. W. D. Jones, *Lord Derby and Victorian Conservatism*, 166.

[8] Hansard, cxix. 889 ff.

[9] Disraeli to Derby, 'private', 1 Sept. 1852 (Derby Papers, 145/2).

[10] Hansard, cxix. 931–2.

ministers were asked in Parliament whether they intended to repeal the Maynooth Act. They tried to evade the question. Disraeli said on 25 March that there would be no attempt at repeal in the present session, and that no pledge could be made regarding a future session as the general election had not yet been held.[11] A week later the earl of Albemarle accused the Government of having no policy on either Protection or Protestantism, and of auctioning them both to the electorate. 'It seemed', he said, that 'the friends and supporters of the noble Earl [Derby] are to go to the Roman Catholic constituencies of Ireland with one set of principles; and to the Protestant constituencies of England with another.'[12] Derby replied that there was no intention of tampering with the 1845 Act, though he did say that recent aggression by the Catholic Church made it difficult to justify the endowment.[13] This reply alarmed some defenders of the grant, and the marquess of Clanricarde asked on 20 April for a plain statement on the matter. Derby repeated that the Government had no present intention of changing the law, but that 'if circumstances should . . . lead . . . to an alteration of their course of conduct', ample notice would be given so that supporters of the grant could form up in defence.[14] Earl Grey then said that the country had the right to a straight answer, since the electoral preparations were much concerned with Maynooth. 'Does the noble Earl', he asked, 'adhere to the [pro-Maynooth] opinions he expressed in 1845?'[15] 'That is a question', replied Derby, 'which the noble Earl has no right to ask of me, or any man'; but he admitted that he was 'greatly disappointed in the result of the measure of 1845'.[16]

On 23 April Spooner said that when his motion came on it would merely seek to inquire into the system of education at Maynooth College: 'he had no intention of making any Motion at present relative to the repeal of the grant to Maynooth'.[17] The muted nature of this demand helped to save the Government from embarrassment. The motion, for a Select Committee of inquiry into the education at Maynooth, was introduced on 11 May. It was seconded by the marquess of Blandford, now holding different views from 1845, when his support for the Maynooth grant had supposedly lost him his seat. Spooner, despite his caution, clearly hoped that an inquiry would lead to removal of the grant. The object of the endowment, he said, had not been realized, for 'the teachers of religion . . . [had] become the leaders and conductors of rebellion'.[18] The offensive doctrines inculcated at Maynooth were said to find fertile soil in the ill-educated Irish peasantry. Among these doctrines Spooner mentioned especially the alleged needlessness of keeping faith with heretics, leading to the lack of firm allegiance to a heretical Government.[19] He himself had supported concession to Catholics in 1829,

[11] Ibid. cxx. 85–6.   [12] Ibid. 582 (2 Apr. 1852).   [13] Ibid. 582–3.
[14] Ibid. 873–82.   [15] Ibid. 882–4.   [16] Ibid.; W. D. Jones, op. cit. 167.
[17] Hansard, cxx. 1029.
[18] Ibid. cxxi. 506. Spooner was quoting a passage from a speech by Russell on 3 Apr. 1845.
[19] Ibid. 511 ff.

but regretted his error as Catholics, he believed, had subsequently disregarded their undertaking not to injure the Protestant Establishment.[20]

Liberals and Peelites were ready to have an inquiry, but not for Spooner's ends; and Spooner's views were countered by Catholics and their sympathizers in the House of Commons. The radical Bernal Osborne said the motion was 'a mean attempt to raise a "No-Popery" cry, with which hon. Gentlemen opposite might go to the hustings . . .' He stated that most of the priests who had sympathized with the rebellion of 1848 were not Maynooth-educated, and asked how the Government could consistently withdraw the Maynooth grant when it subsidized Hindu and Muslim colleges in India: 'What ought the House to think of that odour of sanctity which strained at the Roman Catholic gnat, and swallowed the Brahmin camel?'[21] T. Chisholm Anstey, M.P. for Youghal, introduced a diversionary amendment to consider the removal of all Government aid to religion. This was meant as a challenge to the established Churches, and John Reynolds, a fellow Catholic member, sharpened the threat by raising specifically the abolition of the temporalities of the Church of Ireland.[22] The Anglican opponents of Maynooth naturally could not support this move. Anstey's motion was lost by a large majority on 25 May, the minority consisting largely of Catholics and radicals.[23]

Spooner's motion remained half-heartedly on the cards. Beresford Hope described it as 'a Motion pretending inquiry, but breathing persecution; but when persecution is alleged against it, taking shelter under inquiry'.[24] Bright, who (to the dismay of militant Voluntaries) did not want to revoke the grant despite his adverse vote in 1845, suspected that many members were anxious to avoid a vote.[25] Among these seemed to be the sponsors of the motion. They decided to postpone the debate until 16 June—in order, it was said, to obtain a full House. But Gladstone (who opposed the motion) pointed out that this date would be almost at the end of the session, and Sir Benjamin Hall (another opponent) said that such a course would amount to throwing another question to the electorate.[26] Spencer Walpole, the Home Secretary, insisted that the Government had no connection with Spooner's motion, though he supported it himself; and Disraeli excused the repeated postponements on the ground of more pressing legislative business.[27] The discussion was brought forward to 8 June. Vincent Scully, Catholic member for County Cork, then said that only 300,000 had petitioned for an inquiry, against the 1,500,000 who had petitioned against the grant in 1845.[28] The

---

[20] Ibid. 521.
[21] Ibid. 542, 548-9.
[22] Ibid. 528-32, 842.
[23] Ibid. 1168-70.
[24] Hansard, cxxi. 553.
[25] Bright to George Wilson, 18 May 1852 (G. Wilson Papers). Bright's position was condemned on Voluntary grounds by the *Eclectic Review*, 5th Ser. iii (Jan.–June 1852), 516; iv. (July–Dec. 1852), 120.
[26] Hansard, cxxi. 845-9.
[27] Ibid. 1261 (Walpole, 27 May), 798-9 (Disraeli, 19 May).
[28] Ibid. cxxii. 226 ff.

debate ended in an anti-climax worthy of its history. After 2 a.m. on 15 June it was moved that the debate be adjourned. Newdegate said he should consider a vote for adjournment as equivalent to a vote against an inquiry. The House then divided 103 to 29 against an adjournment—but this vote was used, somewhat surprisingly, as a means of ending discussion of the motion altogether. Spooner said he was satisfied that the division had vindicated his opinions, and therefore he would not press his motion; and Newdegate said he had given notice that this division would be taken as a final decision.[29] In this curious way the Maynooth motion faded out of the current session.

But there was an outcry from Liberals, Peelites, and Irish who felt cheated of victory on the question. They had hoped to defeat the motion or to vindicate their pro-Maynooth opinions through an inquiry. They accused the motion's sponsors of cowardice and the Government of insincerity. William Keogh said that the ministry really wanted to maintain the Maynooth grant, and indeed was supporting parliamentary candidates in Ireland who were not only pro-Maynooth but even prepared to repeal the Ecclesiastical Titles Act. 'Her Majesty's Government', he stated, 'had been, were, and intended to continue to be, playing fast and loose with sincere men who sat behind them'; and he would not be surprised if the Derbyite party broke up in 1853 just as the greater Conservative party had broken up in 1846.[30] Thus Derby and Disraeli were accused in their turn of being 'great parliamentary middle-men', if not yet by erstwhile supporters. Lord Naas, the Chief Secretary for Ireland, denied that the Government was supporting Irish candidates with letters or money. On the other hand, he admitted that Conservative candidates in Ireland were pro-Maynooth, and declared that he himself would not vote to repeal the grant.[31] Philip Howard, a Catholic who was Liberal M.P. for Carlisle, also asked the Government to relinquish a two-faced policy and declare its outlook plainly on the matter.[32] No such clarification was forthcoming, though the Government favoured an inquiry in principle. A Royal Commission was appointed by the Coalition ministry in 1853.

The Government's reserve on the Maynooth question showed its unwillingness to antagonize both the Irish Catholics and its own ultra-Protestant supporters. In addition, it did not wish to repel possible Peelite recruits. It was hoped that Gladstone and Sidney Herbert might be induced to join the Government, and the high-church views of these men perhaps help to explain Derby's connivance at, or unwillingness to obstruct, certain high-church objects. Derby himself was a moderately high churchman,[33] and

---

[29] Ibid. 698–704, 763.   [30] Ibid. 767–8.

[31] Ibid. 769–70.   [32] Ibid. 772–3.

[33] J. T. Ward, 'Derby and Disraeli', in D. Southgate (ed.), The Conservative Leadership, 1832–1932 (London, 1974), 66.

Gladstone wrote that ' . . . the advent of this Government to power affords in respect to Church matters an opportunity for getting something like fair play which may not readily return & which ought not to be lost'.[34]

Blomfield, Wilberforce, and Gladstone discussed the prospect of reintroducing Blomfield's bill to reform the final court of appeal in ecclesiastical causes.[35] Gladstone thought that Derby's advice should be sought. Derby had spoken in favour of Blomfield's bill in 1850, because it transferred power 'from a body who might not be members of the Church, and [conferred] it upon those members of the Church who were authoritatively set forth as the spiritual guides and instructors of the Church'. He had, however, suggested as a modification that episcopal opinions in doctrinal cases, though they would be communicated to the Judicial Committee, would not be binding on that body.[36] Gladstone stated in March 1852 that a proposal embodying Derby's own suggested alteration 'must wear at least a gracious aspect to him'.[37] Blomfield saw Derby, who seemed satisfied with his former suggestion and asked how it would be received:

He enquired what chance there was of unanimity amongst the Bishops. I said that it was impossible to say, for that with respect to some of them, what they agreed upon one day, they might speak against the next: but that I was pledged to do something in the matter, and a great majority of the Clergy were dissatisfied with the constitution of the present Court of Appeal . . . and that I thought they would be tolerably well satisfied with the modification of my Bill which he had proposed . . . He seems very well disposed to do what he can for the Church if he continues in office, about which of course he spoke doubtingly.[38]

The last sentence was crucial, for Derby could not afford to advocate so controversial a measure when he lacked a majority. The current political uncertainty perhaps caused Blomfield to postpone introducing another bill until the next session. On 10 May he announced this intention in the Lords, and said that his new bill would follow Derby's suggestion: the bishops (perhaps acting as the upper house of Convocation) would have doctrinal questions referred to them, and would advise the Judicial Committee on these subjects, but their opinion would not bind the Committee in making a decision.[39] Derby said that he could not promise his support, but would find it difficult to resist a proposal so close to his own.[40] In this matter, however, Derby may well have encountered opposition from some of his own supporters.

A more positive gain for high churchmen was the advance made towards

[34] Gladstone to Bishop Wilberforce, 3 Mar. 1852 (Wilberforce Papers, d. 35).
[35] Wilberforce to Gladstone, 1 Mar. 1852, copy, (ibid. e. 2).
[36] Hansard, cxi. 649, 651–3.
[37] Gladstone to Wilberforce, 3 Mar. 1852 (Wilberforce Papers, d. 35).
[38] Blomfield to Wilberforce, 13 Mar. 1852 (ibid., d. 34).
[39] Hansard, cxxi. 427–8.   [40] Ibid. 428–9.

the revival of Convocation. They were divided over the question of admitting the laity to Convocation, and hindered by the opposition of some powerful evangelicals such as Shaftesbury (formerly Ashley) and Bishop C. R. Sumner. Nevertheless, high church advocates of the revival distinctly progressed in their cliff-hanging ascent to an intermediate toe-hold. During 1851 these advocates had become more confident, despite the actions of the Russell Government. The matter had been formally debated in Parliament for the first time; Phillpotts had held his diocesan synod; and the high-church *Guardian* was hopeful.[41] By the apparently minuscule act of receiving a petition in February 1851, Convocation had made 'the first independent motion outside the established ritual',[42] and ignited something which could not be put out.

In 1852 the champions of Convocation consolidated their position, if not yet with Government acquiescence then at least without Government obstruction. The Convocation of Canterbury made important progress, unlike that of York which, through the action of Archbishop Musgrave, remained closed until 1861. Meeting on 4 February, the Convocation of Canterbury received in this session no fewer than 24 petitions in the upper house and 27 in the lower. Bishop Wilberforce tried to have an address to the Queen adopted, asking for the right to transact synodical business. But Archbishop J. B. Sumner blocked the venture after obtaining legal advice. The archbishop then prorogued Convocation, but did so in a hesitant manner, acting on behalf of the Crown rather than on his own authority. Several eminent lawyers, including Derby's Attorney-General Sir Frederick Thesiger, agreed that Convocation could engage in debates as long as it did not draft canons. But this right was of little use when an unfriendly archbishop could interrupt the debates and prorogue the assemblies at any moment. More significant, therefore, was an opinion obtained by Wilberforce from Thesiger that an archbishop could only prorogue Convocation with the consent of a majority of bishops present in the upper house. These opinions suddenly made an active Convocation a strong possibility. Moreover, the election of a new Parliament required the election of proctors (clerical representatives) for the lower house of a new Convocation, and in 1852 these elections became more than nominal. There were several contested elections, and small but significant numbers of clergymen voted—112 out of 800 in the diocese of Lincoln, 56 out of 330 in the diocese of Hereford, as many as 81 out of 160 in the archdeaconry of Lewes.[43] Before the new Parliament met, the supporters of Convocation were polishing their armour. It remained to be seen how Derby would respond to their moves.

[41] P. J. Welch, 'The Revival of an active Convocation of Canterbury, 1852–5', *JEH* x (1959), 190–1; Stephens, *Hook*, ii. 355.
[42] Chadwick, *Victorian Church*, i. 314.
[43] Ibid. 314–17; Welch, op. cit. 191–2.

High churchmen were also heartened by the failure to persist in an attempt at an official inquiry into the institution of W. J. E. Bennett to the living of Frome-Selwood. This issue was like the Gorham Case in reverse, for in the Bennett affair low churchmen protested against the institution of a Tractarian clergyman. Bennett's previous ministry at Knightsbridge and Pimlico had drawn hooting sacrilegious mobs to his church. Asked by Bishop Blomfield to resign, Bennett had reluctantly complied. With this, asserted Edward Horsman, a Whig M.P., the people of England thought they had seen the last of him as an Anglican pastor. But to the public astonishment, after taking a continental holiday when he had compounded his misdeeds by consorting with friars and attending the Roman mass, Bennett had been appointed to Frome by the dowager marchioness of Bath and instituted by the high-church Bishop Bagot. Instead of being welcomed on his escape from the jaws of Rome, Bennett was blamed for having gone so close. Protests had been made to the patron and the bishop, but without avail. Bagot had replied to the protestors that 'Mr. Bennett has a firm and deep-rooted attachment to our own Church, and to all the doctrines of the Church of England, repudiating all Romish doctrines'.[44] But, to many, this begged the question—which doctrines were Romish and which English? Was the Church of England Protestant or Catholic? Bennett's first act, said Horsman in Parliament, had been to replace his evangelical curate with a Tractarian who had followed him from St. Paul's, Knightsbridge. Horsman concluded his review of the new 'Papal Aggression' at Frome by moving that an address be presented to the Queen, asking that an inquiry be held into the question whether Bennett's institution was in full accordance with 'the Decrees of the Constitution and the Canons Ecclesiastical of the Church of England'.[45]

Ministers would not comply with Horsman's wishes. Disraeli and Sir John Pakington suggested that it would be more satisfactory to appeal to the archbishop. Newdegate and Spooner disagreed with their leaders, but the high churchmanship of Inglis transcended his ultra-Protestantism. He agreed with Disraeli that an inquiry might commence a series of unwelcome investigations into the institution of clergy, and said that the Commons, not being an assembly of churchmen, was not a fit tribunal to decide such a case. Gladstone also spoke against the motion, which was defeated by 100 votes to 80.[46]

The question, however, remained open while the Government inquired into the legality of holding an inquiry. On 17 May Disraeli said that the law officers had deprecated an investigation by Government commission, and advised that redress should be sought under the Church Discipline Act of 1840, which had provided that a judicial inquiry might be held on the authority of the bishop of the diocese. But Horsman said that the members of a

---

[44] Hansard, cxx. 912 (Horsman's speech, 20 Apr. 1852).
[45] Ibid. 895–916, 925–8.   [46] Ibid. 921–5, 932–5, 941–3.

commission would have to be appointed by Bagot, implying that such a commission could not be trusted.[47]

After further discouragement Horsman moved on 8 June that a parliamentary Select Committee be appointed to inquire into the institution of Bennett. He gave details of Bennett's alleged doings abroad, which included not only attending mass but carrying about with him 'a consecrated stone, for an altar', before which he had performed religious services. Stress was laid on the widely believed story that Bennett had been converted to Rome, and the fact that he was still an Anglican was passed over.[48] Towards the end of his long speech Horsman asserted that 'if . . . the House of Commons, as representing the people, was so dissevered from the Established Church that they could not take cognisance of its affairs, then, *a fortiori*, the nation was so dissevered from the Established Church that there should be no Established Church at all'. He did not advocate disestablishment himself, preferring that the Church should be utterly subject to the authority of Parliament.[49] Against Horsman, Gladstone persisted in wanting to have his cake and eat it: ' . . . it does appear to me just possible that we ought to have an Established Church, and yet that this House is not the fitting arena for discussions like the present'.[50] Many of the parishioners of Frome, he said, had shown themselves satisfied with Bennett's ministry; Bagot could scarcely have rejected Bennett without falling foul of the law and being 'sconced [i.e. fined] to a fearful extent'; and Bennett's theology was not as extreme as his opponents said.[51] What was needed, said Gladstone, was an examination of the entire state of the ecclesiastical law and the canonical method of dealing with objections to appointments. This would give a useful turn to Horsman's motion, but with that motion as it stood he could not agree.[52]

Gladstone had the backing of ministers,[53] and Goulburn moved an amendment that the laws of institution should be investigated, rather than Bennett's case in particular.[54] But Horsman's motion was carried by 156 votes to 111, and he had gained a nominal victory. The inquiry, however, was not held. Gladstone moved that, when the committee was nominated, Horsman should be ordered to present written charges against Bagot. Horsman said on 18 June that Gladstone was being obstructive, and announced that he would not press his motion.[55] Thus the Government was rid of another embarrassing question.

The lukewarm attitude of ministers towards the Maynooth and Bennett motions seemed to show that they had little positive regard for no-Popery opinion, and that they preferred a policy of religious neutrality. However, this

[47] Ibid. cxxi. 685 ff. [48] Ibid. cxxii. 245–73. [49] Ibid. 270–1.
[50] Ibid. 277. [51] Ibid. cxxii. 279–91. [52] Ibid. 294–6.
[53] Ibid. 298–303 (Pakington), 318–21 (Disraeli).
[54] Ibid. 326.
[55] Ibid. 938–41; *The Times*, 19 June 1852 (leading article, p. 4).

policy appeared to be weakened when, on 15 June, an ill-timed royal proclamation was issued against the wearing of Catholic vestments and ornaments in public. The reason given by Spencer Walpole in the Commons on 16 June was that a Catholic procession had recently been held with banners, images, and crucifixes, giving 'much annoyance to many of Her Majesty's Protestant subjects . . . actual damage did exist of a breach of the peace'. This had caused the Government to reinforce the twenty-sixth clause of the 1829 Relief Act which banned such processions.[56] The official explanation for the proclamation seemed partly designed to please Protestant opinion, and it might have appeared, on the eve of an election, that the Government hoped to win support in Great Britain by this method. But at the same time the proclamation could only hinder Government from gaining Irish Catholic support, which it was wooing by a defence of the Maynooth grant in Irish constituencies. It is unlikely, therefore, that the proclamation had been issued in order to win electoral advantage. Possibly the Cabinet approached the belief, as Disraeli dramatically claimed in an election speech, that it was necessary to act in order to prevent disturbances 'in more than thirty places at least, which would endanger the life of many of Her Majesty's subjects'.[57]

Unfortunately for the ministers, events occurred a fortnight after the proclamation which were the reverse of their intentions. Catholics in Stockport held a procession on Sunday, 27 June. The Irish population in Stockport was exceptionally high, numbering about 25 per cent of the whole, and was the object of hostility from natives on economic, social, and religious grounds.[58] The Catholics made some efforts to observe the proclamation: 'There were no banners in the procession; the priests did not wear canonical vestments, but appeared in ordinary attire . . . The only badges and symbols that might be supposed to contravene the proclamation were a ball and cross and a gilt dove.'[59] But the incident was provocative, given the heated atmosphere of the time; and although there was no opposition 'beyond occasional groans and hisses' during the procession, many Protestants believed that the procession should not have taken place after the proclamation. The affair became a means of expressing antipathy towards Catholicism and resentment at the economic competition of the Irish, who accepted low wages from employers. On Monday afternoon, 28 June, an argument over the procession led to a fight in a public house, followed by fighting on a larger scale, but this died down. On the Tuesday evening an Irish crowd fought the police and allegedly attacked an Anglican Sunday school.[60] In retaliation, Protestants

---

[56] Hansard, cxxii. 803 ff.   [57] *The Times*, 15 July 1852, p. 2.
[58] Ibid. 1 July 1852, p. 8. For an idea of the long-standing tension between Protestants and Catholics in Stockport, see W. R. Ward, *Religion and Society*, 210.
[59] *The Times*, 1 July 1852, p. 8, reprinting report from *Manchester Guardian*, 30 June. The *Manchester Guardian's* account of the riot also appears in D. Ayerst (ed.), *The Guardian Omnibus, 1821–1971* (London, 1973), 136–41. Cf. *Annual Register*, xciv (1852), 90–3.
[60] *The Times*, 1 July 1852, p. 8.

wrecked 2 Catholic chapels and 24 houses occupied by Irish Catholic labourers. One man was killed, 50 wounded, and 114 arrested—all of these were said to be Irish.[61] There was more rioting on the Wednesday night, but the town's meagre police force had been reinforced by troops and 500 special constables, and the disturbances subsided. A rumour that Catholics were coming over from Manchester and other near-by places did not prove correct. A printed address was issued by 'the Rev. Dr. Turner, Roman Catholic Bishop (so called) of Salford', as *The Times* put it, advising Catholics of the Manchester district to keep the peace.[62] *The Times* had no doubt that 'Papal Aggression' had been partly responsible for the outbreak: 'there is no necessity . . . that Dr. Wiseman should be swollen into a Cardinal Archbishop of Westminster . . .'[63]

On account of the Stockport riots the Government could be accused of having stimulated ultra-Protestant feeling. The pacific intentions of the proclamation were denied or disregarded, and the Government's prospects were seriously affected in the elections which began on 6 July. 'Remember Stockport' reverberated through Erin, and the Government's careful nursing of Irish constituencies came to nought.[64]

ii. THE 1852 ELECTION: MAYNOOTH AND VOLUNTARYISM

Perhaps the most striking impression left by the 1852 election was one of widespread bribery and corruption. The lack of vital public interest in the elections is suggested by the fact that only 212 constituencies were fought, out of 374, and that in many of the contests less than 50 per cent of the electorate voted.[65] Current economic prosperity lent some assistance to Derby, for there was apathy over parliamentary reform and no strong resistance to his anti-democratic declarations. But a prosperous country had, with the exception of some county constituencies, no interest in the revival of Protection which some Derbyites still wanted. Protectionist voters could have little confidence in a party among whose leaders were some who wished to bury Protection. Disraeli declared in an election address that there could be no reversal of the decision of 1846, though measures should be taken to relieve the native producer.[66] The Government's economic uncertainty did nothing to improve its political position, though it is also uncertain whether a clear commercial declaration one way or the other would have done better for it.

Religious issues helped the Government even less. Whereas Irish Catholics denounced the Government's proclamation and the connection of this with the Stockport riots, ultra-Protestants disliked the support of the Maynooth grant by Government candidates in Ireland. The Government

[61] Ibid. 3 July 1852, p. 4.   [62] Ibid. 2 July 1852, p. 5, and 3 July 1852.
[63] Ibid. 3 July 1852, p. 4.   [64] J. H. Whyte, *The Independent Irish Party*, 57–62.
[65] Stewart, op. cit. 198–9.   [66] Disraeli Papers, B/I/D/89.

was trying to please different religious opinions as well as different commercial ones. Religious policies aired in Ireland were different from religious hopes aired in Britain, but 'Remember Stockport' spanned the Irish Sea and the effect on Government fortunes was dismal. Not only did the 'Irish Brigade' gain strikingly where Government had hoped to do so. The Peelites lost a little ground before the ultra-Protestant impetus of Protectionist candidates in England; and for this, among other reasons, were further from joining the Government when the elections were over. Furthermore, a party without a consistent religious policy could not hope to increase its ultra-Protestant support; and anti-Catholic Liberal electors, having been at least partially satisfied by their own party in 1851, had no reason to change their vote. Both Russell's policy in 1850–1 and its own Irish policy had robbed the Derby Government of electoral advantage from no-Popery, and the main religious issue in the elections had little effect on the relative position of the two main parties.

Party deadlock on no-Popery, however, was far from meaning that the question was insignificant in the elections. M.P.s who had opposed the Ecclesiastical Titles Bill had reason to fear for their seats. Sir James Graham's patron at Ripon had told him that he was withdrawing his favour.[67] Roundell Palmer's celebrated speech against the second reading of the bill had, he was told, caused a 'great stir' in his constituency of Plymouth, and a strong evangelical clergyman who had voted for him in 1847 now withdrew his support.[68] Palmer decided to stand again in 1852, but withdrew before the poll after seeing the extent of opposition. However, when one of the successful candidates was unseated for bribery, Palmer was returned at a by-election in 1853.[69]

Ultra-Protestant societies passed resolutions and issued addresses to electors as the 1852 contest approached. The East London Protestant Protection Society issued a placard against the Maynooth grant.[70] The Protestant Association adopted a resolution that men should be returned 'who will make the cause of Protestantism paramount to mere party considerations', so that the number of Protestant M.P.s would be doubled and would 'nullify the power of the Pope's members'.[71] This Association also, in a well-publicized address to electors, warned that reliance could not be placed on party men, for 'both Her Majesty's Government and the leaders of the Opposition, indicate a greater desire to secure the "Irish Vote", than to

[67] Speech of H. D. Seymour, member for Poole, 17 Mar. 1851 (Hansard, cxv. 59); Earl de Grey to Graham, 1 Mar. 1851 (Parker, Graham, ii. 130–1), and Graham's reply (ibid. 131, date not given). Graham was returned for Carlisle.

[68] Dr. James Yonge, Palmer's agent, to Palmer, 21, 23 Mar., 2 Apr. 1851 (Selborne Papers, vol. 1862, fos. 4–9, 14–17); Palmer to Rev. J. Hatchard, 24 Mar. 1851 (ibid., fos. 10–11); R. Palmer, Memorials, pt. I: Family and Personal, 1766–1865 (2 vols., London, 1896), ii. 82–3.

[69] Palmer, op. cit. ii. 132–41, 146–50; The Times, 6 July 1852, p. 4.

[70] The Times, 7 July 1852, p. 3.

[71] Sixteenth Annual Report of Protestant Association, v–vi, 12–13.

legislate on sound Protestant and Constitutional principles'.[72] 'We hold', said the address, 'that the Grant to Maynooth ought to be withdrawn; and that the Papal Aggression should be thoroughly repelled.'[73] An appeal from the managing committee of the recently formed Protestant Alliance concentrated on the Maynooth grant. The Commons had ignored demands for repeal of the grant, and it was hoped that M.P.s would be pressed to demand repeal, together with the subjection of convents 'to the inspection and control of the law'.[74] An address of the Scottish Reformation Society said that Popery had moved from stealthy progress to open aggression. Perhaps as many as 60 or 70 Catholic M.P.s would be returned to the next Parliament, and they needed to be met 'by a larger band of equally determined Protestants'.[75] This society stressed the need to rise above party considerations in order to return firm Protestants. 'Electors!', exhorted the address, 'vote for no man who is not a decided Protestant, prepared to withdraw the Maynooth Endowment, and to resist all national grants to Popery.'[76] 'The one great duty of the new Parliament', echoed the Scottish Free Church *Witness*, 'will be to preserve Britain as a Protestant state.'[77]

Prospective candidates were being sounded on their religious opinions soon after the Derby Government took office. The radical Unitarian John Benjamin Smith, who was a candidate for Stockport, was told in March by the curate-in-charge of St. Peter's church in the town that one who disavowed the absolute and supreme divinity of Christ should not represent 'a professing Christian constituency'. Smith was also asked whether he would support the enforcement of the Ecclesiastical Titles Act and vote for repeal of the Maynooth grant.[78] A placard dated 2 July, addressed to the Protestant electors of Stockport, appealed to the no-Popery opinion which the riots had just displayed. Smith, said the placard, had been asked to give up his seat at the Stirling burghs on account of his pro-Catholic votes, but 'the sample of the "British lion" displayed the other night' promised that Stockport would not give him a berth.[79] Despite this opposition, and a pro-Catholic speech which he delivered at the nomination, Smith was returned after a contest.

The elections did not yield the fruits for which ultra-Protestants hoped. It is true that leading Peelites, whose ecclesiastical liberalism was well known, were hard pressed in the constituencies. While Roundell Palmer retreated

---

[72] *Foreign or Domestic Legislation: an address to the electors, by the Protestant Association* (signed by James Lord; London, 1852), 2–3, printed in *The Times*, 6 July 1852, p. 2.

[73] Ibid.

[74] *The Times*, 22 June 1852, p. 1. Cf. *Witness*, 26 June 1852.

[75] *Address of the Scottish Reformation Society to the Electors of Scotland* (Edinburgh, 1852), printed in *Witness*, 26 June 1852.

[76] Ibid.

[77] 14 July 1852, leading article. Cf. anti-Maynooth speeches at General Assembly of the Scottish Free Church, and report of this Assembly's 'Committee on Popery', *Witness*, 28 May 1852.

[78] Rev. J. M. A. Meridyth to J. B. Smith, 25 Mar. 1852 (J. B. Smith Papers, S. 341).

[79] Printed in *The Times*, 6 July 1852, p. 8.

from Plymouth, Edward Cardwell was defeated at Liverpool after the efforts of the city's Catholic Registration Committee had been overcome by ultra-Protestant opinion stimulated by Hugh McNeile; two Derbyites, Forbes Mackenzie and Charles Turner, were returned after making anti-Maynooth speeches.[80] But in few other constituencies does ultra-Protestantism seem to have been so effective. Gladstone was returned for the second seat at Oxford University, despite opposition. A London committee of members of the University disliked his hostility to the Ecclesiastical Titles Bill and his support of Jewish relief. But they did not succeed in having the ultra-Protestant J. C. Colquhoun adopted as a candidate, and resorted to the more moderate R. B. Marsham, Warden of Merton College, who came third on the poll.[81] 'If it were not for the rejection of Cardwell, and of Roundell Palmer', wrote Aberdeen, 'I do not know that we [Peelites] should have any great reason to complain of the general character of the elections.'[82] This comment was rather too optimistic. The Peelite Philip Pusey withdrew from Berkshire (as Aberdeen mentioned), apparently because he was the brother of Dr. Pusey;[83] and several other Peelites failed in the elections.[84] But some newly elected members showed themselves to be Peelites; some defeated Peelites were returned after petition; and the Peelite strength in Parliament by early 1853 has been calculated as 44, certainly no less than before the elections.[85]

The Liberals had generally better fortune, perhaps because they were less vulnerable to ultra-Protestant feeling on account of their Ecclesiastical Titles Act. Such a reason, however, can scarcely explain the return of Macaulay for Edinburgh in 1852, for he favoured the Maynooth grant in a contest dominated by the anti-Maynooth cry. Questioned by the Scottish Reformation Society on the subject, he would not deign to reply.[86] The four other candidates in this election favoured repeal of the grant, but did so for differing reasons based on varying religious views, and these divisions assisted Macaulay.[87] At Glasgow, however, Lord Melgund, the heir of Minto, with-

[80] Burke, *A Catholic History of Liverpool*, 97–8; Guirron, 'The Ecclesiastical Titles Crisis', 10 ff.; *The Times*, 7 July 1852, pp. 3–4. But Mackenzie, who had voted for the Maynooth Bill in 1845, would not commit himself to introduce a bill to repeal the grant.

[81] S. Northcote, *A Statement of Facts connected with the Election of the Rt. Hon. W. E. Gladstone as member for the University of Oxford in 1847, and with his re-elections in 1852 and 1853* (Oxford and London, 1853), 7–12; letters of Rev. R. Greswell to Gladstone, May–July 1852 (Gladstone Papers, Add. M.S. 44181, fos. 78–135).

[82] Aberdeen to Gladstone, 16 July 1852 (ibid. 44088, fos. 131–2).

[83] *The Times*, 6 July 1852, p. 4. Dr. Pusey wrote a defence of his brother, containing hints which the latter used more briefly in his address to electors. Dr. Pusey's draft is in the Pusey Papers.

[84] *The Times*, 10 July 1852, p. 2 (leading article); J. E. Denison to Earl Fitzwilliam, 12 July 1852 (Fitzwilliam Papers, Sheffield, G 20). Cf. Conacher, *Peelites and the Party System*, 114.

[85] Conacher, op. cit. 118 ff., 233–5.

[86] *Witness*, 3, 9, and 26 June, 3 July 1852; *The Times*, 30 June 1852, p. 8; Craw, 'The Scottish Disruption and its effect on Politics', 30 ff.

[87] Craw, op. cit. 30 ff.; *Witness*, 26 June 1852; *United Presbyterian Magazine*, vi (1852), 383–4.

drew after the poll had commenced rather than face defeat after saying that he opposed repeal of the grant—'the wretched question which so much agitated Scotland'.[88] After the 'Maynooth Paroxysm at Glasgow', wrote Graham, and the defeat of Cardwell at Liverpool, where 'Bigotry reigns triumphant', he believed no popular candidate could succeed unless he took an anti-Maynooth pledge 'which leads directly to voluntaryism in Ireland, and ultimately to the overthrow of all established Churches throughout the realm'.[89] Riots occurred at Wigan during the elections, perhaps stimulated by the news from Stockport: many prisoners were taken, special constables were sworn in, and troops were brought from Preston.[90]

Several of the ministers, with an eye to future policy, detached themselves in election declarations from the no-Popery cry and avoided any commitment on Maynooth. Disraeli noted that the Government supported an inquiry into the College, but did not wish to 'prejudge' the question. 'We have been anxious', he said, 'to subdue the heat of religious controversy, and to deal impartially with all Her Majesty's subjects whether in communion with the Church of Rome or the Church of England; but we cannot sanction an opinion . . . [that] the constitution of this country has ceased to be Protestant.'[91] J. W. Henley said he was determined to defend the position of the established Church, but did not mention Maynooth, and Sir John Pakington and Spencer Walpole merely said that ministers would uphold the Protestant Establishment.[92] R. A. Christopher, Chancellor of the Duchy of Lancaster, was more explicit in saying that he had opposed Catholic concessions since entering Parliament in 1826, and that the results of an inquiry into Maynooth might lead him to vote for repeal of the grant.[93] Lord John Manners, on the other hand, was hampered by his Tractarianism and said that an inquiry into Maynooth must be fair and impartial.[94] Despite these handicaps he was elected. Progressive Conservatives such as Lord Stanley, Derby's heir, were embarrassed by the ultra-Protestant emphasis of some of their colleagues. Stanley thought this was 'a case of playing to the pit'; but, he added, 'reasonable people are tolerant of such measures at election time, and the unreasonable people are mostly with us'.[95] The royal proclamation against Catholic vestments in public had, he believed, won for him the votes of all the ultra-Protestants at King's Lynn; but he thought this movement could be turned 'into a better channel', and hoped the Church might even be persuaded to

[88] *The Times*, 5 July 1852, p. 5; Andrew Bannatyne to John Richardson, 9 July 1852 (Minto Papers, 135/1).

[89] Graham to Aberdeen, 'private', 12 July 1852 (Aberdeen Papers, Add. MS. 43190, fos. 289–92).

[90] *The Times*, 10 July 1852, p. 4.

[91] Printed election address, 2 June 1852 (Disraeli Papers, B/I/D/89).

[92] *The Times*, 3 July 1852, p. 3; 25 June 1852, p. 5; 5 July 1852, p. 5.

[93] Ibid. 26 June 1852, p. 4; 6 July 1852, p. 4.

[94] Ibid. 9 July 1852, p. 3.

[95] Stanley to Disraeli, 19 July 1852 (Disraeli Papers, B/XX/S/554); cf. Stanley's address, *The Times*, 23 June 1852, p. 8.

agree to a reform of church-rates.[96] The young Lord Henry Lennox was more forthright. 'You certainly never overrated the mischief of our horrible No Popery cry', he wrote to Disraeli; ' . . . 4 young men finally declined to write for the Govt which had such a cry. It is too annoying to lose promising young stuff for so absurd & bigoted a piece of folly.'[97]

At least one Government supporter tried to deflect attention from the awkward Protection question on to religious topics. R. P. Warren, standing for the Flint boroughs, was asked by a member of his audience whether he would agree to the reintroduction of Protection. He replied curiously:

The question did not appear to be between protection and free trade, but whether the Queen or the Pope was to be the supreme authority in this country (Cries of 'Answer the question'). With respect to the Maynooth grant, he was of opinion that it had utterly failed in the purpose for which it was intended (A great disturbance arose, because Mr. Warren had not answered the question given above). A gentleman upon the hustings then said to him, 'Will you vote for a 5s. duty, or any duty in fact, upon corn, if proposed by Lord Derby?' Mr. Warren replied, 'I will not pledge myself for or against it' (Great uproar). He was an advocate for the most comprehensive system of religious toleration. He declared himself to be most strongly opposed to the admission of Jews into Parliament.[98]

Warren was defeated. His successful opponent, the Peelite Sir John Hanmer, had declared himself against the Maynooth grant.[99] Another Peelite, Thomas Greene, who condemned the grant (in compensation perhaps for a firm declaration in favour of Free Trade),[100] was initially defeated at Lancaster but returned after petition.

Catholic electors must have found it difficult to choose between a party which had introduced the Ecclesiastical Titles Bill and one which had issued the recent proclamation. The wife of Sir G. C. Lewis said that the Durham Letter and the Titles Act had at first driven Catholics to oppose former Whig ministers, but that some had reverted to giving a Liberal vote because of the proclamation.[101] Catholics could also support radicals who had pursued concession. In the Westminster constituency voters were apparently advised by the Catholic Election Committee for the Metropolitan Boroughs to support William Coningham, a radical, against two Liberal rivals who were unsatisfactory on religious questions. Coningham was unsuccessful, and blamed no-Popery for his defeat.[102] This Catholic Election Committee was also said to have recommended support for Bernal Osborne, who had voted

---

[96] Stanley to Disraeli, 19 July 1852 (see last note). Stanley may have been planning the pamphlet on church-rates which he produced in 1853.

[97] 7 Aug. (?) 1852 (Disraeli Papers, B/XX/LX/8).

[98] *The Times*, 12 July 1852, p. 12.   [99] Ibid.

[100] Ibid. 2 July 1852, p. 5.

[101] Lady Theresa Lewis to Russell, 19 July 1852 (Russell Papers, 10 C, fo. 32).

[102] *The Times*, 7 July 1852, p. 3; 9 July, p. 2.

for the Maynooth grant and against the Titles Bill.[103] With religious consistency, Catholics opposed a radical who had supported the Titles Bill. At Bradford Catholic voters intervened dramatically against Colonel T. P. Thompson, who had voted for the Titles Bill and defended it in an election address. When Thompson seemed near success at the poll, about thirty Catholic voters marched to the booths and plumped for Henry Wickham, a Conservative who had condemned the Maynooth grant.[104] Wickham ousted Thompson from the second seat by 6 votes.

In Britain a tiny Catholic electorate meant that effective action of this kind was rare, but in Ireland Catholics had their own popular party which campaigned against Whigs and Tories alike. In October 1851 Clarendon had said that the Catholic Defence Association was 'a dead failure' and that the influence of the priests was waning; 'though', he added, 'if a general election occurs within a 12 month they will be able to do mischief'.[105] He was right. The Defence Association and the Tenant League between them 'included a great majority of the Liberal electorate: and . . . they included the united ranks of the Catholic clergy, whose political influence was enormous'.[106] The Irish Brigade obtained 48 seats, an increase of 20 since the dissolution. Their success helped not only to reduce the 'Irish Whigs' from 36 to 15 but to restrict the ministerial gain in Ireland to 3 seats (a total of 41).[107] The Government could not have expected much support from staunch followers of the Irish Brigade, but the royal proclamation further reduced the prospect of Catholic support. Catholics saw the proclamation as an attempt to secure the ultra-Protestant vote. 'The Durham Letter', it was said by the *Freeman's Journal*, 'can have no comparison with the Derby Proclamation.'[108] The Stockport riots only allowed the Government's intentions to be presented in an even worse light. 'Never was outrage more deliberately planned', claimed the *Tablet*, 'than the Stockport outrages and murders . . . were planned by Lord Derby and Mr. Walpole . . . when they issued their proclamation against the free exercise of the Catholic religion.'[109] The details of riotous sacrilege at the Stockport chapels were displayed on an election placard in County Tipperary.[110]

The Irish elections were the obverse of the British, a spirited rejection of no-Popery. After the elections, the Brigade condemned the Irish Church Establishment and demanded (with obvious reference to the Ecclesiastical Titles Act and the royal proclamation) the repeal of 'all laws which impose penalties on the ecclesiastics of any Church, or prohibit the performance of

---

[103] P. H. Bagenal, *The Life of Ralph Bernal Osborne, M.P.* (London, 1884), 127; *The Times*, 19 July 1852, p. 3.
[104] Wright, 'Politics and Opinion in Nineteenth Century Bradford', 387–8, 398.
[105] Clarendon to Sir G. C. Lewis, 31 Oct. 1851 (Clarendon Papers, c. 532).
[106] J. H. Whyte, op. cit. 42.   [107] Ibid. 85–6.
[108] Quoted ibid. 58.   [109] Quoted ibid. 59–60.
[110] Printed in J. Lord, *Popery at the Hustings* (London, 1852), 74–5.

spiritual functions, or the exercise of ecclesiastical rights, order, or jurisdiction . . .'[111] Ultra-Protestants replied with accusations that the priests had
abused their spiritual authority for political ends,[112] and could take comfort
in the future from the rapid decline of the independent Irish party. The
Government, for its part, wished to establish good relations with the papacy.
Sir Henry Bulwer, minister at Florence, was sent on a special mission to
Rome, and the electoral extravagance of Irish priests was pointed out in
order to obtain some quietening noises from the Pope.[113]

Dissent added a familiar variation to the main religious theme in this
election. It appears, from a limited correlation of poll-books and church
membership lists, that Dissenters of the older denominations maintained a
strong tendency to vote Liberal. Of 170 members of Fish Street Congregational chapel, Hull (as the list stood in 1850), 64 voted in the 1852 election,
and 56 of them (including the minister) split their vote between the two Liberal candidates, James Clay and Viscount Goderich. Both of these candidates
supported Dissenting claims. One member plumped for Clay, 5 split their
vote between the Conservative candidates, and 2 split between one Liberal
and one Conservative.[114] No members of the chapel who had voted in
1841 displayed a clear party change in 1852.[115] In the 1868 election, also, no
party changes were shown, though among those who had joined the chapel
since 1850 there was more tendency to vote Conservative than among
the older members (8 of the post-1850 members voted Conservative and 19
voted Liberal).[116] The Liberal tendency of Dissenters would vary between
constituencies, depending on local electoral circumstances and the views
of individual candidates. But the tendency was sufficiently marked for the
return of the Congregational Edward Ball as Protectionist M.P. for Cam-
bridgeshire to cause special disgusted comment in the *Nonconformist*.[117]

Voluntary organizations and periodicals hoped, in 1852, to improve on the
basis laid in 1847. It was recognized, however, that the victory of Free Trade
was important, and that this end might not always be served by exclusive
support of Voluntary candidates.[118] The Anti-State Church Association
formed an Election Committee, and advised local committees to bring for-

[111] Quoted Whyte, 88-9.   [112] Lord, op. cit., *passim*.
[113] Monypenny and Buckle, *Life of Disraeli*, iii. 399-401.
[114] Lists of members of Fish St. Congregational chapel (Local History Library, Hull, no. 14);
The Poll-Book . . . for the borough of Kingston-upon-Hull, 8 July 1852, compiled by J. Stark (Hull,
1852; in Local History Library, Hull). Accuracy in identifying the members with voters of the same
name cannot be guaranteed.
[115] List of members, and *The Poll-Book . . . for the borough of Kingston-upon-Hull*, 30 June 1841
(Hull, 1841; Local History Library, Hull).
[116] List of members and *The Poll Book . . . for the borough of Kingston-upon-Hull*, 1868
(Hull, 1868; Local History Library, Hull). It should be remembered that the 1868 election
was mainly concerned with Irish disestablishment, which was not universally popular among
Dissenters.
[117] *Nonconformist*, 28 July 1852, 583.
[118] Minutes of executive committee of Anti-State Church Association, ii. 324-5, 375-6 (12 Feb.,

ward a Voluntary candidate where practicable. Even if candidates could not be persuaded to take a rigorous Voluntary course, 'opposition to all further grants for religious purposes, and to the extention of the State–Church system, should be strenuously insisted upon . . .'[119] The Election Committee distributed placards, handbills, and tracts, but shortage of money made it cautious, and it was resolved that not more than £25 be spent for this purpose. An address to electors was issued by the Association, saying that 'a Church Establishment involves, in regard to men's spiritual interests, all the unnecessary and hurtful restrictions with which Protection but lately fettered their temporal interests'.[120]

Many declarations in favour of Voluntaryism were made by candidates; other candidates advocated the removal of church-rates and the reform of the ecclesiastical courts without going to the length of a Voluntary position.[121] In Wales this election saw an advance in the political activity of the Nonconformist majority. Landlord influence and the absence of the secret ballot were still effective hindrances, but the Baptist magazine, *Seren Gomer*, drew on historic national example to put heart into its readers: ' . . . ballot or no ballot, did the spirit of our forefathers, from the days of Caradog the son of Bran until the days of Llewelyn the Last Prince, remain amongst us, things would not be as they are today'.[122] Dissenters, even including Calvinistic Methodists who had hitherto been Conservative or apolitical, actively campaigned in contests, successfully in Denbighshire but unsuccessfully in the Caernarvon boroughs.[123] 'I have read', wrote one gentleman to a prominent Calvinistic Methodist, that 'your ministers joined heart and hand, soul and voice with the drunkard and the infidel . . . At Denbigh you have fought hand to hand on the same side with Mr. Price the Independent . . . and with a Baptist minister . . .'[124] A second Welsh Dissenting M.P., Walter Coffin (returned for Cardiff boroughs), joined David Morris, who had represented the Carmarthen boroughs since 1837.[125] As yet, however, Dissenting politicians had barely touched the surface of their potential Welsh support.

Scottish Voluntaryism, whose main support came from the United Presby-

---

3 June 1852); Mason, 'The Rise of Combative Dissent', 112 ff. Cf. *Eclectic Review*, 5th Ser. iv (July–Dec. 1852), 123–6.

[119] Election circular issued by Anti-State Church Association, dated 19 June 1852 (copy in Minutes of the Association).

[120] Address to electors by Anti-State Church Association, dated 1 July 1852 (copy in Minutes of the Association).

[121] e.g. Sir Benjamin Hall, Marylebone (*The Times*, 1 July, p. 3); George Scovell, Southwark (ibid. 3 July 1852, p. 5).

[122] Quoted and translated in O. Parry, 'The Parliamentary Representation of Wales and Monmouthshire during the Nineteenth Century, but mainly until 1870' (unpubl. Univ. of Wales M.A. thesis, 1924), 213.

[123] Ibid. 215–26.

[124] B. W. Wynne to Thomas Gee, 31 July 1852 (Thos. Gee Papers, 8309 D, fo. 423).

[125] David, 'Political and Electioneering Activity in South East Wales', 214.

terian denomination, was displayed in the Edinburgh election. Maynooth
was a major issue. The Liberal Independent Committee, which had broken
with the Whigs, nominated Duncan Mclaren, the Lord Provost and a Voluntary. McLaren attempted to obtain Free Church support by saying that he opposed the Maynooth grant on Protestant as well as Voluntary grounds. But Free
Churchmen, being against Voluntaryism in principle, kept their support for
their co-religionist Charles Cowan, the sitting member, and for Alexander
Campbell of Monzie, another Free Churchman and a Conservative.[126] There
was a further Conservative candidate, the Hon. T. C. Bruce. Conservatives,
who had no wish to encourage Voluntaryism, gave some votes to Cowan and
Macaulay when McLaren was second on the poll, thus helping Cowan to win
the second seat. The Whig Macaulay, who had been rejected by the city in
1847 and was described, on account of his studied aloofness, as 'the worst
electioneerer since Coriolanus',[127] triumphed amid all these politico-religious
divisions and emerged head of the poll. The *United Presbyterian Magazine*
blamed the result on Free Churchmen who had refused to support a Voluntary candidate.[128] Ministers, at least, faithfully supported candidates of their
own denomination. Of 9 electors who were Free Church ministers, 1 plumped
for Cowan and the other 8 voted for Cowan and Campbell. Of 7 Church of
Scotland ministers, 4 plumped for Bruce, 2 voted for Bruce and Cowan, and
1 for Bruce and Macaulay. Several United Presbyterian ministers plumped
for McLaren. Only a few ministers voted for Macaulay.[129]

Compared with 1847, the number of Voluntary M.P.s returned seems to
have dropped somewhat. The *Nonconformist* claimed there were 24 firm
Voluntaries, 15 new members who might be Voluntaries, and 25 'sympathizers'.[130] Not all Voluntaries were Dissenters, nor were all Dissenters
Voluntaries, and it has been estimated that 38 Protestant Dissenters were in
the new Parliament.[131] This total included 4 Scottish Free Churchmen and 2
Wesleyans; 1 Free Churchman and 1 Wesleyan, both being new members,
were listed by the *Nonconformist* as possible Voluntaries.[132] The success of
Edward Miall at Rochdale and of George Hadfield at Sheffield compensated
for the defeat of George Thompson at Tower Hamlets and Colonel Thompson at Bradford. The Voluntary successes were a potential challenge to
Whigs, Conservatives, and Peelites alike.

---

[126] *Scotsman*, 9 June 1852; *Witness*, 12, 16, 19, 23, and 26 June 1852; *Nonconformist*, 21 July
1852, p. 569.

[127] Trevelyan, *Macaulay*, 566.   [128] Vol. vi (1852), 383.

[129] *Poll-Book of Election for City of Edinburgh, 1852* (Edinburgh, 1854; list of electors corrected
after appeal court; copy in Guildhall Library, London).

[130] 14 July 1852, 537.

[131] Miall, *Life of Miall*, 171; Mason, op. cit. 113 f.

[132] *Nonconformist*, 4 Aug. 1852, 603; 14 July 1852, 537. This journal gave a total of 33 Dissenting
M.P.s: 13 Congregationalists, 11 Unitarians, 3 United Presbyterians, 2 Baptists, 2 Wesleyans,
1 Quaker, and 1 Plymouth Brother (4 Aug. 1852, 603). The *Eclectic Review* gave a total of 34 (5th
Ser., iv. 381). There were about 50 Catholic M.P.s (ibid. 382).

The prevalence of religious issues in the election was so pronounced that G. J. Harney posed a Chartist query: 'of what interest to the poor and unenfranchised are these fights of rival Churches and rival oppressors ?'[133]

The Government's electoral bid had only slightly paid off. Contemporary estimates of Derby's supporters in the new House varied from 290 to 310; but the Liberals had not greatly diminished, the Peelites were about the same, and Derby did not have a majority. The election had divided leading Peelites farther from the Conservatives (largely over the ultra-Protestant question)[134] and the prospect of a Liberal–Peelite coalition gradually strengthened over the next few months.[135] But Russell's Ecclesiastical Titles Act still rankled, especially with Gladstone, who found Derby's religious attitude more acceptable. Gladstone and Bishop Wilberforce wanted the revival of Convocation and a solution to the problem of church-rates.[136] They had the support of Blomfield, who agreed with a suggestion that registered Dissenters should be exempt from church-rates.[137] Wilberforce thought that the Government would be a lot more sympathetic to their views if Gladstone joined it.[138] Phillpotts, however, vehemently denounced, in a letter to Derby, any alteration in the age-old method of levying church-rates. He clearly feared the prospect of a decision by the House of Lords in the Braintree Case—a decision actually made the following year—that a rate was invalid if not made by a majority of the vestry meeting. Defeat on this point should not be anticipated, he said, by untimely concession.[139]

The church-rate question hung fire for the present, but Convocation made valuable progress. Lord Brougham was spreading the rumour that '"Convocation" was the bait by which Lord Derby intended to catch Gladstone'.[140] Some of the leading Peelites disliked Gladstone's Convocation campaign, and especially Derby's rumoured sympathy with it. Aberdeen said he disapproved of restoring Convocation,[141] and Graham denounced Derby's 'trickery'. If Convocation were allowed to sit and debate, said Graham, there would be 'a large Secession, & probably a Free Kirk . . . The design of this Concession to the High Church Party is a bid for Gladstone & his adherents . . .'[142] Probably no such 'design' existed. Aberdeen said on 24 October that the rumour was 'peremptorily contradicted in the Government Papers', though he

[133] Quoted Wright, 'Politics and Opinion in Nineteenth Century Bradford', 396.

[134] Southgate, *The Passing of the Whigs*, 233; Conacher, *The Peelites and the Party System*, 126–8.

[135] C. H. Stuart, 'The Formation of the Coalition Cabinet of 1852', *Trans. Royal Hist. Soc.* 5th Ser. iv (1954), 64–6; Conacher, op. cit. 124 ff.

[136] Gladstone to Wilberforce, 3 Oct., 2 Nov. 1852 (Wilberforce Papers, d. 35).

[137] Blomfield to Derby, 'private', 19 July 1852 (Derby Papers, 127/6).

[138] Wilberforce to Gladstone, 8 Oct. 1852 (Wilberforce Papers, c. 2); Wilberforce to Archdeacon Robert Wilberforce, 22 Sept. 1852, copy (ibid., d. 19, pp. 12–13).

[139] Phillpotts to Derby, 26 Aug. 1852 (Derby Papers, 142/3).

[140] Aberdeen to Graham, 20 Oct. 1852 (Graham Papers, microfilms, 124).

[141] Ibid.   [142] Graham to Aberdeen, 22 Oct. 1852, copy (ibid.).

still believed there might be some foundation for it.[143] G. C. Lewis told Graham: 'The Convocation scheme is clearly given up—they [the Government] were frightened by [a] broadside in the Times.'[144] The evangelical *Record*, however, claimed on 1 November that Derby intended to advise the Queen that Convocation should have deliberative powers.[145]

Whatever the attitude of the Government, Convocation made a solid advance at the opening of the new Parliament in November. The Convocation of Canterbury met first on 5 November; then again on 12 November, when Bishop Wilberforce moved an amendment to the address to the Crown, desiring that the former powers of Convocation should be resumed. The amendment was carried after alteration. Wilberforce also moved successfully that Convocation should ask the Crown's permission to draft a Clergy Discipline Bill. In the lower house of Convocation a three-day discussion ('the first real debate for 150 years') took place on the question of reviving convocational functions, and a resolution approving this revival was passed. The upper house appointed a committee on clerical discipline, the lower a committee on grievances. Convocation adjourned until the following February, but its success had been sufficient to alarm its opponents. Shaftesbury raised the matter in the Lords, and was assured by Derby that the ministry had no intention of advising the Queen to revive Convocation.[146] Although the advocates of Convocation had been officially discouraged by the Premier, their aim had made real progress during his ministry.

Derby may have hoped to win Gladstone, but the barrier of commercial policy and distrust of Disraeli kept Gladstone firmly away from Derby. On 3 December Disraeli introduced his budget in the Commons, seeking to compensate agriculture and reform the tax system, and the debate produced a notable collision between him and Gladstone. Gladstone's attack was followed by the defeat of the Government by 21 votes on 17 December. Derby resigned later on the same day. He had checked Disraeli's attempt to obtain the help of the Irish Brigade, which was a dubious proposition in any case because the budget extended the income tax to Ireland.[147]

Croker lamented that Derby had gone out on a budget which many Protectionists disliked, instead of on the principle of maintaining the Protestant Constitution, 'round which his friends . . . would have rallied'.[148] Conceivably, however, Derby's Government might have done no more harm to the Protestant Constitution by resigning than by staying in office. Had the Government entrenched itself in power it would have had to face the familiar

[143] Aberdeen to Graham, 24 Oct. 1852 (ibid.). Cf. Russell to Graham, 23 Oct. 1852 (ibid.).
[144] Lewis to Graham, 25 Oct. 1852 (ibid.).
[145] Welch, 'The Revival of an active Convocation of Canterbury', 192.
[146] Ibid. 192–3; Hansard, cxxiii. 277–9, also 247–9. On Shaftesbury's complex attitude, which was not entirely unsympathetic, see Gladstone to Shaftesbury, 8 Nov. 1852, draft (Gladstone Papers, 44300, fos. 11–12); Shaftesbury to Gladstone, 11 Nov. 1852 (ibid., fos. 13–14).
[147] Stewart, 207, 211.   [148] Ibid. 217.

claims of Catholics, Dissenters, and Jews, and in response to these might well have joined the nineteenth-century stream of liberal concession, as happened when Conservatives took office again in 1858. The ministers might have succeeded in restraining their ultra tail more effectively than when Liberals were in power, thus avoiding the Spoonerite anti-Catholic forays of the succeeding years. But the Government was replaced by a Peelite–Liberal coalition, which was followed by a lengthy Liberal domination. Conservatives were therefore, by the beginning of the 1860s, thrown back on Erastianism and Church defence, forces which found an incongruous champion in Disraeli.

CHAPTER VIII

The Tension of Equilibrium, 1852–1859

I. RELIGIOUS TURMOIL IN AN 'AGE OF EQUIPOISE'

THE COMPARATIVE social and political apathy of the 1850s may be explained by the lessening of economic dispute and depression. Commercial prosperity could not silence religious issues, though these also were rather less prominent than in the immediately preceding years. Between 1852 and 1859 the advances made by ecclesiastical movements were not spectacular, controversial episodes were perhaps less frequent, and something of the equipoise visible in other spheres was seen in religion. But the equilibrium was a tense one. The major issues remained seethingly alive. Ultra-Protestants had not been satiated but stimulated to fresh vigilance and endeavour by the Ecclesiastical Titles dispute, and they were alarmed by the Catholic growth caused by Irish immigration. Irish Catholics wished to relieve their humiliation of 1851 by challenging the Church of Ireland. High churchmen, spurred by the Gorham judgement, wanted spiritual government to be conducted by churchmen. Jews still wanted entry to Parliament, and Dissenters' demands persisted. Some of these demands made progress in the 1850s, and the result was the increase of State neutrality in religion. But other demands awaited the more fruitful political background of the next decade.

Evangelicalism enjoyed a belated worldly ascendancy in the 1850s. It acquired (through the ironic countenance of Palmerston) a more official face and greater influence on Government. The revival of 1859 demonstrated that new popular evangelical appeals had not lost their spontaneity and attraction,[1] but the continuous century-old movement was well set in its maturity, and excessively puritanical and negative aspects were well to the fore. One example was Sabbatarianism. Motions by the radical M.P. Sir Joshua Walmsley (representing the radical and secular National Sunday League) to open the British Museum and National Gallery on Sundays after morning service were defeated by 235 votes to 48 in March 1855, and by 376 to 48 in February 1856. Not all the members who opposed the motions were evangelicals, for they included the Tractarian Roundell Palmer and Palmerston himself.[2] Thus ended Walmsley's pious hope that ' . . . thousands, if not tens of thousands, who themselves seldom left their crowded courts and alleys on that day, save for the public-house, would be found with their wives

[1] J. E. Orr, *The Second Evangelical Awakening* (London, 1949).
[2] Hansard, cxxxvii. 915 ff.; cxl. 1053–121.

and families at these sources of instruction . . .'[3] However, a bill of 1855 to stop Sunday trading was abandoned after riots had taken place in Hyde Park.[4]

The ultra-Protestantism of many evangelicals spanned the decade. The official results of the Papal Aggression uproar may have been minimal, but the convictions displayed during the crisis were maintained after it. These convictions sought new channels of expression and popish objects to attack. Charlatan lecturers acting as eloquent prophets of anti-Popery flourished as they could only do in an age when blinkered audiences abounded and when enmity (like love) was blind. Achilli's tales were acclaimed until Newman exposed him. Solid Scots Free Churchmen put their faith in the Rev. Patrick McMenemy, an Irish no-Popery lecturer, until he was arrested for brawling in a Liverpool brothel.[5] The relentless advance of Popery overhung Protestant concern and action. Between 1846 and 1856, reported the *Protestant Magazine*, Catholic places of worship in Great Britain had increased from 629 to 849, 34 convents had increased to 91, and 776 priests to 1,142.[6] In this magazine transgressions of the Ecclesiastical Titles Act were recorded; the arrest of two monks for begging in Liverpool was noted; the Indian Mutiny was seen as a divine retribution to British imperial rule, not only for its oppression but because it had tolerated pagan idolatry in the same way as 'popish superstitions' at home.[7] The journal lamented, however, the decline of the no-Popery impetus with which the decade had started: 'The ebullition of popular feeling in 1851 . . . has been . . . succeeded by comparative inactivity, if not by indifference and apathy.'[8] When the earl of Winchilsea died in 1858, it was regretted that 'out of the one hundred and nine peers who voted against the [Relief] Bill of 1829, only nineteen temporal and two spiritual are now living'.[9] The old Brunswick guard was not being replaced. The battle with liberalism was still being lost, and the outlook was dire.

Anti-Catholicism was endemic in mid-century Britain, and was fed by supposed scandals regarding convents and the confessional.[10] Convents were the especial concern of Henry Drummond, an M.P. who had spoken with outstanding provocation in favour of the Ecclesiastical Titles Bill. He attempted, without success, to pass bills regulating these institutions. The more obvious anti-Catholic demonstrations took place in areas of high Irish immigration. The Stockport riots of 1852 provided one example, and industrial Scotland provided many others. In Scotland were found not only Patrick McMenemy,

---

[3] Ibid. cxl. 1055.

[4] Ibid. cxxxvi. 55–64, 1911 ff.; cxxxix. 368–71; B. Harrison, 'The Sunday Trading Riots of 1855', *Hist. Jl.* viii (1965), 219 ff.

[5] Handley, *The Irish in Scotland*, 245.   [6] *Protestant Magazine*, xviii (1856), 38–40.

[7] Ibid. xx (1858), 141, 134; xix (1857), 125–9.

[8] Ibid. xx (1858), 23.   [9] Ibid. 31.

[10] G. F. A. Best, 'Popular Protestantism', in R. Robson (ed.), *Ideas and Institutions of Victorian Britain* (London, 1967), 127 ff.

the 'Angel Gabriel' and Alessandro Gavazzi, bizarre defenders of Protestantism from Ireland or Italy, but two indigenous and apparently more reliable champions who might well have competed for the title of the Scottish Shaftesbury. These were James Begg, the Free Church leader, and John Hope, an Edinburgh lawyer and member of the Church of Scotland (not to be confused with the Moderate leader in the ten years' conflict). Both of them combined no-Popery and philanthropy in equally ardent proportions.[11] Hope wanted the parliamentary vote to be given to more Protestants, but would refuse it to Papists since 'they were not qualified to rule, not being civilly or religiously free, but in subjection to priests, bishops and Pope'.[12] Begg's *Handbook of Popery* went through several editions and doubtless helped its rough but genial author to win his unwholesome reputation among Scottish Catholics.[13] Proselytizing societies flourished. The Scottish Protestant Society was established in 1854 with John Hope as secretary, and the Scottish Reformation Society, founded in 1850, was still energetic in 1862.[14] In 1856 a recently built Catholic church at Kelso, endowed by the convert James Hope-Scott, was 'attacked by a Protestant mob, set fire to, and burned to the ground, with the schoolhouse and dwelling-house adjoining'.[15]

There were signs that Scottish Protestants saw themselves as more active than the English.[16] But wider British Protestant societies, drawing their membership mainly from England, were also active in the 1850s, pursuing policies which an Anglican opponent had described as 'spelling backward the charter of Englishmen'.[17] These societies included the older Reformation Society and Protestant Association, and the more recently formed Evangelical Alliance and Protestant Alliance. The last-named, founded in 1851, had 49 affiliated local societies a year later.[18] The Protestant Alliance differed from the Protestant Association in that some prominent Liberal Dissenters sat on its committee, and its subscribers included the Voluntary Rev. Thomas Binney as well as the Rev. G. C. Gorham of Brampford Speke.[19] The Protestant Association was in financial difficulties in the mid-1850s. But union with the Alliance was none the less refused in 1856 because of differences between the Liberal Dissenters in the Alliance and the Tory, Erastian membership of the Association;[20] and at the end of the decade the Association

[11] T. Smith, *Memoirs of Begg*, ii. 89–91, 133–5, 161–4, 173–6; D. Jamie, *John Hope, Philanthropist and Reformer* (Edinburgh, 1900), 274–300.

[12] Jamie, 333.

[13] T. Smith, op. cit. ii. 181; Handley, op. cit. 240–1.

[14] *The Position of Popery in Great Britain . . . being the report of operations of the Scottish Reformation Society for 1862* (Edinburgh, 1863), 1–21.

[15] Ornsby, *Memoir of J. R. Hope-Scott*, ii. 215.

[16] e.g. *The Position of Popery in Great Britain*, op. cit. 10.

[17] *Suggestions for a Practical Use of the Papal Aggression: a letter to the Lord Bishop of Manchester, by one of his clergy* (London, 1851), 4.

[18] *The First Annual Report of the Protestant Alliance* (London, 1852), 4.

[19] Ibid. 2, 2–32.

[20] *Protestant Magazine*, xvii (1856), 122, 35–6, 66–9.

was still politically active. The Protestant societies had mutual objects, including missions of conversion to Irish Catholics (both in Ireland and Britain) and exposure of the persecution of Protestants in Catholic countries. In politics their immediate object was withdrawal of the Maynooth grant. But although they had considerable support in Parliament their anti-Maynooth campaign seemed only once to approach success in the Commons, in 1856. Had the Commons passed their bill then, the Lords might well have agreed to it. Gladstone may have been right when he said in 1854: 'We have a parliament which, were the measure of 1829 not law at the moment, would I think probably refuse to make it law.'[21]

With Catholicism under vigorous attack, Puseyism could not escape. The *Protestant Magazine* asked in 1857, 'Has not Tractarianism been a means of leading many to Popery?'[22] Evangelicals and Tractarians clashed sharply in these years, though Pusey said that he had tried at length 'to point out what we [Tractarians] have in common with Evangelicalism'.[23] Tractarian doctrine was disputed in legal cases. After the Gorham Case the main doctrinal *cause célèbre* concerned Archdeacon G. A. Denison's vindication of the Real Presence in the elements of holy communion. Denison preached this doctrine openly in 1853-4, and the pugnacious archdeacon was as anxious to be prosecuted as evangelicals were to prosecute him. Two successive bishops of his diocese refused to indict him, and Archbishop Sumner (though an evangelical) was markedly reluctant to do so. But Sumner was compelled by the Court of Queen's Bench (on the application of Joseph Ditcher, the evangelical vicar of the parish next to Denison's) to hear the case, and in August 1856 the archbishop's court found Denison's doctrine inimical to the Thirty-Nine Articles. Denison refused to recant and was deprived of his living in October.[24] Pusey thought it was vital to defend Denison's doctrine: ' . . . the Low Church, I fear, mean a war of extermination against us'.[25] High churchmen were aroused by the judgement. Seventeen clergymen signed a protest issued by Pusey and Keble, and Gladstone said that those who believed too much were on the unpopular side.[26] Denison himself saw his treatment as a natural result of the doctrinal 'treachery' of the Gorham judgement, and saw the Church 'struggling feebly, and most unsuccessfully, to escape strangling at the hands of the Establishment'.[27]

The sentence against Denison was reversed on appeal by the Court of

---

[21] Quoted Manning, *The Protestant Dissenting Deputies*, 210.

[22] *Protestant Magazine*, xix (1857), 34.

[23] Pusey to Shaftesbury, 17 May 1852 (Pusey Papers).

[24] Chadwick, *Victorian Church*, i. 491-4; Denison, *Notes of My Life*, 222-67; L. Denison (ed.), *Fifty Years at East Brent*, 47 ff.; B. E. Hardman, 'The Evangelical Party in the Church of England, 1855-65' (unpubl. Univ. of Cambridge Ph.D. thesis 1964), 126 ff.

[25] Quoted Chadwick, *Victorian Church*, i. 493.

[26] Gladstone to Bishop Wilberforce, 18, 23 Aug. 1856 (Wilberforce Papers, d. 36). Cf. Gladstone to Aberdeen, 13 Aug. 1856, 'private' (Gladstone Papers, Add. MS. 44089, fo. 196).

[27] Denison to 'a friend', 23 Dec. 1856 (L. Denison, op. cit. 70).

Arches in April 1857, on the technical ground that the suit against him had been brought too late. The indefatigable Ditcher, as relentless as Denison, appealed to the Judicial Committee of the Privy Council, but in the following February this court confirmed the decision of the Court of Arches. The Denison Case, thus foiled of an outcome satisfactory to either side, ended in equilibrium, but had served to intensify attitudes and suspicions. Although the threat of a latitudinarian Establishment did not operate in the non-established Scottish Episcopal Church, the case of Bishop Forbes of Brechin, prosecuted by his fellow bishops for teaching the Real Presence, caused further high-church concern.[28] Forbes, who had moral support at his trial from the presence of Keble, was released with an admonition in February 1860.[29] The formation of Tractarian sisterhoods was naturally attacked. In 1857 John Mason Neale and some of the sisters of his convent at East Grinstead were assaulted after the funeral of one of their members, by a crowd 'who had been told that Sister Amy [the dead sister] had been lured into the community [and] persuaded to leave all her money to it . . .'[30] Finally, there were stormy ritualistic controversies in the recent tradition of W. J. E. Bennett and St. Barnabas' church. Several of these involved the anti-ritualist A. C. Tait, who became bishop of London in 1856. Tait's troubles included a legal wrangle with Robert Liddell, the successor to Bennett's churches, and the prolonged riots at the slum church of St. George's-in-the-East against the ritualism of Bryan King and Charles Lowder. 'Between June 1859 and May 1860 . . . Sunday afternoons at St. George's were the zoo and horror and coconut-shy of London.'[31] Bryan King, the incumbent, eventually left and, like Bennett before him, found a haven in the West Country: he was appointed to a living in the diocese of Salisbury, then ruled by the only Tractarian bishop, W. K. Hamilton.

Such bitter conflicts may have reinforced the warning of W. J. Conybeare, in his article on 'Church Parties' in 1853, that religious discord was promoting scepticism: ' . . . these unnatural hostilities must cease, if we are ever to re-convert the pagans of the factory, or the pantheists of the forum . . . the true battle is . . . between Faith and Atheism'.[32] But not so much a new decade as a new century had to come before hopes of truce and common interest made much progress.

Voluntaryism continued to be a rising contestant in the ecclesiastical stakes

---

[28] Keble to Bishop Wilberforce, 11 Oct. 1857 (Wilberforce Papers, d. 39); Pusey to Gladstone, 5, 8 Dec. 1859 (Pusey Papers); Gladstone to Pusey, 17 Dec. 1859 (ibid.); Wilberforce to Gladstone, 2, 22 Dec. 1859, 3 Jan. 1860 (Gladstone Papers, 44344, fos. 81–8).

[29] For the case see W. Perry, *Alexander Penrose Forbes, Bishop of Brechin* (London, 1939), 78 ff.; M. Lochhead, *Episcopal Scotland in the Nineteenth Century* (London, 1966), 117–28.

[30] Allchin, *The Silent Rebellion*, 98; Chadwick, *Victorian Church*, i. 507.

[31] Chadwick, *Victorian Church*, i. 497–501; R. T. Davidson and W. Benham, *Life of Archibald Campbell Tait, Archbishop of Canterbury* (3rd edn., 2 vols., London, 1891), i. 233–48; *Annual Register*, ci (1859), 125–7; cii (1860), 110–13.

[32] *Edinburgh Review*, xcviii (1853), 341–2.

during the 1850s. Liberal Dissenters could be as anti-Catholic as Anglican evangelicals[33] but anti-Catholic feeling was often displaced by the common interest which both Dissenters and Irish Catholics had in disestablishment. The *Protestant Magazine* complained that political Dissenters had formed an 'unnatural alliance' with 'the extreme Popish party, who . . . are the professed apologists of that very social and ecclesiastical despotism abroad . . . which the Liberals are so loud in denouncing'.[34] Irish disestablishment became a leading demand of English Voluntaries; and its achievement in 1869, to which they contributed, was the peak of their political success.

The confidence of Dissenters was increased by the publication, at the beginning of 1854, of Horace Mann's report on the Religious Census of 1851. The Census may be held as reasonably reliable on a general basis in spite of the criticisms justly made of it,[35] and it showed that about 40 per cent of churchgoers in England and over 75 per cent in Wales attended Nonconformist churches, while in Scotland about 60 per cent of Protestant worshippers attended the Free Church or Dissenting churches.[36] A feature of more importance for the future was the disclosure of large-scale nonattendance, especially among the poor labouring class of the large towns. This was of great concern to many, both churchmen and Nonconformists, but rivalry over the attendance figures distracted attention from the question. The Nonconformist *Patriot* said the Census was a triumph for Dissenting principles, and the elated Anti-State Church Association (called the Liberation Society from 1853) issued a tract propagating the Census results.[37] Bishops Wilberforce and Thirlwall, on the other hand, complained that returns of Dissenting worshippers were exaggerated, and the friction between churchmen and Dissenters prevented a similar census in the future.[38] The Census thus aggravated the Church–Dissenting conflict.

The Liberation Society commenced a new monthly paper, the *Liberator*, in 1855. The society made successful efforts to increase its finances during this decade—in October 1852 it gained some money from spectators who hired its premises in Fleet street to watch the duke of Wellington's funeral procession —but two of its officials proved unsatisfactory and had to be dismissed, and in 1858 it was decided to divide the country into districts, each under a

---

[33] e.g. anti-Catholic articles in *Eclectic Review*, 5th Ser. v (Jan.–June 1853), 189–212; vi (July–Dec. 1853), 33–43.

[34] *Protestant Magazine*, xix (1857), 70.

[35] Cf. G. F. A. Best, *Mid-Victorian Britain, 1851–75* (London, 1971), 176 and refs.; A. Everitt's essay in Cook (ed.), *Local Studies and the History of Education*, 60 n. 8.

[36] For further details from the Census, see above, pp. 6-9, also the Report on the Census, P.P. 1852-3 (1969), lxxxix. 1, esp. p. clvi; Dawson (ed.), *Abridged Statistical History of Scotland*, 1106; Inglis, 'Patterns of Religious Worship in 1851'; Gay, *The Geography of Religion in England*, 55 ff.

[37] *Patriot*, 6 Feb. 1854; Minutes of Liberation Society (executive committee), iii. 32 (19 Jan., 9 Feb. 1854).

[38] Hansard, cxxxv. 23–33; D. Williams, 'The Census of Religious Worship of 1851 in Cardiganshire', *Ceredigion*, iv (1961), 113–14.

financial agent, in an attempt to raise money to pay off debts.[39] The agents received commission on the subscriptions they obtained, as well as a basic salary of about £100 p.a. In 1853 it was decided to set up a Parliamentary and an Electoral Subcommittee. The concern of the latter was with Voluntary efforts in the constituencies. The Parliamentary Committee, chaired by the Baptist Dr. C. J. Foster, was formed to watch all parliamentary topics which concerned Dissenters, to communicate with sympathetic M.P.s, and to promote effective parliamentary action.[40] Its duties came to include the preparation of bills to be introduced in Parliament. An attempt to unite the Parliamentary Committee with the Protestant Dissenting Deputies was a failure. But the Deputies and the Liberation Society remained on amicable terms, the former feeling that free communication was desirable between, as they too rigidly put it, 'the Deputies as representing the Metropolis and the Society the Provinces'.[41] Miall had been returned to Parliament in 1852 as member for the Dissenting stronghold of Rochdale, but he was an unimpressive orator, and in October 1854 the Parliamentary Committee suggested that acquisition of a 'recognized leader' would greatly promote the objects of 'the Voluntary Party' in the Commons. Bright was suggested;[42] but (perhaps looking for a wider field of action) he apparently declined, while still agreeing with general Voluntary aims. Dissent—but not militant Voluntaryism—was to attract the interest and support of bigger political game in the 1860s.

In spite of its efforts in the fifties, the Liberation Society had still not exploited all its potential support. More attention was given to Scotland, the home of modern Voluntaryism, towards the end of the decade. In 1858 it was reported that local committees had recently been established in twelve Scottish towns—including Kilmarnock, Ayr, Greenock, Falkirk, and Jedburgh—and Scottish subscriptions amounted to about £300 at the end of 1859.[43] Wales, despite its large Dissenting population, was neglected in comparison with much of England until a notable Cymric breakthrough was made in 1862. More broadly, it was asserted that the Society in 1861 had only 6,100 subscribers in the whole of Great Britain.[44]

The campaign for disestablishment was still in incubation. But the 1850s were a time of advance for opposition to church-rates, in which the Liberation Society was deeply involved, sometimes drafting bills for presentation to Parliament. Not only had the recently increased numbers of secession Methodists joined older Dissent in opposing the rates, but perhaps Wesleyans

[39] Minutes of Liberation Society (executive committee), ii. 419, 470–3, 492–3; iii. 53–4, 92, and under 9 Apr., 21 May, and 29 Oct. 1858; Mackintosh, *Disestablishment and Liberation*, 53.

[40] Minutes, iii. 34; Mackintosh, op. cit. 57. See D. M. Thompson, 'The Liberation Society, 1844–68', in Hollis (ed.), *Pressure from Without*, 220–2.

[41] Minutes, iii. 39–40, 87–8 (4 Feb., 9 June 1854).

[42] Ibid. 111 (11 Oct. 1854).

[43] Ibid. 26 Nov., 10 Dec. 1858, 21 Jan. 1860.

[44] See below, p. 314. For the neglect of Wales see I. G. Jones, 'The Liberation Society and Welsh Politics', 211 and 215 ff.; and cf. Bright to George Wilson, 31 May 1852 (G. Wilson Papers).

were increasingly reluctant to pay them.[45] Outside the large towns, where compulsory rates had been generally abandoned, church-rate disputes became more frequent after the final decision in the Braintree Case in 1853. This judgement made a rate depend on a majority vote in the vestry meeting, and campaigns therefore began to whip up the necessary majorities to defeat the rate. An incident at Denbigh, in which a noted Dissenter (Thomas Gee) had his goods distrained for non-payment and several persons were imprisoned, was reported to the Liberation Society in December 1854. The executive committee advised the detainees to ask the Home Secretary to investigate the conduct of the magistrates.[46] Seizure of property took place at Wisbech in 1853; St. Neots in Huntingdonshire was exercised by the rate question from 1856 to 1858; and anti-church-rate meetings were held at Norwich in 1858 and 1861.[47] Abundant evidence of disputes had been given to a Select Committee of the Commons appointed in 1851, and the publication of the report and evidence brought forth a variety of proposed solutions in Parliament. Bills for outright abolition obtained increasing support in the Commons from 1855 to 1859. The progressive Conservative Lord Stanley published an influential demand in 1853 that Dissenters should be exempt from the rate. Basing his argument on the ill-feeling caused by the rate, Stanley held that financial support coming only from its own members would be a great moral benefit to the Church of England. He also argued that vestry meetings should consist only of Anglicans, who would then have more freedom to discuss church affairs.[48]

Leading Peelites also discussed a church-rate solution. Sidney Herbert favoured restricting a compulsory rate to churchmen,[49] and this reflected high-church views that only churchmen should run the Church. Gladstone also wanted a settlement for the sake of Church interests.[50] But, like Samuel Wilberforce, he disliked the abolition bills of the 1850s, which aimed to remove the rate altogether while still leaving control over parish churches in the hands of mixed vestries.[51]

On the other hand, the prospect of altering the church-rate law aroused opposition from conservative churchmen who believed that such a concession might encourage Voluntaryism; and this feeling perhaps postponed a settlement of the rate. The Rev. Francis Merewether challenged

[45] Memorandum on Wesleyans and Church Rates, undated [probably 1860s] (Gladstone Papers, 44754, fos. 149-57).

[46] Minutes, iii. 131; printed Biographical Sketch of Thomas Gee, 1895 (in Thomas Gee Papers, 8319 E).

[47] J. C. G. Binfield, 'Nonconformity in the Eastern Counties, 1840-85, with reference to its social background' (unpubl. Univ. of Cambridge Ph.D. thesis 1965), 443.

[48] Lord Stanley, The Church Rate Question Considered (London, 1853), 3-4 ff., 40-1, 51.

[49] Herbert to Gladstone, 10 Apr. 1854 (Gladstone Papers, 44210, fos. 125-6).

[50] Gladstone to Herbert, 31 Oct. 1854, copy (ibid. 44210, fo. 156).

[51] Wilberforce to Gladstone, 10 Jan. 1855, enclosing a plan of Rev. W. J. Butler of Wantage (Gladstone Papers, 44343, fos. 274-7).

Stanley's proposal, claiming that church-rates should be maintained as a homage to the 'inspired, revealed truth' held by the Establishment.[52] Not only Conservatives but some Whigs rallied to the defence of the compulsory rate. Earl Fitzwilliam, apparently forgetting the objections of conscience to ecclesiastical dues, likened church-rates to taxes for maintaining roads and bridges:

... the whole of the inhabitants of the county and of the parish are bound to maintain all the bridges, all the roads, without any plea on the part of John that he never goes over a bridge, or of William that he never travels along such a road ... the same is as fairly predicable of the fabric which is appropriate to the worship of the creator, as of that which is contrived to convey the traveller from the right to the left bank of the river.[53]

Not all supporters of the rates may have found their defence so easy and straightforward as the earl. The complex and pervasive issue of church-rates brought the whole question of a Church Establishment into hot dispute by the end of the decade.

II. THE COALITION AND ECCLESIASTICAL REFORM, 1852-1855

The Aberdeen Cabinet formed in December 1852 comprised 6 Peelites, 6 Whigs, and 1 radical. Peelites took a further 9 places outside the Cabinet, and caused Brougham to marvel that 'a very tiny party has swallowed up the great Whig party'.[54] However, while the 'hard core' Peelite M.P.s numbered only 44, Conservative support for the Coalition was sometimes considerably greater.[55] In terms of existing policy requirements, moreover, a ministry led by a Peelite and with a strong Peelite content might well have been more suitable than a predominantly Whig one. This was certainly the case where Ireland and the Catholics were concerned. In June 1853 Russell gave a reminder of his recent anti-Catholic policy when opposing a motion by an Irish Catholic member, G. H. Moore, to inquire into Irish ecclesiastical revenues. Moore's speech favoured disendowment of the Church of Ireland, and Russell expressed the fear that this might spread to England, going on to allege that the Catholic Church had recently been aiming at political power which was at variance with 'a due attachment to the Crown of this country'.[56] This seemed like the Durham Letter again, and the three Roman Catholics in the Government—Monsell, Keogh, and Sadleir—sent in letters of resignation. These ministers were, however, persuaded to relent, in return for a

---

[52] F. Merewether, *A Reply to Lord Stanley's Pamphlet on Church Rates* (London, 1853), 6 ff., 12.

[53] Fitzwilliam to J. D. Gott, n.d. (Fitzwilliam Papers (Sheffield), G 88).

[54] Quoted Southgate, *The Passing of the Whigs*, 242–3.

[55] Conacher, *The Peelites and the Party System*, 172; J. B. Conacher, *The Aberdeen Coalition, 1852–5* (Cambridge, 1968), 12 n., 36, 556–9.

[56] Hansard, cxxvii. 944–6; part quoted Conacher, *Aberdeen Coalition*, 108.

public letter affirming that the views of Russell were not those of most of the Cabinet.[57]

High churchmen disliked the coalition of high-church Peelites—Gladstone, Newcastle, Herbert, and Viscount Canning—with Erastian Whigs. Gladstone especially was suspected of compromising his principles, and there was strong opposition to his re-election at Oxford University after he took office. Pusey, Keble, and Wilberforce still supported him, retaining their faith in his Church principles. But G. A. Denison opposed him, being unable to countenance his junction with Whigs who supported the 'comprehensive system' of education.[58] W. J. E. Bennett came up from Frome to vote against Gladstone, despite the latter's defence of him in the previous session.[59] But Gladstone won narrowly after a fierce contest. He had repeatedly stated that, unless he had thought the interests of the Church would be as safe under Aberdeen as under Derby, he would not have taken office.[60] Some high churchmen, however, disliked the idea of a Presbyterian Prime Minister, however fair and equitable he might promise to be.[61]

Such men had little cause to worry about Aberdeen. Though a Presbyterian, and more Protestant than some of his Peelite colleagues, he was both less Erastian and less ultra-Protestant than some of his Whig colleagues. On account of his desire to settle the Non-Intrusionist crisis in 1840, and his Benefices Act of 1843, some members of the Church of Scotland saw his Administration as an opportunity to press for the abolition of patronage.[62] Aberdeen favoured latitude in doctrinal matters, and later opposed the deprivation of Denison.[63] It was perhaps the fiercely evangelical *Record* which described him as a 'popishly-inclined-puseyite-presbyterian'.[64] Under Aberdeen the first Tractarian bishop, W. K. Hamilton, was appointed in 1854, after much restless thought by the Premier. The demand for an active Convocation also made, after an initial set-back, notable progress towards its goal.

Samuel Wilberforce was at first unsuccessful in gaining Aberdeen's concurrence in the revival of Convocation.[65] Aberdeen feared that an active

---

[57] Conacher, *Aberdeen Coalition*, 107–10; Graham to Aberdeen, 2 June 1853 (Aberdeen Papers, Add. M.S. 43191, fos. 69–72).

[58] Pusey to Gladstone, 6 Jan. 1853 (Pusey Papers); Denison, *Notes of My Life*, 101, 104, 182–3.

[59] Bishop Wilberforce to Gladstone, 8 Jan. 1853 (Gladstone Papers, 44343, fo. 184); Rev. W. Upton Richards to Gladstone, 9 Jan. 1853 (ibid. 44373, fo. 248). For the election see also Conacher, *Aberdeen Coalition*, 50–1.

[60] Gladstone to Sir William Heathcote, 28 Dec. 1852, copy (Gladstone Papers, 44208, fo. 34); Gladstone to Rev. R. Greswell, 6 Jan. 1853, copy (ibid. 44181, fos. 156–7).

[61] Rev. J. E. N. Molesworth to Gladstone, 18 Jan. 1853 (ibid. 44373, fos. 298–9).

[62] Fleming, *A History of the Church in Scotland*, 124.

[63] Gladstone to Aberdeen, 13 Aug. 1856, 'private' (Gladstone Papers, 44089, fos. 197–8).

[64] Bishop Wilberforce to Archdeacon R. Wilberforce, 21 Dec. 1852 (Wilberforce Papers, d. 19, p. 14).

[65] Welch, 'The Revival of an active Convocation of Canterbury', 194. For Wilberforce's correspondence on Convocation see Ashwell and Wilberforce, *Life of Wilberforce*, ii. 161–240. See also

Convocation might, on account of evangelical opposition, split the Church of England. He reluctantly agreed that Convocation might meet on 16 February 1853 (to which date it had been adjourned) and debate throughout that day but no longer. Accordingly, the Convocation of Canterbury met for one day only (the Convocation of York was still firmly locked out by Archbishop Musgrave), and the plan for revival seemed to have taken a step backwards. Convocation was prorogued until 18 August. On that day Archbishop Sumner did not appear until 3.15 p.m. to open the session, and pronounced it a mere formality, no debates being subsequently held.

By January 1854, however, both Sumner and Aberdeen were rather more amenable. Aberdeen agreed, against the views of Russell, that there might be a two-day meeting in February and even an adjournment, should the amount of business require that length of time. At the meeting on 1 February committees were appointed for various purposes, including the discussion and recommendation of reforms in the constitution of Convocation itself.[66] The committees continued to meet after Convocation had been prorogued, and were strongly disliked by the opponents of synodical action. Convocation itself was adjourned until 20 July 1854, when the reports of committees were presented and adopted. Blomfield stressed the harmony in which the work of the committees had been conducted, and deduced that a revived Convocation would be unlikely to cause the acrimony which many had foretold. He also persuaded Convocation to form two committees (appointed jointly by the upper and lower houses), one to discuss church-rates and the other to consider ecclesiastical discipline. The caution and concord of these developments (and the advocacy of influential prelates) obtained their reward in more official favour, both from Lambeth Palace and Downing Street. On 22 January 1855 Archbishop Sumner asked Aberdeen that Convocation might have a prolonged session to consider the reports of committees, though not more than 'two or at most three days'.[67] It might have seemed in the nick of time. Ten days later the Coalition resigned, and Palmerston—feared to be more forbidding on the subject than Aberdeen, though not, as it turned out, with much foundation—became the new Prime Minister. Aberdeen replied to Sumner, still cautiously, that he did not wish to obstruct 'a proceeding which Your Grace thought essential to the interests and welfare of the Church', but hoped that the sittings might be kept to two days rather than three.[68]

Convocation met in fact from 6 to 9 February. The summit had been reached at last, not least because the aspirations of high churchmen had won

Chadwick, *Victorian Church*, i. 318–24; S. Meacham, *Lord Bishop: the Life of Samuel Wilberforce* (Cambridge, Mass., 1970), 236 ff.

[66] J. H. Overton and E. Wordsworth, *Christopher Wordsworth, Bishop of Lincoln, 1807–85* (London, 1888), 162–4.

[67] J. B. Sumner to Aberdeen, 22, 26 Jan. 1855 (Aberdeen Papers, 43195, fos. 154–6).

[68] Aberdeen to J. B. Sunner, 29 Jan. 1855 (ibid. fo. 158).

the approval of the evangelical archbishop. Sumner, indeed, told Wilberforce in the following October that the assembly might meet for longer if the amount of spiritual business required it.[69] A momentous step in Church government was taken by these concessions. Parliament now had once again an active ecclesiastical partner, with the right to discuss Church liturgy and organization in a more satisfactory atmosphere than that of Parliament. Among the leading questions discussed in early sessions was a reform of the controversial final court of appeal in ecclesiastical cases.[70] Canons agreed by Convocation, however, had still to be submitted for approval by Parliament and ratification by the Sovereign.[71] The Church had become somewhat freer, but was still decidedly subordinate to the State. For many years Convocation seemed, to its proponents, disappointingly passive.

The Coalition ministry was lenient to Catholics and Dissenters as well as to Convocation. During the Government's brief life, over which diplomatic crisis and warfare loomed, many ecclesiastical bills were debated, though mostly defeated, and one substantial measure of religious equality was passed with the eventual agreement of ministers.

In 1853 there was repeated discussion of Maynooth, with no tangible result except to consolidate for the time being (through successive defeats of its opponents) the position of the Government grant. Spooner returned to the fray on 22 February, when he moved for a committee to consider the Act of 1845 with a view to its repeal. The familiar parliamentary alignment re-formed. Ultra-Protestants (but not Conservative ex-Cabinet ministers) supported Spooner, Liberals and Peelites opposed him, and Voluntaries took their customary broad view which was unacceptable to all other parties. Spooner appealed to the principles of 'our blessed constitution in Church and State', condemning the alleged disloyalty of Irish Catholics and especially the electoral activities of priests in 1852.[72] After his speech, William Schole-field (a member for Birmingham) immediately moved a Voluntary amend-ment to consider the removal of all State grants to religion.[73] He was seconded by Sir William Clay, an Anglican Voluntary, and supported by Miall. Lord Stanley, avowing himself a member of the late Government, opposed both Spooner's motion and Scholefield's amendment.[74] The original motion was lost by 30 votes, and the amended motion was crushed by 262 votes to 68.[75]

Spooner was not quite done for the session. He attempted to delete from the supplies a small grant for repairs at Maynooth, but was defeated.[76] In the Lords the earl of Winchilsea proposed that a Select Committee of the

[69] Welch, 'Revival', 196, also 195–6 for details on the revival.
[70] *Journal of Convocation*, ii (Feb. 1856–July 1858), 188–90, 236–7; Overton and Wordsworth, op. cit. 165–9.
[71] *Journal of Convocation*, i (1854–5), 67–72.
[72] Hansard, cxxiv. 414–36.
[73] Ibid. 438–43.
[74] Ibid. 448–51 (Miall), 507–13 (Stanley).
[75] Ibid. 521–3, 889–928.
[76] Conacher, *Aberdeen Coalition*, 106.

House should investigate the nature and results of Maynooth education, basing his demand on the supposed desire of the Roman Church to 'effect a total overthrow and subversion of our Protestant Church and institutions'.[77] Aberdeen suggested that a Royal Commission, with members nominated by the Government, would be more impartial.[78] During the debate Winchilsea freely acknowledged that he wanted the repeal of the Maynooth grant, and said that the Protestant constitution had made the English 'the chosen people of the Christian dispensation'.[79] Aberdeen's proposal defeated Winchilsea's. A Royal Commission was duly appointed, comprising 3 Protestants and 2 Catholics. Its report, submitted in March 1855, recommenced the parliamentary controversy over the College.

Ultra-Protestants mustered enough votes on 10 May to obtain the introduction of a bill by Thomas Chambers, a Liberal M.P., to facilitate the departure of reluctant nuns from convents. Chambers said that Roman Catholic convents in England and Wales had increased from 12 in 1829 to 75 in 1853, and that they had many unwilling inmates. He proposed that the Home Secretary be empowered to investigate suspected cases of restraint, and to use habeas corpus to release the inmates whose restraint was confirmed.[80] Russell strongly opposed the bill, and it was decided to have a Select Committee on the matter. But nothing was done to appoint the Committee that session,[81] and the question was revived the following year.

The advocates of religious equality did rather better than anti-Catholics in 1853, for they obtained vicarious pleasure from the passage of the Canadian Clergy Reserves Bill. This measure allowed the Canadian Legislature to decide on the use of lands (or the monetary produce from the sale of such lands) which had been allotted to the support of clergy of the Churches of England and Scotland, and which had been extended, though not at all equitably, to other Protestants and to Catholics in 1840. Introduced by the Government in the Commons in February, the bill passed the Lords in April.[82] The comfortable majorities were composed mainly of Liberals and Peelites. Most Conservatives opposed the bill on the prescient ground that it would lead to secularization of the lands, and thus encourage the Voluntary principle and its possible application to British Establishments. Inglis, Pakington, Spencer Walpole, and Derby spoke in this sense, and Derby tried unsuccessfully to make the bill apply only to prospective endowments.[83] Gladstone saw the bill as a benefit to colonial freedom and to the Church of England: 'If you want to make the position of the Church of England, which is now honour-

---

[77] Hansard, cxxv. 1291–2.   [78] Ibid. 1301–6.   [79] Ibid. 1345–6.
[80] Ibid. cxxvii. 79–95. E. Lucas, *The Life of Frederick Lucas, M.P.* (2 vols., London, 1886), ii. 41–2.
[81] Hansard, cxxvii. 108–14, 546–88.
[82] Cf. Conacher, *Aberdeen Coalition*, 99–101.
[83] Hansard, cxxiv. 101 (Phillpotts), 148–9 (Inglis), 707 (Derby), 1074 (Pakington); cxxv. 923–39 (Walpole); cxxvi. 381–450 (Derby's amendment).

able, both weak and odious, then combine the maintenance of her claims with the denial of the principle of colonial freedom'.[84] But Phillpotts had expressed surprise that a Government containing Gladstone and others should have introduced a measure which was, he thought, against the interests of the Church.[85] A group of ten high-church Oxford graduates wrote to Gladstone, though not reprovingly, expressing the hope that the ministry would introduce some measures to please 'sincere Churchmen'.[86] One such measure, a Colonial Church Regulation Bill, designed for the self-government of the Church of England in the colonies, passed the Lords in July. Supported by Gladstone, it was negatived in the Commons.[87]

The Voluntaries were not entirely satisfied with the Canadian Act, for the Government had decided to continue a grant from the Consolidated Fund of this country to Anglican and Church of Scotland clergy in Canada. The Liberation Society had opposed this grant, and Miall and Bright challenged it unsuccessfully in the Commons. Gladstone countered this demand by saying that the grant would come into operation only if the reserves were secularized, and then only after a lapse of fifteen to twenty years: Parliament would therefore have the opportunity of altering this provision later.[88] In spite of this reverse, Voluntaries were pleased at the passage of the bill and its sequel. The Canadian Legislature secularized the lands, and the *Nonconformist* said that State-Churchism was 'decaying in its extremities'.[89]

Apart from this success, religious equality secured no positive advance in 1853. On 26 May R. J. Phillimore, member for Tavistock, proposed to settle church-rates by exempting professed Dissenters: such Dissenters would thenceforth have no right to vote in vestry and no other say in church government. But by a majority of 22—a peculiar mixture of Tories and Voluntaries—he was refused leave to introduce a bill. In the debate on this motion Sir William Clay proposed, as an amendment, to abolish church-rates and, in their stead, to use pew-rents and increased yields from church property to maintain church fabrics and services. His motion, reminiscent of Spring Rice's in 1837, was defeated more heavily than Phillimore's (Tories, Peelites, and some Liberals all voting against).[90] A bill to replace the Edinburgh annuity tax with a payment from municipal funds was unacceptable to Voluntaries and was eventually withdrawn.[91] Unlike the church-rate

[84] Ibid. cxxiv. 1138–52, esp. 1148. Cf. Gladstone to Rev. E. Hawkins, 23 Feb. 1853 (Gladstone Papers, 44374, fos. 69–71).

[85] Hansard, cxxiv. 100–1.   [86] Conacher, *Aberdeen Coalition*, 102.

[87] Ibid. 103.

[88] Ibid. 100–1; Hansard, cxxv. 493–5; Minutes of Liberation Society (executive committee), ii. 476–7 (17, 23 Mar. 1853), 501 (4 May 1853).

[89] Miall, *Life of Miall*, 184–5. Cf. protest by Wilberforce in Lords, 25 May 1855 (Hansard, cxxxviii. 1091–3).

[90] Hansard, cxxvii. 567–647; Minutes of Liberation Society, ii. 489 (13 Apr. 1853); *Eclectic Review*, 5th Ser., vi (July–Dec. 1853), 93–9.

[91] Minutes of Liberation Society, ii. 522.

proposals, Jewish relief had Government support, but this question met its usual fate after Russell's successful motion in February for a Committee to consider the matter. A relief bill passed the Commons with the support of a few Conservatives (including Disraeli and Lord Stanley), but was rejected by the Lords in spite of the advocacy of Aberdeen.[92]

In 1854 Parliament sat down to another heterogeneous ecclesiastical breakfast, and digested rather more of it. This was in spite of the fact that the Government was weaker than in 1853 and many reform measures were lost. Among these casualties was a comprehensive bill of Russell's to advance religious equality by abolishing the oath 'on the true faith of a Christian' and other affirmations such as the oaths of supremacy and abjuration. A single oath of allegiance, inoffensive to any religious conscience, was to be substituted. So wide a measure affected not only Jews but Catholics, and invited anti-Catholic opposition not only in Parliament but in provincial meetings, as at Liverpool. A pro-Jew like Disraeli was able to join Newdegate in asserting that the emancipation of the Jews did not require the removal of oaths which affected categories of members already admitted. The second reading was narrowly defeated by 251 to 247.[93]

Rival church-rate solutions were again introduced. On 23 May Sir William Clay, supported by the Liberation Society, successfully moved for leave to introduce a bill for complete abolition of the rate.[94] C. W. Packe, a Conservative M.P. for South Leicestershire, had previously introduced on 9 May a compromise bill, exempting Dissenters from paying for church services but leaving the rate compulsory for the maintenance of fabrics. However, he announced its withdrawal in June because it could not be dealt with in the remainder of the session.[95] The competition with Clay had thus been removed, and the second reading of Clay's bill was debated on 21 June. Goulburn opposed it because many of its supporters wanted disestablishment.[96] Gladstone opposed it because church-rates were not generally disputed in the rural parishes—the great majority of parishes in England. But he suggested that parishes where there was sustained opposition by a majority might, by making a legal declaration, become exempt from the rate.[97] Bright, who was strongly for abolition, said of Gladstone's speech: 'he was as much puzzled, as most of the Members of the House must be, whether the speech was intended to be made for that side of the House or for the other side'.[98] Thus did Gladstone make occasional statements which led Bright to attempt, towards the end of the decade, to draw him into the Liberal party. The second reading of Clay's abolition bill was rejected by 27 votes.

[92] Conacher, *Aberdeen Coalition*, 104-5 (Jewish relief bill); Hansard, cxxvii. 862-955.

[93] Conacher, *Aberdeen Coalition*, 351-2; Hansard, cxxxiii. 272-89, 870-974. At the Liverpool meeting an amendment was carried by Catholics and Nonconformists; Burke, *A Catholic History of Liverpool*, 114.

[94] Hansard, cxxxiii. 805-36; Minutes of Liberation Society, iii. 8.

[95] Hansard, cxxxiv. 139-41.   [96] Ibid. 430-1.   [97] Ibid. 451-5.   [98] Ibid. 459.

Further set-backs for ecclesiastical liberals included the defeat of a Government scheme to extend State payment of prison chaplains to Catholic priests.[99] Spooner and Newdegate led the parliamentary opposition, and resistance was made at a Protestant conference at Edinburgh.[100] This conference also supported another motion by Thomas Chambers in February for inquiry into convents and monasteries. After a debate between ultras on the one hand and Irish Catholic members (supported by Russell) on the other, the motion was carried, and an amendment to quash it was defeated a month later.[101] However, when the names of the committee were proposed, it was objected that 11 out of 15 were anti-Catholic (Henry Drummond, Newdegate, A. Murray Dunlop, and Chambers himself were among the prominent anti-Papists proposed). Frederick Lucas, M.P. for Meath and editor of the *Tablet*, introduced another amendment to stop the committee, saying that the advocates of inquiry had 'nothing but their unworthy suspicions and their intolerable fanaticism, and disease of their own minds, to offer to the House in support of their demand'.[102] Later in the debate Lucas and his fellow Catholics were defended by Lucas's Quaker cousin, John Bright.[103] At length, on 18 May, Chambers said that, on account of numerous obstructive amendments brought by Catholic members against the names proposed for the committee, he would withdraw his motion. Russell expressed pleasure at the quelling of a source of religious bitterness.[104]

A more positive gain for religious liberalism was the inclusion, in Gladstone's and Russell's Oxford University Reform Bill, of James Heywood's clauses, firstly to admit Dissenters to matriculation and secondly to admit them to bachelor's degrees. There was considerable Dissenting agitation for such a reform in the country. Heywood's clauses challenged the concept that education and religion were one and that the Church of England, being the national Church, should control education. On this question Russell began on 17 March by saying that, though he favoured admitting Dissenters, he regarded the matter as a divisive one which was best left to a separate bill, depending perhaps on the decision of the University itself.[105] This view was rejected by Dissenters and their sympathizers, who said that the admittance of Dissenters should be included;[106] and a clash between Dissenters and the Government ensued when Gladstone opposed the Dissenting demand.[107] Party conflict over this demand was more subdued than the intra-Liberal division. Some Conservatives were not unfavourable to the admission of Dissenters; but others were opposed, notably a new member, the high-church Lord Robert Cecil (later marquess of Salisbury), who hit out at the

---

[99] Conacher, *Aberdeen Coalition*, 361.
[100] Handley, op. cit. 112.
[101] Hansard, cxxxi. 53-135, 1411-66.
[102] Ibid. cxxxii. 119.
[103] Ibid. 549-52.
[104] Ibid. cxxxiii. 555-69.
[105] Ibid. cxxxi. 910-11. For this bill cf. Conacher, *Aberdeen Coalition*, 332 ff., esp. 338-43; Mackintosh, 85-8; Minutes of Liberation Society, iii. 58-62, 86-7 (6 Mar., 9 June 1854).
[106] Hansard, cxxxi. 911-14, 933-5.
[107] Ibid. 943-54.

Voluntaries in his maiden speech.[108] Cecil thus commenced a long and prolific career of Church defence in which he was to be sharply at odds with another future high-church Premier, Gladstone. The latter, however, continued to discourage Dissenters' admission at this stage, though saying that he had no objection in principle.[109]

Heywood, M.P. for North Lancashire and a Voluntary, made his first foray into the Government bill on 27 April, when he moved to refer the measure to a Select Committee.[110] If successful, the motion would probably have postponed the bill until the next session. Heywood was therefore supported not only by Miall, Bright, George Hadfield, and others who wanted Dissenters' admission, but also by Disraeli, who did not want such admission but wanted postponement. Miall wanted the question of tests discussed 'honestly and fairly' by a Select Committee, believing this would convert opponents to their removal.[111] But the Government defeated Heywood's amendment by a majority of 82.

Heywood's other strokes were more successful. On 22 June he carried a motion that Dissenters should be admitted through dropping the requirement that all entrants should subscribe to the Thirty-Nine Articles.[112] As his seconder pointed out, Cambridge did not require this subscription at matriculation.[113] Liberal back-benchers and Irish Catholics supported Heywood. Russell spoke against the motion, saying that although Dissenters' admission was desirable it might jeopardize the success of the measure in the Lords.[114] Gladstone argued that Catholics (less attractive claimants than Dissenters, in the current state of public opinion) would have to be admitted along with Protestant Nonconformists and would provide a further challenge to Anglicanism.[115] Frederick Lucas, however, claimed that Catholics would not attend Oxford even if it were opened to them (Newman was then trying to establish a Catholic University of Ireland), and this statement might have won some votes for the motion.[116] On the Opposition side of the House Lord Stanley supported Heywood, to the disgust of other Conservatives.[117] Some ministers who sympathized with Heywood's motion were given permission to abstain from voting,[118] and the remaining opponents suffered a resounding defeat by 252 votes to 161. Liberal back-benchers had defeated ministers, many Conservatives and most Peelites.[119]

So great was Heywood's sense of triumph that he immediately moved a still more contentious clause, to admit Dissenters to all degrees and therefore, by

[108] Ibid. cxxxii. 714.
[109] Ibid. cxxxiv. 547–8.
[110] Ibid. cxxxii. 921–93.
[111] Ibid. 966.
[112] Ibid. cxxxiv. 512–95.
[113] Ibid. 517.
[114] Ibid. 576–85.
[115] Ibid. 543–55.
[116] Cf. Chadwick, *Victorian Church*, i. 481.
[117] Hansard, cxxxiv. 555–63.
[118] Southgate, op. cit. 253–4.
[119] Hansard, cxxxiv. 585–8. See W. R. Ward, *Victorian Oxford* (London, 1965), 195–8.

implication, to a governing capacity in the University; and so great apparently, was Russell's deflation that he said this bold clause might pass without division. But up spoke Spencer Walpole, denying Dissenters a part in University government, and a division was taken which narrowly defeated the clause, 205 to 196.[120] Thirty-four M.P.s, mostly Conservatives, who had voted for the first clause, now voted 'no'. On the third reading Heywood tried again. A diluted version of the defeated clause, opening bachelor's degrees (except in divinity) to Dissenters, was introduced on 29 June. Ministers had now caved in, and the clause passed by 233 votes to 79.[121] In the Lords a division was taken on this clause, but it was comfortably passed, and the bill, incorporating Heywood's clauses, became law in August.

Another privilege of State religion had been loosened. The abolition of University Tests seemed to have drawn nearer, though the hurdles of admission to masters' degrees and fellowships had to be surmounted before non-Anglicans achieved equality with Anglicans at Oxford. Through Heywood's second successful clause proverbially Tory and Anglican Oxford had become more liberal than Cambridge. Legislation in the future was concerned with reforms at Cambridge, then with opening higher attainments to Dissenters at both universities.

Gladstone's advocacy of the Oxford Bill had brought protests from Pusey and Keble, neither of whom wished to see Parliament interfering with the University. Pusey expressed his fears to Gladstone before the bill was introduced[122] and Gladstone sent a strong riposte in which he condemned the 'legal exclusiveness' of the Church of England, which 'has brought her I sadly fear near the day . . . when she shall find that she has bartered freedom for gold and gold for nothing'.[123] After Heywood's clauses had passed, Gladstone protested that 'we did our best to keep them out', in reply to Pusey's criticism that he was 'ever receding, in order to take up a more tenable position; whereas positions are often tenable, if people will but hold them'.[124] Pusey, horrified at Gladstone's eventual consent to Dissenters' admission and his yielding to Heywood's second clause, threatened to stop supporting him at Oxford elections.[125] As before, the friendship recovered, but the difference between the Tractarian professor and the Tractarian politician was to become more marked.

---

[120] Hansard, cxxiv. 588–92.   [121] Hansard, cxxxiv. 883–911.

[122] Pusey to Gladstone, 14 (?), 16 Feb. 1854 (Gladstone Papers, 44281, fos. 117–19, 123–4); Gladstone to Pusey, 15, 17 Feb., 13 Mar. 1854 (Pusey Papers); Liddon, *Life of Pusey*, iii. 399–401.

[123] Gladstone to Pusey, 13 Mar. 1854 (Pusey Papers; copy in Gladstone Papers, 44281, fo. 150).

[124] Pusey to Gladstone, 9 July 1854 (ibid., fo. 163); Gladstone to Pusey, 10 July 1854 (Pusey Papers; copy in Gladstone Papers, 44281, fo. 167).

[125] Pusey to Gladstone, July 1854 (Gladstone Papers, 44281, fos. 171–2).

III. PALMERSTON'S MINISTRY AND RELIGIOUS ISSUES, 1855-1857

By finally agreeing to Heywood's clauses the Coalition had acquiesced in a significant measure of religious liberty. But the Government's main occupation in 1854 was the conduct of a war which brought social disputes and attacks on institutions, seriously interrupting the age of equipoise.[126] Religious institutions and attitudes did not escape this questioning. Although the religious temper of the age and the strength of evangelical religion were shown by the Government's proclamation of public days of 'fast, humiliation and prayer', the second of these days (at the height of shocked reaction to inefficient management in the Crimea) proved inappropriate and provocative, especially to non-Anglicans.[127] Ultra-Protestants cannot have relished a Government decision to pay increased salaries to Catholic chaplains who attended to the spiritual needs of a third of the army,[128] though a request to place Catholic priests on ships was refused: Graham (then First Lord of the Admiralty) said such a ship would become 'a floating Babel of religious discord'.[129]

The war brought a purely Whig Government to office. After Roebuck's successful motion for a committee of inquiry into the management of the war, Aberdeen resigned on 30 January. Derby tried unsuccessfully to form a coalition, then, to Disraeli's disgust, shied at the fence of a pure Conservative ministry. Lansdowne and Russell both failed to form a Government, and the Queen turned distastefully to Palmerston. Peelite ministers (except Newcastle) at first took their former offices in a Palmerston Government, Gladstone consenting with especial reluctance to serve under a minister whom he despised. Disraeli also showed scant respect for the nation's 'inevitable man': ' . . . though he is really an impostor, utterly exhausted, and at the very best only ginger-beer, and not champagne, and now an old painted panataloon, very deaf, very blind, and with false teeth, which would fall out of his mouth when speaking if he did not hesitate and halt so in his talk, here is a man which the country resolves to associate with energy, wisdom, and eloquence . . .'[130] Disraeli led a majority of the Commons in the demand that Roebuck's committee of inquiry should be appointed, and the Peelite ministers resigned on 22 February rather than accept such an inquiry.

Shorn of the high churchmen Gladstone and Herbert, the new Government took from the Prime Minister an air of jaunty Erastianism, mildly

---

[126] O. Anderson, *A Liberal State at War* (London, 1967), 181, also 1-28, 101 ff., 163 ff.

[127] Ibid. 180-1.

[128] Graham to Edward Ellice, 16 Oct. 1852 (Ellice Papers, E 16A, fos. 113-14); Hansard, cxxxi. 314-30.

[129] Graham to Aberdeen, 8 Dec. 1854, copy (Graham Papers, microfilms, 126); Hansard, cxxxii. 994-6.

[130] Disraeli to Lady Londonderry, 2 Feb. 1855 (Monypenny and Buckle, *Life of Disraeli*, iii. 567).

liberal but resting on evangelical approval and paying little attention to the
claims of Dissent. The influence and support of Shaftesbury, Palmerston's
relative, lent the Government religious ballast of an anti-Tractarian kind.
Had Gladstone remained, Palmerston's ecclesiastical appointments might
have been less congruent with Shaftesbury's views, and indeed the nature of
these appointments changed slightly after Gladstone rejoined Palmerston in
1859. But between 1855 and 1858 episcopal and other important clerical
posts were often given to evangelicals, and otherwise to moderate broad
churchmen. By the close of 1856 the Government had appointed five bishops
and two deans, 'three bishops and one dean being staunch Evangelicals, while
the other three were moderate Churchmen'.[131] In 1857 another evangelical
became bishop of Norwich and Henry Alford, prominent in the Evangelical
Alliance, became dean of Canterbury.[132] High churchmen, as in Russell's
ministry ten years before, had no reason to be pleased with such happenings:
Bishop Wilberforce later condemned Palmerston's 'wicked appointments'.[133]

The end of the war in March 1856 removed a Peelite bond of union and
Peelites developed different attitudes to re-union with the Liberals. Herbert
and Cardwell (the latter representing Oxford City, which was more Liberal
than the University) were ready to tolerate Palmerston's leadership in order to
reconstruct the coalition. Aberdeen and Graham preferred Russell as leader
of a revived Coalition. Gladstone (representing Oxford University) was the
most distrustful of Palmerston, and he contemplated a re-union not with the
Liberals but with the Conservatives.[134] Perhaps Derby's high churchmanship,
more appealing to him than Palmerston's latitudinarianism, contributed to
this attitude. Certainly evangelical opinion supporting the Government
thought it highly desirable to exclude Gladstone. Among those consulted on
ecclesiastical matters by Shaftesbury was Alexander Haldane, editor of
the *Record*, a paper which said of Gladstone: '. . . the Evangelical body have
not a more dangerous enemy, nor the Tractarian, or Popishly affected party, a
more zealous, intriguing and powerful friend . . .'[135]

Gladstone received overtures from Derby during 1856, and one in January
1857.[136] The prospect of his yielding to these was worrying to Aberdeen and
Graham, who were striving unsuccessfully to preserve Peelite integrity from
the blandishments of both Liberals and Tories. In November 1856, as
Graham noted sadly, J. A. Stuart-Wortley became Solicitor-General, Newcastle accepted a Lord Lieutenancy, and Cardwell was 'swithering': 'Time,

[131] Hardman, op. cit. 20-8. Cf. Chadwick, *Victorian Church*, i. 469-73; *Protestant Magazine*,
xix (1857), 2-5.

[132] Hardman, 28.   [133] Quoted Hodder, *Shaftesbury*, iii. 191.

[134] Stanmore, *Herbert*, ii. 52 ff.; Graham to Gladstone, 27 Feb. 1856, copy (Graham Papers,
microfilms, 127); Graham to Aberdeen, 11 Nov. 1856, copy (ibid.); Roundell Palmer to Sir A.
Gordon, 9 Nov. 1856 (Selborne Papers, vol. 1872, fos. 86-97).

[135] Quoted *Protestant Magazine*, xviii (1856), 79.

[136] Stanmore, op. cit. ii. 63-4, 70-2; Derby to Gladstone, 25 Jan. 1857, 'confidential' (Gladstone
Papers, 44140, fos. 205-7); Gladstone to Derby, 26 Jan. 1857, 'private', copy (ibid., fos. 208-9).

the great solvent of all difficulties, is rapidly disposing of the scruples of Peel's friends . . . the compactness of the little Band will vanish . . .'[137] By 1 December Graham feared that 'the Session will open with Gladstone on the front bench of the Opposition'.[138] The elevation of an evangelical, Robert Bickersteth, to the see of Ripon reinforced this feeling. 'I suppose', wrote Graham, 'that Bickerstaffe's [sic] appointment . . . has not mollified his [Gladstone's] feelings of ill will towards Palmerston . . .'[139] Indeed Gladstone complained to Wilberforce at this time that 'a haughty and domineering spirit' in Shaftesbury was visible in ecclesiastical appointments.[140] Wilberforce and Sir William Heathcote (Gladstone's fellow member for Oxford University) were stoking his anti-Palmerstonianism.[141] Into his other ear, however, Graham, Aberdeen, Herbert, and Newcastle all poured warnings not to join Derby.[142] Gladstone told Herbert that Palmerston was 'a most demoralising and a most destructive minister for the country'. He delivered an impressive speech against Palmerston's China policy in March 1857, helping to defeat the Government. But Palmerston showed his strength in the country by holding an election which returned him with a comfortable majority.

In the two years before Palmerston went to the polls, Parliament had considered a variety of ecclesiastical matters with little result. In 1855 the topics included attempts to widen the opportunities both for marriage and (in the light of the depressing 1851 Census report) of religious worship. Marriage with a deceased wife's sister was the subject of parliamentary bills from 1849 to 1907, when these marriages were legalized. Heywood's bill of 1855 to legalize such marriages (many of which had taken place before) was opposed on 9 May by high churchmen who claimed that such a provision would violate the degrees of consanguinity prohibited in Leviticus and by canon law, and was supported by evangelicals and broad churchmen who took a different Scriptural interpretation and upheld private judgement. Roundell Palmer, supported by Gladstone, objected to the discussion of this topic in a secular Parliament and held that repeal of an age-old law of the Church would lead to moral anarchy: polygamy, practised by the emergent Mormons, might be legalized next.[143] Spooner, on the other hand, claimed Scriptural sanction for the bill, and Robert Lowe and Cobden supported it, Cobden saying that deceased wife's sisters made particularly affectionate step-

---

[137] Graham to Aberdeen, 22 Nov. 1856 (Aberdeen Papers, 43192, fos. 56–7).
[138] Graham to Aberdeen, 1 Dec. 1856 (ibid., fo. 61).
[139] Graham to Aberdeen, 3 Dec. 1856 (ibid., fo. 66).
[140] Gladstone to Wilberforce, 8 Dec. 1856 (Wilberforce Papers, d. 36).
[141] Heathcote to Gladstone, 11 Dec. 1856 (Gladstone Papers, 44208, fo. 169).
[142] Graham to Gladstone, 3 Dec. 1856 (ibid. 44164, fos. 70–2); Aberdeen to Gladstone, 11, 20, and 30 Dec. 1856 (ibid. 44089, fos. 221, 226–8); Herbert to Gladstone, 19 Dec. 1856, 4 Jan. 1857 (Stanmore, ii. 67, 68); Newcastle to Gladstone, 10, 15 Feb. 1857 (Gladstone Papers, 44263, fos. 4–9, 14–15).
[143] Hansard, cxxxviii. 252–63 (Palmer), 269–80 (Gladstone).

mothers.[144] The second reading passed by the slender majority of 7, but the bill did not get through Committee before the end of the session. A bill of Shaftesbury permitting assemblies of over twenty people to worship in private houses was successful after amendments.

Other religious dishes came out again in 1855 and were sent back to the pantry uneaten. The publication of the Royal Commission report on Maynooth, dated 1 March, revived the question of removing Government support. The report stated that disloyalty was not taught at the College.[145] A professor of theology had informed the Commissioners:

... I firmly believe that nothing could be more pernicious to the Church herself than any attempt to revive the obsolete, the false, and, as I had fondly imagined, the universally abandoned pretension, that the Pope, as head of this Church, possessed any direct or indirect temporal power.[146]

Voting in elections, it was said, was a temporal matter over which priests had no official authority.[147] A teacher at the College said he had impressed on his students that 'the proper place for a missionary priest is his mission ... The rule then is—no political agitation for him ... There may be exceptions to this, but ... even then the priest should enter into the strange sphere with reluctance, act there with meekness and charity, and return back to his own with all possible speed.'[148] However, a former Maynooth student, who had left without finishing his course and had become an Anglican clergyman, said that disloyalty was inculcated at the College, and that hatred of England and Protestantism was strongly felt there.[149]

Thus there was fuel for Spooner in the report as well as for those prepared to maintain the grant. On 1 May Spooner again introduced a motion for a Select Committee to consider withdrawal of the grant. The money, he said, had not been received in the conciliatory spirit which had produced it. In the Commission's report, he claimed, two Maynooth professors 'had declared that it might be a mortal sin to vote for the wrong man ...'[150] But an opponent of Spooner said that the grant should certainly not be removed in time of war: 'the worst enemies of England, even the Czar himself', would only be pleased with a measure which would envenom Ireland and shake the loyalty of numerous Catholic troops.[151] The debate waxed complicated over the Voluntary question. Spooner's seconder, A. M. Dunlop, upheld the motion for Voluntary reasons (which Spooner opposed), but did not wish to support

---

[144] Ibid. 280–2 (Spooner), 265–6 (Lowe), 282–6 (Cobden).
[145] Report of Commissioners into the management and government of Maynooth College, P.P. 1854–5 (1896–I.), xxii. 355.
[146] Ibid. 397 (evidence of Rev. G. Crolly); cf. ibid. 422–3 (Rev. H. Neville), 431 (Rev. C. W. Russell).
[147] Ibid. 401–2, 432, 449.   [148] Ibid. 452 (Rev. Dr. Patrick Murray).
[149] Ibid. 550–2 (Rev. J. O'Callaghan).   [150] Hansard, cxxxvii. 2052–3.
[151] Ibid. 2074.

an amendment by William Scholefield to consider all religious grants with a view to withdrawing them, as he thought this would cause too much opposition.[152] In a division on 18 July a majority of 3 was obtained for adjourning the debate beyond the end of the session. Spooner obtained some solace from the appointment of a Select Committee to inquire into the use of illegal ecclesiastical titles in the Maynooth report.[153]

Church-rates were debated again, but little progress was made. On 29 March Sir William Clay obtained leave to introduce a bill for complete abolition, containing compensatory provisions. Parishes would be enabled (but not compelled) to charge rents for a proportion of their pews and to use them for the purposes now served by church-rates.[154] Henry Drummond described the measure as 'robbing the Church of the rate and cheating the poor of the pews, to which they now have a right', and called on supporters of the motion to admit honestly their supposed object—'that is, to pull down the Established Church (loud cries of "Hear, hear", and "No, no")'.[155] Moving the second reading on 16 May, Clay said his bill provided that a third of the parish church sittings should in any event be kept free; this, he said, might preserve to the poor man more space than before, and would retain for the Church of England ('the poor man's church') the affections of the people.[156] He deprecated the partial solutions which had been proposed: the exemption of all self-declared Dissenters, for example, would encourage hypocritical avowals of Dissent and underline differences of religious opinion between neighbours.[157] Palmerston said that Dissenters should be relieved from paying for church services, but should continue to support church buildings, which were the property of the nation. At present, however, the Government had no solution to bring forward.[158] The second reading obtained a majority of 28. It was the first time a church-rate bill had passed this stage. Clay's measure, however, was abandoned on 25 July because of the late period of the session.

The Liberation Society had been moderately encouraged by the fortunes of Clay's bill, and increased its anti-rate propaganda in the parishes.[159] During 1856 three church-rate solutions were discussed in Parliament, including a Government proposal. First, on 5 February, C. W. Packe introduced a bill to relieve Dissenters of payment for church services, but not of payment for church buildings, and to arrange for the collection of the rate in a different way.[160] Clay introduced another bill for complete abolition, but omitted the proposal of the previous session regarding pew-rents.[161] When the second

[152] Ibid. 2070–3.
[153] Ibid. 2077 ff.; cxxxviii. 1488–1533; cxxxix. 238–71, 1019–20, 1270–4.
[154] Ibid. cxxxvii. 1355–69.   [155] Ibid. 1362.
[156] Ibid. cxxxviii. 667.   [157] Ibid. 671–2.
[158] Ibid. 688–90.
[159] Minutes of Liberation Society, iii. 195–6 (1 Sept. 1855).
[160] Hansard, cxl. 253–6.   [161] Ibid. 1869.

reading of Clay's bill was discussed on 5 March, the Home Secretary, Sir George Grey, suggested on behalf of the Government that rates should be abolished completely only in parishes which had refused them for a certain period, but that Dissenters could claim exemption whenever the rate was levied. Government, Grey said, would support the second reading of Clay's bill and would introduce appropriate amendments in Committee.[162] Russell, out of office, opposed both the Government's suggestion and Clay's proposal, and went on, not untypically, to attack high churchmen for wanting to exclude Dissenters from managing the parochial affairs of the Church. He would prefer to have Dissenters continue to pay the rate than to see them excluded from vestry meetings and a 'sectarian Establishment' created.[163]

Clay's second reading passed by 43 votes with ministerial support.[164] But Packe still ran his bill against Clay's, and moved the second reading on 21 May. The Congregationalist George Hadfield, who represented Sheffield, remarked that Packe's solution would revive the rate in places (including Sheffield) where it had been dead for many years.[165] Sir George Grey, for the Government, agreed with Hadfield's objection and raised another against a legal provision of Packe's bill. Packe then withdrew the bill.[166] Clay's was also withdrawn because the Government did not appoint a time for its further discussion. The executive committee of the Liberation Society then declared itself free from having to support the Government amendments, and returned to 'simple and unconditional' abolition.[167] The web of solutions had disappeared.

In this session an attempt to admit Jews to Parliament by abolishing the oath of abjuration (including the words 'on the true faith of a Christian') succeeded in the Commons but not in the Lords.[168] On the other hand, religious equality made a slight advance with the passage of a Cambridge University Bill, Clause 44 of which opened all non-theological degrees (but not membership of the Senate) to non-Anglicans. L. T. Wigram, a member for the University, moved to reduce the provision to B.A. degrees only and thus make Cambridge level with Oxford. Milner Gibson countered with a plea that Cambridge should be allowed to regain its 'enlightened and liberal' superiority, and Heywood carried an amendment allowing non-Anglican M.A.s to sit in Senate.[169] But this amendment was rejected in the Lords, and, after further debate in the Commons, the bill was passed without it.[170] Thus Cambridge still barred non-Anglicans from University government but allowed them to be M.A.s. In this year also Dissenters were relieved of the irritation of having to notify their marriages to the Poor Law Guardians,

---

[162] Ibid. 1896–1904.   [163] Ibid. 1912–16.   [164] Ibid. 1919–22, 1924–7.
[165] Ibid. cxlii. 474.   [166] Ibid. 475–6.
[167] Minutes of Liberation Society, iii. 252–3, 290 (19 Mar., 3 July 1856).
[168] Hansard, cxlii. 595–605, 1165–97, 1772–1807.
[169] Ibid. 1749–58.   [170] Ibid. cxliii. 309–19, 1042–5.

though the registrars still had to be present at marriage ceremonies in their chapels.[171]

Spooner's anti-Maynooth campaign made progress this year. Introducing his usual motion for a Committee on 15 April, Spooner claimed that the Maynooth Commissioners had let themselves be deceived by the professors and had ignored examples of disloyalty at the College. Against Spooner, references were made to conspicuous loyalty by the numerous Catholic soldiers in the Crimean war and to the Catholic faith of our French allies.[172] A member for Co. Cork noted that the leaders of both Government and Opposition were absent from the House: 'every man who had felt, or who thought himself likely to feel, the responsibility of a Minister refrained from connecting himself with this proposition'.[173] Newdegate, supporting Spooner, said that the curriculum at Maynooth had been getting more Ultramontane in recent years.[174] For the first and only time Spooner obtained a majority (of 26 votes)—though most Voluntaries in the House supported him for their own ulterior motives, with which he emphatically disagreed.

Spooner then built on his success, obtaining leave to introduce a bill repealing the grant. The second reading was agreed to in the early hours of 26 June by a majority of 6. But Spooner's opponents, encouraged by this small majority, used 'talking out' tactics to thwart him. First George Bowyer, Catholic M.P. for Dundalk, and then Henry Herbert, member for Co. Kerry, moved to adjourn the debate so that further discussion could take place before the second reading. Herbert 'continued to speak till the hands of the clock pointed at a quarter to six [a.m.], when, according to the rules of the House, all proceedings on an opposed Motion are suspended'.[175] The House then adjourned. Later on the same day, instead of pressing the second reading, Spooner moved that the reading be abandoned, which meant that his bill would be dropped. He had been met, he said, with 'a most extraordinary and very nearly unparliamentary opposition', and had been defeated by a trick. There was no point in trying to carry the measure further that session, but he was satisfied with the stage it had reached. He would reintroduce the bill on the first notice day of the next session.[176] The *Press*, an organ of progressive Conservatism, called Spooner a 'dreamer' and a 'parliamentary impracticable', and said that no Conservative Cabinet could agree to remove the grant.[177] But the *Protestant Magazine* said that, though Spooner was opposed by some Conservatives as well as Liberals, he had the backing of 'a party in the nation, composed of some of all parties, and stronger than any party'.[178]

Disendowment of the Church of Ireland was in one way a contrast to anti-

---

[171] Manning, *The Protestant Dissenting Deputies*, 280–3.
[172] Hansard, cxli. 1049–74.   [173] Ibid. 1082.   [174] Ibid. 1090–1.
[175] Ibid. cxlii. 1906 ff., 1965.   [176] Ibid. 2046–7.
[177] Quoted *Protestant Magazine*, xviii (1856), 183.
[178] Ibid. 180–1.

Maynooth feeling, but to Voluntaries it was a logical extension of it. Irish disendowment, last raised by G. H. Moore in 1853, was debated again in 1856. A forthcoming motion by Miall on this subject had been discussed in November 1855 by the Liberation Society's Parliamentary Subcommittee, which planned to stir up M.P.s in its favour.[179] On 8 February this committee agreed on the wording of Miall's motion, that a Committee of the whole House should consider 'the temporal provisions made by the law for religious teaching and worship in Ireland'.[180] Speaking on 27 May, Miall found a major justification for his motion in Spooner's anti-Maynooth bill: how could Irish tranquillity be preserved if endowments were withdrawn from Catholics but not from Protestants?[181] 'Concurrent endowment' was too strongly opposed, so equity must be established by disendowment and disestablishment.[182] Miall thus appealed to expediency rather than the unvarnished Voluntary principle. Voluntaries were against concurrent endowment whether public feeling opposed it or not, and wished to disestablish the Church of England, an aim which Miall denied as a purpose of his motion; he claimed, on the contrary, that the Establishment would last longer in England if its unpopular Irish branch were removed.[183] Miall claimed a precedent for his wishes in the Irish Church Temporalities Act of 1833, saying that this had already partially disendowed the Church. To operate his scheme, he proposed to set up a court to take possession of all State ecclesiastical endowments in Ireland, including those made to Catholics and Presbyterians as well as the Church of Ireland. Landowners could redeem the rent-charges payable to the Church. The court would make grants from its funds to the Church of Ireland commensurate with the Church's size and usefulness, and the Church would keep its buildings. The surplus funds would best be employed in providing hospitals, reformatories, and public works in Ireland.[184] The appropriation question of the 1830s had returned, and similar political divisions had returned with it: Dissenters were supporting Irish Catholics against firm Establishmentarians.

Miall, being so firmly connected with militant Voluntaryism, was the last man in the Commons to persuade the House to accept such a motion. His arguments were opposed by G. A. Hamilton, Conservative member for Dublin University, on the ground that 'it was the duty of a State to acknowledge some definite system of religious truth'.[185] An Irish Presbyterian member opposed the motion because it would remove the *regium donum* of £40,000 a year to Irish Presbyterian ministers.[186] Palmerston said that the temporalities of the Church of Ireland were secured by the fifth article of the Act of Union, and that the motion was really aiming at disestablishment all

---

[179] Minutes of Liberation Society, iii. 209 (30 Nov. 1855).
[180] Ibid. 237.   [181] Hansard, cxliii. 715-18.   [182] Ibid. 724.
[183] Ibid. 732-3.   [184] Ibid. 728-9, 734-7.   [185] Ibid. 753.
[186] Ibid. 737-9.

round. An established Church, he said, was essential to the well-being of a community, and only one denomination should be established.[187]

In the division Miall had 93 supporters, and lost by a majority of 70.[188] However, there was a positive result in the development of co-operation between the Liberation Society and Irish Catholics in support of disestablishment. The Society's Printing Subcommittee decided to send 5,000 copies of the *Liberator* (the society's organ) to Catholic priests.[189] On 8 September Miall reported to the executive committee that a large and important anti-State Church meeting had taken place at Clonakilty (Co. Cork) on 15 August, arranged by William O'Neill Daunt. The latter had written to Miall suggesting co-operative efforts against the Irish Church Establishment, and Dr. C. J. Foster reported that he had already visited Ireland to confer with Daunt.[190] At another meeting of the executive committee on 17 November Foster stated that 'Mr. Daunt appeared fully disposed to rely on the good faith, ability and energy of the Society, and to act on his reliance'. A paper by Miall, presented by Foster, urged that Voluntaries should work for the same object as Irish Catholics but through their own organization, thus recognizing the difficulties of immediate political solidarity between Roman Catholics and dedicated Protestants. In particular, there were different attitudes to the Maynooth grant, which British Voluntaries attacked but which Irish Catholics wished to retain as long as the Church of Ireland kept its State endowment. 'It is to be understood', said Miall and Foster's paper, 'that both sides pursue their own course respectively as to Maynooth . . .'[191] The executive committee approved of this paper on 1 December, welcomed moves to obtain Irish co-operation, and hoped that Irish Catholics would organize their own movement for disestablishment.[192] It was eight years before such an Irish organization was formed, and six years before the Maynooth obstacle to united action was removed by the Liberation Society's agreement to suspend opposition to the grant.[193] But the first steps had been taken towards what became, ten years later, an important concerted force.

Other topics of religious controversy in the session of 1856 included Russell's proposals to extend education by imposing a school rate in districts found to be educationally inadequate. In schools supported by rates the Bible was to be read daily, and other provisions for religious instruction could be made by the school committees, but children could be withdrawn from such instruction on grounds of conscience.[194] Objections came from the usual quarters. Roebuck and Milner Gibson wanted completely secular education.

---

[187] Ibid. 765–70.   [188] Division list ibid. 770–2.
[189] Minutes of Liberation Society, iii. 281 (9 June 1856).
[190] Ibid. 291; Mackintosh, 78–9.
[191] Minutes, op. cit. 311–12.   [192] Ibid. 316.
[193] E. R. Norman, *The Catholic Church and Ireland in the Age of Rebellion, 1859–73* (London, 1965), 178–9.
[194] Hansard, cxl. 1965 ff.

Doctrinal attitudes, said Roebuck, could not be divorced from Bible-reading; provision for such reading would 'shut out every Catholic and render education anything but national'.[195] Thus the desire for open entry to education by children of different denominations led to the demand for a secular system. High churchmen, in contrast, objected to the lessening of doctrinal influence, and Voluntaries opposed the threatened Government encroachment on Voluntary education.[196] There was lengthy debate, and further discussion in committee, but nothing resulted. Religious differences over Scottish education were shown in connection with a bill of the Lord Advocate allowing Dissenters to become parochial schoolmasters. Some M.P.s supported the bill; some opposed it as a threat to the Scottish Establishment, and (in the view of Newdegate) as a threat to the English Establishment as well; and some wished the posts to be limited to Presbyterians though not to members of the Church of Scotland.[197] The bill easily passed the Commons, though a majority of the Scottish county members were against it.[198] The Lords weakened the bill by amending two clauses, and the Commons refused to accept this condition. The bill therefore fell between two Houses.

The 1856 session had seen much religious debate, and one or two sparse but significant achievements had emerged. The large ecclesiastical questions had been discussed more comprehensively than usual, but remained to be discussed comprehensively again. Thus the mid-century stalemate made its slow unwieldy progress. Palmerston's foreign exploits, however, proved more than an adequate distraction from domestic barrenness at a time of comparative apathy over reform, and the 1857 session was broken in March by his defeat over the affair of Canton.

Before this happening, various questions were raised in Parliament, but they had to be shelved because of the crisis. Government bills were introduced by the Lord Chancellor, Cranworth, to transfer the probate and divorce jurisdiction of ecclesiastical courts to lay courts. The English Divorce Bill—a previous version of which had passed the Lords in 1856 but had not reached the Commons in time to be discussed—proposed to increase the facilities for divorce *a vinculo matrimonii* by opening suits to the public on grounds of adultery. The suggested reform naturally aroused the hostility of high churchmen who were anxious to vindicate the sacredness of the marriage bond. Bishop Wilberforce obtained Derby's support for an amendment to prohibit the intermarriage of the guilty parties in a divorce suit. This amendment had been adopted in 1856, but Cranworth now wished to exclude it. In opposing the second reading, Wilberforce 'assumed that in all legislation upon this subject the first obvious principle . . . was to surround

---

[195] Ibid. 1995.

[196] Rev. R. Greswell to Gladstone, 9 Apr. 1856 (Gladstone Papers, 44181, fo. 190); Hansard, cxl. 941-53 (Gladstone), 2011-12 (Hadfield), 841-51 (Graham).

[197] Ibid. cxli. 663-74; cxlii. 885-96; 1464-71; cxliii. 372-4.

[198] Ibid. 731.

marriage with every new fence and every guard that could be devised'—this bill, however, seemed to be based on a totally different principle.[199] The second reading passed on 3 March, but on that day Palmerston was defeated in the other House and Parliament was soon dissolved, so the bill had to pass the Lords again in the new Parliament and then re-enter the Commons.

In February Spooner, encouraged by his near-success in 1856, produced his Maynooth motion again—the 'demon whoop of intolerance', as the *Catholic Institute Magazine* called it. Astonishingly, the motion was opposed by Henry Drummond, who said that German speculative theology was a bigger menace than Catholic superstition.[200] The *Record* was disgusted, and an Irish Catholic commented that Drummond's case was 'the second in the history of the world in which a prophet intending to curse the people of God had been obliged to bless them . . .'[201] The Voluntary M.P.s supported the motion, which was lost by 8 votes: the anti-Maynooth campaign was beginning to lose impetus. A measure with an opposite, pro-Catholic intention was W. T. Fagan's bill to abolish 'ministers' money'—a tax paid by the inhabitants of eight Irish towns, including Catholics, for the benefit of the Church of Ireland. The second reading passed on 18 March (three days before the dissolution), and the bill passed in the new Parliament. Thomas Meagher, supporting the measure, had suggested that the electoral strength of the towns concerned would be useful to the Government, and had anticipated the backing of Scottish members opposed to the similar annuity tax in Edinburgh and Montrose. Edward Horsman, Chief Secretary for Ireland since 1855, had expressed Government agreement with the bill, and Adam Black and Charles Cowan (M.P.s for Edinburgh) seized on Meagher's hint and condemned the annuity tax.[202] Thus religious liberty causes from Ireland and Scotland piped out the old Parliament.

IV. PALMERSTON'S DEFEAT AND RETURN, 1857

On 25 February 1857 a motion by Disraeli against the budget, supported by Gladstone, radicals, and Irish, was trounced by 80 votes. But a few days later Palmerston sank in his own gunboat diplomacy, being attacked in both Houses (though unsuccessfully in the Lords) for the bombardment of Canton, to which he gave full support after the event. These issues might have seemed purely economic in the one case and purely chauvinistic in the other, but current religious divisions were justly claimed to have invaded them. The evangelical *Record* claimed, though perhaps with exaggeration, that on the financial motion ten 'Conservatives' had voted with Palmerston 'to mark their sense of the upright, sagacious, and disinterested manner in

---

[199] Wilberforce to Derby, Mar. 1857 (Derby Papers, 156/3); Derby to Wilberforce, 2 Mar. 1857 (Wilberforce Papers, c. 5); Hansard, cxliv. 1685-1721.

[200] Hansard, cxliv. 909.

[201] *Record*, 28 Feb. 1857; Hansard, cxliv. 909.

[202] Hansard, cxliv. 2423 ff.

which he has dispensed the patronage of the Church'.[203] The *Record* lamented the alliance of Conservatives with Peelites and some radicals against the Government, and approved of Conservative M.P.s who were prepared to support the Premier against Derby: 'we fear that Lord Derby's principles of Churchmanship are allied to those of Mr. Gladstone, in all but that intense earnestness which makes the Rt. Hon. Commoner so dangerous a statesman'.[204] But most ultra-Protestants supported Cobden's vote of censure on 3 March, which was carried by 263 to 247. Palmerston's supporters included a few Tories, some of whom had praised his Protestantism in the debate.[205] But Spooner and Newdegate joined the great majority of Conservatives behind Cobden and Disraeli. Palmerston's pro-Maynooth policy had probably induced them to vote alongside high churchmen like Lord John Manners and Lord Robert Cecil and liberal Conservatives like Lord Stanley, not to mention Peelites such as Gladstone, Graham, Herbert, and Roundell Palmer.[206]

The Liberals were also divided, 48 of them (according to the *Record*) voting against Palmerston.[207] The pro-Palmerston *Daily Scotsman*, however, claimed that Liberals were more united on this than on almost any question for many years. The dissentient Liberals who supported Cobden, said this paper, consisted of about 10 trouble-making Irish, 19 Cobdenites of the 'Manchester school', 16 'malcontent' and unattached radicals such as Roebuck and Layard, and finally Lord John Russell and 2 followers.[208] Voluntaries were not mentioned as a category, but the inclusion in Cobden's lobby of Miall, Hadfield, W. J. Fox, Apsley Pellatt, and William Williams indicates the partial contribution of this body to Palmerston's defeat. It is impossible to decide how far pacifism and anti-imperialism, rather than Voluntaryism, decided their vote. But the growing impatience of Voluntaries with Palmerston's Government, based on its unsatisfactory attitude to religious equality questions in 1856, was a significant political factor. This is clearly shown by an extract in the Liberation Society minutes (the possible political importance of which has already been noted):[209]

The Chairman [of the Parliamentary Sub-committee], Dr. Foster, then brought under the notice of the Committee the fact that they had been opposed or hindered by the Government in all their proposals relative to religious freedom, particularly the Church Rate Bill ... He thought ... that a union now affected among a few M.P.s (from 10 to 20) for the purpose of acting together adversely to the

---

[203] 25 Feb. 1857.
[204] *Record*, 4 Mar. 1857. The high-church *Clerical Journal* (9 Mar. 1857) defended Derby.
[205] Speech of W. Kendall, 3 Mar. 1857 (Hansard, cxliv. 1744–5).
[206] Divison list, ibid. 1846–50; analysis of voting in the *Record*, 6 Mar. 1857.
[207] *Record*, 6 Mar. 1857.
[208] 3 Mar. 1857.
[209] Vincent, *The Formation of the Liberal Party*, 75.

Government, on the next party vote, if avowed, would have the effect of altering the present policy of the Government on the next questions.[210]

Dr. Foster must have been gratified by the downfall of Palmerston's Government so soon after his statement, but the extent of Voluntary support for Cobden in the division must have disappointed him, and any connection between the statement and the downfall is far from clear. Although some of the 'hardest' Voluntaries were with Cobden, Sir John Bowring, Governor of Hong Kong (who had ordered the bombardment of Canton), was a Voluntary himself, and many Voluntaries or sympathizers voted with Palmerston. These included Adam Black, Sir William Clay, Charles Cowan, L. Ll. Dillwyn, George Duncan, Sir Benjamin Hall, William Scholefield, and Sir Joshua Walmsley.[211] Cobden also mentioned two Voluntaries who abstained: 'Kershaw & Hindley . . . are not people to go tiger-hunting with'.[212]

The defeat of Palmerston encouraged the hope that Gladstone, who had made a powerful speech for the motion, would rejoin the Conservatives.[213] But Gladstone continued to gratify Herbert and Aberdeen by sitting on the fence.[214] He had voted not only with Conservatives but with pacifist radicals, and his dislike of Palmerstonian aggression, together with his Free Trade convictions, kept open an alternative Liberal channel for the future. Curiously however, it was under Palmerston that he was to join the Liberals.

Palmerston resigned after his defeat, and a general election was held in late March and early April. The accumulated religious issues of recent years were displayed in the contests. The *Record* plumped for Palmerston because of his energetic and 'just' foreign policies and his protection of 'Christian interests'. True, he upheld the Maynooth grant, but so did Derby, Disraeli, Gladstone, and Russell. Palmerston was a far more reliable Protestant than Derby: 'A greater calamity than a Government conducted by such a man as Lord Derby, on such principles as those of the Bishop of Oxford [Wilberforce] and Mr. Gladstone, could scarcely, we believe, be inflicted upon our country.'[215] The Protestant and evangelical cause could hardly be entrusted to 'a nobleman who lowers his commanding station by all the degrading associations of the turf . . .'[216] The electors must prevent such a catastrophe. The *Record* averred that 'the mortal struggle is between High Church and Low Church', that Gladstone opposed not Bowring but Bickersteth, and was fighting a high-church battle on Chinese ground.[217]

[210] Minutes of Liberation Society, iii. 329 (16 Feb. 1857); Vincent, op. cit. 75.
[211] Division list, Hansard, cxliv. 1846 ff.; *Record*, 6 Mar. 1857.
[212] Cobden to Bright, 6 Mar. 1857 (Cobden Papers, Add. MS. 43650, fos. 243-4).
[213] Sir Eardley Wilmot to Gladstone, 5 Mar. 1857 (Gladstone Papers, 44387, fos. 115-16).
[214] Gladstone to Sidney Herbert, 22 Mar. 1857, copy (ibid. 44210, fos. 306-10); Aberdeen to Gladstone, 8 Apr. 1857 (ibid. 44089, fos. 260-1).
[215] *Record*, 6 Mar. 1857 (leading article).
[216] Ibid. 11 Mar. 1857.
[217] Ibid. 9 Mar. 1857 (leading article).

But the electoral reality was wider than this, as the *Record* admitted. Some Liberal candidates—for example, Lords Althorp and Melgund[218]—were sound Palmerstonians although supporting causes which were unpalatable to the *Record*, such as church-rate abolition, the Maynooth grant, Jewish relief, Sunday amusements, and the abolition of tests for Scots parochial school posts. The *Record* had to warn electors not to vote for such Palmerstonians as the radicals Sir Benjamin Hall and Sir Joshua Walmsley, as being opposed to the true interests of the Church.[219] Although Palmerston himself and most Palmerstonians supported the Maynooth grant, this paper recommended that all candidates be pressed to vote for the grant's removal.[220] Anti-Maynooth campaigns were also waged by the Protestant Association—whose electoral efforts, however, were straitened by penury[221]—and by the Scottish Reformation Society, and Maynooth was a constant theme in election speeches.[222]

More important to many voters than such matters may well have been a candidate's attitude to Palmerston and national glory. The Palmerstonian umbrella was capacious and nondescript enough to allow Liberals of various opinions to creep into Parliament beneath it. The diversity of his party on religious questions weakened the credibility of Palmerston as a champion of Church defence; and the Conservatives were soon to strengthen themselves in this role, taking an opposite line from Palmerston's embarrassing Dissenting followers.

In view of Palmerston's importance in the elections, and the scattering of his foes, it may seem surprising that the Voluntaries recorded an increase in parliamentary support.[223] But the gain was on account of the new members returned. This gain may have been partly the result of an electoral drive by the Liberation Society, which had been proceeding since June 1856 and was concerned with the registration of voters in selected county seats. The Society also spent £362 on circulating 75,000 copies of an election circular.[224] The gain in new members for 'religious liberty' (which cannot be equated with strict Voluntaryism) was calculated, by the Liberation Society's electoral committee, at no less than 36.[225] But this could be only a tentative estimate, depending for substantiation on the parliamentary voting of the members concerned. The number of *re-elected* 'religious liberty' members showed a decline. Forty of these members were listed, and seven of them had opposed

---

[218] *The Times*, 1 Apr. 1857, p. 6 (address of Althorp); *Daily Scotsman*, 11, 13 Mar. 1857 (addresses of Moncreiff, Lord Advocate, and Melgund).

[219] *Record*, 9 Mar. 1857.

[220] Ibid.

[221] *Protestant Magazine*, xix (1857), 74, 80–1; xx (1858), 30–2.

[222] e.g. in Berks., North Warwicks. (Newdegate), Herts., and South Wilts. (*Times*, 1, 2, and 4 Apr. 1857).

[223] Minutes of Liberation Society, iii. 341–7 (6 Apr. 1857).

[224] Ibid. 288–9 (30 June 1856), 333–4, 338 (9, 23 Mar. 1857), 341 (6 Apr. 1857); Vincent, 72–3; D. M. Thompson, 'The Liberation Society, 1844–68', in Hollis (ed.), *Pressure from Without*, 223.

[225] List of names in Minutes of Liberation Society, iii. 342–6 (6 Apr. 1857).

Palmerston on the China vote.[226] Five 'religious liberty' members who had voted against Palmerston were defeated—Miall, Pellatt, W. J. Fox, Layard, and James Bell (Bright was also defeated, but had been absent from the debate).

How far does this show that a vote for or against Palmerston on China was a crucial test in the elections? That it was a contributory factor there is no doubt, but the strength of its contribution differed between constituencies. Miall, for one, was defeated by other (or at least additional) factors. He lost his seat at Rochdale by only 44 votes, and 50 of his supporters had been given a free trip to Southport and Liverpool on polling day by an enterprising free-lance Tory agent.[227] Local circumstances of this kind, including the relative strength of a variety of issues, would need to be investigated for the other defeated members. Moreover, about ten 'religious liberty' men who had abstained or voted for Palmerston (including Sir William Clay) lost their seats. The Palmerston test was important but by no means infallible.

The Times gave Palmerston a majority of 105,[228] and both radicals and Peelites had gone down in the slaughter. Probably only about five Peelites were left in the Commons. The loyalty of even these to the median way was doubtful, considering the different inclinations of Herbert (who in spite of an anti-Palmerston vote seemed determined to become a Liberal) and of Gladstone. However, Gladstone was anxious that he and Herbert should not divide, and an uncertain unity survived among the diminished band.[229]

The election could be counted a moderate success for evangelicalism against high-church interests. Nicholas Kendall, a Tory who was re-elected for East Cornwall, said dramatically in an election speech:

He felt it to be necessary to watch narrowly the High Church party (Hear, hear). In the course of the Russian war he had observed in all parts of the House certain persons who were sure to join against Lord Palmerston's Government. These were members of the extreme High Church party. In all other questions it was the same. There was a party the object of which was to form an Administration based on extreme High Church principles . . . and when he saw that combination of the other day—and there was not a man known to be of extreme High Church principles who did not join in—he did not hesitate one moment to give his support to Lord Palmerston (Cheers).[230]

In the West Country, at least, anti-Puseyism was a marked electoral feature. Stafford Northcote told Gladstone that it had helped to cause his defeat in

---

[226] Ibid. 342; division list, Hansard, cxliv. 1846 ff.; Record, 6 Mar. 1857.

[227] Vincent, 111–13. Miall was also unpopular with some rich and influential Liberals in Rochdale, who perhaps disliked his militant Voluntaryism; Cobden to Bright, 16 June 1857 (Cobden Papers, 43650, fo. 246).

[228] 13 Apr. 1857, p. 7.

[229] Herbert to Gladstone, 18 Mar., 13 Apr. 1857 (Gladstone Papers, 44210, fos. 314–16); Gladstone to Herbert, 17 Apr. 1857, copy (ibid., fos. 320–3).

[230] The Times, 7 Apr. 1857, p. 5.

North Devon; considering going abroad to replenish his finances, he thought of going to Geneva to clear himself of 'the Puseyite taint'.[231] Another correspondent of Gladstone said that clergy at Tiverton (where Palmerston was returned unopposed) had praised the Premier's 'excellent episcopal appointments' and had expressed the hope that an evangelical would soon succeed Phillpotts at Exeter.[232] Phillpotts was nearly 80, but held the see for twelve more years.

The views of Nicholas Kendall were doubtless held privately by other Conservative M.P.s who had not voted for Palmerston but to whom Protestantism, patriotism, and Erastianism were similarly important. But the Erastian value of Palmerston was weakened by his own liberal views, his flourishing Voluntary or 'religious liberty' wing, and his taking high-church Peelites into the Government. The political changes of the next few years, when even Gladstone took office under Palmerston, helped to clear party confusion by driving Conservative Establishmentarians to find leadership in their own party.

V. THE DIVORCE CONTROVERSY, 1857

The opening of the new Parliament on 30 April 1857 allowed the discussion of ecclesiastical measures to be resumed. The large Liberal majority was dismal for Spooner, but on 21 May, after presenting 50 anti-Maynooth petitions from Scotland, he moved doggedly for a Committee on the Maynooth Act with a view to its repeal. He declared his regret at having supported Catholic emancipation in the 1820s, for (he said) since they had gained entry to Parliament Catholics had been striving to win ascendancy over Protestants.[233] But Spooner's cause was waning in Parliament. The motion was lost by 125 votes to 91, and Roebuck congratulated the House on 'having escaped the dreary miseries of a Maynooth debate'.[234] Apart from this negative victory, a minor advance for religious liberty in this session was the passage, with Government agreement, of Fagan's bill to abolish 'ministers' money' in Ireland.[235] But this was a rare fillip. A bill to abolish the Edinburgh annuity tax was withdrawn, and a Government attempt at Jewish emancipation was rejected by the Lords after passing the Commons.[236] Government, moreover, did not fulfil an undertaking to introduce a church-rate bill. Its declared intention to do so had caused Sir John Trelawny, who succeeded the defeated Clay as the promoter of abolition measures, to withdraw his own motion, so this matter was avoided for the session.[237] The Burial Acts Amendment Act enabled more unconsecrated burial ground to be opened for the use of

[231] Northcote to Gladstone, 4 Apr. 1857 (Gladstone Papers, 44217, fos. 20–1).
[232] Sir J. Maxwell to Gladstone, 9 Apr. 1857 (ibid. 44387, fo. 202).
[233] Hansard, cxlv. 644–63.   [234] Ibid. 671.
[235] Ibid. 281–4, 542–621, 1960 ff.
[236] Ibid. cxlvi. 1207–9; Minutes of Liberation Society, iii (27 July 1857).
[237] Minutes of Liberation Society, iii. 368 (15 June 1857) and 27 July 1857.

Dissenters, but merely stimulated afresh the Nonconformist desire to bury their dead with their own rites in consecrated parochial ground.[238] Such a demand was resisted by defensive churchmen because it was believed to aim at sharing not just the churchyard but the church building too.[239]

This session was concerned with divorce as well as burial. The Lord Chancellor's bill permitting divorce *a vinculo* (for adultery only) re-entered the Lords. Its second reading passed on 19 May, 10 bishops being in favour and 5 against. The Lords then discussed the bill in Committee and sent it to the Commons. There the second reading passed easily at the end of July. The opponents were a mixed bag—Spooner and Newdegate voted alongside Gladstone and Roman Catholic members.[240] The bill, after a fortnight's discussion in Committee where important amendments were made, passed the Commons on 21 August, and some further slight changes to the Commons' amendments by the Upper House were accepted by the Lower.[241]

At all stages this measure was resisted by prominent high churchmen, with Roman Catholics such as the duke of Norfolk and George Bowyer making a contribution. Bishops Hamilton and Wilberforce insisted that there was no Scriptural or patristic sanction for divorce *a vinculo matrimonii* (such sanction being restricted to divorce *a mensa et thoro*, which left the parties married though separated).[242] But differences of opinion were naturally found between the bishops. Archbishop Sumner held that divorce for adultery was allowed by the New Testament, but not the remarriage of the guilty party, which he tried (almost successfully) to prevent. Tait, the new bishop of London, was more liberal and Protestant in tone, believing that the bill should go further and allow other grounds for divorce than adultery alone.[243]

In the Commons resistance came chiefly from Gladstone, Lord John Manners, and Sir William Heathcote, all high churchmen whose sensitiveness in doctrinal matters was aggravated by the current Denison Case.[244] Undeterred by his previous sympathetic (and picaresque) involvement in the divorce of his friend the duke of Newcastle, Gladstone threw himself eagerly into battle with Government on the issue. He spoke at length, wrote an article for the *Quarterly Review*, and conducted an intense correspondence with supporters.[245] Some clergymen sent petitions for Gladstone to present; one apologized for the scarcity of signatures by saying that he did not want to

[238] Ibid., 14 Aug. 1857; Mackintosh, 108–9.
[239] e.g. Sir. C. Anderson to Bishop Wilberforce, Mar. 1857 (Wilberforce Papers, d. 28).
[240] Division list, Hansard, cxlvii. 892–4.
[241] *Annual Register*, xcix (1857), 169–75.
[242] Hansard, cxlv. 516–22 (Hamilton), 523–31 (Wilberforce).
[243] Ibid. 495, 828 (Sumner), 531–3 (Tait); Chadwick, *Victorian Church*, i. 482–3.
[244] Hansard, cxlvii. 383–95, 825–56 (Gladstone), 767–73 (Manners), 736–42 (Heathcote).
[245] e.g. Gladstone to Graham, 12, 20 June, 4 Sept. 1857 (Graham Papers, microfilms, 127); Graham to Gladstone, 31 Aug. 1857 (Gladstone Papers, 44164, fo. 115); letters to Gladstone from Rev. T. W. Perry, 26 June 1857 (Gladstone Papers, 44387, fos. 328–31), Rev. H. A. Woodgate, 13, 17 July 1857 (ibid. 44388, fos. 45–50, 66–9), Rev. James Fraser, 29 July 1857 (ibid., fos. 95–9).

tempt his parishioners into marital infidelity by mentioning the subject to them.[246] Gladstone himself claimed to speak for the majority of public opinion, and held that the clergy who opposed the bill (a petition was signed by over 6,000 of them) represented not one party alone but 'the general mind of the clerical order on this subject'.[247] On the other hand, one of his correspondents thought that at least half the clergy were generally in favour of the bill.[248]

Opponents of the bill contended especially for the right of clergy to refuse to solemnize the marriages of divorced persons. Wilberforce moved an amendment in the Lords for this purpose, but it was opposed by Bishop Tait and Lord Chancellor Cranworth and lost by many votes.[249] In the Commons such an amendment was strongly discouraged by the Attorney-General, Sir Richard Bethell. None the less, the amendment was proposed, and Bethell reluctantly said that the Government had decided to accept it for the re-marriage of guilty parties only. He himself deplored the discord such a concession might cause.[250] The qualified amendment was adopted. But in return the Government wanted to insert a provision that in the case of refusal to remarry, the ceremony might be performed in the same church by another clergyman of the same diocese. This clause was strongly resisted by Heathcote, Manners, and others, but passed by 73 votes to 33.[251] In the Lords the clause was resisted unsuccessfully by Redesdale, and was included in the new Act.[252] The concession was still a significant gain for high church-men. But to Gladstone, among others, there were religious obstacles to the spiritual remarriage of even innocent parties, and he was less liberal on this point than Pusey.[253] Gladstone had fruitlessly suggested a civil marriage only for divorced persons.

The Divorce and Probate Acts removed much work from ecclesiastical courts to civil, and thus meant a further reduction in the direct authority of the Church. More worrying to high churchmen was the disregard of strict doctrinal beliefs implied in the general allowance of divorce *a vinculo*. Beyond this, an unpalatable law was, in their view, being forced on the Church by Parliament. This civil threat to spiritual authority seemed (because it was a parliamentary statute) even clearer than the Gorham judgement, and high churchmen reacted the more strongly because of their permanent suspicion of the State. The confrontation between civil and spiritual claims was sharply displayed when the Attorney-General said: 'The true notion of

---

[246] Rev. J. H. Blunt to Gladstone, 4 Aug. 1857 (ibid., fos. 108–9).
[247] Hansard, cxlvii. 388, 825–7.
[248] Rev. C. C. Domvile to Gladstone, 29 July, 3 Aug. 1857 (Gladstone Papers, 44388, fos. 93–4).
[249] Hansard, cxlv. 912 ff.
[250] Ibid. cxlvii. 734–5, 1796 ff.; *Annual Register*, xcix (1857), 163–4, 171–3.
[251] Ibid. 173.   [252] Ibid. 175.
[253] Gladstone to Pusey, 8 Sept. 1857 (Pusey Papers); Pusey to Gladstone, 29 Sept. 1857, copy (ibid.).

the supremacy of the Crown consisted in this, that the Church, like every other body, should submit to the civil law of the land'.[254] Gladstone, on the other hand, insisted that Parliament should not 'take upon itself by its sole authority to determine religious and spiritual matters'.[255] In the lower house of the Canterbury Convocation in the following February, voices were raised against Parliament's alteration of Church doctrine and discipline without obtaining the consent of the spiritualty in Convocations or Synods.[256]

Ardent high churchmen believed that the Divorce Act separated Church law from State law.[257] In view of this alienation, which might be extended by future measures, could churchmen of principle still subscribe to the Establishment? In an impassioned diatribe against the Act, on the ground that it promoted 'no morality', G. A. Denison impugned the religious indifference of a Government which maintained civil and religious liberty 'in all the unbridled licence of private judgement': 'great as is the blessing of the Establishment, I cannot regard it as worth preserving under the conditions of the Divorce Act...'[258] The prospect of Tractarian secession reopened. Keble doubted whether he could continue to hold temporalities in a Church which abandoned the indissolubility of marriage, and Pusey pointed to the example of Scottish disruption over a different principle.[259] More dangerous than disestablishment, wrote Gladstone, was 'the loss of those elementary principles of right and wrong on which Christianity itself must be built':

The present position of the Church of England is gradually approximating to the Erastian theory that the business of an Establishment is to teach all sorts of doctrines, and to provide Christian Ordinances by way of comfort for all sorts of people to be used at their own option. It must become, if uncorrected, in lapse of time a thoroughly immoral position.[260]

Thus high churchmen were in doctrinal conflict with Palmerston's ministry as they had been formerly with Russell's. Gladstone was separated as deeply from Palmerston over divorce as over China. The prospect of his joining a Liberal Government seemed, in the autumn of 1857, to have become very faint. Yet was there any other possible ministry, satisfactory on ecclesiastical or other grounds, which he could support?

A familiar parade of ecclesiastical measures faced the new parliamentary session, which opened in December 1857. But only church-rate abolition made some progress before the Government fell in February. The Liberation Society was disappointed by a statement of Palmerston's that the Govern-

[254] Hansard, cxlvii. 732.   [255] Ibid. 851.
[256] The Chronicle of Convocation, 10-12 Feb. 1858 (London, 1859), 96-101.
[257] Speech of Bishop Hamilton of Salisbury in the Lords, 19 May 1857 (Hansard, cxlv. 520).
[258] G. A. Denison, The Public Sin of the Divorce Act: a sermon (London, 1857), 7-8, 19-20, 25, 28.
[259] Keble to Bishop Wilberforce, 6 Aug. 1857 (Wilberforce Papers, d. 39); Pusey to Gladstone, 7 Sept. 1857, copy (Pusey Papers).
[260] Gladstone to Wilberforce, 2 Nov. 1857 (Wilberforce Papers, d. 36).

ment, while intending to bring in a church-rate bill, could not pledge itself to do so that session.[261] On 27 January 1858 a deputation of 140 organized by the Society, including 11 M.P.s, asked Palmerston to take the matter in hand more decisively, but left empty-handed, having been given no specific pledge about the introduction of a bill. Consequently they felt that any measure initiated by Government would be unsatisfactory.[262] The deputation immediately passed a resolution to introduce another bill for total abolition of the rate. They also resolved to stir up opposition in the parishes, even where opponents were in a minority—'it being a matter of common experience that even the opposition of a minority may practically prevent the levying of a church rate'.[263] Before long this campaign produced an unwelcome reaction in defence of the rate and of the Establishment generally. But in the meantime an abolition bill, drawn up by the Liberation Society,[264] was introduced by Sir John Trelawny. This passed the second reading on 17 February by 54 votes—the highest majority so far obtained—against Conservatives (led by Lord Robert Cecil) and a few Peelites and Liberals, including Sir George Grey (Home Secretary) who argued again for a compromise which would exempt Dissenters and allow pew-rents as a substitute.[265] Cecil's speech presaged the terms of the deeper struggle which was soon to develop, partly through his initiative, for he opposed the bill as a first step to disestablishment. He showed, from recent returns, that out of 7,327 parishes in England church-rates had been refused in only 357 (under 5 per cent), and in 17 per cent of Welsh parishes.[266]

Two days later, ironically, Palmerston was defeated for not being chauvinistic enough in the face of heated French demands after the Orsini bomb incident. Eighty-four Liberals voted against Palmerston, and on 21 February Derby, who had joined them, agreed to form a Government.

VI. DERBY, CHURCH-RATES, AND JEWISH RELIEF

As in 1852 Derby was in a minority and had shaky prospects, not least on account of the divisions among his own supporters. An immediate effort to win the services of Gladstone was well timed in view of the latter's feeling over the Divorce Act; but it showed little indulgence by Derby of his ultra-Protestant followers, to whom Gladstone was a *bête noire*. The effort failed,[267] but Derby thought it worth reviving in May (again unsuccessfully) when there was a vacancy at the India Board, and Russell imagined that he might try and 'chain Gladstone by a few High Church appointments in the Church'.[268] Derby had few such appointments to make during his brief term,

---

[261] Minutes of Liberation Society, iii (18 Dec. 1857).

[262] Ibid., 30 Jan. 1858. [263] Ibid. [264] Ibid., also 5 Feb. 1858.

[265] Hansard, cxlviii. 1553–85. [266] Ibid. 1560–4, 1583–5.

[267] Gladstone to Derby, 21 Feb. 1858, copy (Gladstone Papers, 44140, fos. 237–9); W. D. Jones, *Lord Derby and Victorian Conservatism*, 226–7.

[268] Russell to Graham, 4 Mar. 1858 (Graham Papers, microfilms, 127).

but he certainly had no wish to appoint well-known ultra-Protestants. He refused requests from his Solicitor-General, Sir Hugh Cairns, that Hugh McNeile, the militant Liverpool evangelical, should be given the deanery of Ely in November 1858, and that he should become bishop of Bangor in April 1859.[269]

Although the Government was without the possibly strengthening, possibly embarrassing, presence of Gladstone, it embraced the ill-matched attitudes of progressives like Disraeli, Stanley, and Pakington and traditionalists such as Henley, Manners, and Walpole. The Conservatives had to face the same problems as the Liberals and, being in a minority, were more inclined to positive reform than Palmerston's Government had been. Reforms were desirable to emit confidence and gain support, and Derby, now more progressive than six years before, told the Lords a week after kissing hands that a Conservative ministry need not be a stationary one.[270] At this early stage it was promised that attention would be given to parliamentary reform. But the eventual Reform Bill of 1859, although moderate, split the Cabinet and caused Henley and Walpole to resign. Church matters were equally sensitive, and Derby could be neither too rigid nor too liberal on these without causing strains in his Government and party.

The Maynooth question still divided Conservatives, and the Protestant Association was still campaigning against Government money for the College. But the winning of Catholic votes—a continuing possibility, commenced by Russell's Ecclesiastical Titles Act—was important to Derby, as well as the necessity of keeping ultra-Protestant support. His reply to a large deputation from Protestant societies on 27 April represented a manful attempt to have both. To the deputation (which included Spooner, Newdegate, James Lord, and Anglican, Wesleyan, and Scottish clergy), he said he could not deprive Maynooth of its moneys: this would encourage Voluntaryism, threaten the Church of Ireland, and antagonize the Irish Catholics. But he was anxious to offer compensation in return for cancellation of future annual grants.[271] Spooner was dissatisfied with this, but his usual motion in the Commons two days later was beaten by 210 votes to 155.[272] The *Protestant Magazine* could find only two M.P.s who had changed to voting against the motion, and one who had changed to favour it,[273] but the cause was making no progress.

If Maynooth was in the doldrums, the Church Rate Abolition Bill— pressed by an opposite ecclesiastical group and strongly denounced by the Protestant Association[274]—advanced to a third reading in the Commons for the first time, passing by 63 votes on 8 June. Graham had announced his support for the bill, though preferring a compromise, and Spencer Walpole

269 Derby to Cairns, 14 Nov. 1858, 25 Apr. 1859 (Cairns Papers, 30/51/8).
270 Quoted W. D. Jones, op. cit. 231.
271 *Protestant Magazine*, xx (1858), 60–4. See also ibid. 166–8.
272 Hansard, cxlix. 1990–9.   273 *Protestant Magazine*, xx (1858), 73 ff.
274 Ibid. 13.

(Home Secretary), though opposing the bill and warning that ulterior Voluntary forces were at work, advised that a charge on landowners should be substituted for the rate.[275] This was approaching the views of liberal Conservative ministers such as Pakington, who wanted to exempt Dissenters from payment.[276] Gladstone also affirmed his agreement with the exemption of Dissenters, but rejected complete abolition, saying that church-rates were still unopposed in most parishes and that the dispute could only be settled by compromise.[277] In the Lords the second reading was moved by the duke of Somerset, a pronounced broad churchman. Derby gave an adroit perform-ance, opposing the bill but hinting at compromise. A settlement might be reached, he said, if Dissenters would agree to a commutation which would leave the Church an equivalent sum.[278] The bill failed by 187 votes to a mere 36.

The church-rate question appeared to be entering a pattern similar to that of Jewish relief, with the Upper House blocking the demands of the Lower. But its fate was to be more chequered. Whereas the Jewish question was resolved this year, church-rate abolition did not retain even its Commons majority for long. The reasons for this were already looming. The Liberation Society, whose dedication to disestablishment was well known, tightened its anti-rate campaign after the parliamentary encouragement of 1858; this had the effect of toughening Church resistance, not only to abolition of the rate but to the Society's broader desires.

The Liberation Society had appointed, on 6 July, a Church Rate Sub-committee, which immediately suggested propaganda of various kinds in order to increase opposition to the rate. It was proposed that £50 should be spent on newspaper advertisements, and that local conferences should be held over the winter.[279] More should be made, it was suggested, of the general question of disestablishment. The following ingenious, but extremely contentious, suggestion was made for the purpose of hastening abolition of the rate:

That, having regard to the fact that the continuance of Church Rates is advocated on the grounds that the Churches are national edifices, there be prepared a Bill for vesting the control of the parish churches in the parish vestries, instead of the incumbent, with a view to the same being used for other purposes than the worship of the episcopalian body exclusively.[280]

Dr. C. J. Foster was accordingly deputed to approach M.P.s in order to introduce in the next session a bill 'to transfer the freehold of the parochial churches from the Parson to the representatives of the parish',[281] and the

[275] Hansard, cli. 1719–22.
[276] Pakington to Disraeli, 31 Mar. 1858 (Disraeli Papers, B/XX/P/38).
[277] Hansard, cl. 1724–7.   [278] Ibid. cli. 824–37.
[279] Minutes of Liberation Society, iii (16 July 1858).
[280] Ibid.
[281] Ibid., 21 July 1858.

radical T. S. Duncombe gave notice of such a bill before Parliament was prorogued at the end of the 1858 session.[282] The 'representatives of the parish'
might include people of any religious persuasion or of none, and the initiation
of such a provocative measure by the Liberation Society was unlikely to assist
their causes. While intending to remove resistance to abolition of the rate,
it could also have the opposite effect. There had existed since 1856 a Committee of Laymen of the Church of England, dedicated to church-rate defence,
and this set about exposing the Liberation Society:

> It cannot be too clearly seen that the abolition of Church-rates is inevitably to be
> followed by steps . . . for the entire separation of the Church from the State: and
> this is not at the call of constituencies, whose consciences are aggrieved, but at the
> dictation of a political body who have been for the last fourteen years, as they
> avow, disseminating their pernicious views . . .[283]

On such mutually fractious terms was the battle joined.

A Conservative Government had not stopped the advance against church-
rates. The same Government also agreed to Jewish relief, the most symbolic
religious liberty measure of the 1850s. Derby's reluctant agreement to this
reform was the fruit not only of his being in a minority but of the fact that
several powerful colleagues supported the change.

It was in a peculiarly tortuous way, however, that Parliament (with great
reluctance, as it would seem) relinquished one of its chief talking points for
nearly thirty years. On 10 December 1857 an Oaths Bill was brought in by
Russell, the main object being to admit Jews to Parliament. This bill was
allowed through its early stages with little opposition. Russell defeated, by a
huge majority, an amendment to enable Catholic M.P.s to take the same oath
as others: the amendment, he said, would only frustrate his attempt to relieve
the Jews. Another large majority of 153 disposed of an amendment by Newdegate, seconded by Spooner, to strike out the core of the bill—the fifth
clause, allowing Jews to take the entrance oath without the words 'upon the
true faith of a Christian'.[284] Newdegate raked up old arguments against the
Jews and in favour of an exclusively Christian Parliament, and, to strengthen
his case, alleged there was a great similarity between Jews and Roman
Catholics.[285]

The bill duly passed the Commons and was debated in the Lords in April.
Derby said he would support opposition to the crucial fifth clause if such
opposition were shown in Committee. But Earl Grey warned that if the Lords
threw out the bill this time, conflict with the Lower House would result and
the Commons would enforce their will against the Lords. The second reading

---

[282] Ibid., 15 Aug. 1858.

[283] Tract No. 9 of Committee of Laymen, entitled 'Church Rates' (London, 1858), 4.

[284] Hansard, cxlix. 465–83, 490–550. For the settlement cf. M. C. N. Salbstein, 'The Emancipation of the Jews in Britain' (unpubl. Univ. of London Ph.D. thesis 1974), 409 ff.

[285] Hansard, cxlix. 500–1.

was allowed to pass on 22 April, but five days later Lord Chancellor Chelmsford (formerly Sir Frederick Thesiger) repeated Newdegate's effort to omit the fifth clause. His amendment was carried, by 119 votes to 80, perhaps less on account of anti-Jewish feeling than of his eloquent appeal to resist dictation by the Commons—they would be left, he said, as 'nothing more than a registry-office for the decrees of the House of Commons'.[286] Thus the Lords rejected the bill's main object, and, not surprisingly, the Commons re-inserted the bill's stuffing when it was sent back to them. Chelmsford's amendment was rejected, and it was decided that reasons for disagreement with the Lords were to be drawn up by a committee, of which (after a division) Lionel de Rothschild was made a member in spite of his official exclusion from the Commons.[287] The reasons for disagreement were delivered at a conference with the Lords on 18 May. The Houses were back to square one.

The impasse was relieved by Conservative initiative. The Conservative earl of Lucan proposed a skilful amendment in the Lords on 31 May, that each House should be enabled to alter the oath as regards its own members. He avowedly recognized the force of repeated demands from the Commons. Derby was not convinced that these represented an increased desire in the country for Jewish admission, but left the way open for compromise: he would not entirely rule out Lucan's amendment. But Lyndhurst, another Conservative, who had long advocated Jewish relief, wished the Lords to give way and let the whole of Russell's bill through. It was agreed that both Lucan and Lyndhurst should prepare compromise bills.[288] Thus two Conservatives were preparing relief bills, while two other Conservatives— Spooner and Newdegate—whipped up resistance at the annual meeting of the Protestant Association on 17 June, Newdegate saying that the threatened concession was 'one of the greatest dangers that ever assailed this country'.[289] On 1 July both bills were considered. Lyndhurst's solution was the wider, suggesting that each House be empowered to admit not only Jews but all non-Christians. Derby preferred Lucan's measure, and Lyndhurst agreed that Lucan's bill should be given a prior chance to pass. In the subsequent debate Bishop Wilberforce said that, if reform were imperative, he preferred Lyndhurst's bill to Lucan's on the ground that Mahomedans were more sympathetic to Christianity than Jews.[290] But the second reading of Lucan's bill was carried by a majority of 46, Derby and other ministers voting in favour. Seven bishops assented and 11 opposed, the latter including both evangelicals and high churchmen.[291] Shaftesbury had decided to abstain, yielding 'to force, not to reason'.[292] He could not see, as he had written before,

[286] Ibid. 1767-8.   [287] Ibid. cl. 336-54, 430-43.   [288] Ibid. 1139 ff.
[289] Protestant Magazine, xx (1858), 84, 103-4.
[290] Hansard, cli. 724.   [291] Ibid. 727-30.
[292] Hodder, Shaftesbury, iii. 75.

how this ministry could claim to be Conservative,[293] and his annoyance was general amongst ultras.

On 12 July the Lords passed limited Jewish emancipation at last. Although the measure was not his own bill as passed by the Commons, Russell decided to adopt it, and moved its second reading in the Lower House on 16 July.[294] Newdegate moved against it, supported by Spooner and others who castigated the Lords for a concession 'worse than 1846', but Henry Drummond said this bill was the least mischievous mode of resolving an inescapable problem.[295] Newdegate was defeated, the second reading passed though most ministers in the Commons opposed it, and the third reading passed on 21 July.[296] Lucan's measure had succeeded. It remained to apply it to Lionel de Rothschild, who had been returned for the City of London in every general election since 1847 but hitherto kept out of his seat, and if possible to extend its provision to cover all Jews seeking entry. On 26 July Russell moved a resolution that any Jew might take a modified oath which would allow him to sit in the Commons. The die-hards spoke out again, but the resolution was carried by 69 votes to 37. Rothschild then took the oath on the Old Testament, omitting the words 'upon the true faith of a Christian', and took his seat on the Opposition benches.[297] Consolidation of the ground thus gained was left to a future session.

Jews had done better than deceased wife's sisters. Another bill to permit marriage with these by their former sisters' husbands passed the Commons, but was not granted similar indulgence by the Lords. Arguments on canonical grounds were urged against it, and Phillpotts, when reaching his peroration, dashed his copy of the bill to the floor.[298]

Jewish relief might have seemed an impressive bow to toleration, a concession to principle rather than political pressure, had not the settlement been so long in coming. Fortuitous political circumstances—the combination of renewed demands from a majority Liberal Opposition and the concessionary temper of a minority Conservative Government—had produced the settlement after all. The concession, however, represented the collapse of an important though badly eroded landmark in the relations of the State and religious groups. The reform could only encourage the demands of more powerful aspirants, of whom Nonconformists were currently the most active.

Dissenters also gained some satisfaction in connection with another 1858 measure, the Government's India Act. In the Lords Derby stated that 'nothing could be more . . . dangerous on the part of the State than any open and active assistance to any [sect], or any attempt to convert the native population from their own religions, however false and superstitious'.[299]

[293] Quoted in W. D. Jones, 243.
[295] Ibid. 1614–31.
[297] Ibid. 2105–15.
[299] Ibid. 2012.

[294] Hansard, cli. 1614.
[296] Ibid. 1879–1960.
[298] Ibid. 1995.

This was an almost identical, if coincidental, repetition of a Liberation Society minute of November 1857, resolving that the Government should not establish or finance any missionary organization as a State body, and should grant the fullest liberty of worship and teaching to all the native Indian religions and prevent any persecution or unequal treatment.[300] The Voluntaries were calling in the empire to redress the balance of the mother country.

Jewish relief and the passage of a Church Rate Abolition Bill by the Commons were promising breaks in the stalemate of the 1850s, and Dissenters planned a busy parliamentary programme for 1859. The Liberation Society promoted the reintroduction of Trelawny's abolition bill, and gave their support to a bill allowing Dissenters to sit on the boards of endowed schools, to an Annuity Tax Bill (which had been defeated by one vote on its second reading in 1858), to the abolition of the *regium donum* to Irish Presbyterian ministers, and to a bill allowing Catholic M.P.s to take the same oath as Protestant M.P.s.[301] A sign of opposition from Church defenders was the presentation of a petition for maintaining church-rates to the Canterbury Convocation when it met at the opening of Parliament.[302] Of the Dissenting programme, only an Oaths Bill for Catholic M.P.s and an Annuity Tax Bill were introduced before the ministry was defeated over its Parliamentary Reform Bill on 31 March, and a dissolution and general election took place.

The elections were held at the end of April and in early May. The Government, seeking a majority, was unfortunate in that there was little support in the country for its parliamentary reform measure, while support for Sardinia in the war with Austria (which broke out during the election campaign) benefited Palmerston—who extolled Italian liberation in his election address —rather than Derby who was thought to be pro-Austrian. Compared with these issues, a minor role was played by ecclesiastical questions. The Maynooth grant and church-rates remained the leading ones, and demands for the removal of each were advanced by the usual contrasting bodies. An address of the Protestant Association condemned grants to popish schools and army chaplains as well as to Maynooth, and called on Protestant electors to counteract the baleful influence of 'a strong Popish phalanx in the H. of Commons'.[303] Candidates were sometimes attacked for their pro-Maynooth views.[304] Progressive Conservative ministers remained anxious to attract the Catholic vote which Russell had opened to them in 1851 and which Palmerston (by doing nothing for Ireland and passing the 1857 Divorce Bill) had left unreclaimed. Irish Catholics were ready to support either party. In 1859 some minor concessions from the Government (such as the payment of

---

[300] Minutes of Liberation Society, iii (18 Nov. 1857).

[301] Ibid., 4 Feb. 1859.

[302] *Chronicle of Convocation*, sessions of 9–11 Feb. 1859 (London, 1859), 1–2.

[303] *Protestant Magazine*, xxi (1859), 50–1.

[304] e.g. W. L. Guttsman, 'The General Election of 1859 in the Cities of Yorkshire,' *International Review of Social History*, ii (1957), 245.

Catholic prison chaplains) and the papal opposition to Italian nationalism tipped some of them towards Derby. Conservatives had Wiseman's support, and they obtained most of the Irish seats with a net gain of at least eight. Even the Conservative victory in South Lancashire was attributed to Catholic electors.[305]

The Liberation Society had little time to prepare for this election, and was unable to secure Miall's adoption as a candidate. But its Electoral Sub-committee sat daily from 6 April at 2 Serjeant's Inn, Fleet Street, and nearly 5,000 circulars and 5,000 copies of *Hints to Electors* were distributed.[306] The abolition of church-rates, the Society's leading current topic, was demanded by several candidates, including not only Voluntaries but Lord John Russell (a recent convert to abolition) and other Liberal Anglicans.[307] E. A. Freeman, the historian of early medieval England, who stood at Wallingford but withdrew before the poll, said he wanted, in addition to the ballot and a wide franchise, 'the total repeal of the church-rates, as an impost at once unjust on the Dissenters and tending to bring the Church—to which I myself belong—into odium'.[308] Some Conservative candidates favoured a compromise settlement.[309] The desire for disestablishment was also occasionally raised; but such a matter, and the effect of the anti-church-rate campaign on promoting it, brought determined resistance from the Anglican Committee of Laymen in an electoral address.[310] In a notable incident in Merioneth twelve Nonconformist tenants were evicted by their landlords for abstaining or for voting in favour of an unsuccessful candidate who wanted to abolish church-rates, standing against a Conservative who was disliked for his Tractarian views.[311]

The 1859 election was a stagnant one for Voluntaries, who made no gains, and beneficial to the Conservative Government, which gained about 30 seats.[312] But this was not enough to keep the latter in office, and on 11 June the Conservatives were defeated, on a vote of no confidence, by the tiny majority of 13 in a huge House. Derby resigned, and Palmerston resumed office. Gladstone had first voted to keep Derby in, but then accepted office in the Government formed by Palmerston.

[305] See Hoppen, 'Tories, Catholics, and the General Election of 1859'; Vincent, 261-7. Cf. A. Brewster to Graham, 29 May 1859 (Graham Papers, microfilms, 128).

[306] Minutes of Liberation Society, iii (8, 27 Apr. 1859); *The Times*, 22 Apr. 1859, p. 3 (advertisement).

[307] *The Times*, 30 Apr. 1859, p. 5 (Russell), 27 Apr. 1859, p. 12 (W. D. Seymour), 29 Apr. 1859, p. 8 (E. S. Ruthven).

[308] Ibid., 27 Apr. 1859, p. 12.

[309] Ibid., 22 Apr. 1859, p. 7 (T. Bromley), 25 Apr. 1859, p. 5 (J. H. Maxwell), 4 May 1859, p. 8 (G. J. Noel).

[310] Ibid., 26 Apr. 1859, p. 3.

[311] Detailed account in I. G. Jones, 'Merioneth Politics in Mid-Nineteenth Century', *Journal of the Merioneth Historical and Record Society*, v (1965-8), 301-12.

[312] Mason, 'The Rise of Combative Dissent', 120-1; Guttsman, op. cit. 236; also Morley, *Life of Gladstone*, i. 622.

Gladstone's joining the Liberals provides scope for endless debate.[313] A cynic might say that he was only awaiting the election result before deciding which way to jump. Morley, who was no cynic, implied that Gladstone joined Palmerston because Palmerston was like Derby.[314] But this does not explain why he would not join Derby, and tends to ignore his vehement denunciations of Palmerston during the last four years. During a period of eighteen years Gladstone had developed considerably in a liberal direction. He had adopted many reforms against the opposition of ultra-Conservatives, and he contemplated other reforms which they resisted. But his progress in domestic reform by 1859 had taken him no further than progressive Conservatives, and he was less liberal than some of these in certain respects. For example, over church-rates he was less advanced than Lord Stanley. Gladstone was able to make his decision in unexpected favour of Palmerston because he was intensely interested in the burning question of the hour—Italian liberation—and this question did clearly separate Palmerston from the Conservatives. 'The most brilliant stroke made', wrote Aberdeen to Graham, 'was Palmerston's speech at Tiverton. His declared wish to see the Germans turned out of Italy by the war, has secured Gladstone, who is ready to act with him, or under him, notwithstanding the thousand imprecations of late years.'[315] Gladstone's involvement in the Italian question was a central feature of his political development, a product of his revulsion in 1850 from Neapolitan tyranny, which he had described as 'the negation of God erected into a system of government'.[316] But this matter could serve as a pretext, as well as a positive reason, for joining the Liberal party. Then verging on the age of 50, he was anxious to end his isolation and acquire a firm future in politics. His close Peelite associates had had less objection to Palmerston than he had,[317] and had practically aligned themselves with the Liberals. If friendship could draw him in one direction, enmity could seal off another. His dislike (and perhaps jealousy) of Disraeli helped to block the alternative opening.

Having joined Palmerston, Gladstone was linked to a man with whom he had little in common, whom he had denounced habitually, and with whom tension was practically inescapable. The difference of viewpoint within parties was such that Gladstone, the erstwhile Conservative, was closer to the radicals than to Palmerston in some respects, particularly in his desire to press Free Trade to a conclusion at the expense of defence. With radical ecclesiastical views his sympathies were not so clear. His anti-Erastian high

[313] See the interesting discussion in A. O. J. Cockshut, *Truth to Life—the Art of Biography in the Nineteenth Century* (London, 1974), 183–6.

[314] Morley, op. cit. i. 631; quoted Cockshut, op. cit. 185.

[315] Aberdeen to Graham, 27 May 1859 (Graham Papers, microfilms, 128). Cf. Gladstone's own explanations (Morley, i. 627–8).

[316] D. M. Schreuder, 'Gladstone and Italian Unification, 1848–70: the Making of a Liberal?', *EHR* lxxxv (1970), 478–88, 496–501; Morley, i. 389–402; ii. 1 ff.

[317] Newcastle to Gladstone, 10, 15 Feb. 1857 (Gladstone Papers, 44263, fos. 4–9, 14–15); Sidney Herbert to Russell, 17 May 1859, copy (ibid. 44211, fos. 53–4).

churchmanship gave him sympathy with the desire of non-Anglicans to rid themselves of the remaining State restrictions. He wanted also a purer and more popular Church, and therefore wanted to reduce the opposition to it. But, provided the established Church could be freer and purer, he wished it to remain established—looking longingly, perhaps, to the looser State connection north of the border—and so he was unwilling to entertain a Voluntary solution so far as England was concerned.

Gladstone's junction with the Liberals helped to develop an alliance between firm Erastians and the Conservative party. But Gladstone did not make the Liberal party more liberal by taking any new ideas into it with him. Rather did he, with his searching, open mind and interest henceforth in building Liberal strength, become more liberal in religion and other matters through his association with the party.

This development lay in the future. Gladstone did not mention any religious reasons for joining Palmerston. Indeed he had not any. The Liberal Government of 1859 brought no progressive change in the ecclesiastical situation—rather did conservative reaction help to retard reform for some years. Ecclesiastical questions remained in stalemate throughout the life of the new Government. Those before cried onward, those behind cried back, and between them the Government did nothing.

CHAPTER IX

The Hardening of Conflict: Dissenters and Church Defenders, 1859-1865

I. CHURCH APPOINTMENTS AND THE LIBERAL GOVERNMENT

THE 1859 election and the formation of Palmerston's second ministry promised no great change in ecclesiastical politics. The campaigns to remove the Maynooth grant and to abolish church-rates had received little encouragement from these events. The new Government had no intention of altering the Maynooth endowment, and Dissent had not gained in the election. In July 1859, however, when church-rates were first discussed in the new Parliament, Palmerston supported abolition of the rate for the first time; and the issue was made an 'open question' in the Government, several other ministers being willing to abolish the tax. But a fierce conflict developed in the country between Voluntaries and defenders of the Establishment, and the effect of Church counter-attack was shown in a reversal of the parliamentary trend on church-rates—culminating in 1864, when, for the first time since 1852, no church-rate abolition motion was brought before the Commons. The parliamentary anti-rate campaign had turned full circle in twelve years, without result.

Underlying liberal tendencies were later to emerge, working to achieve both the abolition of compulsory church-rates and the abolition of the Maynooth grant (the latter only in harness with Irish disestablishment, which anti-Maynooth opinion abhorred). These tendencies were linked with Gladstone's liberal progress. But in 1859 Gladstone's future was unknowable. Bishop Wilberforce said that his re-election at Oxford was 'of great importance for conservative opinions of which he is the key in the Cabinet', and for Church security, and that his joining Palmerston was a mere 'mistake in judgement' for which it would be unjust to turn out one who had made great sacrifices for the Church of England.[1] Gladstone thus appeared to his Oxford followers, and doubtless to many others, as a staunch defender of orthodoxy and the Establishment against latitudinarians and Nonconformists. He seemed far removed from the alliance with Dissenters and Catholics which he reached a few years later. But an unfavourable view of Gladstone (that of Bagehot, published in July 1860) attributed to him a mind which was

[1] Wilberforce to Rev. Austen Leigh, 25 June 1859 (Wilberforce Papers, d. 40).

basically 'impressible, impetuous and unfixed' and which had departed so far from its youthful moorings as to have lost all sense of consistency.[2]

Gladstone was expected to care for the Church's interests—and, more specifically, high-church interests—in regard to episcopal appointments. The continued evangelical tendency of Palmerston's appointments was illustrated when Dr J. C. Wigram became Bishop of Rochester and Samuel Waldegrave bishop of Carlisle, both in 1860, and Francis Jeune bishop of Peterborough in 1864. The Tractarian Bishop Hamilton of Salisbury, in whose diocese Waldegrave had served for many years, said that his relations with Waldegrave had been more difficult than with almost any other of his clergy,[3] and Bishop Wilberforce was highly offended by Waldegrave's advancement.[4] But after 1860 there was a wider approach to the filling of sees. Not high churchmen but moderate orthodox clerics were appointed (for example William Thomson to Gloucester and Bristol in 1861 and to York in 1862). Conciliatory high churchmen like Gladstone could approve of them, while Shaftesbury on the other hand could find little to disapprove in them.[5]

Gladstone, however, obtained nothing more positive from Palmerston regarding his desires for the increased prosperity of the Church. Palmerston told him that he could not create any new bishoprics: 'There would be no Difficulty in finding any additional Number of Bishops, but I do not know where we should find additional Salaries . . .'[6] Early in 1862 Palmerston said that a candidate for the provostship of Eton was recommended 'by the high Church party, whose recommendation rather tells against him';[7] and in 1864 both high churchmen and evangelicals disliked the appointment of A. P. Stanley, the prominent broad churchman, to the deanery of Westminster. A correspondent wrote fearfully to Gladstone that this would mean having a dean who believed the New Testament contained no doctrine, and Pusey said that Stanley, as a professor of ecclesiastical history, had 'sent students miserably adrift as to faith'.[8]

Gladstone himself was showing a liberal approach to appointments. In September 1862 he recommended Longley, archbishop of York, for appointment to Canterbury on the ground that the new Primate should be 'some one who from moderation as well as piety and learning should carry real

---

[2] 'Mr. Gladstone', in *National Review*, ii (July 1860), 219 ff.; reprinted N. St. John-Stevas (ed.), *Bagehot's Historical Essays* (London, 1971), 260–1.

[3] Hamilton to Roundell Palmer, 3 Dec. 1860 (Selborne Papers, vol. 1862, fos. 110–11). Cf. Waldegrave to Palmer, 26 Nov. 1860 (ibid., fos. 104–6).

[4] Wilberforce to Gladstone, 20 Aug., 28 Sept. 1860 (Gladstone Papers, 44344, fos. 120–3).

[5] Gladstone to Palmerston, 29 Aug. 1861 (P. Guedalla (ed.), *Gladstone and Palmerston, 1851–65* (London, 1928), 189). Cf. Hardman, 'The Evangelical Party in the Church of England', 33 ff. But see also Newcastle to Palmerston, 22 Aug. 1861 (Martineau, *Life of Newcastle*, 329–30).

[6] Palmerston to Gladstone, 2 Sept. 1861 (Guedalla, op. cit. 189).

[7] Palmerston to Clarendon, 3 Feb. 1862 (Clarendon Papers, c. 524).

[8] Rev. Arthur Russell to Gladstone, 11 Nov. 1863 (Gladstone Papers, 44401, fos. 179–80); Pusey to Gladstone, 9 Nov. 1863 (Pusey Papers).

weight not with any party in particular but with the Church at large'.[9] Longley having been chosen for Canterbury, York then had to be filled. Gladstone wrote to Palmerston recommending Wilberforce as being probably the foremost preacher and the most hard-working bishop in the Church. But he was doubtful whether his recommendation (which was expressed tentatively enough) would succeed;[10] and indeed it is doubtful whether Gladstone really wanted it to succeed. He had serious misgivings whether Wilberforce was liberal enough for the age, and no doubt he disliked the fact that Wilberforce was acting as chairman at Church propaganda meetings addressed by Disraeli.[11] He wrote to Wilberforce on 2 October:

Part of the special work of this age ought to be to clear the relations between Church and State. It is needless for me to point out to you ... the multitude of questions, each of which presents a separate knot as yet untied ... there is Church Rate: there is national Education: there is the law of Marriage & Divorce : there is Clergy Relief (however dubiously so called): there is the Court of Appeal: there are Oaths and Declarations of Roman Catholics and Dissenters: there was and in some sense still is the admission of Jews and others to the Legislature: there is Clergy Discipline ... I think the State has a right to expect from the Church that its Episcopal Rulers, at least that the leading governing spirits among them, shall contribute liberally and even sometimes boldly to the solution of these questions.

... You have opposed many changes which you thought injurious; and, as regards many of those you have opposed, I certainly am in no condition to find fault with you.

But I think I should be puzzled were Lord Palmerston to say to me 'I will not dwell on ... which of the changes asked for he has opposed, but I will desire you to tell me of which of these problems [he] has, as a leader of the clergy, publicly *and* at his own risk, promoted the solution?

... I seem to observe that the character you have got with politicians among whom I live is that of a most able Prelate getting all you can for the Church, asking more, giving nothing ...[12]

Wilberforce admitted that he had 'not much to point to' in the way of agreement with liberal concessions, but named support of the Oxford University Bill in 1854, advocacy of a church-rate settlement on compromise lines, and defence of 'the liberal education view in the National Society'.[13] Gladstone said 'the Oxford Bill is a very good case',[14] but Thomson got the appointment. To console Wilberforce, Gladstone sent him a copy of his letter recommending

[9] Gladstone to Palmerston, 7 Sept. 1862 (Guedalla, 231–2).

[10] Gladstone to Wilberforce, 10, 23 Sept. 1862 (Wilberforce Papers, d. 37); Gladstone to Palmerston, 28 Sept. 1862 (Guedalla, 236–8).

[11] See below, p. 317.

[12] Gladstone to Wilberforce, 2 Oct. 1862 (Lathbury, *Correspondence of Gladstone*, i. 196–8, part quoted Meacham, *Life of Wilberforce*, 267–8).

[13] Wilberforce to Gladstone, 4 Oct. 1862 (Wilberforce Papers, d. 37).

[14] Gladstone to Wilberforce, 8 Oct. 1862 (ibid.).

him. Wilberforce expressed heartfelt gratitude for the praise therein,[15] but he soon showed dislike of some of Gladstone's policies towards the Church.

Gladstone's letter of 2 October 1862 reveals the importance which 'religious equality' questions had come to possess for him, and shows the developing mentality behind the measures he urged and effected for the benefit of Nonconformists and Catholics during the 1860s. This progression was doubtless stimulated by, and in its turn stimulated, his other approaches to radicalism, through repeal of the paper duties and parliamentary reform.

If Gladstone's alliance with Dissent was far away in 1859, so was the reconciliation of Catholics with the Liberal party. On the Italian nationalist question, so prominent in that year, Catholic opinion was more pro-papal in Ireland than in Great Britain.[16] In Liverpool, division among Catholics was shown. A Catholic view in support of the nationalists was expressed by the *Liverpool Daily Post*, which was taken to task by the more Ultramontane and 'Irish' *Northern Press* (edited by a convert from Anglicanism, S. B. Harper): 'Victor Emmanuel is applauded, Garibaldi is raised to the gods, and the Pope may fall to the ground, for all these liberal minded Catholics care'.[17] Support for the Pope against the nationalists was shown by special collections of Peter's Pence in Catholic churches in the city, and the bishop of Liverpool went to Rome to present addresses and money. The *Liverpool Mercury*, with Liberal views, joined more ultra-Protestant opinion in denouncing the Pope.[18]

The Italian issue was still very much alive in this region, and in London, in 1862. Many Irish labourers then gathered in Birkenhead to stop a debate by an Anglican society on the patriotism of Garibaldi. A thousand constables were sworn in, but had little effect against the mob.[19] Catholic voters in a by-election at Preston in April 1862 refused, under the leadership of a chemist named Cornelius Satterthwaite, to vote for the Liberal candidate, George Melly, because he was identified with Palmerston's foreign policy; and this candidate lost the contest.[20] Catholic M.P.s had also shown their continued dissatisfaction with the Liberals. Bright wrote in December 1859: 'They have not forgotten the Durham Letter, & the stupid habit of attacking the Pope which seems inseparable from a speech on Italian affairs from Lord Palmerston or Lord John Russell only adds to their ill-will.'[21] Disraeli tried to

---

[15] Gladstone to Wilberforce, 8 Nov. 1862 (ibid.); Wilberforce to Gladstone, 13 Nov. 1862 (ibid.).

[16] Norman, *The Catholic Church and Ireland*, 38–51.

[17] Burke, *A Catholic History of Liverpool*, 144–5.

[18] Ibid. 143, 146.

[19] Ibid. 154–5; see also ibid. 159–60. For the London and Birkenhead disturbances see S. Gilley, 'The Garibaldi Riots of 1862', *Hist. Jl.* xvi (1973), 697–732.

[20] H. A. Taylor, 'Politics in Famine-Stricken Preston, 1861–5', *Transactions of the Historic Society of Lancashire and Cheshire*, cvii (1955), 121 ff. See also George Melly Papers, 2nd Ser., V, esp. fo. 1326a.

[21] Bright to Edward Ellice, 16 Dec. 1859 (Ellice Papers, E4, fo. 82).

obtain, or retain, the Catholic vote which the Liberals had lost;[22] though he was hampered in this not only by ultra-Protestant Tory back-benchers but also by his own emphatically pro-Establishment policy shown from 1859 onwards.

II. THE FAILURE OF RELIGIOUS EQUALITY

Familiar ecclesiastical questions were before the country and Parliament from 1859 to 1865, and there was little approach to solutions. Thomas Chambers, speaking at the annual meeting of the Protestant Association on 1 June 1859, despaired of ultra-Protestant ends being gained in politics. Both parties had betrayed Protestantism, and 'the present meeting was a proof of the want of interest in the matter. Out of one thousand ministers of the Church of England and other bodies in the metropolis, he did not see more than ten present. Was Protestantism a thing of no value to them?' We were threatened with a Catholic Establishment, he said, endowed by the State alongside the Protestant one—in the form of Catholic chaplains in workhouses, penitentiaries, gaols, and the armed forces, and grants to Catholic education.[23]

The declining fortunes of the anti-Maynooth campaign in Parliament seemed to bear out Chambers's pessimism. Spooner moved in February 1860 for a Committee of the whole House to consider the withdrawal of the Maynooth endowments. Both parties, he said, were too lenient to Catholics, both 'tried too much to reconcile those who would never be reconciled . . .' He himself had supported Catholic Emancipation in the 1820s, 'in ignorance of that priestly domination in which another generation had been nursed up, and the doctrines subversive of everything loyal that had been taught from Maynooth to the deluded Papists of Ireland'.[24] Spooner's motion was no more appealing to leading Conservatives who were seeking the Catholic vote that it was to Liberal ministers. He had the support of only 128 members in the division and was defeated by a majority of 58. As a further insult, Parliament passed in this session a bill of Cardwell's (Chief Secretary for Ireland) permitting the transfer of endowment funds from some Maynooth students in order to finance repair of the buildings. Spooner and Newdegate fought the new bill to no avail, obtaining only 57 votes to support them.[25] In 1862 G. H. Whalley, Liberal M.P. for Peterborough but strongly anti-Maynooth, objected to an address of condolence from Maynooth College to the Queen on the death of the Prince Consort. This, he said, gave the College an undeserved patina of loyalty: the students in fact were the reverse of loyal.[26] On 6 May that year Whalley moved, 'amidst much interruption', for a Committee to consider abolishing the Maynooth grant, but after a very brief

[22] Cf. Vincent, *The Formation of the Liberal Party*, 261–3.
[23] *Protestant Magazine*, xxi (1859), 79–80.
[24] Hansard, clvi. 1038–47. [25] Ibid. clix. 1606–8, 2277–87.
[26] Ibid. clxv. 1027–30 (4 Mar. 1862).

debate was defeated by 82 votes.[27] In June 1863 he tried again, but the motion was briefly disposed of by a majority of 98, after Voluntaries as well as ultra-Tories had voted for it.[28] There was no anti-Maynooth motion in 1864 or 1865. The parliamentary anti-Maynooth campaign, a regular feature since 1852, had, like church-rate abolition, described a large and fruitless circle. In such matters Parliament would go neither backward nor forward.

Liberal ecclesiastical measures also fared badly during Palmerston's second ministry. This was the combined effect of larger Conservative representation and a moderate Liberal Government which would not give way completely to the demands of its Dissenting, radical left. Many Liberals put up only a half-hearted resistance to the 'Church defence' attitude of the Conservatives and this increased the frustration of Dissent with the Liberal party.

The ministry, however, was not completely barren of religious reform: Scottish Dissenters, Jews, and Catholics all gained a little something. An abortive attempt to abolish the Edinburgh annuity tax in 1859 was followed by positive Government steps towards a solution, and in 1860 a compromise bill was brought in by the Lord Advocate. In place of the tax, the town council would levy an assessment on householders of 8d. in the pound for fifteen years, at the end of which time a sufficient sum would have accumulated to pay 13 ministers (to be reduced to this number from 18) £600 p.a., leaving a surplus in the hands of the council.[29] Voluntaries were divided over the bill. The Liberation Society thought it would merely create 'a new & permanent endowment in favor of the Established Kirk of Scotland', and George Hadfield moved to reject it as being contrary to the principle of voluntary support.[30] But Adam Black (an M.P. for Edinburgh) and other Scottish Voluntary members thought it in the best interests of Edinburgh to accept the offer, after slight modification. Hadfield, finding no Scottish support, withdrew his amendment, and the bill passed both Houses.[31] The arrangement, however, still produced opposition on Voluntary grounds.

A more satisfactory settlement was achieved in 1860 for Jewish relief. A bill was introduced by T. S. Duncombe to make Jewish entrance to Parliament more secure than was allowed by the temporary resolutions provided in 1858. Newdegate, seconded by Spooner, moved to reject the bill on the ground that the bitter constitutional dispute of two years before should not be reopened, but he was defeated by 117 to 75.[32] The Lords amended the wording of the measure. After it had received the royal assent, Duncombe moved that the sessional resolution, allowing Jews to omit the words 'upon the true faith of a Christian' from their oaths, should become a standing order of the House, and this was agreed. The question of Jews in the

[27] Hansard, clxvi. 1292–1303.   [28] Ibid. clxxi. 251–61.   [29] Ibid. clv. 275–7.
[30] Minutes of Liberation Society, iii (3, 10 Feb., 9 Mar. 1860); Hansard, clviii. 1348–9.
[31] Hansard, clviii. 1350–64; clix. 2013–14.
[32] Ibid. clvii. 960–3, 1916–19.

Commons had been laid to rest. Duncombe congratulated the House 'on the destruction of the last shred of persecution for religion's sake, as far as that House was concerned';[33] but secularists, still debarred from Parliament, would have disagreed with this verdict.

Roman Catholics also obtained, against popular prejudice, a concession from the Government—though it was but a very slight bow to the wide pro-Catholic programme which Archbishop Cullen had hoped that the Liberal Government would adopt, and no answer at all to the demands and discontent of Irish Catholicism.[34] A bill, introduced by the Home Secretary, was passed in 1863 improving the facilities for non-Anglican prisoners in England and Scotland to receive the ministrations of chaplains of their own faith, and thereby lessening the prospects of proselytization. The magistrates were enabled to recommend such chaplains, who would be paid out of the rates. Lord Edward Howard, then 'the sole Roman Catholic representative of an English or Scottish constituency', naturally spoke for the bill,[35] and Liberals were generally in favour. The division was again revealed between ultra-Tories and progressives in the Conservative party—Newdegate and others opposed the bill (which was also condemned by the Scottish Reformation Society)[36] but Derby, Disraeli, Henley, and Pakington were in favour.[37] Derby thought it necessary to deny that the bill commenced 'placing the Roman Catholic Church on an equality with the Establishment'.[38] After the bill had passed, the Liverpool magistrates selected a Catholic prison chaplain at a salary of £300 p.a.; but the appointment had to be approved by the town council, and ultra-Protestant councillors tried to obtain refusal of payment. The dispute was ended by the intervention of the Home Secretary, who said that the chaplain's salary could come from fines and court fees and not from the council.[39]

This measure was a response to the increasing number of Catholic inmates of British gaols which Irish immigration had brought about. In 1862, it appeared, there were between 3,000 and 4,000 Catholic prisoners in English county and borough gaols, and about 1,500 in convict prisons.[40] The Act officially included Protestant Dissenters too, but there may have been fewer Nonconformist prisoners than Catholic.

Dissenters achieved very little during Palmerston's second Government, and were particularly disappointed by a swing of parliamentary opinion against church-rate abolition, which had seemed so close to success. Opposition to the rate continued in the country, encouraged by the Liberation Society and manifested by secularists as well as Dissenters (G. J. Holyoake

[33] Ibid. clx. 1346–7.   [34] Norman, op. cit. 37, 51–86.
[35] *Annual Register*, cv (1863), 71.
[36] Dundee Town Council Minutes (general committee), v (29 Apr. 1863).
[37] *Annual Register*, cv (1863), 71–3.
[38] Ibid.   [39] Burke, op. cit. 157.
[40] *Annual Register*, cv (1863), 71.

had lost an eight-day clock for non-payment in 1855, and Bradlaugh resisted the rate in 1859 and 1860).[41] In the Government the matter had become an 'open question'. Russell now supported abolition, as did Palmerston, Graham, Grey, Lewis, Cardwell, and other ministers. But when Roundell Palmer accepted office as Solicitor-General in 1861 he was permitted to continue expressing his pro-rate opinions.[42] Gladstone continued to oppose complete abolition, but was still looking for a chance to promote 'some tolerable adjustment'.[43] In May 1860 he sent to Bishop Wilberforce a plan for settlement. This suggested that a rate should no longer be levied in places where none had been imposed for the past seven years, or where a rate should be refused in two successive years in the future. Moreover, where a rate was still levied, any payer might receive exemption on conscientious grounds, but would then have no say in church management.[44] These were generous proposals, a significant indication of the tendency which led Gladstone to advocate abolition of the compulsory rate by 1866.

But in the parliamentary session of 1859 Gladstone had remarked on the 'wretched division' in the Commons against church-rates: '193 to 273 [263 was meant], nearly the same majority as in the last Parliament, notwithstanding the gain of 25 seats = 50 votes to Lord Derby!!'[45] This was indeed only a slight decrease from the majority obtained before the 1859 election, but the decline accelerated in succeeding years. The abolition bill progressed no further in 1859. The Liberation Society was being increasingly countered by Church defence. In December 1859 the Society feared that this might increase the vote in favour of church-rates in the Commons.[46] Its prophecy proved correct. In 1860 Trelawny's bill was opposed by several fighting speeches in defence of the Establishment and its privileges. The second reading passed by a mere 29 votes (though only one member, Townsend Mainwaring, Conservative M.P. for Denbigh boroughs, appears to have changed his vote to opposition), and the third reading passed by only 9 votes.[47] In the Lords the duke of Newcastle (a Cabinet Minister) announced his conversion to abolition, but the bill was lost on the second reading by the overwhelming majority of 128 to 31.[48]

The Liberation Society, confronted with this recession, put on a brave face. It was noted that exactly the same number of M.P.s (263) had supported the second reading in February 1860 as in July 1859, and that the lower

[41] E. Royle, *Victorian Infidels* (Manchester, 1974), 267.

[42] Palmer to Henry Brand, 1 July 1861 (Selborne Papers, vol. 1862, fos. 133–4); R. Palmer, *Memorials, Family and Personal*, ii. 367.

[43] Gladstone to Keble, 24 Mar. 1860 (Keble Papers, E. 90).

[44] Gladstone to Wilberforce, 2 May 1860 (Wilberforce Papers, d. 36). Cf. some draft solutions by Keble at this time (in Keble Papers, E. 90, some dated Apr. 1860).

[45] Gladstone to Wilberforce, 13 July 1859 (Wilberforce Papers, d. 36). Cf. division list, 13 July 1859 (Hansard, cliv. 1183–6).

[46] Minutes of Liberation Society, iii (9 Dec. 1859).

[47] Hansard, clvi. 634–86; clviii. 259–301.

[48] Ibid. clix. 618–65.

majority had resulted from the increase of voters on the other side.[49] This seemed accurate: the opposition to the second reading had jumped from 193 (July 1859) to 234 (February 1860). But the Society's executive committee was impressed by 'the recent strenuous exertions of the upholders of Church Rates', and remarked especially on the need to obtain the votes of absent M.P.s in order to 'defeat the threat'.[50] The Society launched a strenuous petitioning campaign between the second and third readings in 1860, and was gratified by the presentation of 5,447 petitions containing 600,699 signatures. Against the bill, it was said, there were presented 5,459 petitions containing only 193,375 signatures.[51] The signatures in favour of the bill, it was claimed, came from a wide range of Dissenters. But in fact the largest numbers of petitions with a denominational ascription (as opposed to general 'ratepayers' and 'inhabitants', who presented 1,908 petitions) came, fairly predictably, from Baptists (819) and Congregationalists (728). Wesleyans, it seems, were not anxious to petition against the rates. Though they were more numerous than either Baptists or Congregationalists, Wesleyans petitioning as such produced only 135 petitions. Calvinistic Methodists similarly produced only 108. The secession Methodists produced far more. Primitive Methodists accounted for 265 petitions, the United Methodist Free Churches (a body formed by the union of two secession groups in 1857) for 164, and the Methodist New Connection for 97. Roman Catholics produced a mere 27, against the 61 forwarded by the much less numerous Quakers.[52] This may have indicated how little the Catholics combined in political action with Protestant Dissenters; but it may also have reflected the concentration of Catholics in large towns where the rate was no longer levied. In any case, in regard to the above figures, the numbers of petitions are no clear guide to the numbers of signatures.

After the defeat of 1860, the Liberation Society's Church Rate Committee renewed its efforts in preparation for the next session. In the autumn anti-church-rate conferences were held at Bristol, Taunton, Liverpool, Birkenhead, Preston, and Ashton-under-Lyne.[53] In December the Society urged electors to memorialize their M.P.s on the need to vote in every division, and authorized that £1,000 be spent in an attempt to carry the bill.[54] Special agents were sent to promote the memorials to M.P.s, and a large anti-rate conference was organized at the Freemasons' Hall on 12 February 1861: nearly 800 persons attended from 330 places, and William Scholefield, M.P., presided.[55] But disappointment followed. Another reduced majority (of only 15) passed the second reading of Trelawny's bill on 27 February.[56] The

[49] Minutes of Liberation Society, iii (10 Feb. 1860).
[50] Ibid.   [51] Ibid. 30 Mar., 27 Apr. 1860.
[52] Analysis of petitions ibid., 27 Apr. 1860; part printed in Vincent, op. cit. 70.
[53] Minutes of Liberation Society, iii (29 Sept., 30 Nov., 21 Dec. 1860).
[54] Ibid., 21 Dec. 1860.   [55] Ibid., 18 Jan., 22 Feb. 1861.
[56] Hansard, clxi. 1053–7.

Liberation Society noted that, in the fullest House which had ever voted on the question, whereas 18 more members had voted for abolition than ever before (a total of 281),[57] votes against the bill had risen even more steeply (to 266). But only two members (Hon. R. H. Dutton and Sir E. Lacon) had changed their votes to oppose the bill, and the increase in opposition came from former absentees. On the third reading on 19 June, after fruitless suggestions for compromise had been made by Sir G. C. Lewis and by Newdegate,[58] the voting trend broke even and the House reached a remarkable tie at 274 votes on each side. The decision therefore lay with the Speaker, who said: ' . . . it seems to me the general opinion of the House is in favour of some settlement of this question different from that which is contained in this Bill . . . I therefore give my vote with the "Noes".'[59] For the first time since 1854 a Church Rate Abolition Bill had been defeated in the Commons. Seven fewer members had supported it than on the second reading, and eight more had opposed it.[60] The swing was taking place mainly through the voting of opponents who had previously abstained, and through the abstention of previously active supporters. The initiative had passed from Dissenters to Church defenders.

The Liberation Society committee consoled itself with the reflection that Conservatives were seeking rejection of the bill as 'a trial & triumph of party strength'. The committee reaffirmed its support for complete abolition, and not for a compromise which might only exempt Dissenters. But disappointment continued in 1862, when Trelawny's bill failed on the second reading by a majority of one, 287 to 286.[61] The Liberation Society committee computed that only two M.P.s—Lord Ernest Bruce and H. B. Baring, Liberal members for the pocket borough of Marlborough—changed to opposition in this division, but that twenty 'supporters' were absent (a few of them being ill or abroad).[62] Most of the ministers had voted for the bill, Gladstone and Roundell Palmer being among the exceptions.[63]

In April 1863 Trelawny, now avowedly weary of his unpromising annual task and seeking release from it, saw his bill defeated on the second reading by ten votes, 285 to 275, a result which was met by Conservative cheering. Twenty-nine 'supporters' were absent from the House, a sign of growing despair or indifference.[64] As a result, there were no abolition bills in the two succeeding years. But offers of compromise were made, even by strong opponents of abolition. Newdegate introduced every year from 1862 to 1865, and beyond, a bill to commute the rate to a fixed charge on realty, but had no

[57] Minutes of Liberation Society, iii (8 Mar. 1861).
[58] Hansard, clxiii. 1301–7.   [59] Ibid. 1322.
[60] Minutes of Liberation Society, iii (21 June 1861).
[61] Hansard, clxvi. 1727–35.
[62] Minutes of Liberation Society, iv. 42 (16 May 1862).
[63] Ibid.
[64] Ibid. 108–9; Hansard, clxx. 974–8.

success.[65] Abolitionists would not support this measure, and Sir George Grey advised that the whole matter should be left to the opinion of the voters at the next general election.[66] In 1864, however, the anti-raters did have the satisfaction of seeing the withdrawal of a Church Building Acts Consolidation Bill, which would have extended the rate to newly created parishes.[67]

The anti-church-rate cause, which had seemed so hopeful in 1859, was now waiting passively for the demise of the current Parliament and the election of a new one. Other 'religious equality' causes in which Dissenters were interested had fared no better. Apart from church-rates, Dissenting grievances considered by Parliament between 1859 and 1865 comprised endowed school trusteeships, declarations required from public officials, burial in churchyards with Dissenting rites, and University Tests. In 1860 a bill was introduced in the Lords by the Lord Chancellor, Cranworth, to regulate the qualifications of endowed school trustees, and included a provision that Dissenters might be elected as trustees unless they were expressly excluded by the trust deed. This provision implied possible changes in school curricula in accordance with Dissenting views, and churchmen resisted it. The bill only passed after the provision had been struck out.[68] On 26 January 1860 a similar bill was introduced in the Commons by Lewis Llewellyn Dillwyn, but this was rejected.[69] Dillwyn's bill again did not pass the Commons in 1863.[70] Somewhat more successful, though still not reaching enactment, were George Hadfield's bills to abolish the (allegedly spurious) declaration, required of Dissenting officials by the Act of 1828, that they would do nothing to injure the Church Establishment. A bill for this object passed the Commons in 1860 but not the Lords.[71] Similar bills passed the Commons in every session from 1861 to 1863, and again in 1865, but all were rejected by the Lords.

A Dissenters' Burials Bill was brought in without success in 1861, 1862, and 1863 by Sir Samuel Morton Peto, a leading Baptist who represented Finsbury. Peto claimed the right of burial with Dissenting services in parish churchyards, and sought to allay Anglican fears by saying that Nonconformists only wanted equal rights.[72] But in 1863 the measure was crushed by 221 votes to 96. Apart from strong Conservative opposition even Trelawny spoke against it. By enabling Dissenters to hold their own services in parish churchyards, he stated, the measure would give Dissenters some benefit from church-rates and would therefore weaken their case against the rate.[73] Gladstone, however, had already supported the Burials Bill in 1862, and in

---

[65] *Journals of the House of Commons*, cxvii (1862), 44, 324; cxviii (1863), 45, 205; cxix (1864), 46, 198; cxx (1865), 86, 254; *Annual Register*, cv (1863), 79; cvi (1864), 158; cvii (1865), 94.
[66] Ibid. cvii. 94.
[67] Minutes of Liberation Society, iv. 200–8 (29 Apr., 20 May, 3 and 17 June 1864).
[68] *Annual Register*, cii (1860), 190–2.   [69] Hansard, clvi. 162–3; clvii. 965–93.
[70] Ibid. clxxi. 1004–8.
[71] Ibid. clvi. 179–80, 441–3, 2008–9; clvii. 1007–16.
[72] Ibid. clxi. 652, 654–5 (19 Feb. 1861).   [73] Ibid. clxx. 159.

1863 (a year in which he also spoke in favour of Hadfield's bill)[74] he said that it was inconsistent with civil and religious freedom to exclude a Nonconformist's remains which had not had the Anglican service read over them.[75]

Gladstone's declaration was far more significant for religious liberty in the future than for the present. In the meantime the legislative failures continued. A bill of J. G. Dodson, M.P. for East Sussex, to admit non-Anglicans to M.A.s at Oxford (also to give non-Anglican M.A.s a vote in the University Convocation, and to allow them certain other benefits) was defeated by two votes in 1864.[76] When the same bill was revived by G. J. Goschen in 1865 its second reading was carried despite the opposition of Gladstone and Lord Robert Cecil, who wished to keep the governing bodies of the University exclusively in Anglican hands. But the bill did not proceed further because of the lateness of the session.[77]

Among other failures, the reviving demands of Irish Catholics were the most important. Attempts of various kinds had been under consideration since 1854 to remove the special oath which the 1829 Relief Act required of Catholic M.P.s, and which included the denial of any intention to subvert the Church Establishment or otherwise to disturb the Protestant religion and Government. William Monsell, M.P. for Co. Limerick, obtained leave in March 1865 to introduce such a bill. He was opposed by Newdegate, who said it was a particularly inopportune moment for making the change when the Syllabus of Errors showed growing papal assertiveness.[78] In the subsequent debates the recent formation of the National Association of Ireland, aiming at disestablishment of the Irish Church, was cited as a reason for resisting the measure; Catholic M.P.s, it was implied, would attack the Irish Establishment more assiduously once they had got rid of this oath.[79] The second reading passed by 66 votes but, when it had gone through the Commons, Lord Derby succeeded in obtaining its rejection by the Lords.[80] Opposition to this measure showed the belief that the Irish Establishment needed defence against reviving attacks which were seen both in Ireland and in Parliament. Dillwyn had moved in May 1863 for a Select Committee to inquire into the desirability of redistributing Irish religious endowments in a manner 'most conducive to the welfare of all classes of Her Majesty's Irish subjects'.[81] He described the Church of Ireland as a source of national weakness rather than strength. This motion was withdrawn. But on 26 June 1863 Bernal Osborne had brought in a similar motion and called, with the aid of numerous statistics, for swingeing reforms in the Irish Church in the

---

[74] Ibid. clxix. 1047–50.   [75] Ibid. clxx. 153.
[76] Ibid. clxxvi. 678–80; W. R. Ward, *Victorian Oxford*, 244–6.
[77] Hansard, clxxx. 185–250; W. R. Ward, op. cit. 247.
[78] Hansard, clxxviii. 31–5.
[79] Ibid. clxxix. 432–3 (Anthony Lefroy, M.P. for Dublin University).
[80] Ibid. clxxx. 772–92, 802–3, 821–2. See also Norman, *The Catholic Church and Ireland*, 293–4.
[81] *Annual Register*, cv (1863), 95; Hansard, clxx. 1968 ff.

manner of 1833. The dioceses should be reduced to six and their incomes halved; the parochial clergy should be reduced and their incomes made more equal.[82] Members of the Government opposed the motion, Sir Robert Peel (Chief Secretary for Ireland) saying that it was a revival of the dreaded appropriation and, if carried, would encourage similar treatment of the Church of England (thus reviving a common complaint against appropriation in the 1830s).[83] This motion too was dropped.

Dillwyn had remarked that the Irish Catholics were currently apathetic on this question,[84] but this was not a view which could be held much longer. The formation of the National Association on 29 December 1864, dedicated to disendowment of the Church of Ireland and the application of its revenues to 'purposes of national utility', compensation for tenants' improvements on their land, and equality of denominational education, denoted the resurgence of Irish constitutional aims, just as Fenian activities denoted the revival of unconstitutional ones. Disendowment was a matter on which British Voluntaries, now that they had officially abandoned the desire to abolish the Maynooth grant *per se*, wholeheartedly joined the Irish Catholics.[85] On 28 March 1865 Dillwyn raised the Irish Church question again, in a motion to the effect that the Establishment was unsatisfactory and called for the early attention of Government. Though it was defeated, the motion obtained sympathy from Gladstone. The latter strongly criticized the Church of Ireland as an Establishment and opposed the motion only because it was premature at that stage, not because it was intrinsically undesirable.[86] Palmerston was alarmed at Gladstone's attitude,[87] and indeed the chain of events which led to Irish disestablishment was now beginning.

Meanwhile the aims of Dissenters and Catholics continued to have a barren time. One should add to the list of 'religious equality' failures the rejection (in 1861 and 1863) of Secular Affirmation Bills, supported by Dissenting and Catholic M.P.s, designed to allow secularists to give evidence in law courts by exempting them from the Christian oath.[88]

III. CHURCH DEFENCE AND DISRAELI

Behind the rising votes against church-rate abolition and the successful opposition to other 'religious equality' bills was a Church defence movement of notable proportions. It took effect through various channels—associations of Anglican clergy and laymen, journalism, and political campaigning inside and outside Parliament. In this way the conflict of Church and chapel reached a new pitch of intensity.

[82] Ibid. clxxi. 1560 ff.
[83] Ibid. 1686, 1695.
[84] *Annual Register*, cv (1863), 95.
[85] Norman, op. cit. 135 ff.
[86] Hansard, clxxviii. 420–34; Morley, *Gladstone*, ii. 141–3, 239–40; W. E. Gladstone, 'A Chapter of Autobiography', in *Gleanings of Past Years* (7 vols., London, 1879), vii. 130–4.
[87] Palmerston to Gladstone, 27 Mar. 1865 (Guedalla, 326–7).
[88] Royle, op. cit. 268–71.

The aim of Church defenders was to defeat the Liberation Society and its Voluntary aims. The House of Lords had appointed a Select Committee on church-rates in 1859, and witnesses before this Committee (Samuel Morley and Dr. C. J. Foster) had admitted to a wish for disestablishment. Lord Robert Montagu drew attention to this in the Commons in February 1860, saying that the 'agitation for the abolition of Church rates is merely a political movement, and . . . the ultimate aim of that movement is the destruction of the Church Establishment . . .'[89] By this time the connection between church-rate abolition and Voluntaryism was being constantly noted.

The Committee of Laymen of the Church of England, founded in 1856, issued a series of Church defence tracts. The thirteenth tract, published in 1859 and entitled 'Church Rates', said that the time had come 'for a determined rally . . . on the part of the friends of the Constitution, for the maintenance of the principle of the ancient Rate, as involving that of the continuance of an Established Church . . .'[90] Clerical defence was often expressed. In the lower house of the Canterbury Convocation church-rates were debated in June 1859: Canon Christopher Wordsworth said that the rates were 'a part of the royalty of Christ our Saviour', and Archdeacon Hale of London said that Voluntaries wished to use the abolition of the rate 'as the first step towards the annihilation of our Church as the national religion'.[91] Archdeacon Denison wrote in the autumn to Archdeacon Hale that they should be ready 'in our several Archdeaconries, with a great mass of Petitions when Parliament meets'.[92] Denison placed pro-church-rate resolutions before a large public meeting in November, and they were carried unanimously.[93] In the following January the archdeacon of Buckinghamshire, Edward Bickersteth, appealed to his clergy for 'a firm & united resistance' and a concerted petitioning movement in favour of maintaining the rate. He suggested a form of petition to the Commons which stated 'that measures of late introduced into your Honourable House for the Abolition of Church Rates, would be inconsistent with the principle of an Established Church'.[94] But the response to his appeal was disappointing.[95] The Rev. Francis Merewether, still ardently pamphleteering, published in 1862 a letter to the members of both Houses, entitled *Establishment or non-establishment?* The national Church, he said, came nearest 'to the rule of Christ and His Apostles in the

[89] Hansard, clvi. 647–57; Miall, *Life of Miall*, 225 f. Reports of the Select Committee of the House of Lords . . . [on] the assessment and the levy of church rates, with evidence, etc.; 1859 (179. Sess. 2.) v. 15, 1860 (154), xxii. 159.

[90] Tract No. 13 of Committee of Laymen (London, 1859).

[91] Overton and Wordsworth, *Christopher Wordsworth*, 170; *Chronicle of Convocation*, sessions of 22, 23, 24, and 30 June 1859 (London, 1860).

[92] Denison to Hale, 11 Nov. 1859 (L. Denison (3d.), *Fifty Years at East Brent*, 76–7).

[93] Ibid. 82–3.

[94] Circular dated 10 Jan. 1860, encl. in Ven. E. Bickersteth to Disraeli, 10 Feb. 1860 (Disraeli Papers, B/XXI/B/483).

[95] Bickersteth to Disraeli (ibid.).

matter of Church Government', and the influence of the aristocracy through the Establishment was 'a valuable component part of Christian society'.[96] The 'non-Establishment' by contrast was an undignified mêlée of Dissenting sects which had not succeeded in attracting a majority of the population. The national Church remained the people's Church, and was entitled to keep its rates.[97] But not all clergymen defended church-rates, and not only broad churchmen advocated their removal. The extreme high churchman W. J. E. Bennett printed an appeal for abolition in 1861, saying that the rates were increasingly anachronistic in an age of liberal concession.[98]

Attempts to organize clerical defence of rates and Church Establishment on a nationwide basis were made by the Church Institution. This was formed in December 1859 on the initiative of Henry Hoare, a wealthy and devoted layman who had been prominently concerned in the revival of Convocation. From 1871 the society was known as the Church Defence Institution. Hoare was treasurer of the society, and its executive committee, consisting of twenty-nine laymen, included Lord Robert Cecil, A. J. Beresford Hope, C. G. Merewether, and Lord Robert Montagu. The rules of the association, which received the approval of the archbishop of Canterbury and several bishops, stated that questions of doctrine were to be avoided at the meetings, which aimed at harmony.[99] A prime motive of the Institution was defence of the union between Church and State, and the Liberation Society was named as the main enemy.[100] 'The critical moment', said Hoare on one occasion, 'has arrived. It must be now or never and the watchword was "Up Guards, and at 'em".'[101] A 'central council' of clergy and laymen, of varied religious opinions, headed the organization. The council issued, from 5 March 1862, the *Church Institution Circular* (published weekly and costing a penny) containing information and advice aimed at promoting the society's political objects.[102] Extension throughout the country was to be through local associations (consisting of clergy and laity) formed first in the rural deaneries and then in the parishes. Thus the Church Institution attempted to exploit the political potential of country rectories in the same way as the Liberation Society and the *Nonconformist* sought out Dissenting manses. In April 1863 it was said that 470 rural deaneries in England and Wales had formed local associations connected with the Institution; nevertheless, 'the principle . . . is as yet only in its infancy . . . the strength of the Church cannot be known until not only every Deanery, but every *Parish* has its Association . . . [then] the voices of

---

[96] F. Merewether, *Establishment or non-Establishment?* (London, 1862), 30–2.
[97] Ibid. 35 ff.
[98] W. J. E. Bennett, *Why Church Rates should be abolished* (London, 1861), 41.
[99] Sweet, *Henry Hoare*, 445–51; M. A. Crowther, *Church Embattled* (Newton Abbot, 1970), 195–7; *The Principles and Objects of the Church Defence Institution* (London, n.d. [1871]), 1.
[100] *The Principles and Objects* . . ., op. cit. 4; Sweet, op. cit. 450–1.
[101] Mackintosh, *Disestablishment and Liberation*, 110.
[102] *Church Institution Circular*, 5 Mar. 1862.

10,000 Parishes will be heard . . . by Parliament itself'.[103] The local associations had lay agents in London, each of whom sat on the central council.[104] An Association of Churchwardens was formed in 1860 with a purpose similar to that of the Institution, and (a reflection of the 1830s) Operative Church Associations were formed in Manchester, Oldham, Mossley, and other industrial localities.[105]

Church Institution meetings applauded the anti-church-rate decline in the Commons. The decline was credited in no small measure to the work of the local associations.[106] 'Religious equality' measures in Parliament were denounced. Parliament, said a speaker at a Church Institution meeting at Northampton, was now dangerously unrepresentative of the Church; Convocation represented only the clergy, and so the Institution provided much-needed representation for the Anglican laity.[107]

The Liberation Society was under constant fire from the Church Institution, and the importance of this Society in indirectly promoting the Institution is shown by a lecture delivered to the Bristol Church Defence Association in 1861. The speaker, a local clergyman named J. B. Clifford, stated that his lecture resulted from a visit by members of the Liberation Society in the previous year. Much of the lecture was an attempt to prove that the Liberation Society was weaker than it looked. The Society's last report, said the speaker, showed that it had only 6,100 subscribers in the whole country; and there were, he maintained, only 180 subscribers in Bristol and its neighbourhood.[108] The Society had little positive support even from Dissenters, and 'the importance of the society ought to be but lightly esteemed by our Houses of Parliament'.[109] Parliamentary opposition to church-rates was commendably declining, and other Dissenting bills were being rejected. Dissenters were inconsistent in their attitude to State endowments, as was shown by the fact that the London Missionary Society, a Dissenting body, wanted Government support for religion in the South Sea islands.[110] The Church Establishment, unlike the Liberation Society which tended to promote national infidelity, was well worthy of support, as was shown by its remarkable revival in the last few decades: it was 'a glorious instrument for the promulgation of the truth . . . the bulwark of our common Protestantism . . . the greatest barrier to infidelity . . . the strong foundation on which our constitution and liberties are based . . .'[111]

---

[103] Ibid. vol. II, No. xxxi (Apr. 1863), 181–2; vol. II, No. xxxv (Aug. 1863), 285.

[104] *Church Institution meeting of united deaneries of Northampton, Preston and Brackley north-east, 15 Nov. 1862* (Northampton, n.d.; pamphlet in British Library, 4108 de. 14), 2.

[105] *Church Institution Circular*, vol. III, No. xxxviii (Jan. 1864), 63.

[106] *Church Institution meeting at Northampton . . .*, op. cit. 2 ff.

[107] Ibid. 7.

[108] Lecture on *The Dissenters, the Liberation Society and the Church of England*; Bristol Church Defence Association Tracts (Bristol, n.d.), 5.

[109] Ibid. 12.   [110] Ibid. 13.   [111] Ibid. 22.

Yet the Church Institution found it difficult to compete financially with the Liberation Society, in spite of the greater clerical wealth which it could have expected to tap. In the fourth year of its existence (1863) the Institution's income was hardly a third of the Liberation Society's.[112] There was a lack of direct political activity by the Institution, and churchmen were urged to act with the same committed fervour as Liberationists at the next election.[113] Protection of the established status of the Church of Ireland concerned Church defenders. Hugh McNeile, T. R. Birks, and Sir Hugh Cairns delivered addresses at the Irish Church Missions' Anniversary Breakfast in 1864, and Cairns emphasized the unity of the two Establishments: a threat to the one half equally endangered the other.[114]

The Liberation Society was far from undisturbed by Church defence activities. Its executive committee noted in November 1860 that the Society was 'deficient in its provisions to meet the numerous & various efforts made . . . to excite, propagate, & direct public opinion against it'.[115] The committee therefore recommended that £200 p.a. (later raised to £300) should be provided for 'a suitable person' to combat the propaganda of Church defenders, both nationally and locally. Herbert S. Skeats was selected. He was to draw up a register of every scrap of information which might be of use to the Society. This would provide 'a well digested repertory of an immense mass of local details, always useful both in its general & local effects'. He should also start to collect a library of controversial, historical, legal, and parliamentary works on all subjects of interest to the Society.[116]

Attacks on Voluntaryism came from other quarters beside the Church Institution. In 1864 Richard Masheder, a Fellow of Magdalene College, Cambridge, published *Dissent and Democracy: their mutual relations and common objects*—an attack on the connected claims for Dissenting equality and parliamentary reform, doubtless stimulated by the revival of the latter cause at that time. A widening democratic system, he said, would encourage Voluntary aims by increasing the political power of Nonconformists: 'It is by way, first of a £6 borough franchise, then of universal suffrage, the ballot, annual parliaments, equal electoral districts, and "a reasonable remuneration to members of Parliament", that Dissent calculates upon reaching the goal proposed—the separation of Church and State.' To resist this progression, churchmen should defend the existing parliamentary constitution as eagerly as they championed the Church.[117]

Periodicals also took up the cause of Church protection—notably the *Quarterly Review* and *Saturday Review*. Among the contributors to these

---

[112] *Church Institution Circular*, vol. II, No. xxxv (Aug. 1863), 287.
[113] Ibid.
[114] *Addresses* . . . at the Irish Church Missions' Anniversary Breakfast (London, 1864), 4 ff.
[115] Minutes of Liberation Society, iii (30 Nov. 1860).
[116] Ibid.
[117] R. Masheder, *Dissent and Democracy* (London, 1864), 3–4, 312 ff.

papers was Lord Robert Cecil, who wrote extensively on Church defence.[118] Writing in the *Quarterly* in 1861, Cecil anticipated Masheder by saying that the attack on the Church Establishment was not isolated, but showed a desire to advance along 'the whole revolutionary line', and he advocated that vestry membership should include only landlords (not occupiers), because landlords were more willing to pay church-rates.[119] An anonymous article in the *Saturday Review* in March 1860 inveighed against the Liberation Society's alleged desire for 'joint-possession' of the parish churches: 'The tendency is not to disestablish the Church alone, but to establish Dissent'.[120] Anglicanism, though not perfect, was preferable to its rivals: ' . . . whatever people may think of chants & copes, we are not going to pull them down to put Little Bethel in their stead. A Tower Hamletized Church would be something more serious and more lasting than even Mr. Bryan King's unwise experiments in chasubles.'[121] Another article counselled, in the same tone: ' . . . it is better to resign ourselves to the tyranny under which we already suffer so much than to chance a future directed by Mr. Dawburn of Wisbeach and the Rev. H. Capern of Bugbrook'.[122] The article of March 1860 was prepared to see Dissenters relieved of church-rates, provided they took no part in managing the parish churches by attending vestry meetings. This solution would surely satisfy the many Dissenters who had sincere, conscientious scruples against the rate.[123]

For the political realization of their desires, defenders of the Church looked to the Conservative party, as Cecil urged them to do in a *Quarterly Review* article of 1865.[124] Although Palmerston's Government had no wish to destroy the Establishment, it had made church-rate abolition an 'open question', and Palmerston himself had voted for abolition. Gladstone was prepared to compromise on the rate question, and sympathized with some other Dissenting claims, giving his support to Hadfield's and Peto's bills. Conservative leaders, while still interested in winning Catholic support, were ready to try and detach Erastian support from Palmerston. Disraeli was later, when in office, to show himself susceptible to compromise on such matters as church-rates. But at this juncture he fully appreciated the political value of the Church reaction, and was both willing and able to take the part of Church champion—appearing so ardent at times as to cause embarrassment to Derby.[125] The established Church, he held, should be defended not

[118] See list of Cecil's articles in M. Pinto-Duschinsky, *The Political Thought of Lord Salisbury, 1854–68* (London, 1967), 157 ff. For examples of Cecil's Church views in these articles see P. Smith (ed.), *Lord Salisbury on Politics: a selection from his articles in the Quarterly Review, 1860–83* (Cambridge, 1972), 288–9, 319–20, 323–6.

[119] Article on 'Church Rates', *Quarterly Review*, 110 (1861), 545, 558–9, 566–72.

[120] *Saturday Review*, ix. 304 (10 Mar. 1860).

[121] Ibid. 395.   [122] Ibid. xi. 445–6 (4 May 1861).

[123] Ibid. ix. 304 (10 Mar. 1860).

[124] 'The Church in her Relations to Political Parties', *Quarterly Review*, 118 (1865), 212 ff.

[125] Derby to Disraeli, 12 Dec. 1860 (Disraeli Papers, B/XX/S/277).

only as part of our national heritage but as a natural institution for a believing population.

Disraeli's own archdeacon in Buckinghamshire, the Ven. Edward Bickersteth, helped to link him with Church affairs. In April 1860 Bickersteth asked Disraeli to attend a lay and clerical conference of some 50 people at High Wycombe on the subject of church-rates.[126] Church extension and efficiency, he later told Disraeli, would bring political strength: ' . . . the best way to strengthen the Church party in the country is to set the Clergy vigorously to work in their parishes, especially in preparing their young people for confirmation, & training them up regularly to be communicants . . . if this were effectively done their Radicalism & Dissent would be gradually undermined . . . this never can be done without a considerable increase of our Home Episcopate'.[127] Bickersteth asked Disraeli to second resolutions at an Aylesbury meeting in July 1861 (at which Bishop Wilberforce presided), on behalf of the Diocesan Church Building Society;[128] and in October 1862 he expressed pleasure that Disraeli was to speak at High Wycombe in favour of the Small Benefices Augmentation Association—a meeting which was reported in the *Church Institution Circular*.[129] When, in 1865, Queen Emma of Hawaii was to attend an Aylesbury meeting to promote Church missions abroad, Bickersteth again tried to obtain Disraeli's participation.[130]

Several of Disraeli's speeches to clerical gatherings in Buckinghamshire stressed the need to maintain church-rates and avoid a compromise, for the sake of preserving the Establishment. Such opinions he delivered at a ruridecanal meeting at Amersham in December 1860. Derby was alarmed at the way he was closing the door to compromise, and wrote after this speech:

I see you have come out very strong on the subject of Church Rates . . . I entertain a fear that you have even spoken too decidedly . . . the present law is, if not so objectionable in itself, so difficult of enforcement, that if an amendment could be obtained by some concession, I think it would be worth the sacrifice . . . I am afraid that we shall now be open to the retort that we insist absolutely on the maintenance of the law exactly as it stands. This may, I fear, increase the majority against us in the Commons . . .[131]

Disraeli did not reply to this for six weeks, and Derby thought he might be annoyed.[132] When Disraeli eventually set pen to paper on the subject, he emphasized the political benefits which he expected his standpoint to bring:

---

[126] Bickersteth to Disraeli, 10 Apr. 1860 (ibid. B/XXI/B/484).
[127] Bickersteth to Disraeli, 21 Mar. 1862 (ibid. 490).
[128] Bickersteth to Disraeli, 31 July, 23 Oct., and 9 Nov. 1861 (ibid. 486-9).
[129] Bickersteth to Disraeli, 4 Oct. 1862 (ibid. 491); *Church Institution Circular*, Nov. 1862, p. 64.
[130] Bickersteth to Disraeli, 13 Oct. 1865 (Disraeli Papers, B/XXI/B/498).
[131] Derby to Disraeli, 12 Dec. 1860 (ibid. B/XX/S/277; part quoted Monypenny and Buckle, *Life of Disraeli*, iv. 357).
[132] Derby to Disraeli, 27 Jan. 1861 (Monypenny and Buckle, iv. 357-8).

As for Church rates, I took the step after great inquiry and reflection; and I think if I had not taken it our counties would have slipped away. The moment was more than ripe. The enclosed will give you some idea how it worked in Wales, where the clergy, and the Church generally, are weakest. It will work more powerfully in Wiltshire, and, from the numerous communications which reach me, I think I shall have effected my purpose.[133]

Disraeli's speeches in the country had the strong approval of Archdeacon Bickersteth, who was at hand to congratulate, to encourage publication and to advise alterations.[134] Lord John Manners and the Rev. Francis Merewether also wrote praising the speeches.[135] These orations reflected Disraeli's sustained efforts in Parliament against church-rate abolition and other concessions. He spoke against the second reading of Trelawny's bill in February 1860, saying that church-rates were not so much a practical grievance as a pretext for demanding disestablishment, and that it would be 'tyrannical interference' for the State to overturn the parochial constitution.[136] He condemned the bill in 1861 as an assault on parochial independence, and said that a Dissenter had no longer any grievance, in regard to the rate, but that of having to submit to a majority in the vestry.[137] The defeat of the 1862 bill by a majority of 1 was preceded by another speech from Disraeli. Church-rates in each parish, he repeated, were adopted by a majority, and government by a majority was 'the rule and spring of our political life'.[138] Other bills to relieve Dissent met his opposition; and, still desiring Catholic support for his party, he was displeased that Catholics combined with Protestant Dissenters to oppose the established Church. 'Peto's bill comes on next Wednesday; most offensive to the English clergy', he wrote on 10 April 1863. 'It would be wise in the Catholic members, and would greatly assist me in my conscientious efforts on their behalf, if they did not mix themselves up with these Pedo or Peto Baptists, or whatever they may be.'[139]

In spite of his desire to win the Catholics, Disraeli would not support pro-Catholic measures when they seemed to represent threats to the Establishment. In 1865 he resisted Monsell's bill to change the Catholic M.P.s' oath. Referring to the unwelcome formation of the National Association, and its policy of disendowment of the Church of Ireland, he said that pro-Catholic reforms must be given in a spirit of conciliation and not extracted by threats.[140]

---

[133] Disraeli to Derby, 28 Jan. 1861 (ibid. 358; original in Derby Papers, 146/1). 'The enclosed' is not placed with the letter in the Derby Papers.

[134] Bickersteth to Disraeli, 9 Feb. 1860, 1 and 6 Nov. 1862, 30 Nov., 1 and 4 Dec. 1864 (Disraeli Papers, B/XXI/B/482, 493–7).

[135] Manners to Disraeli, 13 Dec. 1860 (Disraeli Papers, B/XX/M/117); Merewether to Disraeli, 30 Jan. 1861 (ibid. 336).

[136] Hansard, clvi. 672–6.   [137] Monypenny and Buckle, iv. 359.

[138] *Annual Register*, civ (1862), 33–4.

[139] Disraeli to Viscount Campden, 10 Apr. 1863 (Monypenny and Buckle, iv. 367).

[140] Hansard, clxxx. 56, 64. Derby's speech in the Lords was similar (ibid. 772 ff.).

The odium which was cast on the Liberation Society and on Voluntaryism caused some Liberals and Dissenters to deny connection with them. In the face of repeated allegations in the Commons that church-rate abolitionists were spokesmen for the Liberation Society, Trelawny assured the House that he was not connected with the Society though he greatly respected some of its leading members.[141] Cecil congratulated Trelawny and others on making such declarations.[142] Similarly, Peto denied, when advocating his Burials Bill in 1861, that he was attached to the Liberation Society.[143] But this was less convincing: both the *Saturday Review* and Cecil in the Commons pointed out that he had been a leading member of the Society in 1859.[144]

How did Church defenders react to Disraeli's political campaign on their behalf? A writer in the *Saturday Review* in December 1860 found his new-found zeal 'a shade too strong', and preferred compromise—the acceptance of a suggestion made (among others) by the Lords' Select Committee of 1859, that Dissenters and others desiring it should receive exemption from the rate, and should not thenceforth take part in vestry meetings. Disraeli's object, said the article (not without justice, considering Disraeli's own admission to Derby),[145] was transparently political. He was patronizing the pro-rate movement 'in the hope of winning back the counties, through the help of clerical canvassers, on a cry which should develope [*sic*] the *odium theologicum* into a political vendetta . . .' The result of this policy might be that 'the seeds of all old political bitterness will be revivified, the good work of a quarter of a century will be undone, the Church will again become the object of popular hatred . . .'[146]

This article may have underestimated the resilient capacity for compromise which Disraeli was to demonstrate again when political times were different and when he had left Opposition for office. In the meantime, the object of Disraeli's artificially adamant stance on one side of the Church–Dissent controversy was to render his political opponents vulnerable by presenting them in an equally extreme light on the other side. The attempt did not succeed electorally in 1865, for it was very difficult to make Palmerston appear radical. But Disraeli at least made Gladstone look left-wing, because Gladstone could only strengthen his own political force by appealing to radicalism and Dissent.

IV. NONCONFORMITY AND GLADSTONE

The Liberation Society in the 1860s, being confronted with declining political success, undertook some vigorous soul-searching with regard to its future. Although the amount of subscriptions exceeded £3,500 in 1859–60, and

[141] Ibid. clvi. 682.   [142] Ibid. clxiii. 1291–2.   [143] Ibid. clxii. 1024.
[144] Ibid. clxiii. 1292; *Saturday Review*, xi. 445–6 (4 May 1861).
[145] Disraeli to Derby, 28 Jan. 1861 (Monypenny and Buckle, iv. 358).
[146] *Saturday Review*, x. 760.

the number of subscribers reached approximately 5,500 in the same year,[147] finance continued to be a problem. In 1861–2 the Society had a deficit of £330 and in 1862–3 one of £829.[148] Far more uncertain were the Society's political prospects and the parliamentary tactics it should decide to adopt. The current trough was blamed on the previous heights attained: it was said, in a minute of February 1862, to be 'an effect of past successes, in the fears & the anger of the supporters of Church Establishments . . .'[149] What, then, should the Liberation Society do? *Reculer pour mieux sauter*, it was thought, was the best maxim for parliamentary behaviour in the near future. It seemed better to husband resources rather than carry on assaulting the same apparently impenetrable objects, and to await a more propitious time before resuming bold action. In the meantime, fresh efforts should be made to gain public support. Among specific objects which it seemed still worth while to press, special consideration (said a minute of 19 September 1862) should be given to disestablishment in Ireland, Wales, and Scotland. These were countries which the Society had neglected hitherto; and in them disestablishment would—on account of Dissenting strength—be a more formidable cause than in England, whose case for a Voluntary system was hardly worth while laying before Parliament in 'a like direct & comprehensive manner'.[150] Thus the attention of these particular radicals was already being focused on the Celtic fringe.

Before this minute was drawn up, hopes had been expressed that a Scottish conference might be held in November 1862. The formation of a separate society for Scotland, or a special branch of the Liberation Society, was discouraged, but it was thought that members of the Society's council who lived in Scotland might meet at stated times for discussion of relevant problems in that country, that they might appoint their own secretary, and that a liaison officer might function between Scotland and the central committee. Such suggestions, it was hoped, would 'meet the objection that the Society now confines itself exclusively to English questions'.[151] On the Society's behalf, a Mr. Oulton met Voluntary Committees at Edinburgh, Glasgow and Dundee in order to arrange the conference, but difficulties prevented the conference being held.[152] After further difficulties, a financial agent (Rev. Anderson Drysdale, a United Presbyterian minister) was appointed for Western Scotland in July 1863, but a year later his engagement was terminated as having been insufficiently remunerative.[153] This result was as disappointing as that which had followed the appointment of a salaried person in November 1861 to raise more subscriptions from Wesleyans.[154]

[147] Minutes of Liberation Society, iii (3 Aug. 1860).
[148] Ibid. iv. (26 June 1863).   [149] Ibid. iv. 14 (5 Feb. 1862).
[150] Ibid. 66–8 (19 Sept. 1862).   [151] Ibid. 59–62 (1 Aug. 1862).
[152] Ibid. 71, 77 (17 Oct., 14 Nov. 1862).
[153] Ibid. (13 Feb., 10 July 1863, 15 July 1864).
[154] Ibid. iii. (15 Nov. 1861); iv. 57–8 (1 Aug. 1862).

The Society's foray into Wales in the autumn of 1862 was more successful. Here the ground was promising, for Nonconformists were truly thick upon it —a fact which had been lamented by a dean of Jesus College, Oxford, when he appealed to Gladstone in 1853 for Welsh-speaking bishops to be appointed in Wales in order to make the established Church more popular.[155] Even landlord domination could have indirect effects on promoting Voluntaryism. In Merionethshire the evictions after the 1859 election had initiated a more militant approach to radical and Dissenting politics. Whereas a visit by the Society to Merioneth towns in 1851 had been unfruitful, another visit in 1860 had profitable results.[156] Articles in the *Baner ac Amserau Cymru* coincidentally encouraged a Liberation Society effort by attacking the current Welsh representation at Westminster as being too English and Anglican, regardless of whether it was Whig or Tory.[157]

North Wales was left until 1866 before a vigorous approach was made. But a successful conference was held at Swansea on 23 and 24 September 1862, convened by forty residents of South Wales to receive a deputation consisting of Miall, Henry Richard, and Carvell Williams (secretary of the Society). Two public meetings, one conducted in English and the other in Welsh, were arranged as part of the proceedings.[158] A gathering of 200 delegates heard, among other speakers, Lewis Dillwyn, member for Swansea and spokesman for Dissenting causes, probably the only Welsh M.P. considered worthy of support. A paper read by Carvell Williams reported, among other matters, that most Welsh M.P.s had opposed Peto's Burials Bill; and the conference passed a resolution saying that Welsh Nonconformity was inadequately represented in the Commons.[159] The report of proceedings at the conference was published in English and Welsh, and results of the conference were the establishment of a Committee for South Wales at Cardiff, the appointment of a new district agent (Rev. John Rees of Swansea), and the dispatch of copies of the Society's publications to Welsh Dissenting periodicals.[160] The potential Voluntary strength of Wales, long hindered by interdenominational differences and landlord influence, was now beginning to be exploited by a London-based organization. When it had gathered strength, the movement for Welsh disestablishment was to assume a more nationalist colouring, but the English initiative in 1862 was important to its development.

---

[155] Rev. Robert Owen to Gladstone, 12 Jan. 1853 (Gladstone Papers, Add. MS. 44373, fos. 266–74).

[156] I. G. Jones, 'Merioneth Politics in Mid-Nineteenth Century', 306–16; Minutes of Liberation Society, iii (19 Oct. 1860).

[157] e.g. article of 2 Apr. 1862; Parry, 'The Parliamentary Representation of Wales and Monmouthshire', 248–9.

[158] Minutes of Liberation Society, iv. 63–4 (5 Sept. 1862).

[159] C. S. Miall, *Henry Richard, M.P.* (London, 1889), 119–23. For the conference see also I. G. Jones, 'The Liberation Society and Welsh politics', 216–18.

[160] I. G. Jones, op. cit. 218; Minutes of Liberation Society, iv. 69–70 (3 Oct. 1862).

The Society's connections with Irish Catholicism were also strengthened at this period. At a meeting of the executive committee on 31 October 1862 a letter from O'Neill Daunt was read, urging the Society to abandon opposition to the Maynooth grant in order to form a united movement against the Church Establishment in Ireland.[161] The committee's reply was affirmative.[162] But the Society's current political defeatism prevented it in 1863 from even supporting Irish efforts to stimulate petitioning against the Establishment; and in regard to the Irish Church a more vigorous policy was only adopted in 1865, in response to a move from the Irish Catholics themselves, shown in the establishment of the National Association.[163]

The Society's Welsh effort helped to sustain it during this arid period. But this was not the only sign of action. In December 1862 a West Riding Committee was formed, following a successful conference of about 200 persons in that area.[164] That year had also seen a spiritual renewal of confidence from the bicentenary commemoration of the ejection of 2,000 non-conforming ministers on St. Bartholomew's Day, 1662. This helped Dissenters, at least those of the older denominations, to recall their brave seventeenth-century past. The same reverent zeal caused the formation of a Central United Bartholomew Committee which the Liberation Society supported.[165] This committee admitted that the ejected ministers had not been Voluntaries,[166] and the *Church Institution Circular* seized on the differences between the attitudes of 1662 and 1862, including the fact that many of the ejected ministers had not objected to episcopacy. The commemoration, said this journal, was a false one, staged by Miall and the Liberation Society for their own purposes.[167]

Events in 1862 had shown that, while the Liberation Society had considerable, indeed increasing, support in the country, its parliamentary impetus had not revived. In 1863 the Church Rate Bill suffered another defeat, and there followed Sir John Trelawny's relinquishment of his active advocacy and the emigration of Dr. C. J. Foster, the energetic chairman of the Parliamentary Subcommittee, to New Zealand.[168] The Society's minutes in the late summer and autumn of 1863 reveal its continuing restless dilemma. On the one hand, in August it was resolved to extend the anti-rate agitation in the parishes, and for this purpose to supply legal information and publications for distribution.[169] On the other hand, a lengthy survey of the political situation was undertaken by the Parliamentary Subcommittee, and presented in an important memorandum of 23 October 1863. The decline in parliamentary fortunes

[161] Ibid. 76 (31 Oct. 1862).   [162] Ibid. 78 (14 Nov. 1862); Norman, op. cit. 179.

[163] Norman, 179–80; Minutes of Liberation Society, iv. 234–5 (6 Jan. 1865).

[164] Minutes of Liberation Society, iv. 82–3 (19 Dec. 1862).

[165] Ibid. (17 Jan., 28 Feb. 1862).

[166] D. M. Thompson (ed.), *Nonconformity in the Nineteenth Century*, 171–2.

[167] Quotation from the *Standard* of 10 Apr. 1862, in *Church Institution Circular*, 23 Apr. 1862, pp. 127–8; also ibid., 6 Sept. 1862, pp. 6–7.

[168] Mackintosh, op. cit. 122.

[169] Minutes of Liberation Society, iv. 127–8, 130–1 (7 Aug., 4 Sept. 1863).

was dated from the 'tie' vote of 1861. Since then, bills had been opposed 'on account of our supposed connection with or interest in them', and (referring to Peto) 'members, who had charge of them, in some instances went out of their way to disclaim us'. Moreover, the loss of votes was not recompensed by able parliamentary leadership: '. . . we do not make up for our inferiority in the division list, by our superiority in debate—but rather the reverse'. There was 'an utter want of commanding qualifications for the successful lead even of a forlorn hope'.[170]

What, then, must be done, in order to 'plant in the heart of present difficulties the germ of future power'? The dry bones must receive new life, and must become no less than 'an independent political party, strong in its own strength, capable of indefinite expansion, & vitalized & united by the broad principle which the society aims to embody in legislation'. A defensive policy should be maintained during the present Parliament; but the Society should immerse itself in electoral activity in order to ensure that the next Parliament would be more amenable to religious equality.[171] Liberationists should put their own special principles first, and the interests of the Liberal party second, for a more self-effacing policy in the past had not been very successful:

. . . in return for the preponderance given by our support to the Liberals in Parliament, we have exacted from them some few concessions. With our aid they have at length achieved all those changes in the domestic policy of the country which they deemed to be necessary to its welfare. As a party, they have nothing more to offer, whilst we who have followed them, & worked with them, have almost everything yet to gain . . . Such being the case, might not they who are in pursuit of religious equality reverse the rule of their political action by giving primary importance to their object, & only subordinate importance to the ascendancy of the Liberals?[172]

Such a policy might be carried out by requiring the Liberal party to give more practical recognition to the strength of Voluntaryism: 'For instance, if, in a constituency returning two members, we contribute the larger number or a full half of the votes, which give them their seats, we are entitled to claim for ourselves the nomination of one of the two accepted candidates'. As a rule, 'we should act with the Liberal Party in future elections on the indispensable condition, that up to the measure of our strength on the local register the objects about [sic] which we are interested shall be advanced by the election'. If this condition were denied, 'we should resolutely withhold our cooperation —our "vote & influence"—whatever may be the consequences of our abstention to the Liberal Party'.[173] It was a good time to take this stand, continued the memorandum, because the Liberals then had no other policy for which it was worth making sacrifices.[174]

---

[170] Ibid. 141–6 (23 Oct. 1863).   [171] Ibid. 147–51.   [172] Ibid. 152.
[173] Ibid. 153–4.   [174] Ibid. 156.

This was the core of the memorandum—a declaration of independent political action if thought necessary, not a novel possibility but one now stated with new emphasis .A start was made towards carrying the plan into action. The Subcommittee recommended that a select conference of the Society's friends should be convened to discuss the electoral scheme. These suggestions were adopted by the executive committee, and a conference of chosen friends was held in London on 11 November 1863.[175] The conference resolved that traditional party claims should be subordinated to the advancement of Voluntary principles. Conferences at Manchester and Bristol, on 18 and 25 November respectively, also approved the recommended electoral policy.[176] The executive committee then decided that a paper should be issued describing the policy, and that Herbert Skeats should collect information on the current state of the constituencies and on the best means of influencing them.[177]

But perhaps not even the executive committee itself was serious in its threat to desert the Liberal party, for in May 1864 the council of the Society expressed confidence that the policy would not lead to separation between that party and the Dissenters.[178] There was obviously a preference for doing everything possible to persuade the Liberal party to adopt the Society's priorities, and the 1865 election brought little increase of parliamentary strength to the Dissenters. However, the Society had fixed on a morale-boosting policy tailored to its current political condition, combining present defensiveness with aggressive intentions for the future.

The prospect of a rift with the Liberal party was in fact beginning to recede, for in one important respect the party was becoming more amenable to Nonconformist claims. The most dynamic Liberal minister, then clearly in the process of rising to leadership of the party, was becoming increasingly interested in religious liberty. The October memorandum of the Liberation Society had bemoaned 'the utter want of commanding qualifications' for successful leadership of the cause at that juncture. The failure of Miall, despite two attempts at the polls, to return to Parliament since 1857, and Trelawny's declining to introduce further bills, had left a political void. While the Liberation Society never found the outstanding parliamentary champion of the Voluntary principle whom they would perhaps have preferred, the void was partially, if not wholly satisfactorily, filled in the course of the 1860s from an unexpected source—a high-church minister of the Crown. Gladstone's interest in these matters was perhaps a natural concomitant of his political position since 1859 and the increasingly pronounced Liberalism which he was taking up, partly under the pressure of Disraeli's current emphasis on Conservative reaction. It was paradoxical that Gladstone, a strong churchman and apparently more dogmatic and 'serious' in religion

175 Ibid. 164, also under 11 Nov. 1863.   176 Ibid. iv. 174 (27 Nov. 1863).
177 Ibid. 176 (11 Dec. 1863).   178 Mackintosh, 123.

than Disraeli, should have taken a liberal, pro-Dissenting line; and that Disraeli, having experienced diverse religious influences in his life, should pursue a strongly pro-Church and Erastian policy. One feels that their roles in this, and in other matters, might have been reversed. Interchangeability was perhaps a strong ingredient in their intense rivalry.

Yet Gladstone's anti-Erastianism, though not extreme enough to satisfy Voluntaries, was deep-rooted and sincere. Within limits—which were capacious enough to permit even disestablishment in special circumstances—he had been convinced by Tractarian influence that faith was a superior consideration to the State connection, that the Church's foundations were 'on the holy hills', and that 'her charter is legibly divine'.[179] The march of time and the spread of toleration had shown him the untenability of his ideal of 1838 that the State should support only the true faith (or one of proved spiritual worth which it had already contracted to support). Indeed, after 1838 he had agreed to a State grant to another religion and had assisted the entry of Jews, Nonconformists, and Catholics into institutions of the State or of the established Church which would, on the exclusive theory, have admitted only Anglicans. By 1863 Gladstone was linking his religious anti-Erastianism, his desire for ecclesiastical self-government, with liberalism to Dissent: 'A liberal and kindly treatment of the Church by the State, and of Dissenters by the Church, is what I desire to see'.[180] His view that faith was superior to temporalities was compatible with the opinion that temporalities could be shared with the heterodox. This was going beyond the view of some Tractarians in the 1830s that Nonconformists should be given civil equality so long as they did not encroach on the possessions of the established Church.[181] Gladstone was now prepared, in some respects, to permit such an encroachment. This was seen in his support of Peto's Burials Bill, and it was over this matter that he encountered opposition from high churchmen at Oxford who did not have his Liberal political commitment, and who found it more difficult than Gladstone himself to separate encroachment on temporalities from encroachment on beliefs. Pusey was indignant that a representative of the University, particularly a high churchman whom he had long supported, could acquiesce in such a measure. He wrote several letters of rebuke to Gladstone on this topic. On 10 June 1862 he even hinted at a possible high-church secession:

I have been very grieved to hear that you [i.e. the Commons] have ... a clause ... [in] Sir M. Peto's Bill, to the effect that Clergymen might give leave to Dissenters to perform the Burial Service in our Churchyards ... it is very hard on [the Church], to give power to individual Clergymen to compromise her by an ill-considered and often ignorant approbation of the religious or unreligious

---

[179] Gladstone, *The State in its Relations with the Church* (1838 ed.), 4.
[180] Gladstone to Rev. Antony Buller, 4 Apr. 1863 (Gladstone Papers, 44400, fo. 155).
[181] See above, p. 84.

services of Dissenters, Socinians, Deists, etc. Such quasi-approbation of the Services even of Wesleyans might go hard to involve us in heresy.

Then from the Churchyard there is only a step, religiously as well as physically, to the Church. It will be much more difficult to resist than this first step.

. . . If Church-rates, Church-yards, Tithes, Houses, were to go, it would be hard upon our people, but we should, by God's blessing, recover. But a fraternising and mixing ourselves up with Dissenters we could not recover. Those of us of the so-called High Church, who should live to see it, would, I suppose, bodily be compelled to leave her.

. . . These tidings of your measure make one feel like one living in a house with notice to quit.[182]

In another letter, Pusey complained: 'What the Dissenters really want . . . is not that they should be buried in our Church-yards, but that everything which the Church has, should be divided with them . . .'[183]

Gladstone, however, continued on his concessionary course, in 1863 supporting Peto's bill again, also Hadfield's bill to remove the declaration required of officials that they would safeguard the position of the Establishment.[184] The *Church Institution Circular* said that by supporting Hadfield's bill Gladstone had 'out-Heroded Herod';[185] and Bishop Wilberforce seemed to think this reform was demanded by men who were 'banded together to put an end to the Union between Church & State'.[186] But Gladstone thought that judicious concession was more in the Church's interest than outright resistance. The Church, he said in a highly significant letter to Wilberforce, 'should rest on her possessions & her powers, parting with none of them except for equivalents in another currency, or upon full consideration of prudential *pros & cons*: but outside of these, she should avoid all points of sore contact with Dissenters'. His own vote for Hadfield's bill was an example of actions which would 'weaken the invading army'.[187] Gladstone's argument was basically an old one, which had been used over Catholic emancipation in the 1820s: the established Church would become stronger and freer by granting concessions, not by resisting them, for concessions would remove its opponents' grounds of attack.

On church-rates, Gladstone's increasingly concessionary attitude came from long cogitation, and represented no sudden or fundamental change at this time. In March 1863 he told Wilberforce that, while 'the abolition or disuse of the Church Rate in many parishes in England has been for the relative advantage of the Church', he wished to retain the rate 'in our rural parishes,

---

[182] Pusey to Gladstone, 10 June 1862 (Pusey Papers); quoted G. I. T. Machin, 'Gladstone and Nonconformity in the 1860s: the Formation of an Alliance', *Hist. Jl.* xvii (1974), 350.

[183] Quoted ibid. Cf. Pusey to Gladstone, 14 June 1862 (Pusey Papers).

[184] Hansard, clxix. 1047–50; clxx. 153.

[185] Vol. II, No. xxxi (Apr. 1863), 188–9.

[186] Gladstone to Wilberforce, 21 Mar. 1863 (Wilberforce Papers, d. 37); printed with omissions in Ashwell and Wilberforce, *Life of Wilberforce*, iii. 80–4.

[187] Ibid.

where Dissenters are few & other resources small'.[188] But by April 1865 he believed, as he told his son W. H. Gladstone, that the general abolition of the compulsory rate might actually strengthen the Establishment, and he repeated this view in August.[189]

On the question of disestablishment of the Church of Ireland Gladstone was also becoming more liberal. Again, however, this was a matter of a lengthy mental development being thrust by circumstances to the surface level of political action—notably, in this case, by Fenianism and the need for a Liberal revival in 1867–8. Gladstone's departure from strict defence of the Church of Ireland as an Establishment dated from about 1845, when he had supported the Maynooth grant. Yet, although he was a 'Catholic Anglican', his alliance with Catholicism was less natural than his alliance with Nonconformists. His progress towards Liberalism divided him in some ways from Catholics (except Liberal ones): this was seen in his support for Italian nationalism and his lack of sympathy for denominational education in Ireland. However, his adoption of Irish disestablishment was obviously pleasing to Irish Catholics, and both he and Irish Catholics urged this policy while holding the *concept* of religious Establishment in reserve.

A hint of Gladstone's future policy on the Church of Ireland was given in his speech on Dillwyn's motion on Irish ecclesiastical revenues on 28 March 1865. In this speech Gladstone criticized the established status of the Church of Ireland on the ground of its wealth and minority status, and said that he would oppose the motion only because he considered it untimely.[190] Six weeks before he had stated flatly: ' . . . I am not loyal to it [the Church of Ireland] as an Establishment . . . I could not renew the votes and speeches of thirty years back . . . I look upon its present form of existence as no more favourable to religion in any sense of the word, than it is to civil justice and to the contentment and loyalty of Ireland'.[191] In the next few years, thanks to Gladstone's policy, a *rapprochement* occurred between Irish Catholics and the Liberals which at length, after rebutting persistent Conservative competition, erased the political effects of 1850–1. The Liberal party gained about 20 Irish seats between 1864 and 1869.[192]

The support of Dissenters was important to Gladstone, and Gladstone's advocacy was no less attractive to Dissent. Common spiritual fervour formed an excellent social solvent and promoter of political understanding between a zealous high churchman and zealous Dissenters. The Rev. Henry

[188] Ibid.

[189] Gladstone to W. H. Gladstone, 16 Apr. 1865 (Morley, *Gladstone*, ii. 159–60; Lathbury, ii. 170–2); Gladstone to Sir Stafford Northcote, 9 Aug. 1865 (Lathbury, i. 142).

[190] Hansard, clxxviii. 420–34; W. E. Williams, *The Rise of Gladstone to the Leadership of the Liberal Party, 1859–68* (Cambridge, 1934), 158–9. Cf. Rev. W. N. Molesworth to Gladstone, 1 Apr. 1865 (Gladstone Papers, 44406, fos. 1–2); Rev. W. Mazière Brady to Gladstone, 11 Apr. 1865 (ibid., fos. 29–30).

[191] Gladstone to Sir R. Phillimore, 13 Feb. 1865 (Morley, *Gladstone*, ii. 141–2).

[192] Vincent, *The Formation of the Liberal Party*, 50–1.

Allon, Congregationalist editor of the *British Quarterly Review*, told Gladstone that Dissenters 'have . . . confidence in the deep feeling of religiousness which appears to imbue your public life and to make it a great and sacred responsibility . . . [no] public man of late years, has inspired anything like the confidence & . . . enthusiasm among Nonconformists that you now command'.[193] Gladstone's understanding with Nonconformists was consolidated in a more intimate and personal ambience than the floor of the House of Commons. While Edward Bickersteth nourished Disraeli's alliance with the Establishment, Gladstone's relations with Dissent were strengthened by the special efforts of Christopher Newman Hall—a prominent Congregational minister and author of the best-selling evangelical tract, *Come to Jesus*. One of Newman Hall's chief attributes as a negotiator was his moderation. Though in 1860 he had declared himself an admirer of Miall, he was no conspicuous figure in the Liberation Society. Being without militancy or political prominence, he was more fitted than the leaders of 'political Dissent' to win gradually the support of Gladstone. His approach reflected that of the *Eclectic Review* in 1863, advising less political militancy and more spirituality.[194]

Newman Hall's correspondence with Gladstone, which had begun slightly earlier, became important in 1864. Hall employed tactics of mild persuasion and flattery to draw Gladstone into Nonconformist circles, and his success, given Gladstone's pre-existing desire to be persuaded, was not surprising. In May 1864 Gladstone wrote to thank Hall for the promised gift of an address by the current chairman of the Congregational Union (Henry Allon) and said: 'Myself in profession at least a somewhat stiff Churchman, I value beyond all price the concurrence of the great mass of Christians in those doctrines and propositions of religion which lie nearest the seat of life.'[195] On 10 November 1864 Hall suggested that Gladstone meet some leading Nonconformists at his house a few days later. 'There is no public man to whom we look with greater hope', he pressed. 'I thought that in the very important part you will have to take as the Leader of wise and safe Liberalism, you yourself might not deem an hour or two unprofitably spent in more thoroughly understanding the views and motives of religious and thoughtful men who represent a large and not uninfluential section of the great Liberal party.'[196] Gladstone, after a precautionary interview with Hall,[197] accepted the invitation. Hall invited 14 other guests, 13 of whom he named to Gladstone before the meeting—10 Congregational ministers, professors, and journalists, 2 Baptist ministers, and 1 Wesleyan minister.[198] The absence of Edward Miall

[193] Allon to Gladstone, 6 July 1866 (Gladstone Papers, 44095, fos. 304-5).
[194] *Eclectic Review*, 8th Ser. iv (Jan.–June 1863), 96-7.
[195] Gladstone to Hall, 14 May 1864 (Hall, *Autobiography*, 265).
[196] Newman Hall to Gladstone, 10 Nov. 1864 (Gladstone Papers, 44188, fos. 20-2).
[197] Gladstone to Hall, 11 Nov. 1864, copy (ibid., Letter-books, 44534, p. 309).
[198] For the names see Machin, op. cit. 355 n.

and the presence of the Wesleyan (William Bunting, son of Jabez Bunting) show Hall's obvious concern with delicacy and tact, with avoiding 'points of sore contact', in winning Gladstone's sympathy.

The meeting was held at 9 p.m. on 15 November at Hall's house in New Finchley Road, Hampstead. In a letter apparently dated 26 (but perhaps really 16) November the host sent Gladstone some 'supplementary remarks', as the discussion had not been so full as he intended. This letter reminded Gladstone that the numerous Wesleyan body was 'not kept out of the Church of Engd. by any objection to the Establishment principle',[199] and indeed Hall minimized to an incredible degree the political aims and activity of Dissent. He claimed that 'while hoping for the ultimate recognition of the Free Church Theory, they [Dissenters] are not expecting it at present, they meditate no political action to bring it about, they make it no question on the hustings, and look for it more as the result of influences within the Church of England than of efforts from without'.[200] He emphasized the more limited aims of Dissenters—educational reform, church-rate abolition, disestablishment of the Church of Ireland—and stressed the benefits which such reforms would bring to the Church of England.[201]

Gladstone was more reluctant to yield to equality for non-Anglicans in the universities than to other Dissenting demands. For this he had no obvious political reason, apart from his relations with his Oxford constituents, and was perhaps more affected by the belief that such a concession would entirely separate religion from education in his old university. Hall in later letters was particularly mild in his persuasiveness on this issue, though he had no rapid success.[202] In 1864 and 1865 Gladstone spoke against bills to admit Dissenters to the M.A. degree at Oxford.[203]

In the thirteen months after the first meeting Gladstone found it inconvenient to accept two further invitations from Newman Hall.[204] But this did not mean that his interest in Nonconformist desires was waning, and on another invitation from Hall he visited his house on 25 January 1866, when among those he met were Edward Baines, R. W. Dale, and Samuel Morley.[205] The meetings were still being held ten years later.[206] The alliance was rapidly consolidated by the succession of events from 1865 to 1869—Gladstone's

---

[199] Hall to Gladstone, 26 Nov. 1864 (ibid., fo. 30).

[200] Ibid., fos. 30–2.

[201] Ibid., fo. 31.

[202] G. I. T. Machin, 'Gladstone and Nonconformity', 356–8. On the University Test question see also Gladstone to the Vice-Chancellor of Oxford, 24 July 1863 (Gladstone Papers, 44401, fos. 39–41); Gladstone to Rev. Baldwin Brown, 29 July 1865 (Lathbury, i. 219–20).

[203] *Annual Register*, cvi (1864), 152; cvii (1865), 79–80.

[204] Newman Hall to Gladstone, Feb. 1865 (Gladstone Papers, 44188, fos. 34–7); Gladstone to Hall, 4 Feb. 1865 (Hall, *Autobiography*, 266); Gladstone to Hall, 22 Dec. 1865, copy in letter-book (Gladstone Papers, 44535, p. 330).

[205] Hall to Gladstone, 25 Jan. 1866 (Gladstone Papers, 44188, fos. 61–2).

[206] Hall, *Autobiography*, 272.

defeat at Oxford, the parliamentary reform crisis, church-rate abolition, and Irish disestablishment.

Events in 1865 hastened Gladstone's political evolution. The general election of July 1865 saw his defeat at Oxford University—a logical stage in a development in which he had recently shown none of the obvious signs of Church defence, except his desire to continue university inequality. Recent complaints of his 'apostasy' had been emphatic, and it was hoped that Oxford would reward him justly by defeating him. 'We apprehend', said the *Church Institution Circular* in April 1863, 'that it is now quite certain that Mr. Gladstone will never again be elected for the University of Oxford'.[207] Gladstone's vote for Hadfield's bill had produced a protest from Oxford University in March 1863. This address began by praising Gladstone's recent influence on episcopal appointments, but then asked him to explain his support for Hadfield's bill and said that if the State were thus to remove the Church's securities it should allow, in proportion, more freedom of government to the Church.[208] Gladstone replied, with justice, that the revival of Convocation (which he had so strongly advocated) had been an example of liberal treatment of the Church, 'though the fruit may not thus far have been great as the body has not shewn all the working power that might have been desired'.[209] Gladstone's policies, however, were far from pleasing Church defenders, particularly in the militant atmosphere then prevailing. In the 1865 election G. A. Denison organized the opposition to Gladstone and helped to obtain over 1,000 signatures asking G. Gathorne Hardy to oppose him. 'I had more to do with the unseating of Mr. Gladstone', he wrote proudly, 'than any other elector for the University.'[210] 'You were too great for them', was Wilberforce's consolation to Gladstone on his defeat. The ejection would surely not have occurred, he said, if half the electors 'had known what I know of your real devotion to our Church . . .'[211] Old Bishop Phillpotts, despite political differences, added another warm high-church tribute to Gladstone: 'How much I honor, esteem & love you, I shall not attempt to say. You have my warm gratitude & my earnest prayer'.[212]

But to Newman Hall, Gladstone's fate at Oxford was a welcome sign of his liberation, as was his return four days afterwards for South Lancashire, a modern industrial constituency apparently far more suitable as an electoral base for Gladstone's activities and Hall's hopes. 'I . . . rejoice', Hall wrote, 'that our Chief leader of Progress is now connected with a Constituency which looks onward, rather than with one which looks back-

207 Vol. II, No. xxxi (Apr. 1863), 189.
208 Enclosed in Rev. Antony Buller to Gladstone, 24 Mar. 1863 (Gladstone Papers, 44400, fos. 133–4).
209 Gladstone to Rev. A. Buller, 4 Apr. 1863 (ibid., fo. 154).
210 Denison, *Notes of My Life*, 183, 334 ff.
211 Wilberforce to Gladstone, 18 July 1865 (Gladstone Papers, 44345, fos. 15–17).
212 Phillpotts to Gladstone, 6 Feb. 1866 (ibid. 44409, fo. 180).

ward.'[213] If Hall had remembered the strength of no-Popery in Gladstone's new constituency he would not have been so ready to call it progressive.

The Liberation Society, showing the renewed determination of the last two years, had worked hard for these elections through its Electoral Sub-committee. In October 1864 this committee had asked that 'a thoroughly efficient Special Agent' be engaged to visit constituencies before the election, and Mr. J. M. Hare had been appointed.[214] The Electoral Subcommittee had appointed a subcommittee of its own to examine the state of constituencies. This second subcommittee reported that efforts by the Society would be of little use in 167 out of 200 English boroughs: in some of these Conservatives were firmly ensconced, in others supporters of the Dissenting claims were safely seated, and in a third category intervention might weaken the chances of a 'firm friend'. In the remaining 33 English boroughs, however, the Society might profitably intervene: unsatisfactory 'supporters' might be turned out or made to pledge themselves more firmly to religious equality. The electoral committee decided that Mr. Hare should visit some of the boroughs.[215] Before and during the election campaign, the Society was very active. Adver-tisements were placed in journals, urging friends of religious equality to register as electors; the *Nonconformist* printed the promises and opinions of candidates, and the votes of M.P.s on ecc esiastical questions in the previous session were recorded. H. S. Skeats published a volume giving details of elections in every constituency during the last thirty years.[216]

Dissenting fortunes in the election were mixed, and little over-all advance was made. Miall failed to be adopted as a candidate at Manchester: 'Miall is a noble fellow', wrote a correspondent of George Wilson, 'but the victory if won by him would only be the victory of a *section*, the Anti-State Church Party . . .'[217] A suggestion was made in 1866, though not taken up, that he should stand for Co. Tipperary—a product of the strengthening alliance between Voluntaries and Irish Catholics.[218] Voluntaries were pleased by the return of Duncan McLaren for Edinburgh, representing dissatisfaction with the annuity tax settlement of 1860;[219] and a stormy election at Nottingham, where mobs cried 'the Church in danger!' and Church defence placards were displayed, resulted in the return of Samuel Morley, though he was unseated on petition the following April.[220] In Wales, although more Liberals were returned, the Liberation Society had no direct electoral success to sustain the promise of its South Wales intervention in 1862. In Cardiganshire (where

[213] Hall to Gladstone, 25 July 1865 (ibid. 44188, fo. 49).
[214] Minutes of Liberation Society, iv. 222–3 (7, 21 Oct. 1864).
[215] Ibid. 228–9 (18 Nov. 1864), 276–7 (21 July 1865).
[216] Ibid.; Mackintosh, *Disestablishment and Liberation*, 123.
[217] R. Cooper to George Wilson, May 1865 (G. Wilson Papers).
[218] Norman, *Catholic Church*, 180 n. 5.
[219] Mackie, *The Life and Work of Duncan McLaren*, ii. 39–49.
[220] Hodder, *Life of Samuel Morley*, 209–14.

admittedly the Society had made hardly any impact), first Henry Richard withdrew through lack of adequate Nonconformist support, and secondly David Davies, a Calvinistic Methodist entrepreneur, was defeated by a Whig after failing to receive the support of members of other Dissenting denominations.[221] The Liberation Society claimed, somewhat dubiously, several successes in English seats: in Bury, Lichfield, Northallerton, and East and West Norfolk Liberals who were unsatisfactory to the Society had been defeated, though usually only by Conservatives who can scarcely have been more satisfactory.[222] Of all the Liberals returned, only 8 or 10 were said to oppose complete abolition of church-rates, Gladstone and Roundell Palmer being among these.[223]

To the extent that the Liberation Society had opposed unsatisfactory Liberals even when this allowed Conservatives to take the seats, the Society cannot be said to have contributed to Liberal success in the election, though it did help to give more weight to radicalism in the Liberal representation. The election nevertheless was successful for the Liberal party, which easily held its own with a majority of 70. Seventeen members of the Liberation Society were among the M.P.s returned (one or two of them being Anglican), and it was said that 22 Dissenters who did not subscribe to the Society had also been returned.[224] Allowing for exaggeration, the number of Protestant Nonconformists in the new Parliament was probably about 30. This was certainly not a spectacular advance for 'religious equality' supporters, but the Liberation Society was cautiously optimistic and was ready for a new campaign against church-rates.[225] 'The new Parliament', it was said, 'will be free from the reproach attaching to [the last], that it confined its attention exclusively to the material interests of the nation, & did not pass a solitary measure for the extension of religious liberty.'[226] It was realized that parliamentary reform would be the main topic in the first session of the new Parliament, and it was naturally urged that a Reform Bill should be supported on account of the increased Dissenting strength anticipated from it.[227]

The continuing conflict between Voluntaries and Church defenders in these years was not salved at all by the concurrent growth of an outside threat in the shape of unorthodox doctrinal views. This threat came from the seven contributors to *Essays and Reviews* and from Bishop Colenso of Natal. The Church of England was greatly troubled by these tendencies. When Rowland Williams and H. B. Wilson, two of the contributors to *Essays and Reviews*, were acquitted on appeal by the Judicial Committee of the Privy Council in

---

[221] Machin, 'A Welsh Church Rate Fracas', 468; Minutes of Liberation Society, iv. 284–5 (21 July 1865). See also I. G. Jones, 'Cardiganshire Politics in the Mid-Nineteenth Century—a study of the elections of 1865 and 1868', *Ceredigion*, v (1964), 15–27.

[222] Minutes of Liberation Society, iv. 278–9 (21 July 1865).

[223] Ibid. 282.   [224] Ibid. 282–3.

[225] Ibid. 326–8 (17 Nov. 1865).   [226] Ibid. 285 (21 July 1865).

[227] Ibid. 328 (17 Nov. 1865).

February 1864, this seemed another example, in line with 1850, of unpalatable doctrinal latitude by a State organ. Widespread clerical and lay protest resulted.[228] The Judicial Committee then consolidated its reputation by acquitting Colenso in 1865, though acting in a purely secular capacity and not treating the matter as an 'ecclesiastical cause'. Gladstone claimed that 'this sentence of the Privy Council amounts to the utter destruction of the Supremacy in S. Africa by the hands of the Crown itself'.[229] High churchmen were led to consider again a reform of the judicial system in ecclesiastical cases, and Keble mentioned, as an alternative, secession from the Establishment.[230]

Orthodox purists also disliked the attempts made in Parliament to relax the rules of subscription to the Thirty-Nine Articles and the Act of Uniformity, and to effect liturgical revision, in order to make the Church more comprehensive, forward-looking, and attractive to prospective ordinands. These attempts were made by Lord Ebury (the former Lord Robert Grosvenor) in the Lords and by E. P. Bouverie and Charles Buxton in the Commons.[231] Among those who spoke against them were Bishop Wilberforce, who denied that a revision of the liturgy would reunite Dissenters to the Church.[232] Other opponents were Gladstone, Disraeli, Cecil, and Spencer Walpole.[233] Disraeli said that 'a Church might be so comprehensive that nobody knew what it comprehended', and that 'if there was to be a Church, it must have symbols of union among those who were in communion with it'.[234] However, a Royal Commission was appointed in 1864 to consider the declarations and forms of subscription required of Anglican clergy; and as a result of its almost unanimous recommendations (Sir William Heathote alone dissenting) the old form of subscription was replaced by a more general one by means of the Clerical Subscription Act passed in 1865.[235]

The threat to orthodoxy even showed temporary signs of drawing high churchmen and evangelicals together. After the acquittal of Williams and Wilson, Pusey took an unusual step by writing to the evangelical *Record*, calling on all Christians to shelve minor differences 'in mutual resistance of [sic] the great doctrinal errors of the day'.[236] Shaftesbury took the opportunity to pen a rare letter to Pusey, his relative: 'We have to struggle, not for Apostolical Succession or Baptismal Regeneration, but for the very Atonement itself . . . let all who love our blessed Lord . . . show that, despite our

---

[228] Bowen, *The Idea of the Victorian Church*, 166–82; Chadwick, *Victorian Church*, ii. 83–4.

[229] Gladstone to Miss Burdett Coutts, 22 Apr. 1866, copy (Gladstone Papers, 44410, fos. 80–3).

[230] Pusey to Gladstone, 18 Feb. 1864 (Pusey Papers); Keble to Gladstone, 27 Mar., 11 Apr. 1864 (Gladstone Papers, 44402, fos. 217–22, 245–7); Keble to Sir Roundell Palmer, Easter 1864 (Liddon Papers, 1864, 9); Derby to Wilberforce, 25 Apr. 1864 (Wilberforce Papers, c. 5).

[231] *Annual Register*, cii (1860), 196–7; ciii (1861), 163; civ (1862), 37–8; cv (1863), 82–92.

[232] Ibid. cii (1860), 197.   [233] Ibid. cv (1863), 85–7.   [234] Ibid. 87.

[235] Ibid. cvii (1865), 77–8; Crowther, *Church Embattled*, 146–9; Chadwick, *Victorian Church*, ii. 133.

[236] Hodder, *Shaftesbury*, iii. 166.

wanderings, our doubts, our contentions, we may yet be one in Him'.[237]

Cecil, writing in the *Quarterly Review*, regarded the 'latitudinarian attack' as a more insidious one than that of Voluntaries, threatening to bring about 'a Church purged of dogma, disembarrassed of belief, embracing every error and every crotchet within its fold but retaining its influence for purposes of high police, and devoting all its energies to the foundation of mechanics' institutes . . .'[238] The *Record* had seen a sinister connection between the latitudinarian and Voluntary movements: Miall, it had said, 'throws his shield over . . . the assailants of [biblical] inspiration, and holds forth as exclusive bigots those who dwell on the evils of departing from the great truths of the Gospel'.[239]

Thus it was feared that the growth of latitudinarian opinion, with the political liberalism which seemed firmly attached to it, would weaken the Establishment. The threat was the more serious because efforts at reform seemed to be encouraged afresh by the events of 1865, which were rounded off by the death of Palmerston in October. 'Thus goes the "Ultimus Romanorum"', wrote Shaftesbury despairingly, 'and now begins, be assured of it, the greatest social, political, and religious revolution that England has yet endured. What an instrument he has been in the hands of God the Almighty.'[240] From the opposite viewpoint Bright wrote that Palmerston had 'stood for some years between "the old & the new", & his removal will make a real & probably not a small revolution . . . Russell & Gladstone are now the Govt., & it is quite impossible for them to go on without some honest attempt on the suffrage question.'[241] The restrained Liberalism which had held the Opposition in check was replaced by greater reforming ardour, and it seemed that Government and Opposition would move into mutual antagonism when projected reforms were announced. The franchise plans of Russell and Gladstone were naturally supported by leading Dissenters. The moderate Reform Union, founded in April 1864, had several Dissenters among its vice-presidents, including Thomas Barnes, Rev. G. W. Conder, John Crossley, Alfred Illingworth, and Samuel Morley.[242] Thus there revived, as questions of practical politics, the extension of parliamentary democracy and the weakening of the Church Establishment. Though the connection between these two aims became less obvious in later years, in the mid-1860s they seemed inseparable.

[237] Shaftesbury to Pusey, 26 Feb. 1864 (ibid. 166–7); Pusey to Shaftesbury, 28 Feb. 1864 (ibid. 167).

[238] *Quarterly Review*, cxviii (1865), 205.

[239] *Record*, 27 Feb. 1857.

[240] Shaftesbury to Alexander Haldane, 18 Oct. 1865 (Hodder, op. cit. iii. 185). Shaftesbury gave strong testimony to the curious intimacy between Palmerston and himself: 'To none will the loss [of Palmerston] be as it is to myself. I lose a man who, I know, esteemed and loved me far beyond every other man living.' (ibid. 146).

[241] Bright to J. B. Smith, 28 Oct. 1865 (J. B. Smith Papers, S. 344).

[242] List of committee, with Constitution of the Reform Union, 20 Apr. 1864 (G Wilson Papers).

CHAPTER X

Religious Politics, 1865-1868: Gladstone, Disraeli, Church-rates, and Ireland

THREE years of intense political activity and confusion followed Palmerston's death until, at the end of 1868, Gladstone—the rather elderly *enfant terrible* of the Liberal party, or, to many, its rising hope—was safely in power with a larger majority than Palmerston had obtained in 1865. In the meantime, the splitting of the Liberals over the 1866 Reform Bill had robbed them of continuous office for the full parliamentary term. But Gladstone compensated for this set-back by adopting Irish disestablishment, a popular radical policy which Disraeli, having already staged the daring radical *coup* of 1867, now failed to trump and had little choice but to resist.

Derby had prophesied to Disraeli, as early as November 1865, that the Liberal Government would 'bribe the R. Catholics' by 'the sacrifice of the Irish Protestant Church'. This policy, he insisted, was one which the Conservatives could not touch themselves, since they were bound to maintain Church Establishments. The Irish and English Churches were so closely linked that 'the one in sinking will drag the other with it'.[1] Somewhat surprisingly for one who had previously been reproved by Derby for the intransigence of his pro-Church speeches, Disraeli seemed less attached to the Irish Establishment than his chief. 'It is a very unpopular cause', he wrote, 'even with many of our best men'.[2] However, unlike parliamentary reform, Irish disestablishment was not to be passed by Conservatives. The feat may not have proved impossible, but it would have been extremely difficult to persuade Tory ultra-Protestants to accept it. 'You well know', a speaker told the Bristol Church Defence Association in 1866, 'that if one limb is injured the whole body suffers; and depend upon it if the enemies of our constitution in Church and State succeed in overthrowing the Church of Ireland, they will attempt . . . also to overthrow the Church of England.'[3] Gladstone, not the Conservative leader, was to demonstrate how it was possible to carry out surgery on one limb without damaging the rest of the body.

---

[1] Derby to Disraeli, 21 Nov. 1865 (Disraeli Papers, B/XX/S/337). Cf. Derby to Disraeli, 10 Mar. 1865 (ibid. 332).

[2] Disraeli to Derby, 'private', 24 Nov. 1865 (Derby Papers, 146/1).

[3] *Report and Addresses of Bristol Church Defence Association* (London and Bristol, 1866), 24. The speaker was C. G. Prideaux, author of *A Practical Guide to the Duties of Churchwardens.*

I. RELIGIOUS LIBERALISM IN 1866

Reform measures, and not merely ones concerned with parliamentary representation, were naturally expected from the Russell–Gladstone ministry. In the 1866 session, despite parliamentary preoccupation with franchise reform, both Catholics and Dissenters made legislative gains. Following the narrow defeat of Monsell's Oaths Bill in 1865, a similar Government bill to deal with part of the Catholic oaths grievance was introduced by Sir George Grey, the Home Secretary, in March 1866. The bill proposed to replace the unpalatable oath of 1829 with a simple oath for M.P.s. The second reading in the Commons passed by a huge majority, as few as 5 members voting against it, and the bill was accepted by the Lords, becoming law at the end of April.[4] Many Conservatives had disregarded Newdegate's warning that a period when Fenianism was spreading was no time to abolish part of the oath of supremacy. Disraeli carried an amendment that the new Act should reaffirm the succession to the Crown as laid down in the reign of William III, but failed narrowly to carry another amendment, aimed against papal authority in the country.[5] On 30 April, the day this bill received the royal assent, it was announced that the Government intended to issue a commission to inquire into further aspects of the Catholic oaths grievance. These comprised oaths taken by Catholic office-holders, including a declaration against transubstantiation, and an oath taken by students, officers, and servants at Maynooth. The report of the commission, appearing in 1867, recommended a drastic reduction in the number of persons required to take an oath. The declaration against transubstantiation was abolished in 1867, and the Promissory Oaths Act of 1868 greatly reduced the number of officials who had to take an oath. These reforms eased the consciences of Catholics who wished to attack the established status and endowments of the Church of Ireland. To this extent the reform justified the fears of Protestants who had wished to keep the oaths as they were.[6]

The question of the Irish Church itself was raised again in Parliament during 1866, and was raised with increasing insistence in the three subsequent sessions. In 1866, however, nothing materialized from the debates. In the Upper House, proposals by Lord Lifford for appropriation of Church revenues and State support of the Catholic priesthood were debated without result; and a motion of Earl Grey for a comprehensive review of the state of Ireland was negatived after opposition by Government spokesmen (Grey himself favoured, among other proposals, appropriation of Church revenues and repeal of the Ecclesiastical Titles Act).[7] In the Commons in April Sir John Gray, member for Kilkenny and a leader of the National Association,

---

[4] *Annual Register*, cviii (1866), 23–5; Norman, *The Catholic Church and Ireland*, 294–5.
[5] *Annual Register*, cviii (1866), 24; Hansard, clxxxii. 297–311.
[6] Norman, op. cit. 295–6.   [7] *Annual Register*, cviii (1866), 35–41.

moved that the Church of Ireland, being a just cause of dissatisfaction, should be taken into consideration by Parliament. But discussion of the motion was dropped because priority was given to the Parliamentary Reform Bill.[8]

Protestant Dissenters also had mixed fortunes in this first session of the new Parliament. The passage of Hadfield's Qualification Bill in May after so many previous attempts might have seemed the beginning of seven fat years after seven lean ones.[9] They were not seven fat years, as it turned out, but only five or six, since they did not stretch beyond the University Tests Act of 1871, and began to peter out with Nonconformist dissatisfaction over the 1870 Education Act. Moreover, the new dispensation was slow to mete out its benefits. The primacy of the Reform Bill had been fully recognized by the Liberation Society, which had decided to limit its own direct efforts in the 1866 session to a Church Rate Abolition Bill. The Society also agreed, however, to support the efforts of others over Hadfield's bill, University Tests abolition, reform of parliamentary oaths, and disendowment of the Irish Church.[10] The Liberals' Reform Bill suffered defeat in June, and the Government's consequent resignation was no comfort to the Dissenters. In the meantime, other 'religious equality' questions had been subordinated to the unsuccessful Reform. A bill of J. D. Coleridge (M.P. for Exeter) to open masters' degrees at Oxford to Dissenters easily passed its second reading, but was dropped because not enough parliamentary time could be found for it.[11] The same reason caused the abandonment of a bill of E. P. Bouverie enabling Protestant Dissenters to hold college fellowships, though this bill also passed its second reading.[12] Gladstone was still discouraging to Dissenters on this matter: he said in July that such bills seemed unlikely to open the way to a solution of the question.[13] However, in the autumn he began to think of resigning himself to a change. 'The present state of things was unmaintainable', he said, and a moderate reform at this time might forestall a more fundamental change later. An acceptable compromise might be the reservation of half the fellowships in each college for Anglican clergy.[14]

More encouraging to Dissenters in 1866 was Gladstone's sponsorship of a legislative solution to the church-rate question. This emerged from the second reading, on 7 March, of an abolition bill introduced at the request of the Liberation Society by J. A. Hardcastle, a Liberal Anglican M.P. for Bury St. Edmunds. Hardcastle had stated that a settlement of this question

---

[8] Ibid. 41–3; Hansard, clxxxii. 973 ff.

[9] Ibid. clxxxi. 1239–57; *Journals of the House of Commons*, cxxi (1866), 284.

[10] Minutes of Liberation Society (executive committee), iv. 327–8 (17 Nov. 1865).

[11] Hansard, clxxxii. 659–715; clxxxiv. 307–44.

[12] Ibid. clxxxi. 1257–64.

[13] Gladstone to the editor of the *Patriot*, 'private', 13 July 1866 (copy in Letter-book, Gladstone Papers, Add. MS. 44536, pp. 139–40).

[14] W. R. Ward, *Victorian Oxford*, 253–4.

was overdue: 36 parliamentary attempts had been made since 1834, he said, and 20 divisions had been taken.[15] Abolition of the rate would strengthen the Church by removing hostility to it, and, he claimed, would not threaten the union of Church and State.[16] Spencer Walpole, however, moved to postpone the reading (i.e. reject the bill) on the familiar grounds that advocates of abolition of the rate really wanted complete disendowment of the Church, and that only in comparatively few parishes was the rate now refused.[17]

Walpole's seconder, Charles du Cane, warned the House against abolishing the rate at a time when the Reform Bill was proposing to widen the franchise: such an extension of democracy was just what Miall was looking for in order to enhance his aims.[18] Dissent and democracy were seen as twin causes. This fear must have been compounded when Gladstone, the champion of the Reform Bill, announced in the debate that in his view, as in Hardcastle's, the church-rate question should be settled, and that he had a compromise scheme ready: 'the abolition of church rates would remove the occasion of controversy on many sore points . . .'[19] Du Cane's reference to the Reform Bill, he said, meant that 'the Church is safe within these walls so long as you keep the nation out of them'.[20] In this way Gladstone appealed again to his hardening opinion that the Church's safety lay in concession. He was reproducing, in a more extreme way, the Whig attitude of the 1830s which he had then combated.

Gladstone's announcement on church-rates can have come as no surprise to those who had observed his growing understanding with Nonconformists in recent years, or who knew that he had favoured a compromise settlement since 1849.[21] His idea of a compromise had, since 1854, taken the form of a proposal that church-rates should be levied only in parishes where a majority was willing to pay.[22] This suggestion was intended to retain the rate in rural parishes where there were comparatively few objectors and scant alternative methods of support. Now, in 1866, he suggested a different compromise, though with the same end in view—to achieve voluntary payment of the rate, while still attempting to protect the time-honoured levy in the rural parishes. The increased support for church-rate reform in this Parliament, and the chance of obtaining the closer political alliance of Dissenters who were already attached to the Reform Bill, led Gladstone now to urge a practical solution.

Gladstone had drafted a scheme three days before he explained it to the House. The plan provided that payment of the rate would become completely voluntary, but that those who did not wish to pay would be disqualified from any say in church management. This idea was not new: a scheme resembling

---

[15] Hansard, clxxxi. 1633.　　　　[16] Ibid. 1636.　　　　[17] Ibid. 1643–55.
[18] Ibid. 1659.　　　[19] Ibid. 1662.　　　[20] Ibid.
[21] O. Anderson, 'Gladstone's Abolition of Church Rates: a minor political Myth and its historiographical Career', *JEH* xxv (1974), 186–7; also see above, pp. 259, 266.
[22] Anderson, op. cit. 186–7.

it had been suggested by William Page Wood in 1849,[23] and similar proposals had been made later. The plan also proposed that vestries be enabled to make extra charges for burials and pews on those who refused to pay the rate.[24] But this part of the scheme was later dropped—indeed it conflicted with Gladstone's own advocacy of Dissenting burials in parish churchyards.

There were diverse reactions to the scheme in the Commons. Beresford Hope wanted Hardcastle to withdraw his bill in order that a compromise measure, based on Gladstone's plan, could take its place.[25] Bright, on the other hand, disliked any compromise on the issue: abolition should be absolute, and the Church would be none the worse for it—he offered the comfort that 'as a political institution, in all probability it is destined to many years of life'.[26] Samuel Morley, however, welcomed the bill.[27] Miall declared at the annual meeting of the Liberation Society council on 5 May that Gladstone's general compromise was acceptable.[28] The Liberation Society strengthened its determination to abolish the compulsory rate by conducting an inquiry into the payment of church-rates. Returns were received from 1,510 parishes: in 900 of these the rates had been already abandoned, in 200 the expenses were paid out of endowments, in 284 the rate was levied but not enforced, and in only 150 was payment compulsory.[29] These figures could be used in favour of the case for abolition, and they were given to Hardcastle so that he could employ them when he reintroduced his bill in the next session.[30]

The debate on 7 March ended with the passage of Hardcastle's bill by a majority of 33; Gladstone had voted for the bill after Hardcastle had said he would consider his suggestions. This result signified a notable revival of the cause, and of Dissenting interests in general, after the adverse divisions of recent years. The Liberation Society committee went sedulously through the division list, finding that 11 Liberals had voted against the bill and 4 Conservatives (including Lord Stanley) in favour; and that 24 Liberals were unaccounted for, not being ill, abroad, or expected 'neutrals'[31]. Gladstone tried to win support for his own scheme from Conservatives, Anglican Liberals, and Dissenters. To the high-church Sir William Heathcote, formerly his co-member for Oxford University, he wrote: 'What weighs with me is the gt. advantage the Church will gain fr[om] this measure as a real effective surrender of the priceless old fabrics of our Churches into the hands of Churchmen. I think . . . that under this plan the rate wd. *revive* in many

[23] Hansard, ciii. 650-1 (13 Mar. 1849).
[24] Ibid. clxxxi. 1666-7.   [25] Ibid. clxxxi. 1668-72.
[26] Ibid. 1678.   [27] Ibid. clxxxi. 1688-9.
[28] Mackintosh, *Disestablishment and Liberation*, 171.
[29] Ibid.; Minutes of Liberation Society, iv. 377-8 (8 June 1866).
[30] Minutes of Liberation Society, iv. 377-8 (8 June 1866).
[31] Ibid. 354-5; division list, Hansard, clxxxi. 1691-5.

places.'[32] Heathcote saw hazards in the scheme. While seeing that obstacles to the churchyard burial of non-payers of the rate might be a 'gain', in that Dissenters might be led to give up the claim to churchyard burials, he pointed out that 'a malcontent' might not declare himself exempt from the rate but merely defy the authorities to levy it, and then:

... being still on the list of those who are supposed to be liable he will retain his right to elect churchwardens, interfere in expenditure, etc., etc. From this it follows that ... at the least, you must provide that a failure to pay within a given number of days after the publication of the rate shall be taken to be by law a declaration of refusal, & a surrender of all Church privileges.[33]

Gladstone decided to introduce his plan in the form of a separate bill, rather than try to amend Hardcastle's bill. On 12 April he submitted a draft measure to Sir Robert Phillimore, Sir George Grey, and Roundell Palmer, and on Palmer's advice he abandoned the suggestion that non-payers should be charged extra for burials and pews.[34] This alteration, however, made it even less likely that Heathcote would approve of the bill. Gladstone asked him, on 25 April, to try and gain the support of Conservatives for the scheme, but Heathcote replied that he could not 'see in them [Gladstone's proposals] any concession of a real advantage such as you hoped to secure, in lieu of what is to be given up'.[35]

Beresford Hope, another high churchman, was more encouraging. He suggested that 'regulation' would be a better word than 'abolition', in order to affirm continuity of the 'immemorial institution' of the rate.[36] The bill, he said, should not only enable parishes and districts to make a rate as hitherto (the rate should be voluntary), but should make the rate recoverable in the County Court from persons who had declared themselves willing to pay.[37] In the end Hope found that Gladstone's bill did not meet his stipulations, and he opposed the measure. Archdeacon Denison was more decidedly for maintaining the existing system, and was ready to appeal to Convocation and public opinion in an effort to save it.[38] But some Conservatives were becoming inclined to accept a compromise.

To minimize the concept of 'abolition' in the bill in order to win the acquiescence of churchmen was to risk disappointing Dissenters. Militant Nonconformists preferred total abolition of the rate as a purer manifestation of the Voluntary principle. Initially, however, Gladstone had considerable success in winning the agreement of Dissenters. This might have reflected a

[32] Gladstone to Heathcote, 16 Mar. 1866, copy (Gladstone Papers, 44209, fo. 174).
[33] Heathcote to Gladstone, 18 Mar. 1866 (ibid. fos. 176–7).
[34] Anderson, 187.
[35] Gladstone to Heathcote, 25 Apr. 1866 (copy in Letter-book, Gladstone Papers, 44536, p. 87); Heathcote to Gladstone, 28 Apr. 1866 (ibid. 44209, fo. 181).
[36] A. J. Beresford Hope to Gladstone, 30 Apr. 1866 (ibid. 44213, fos. 332–3).
[37] Ibid. fo. 334. See also Hope to Gladstone, 3 May 1866 (ibid. fos. 335–6).
[38] Denison to Gladstone, 25 May 1866 (ibid. 44140, fos. 67–8).

cautious rallying to Gladstone in the face of Conservative and Adullamite opposition to the Reform Bill. Newman Hall confidently told him on 23 March that 'all Dissenters and Dissenting papers I have met with most willingly accept your "compromise"'.[39] Perhaps he exaggerated in saying this and he added a sentence, worded with typical skill, which hinted that he himself hankered after total abolition: 'The only objection has come from some Churchmen who think that the continuance of the *forms* of a compulsory rate, will hinder that development of generous voluntaryism which would have resulted from the total & unqualified abolition of even the outward semblance of compulsion.'[40] Gladstone also had the support of Samuel Morley and of Hardcastle (who agreed to postpone his own bill, as he announced in the Commons on 4 May).[41] Through their aid the support of the Dissenting Deputies and the Liberation Society was officially obtained.[42] But this co-operation was only granted on condition that alterations were made in the bill, mainly in order to restrict the disqualification of non-paying parishioners in vestry matters to the making and application of the rate.[43] Gladstone agreed to these alterations, but some militant Dissenters were still reluctant to support his plan.[44]

Armed with considerable support, Gladstone sought leave on 8 May to introduce his bill for abolition of compulsory church-rates—a measure which had Government sponsorship. The bill, he stated, would enable a voluntary rate to be legally assessed on those who agreed to pay, and to be used for any of the purposes on which church-rate had hitherto been expended. Discussion of a voluntary rate in the vestries would be limited to those who intended to subscribe to it. Non-payers could not be ecclesiastical churchwardens, but could be churchwardens in a secular capacity, performing non-religious duties.[45] Among Gladstone's opponents in the ensuing debate were some who reflected the 'die-hard' vindication of the rate showing itself in Church defence associations in the country.[46] Newdegate raised an important consideration regarding the proposed exclusion of non-payers from making and applying the rate—a consideration which was doubtless motivated by the fear that Tractarianism would become dominant in certain parishes:

He feared that, by this proposal, a minority in a parish might acquire power to sanction a manner of conducting the services of the Church which was disagreeable and offensive to the majority; and that the means of introducing variations of the services in the different parishes would be obtained. One argument in favour of

---

[39] Rev. C. Newman Hall to Gladstone, 23 Mar. 1866 (ibid. 44188, fo. 68).
[40] Ibid.
[41] Anderson, 187; Gladstone to J. A. Hardcastle, 25, 28, and 29 Apr. 1866 (copies in Letter-book, Gladstone Papers, 44536, pp. 88–9); Samuel Morley to Gladstone, 28 Apr. 1866 (ibid. 44410, fo. 110).
[42] Hansard, clxxxiii. 438.   [43] Anderson, 187.   [44] Ibid. 188.
[45] Hansard, clxxxiii. 623–4.
[46] e.g. *Report and Addresses of Bristol Church Defence Association*, 21–2.

church rates among Churchmen was this—that if a congregation disapproved the manner in which the services were conducted, they had the remedy in their hands by withholding the rate. This Bill would considerably impair that power.[47]

This discussion ended with Gladstone's obtaining leave to introduce the measure. But political crisis intervened to hinder the bill's progress. On 18 June the Government was defeated on an Opposition motion to alter the proposed new parliamentary franchise, and the resignation of the ministry was announced on 26 June. Derby formed a minority Government, and Gladstone, having suffered a major reverse over his foremost measure, now saw the prospects for his Church Rate Bill receding as well. However, the new Government undertook not to oppose the second reading, on condition that the bill was taken no further in that session so that the details of a solution could be fully considered in the recess. Disraeli stated: 'The Government . . . do not accept the principle of the Bill, nor do they mean to vote for the second reading, but will not vote against it.'[48]

After this declaration, Conservatives stated their objections to the measure. Newdegate opposed it because he thought it did not provide an adequate substitute for the rate. He found more satisfaction in his own Church Rate Commutation Bill, which had been placed before the House again that session, but which does not appear even to have been debated. He also said that Gladstone's provisions would exclude the poor (who would be among non-payers of the rate) from having a say in the rate's application, and would confine such matters to a minority in the parish, perhaps consisting exclusively of high, low, or broad churchmen. In this way the Church's fearful divisions would be strengthened.[49] Charles Neate, Liberal M.P. for Oxford City, then stated his preference for yet another bill, presented to the House on 11 June by William Bovill, who had since become Conservative Solicitor-General. This proposed to continue the old rate, while allowing unwilling persons to exempt themselves by a declaration—a means of 'contracting out' rather than 'contracting in' which was likely to result in more people continuing to pay the rate than if payment was left to individual initiative. Neate wanted the State to make some assured provision for maintaining church buildings (he suggested that the funds of the Ecclesiastical Commission might be used), and he moved an amendment for this purpose.[50] Beresford Hope also preferred Bovill's bill to Gladstone's because it continued the old rate; but, as an anti-Erastian, he feared that Neate's amendment might place the churches too much under State control, resulting perhaps in the same church building being let out to different denominations at different times.[51]

Roundell Palmer interrupted these criticisms by praising Gladstone's bill and saying that its proposals should be adequate for the Church to support itself.[52] But criticism was immediately resumed in the debate, which was

[47] Hansard, clxxxiii. 625-6.   [48] Ibid. clxxxiv. 1029-32.   [49] Ibid. 1032-6.
[50] Ibid. 1036-41.   [51] Ibid. 1041-6.   [52] Ibid. 1046-51.

adjourned to 24 July and then to 1 August. Manners stated that a voluntary rate would be insufficient for the Church's needs; Newdegate repeated his objection that the exclusion of many from managing the churches would 'destroy the national characteristics of the Church of England'; and Bovill claimed that the bill, rather than being a compromise, was 'an absolute concession to the Dissenters, without a single redeeming feature in favour of the Church'.[53] However, in accordance with the Government's policy, the second reading of Gladstone's bill was passed without a division, and was to be committed a month later (i.e. after the end of the session).[54] In the general clearing up of the session's tangled efforts, Hardcastle's, Newdegate's, and Bovill's bills were withdrawn on the same date of 1 August.

The somewhat contradictory end to the debate showed that the form of a settlement was still extremely problematical, and the continued domination of parliamentary reform in 1867 postponed an agreed interparty solution until 1868. It did seem, however, that the Conservative Government was inclined to adopt a compromise settlement, even if not Gladstone's. The advent of another minority Conservative ministry, needing to gain support in the country, had promised that concession would not be ignored. Disraeli's recent role as an ardent defender of Establishment privilege had to be modified.

II. CONSERVATIVE REFORM AND CHURCH-RATE SETTLEMENT, 1867–8

Even Disraeli's most ardent Church defence associates and admirers of the past few years must have realized the unlikelihood of his maintaining intact, on resuming office as Chancellor of the Exchequer in June 1866, the principles and policies he had so frequently and emphatically proclaimed in Opposition. Disraeli's ecclesiastical dilemma was soon revealed. Early in July Sir George Bowyer, Catholic M.P. for Dundalk, wrote to him: 'I hope you will take such a course to enable the R.C. Members to support you. I am most desirous of supporting you if I *can*. This must depend on your measures. You have a great opportunity of taking the wind out of the sails of the Whigs, without doing anything that *reasonable* Protestants can complain of.'[55] But policies which would be sufficient to deflate the Whigs naturally ran the risk of colliding with ultra stolidity—some of Disraeli's back-benchers not being 'reasonable' in Bowyer's meaning of the term. The well-established tendency of Conservatives to divide over progressive measures was displayed again over parliamentary reform in 1867, but not so obviously over ecclesiastical questions during this ministry because Gladstone seized the most important of these, the Irish Church, from Disraeli's necessarily uncertain grasp.

[53] Ibid. 1862 f., 1874–9.   [54] Ibid. 1884.
[55] Bowyer to Disraeli, 5 (?) July 1866 (Disraeli Papers, B/XXI/B/714).

In the meantime, however, Church defenders were not at all sure that Disraeli would hold to his recent course sufficiently even to maintain church-rates. A. C. Tait, bishop of London and soon to become archbishop of Canterbury, said that a compromise was wanted by the bishops and 'the Church generally', but had not been pressed because 'Dizzy humbugged old [Archdeacon] Hale and some others into the belief that he was the Church's all-powerful friend, and wd. maintain Church rates with no surrender. Surely the Govt. who have led us into this mess by playing on the folly of the Clergy will not be so dastardly as to abandon us.'[56] Similarly, doubts were expressed by Cranborne, Manners, and Denison about the Government's adherence to strict Church views on education.[57] It was objected particularly that Pakington, who had joined the Conservative Cabinet, strongly favoured the 'Conscience Clause' allowing the children of Dissenters to be absent from Anglican instruction in National Society schools.[58] Denison had similar objections (though these were apparently misplaced) to the appointment of Lord Robert Montagu as Vice-President of the Education Committee in March 1867, believing that the appointment would lead to attempts to please 'the political Nonconformists'.[59] In these circumstances, Denison can scarcely have been comforted by the decline of educational voluntaryism among Nonconformists. This cause, which had been deserted already by Miall and Morley, was severely shaken when Edward Baines, its foremost champion, announced at a meeting of the Congregational Union at Manchester in October 1867 his conversion to a system of schools supported and inspected by the State. Voluntaryism in education had run parallel, though remotely, to Denison's own aversion to State control; and Baines's capitulation encouraged Denison's chief fear—a national educational reform on latitudinarian, non-denominational lines. The parliamentary enfranchisement of 1867, which the Conservative Government carried, urged forward educational extension, and a broad liberal method seemed the only practical way of attaining this extension in a society of many denominations and standpoints.

But Voluntaryism, even though it was prepared to compromise in its educational policy, showed no slackening in its 'religious equality' aims. Contributing to Dissenters' confidence at this time was the conviction that their proportion of the population was continuing to increase. There was no second Religious Census in 1861 to confirm this assumption, but the

---

[56] Tait to Bishop Wilberforce, 8 Aug. 1867 (Wilberforce Papers, d. 47, fos. 103–4). Hale was archdeacon of London.

[57] Cranborne to Disraeli, 29 June 1866 (Disraeli Papers, B/XX/Ce/6); Manners to Disraeli, 24 Oct. 1866 (ibid. M/138); G. A. Denison to Disraeli, 5 Apr. 1867 (L. Denison (ed.), *Fifty Years at East Brent*, 93–4).

[58] Cranborne to Disraeli, 29 June 1866 (Disraeli Papers, B/XX/Ce/6).

[59] Denison to Disraeli, 5 Apr. 1867 (L. Denison, op. cit. 93–4). Disraeli in reply said that Montagu disclaimed having made the speech which led Denison to attribute these views to him (ibid.).

Nonconformist, in its issues of 15 November and 13 December 1865, gave figures for church accommodation in London which showed that the proportion of non-Anglican accommodation had grown by 6 per cent since 1851. The *British Quarterly Review*, reprinting the figures, stressed that this increase had been achieved by Churches 'which receive not a shilling of State endowment or an iota of State favour', though it was admitted that the Church of England was sustaining its strenuous efforts in the metropolis.[60]

The Liberation Society was extending its efforts at this time. Special concentration was placed on the young, and on Scotland and Wales. A young men's conference was held by the executive committee on 9 January 1867; 359 people were present, and a resolution was passed that it was 'the duty of those who believe in the spirituality of Christ's Kingdom & desire to secure religious equality for the people, to labor with increased energy to hasten the legislative adoption of their principles'.[61] By early 1868 similar young men's conferences had been held in twenty-four towns, where local committees or young men's associations were now receiving instructions from the Society's executive committee.[62] This enthusiasm must have compensated for the refusal of the Manchester Nonconformist Defence Association, founded in 1864, to add its own special fund to a Liberation Society fund of £25,000 inaugurated in 1865.[63] Subscriptions were clearly growing; in 1869 the Society had about 10,000 subscribers, the largest number to date, and the amount they subscribed (£8,913) was the largest annual figure so far raised.[64]

This increase was partly a result of the special attention given to Wales in 1866. Little had been undertaken or achieved by Welsh radicals in the 1865 election; but in May 1866 the Society's executive committee planned a new Welsh programme as a successor to the 1862 campaign in South Wales. At a committee meeting on 25 May it was noted that the Society's prospectus had been translated into Welsh. It was decided to issue a series of tracts in Welsh, and to publish Henry Richard's recent articles in the *Morning Star* in the form of a book. These articles appeared in 1867 as *Letters on the Social and Political Condition of the Principality of Wales*, a work which had much political influence.[65] The meeting of 25 May 1866 also decided that six Welsh county conferences should be held in the following autumn; and by September conferences had been arranged in Denbighshire (at Denbigh), Merionethshire (at Bala), Montgomeryshire (at Newtown), and in Cardiganshire.[66] The Bala meeting was addressed by Miall, Henry Richard, and Carvell Williams, and—a departure from former indifference to political agitation—

---

[60] *British Quarterly Review*, xliii (Jan.–Apr. 1866), 145–6.
[61] Minutes of Liberation Society, iv. 416 (11 Jan. 1867).
[62] Mackintosh, op. cit. 121–2.   [63] Ibid. 120.   [64] Ibid.
[65] K. O. Morgan, *Wales in British Politics, 1868–1922* (2nd edn., Cardiff, 1970), 21.
[66] Minutes of Liberation Society, iv. 370–1, 392–3 (25 May, 7 Sept. 1866).

many Calvinistic Methodists, including students, took part in the demonstration.[67] At each of the conferences a county committee was appointed.[68] Welsh grievances and aspirations, whether they were concerned with the rejection of landlord influence, the abolition of church-rates, or outright disestablishment of the Church, provided a ready welcome for the Society. The executive committee remarked in May 1867 that it had found in Wales 'a soil which will ultimately repay diligent culture'.[69] The current satisfaction of the Society with the policies of the Liberal party was shown by the direct connection between the Society's efforts and the growth of Liberal organization in Wales. Miall, Richard, and Williams, as members of the Society's Welsh Subcommittee, consulted people at Swansea about the formation of a Liberal Registration Society for South Wales. Samuel Morley, perhaps the Society's wealthiest member, had offered to give £500 to this venture, and the Liberation Society planned to give some money itself.[70] Following a conference at Carmarthen, a South Wales Liberal Registration Committee was founded.[71] The Welsh Reform Association, started in July 1868 after a meeting at Liverpool, also received aid from the Society.[72]

Scotland was also of interest to the Society. In the autumn of 1867 the Secretary, Carvell Williams, attended meetings at Glasgow, Edinburgh, Paisley, Perth, Dundee, and Greenock, and told the executive committee that more space for Scottish questions in the *Liberator* had been requested.[73] This was a crucial year for Voluntaryism in Scotland, for developments took place which ultimately decided the fate (at this stage, though not for the future) of negotiations for union between the Free Church and the United Presbyterian Church. Sir George Sinclair, who had tried to prevent the Disruption in 1843 and had joined the Free Church in 1851, had bent his strenuous efforts since 1854 to the union of Presbyterians who were outside the established Church.[74] A parallel United Presbyterian pioneer of union was the Rev. John Cairns, who had optimistically announced at Newcastle on 28 January 1863 that 'the time for union between the Free and the United Presbyterian Churches had now arrived . . . the only existing divergence between the two Churches, a different view of the civil magistrate's duties in regard to religion, need not be a hindrance, as neither Church made this a term of communion'.[75] The distinction, however, was crucial. It proved an insuperable barrier for many years between some Free Churchmen who held that the Church might accept the temporal support of civil Government

---

[67] I. G. Jones, 'Merioneth Politics in Mid-Nineteenth Century', 317.
[68] Minutes of Liberation Society, iv. 397 (5 Oct. 1866).
[69] I. G. Jones, 'The Liberation Society and Welsh Politics', 222.
[70] Minutes of Liberation Society, iv. 449 (7 June 1867).
[71] Ibid. 455 (5 July 1867).   [72] Ibid. v. 65 (12 June 1868).
[73] Ibid. iv. 489 (15 Nov. 1867).
[74] e.g. *A Letter addressed to the non-established Presbyterian Communions of Scotland.*
[75] MacEwen, *The Life and Letters of John Cairns*, 502; Fleming, *A History of the Church in Scotland*, 134.

provided that entire spiritual independence was retained, and United Presbyterians who held that civil Government, being unable to judge of religious truth, could not make financial provision for religion.

In May 1863 both Churches agreed to form committees to confer together on union. Articles of agreement were eventually drawn up by a joint committee in 1867, affirming the right of the Church to conduct its government without civil interference, and the obligation of Christians to support the Church with their own financial offerings. In May 1867 the Synod of the United Presbyterian Church accepted these articles and the General Assembly of the Free Church voted to continue discussions on union. But a dissident element in the Free Church, led by Dr. James Begg, began to show itself in this Assembly; and the opposition of this group, though it always remained a minority in the Assembly, was sufficient to cause the union negotiations to be abandoned in 1873.[76] However, this failure was not foreseen in 1867, when a likelier result seemed to be a successful union and the consequent strengthening of British Voluntaryism.

Ironically, the Conservative Government bestowed on Dissent a great indirect boost to its political confidence—the Reform Act of 1867, with its radical amendments making household suffrage a reality in the boroughs. This Act, while holding out the hope of some working-class support for the Conservatives, also enfranchised many likely supporters of Gladstone— Dissenting small tradesmen and skilled workers who had been reared on the shibboleths of radicalism and disestablishment. It was an essential safeguard for Conservatism that redistribution of parliamentary seats should not march in step with the enfranchisement, so there was no large-scale transfer of seats from counties and small boroughs to large towns.[77] The absence of such a rearrangement assisted Whigs as well as Conservatives, and limited both the increase of Nonconformist M.P.s and the decline of traditional representation by the Whig landowning classes. But in spite of such restrictions the increase in electoral weight given to Dissenters seemed of great long term significance, and it was confidently reported by the Parliamentary Committee of the Liberation Society that the reform 'cannot but greatly increase their political influence, & put within their reach the realization of results which, under the existing political system, they have not ventured to contemplate'.[78] It had already been decided to assess the strength of Voluntaryism in individual counties in preparation for the next general election.[79] Only the future could tell, however, whether the newly enfranchised workers

---

[76] For detailed accounts of the negotiations between 1863 and 1873 see MacEwen, op. cit. 498 ff.; Fleming, op. cit. 130 ff., 176 ff.; T. Smith, *Memoirs of James Begg*, ii. 494-513; A. L. Drummond and J. Bulloch, *The Church in Victorian Scotland, 1843-74* (Edinburgh, 1975), 315 ff.

[77] See F. B. Smith, *The Making of the Second Reform Bill* (Cambridge, 1966), 225, 237-40.

[78] Report dated 21 Aug. 1867, in Minutes of Liberation Society, iv. 475; quoted Machin, 'Gladstone and Nonconformity in the 1860s', 359-60. Cf. *Nonconformist*, 29 May 1867 (p. 437).

[79] Minutes of Liberation Society, iv. 459-60 (19 July 1867).

would keenly support the objects of the Liberation Society (as the Society attempted, by means of association with trade union leaders, to ensure that they would), or whether they would prefer to concentrate on different legislative aims.

Many Dissenters must have regretted that it was Disraeli and not Gladstone who was responsible for the Reform Act.[80] Newman Hall wished that Gladstone would 'plainly . . . pronounce for Household Suffrage', which would be 'accepted, *now*, by the manhood suffrage party as a *settlement*'; he should 'head the tide rather than be overtaken by it'.[81] A copy of a sonnet by Hall, accompanying this letter, denied that 'mere ambition' (presumably personified by Disraeli) could safely steer the State to the haven of a 'safe, contented Freedom'. 'A Captain, able, brave, sincere' was needed, namely Gladstone himself.[82] The alliance of Dissent with the Liberal party easily survived the events of 1867, for a cohesive policy was soon initiated by Gladstone.

In spite of parliamentary preoccupation with Reform several 'religious equality' issues were aired in 1867 and some were successful. The list of topics to which the Liberation Society gave its blessing displayed the current firm alliance of Voluntaryism and Irish Catholicism. Apart from abolition of church-rates, of University Tests, and of the Edinburgh annuity tax commutation, the Liberation Society supported two bills of Sir Colman O'Loghlen, M.P. for Co. Clare. One proposed to remove the declaration against transubstantiation. The other proposed to relax religious tests for public office and included a provision that persons of any denomination might become Lord Chancellor or Lord Lieutenant of Ireland.[83] The declaration against transubstantiation was duly abolished, and the other bill was passed after an amendment to omit the Lord Lieutenancy.[84] Reform of the Church of Ireland also seemed somewhat nearer. Sir John Gray was unsuccessful in proposing, on 7 May, a motion similar to his one of the previous year, that a Committee of the whole House should consider the temporalities and privileges of the Church of Ireland.[85] Gladstone agreed with his views on that Church, but said that a firm and just policy for dealing with the question had still to be worked out.[86] In the Lords on 24 June Russell (back on familiar ground of the 1830s) succeeded in obtaining an address for a Royal Commission to investigate the revenues of the Church of Ireland. This Commission's terms of reference, however, were much more restricted than Russell had intended,

---

[80] Cf. comments of the *Nonconformist*, 20 Mar. 1867 (p. 234), 27 Mar. 1867 (p. 254), 3 July 1867 (p. 546). But at least one Dissenting M.P.—J. B. Smith (member for Stockport)—enthusiastically supported Disraeli; letter of Smith dated 28 May 1867 (J. B. Smith Papers, S. 341).

[81] Newman Hall to Gladstone, 16 May 1867 (Gladstone Papers, 44188, fos. 73–4). Cf. Henry Allon to Gladstone, 17 Apr. 1867 (ibid. 44095, fo. 308).

[82] Hall to Gladstone, 16 May 1867, encl. (ibid. 44188, fo. 74).

[83] Minutes of Liberation Society, iv. 426 (8 Feb. 1867).

[84] *Annual Register*, cix (1867), 161–2.   [85] Hansard, clxxxvii. 96 ff.

[86] Ibid. 121–31.

the Lords having rejected that part of his motion which contained the words 'with a view to their [the revenues'] more equitable application for the benefit of the Irish people'.[87] Russell himself had suggested that Church funds should be used for the concurrent endowment of different Churches in Ireland.

On the subject of church-rates, Gladstone regretted that Hardcastle intended to reintroduce his bill for unconditional abolition.[88] Hardcastle brought it into the Commons on 12 February. The Government opposed the bill, but it was supported by the Liberals and the second reading was carried by 263 votes to 187, the largest majority ever obtained by a church-rate abolition measure.[89] This was a forceful revival of the anti-church-rate cause, and no doubt it encouraged an agreed interparty solution. But, after the third reading had been passed in a much smaller House, the bill went to the Lords and was there defeated by 82 votes to 24. The relentless Newdegate had again brought in his bill to commute the rate to a charge on property, payable by the landlords. He desired that control over the churches should not be wholly transferred from the laity to the clergy—'a result which clergymen with high ritualistic tendencies would be glad to see'. But his bill obtained only 45 votes and was defeated by a majority of 132.[90] On the question of University Tests, the bills of J. D. Coleridge (to open M.A.s at Oxford, extended to include other benefits) and of E. P. Bouverie (to open college fellowships to Dissenters) were successful in the Commons but defeated when they were sent to the Upper House.[91] A bill to abolish the Edinburgh annuity tax arrangement did not reach a second reading in the Commons.

For Dissenters, however, set-backs seemed more than balanced by success in 1867. In the next year this progress was strikingly maintained. Admittedly, a broad University Tests Bill of J. D. Coleridge had to be dropped through lack of time after its second reading had passed by a handsome majority.[92] But major successes were either achieved or were promisingly in the making. Not only were church-rates settled, but the Liberals decided on a broad plan for the Irish Church which, thanks to electoral victory, they were later able to carry as a Government.

Both church-rates and the Church of Ireland had been political questions since the early 1830s. The former had consumed much more of the time and energy of Dissenting politicians. But by the mid-1860s church-rates were becoming less important than the Irish Church question, which combined a greater number of interests and could be held to have a more significant bearing on the position of Church Establishments in general. Nevertheless, an attempt to settle the rate problem had similar political implications for

[87] Ibid. clxxxviii. 354-423.
[88] Gladstone to Roundell Palmer, 25 Jan. 1867 (Selborne Papers, vol. 1862, fo. 250).
[89] Hansard, clxxxvi. 215-50.   [90] Ibid. clxxxvi. 250-66.
[91] W. R. Ward, *Victorian Oxford*, 254.   [92] *Annual Register*, cx (1868), 160-3.

Gladstone as an attempt to deal with the Irish Church. A solution to the rate question sponsored by himself would help to rally the ranks of Liberalism after their defeat and division of 1867, and would consolidate the support of Dissenters whose electoral strength had recently increased. On the Government side, it was also important to participate in an agreed church-rate solution, for such action might help to wean Protestant Dissenters from alliance with Irish Catholicism over the Church of Ireland question. So it was that church-rates were finally settled by a consensus—a tacit agreement between the leaders of each party. Some militants among both churchmen and Voluntaries were left dissatisfied by the solution. But the majority on each side was rendered acquiescent, especially when the solution was altered by amendments which, oddly enough, pleased many churchmen as well as Dissenters.

On 28 November 1867, nine days after the session opened, Gladstone obtained leave to introduce a revised bill to abolish the compulsory rate. The bill had been altered in order to make it more acceptable to churchmen, and in December Hardcastle told Roundell Palmer, a co-sponsor of the bill, that Voluntaries had important objections. They disliked Clause 6, which enabled churchwardens to recover, by legal process, amounts which had been promised towards the rate; and Clause 8, which barred non-payers from acting as churchwardens 'except for secular purposes only'.[93] Hardcastle said that he did not oppose these provisions himself, but that he believed his associates in this matter would oppose them.[94] This implied that the opposition came from the executive committee of the Liberation Society, with whom he was then working in close conjunction. Palmer said that he had supplied Clause 6, which he considered an essential provision 'to enable Churchwardens to give any orders, or make any contracts, on the faith of any vote for a voluntary Church Rate'.[95] The other disputed provision, restriction on churchwardenship, Palmer was ready to give up: he 'attached no great value to it', and its omission would simplify the working of the bill.[96]

The objections of Liberationists to the 'legal contractual' side of the proposed voluntary rate were explained in a report of the Parliamentary Committee of the Society, presented on 7 February. The fifth clause of the bill, it was alleged, provided that 'before any one can vote on making a voluntary Church Rate, he must sign a declaration that he is willing to pay his share of such a Rate should one be made'; consequently, 'even those who have voted against such a rate will be called upon to pay it'. Dubious though the

---

[93] Palmer to Gladstone, 21 Dec. 1867, and encls. (Gladstone Papers, 44296, fo. 101). See the objections of the *Nonconformist*, 18 Jan. 1868 (pp. 49–50).

[94] Palmer to Gladstone, 21 Dec. 1867, and encls. (Gladstone Papers, 44296, fo. 101).

[95] Ibid., fos. 102–3. But cf. Palmer's letter to Gladstone, 21 Jan. 1868, where he repeated his opinion on the clause but said 'with respect to the Church Rate Bill, I will do as you think best' (ibid., fo. 111).

[96] Palmer to Gladstone, 21 Dec. 1867 (ibid., fo. 103).

provision was, it might be allowed to pass if nothing was done to enforce recovery by legal process. In Gladstone's previous bill the clause had stood alone, but in the new bill Clause 6 stated that agreements might be made to enforce payment 'in the same manner as other Contracts of a like nature might be enforced in any Court of Law or Equity'. Since the whole object of the bill was to abolish compulsory rates, and since its preamble stated that the power to compel payment by any legal process should be removed, it seemed inconsistent to create a contract for payment of a voluntary rate, and to permit enforcement of such a contract in a law court.[97] A joint deputation from the Dissenting Deputies and the Liberation Society (including Hardcastle, Miall and Carvell Williams) discussed these worries with Gladstone on 15 February. But Gladstone, as well as warning them that the Government might oppose a stronger bill, told them there was no intention of compelling payment from the unwilling but only from those who had said they wished to pay.[98] Thereafter the *Nonconformist* came round, though reluctantly, to support the bill.[99]

On 19 February Gladstone introduced the second reading of the bill in the Commons. He was at pains to conciliate both right and left. First he said that Hardcastle had made sacrifices in order to obtain Conservative support for a solution, and thanked many Conservatives for being willing to consider the bill.[100] Next he sought to allay the fears of Dissenters who thought that compulsion had been partially sanctioned in the present bill. There was 'no foundation whatever for that idea', and the object of Clause 6 was only to enable a churchwarden, in the same way as a treasurer of a Dissenting chapel or a hospital, to safeguard his personal liability for meeting expenses by recovering promised contributions by law if necessary.[101] In fact, he stressed, since 1866 the bill had been made more rather than less conciliatory to Dissenters. The last disability to be removed from the bill (perhaps because of Palmer's willingness to abandon it) was that restricting service as a churchwarden. On this point he skilfully stated: ' . . . on consideration we have felt that all we could reasonably ask of the House was, that those who subscribe to the fund under this Bill should have the management of the fund, and if they chose to appoint for that purpose a person who had not subscribed it is not our business to interfere with them'.[102] This meant that subscribers to the rate were being empowered, for the sake of satisfying Dissenters, to do that which they were most unlikely to do.

Lastly, Gladstone sought support by stating how his measure was preferable to complete abolition. The difference was small in theory, but great in practice, 'between a system which entirely and rudely shivered to fragments

[97] Minutes of Liberation Society, v. 19–20 (7 Feb. 1868).
[98] Cf. Mackintosh, 173; Anderson, 189.
[99] *Nonconformist*, 22 Feb. 1868 (p. 169), 14 Mar. 1868 (p. 241).
[100] Hansard, cxc. 958.   [101] Ibid. 960.   [102] Ibid. 959.

the existing machinery of church rates, and a system which leaves that machinery to operate, although upon a basis that is known and understood to be voluntary and free'. It was also desirable that a clergyman alone should not have to collect funds for a church, but that there should be a vestry and churchwardens to perform this function. Gladstone then tried to reassure those who feared that surrender of the age-old principle of a church-rate would lead to surrender of the age-old principle of an established Church. He said that the Church would become stronger and safer by the removal of such an irritation, and undoubtedly spoke his true belief. But in his method of doing so he seemed to forget himself:

... unless the vestry-cess in Ireland had been healed and closed up [in 1833] ... by the resolute action of Lord Derby, when he, by the Church Temporalities Act, destroyed the principle of a Church Establishment for Ireland—so far as that principle is involved in a rate for the maintenance of the fabric and for the services —it is highly probable that the Irish Church Establishment would not be in existence at this moment ...[103]

He seemed to be repeating unthinkingly the plea he had made to Sir Stafford Northcote in 1865: 'I think it *clear* that in Ireland the Establishment has been infinitely relieved and made far safer by the abolition of Church cess ... That *some* of the anti-Church Rate people look upon this measure as a blow to the Establishment only shows me their feebleness and their Brobding- nagian estimate of Lilliputian proceedings ...'[104] Matters had changed since 1865, and not least because Gladstone himself was contemplating radical treatment of the Irish Church. In citing the Church of Ireland as an illu- stration of a strengthened Establishment, he was almost inviting the response which Newdegate very soon made in the debate:

he ... begged to ask the right hon. Gentleman whether he considered the position of the Church of Ireland safe at present? He would beg to refer the right hon. Gentleman to those who were urging him forward in his present course in seeking to abolish church rates unconditionally, whether they considered the Establish- ment of the Church of Ireland safe; every one knew that they would tell the right hon. Gentleman that the Establishment of the Church in Ireland was condemned, was tottering to its fall, and that they rejoiced in the prospect of its destruction. That was, indeed, a most pregnant illustration.[105]

The ineptitude of the illustration, as well as its invertedly prophetic nature, was glaringly revealed less than a month later, when Gladstone announced in Parliament his policy of disestablishing the Church of Ireland. But this new development did not prevent the Lords from passing his Church Rate Bill, or the Government from agreeing with this action. Indeed, Gladstone's Irish

---

[103] Ibid. 963–4.
[104] Gladstone to Northcote, 9 Aug. 1865 (Lathbury, *Correspondence of Gladstone*, i. 142–3).
[105] Hansard, cxc. 971.

Church policy may have made a consensus solution of the church-rate question more necessary, in order to make the most of no-Popery feeling among Dissenters.

In the debate, Charles Gilpin, a Quaker who sat for Northampton, objected to legal provision for recovery of the rate.[106] A. S. Ayrton, M.P. for Tower Hamlets, said that an official procedure for raising and collecting the rate might enable wealthy Tractarians to gain control of churches and to introduce 'practices repugnant to the Protestant feeling of the country'.[107] Most Conservatives were probably content to accept the proposals. Cranborne (formerly Lord Robert Cecil), one of the foremost Church defenders, thought that adamant resistance would only result in a more extreme and unpalatable reform: 'We may go further and fare worse'.[108] Hardcastle welcomed Cranborne's conciliatory speech, and J. G. Hubbard also gave a general support to the measure.[109] Three other familiar bills had also been introduced—Hardcastle's (for total abolition), Hubbard's (for exempting Dissenters), and Newdegate's (for substituting a charge on property). But, having been read a second time, these bills were postponed while Gladstone's, having passed the second reading without a division, went into Committee. At the Committee stage (11 March) some minor changes were made to the bill but its main provisions were retained.[110] On 24 March the third reading was passed after Newdegate and others had made a last stand. Newdegate's motion to adjourn the House was negatived without a division, and a motion by Charles Schreiber, Conservative M.P. for Cheltenham, to adjourn the debate was defeated by 131 votes to 28. This was the last division in the Commons on the over-familiar question of church-rate. After the division, the Speaker put the question and declared that the Ayes had it.[111]

The Lords altered the bill, but did so in a manner which made it more liberal to Dissenters. Naturally this was not the object of their Lordships' amendments—indeed, the aim was to give the bill more of an Erastian emphasis and not less of one. Gladstone told Bishop Wilberforce on 30 March that 'the 8th. clause for the first time deprives Dissenters, or rather non-contributors, of the power which they now possess to interfere with the disposition of voluntary contributions . . .'[112] But the Lords seemed less influenced by the possible attractions of this clause than by the possible danger that it would make the Church less Erastian by tending to confine its control to enthusiastic high churchmen. In the Lords' debate on the bill on 23 April Bishop Tait dwelt on the current menace to religious Establishments, and emphasized the Tractarian part in it: ' ... they could not be blind to

---

[106] Ibid. 964–7. [107] Ibid. 976.
[108] Ibid. 970; quoted Pinto-Duschinsky, *Political Thought of Salisbury*, 147–8. Cf. Cranborne to Carnarvon, 27 Feb. 1868 (Salisbury Papers, D/31/14).
[109] Hansard, cxc. 973–5. [110] Ibid. 1415–30.
[111] Ibid. cxci. 206–8; Mackintosh, 174–5.
[112] Wilberforce Papers, d. 37.

the fact that there were certain members of the Church of England—visionary theorists they might be called—who were in favour rather of a so-called free than of an Established Church.'[113] This was, in effect, the same as Newdegate's warning that the proposed church-rate alterations should not be allowed to turn churches over to Tractarian control. Tait and others supported a suggestion that the bill should be referred to a Select Committee of the House, in the hope that amendments might be made. After the second reading had been allowed to pass without division, a motion for a Select Committee was accepted on 30 April.

In the Select Committee Lord Cairns, the fervent evangelical Lord Chancellor, played a prominent part in suggesting amendments which accorded with Tait's views.[114] These amendments removed the legal procedure for recovering sums which had been promised to the rate, and, more pertinently, struck out the provision whereby only contributors could take part in making and administering a future rate. When the whole House considered these amendments on 3 July, they proved acceptable to those prelates and laymen who were anxious to preserve a broadly based, Erastian Establishment, open and welcoming to all with the slightest glimmer of interest in it. It was not surprising that the aggressively broad-church Russell had no criticism to make of them.[115] Archbishop Thomson expressed his approval.[116] Strong opposition came from Bishop Wilberforce, who moved to restore both the machinery for recovery of promised amounts and restriction of the management of the rate to payers. But his effort was negatived.[117] The bishop of Gloucester and Bristol, C. J. Ellicott, also criticized the amendments as being likely to weaken the Church, but Cairns insisted to the contrary that the altered measure provided a satisfactory solution which could only benefit the Church Establishment.[118]

The bill was then passed and returned to the Commons. When the Lords' amendments were considered on 24 July Gladstone reluctantly accepted them,[119] and seven days later the bill received the royal assent. The other three proposed church-rate measures were withdrawn.

It was rare for an ecclesiastical reform to please both Dissenters and churchmen, and until the last two years such a conclusion would scarcely have been predicted for the bitter and protracted church-rate contest. The final amended solution may have helped to preserve the national character of the Church of England, and this was particularly important at a time when the Irish branch of that Church was under fierce attack on the ground that it was against national interest. In removing legal compulsion, the settlement also held a high place in the line of liberal reform. The Liberation Society

[113] Hansard, cxci. 1120.
[115] Hansard, cxciii. 594–6.
[117] Ibid. 604–6, 896–903.
[119] Ibid. 1773; Anderson, 190–2.

[114] *Annual Register*, cx (1868), 149.
[116] Ibid. 602–3.
[118] Ibid. 1099–1101.

declared its pleasure at the outcome as encouraging the principle of voluntary support: the executive committee hoped that 'the Church of England will acquire such increased experience of the power & sufficiency of Christian willinghood, as a means of sustaining Christian agencies, as will encourage them to rely upon it unreservedly for the future maintenance & extension of their Church'.[120] The politics of the settlement showed that neither party wished to alienate the growing strength of Dissent. Gladstone, who initiated the settlement, wanted to consolidate his alliance with an important section of the Liberal party. The Government gave its acceptance in order to prevent this alliance becoming too exclusive—an important consideration to Conservatives, especially when Gladstone was espousing a policy which by no means all Dissenters would favour. Wesleyans had been irritated by having to pay church-rates, though they had not usually joined the outcry against them. They, and perhaps others, would more readily support the Conservatives against a 'pro-popish' policy if the Conservatives had agreed to abolition of the compulsory rate.

The church-rate settlement eminently showed how Dissenting grievances which had been urged since the 1830s were finding a favourable climate for solution in the later 1860s. Yet, despite the removal of general compulsion, had the last been heard of church-rates? Various local Acts had escaped the 1868 measure, and the imposition of rates under these Acts engaged the attention of the Dissenting Deputies and the Liberation Society for many years afterwards.[121] Moreover, C. G. Prideaux, in the twelfth edition of his *Practical Guide to the Duties of Churchwardens* (published in 1871), gave an emphatic negative to any suggestion that church-rates had become illegal. The 1868 Act had, in its ninth clause, enabled parishes to appoint trustees to receive moneys, and these trustees could pass on funds to the churchwardens.[122] This was, in Prideaux's view, a remedy for the 'mischief' of the earlier sections: the statute expressly recognized church-rates and contemplated their continuance.[123] Prideaux advised churchwardens to endeavour to collect a voluntary rate from the occupants, though they could do no more than this.[124] Even in the most urbanized of parishes, in the later twentieth century, church-rate notices could be received, and the occupant—unless he remembered the Compulsory Church Rate Abolition Act of 1868—may have assumed that payment was essential.

III. THE IRISH CHURCH CRISIS, 1868

Irish disestablishment was the decisive political question of 1868, the issue which helped Gladstone to enjoy some of the fruits of Disraeli's parliamentary reform and to return to power with a large majority. The question

---

[120] Minutes of Liberation Society, v. 79 (7 Aug. 1868).
[121] Manning, *The Protestant Dissenting Deputies*, 195–8.
[122] *Practical Guide . . .*, op. cit. 90.   [123] Ibid. 94–5.   [124] Ibid. 214.

had revived strongly in recent years, especially since the formation of the National Association of Ireland, and had been discussed in the Commons in 1865 and in both Houses in 1866 and 1867. A Royal Commission on the revenues and administration of the Church of Ireland had resulted from a motion of Earl Russell in June 1867, and its report was still awaited when the crucial debates of 1868 took place.

The committee of the Liberation Society believed that Parliament would soon feel compelled to deal with the Irish Church, and recommended that plans should be drawn up in the autumn of 1867, 'specially adapted to turn to account the present favorable [sic] opportunity for settling the Irish Church question'.[125] It was also decided that the Secretary, Carvell Williams, should visit Ireland 'to confer with the Society's friends'.[126] The Society wished to consolidate its alliance with the National Association and the Irish Catholics. Williams undertook the visit and had interviews with the committee of the National Association, six Catholic bishops, several M.P.s, leading journalists, and Dissenting ministers. He urged the firmest co-operation between Irish Catholicism and the Liberation Society, and insisted that the means of settlement should be complete and impartial disendowment rather than concurrent endowment.[127] He expected that resolutions against accepting any of the endowments of the Church of Ireland would be adopted at a meeting of the Catholic bishops commencing on 1 October in Dublin. This three-day meeting passed firm resolutions in favour of disendowing the Church of Ireland and against accepting any endowment for the Irish Catholic Church.[128] The Liberation Society committee built on this encouragement: it persuaded the National Association to issue an address, circulated anti-endowment publications, and gave special attention to the topic at winter meetings and lectures.[129] The Society's absorption in this campaign was to last until disestablishment was safely carried in 1869.

The confirmation of official Catholic resistance to State support gratified the Liberation Society. The executive committee had previously recorded its strong objection to a solution based on the transfer of some Irish Church endowments to Catholics, such as Russell had suggested in the Lords.[130] Williams's insistence on complete disendowment when visiting Ireland doubtless resulted from the executive committee's declaration that concurrent endowment had been suggested as a diversionary move to buoy up the English Establishment.[131] The Liberation Society's determination was transmitted by Williams to the bishops and doubtless encouraged them to pass their resolutions on disendowment.

[125] Minutes of Liberation Society, iv. 454, 460 (5, 19 July 1867).
[126] Ibid. 463 (19 July 1867).
[127] Ibid. 479-80 (4 Oct. 1867); Norman, Catholic Church, 328-30.
[128] Minutes of Liberation Society, iv. 483 (18 Oct. 1867).
[129] See Norman, 333-4.   [130] Annual Register, cix (1867), 146.
[131] Minutes of Liberation Society, iv. 454-5 (5 July 1867).

Complete disendowment as an accompaniment to disestablishment of the Irish Church was the hope of Dissenting politicians and the radical Dissenting Press.[132] But some Catholics—Aubrey de Vere, Bishop Moriarty of Kerry, William Monsell, and Ambrose Phillipps de Lisle—strongly favoured concurrent endowment.[133] The National Association and most Catholic bishops had committed themselves to disendowment, which strengthened the Liberation Society's hand. But the bishops may not have seemed entirely reliable advocates of this policy, for they wished to retain the Maynooth grant and were negotiating for a new State subvention in the form of a grant to a Catholic university. It was also questionable how far the Catholic laity were prepared to agitate for disestablishment. Carvell Williams had excused the absence of a popular Irish movement against the established Church by stating that Fenianism was a distraction, and had said that widespread agitation on the subject was unlikely.[134] The organization for Irish disestablishment came more strongly from English Voluntaries than from the Irish. This was partly because the Liberation Society committee were perpetual political organizers and the Catholic bishops were not.

Liberal politicians needed more incentive to adopt Irish disestablishment than the goading of a farouche minority group like the Liberation Society. Disestablishment revived all the problems and prospects of the appropriation policy in the 1830s. Some Whig aristocrats were by no means anxious to adopt a policy which might be applied to the English Church, or to overthrow an institution if other institutions became shakier in consequence.[135] Russell, though he had urged appropriation of Irish Church revenues, preferred the sharing of resources to complete disendowment. He had long suggested endowment of the Irish Catholic priesthood, and continued to advocate distribution between denominations though he gave his support to disendowment as second best.[136]

Gladstone, for his part, was eventually committed to disendowment by external influences. His mind had long been moving towards an Irish Church settlement, but he did not urge one until political circumstances enticed him. The Liberal débâcle over parliamentary reform and the need to rally his party around a fresh political aim pushed him towards Irish Church reform in 1867–8. It was clear from his speech in the Commons on 7 May 1867 that he was ready to reform the Irish Establishment on the ground that it was unacceptable to the great majority.[137] This Warburtonian view revealed how far he had moved from his position of 1838, when truth was to be upheld regardless of

---

[132] e.g. The *United Methodist Free Churches' Magazine*, xi (1868), 484–5.
[133] Norman, 301–19; de Lisle to duke of Rutland, 6 May 1868 (Purcell, *Life and Letters of de Lisle*, ii. 297–8).
[134] Minutes of Liberation Society, iv. 480 (4 Oct. 1867).
[135] Cf. Southgate, *The Passing of the Whigs*, 337.
[136] Prest, *Russell*, 417; *Annual Register*, cx (1868), 74, 77.
[137] Hansard, clxxxvii. 121–6.

numbers. But he was no positive Voluntary, and in July 1867 he said he would support concurrent endowment if the Irish Catholics wished it.[138] He had to think about Whigs as well as radical Dissenters, and his own past opinions made him seem more favourable to a shared provision than to disendowment.

Gladstone and the Voluntaries had approached the Irish Church problem from different historical directions. Voluntaries had strongly opposed the Maynooth grant in 1845; in the later 1860s they still wished to remove the grant and to prevent its extension in the form of concurrent endowment. Gladstone's decision to support the 1845 grant, on the other hand, had weakened his defensive championship of the Irish Establishment; and this decision was his basic justification (as he affirmed to Bright in December 1867) for considering reform of this Establishment.[139] Since the Maynooth grant was the start of his reforming career in this particular, it might have seemed that concurrent endowment would be its terminus. Clearly, as an individual he could have adopted this policy as easily as disendowment, and he admitted that he was willing to turn either way.[140] But the resolutions of the Catholic bishops in October persuaded him to adopt disendowment, a policy which would also strengthen his alliance with Nonconformity. In February 1868 he told Russell that while he personally preferred redistribution of endowments to complete disendowment, Nonconformists would fiercely resist the former, 'and the Roman Catholics would have to follow suit'.[141] Added to this was the possibility that Disraeli's Government would adopt concurrent endowment: this prospect made disestablishment and disendowment a promising means of ousting the Conservatives. There was no religious obstacle to hinder Gladstone's taking up such a policy, for he held the Tractarian belief that a Church might become stronger by relying on her spiritual resources alone—and some years after disestablishment he drew satisfaction from the increased prosperity of the Church of Ireland.[142]

Political interest in the Church and other Irish problems was intensified by Fenian activities in both Ireland and Britain. Tension and rioting between Catholic and Protestant was encouraged in Wolverhampton and Birmingham in June 1867 by a series of anti-Catholic lectures given by William Murphy, an Irish Protestant.[143] Trouble was also shown in South

---

[138] Norman, 332.

[139] Gladstone to Bright, 10 Dec. 1867; quoted Lathbury, op. cit. i. 154-5, and W. E. Williams, *The Rise of Gladstone*, 162. For Gladstone's explanation of his changing attitude to the Irish Church see also his 'Chapter of Autobiography' in *Gleanings of Past Years*, vii. 97-151; and Lathbury, i. 149-50. On this matter see also P. M. H. Bell, *Disestablishment in Ireland and Wales* (London, 1969), 76 ff.

[140] Norman, 332.

[141] Gladstone to Russell, 21 Feb. 1868 (Gooch, *Correspondence of Russell*, ii. 366). Cf. Gladstone to Clarendon, 17 Feb. 1868 (Clarendon Papers, c. 523).

[142] Lathbury, i. 153. Cf. opinion of the *Guardian*, 1 Apr. 1868, p. 372.

[143] *Annual Register*, cix (1867), Chronicle, 79; *Nonconformist*, 19 June 1867 (p. 511); W. L. Arnstein, 'The Murphy Riots: a Victorian Dilemma', *Victorian Studies*, xix (1975-6), 51-71.

Lancashire—an area which was both Derby's home and Gladstone's constituency. The historian of Catholic Liverpool tells us that many hundreds of Irishmen in the city belonged to the Irish Republican Brotherhood (the official name of the Fenian organization), and that thousands of others were warmly sympathetic.[144] In November Liverpool Catholic demonstrations in sympathy with the 'Manchester martyrs' were reluctantly abandoned on the advice of clerical leaders, and a clash with Orange counter-demonstrators was thereby averted.[145] Also in Liverpool, in April 1868, a fracas erupted over an attempt by an Orangeman to replace a retiring Catholic member on the Board of Guardians; the Catholic candidate was finally returned by a narrow majority.[146] Early in January Derby had written to Disraeli about a religious disturbance at Warrington:

You saw the account of the attempt to blow up the gas-works at Warrington. An Irish priest is trying to make out that it was all a hoax; but all the R. Catholic workmen have been dismissed; and one of the managers was imprudent enough to tell the Priest that they were so dismissed on account of their Religion! Four Irish Workmen (Protestants) have been kept on . . . In England the feeling is so strong that I believe we shall have to resist a popular pressure for ultra-constitutional measures of repression as applied to *this* Country as well as Ireland.[147]

Gladstone's move towards Irish reform may have been affected by such developments in his constituency. On 19 December 1867 he had publicly told some of his constituents at Southport that he intended to reform Irish Church, land, and education.[148]

The Government showed little attempt to forestall Gladstone in making offers of reform to Ireland. Government policy comprised both extended coercion (in February 1868) and tentative suggestions for ecclesiastical equity. When Russell asked in the Lords on 24 February why the Government proposed no conciliatory measures, especially in regard to the Church, Lord Hardwicke hinted in reply that something might be done to raise Catholics to the same level as Protestants.[149] When Disraeli succeeded Derby as Prime Minister he told a meeting of ministers on 26 February that he desired a liberal treatment of Ireland, but left concrete proposals for the Irish Secretary, Lord Mayo, to make in a Commons debate to be held in March.[150] The Government was no doubt wary of the ultra-Protestant feeling among its own supporters. As Cranborne had written to Disraeli on 5 October 1866, 'there are very few points in which we can please the Catholics without offending the Protestant Conservatives in England & the North of Ireland'.[151] Disraeli could not force another sweeping reform on

---

[144] Burke, *A Catholic History of Liverpool*, 179.
[145] Ibid. 179–80.   [146] Ibid. 181–2.
[147] Derby to Disraeli, 3 Jan. 1868 (Disraeli Papers, B/XX/S/470).
[148] Morley, *Life of Gladstone*, ii. 243.   [149] *Annual Register*, cx (1868), 6–8.
[150] Ibid. 9–10.
[151] Disraeli Papers, B/XX/Ce/10; copy in Salisbury Papers, D/20/15.

Tories just after they had swallowed the Act of 1867. It was only in a tentative and scarcely convincing fashion that the Government entertained even concurrent endowment as one of its remedies for Ireland. This caution is demonstrated by its attitude to the question of a chartered and endowed Catholic university.

The Catholic bishops had been negotiating on the subject of Catholic university education since 1865, first with the Liberal and then with the Conservative Government.[152] From May 1867 to March 1868 Archbishop Manning acted as a mediator between the Irish Catholic prelates and Disraeli.[153] On 19 February 1868 Disraeli offered Manning a charter for a Catholic university, but no endowment, and wanted admission of Catholic laymen to its governing body with the intention of restricting sacerdotal influence. Manning urged acceptance of this plan, though, as soon appeared, it was not satisfactory to some of the Irish bishops. Manning hopefully stated that a Government endowment might be granted later.[154] Indeed, the Government did show some willingness to offer financial aid to a Catholic university. At an important Cabinet meeting on 2 March, when Mayo's forthcoming statement was planned, it was decided to hint that financial support might be given for buildings. When Mayo actually made his speech on 10 March an initial grant was offered for scholarships.[155] Beyond the halfhearted nature (by Irish Catholic standards) of these educational proposals, it was unlikely that the restriction of a definite offer of reform to the narrow sphere of higher education would be at all adequate to quieten Ireland. On 2 March, the day when the Cabinet decided on this policy, Bishop Moriarty wrote to William Monsell that the education question 'can never be a cause of popular disaffection, because it touches only a class which is not disaffected, and because those who want education most feel the want least'.[156] Monsell gave Moriarty's letter to Gladstone,[157] and thus helped him to seize the question of Irish reform from Disraeli's hands.

Gladstone profited both from the Government's failure to offer a clear policy of Irish Church (or land) reform and from its unwillingness to endow a Catholic university. He filled the gap by suggesting his own radical Church reform. On 16 March, at a late stage in the lengthy debate in which Mayo had made his statement of Government policy, Gladstone declared that the Church of Ireland must be disestablished, and promised appropriate resolutions.[158] Disraeli had heard at least three days before that Gladstone intended to propose entire disendowment[159]—though this was not done as yet. In the

[152] Norman, 190 ff.
[153] Ibid. 242 ff.; Manning to Disraeli, 4 May, 20 Aug. 1867 (Disraeli Papers, B/XXI/M/161, 165).
[154] Norman, 256.
[155] Ibid. 261.
[156] Quoted ibid. 258-9.
[157] Ibid. 259.
[158] Hansard, cxc. 1744-71.
[159] Disraeli to Derby, 13 Mar. 1868 (Derby Papers, 146/4).

same speech Gladstone appealed to liberal opinion on education by condemning the idea of a State-endowed denominational university; though ministers, both now and in later parliamentary debates,[160] denied that their scheme amounted to endowment. In order to achieve a coherent Liberal policy of denominational disendowment (which included abolition of the Maynooth grant), and to divide the Conservatives, Gladstone continued to berate ministers for their supposed endowment tendencies even though ministers themselves denied them.[161] In doing so he was appealing to Dissenters. As for Irish Catholics, he could afford to condemn their educational endowment because he had pledged himself to a policy far more attractive to them.

Gladstone had responded more broadly than Mayo to the Irish Catholic motion which had commenced the crucial debate of 10–16 March. This was a motion of J. F. Maguire, M.P. for Dungarvan, for a Committee of the whole House on the state of Ireland, introduced by a speech calling for disestablishment and disendowment of the Irish Church as well as land and educational reform.[162] After Gladstone's declaration of intent, Maguire withdrew his motion. Gladstone's plan gained rapid success in the Commons from the enthusiastic support of the suddenly revivified Liberal majority in that House. On 23 March he presented his resolutions. Primarily, he would propose that the Church of Ireland should cease to be established, due regard being shown to all personal interests and rights of property. As corollaries, he would propose to suspend the making of appointments through public patronage in that Church, to restrict the operations of the Irish Ecclesiastical Commissioners, and to ask the Queen to place at Parliament's disposal her interest in the Church's temporalities.[163]

Disraeli's reply was that legislation on so important a matter should not be attempted until a Parliament had been elected under the new, wider franchise.[164] He wrote to Cairns on 19 March:

I think we ought to hold that the whole question of national establishments is now raised; that the Irish Ch: is but a small portion of the question ... But we must detach the Irish Ch: as much as possible from the prominent portion of the subject, for, there is no doubt, it is not popular. I think, if the principle, that the State should adopt & uphold religion as an essential portion of the Constitution, be broadly raised, a great number of members from the north of England & Scotland, called Liberals, wd. be obligd. to leave the philosophic standard.

Therefore, he added, he was inclined to an amendment which 'while it is [sic] admitted that the present condition of the Ch: in Ireland was susceptible

[160] *Annual Register*, cx (1868), 94–5.
[161] Norman, 264–7; *Annual Register*, cx (1868), 96.
[162] Hansard, cxc. 1288–1314.   [163] Ibid. cxci. 32–3.
[164] Cairns to Disraeli, 2 Mar. 1868 (Disraeli Papers, B/XX/Ca/17); Disraeli to Derby, 4 Mar. 1868 (Derby Papers, 146/4); Derby to Disraeli, 6 Mar. 1868 (Disraeli Papers, B/XX/S/484); Cairns to Disraeli, 23 Mar. 1868 (ibid. B/XX/Ca/22).

of improvement; while it might be desirable to elevate the status of the unendowed clergy of that country; still declared it was the first duty of the State to acknowledge & maintain the religious principle in an established form, etc.'[165]

The amendment with which the Cabinet decided, on 24 March, to meet Gladstone's forthcoming motion, proposed that considerable changes in the Irish Church temporalities might be required when the current Lords' inquiry had made its report, but that any motion for disestablishment or disendowment should be reserved for a new Parliament.[166] Lord Stanley was appointed to move the amendment. He had already advocated postponement at a banquet to Cabinet ministers at Bristol on 22 January;[167] and he, along with Pakington in the Cabinet, believed that Irish disestablishment should not be resisted.[168] But the amendment was anathema to Derby and other Conservatives who upheld the inalienability of Irish Church revenues— the point on which Derby had left the Whigs in 1834 and to which he still firmly adhered.[169] Cranborne, bitterly distrustful of Disraeli since his experience over parliamentary reform in 1867, had already given his opinion that 'Dizzy intends to pursue the old game of talking Green in the House and Orange in the lobby'.[170] He thought that the choice of Stanley to move the amendment heralded another betrayal of Conservative principle, and delivered a hostile speech refusing to support a policy whose object seemed 'merely to gain time and to enable the Government to keep the cards in their hands for another year to shuffle as they please'.[171]

The divisions among Conservatives were potentially more dangerous than the objections which Gladstone's policy encountered from Liberals like Roundell Palmer and Earl Grey.[172] If Disraeli had tackled the Irish Church question on the lines of concurrent endowment the split in his ranks would have been severe. But Disraeli helped to disarm his critics by delivering, towards the end of the debate on Gladstone's motion on 3 April for a Committee of the whole House, a strong defence of the principle of an established Church as a means of maintaining the link between religion and political authority. If that connection were severed in Ireland, he asked, might not a

[165] Cairns Papers, 30/51/1; cf. Bell, op. cit. 86.

[166] Disraeli to Derby, 25 Mar. 1868 (Derby Papers, 146/4). W. E. Forster had suspected that Disraeli might try to delay legislation until the new Parliament; Cardwell to Gladstone, 23 Mar. 1868 (Gladstone Papers, 44118, fos. 268-9).

[167] Annual Register, cx (1868), 3.

[168] Blake, Disraeli, 498; Pakington to Disraeli, 14 Mar. 1868 (Disraeli Papers, B/XX/P/94).

[169] Derby to Disraeli, 3 Mar. 1868 (Disraeli Papers, B/XX/S/483); W. D. Jones, Lord Derby and Victorian Conservatism, 337-8.

[170] Cranborne to Carnarvon, 6 Mar. 1868 (Salisbury Papers, D/31/15).

[171] Hansard, cxci. 540.

[172] R. Palmer, Memorials, Personal and Political, i. 77 ff.; Cardwell to Gladstone, 5 Nov. 1867, 9 Apr. 1868 (Gladstone Papers, 44118, fos. 235, 271-2); Journal of Earl Grey, 1868 (Grey Papers, C3/22).

like disjunction take place in Wales, Scotland, even England?[173] He hinted at a shady conspiracy of Tractarians and Irish Ultramontanes to demolish Establishments, though when the problem arose later of whether to support an anti-ritualist bill of Shaftesbury, the Government succeeded in putting off such an attempt until a later session.[174] Gladstone had already, in his opening speech, taken the opposite view that the Church of England would be strengthened rather than weakened by vigorous treatment of its Irish arm; he now repeated this opinion by saying that Irish disestablishment was the most effectual means of maintaining religious Establishments elsewhere.[175] The division in the Commons resulted in an unexpectedly decisive victory for Gladstone. Stanley's amendment was defeated by 60 votes, and Gladstone's motion was carried by 56.

In the remainder of the session there were further lengthy debates on the issue, and familiar arguments were rehearsed, including the supposed threat of Gladstone's resolutions to other Establishments besides the Irish. The first, and crucial, resolution on disestablishment was carried by a majority of 65 in the Commons on 1 May.[176] Three days later it was stated, to the anger of the Liberals, that ministers would remain in office until a dissolution of Parliament, which might be in November. The Government allowed Gladstone's two subsidiary resolutions to pass without dividing the House; and the Queen gave a favourable answer to the address presented to her, in pursuance of the third resolution, that she would place the Crown's interest in Irish Church temporalities at the disposal of Parliament.[177] Gladstone then introduced a Suspensory Bill on 14 May, in order to prevent new appointments in the Church of Ireland until 1 August 1869 and to restrict the proceedings of the Ecclesiastical Commissioners for the same period. The Commons passed the bill after an amendment concerning new appointments at Maynooth; but the Lords, after an energetic three-night debate on the entire Irish Church question, threw the bill out by 192 votes to 97 on 27 June.[178] Gladstone could only hope that the general election results would cause the peers to change their tune.

While the House of Commons was thus deciding on the main lines of policy in accordance with Gladstone's resolutions, the former prospect of understanding between Disraeli and the Irish Catholic prelates over a university charter had faded out. Manning had transferred his support to the wider scheme of his old friend Gladstone. After a hopeful interview with Disraeli on 14 March, he had asked the latter, on the fifteenth, 'Why not try

---

[173] Hansard, cxci. 917–20; Blake, *Disraeli*, 500.

[174] *Annual Register*, cx (1868), 163; Cairns to Disraeli, 5 June 1868 (Disraeli Papers, B/XX/Ca/34); Manners to Disraeli, 13 June 1868 (ibid. B/XX/M/151).

[175] Hansard, cxci. 928–30. Cf. Gladstone to Roundell Palmer, 4 Apr. 1868 (Lathbury, i. 155–6).

[176] Hansard, cxci. 1675–9.   [177] *Annual Register*, cx (1868), 90–4.

[178] Ibid. 94–107.

at last to make Ireland like the Rhenish Provinces, a happy & prosperous Catholic country? Surely this is a policy worthy of a Statesman.' But on 24 March he wrote to Gladstone: 'I am thankful that you have laid the axe to the root'.[179] He continued to write such letters, stoking Gladstone's ardour in the effort to pass his parliamentary resolutions. On 28 March, for instance, he wrote: 'I don't think it [disestablishment] a leap in the dark, but a step onwards into the light'; and on 8 April: 'It is necessary that the supporters of the Resolutions should follow [the victory] up, & turn it to practical purposes'.[180]

There was of course no parallel correspondence with Disraeli after the middle of March,[181] and it was only in December, when Gladstone had come into power and Church reform was virtually assured, that Manning felt free to communicate with Disraeli again:

I have felt that a ravine, I will not say a gulf opened between us when the resolutions on the Irish Church were laid upon the table of the House. I regretted this as I had hoped to see the scheme of the Catholic University happily matured: but with my inevitable convictions as to the Irish Church I felt that I ought not to trespass upon your kindness . . .[182]

But Disraeli was unreceptive to such an apology: not only had Manning apparently changed horses, but the fate of the university question showed that his representation of Catholic bishops' views on the matter had been over-optimistic. Gladstone's formidably attractive counter-plan had lessened Catholic inclinations to compromise with Disraeli. With Manning no longer striving for an agreed solution between Government and Catholic prelates, the latter had demanded more clerical control over the proposed university. The Government had been unable to entertain these conditions; it was being forced by Gladstone's assault to abandon its old policy of wooing Catholic votes and to appear more anti-popish and anti-sacerdotal before the country. Gladstone, in fact, had redeemed at last the political legacy of 1851. Mayo had rejected the bishops' conditions on 11 May. The negotiations ceased, and at the end of June, to Cullen's disappointment, Mayo refused to reopen them.[183] Disraeli believed Manning had been guilty of duplicity, and later took consolation in portraying him as Cardinal Grandison in *Lothair*.

If Gladstone's Irish policy had tied Catholic support to the Liberals, it had also firmly attached most Protestant Dissenters. The militant demands of the Liberation Society could unite with the stealthier approach of moderate Voluntaries behind Gladstone's policy and behind the attempt to ensure that

[179] Manning to Disraeli, 15 Mar. 1868 (Disraeli Papers, B/XXI/M/171); Manning to Gladstone, 24 Mar. 1868 (Gladstone Papers, 44249, fos. 31-2).
[180] Manning to Gladstone, 28 Mar., 8 Apr. 1868 (Gladstone Papers, 44249, fo. 34 ff.).
[181] Blake, *Disraeli*, 497.
[182] Manning to Disraeli, 2 Dec. 1868 (Disraeli Papers, B/XXI/M/173).
[183] See Norman, 267-81.

this policy included complete disendowment in Ireland. Thus the restrained Dissenting Deputies suggested that the less inhibited Liberation Society should join them in sending a deputation to the Liberal leaders, deprecating concurrent endowment as a solution.[184] On 27 March the Liberation Society's executive committee urged the friends of religious liberty to give 'prompt & energetic' support to Gladstone and his resolutions.[185] Preparations for a general election had already begun, and the Society's Parliamentary Committee reported on 27 March that letters had been sent to 100 boroughs, requesting that meetings of Liberal electors should be held to pass resolutions in support of Gladstone's policy.[186] In an effort to encourage the increasingly significant workers' associations to campaign for disestablishment, the Society agreed to a request from the London Working Men's Association for a grant of £40 towards the expenses of a meeting in support of Gladstone.[187]

On a more intimate level Gladstone was being assured by his Nonconformist correspondents of their confidence, in terms of goodwill to Anglicanism which he would surely appreciate. Henry Allon wrote on 5 May, after leaving some resolutions for him to see:

... Judging from my own experience of voluntary churches, none will rejoice in such a settlement more than episcopalians themselves—after a little while.

It may interest you to know that in the public prayers which in nonconforming churches are offered for the nation and its rulers and statesmen, the divine blessing has been very generally implored upon you and your proposal, of course in general but yet unmistakable terms. Since the agitation of the slavery question such a thing I imagine has scarcely occurred.[188]

Similarly, Newman Hall averred in typically diplomatic terms: 'However great the tax on your personal comfort, it is worth it to carry a measure so calculated to tranquillise Ireland, and by putting an end to a wrong done to Popery, to promote the cause of Protestantism.'[189] Political circumstances had brought not only Gladstone but Manning into Newman Hall's parlour. The Catholic and the Nonconformist leader were in hearty agreement on complete disendowment as a solution to Irish religious problems. Hall wrote to Henry Allon, perhaps in July: '"Archbishop" Manning is coming for a quiet cup of Tea & chat tomorrow at 7 (Saturday) . . . will you & Mrs Allon give us the pleasure of your company . . . quite informal. I have only just heard from Manning—who in effect asked to be better acquainted & wants to know more of us.'[190] It was probably of this meeting that Hall informed Gladstone on 1 August: 'Dr. Manning spent an evening here lately & assured us that his Church would refuse endowment, as not needed, as

[184] Minutes of Liberation Society, v. 31–2 (20 Mar. 1868).
[185] Ibid. v. 34.   [186] Ibid. 35.   [187] Ibid. (27 Mar. 1868).
[188] Gladstone Papers, 44095, fos. 310–11.
[189] Hall to Gladstone, 1 Aug. 1868 (ibid. 44188, fo. 82).
[190] A. Peel (ed.), *Letters to a Victorian Editor* (London, 1929), 319.

injuring the present sources of revenue, and as lessening their moral power.'[191]
No doubt Hall sardonically described Manning to Allon as 'Archbishop', and
to Gladstone as Dr., on account of the Ecclesiastical Titles Act whose passage
in 1851 Hall had opposed, and which remained law despite a recent move to
repeal it.[192]

Wesleyans were far less certain supporters of disestablishment than the
radical Dissenters, who included the Methodist secession groups. The
traditional conservative, Protestant view was still highly influential among
Wesleyans, though a tendency to political liberalism was also present. A
correspondent of Disraeli even alleged that 'among their ministers there is a
strong party of Radical & almost Republican views'.[193] Newman Hall told
Gladstone, on the testimony of Wesleyans, that they 'would all vote for Total
Disendowment rather than for any measure involving endowment of
Popery . . .',[194] though this begged the question whether they would all
support disestablishment in the first place.

Indeed, not all Dissenters, even among Congregationalists or Baptists,
could be persuaded to resolve their mental dichotomy between anti-Catholicism and disestablishment in favour of the latter. Hall warned Gladstone
against a Congregational minister and well-known anti-secularist lecturer,
the Rev. Brewin Grant, who had published a talk he had given at Blackburn
on 8 July, entitled *The Irish Church, an English Dissenter's View of it, or Mr.
Gladstone's Missing Link*. Grant said that, although a Voluntary, he defended
the Irish Church Establishment because the attack on it was 'Romanish'.
Gladstone's vague parliamentary resolutions had left the door open for the
endowment of the Catholic Church, though in Ireland itself there was 'no
excitement . . . on the Irish Church except as the echo of the Liberation
Society in England'.[195] He challenged the current Dissenting worship of
Gladstone: 'This surrender to a man, into whose principles and purposes it is
profane to pry, is the perfection of political adulation and fanaticism.'[196]
Instead of being blinded by Gladstone, Dissenters should look for protection
to his rival: Grant advised the new electors to vote for 'the man who gave
them the legal right to vote, and surpassed the self-styled "Liberals" in real
Tory liberality'.[197] He concluded with a ringing declaration: ' . . . there will
be found thousands of Dissenters who will stand like a wall in front of the
Church, and while the Church stands behind them as a tower of strength,
Dissent will be as the earthwork in front . . .'[198]

[191] Gladstone Papers, 44188, fo. 83.   [192] *Annual Register*, cx (1868), 45-6.
[193] G. Mee to Disraeli, 29 Aug. 1868 (Disraeli Papers, C/III/a/48y). Cf. William Evans to George
Wilson, 12 Aug. 1868 (Wilson Papers).
[194] Hall to Gladstone, 1 Aug. 1868 (Gladstone Papers, 44188, fo. 83).
[195] *The Irish Church, an English Dissenter's view of it* . . . (London, 1868), 2, 4, 7-8.
[196] Ibid. 10.   [197] Ibid. 14.
[198] Ibid. Cf. the hopes placed in Protestant Dissenters by 'a Winchester Churchman' in *The
Irish Church Question Considered* . . . (London, n.d.), 37-8.

This was in sharp contrast to the politics of Newman Hall, and the latter was at pains to disabuse Gladstone of any idea that Grant's views were typical of Congregationalists:

You should know that although an Independent Minister he has no standing amongst us. He was always an Arab, always quarrelling with his Brethren. Some years ago he wrote a pamphlet charging me & others who had the honor [sic] of meeting you here, with heresy, but I never took the trouble to read it. He has never been successful as a Pastor. The party taking him up may try to make capital out of his being a 'Dissenter', but in no sense does he represent Dissenters.[199]

If Dissenters were divided over Irish disestablishment, churchmen showed greater division. The strongest opposition came from Anglican evangelicals, in whom anti-Catholicism and Erastianism combined to cause fierce resistance. For political reasons Disraeli had to appeal to this group. In Church appointments, Conservative agents and others urged to him to satisfy evangelical claims. He was advised to appoint one of the most outspoken anti-Catholic evangelicals, Rev. Hugh McNeile, to the bishopric of Hereford in succession to R. D. Hampden.[200] Disraeli demurred, and the Hereford bishopric was spared the publicity of another national controversy. But he appointed McNeile dean of Ripon in August 1868—a bold enough stroke, which, he told Derby, would surely 'put an end to the Low Church discontent & murmurs'.[201] Lord Cairns said that 'nothing more politic could occur at the present time', and Disraeli thought that 'the Deanery of Ripon has been a *coup*. I was really surrounded by hungry lions & bulls of Bashan till that took place, but since, there has been a lull ... Probably, they were all astounded.'[202] The Church Institution did much to stimulate churchmen against Gladstone's intentions, issuing pamphlets and organizing lectures in defence of the Irish Church Establishment and, by natural association, that of England.[203] Broad churchmen were divided in their reactions to the topic of the moment. Tait, whom Disraeli appointed with some reluctance to the see of Canterbury in November, was against disestablishment;[204] but many broad churchmen favoured it as a means of justice to Ireland. On 23 June there was presented to the Lords a petition for Irish disestablishment signed by 261 liberal churchmen, including Maurice, Kingsley, Jowett, and Dean Alford.[205]

High churchmen were also divided, as might have been anticipated from their diverse attitudes to Establishment. Gladstone himself was represented

[199] Hall to Gladstone, 1 Aug. 1868 (Gladstone Papers, 44188, fo. 83).
[200] James B. Barnes, Conservative agent in Berkshire, to Disraeli, Aug. (?) 1868 (Disraeli Papers, C/III/a/42); C. H. Frewen to Disraeli, 27 Apr. 1868 (ibid. 47j).
[201] Disraeli to Derby, 23 Aug. 1868 (Derby Papers, 146/4).
[202] Cairns to Disraeli, 22 Aug. 1868 (ibid. C/III/A/48r); Disraeli to Derby, 18 Sept. 1868 (Derby Papers, 146/4).
[203] P. T. Marsh, *The Victorian Church in Decline, 1868-82* (London, 1969), 23.
[204] Disraeli to Derby, 2 Nov. 1868 (Derby Papers, 146/4); Marsh, op. cit. 24-5.
[205] Mackintosh, *Disestablishment*, 147. Cf. Marsh, 25-6.

by *Punch* as a Tractarian Guy Fawkes seeking to blow up the Protestant Irish Church.[206] W. F. Hook contemplated with apparent equanimity the possible effects of Irish disestablishment on the Church of England: ' . . . I have given all my sons to the service of our God, & the ministry of his Church. They know that, in the disestablishment of the Church of England, which *must* follow, they are choosing a path which will lead to beggary & persecution, —but they are hearty in the cause.'[207] Bishop Hamilton of Salisbury told Gladstone that 'I have always looked on [disestablishment] as a means of escape from what I have ever thought was our Church's greatest danger, namely Erastianism.'[208] Denison, on the other hand, was flatly opposed to Gladstone's policy, wrote pamphlets condemning it, and organized a Church and State Defence Society against it.[209] Like evangelical pamphleteers, he saw disestablishment as an encouragement to, or even a result of, the growth of unbelief. He wrote: 'To say that a branch of the Reformed Catholic Church shall cease to be the National Church . . . because it is not the Church of the majority, is to separate Truth and Religion, and to put in its [*sic*] place man's disbelief or man's corruption as the rule of the National Life'.[210] Wilberforce also was strongly opposed to disestablishment, but was caught between dislike of Gladstone's policy and dislike of Disraeli's appeal to low churchmanship.[211] Political interest and conviction and doctrinal principle had brought together, in support of Irish disestablishment, people of opposite religious beliefs who could not have been similarly allied over any other cause.

From the moment the Irish Church became the leading parliamentary concern it engaged close attention in the country, with preparation for the general election being the main purpose of propaganda. In addition to newspaper and pamphlet persuasion by the different sides, a great many rival meetings were held from April to June, providing a vocal national background to the parliamentary arguments. Meetings in favour of Irish disestablishment were held on 31 March at Glasgow, Liverpool, Newcastle upon Tyne, and at the Freemasons' Hall, London, where the assembly was convened by the London Working Men's Association;[212] on 1 April at the Free Trade Hall, Manchester, at Sheffield (where 7,000 or 8,000 were said to have attended), and at St. Helens;[213] on 2 April at Leeds; on 15 April at London, Leith, and Godalming; on 16 April at Burslem; on 22 April at the Baptist Metropolitan Tabernacle, where a gathering of 7,000 was addressed by Bright; on 24 April at Dundee, Stirling, and Lauder; on 27 April at

---

[206] *Cartoons from 'Punch'* (4 vols., London, 1906), ii. 295.
[207] Hook to Gladstone, 8 June 1868 (Gladstone Papers, 44213, fos. 144-5).
[208] W. K. Hamilton to Gladstone, 25 Aug. 1868 (ibid. 44183, fos. 369-70).
[209] Marsh, 22-3.
[210] Denison to earl of Carnarvon, 27 June 1868 (L. Denison (ed.), *Fifty Years at East Brent*, 102).
[211] Meacham, *Samuel Wilberforce*, 283-9.   [212] *The Times*, 1 Apr. 1868, pp. 5, 10, 12.
[213] Ibid. 2 Apr. 1868, pp. 5, 12.

Edinburgh; and on 28 April at Bradford.[214] In May pro-disestablishment meetings gathered at Middlesbrough, Preston, and London.[215] The Reform League arranged a meeting in defence of Gladstone's resolutions at St. James's Hall, London, on 12 May; Edmond Beales and George Odger addressed the assembly.[216] On the next day Beales and George Potter addressed a meeting with the same object in Trafalgar Square, arranged by the committee of the London Working Men's Association; resolutions were passed in favour of Irish disestablishment and against the Government's decision to stay in office.[217] On 19 July a working men's demonstration against the Irish Establishment took place in Hyde Park.[218]

An important meeting to support disestablishment had been organized by the Reform Union and was held at St. James's Hall on 16 April. Russell presided, and said that he submitted to complete disendowment in deference to much British opinion and to the wishes of the Irish Catholics themselves. Miall was prominent in the proceedings, and expressed his gratified surprise that a cause he had so long advocated had suddenly become popular.[219]

On the next evening the same hall was used for an opposite purpose—defence of the Irish Establishment—at a meeting organized by the United Protestant Defence Committee. The chairman, J. C. Colquhoun, a veteran leader of the Protestant Association, said that he had been through Ireland and had 'never heard there but one voice—that they respected and loved the Irish Protestant clergy'.[220] On 6 May a great clerical meeting condemned disestablishment, also at St. James's Hall. This was attended by the two Church of England and the two Church of Ireland archbishops, several bishops, deans, and other clergy, peers, M.P.s, and the Lord Mayor of London. The maintenance of the English Establishment as well as the Irish was demanded. Archbishop Longley, who presided, referred pointedly to Gladstone's assertion in *The State in its Relations with the Church* that 'the union of Church and State was in conformity with the will of God, and was essential to the advancement of the best interests of Christianity'.[221] The Lord Mayor moved a resolution 'that the union of Church and State should be maintained . . .'[222] Wilberforce seconded this resolution, and Bishop Tait moved another, that Irish disestablishment 'would be a serious blow to the Reformed Faith in the United Kingdom, and would directly tend to promote the ascendancy of a foreign power within her Majesty's dominions'.[223] A third resolution, however, was more conciliatory; moved by Dean Stanley and seconded by

---

[214] Ibid. 3 Apr. 1868, p. 12; 16 Apr., p. 10; 17 Apr., p. 5; 18 Apr., p. 12; 23 Apr., p. 5; 27 Apr., p. 9; 28 Apr., p. 12; 29 Apr., p. 9.

[215] Ibid. 7 May 1868, pp. 5, 9; 13 May, p. 5.   [216] Ibid. 13 May 1868, p. 5.

[217] Ibid. 12 May 1868, p. 8; 14 May 1868, p. 7.   [218] Ibid. 20 July 1868, p. 12.

[219] Ibid. 17 Apr. 1868, p. 5; *Annual Register*, cx (1868), 73-5.

[220] Ibid. 75-6; *The Times*, 18 Apr. 1868, p. 12.

[221] *Annual Register*, cx (1868), 89.   [222] Ibid.

[223] Ibid. 89-90.

Lord Colchester, it declared that, whereas the contemplated reform measure would 'work great wrong', 'all changes in the Irish branch of the United Church of England and Ireland which shall upon fair examination be found necessary shall be carried out'.[224] All these resolutions were carried.

Other meetings against Irish disestablishment included one held by the Liverpool Conservative Working Men's Association on 1 April; one at Birmingham on 16 April, where there was an attendance of over 4,000 and where Newdegate seconded one of the resolutions; and one at Leeds on 27 April, where, however, there was so much opposition and uproar that the meeting was closed within half an hour.[225] A conference of clergy in the archdeaconry of Stafford on 8 May, a London meeting on 18 May where the Lord Mayor gleefully read extracts from Gladstone's book of 1838, another London meeting on 9 June where similar extracts were read, an assembly at Bury St. Edmunds on 10 June, a meeting of Liverpool 'Constitutionalists' on 20 June, and a gathering at the Crystal Palace on 17 August—all these were further examples of opposition to the disestablishment of the Irish Church, though not necessarily to the reform of that Church.[226] The Church of Scotland differed from Scottish Dissenters, and to a lesser extent from Scottish Free Churchmen, in making a stand for the Irish Establishment. On 26 May the General Assembly resolved by a large majority to petition Parliament against Irish disestablishment. The Church of Scotland Presbytery of Edinburgh had declared against disestablishment, and the Synod of Merse and Teviotdale, meeting at Jedburgh on 14 April, had agreed—though only by the casting vote of the Moderator—to petition Parliament for the same object.[227] Some meetings against disestablishment were picturesque and some were rumbustious. At an Orange meeting held in the Hanover Square Rooms, London, on 23 June, the procession was headed by two Chelsea pensioners with drawn swords, and others in the procession carried Bibles on cushions; the chairman called for the formation of an Orange Association for women, 'for the purpose of promoting every anti-Papal, anti-Puseyite, and anti-infidel movement inaugurated in these countries'.[228] At a meeting in the Lecture Hall, Greenwich, on 29 April, a Baptist minister asked leave to move an amendment, but 'some of the persons who had got up the meeting immediately set upon [him], knocked him down, tore his coat to shreds, and hustled him out of the hall'.[229]

[224] Ibid.

[225] *The Times*, 3 Apr. 1868, p. 12; 18 Apr., p. 12; 28 Apr., p. 12.

[226] Ibid., 9 May 1868, p. 9; 19 May, p. 10; 10 June, p. 5; 12 June, p. 9; 22 June, p. 6; 18 Aug., p. 7.

[227] Ibid., 29 May 1868, p. 11; 16 Apr., p. 10. Minutes of Church of Scotland Presbytery of Edinburgh, CH2/121/26, p. 499 (29 Apr. 1868). For the views of United Presbyterians and Free Churchmen see *The Times*, 18 May 1868, p. 5; 19 June, p. 11; also Minutes of U.P. Presbyteries of Edinburgh, 7 Apr. 1868 (CH3/111/33, pp. 456–8) and Dundee, 21 Apr. 1868 (CH3/91/7), and Minutes of Free Church Presbytery of Edinburgh, 19 July 1868 (CH3/111/29, p. 178).

[228] *The Times*, 24 June 1868, p. 12.   [229] Ibid., 30 Apr. 1868.

But far worse violence than this occurred during the Irish Church controversy, as a result of the lectures and publications of William Murphy. After his successful agitation in the Midlands in 1867, Murphy turned his attention to the Lancashire industrial area with its large Irish immigrant population. There he proceeded to cause immense damage to property, human relations, even lives, in the most concentrated series of religious riots in nineteenth-century Britain. Murphy's sponsors were the Protestant Evangelical Mission and Electoral Union, among whose anti-popish objects (as stated in 1872) was the repeal of the Relief Act of 1829.[230] In the early months of 1868 Murphy and his followers caused disturbances at Bacup and Rochdale.[231] On 10 May, following his lectures, rioting broke out at Ashton-under-Lyne, where anti-Catholic eruptions had already occurred during the cotton famine. Protestant processions from Dukinfield, Stalybridge, and Ashton joined forces, and numerous houses in the Irish district of Ashton were attacked, together with two Catholic chapels and their schools. Order was at length restored by the magistrates, county police, and special constables. But on the evening of 11 May the rioters struck again. Houses in Reyner Row, an Irish locality, were sacked: 'The rioters met with little or no opposition . . . the window frames and doors were smashed to atoms, and the furniture and bedding were hurled into the street, where they were burnt. Tables, chairs, sofas, pictures, chimney-glasses, ornaments, carpets—all were thrown into one heterogeneous mass, and consumed by the flames.'[232] Far worse than this, an elderly woman was trampled to death. The magistrates summoned troops, the 6th. Enniskillen dragoons and two companies of the 70th. Foot. By 2 a.m. on 12 May everything was reported quiet, and a committee of the magistrates was appointed to take care of those injured in the riots. On the following night another Catholic chapel was attacked but the police prevented further damage, and an attempt to spread the riots to Stalybridge had little success.[233]

A day or two afterwards Murphy set up his 'Protestant tent' in an Irish district of Bury; a violent clash occurred, and eventually ended after the police had charged the combatants.[234] Oldham soon witnessed a similar connection between Murphy's lectures and violent upheaval. On the night of 25 May a crowd gathered to attack a Catholic chapel. On 26 May a crowd formed again in the evening, attacked more property, and stoned policemen and members of the Watch Committee. An 'Irish' body from Oldham, presumably in retaliation but perhaps lacking in political discernment, broke the windows of a Congregational and a Baptist chapel at Hollinwood. Special constables prevented another outbreak at Oldham on the evening of 27 May,

[230] H. J. Hanham, *Elections and Party Management : Politics in the time of Gladstone and Disraeli* (London, 1959), 306.
[231] Ibid. 304–5; Arnstein, op. cit. 59 ff.   [232] *Annual Register*, cx (1868), pt. II, Chronicle, 56.
[233] Ibid. cx (1868), pt. II, 57–8.   [234] *The Times*, 15 May 1868, p. 12.

but on the twenty-eighth some workers at Platt Brothers' ironworks were found making pike-heads.[235]

The climax of the Lancashire riots occurred at Manchester in September. Murphy had been arrested after arriving in the city, but had been released on bail. He then issued an address offering himself as a Protestant candidate at the forthcoming parliamentary election, and called an open-air 'election meeting' on 5 September. A crowd of five or six thousand gathered, and 'a formidable phalanx of Irishmen' made free with sticks and stones. Order was restored by about a hundred city police who made several arrests. Murphy then appeared on a waggon and addressed the multitude, to the obvious distaste of the Catholics. A resolution was passed that he was a fit and proper person to represent the Protestant interest in Parliament, and after three cheers for the Crown and Prince William of Orange, and three groans for Popery, Murphy was 'carried shoulder-high out of the reach of danger'.[236] He did not stand as a candidate, however, and took to addressing 'respectable' audiences indoors—where he was relatively inconspicuous and relatively safe until, in 1871, he was assaulted by Irish miners at Whitehaven and later died of his injuries.[237]

Murphy was strongly supported by ultra-Protestant Anglican clergy, some of whom denounced Gladstone all the more fiercely because of Murphy's inflammatory impetus.[238] The riots must have greatly increased the current tension, in which preparations were being made for a general election to decide the fate of Disraeli's Government and Gladstone's plan.

IV. THE 1868 ELECTION

The election campaign in 1868 was long and intense. The contest was antici-pated for about a year before it took place in November, and election speeches were being given as early as May.[239] Gladstone's Irish policy, and the reactions to this and to Fenianism, provided a heated background to the struggle; but other questions, differing between areas, were equally or more important. Cotton operatives in South-East Lancashire were drawn to Con-servatism through friction with the dominant Liberal manufacturing élite as much as through anti-Irish feeling or Murphy-mania;[240] though in Glad-stone's constituency of South-West Lancashire probably a more deeply rooted anti-Catholicism prevailed. Welsh rural electors who voted radical were actuated by traditional economic opposition to landlords (who were often non-resident) as much as by dislike of the established Church.[241] But

---

[235] Ibid., 29 May 1868, p. 5.

[236] *Annual Register*, cx (1868), pt. II, 116–18; Hanham, 307.

[237] Hanham, 306; Arnstein, 70.

[238] Letter of G. H. Whalley, M.P., in *The Times*, 29 May 1868, p. 5; Hanham, 307–8.

[239] e.g. *The Times*, 9 May 1868, p. 5.   [240] Hanham, 308.

[241] Cf. ibid. 176.

the Irish Church question was a unifying factor which affected every contest in some degree. In general it simplified political standpoints, for disagreements over the object of disestablishment were submerged in the immediate aim of carrying this reform.

The Liberal majority gained in the election owed a great deal to the votes of British Dissenters and Irish Catholics. The public speeches of Gladstone and other Liberals were paralleled by prodigious activity on the part of the Liberation Society. On 12 June 1868 the executive committee decided to issue a circular urging that as many friends of religious liberty as possible should register as electors, also that information be gathered from the constituencies and a list of possible candidates be drawn up.[242] Irish disestablishment, it was stated, should be the one and only point to be insisted on at the elections, all other matters of religious equality (even compulsory church-rate abolition, if it should not pass that session) being regarded as subordinate to it.[243] Concentration on Irish disestablishment enabled the Society to attain closer union than usual with the Liberal party. It was remarked, after the election, that the Society had not found it necessary as in previous contests to find suitable candidates or to obtain satisfactory pledges—'the energy of the Liberal Party, local or central, having sufficed for the supply of candidates, & the readiness of such candidates to support Mr. Gladstone's ecclesiastical policy having made any pressure on the part of the Society's supporters altogether needless'.[244]

Irish disestablishment had the ability thus to combine militant Voluntaries with the majority of the Liberal party. Once the cause had been gained, differences were liable to become prominent again: it was appreciated that most of the newly elected Liberal M.P.s did not support the Society's more extreme aims.[245] Despite this, the Society claimed that its contribution to the Liberal victory had been of the greatest importance, that it had done more than 'any other of the organisations which have been engaged in agitating for the abolition of the Irish Establishment', and that, 'essential as may be the leadership of the Liberal Party to accomplish Disestablishment in Ireland, that party has to a large extent still to rely on the Society and its supporters for those tuitional efforts which are needed to influence the minds, and the political action, of the masses of the population'. Certainly the Society had attempted much by speech and word: between December 1867 and November 1868 it had sponsored 515 lectures, many of them in places previously unvisited, and had distributed about 1,060,000 copies of publications. A total of £3,145 had been spent on the campaign since the end of 1867.[246]

The Society was gratified by the enlarged Liberal majority of 110 which was obtained in the elections. About 53 Protestant Dissenters were returned,

[242] Minutes of Liberation Society, v. 61–2.
[244] Ibid. 103 (4 Dec. 1868).
[246] Ibid. 103–4, 108.

[243] Ibid. 62.
[245] Ibid.

a larger number than ever before.[247] It was noted that about three-quarters of the Liberal majority was contributed by Ireland, Scotland, and Wales—'those parts of the kingdom', it was claimed, 'in which the [Irish Church] question was dealt with on its merits, rather than as affecting the stability of the English Establishment'.[248] This was rather a misleading assessment. Irish disestablishment was not considered purely 'on its merits' in Wales, where the future of the Anglican Establishment in that country was a related and fundamental concern. Nor was Irish disestablishment an abstract consideration in Scotland, where Voluntaries were interested in the linked question of overthrowing the established status of the Church of Scotland, and looked as though they would obtain (on account of the union negotiations) the support of most Free Churchmen for their ends. Conservative candidates in Scotland defended the Scottish and English Establishments as well as the Irish;[249] and the electoral division between Church of Scotland Ministers on the one hand, Dissenting and Free Church ministers on the other, was extremely clear-cut. In the Scottish university elections (the first time they were held) Church of Scotland ministers voted Conservative by the huge majority of 1,221 to 67, and Free Church and United Presbyterian ministers voted Liberal by 1,081 to 34.[250] Denominational divisions help to explain why only 8 of the 60 Scottish M.P.s returned were Conservatives.

In Wales, similarly, only 10 Conservatives were returned (out of the 33 members);[251] and the Liberation Society was particularly pleased with the Welsh results, which it ascribed 'in no small degree . . . to the Conferences & meetings held in the Principality at the instance of the Society'.[252] These meetings, the Society's assistance to Welsh radical associations formed in 1867 and 1868, and the recent franchise reform, had all contributed to the results. The questions of Irish disestablishment and disendowment (and of land and educational reform) were strikingly appropriate to the particular demands of Wales. Watkin Williams, the successful Liberal Anglican candidate for the Denbigh boroughs, had written on 25 May to Thomas Gee, the busy and effective radical organizer:

It strikes me that the time has now come when the Welsh people if they are only united & resolute have an opportunity of carrying out for Wales the same measure of religious equality which Gladstone has proposed for Ireland . . . The Welsh ought to strike while the iron is hot . . . I mean to insist upon the right of the Welsh to be relieved of the anomaly of the endowment & establishment amongst them of the Established Church of England . . .[253]

[247] List of 'Dissenting members of the House of Commons', 1869 (Gladstone Papers, 44612, fos. 138–9). But cf. Miall, *Life of Miall*, 263–4.
[248] Minutes of Liberation Society, v. 106.   [249] The *Scotsman*, 10 Aug. 1868, p. 1.
[250] Figures quoted in Vincent, *Formation of the Liberal Party*, 49.
[251] K. O. Morgan, *Wales in British Politics*, 25.
[252] Minutes of Liberation Society, v. 106 (4 Dec. 1868).
[253] Thomas Gee Papers, 8309D, fo. 378.

Gee, no doubt thinking of the diverse reactions of Liberals to the disestablishment of Anglicanism in Wales, advised him to be cautious. The advice was taken, though Williams repeated in July his promise 'to promote liberal measures & in particular to bring about thorough religious equality throughout the whole kingdom'.[254] In addition to Williams's return, Evan M. Richards, a Baptist (though rather reticent on disestablishment) was returned for Cardiganshire;[255] and the electorate of Merthyr Tydfil, now ten times its former size, returned a leading Voluntary and workers' champion, Henry Richard.[256] These victories were important as a precedent. But, in spite of Lloyd George's claim that they 'woke the spirit of the mountains', this Nonconformist spirit (if such it was) remained to be stirred much more effectively in the future.[257] Dissenting ambitions still had to contend with powerful landlord opposition, including that of Liberals as well as Tories.[258] Undeterred by radical threats, Welsh landlords carried out more evictions after the elections—though this in turn spurred further radical action and the demand for the secret ballot.[259]

The Liberation Society had decided to leave the Irish elections to take care of themselves;[260] and Irish Catholicism fulfilled the hopes placed in it by gaining some seats for the Liberal party, to which it was temporarily wedded once more through the disestablishment policy. Manning told Gladstone that the only Catholics who had voted Conservative were those who feared Liberal educational policy.[261] The Catholic bishops became electioneering agents, working hard to find suitable candidates and urging electors to vote Liberal. After the elections some bishops and clergy were found guilty of having exerted undue influence. At Drogheda a Catholic mob led by a priest had stoned electors who would not vote for the right candidate.[262] Sir George Bowyer, a Catholic who had supported the Government, lost the seat at Dundalk which he had held since 1852. 'Gladstone & Bright sent a joint

---

[254] Watkin Williams to Gee, 4 July 1868 (ibid., fo. 385). For the Denbigh Boroughs and Denbighshire elections, see Jane Morgan, 'Denbighshire's *Annus Mirabilis*: the Borough and County Elections of 1868', *Welsh HR* vii. 1 (1974), 63–87.

[255] See I. G. Jones, 'Cardiganshire Politics in the Mid-Nineteenth Century', 29 ff.; also Henry Richard to Thomas Gee, 25 Aug. 1868 (Gee Papers, 8308D, fo. 296); Henry Richard to John Matthews, 22 Aug. 1868 (Matthews Papers, 8231E, fo. 69); E. M. Richards to John Matthews, 17 Aug. to 30 Nov. 1868 (ibid., fos. 72–82).

[256] On this election see I. G. Jones, 'The Merthyr of Henry Richard', in G. Williams (ed.), *Merthyr Politics* (Cardiff, 1966), 31–55; I. G. Jones, 'Dr. Thomas Price and the Election of 1868 in Merthyr Tydfil: a Study in Nonconformist Politics', pts. 1 and 2, *Welsh HR* ii. 2 (1964), 147–72, ii. 3 (1965), 251–70; Henry Richard to Thomas Gee, 25 Aug. 1868 (Gee Papers, 8308D, fo. 296).

[257] K. O. Morgan, op. cit. 22.

[258] H. R. Davies to Thomas Gee, 1 July 1868 (Gee Papers, 8310D, fo. 431).

[259] K. O. Morgan, 25–7.

[260] Minutes of Liberation Society, v. 80 (7 Aug. 1868).

[261] Manning to Gladstone, 24 Nov. 1868 (Gladstone Papers, 44249, fos. 68–9). The *Tablet* condemned this educational policy and stressed the political independence of Catholics; 7 Nov. 1868, p. 2.

[262] See Norman, 347–50.

letter *denouncing* me', he told Disraeli, 'and they used *every* influence against me.' Archbishop Kieran had 'allowed his curates to canvass' against Bowyer, and had resisted Cullen's appeals for leniency.[263] The moderate Bishop Moriarty of Kerry illustrated the current 'union of hearts' between Gladstone and the Catholics when he wrote to Bowyer after the election:

> The Dundalk election gave me *pain* . . . [but] I blamed you somewhat. The nation is making a great and exceptional effort to reverse the policy of three centuries.
>
> We are all, myself among the number, called upon, for the public good, to hide our individual views and party predilections, and to unite for the carrying of a great measure under the leadership of one man. No statesman before Gladstone ever acknowledged the rights of Ireland. You should have, in the present circumstances, joined his standard. Our people are persuaded that you are a D' Israelite. With that conviction it would be impossible to return any man—even the Pope himself—for a Liberal Irish constituency.[264]

Dundalk was only one of several northern Irish boroughs where the Conservatives lost seats, and it was clear that many Presbyterians had voted the same way as the Catholics.[265] In Ireland as a whole there were 10 Liberal gains, resulting in 65 Liberal and 40 Conservative seats.

Anti-Catholic feeling was more obvious in Lancashire than in Ulster. Gladstone's Irish policy had helped to turn Lancashire over to Disraeli. In the industrial south-east of the county, which was stirred by Murphy and distracted by conflicts of interest between employer and worker and between Liberal and Liberal, 8 Conservatives and 7 Liberals were returned in 1868, whereas 11 Liberals and only 1 Conservative had been returned in 1865.[266] At Blackburn, which returned two Conservatives as in 1865, Murphy-like rioting began on 30 October, as a result of municipal elections which coincided with the general election campaign. Two meetings of rival municipal candidates were held in the Nova Scotia district in the town, and the rival audiences, the worse for drink supplied by the candidates, collided in the streets afterwards. A moonlit riot took place, involving several hundred persons. The 'Tory' mob broke all the windows of the Ivy Inn, where the Liberal candidates had their committee rooms, and performed a similar service at St. Mary's Catholic church. The Liberal supporters retaliated by attacking an inn where the Conservatives met. On the following day troops arrived from Preston to protect the municipal polling booths, and a hundred special constables were engaged. Much fighting occurred none the less, involving a thousand persons, and voting was interrupted for hours at a stretch until the police and military at length succeeded in restoring order.[267]

---

[263] Bowyer to Disraeli, 25 Nov. 1868 (Disraeli Papers, B/XXI/B/717).

[264] Moriarty to Bowyer, 4 Dec. 1868; encl. in Bowyer to Disraeli, 7 Dec. 1868 (ibid. B/XXI/B/719).

[265] Norman, op. cit. 351.   [266] Hanham, 308-13.

[267] *Annual Register*, cx (1868), 135-6. Cf. J. C. Lowe, 'The Tory Triumph of 1868 in Blackburn and in Lancashire', *Hist. Jl.* xvi (1973), 742-3.

During the general election outbreaks of rioting occurred at other places, including Wakefield and Ladybank in Fife.[268]

Gladstone himself could scarcely have stood in a more unsuitable constituency than South-West Lancashire. A virtuoso popular speech-maker, he preached impressively to the converted in the country as a whole, but there was a comparatively low proportion of these in South-West Lancashire. The support of Dissenters would have been his, regardless of Irish disestablishment, and this cause transferred Catholic support from Conservative to Liberal. Most Catholic landowners in the constituency gave their influence to the Liberal side, though some (such as Lady Scarisbrick) needed delicate persuasion before they would leave their Conservative allegiance.[269] Whigs in the constituency (as elsewhere) were extremely apprehensive about Gladstone's Irish policy.[270] This was notably the case with the earl of Sefton, a powerful landowner. Sefton was only persuaded to continue giving to the Liberals his influence and money (eventually he gave £2,000) by the fact that his moderate cousin H. R. Grenfell stood as Gladstone's fellow candidate.[271] But Orange feeling, very strong in an area which was adjacent to Liverpool, defeated Gladstone and Grenfell at the poll. The Manchester cathedral bells were rung in celebration. Gladstone, who had been compelled to change his seat only three years before, now had to transfer his attentions once again. Fortunately, the borough of Greenwich had already returned him. Newman Hall assured him that he would be regarded as 'the Representative . . . of the whole of the United Kingdom', and asked him to come for another evening.[272]

Gladstone's firm alliance with Liberal Nonconformity during the elections was shown both by Liberation Society propaganda and the encouraging letters he received from Newman Hall and Henry Allon.[273] The Conservatives, on the other hand, looked to churchmen for support, and this could be a tricky matter because of Church divisions. In August a letter had reached Disraeli's eyes, complaining that Conservatives were neglecting the clergy: it would be 'so much positive strength deducted from the Conservative cause', it was said, unless the clergy were given political reward and encouragement.[274] Soon afterwards Disraeli heard that McNeile's appointment would 'induce many of our Conservative Clergy to take an active part in the elections'.[275] But the hazards of thus pleasing one clerical party and not another were revealed in a letter from a Conservative agent to Montagu Corry, Disraeli's private secretary, about the South Derbyshire election.

---

[268] The *Scotsman*, 19 Nov. 1868, p. 6; 21 Nov. 1868, p. 2; 27 Nov. 1868, p. 6.

[269] P. Searby, 'Gladstone in West Derby Hundred: the Liberal Campaign in South-West Lancashire in 1868', *Transactions of the Historic Society of Lancashire and Cheshire*, cxi (1960), 151–2.

[270] Southgate, op. cit. 332–3, 341–2.   [271] Searby, op. cit. 148–51.

[272] Hall to Gladstone, 25 Nov. 1868 (Gladstone Papers, 44188, fos. 87–8).

[273] e.g. Allon to Gladstone, 25 Nov. 1868 (ibid. 44095, fos. 317–18).

[274] R. Gregory to W. H. Cooke, 11 Aug. 1868 (Disraeli Papers, B/IX/G/12b).

[275] G. Mee to Disraeli, 29 Aug. 1868 (ibid. C/III/a/48y).

The dean of Lichfield, the diocese in which the constituency lay, had died, and it was suggested that Disraeli should delay appointing a successor until after the contest:

The High Church party lay & clerical who are all Conservatives here, have for the good of the cause consented to support Mr. Rowland Smith [the successful Conservative candidate] who is a remarkably Low Church Puritan . . . and if they fancy that the Government are likely to promote Low Churchmen like Dr. McNeile, they will become lukewarm, & leave the cause to take care of itself. This consideration would also affect their votes in the University election. On the other hand a very High Church appointment might alienate a few ultra-Protestants . . . when talking it over in Committee yesterday we agreed that it was rather unfortunate that the Dean had not lived a week or two longer.[276]

The same correspondent reported an exception, at Derby, to the clerical alignment against Irish disestablishment. This exception was 'a very clever & leading Evangelical Clergyman, always a great Radical, who is now lecturing & writing against the Irish Church. He is Vicar of St. Werburgh's Derby, a Lord Chancellor's living, and I heartily wish he might be promoted to some out of the way country living where he can do less harm than in a large town . . . A good sound Conservative Clergyman would be invaluable to the cause here.'[277] Another exception was 'A Protestant Churchman'. In a pamphlet entitled *A Protest for Protestant Electors* this author advanced an old argument, put forward by Chalmers in defence of Catholic Emancipation in 1829, that Protestantism did not need legal privilege to help it: 'we protest . . . that it is an insult to the Protestant Episcopal Church in Ireland, to suppose that it must perish if the aid and patronage of the State is withdrawn'.[278]

Among Conservative politicians Lord Stanley was an independent spirit who refused to follow Disraeli into the rigid opposition to Irish disestablishment and disendowment which the Premier had been compelled, probably against his personal inclination, to adopt. On 23 September Stanley criticized Disraeli's election address because it seemed 'not in express words, but by implication, to reject absolutely the idea of any compromise as regards the revenues [of the Church of Ireland] . . . My view is, and long has been, that a compromise ought to be effected as to the endowments...'[279] On the following day he wrote more bluntly: 'Does any man suppose, who has considered the matter at all, that it is possible to save the whole of the endowments, or to maintain the thing as it stands?'[280] He claimed that as many as two-thirds of the Conservative party favoured a compromise,[281] and a few days later he

[276] John Borough to Montagu Corry, 10 Oct. 1868 (ibid. B/IX/G/19).
[277] Borough to Corry, 4 Nov. 1868 (ibid. G/55).
[278] *A Protest for Protestant Electors*, by Esse Quam Videri ('A Protestant Churchman') (London, 1868), 6.
[279] Stanley to Disraeli, 23 Sept. 1868 (Disraeli Papers, B/XX/S/817).
[280] Stanley to Disraeli, 24 Sept. 1868 (ibid. 818).
[281] Ibid.

wrote expressing his regret that Disraeli thought compromise impossible.[282] Derby was apprehensive about what his son would say to his constituents at King's Lynn, fearing that he 'might throw such a shell in the Conservative ranks as to be fatal to the existence of the Government'.[283] But he noted thankfully on 14 November that Stanley had been cautious;[284] he had said that, while the Irish Church contained 'indefensible anomalies', it should be reformed rather than destroyed.[285]

On 7 December Sir George Bowyer also wrote two letters to Disraeli about the desirability of compromise, in order to 'take the wind out of Gladstone's sails'. He suggested that the Protestants might be induced to make 'a handsome offer', and that he himself would attempt to influence the Catholic bishops.[286] But this was unrealistic, given the stance which Disraeli had taken up, and could now do nothing to keep him in power. Disraeli had resigned before meeting Parliament, and Gladstone had already, on 1 December, received the Queen's commission to form a Government. The way had been cleared for the most radical act of ecclesiastical policy for two hundred years.

[282] Stanley to Disraeli, 29 Sept. 1868 (ibid. 824).
[283] Derby to Disraeli, 29 Oct. 1868 (ibid. 502).
[284] Derby to Disraeli, 14 Nov. 1868 (ibid. 504).
[285] *The Times*, 18 Nov. 1868, p. 7 (address of Stanley).
[286] Bowyer to Disraeli, 7 Dec. 1868 (first letter) (Disraeli Papers, B/XXI/B/719).

CHAPTER XI

Conclusion: The Opening of an Era?

THE PERIOD studied in this book witnesses the extension of religious plurality in a non-authoritarian society, and the natural strains and problems to which this gave rise. Traditional religious beliefs, forms of worship and of Church government had been under criticism and challenge in Europe since the sixteenth century and before. Differences which, before the Reformation, had existed within one of the Church's two branches, had since that time formed the ground of separation between numerous Churches, which might proceed to disintegrate in turn or to survive through compromise. In Great Britain the growth of Churches outside the Establishments was not very pronounced before the end of the eighteenth century, but since then the growth of population had coincided with the expansion of non-established denominations. Protestant Nonconformity grew prodigiously, and Irish immigration brought Roman Catholic expansion.

Sixteenth-century English Governments had aimed to create a 'single-Church' State, but the persistence of Catholicism and the appearance of Protestant Dissent had weakened this hope. Toleration had partially triumphed by revolution in 1688. The Toleration Act of 1689 and the Scottish Church settlement of 1690 had each shown a diversified approach, though this stopped short of tolerance to Catholics until many years later. The comparative tolerance and liberalism of the mid-nineteenth century, in which reactionary attitudes clearly existed but had little substantive effect, amounted to a reversal of the idea of a one-Church State. Besides the many acts of ecclesiastical concession in this period, constitutional restrictions limiting the political action of Dissenters (among others) were relaxed by two major pieces of parliamentary reform. Thus, both directly and indirectly, by deliberate acts of policy, the privileged Establishment was being rejected.

The political problems of religion in the period were questions of liberty posed by the growth of non-established religion, and questions of control within the established Churches themselves. Dissenters had moved from a quiet but major victory regarding civil equality in 1828 to other demands for civil and educational equality, extending to a demand that established Churches should be sacrificed. Roman Catholics similarly demanded concessions in Ireland, including disestablishment of the Irish Church, and on the latter question Catholic and Dissenting interests coincided. These claims were supported by pressure groups such as the Liberation Society and the

National Association of Ireland. Governments made discriminating concessions in accordance with a generally liberal approach to rule and a concomitant desire to retain Establishments. This approach was common, in
differing degrees, to both parties, despite the ultra element among the Conservatives and the radical Dissenting element among the Liberals. Given the
dual nature of Government policy, it was not surprising that concessions
were granted more readily to those with political force to back up their
demands—namely, Roman Catholics and Dissenters. Others—Jews,
Tractarians, declared unbelievers—obtained their relief more tardily, in the
case of Tractarians only after positive attempts had been made to restrict
them.

The winning of civil equality was one outcome of religious diversity. On
account of the dissipation of resources among a host of competing religious
bodies, and the obvious failure of these resources to reach the entire nation,
this diversity also contributed to the growth of social provision and control
by the secular State. Governments extended their control not only over
purely secular matters such as public health and factory labour, but over
matters which had been (or were partly still) under religious surveillance—
poor relief, education, marriage. Retreating from the control of religion itself,
Governments were encroaching on some of religion's spheres. *Laissez-faire* in
one sphere was paralleled by increasing State intervention in others.

Growing State control in matters of Church interest produced conflict
with strict churchmen, particularly since the Legislature was becoming
more and more diverse in religious composition. Before 1829 there had been
only the occasional Dissenting M.P., but Catholic emancipation had opened
the way to a much larger group of members who did not belong to the established Churches, and the number of protestant Dissenting M.P.s gradually
increased after 1832. The concern of Catholic and Dissenting M.P.s with
their own ecclesiastical interests and with reform of the Establishment produced natural reactions in the form of high-church and ultra-Protestant
movements in the Church of England and Chalmers's Non-Instrusionist
movement in the Church of Scotland. The Tractarians were opposed to the
maintenance of Erastian control by an untrustworthy heterodox Legislature,
and sought greater self-government by the Church. In particular they reacted
against religious decisions which were made by a lay judicial body created by
the State, and disliked the fact that such a body could make religious decisions
at all. Demanding liberty for themselves from the Legislature, some high
churchmen were led into coincidental alliance with Nonconformists and
Roman Catholics whom the Tractarian movement had been formed to
resist. This was one example of the difference which appeared between
political and theological lines of division when similar political aims might
assist different forms of religion. High churchmen might even support disestablishment. Gladstone's ecclesiastical liberalism was a product of his high

churchmanship as well as of his political development. His faith in a self-governing Church, together with his political understanding with Nonconformity, gave him a certain sympathy with Voluntaryism, though his regard for the English Establishment made it unlikely that he would advance the Voluntary case very positively in England. In March 1869 he wrote to Matthew Arnold (paradoxically acknowledging a copy of *Culture and Anarchy* with its aspersions on Nonconformists):

... I am one of those who think that when we pass away fr[om] the present Church Est[ablishments], they will be succeeded, not by a new fashion of the like species, but by what is termed the Voluntary system. I can contemplate this result with[out] great uneasiness; not because I think it absolutely good, but because it may be the best & safest of the alternatives before us, as the most likely to keep in a state of freshness the heart & conscience of man.[1]

By the end of 1868 the forces of religious liberalism seemed to be moving relentlessly from one triumph to the next. As well as political concession there was growing intellectual latitude which questioned traditional beliefs and was apparently condoned by the State. After German biblical criticism had come geological explanations of the world and evolutionary explanations of man, culminating in the hotly debated Darwinism of the 1860s. Such intellectual questioning influenced Christianity in general without discriminating between denominations. Nor did the bounds of 'intellectual liberty' coincide with those of 'religious liberty'. Roman Catholics usually resisted the former but, in the United Kingdom, claimed the same political equality as other non-established groups.

The main threat to Church Establishments still came from Nonconformity rather than from the broad, exterior questioning of faith. The spectre of general disestablishment, not that of general loss of faith, loomed in 1868–9. Protestant Dissent had lost most of its practical grievances, notably the major one of church-rates, and was united with Catholics to bring about the disestablishment of an important branch of the Anglican Church. Would this lead to renewed assaults on Establishment in England, Wales, and Scotland, with the connivance or acquiescence of concessionary Governments? Practical persons were not lulled by protestations such as Miall's at the Bradford election in 1868, that general disestablishment 'is not one of those practical questions in the solution of which the next Parliament will be engaged'.[2] Miall himself brought in motions for disestablishment in 1871, 1872, and 1873. Clarendon, writing to Russell in November 1868, hazarded that the English Church Establishment would 'perhaps last till the end of the century'.[3]

---

[1] Gladstone to Arnold, 30 Mar. 1869 (copy in Letter-book, Gladstone Papers, Add. MS. 44536, p. 274).
[2] Miall, *Life of Miall*, 286.
[3] Sir H. Maxwell, *Life and Letters of ... fourth earl of Clarendon* (2 vols., London, 1913), ii. 351.

It remained to be seen, however, whether the other established Churches would suffer the fate of the Irish. Would Gladstone's removal of 'points of sore contact' have a reverse effect by strengthening the English Establishment, or would he move further towards general disestablishment in order to please his radical, Dissenting followers? Gladstone's decision on the Irish Church in 1868, and the subsequent carrying of his policy, might remain an isolated episode or might lead to similar developments in Great Britain. The powerful trends of the period could not be contained within it. How much influence would they have beyond it?

Appendix

CONTRASTS IN CHURCH ATTENDANCE, 1851: BATH AND
STOCKPORT
(from Religious Census, P.P.1852–3, lxxxix, pp. cclii and cclxix)

BATH (population 53 240)

	Attendances		
	Morning	Afternoon	Evening
Church of England	13 704	3974	8737
Independents	1440	——	1206
Particular Baptists	1288	100	1645
Friends	47	——	21
Unitarians	175	——	120
Moravians	390	——	200
Wesleyans	886	85	982
Primitive Methodists	437	——	530
Wesleyan Association	95	——	89
Wesleyan Reformers	770	70	556
Lady Huntingdon's Connection	500	60	930
New Church	150	——	——
Brethren	30	——	12
Isolated congregations	1050	——	500
Roman Catholics	645	580	170
Catholic and Apostolic Church	110	96	——
Latter Day Saints (Mormons)	70	120	250
Jews	15	29	28
TOTALS	21 802	5114	15 876

STOCKPORT (population 53 835)

Church of England	4010	1920	3270
Independents	1598	——	1716
Particular Baptists	349	——	405
General Baptists, New Connection	30	——	40
Unitarians	250	——	150
Wesleyans	2600	110	2201
Methodist New Connection	640	——	672
Primitive Methodists	253	137	420
Wesleyan Association	250	——	120
Independent Methodists	50	30	175
Isolated congregations	——	——	173
Roman Catholics	2000	——	——
Latter Day Saints	80	140	160
TOTALS	12 110	2337	9502

Bibliography

I MANUSCRIPTS

Aberdeen Papers, British Library Add. MSS. 43039–358.

Baptismal Registers, Public Record Office, R.G.4 (selected):

  Kingston-upon-Hull: Fish Street Independent Chapel (3388); Mill Street Primitive Methodist Chapel, 1823–37 (3713);

  Liverpool: Byron Street Baptist Chapel, 1783–1837 (1479); Great George Street Independent Chapel (1478);

  Manchester: Grosvenor Street Independent Chapel (2693); St. George's Road (Oxford Street) Baptist Chapel (2692);

  Merthyr Tydfil: Bethel Baptist Chapel, Georgetown (3499); Pennsylvania (or Pontmorlais) Calvinistic Methodist Chapel (3888);

  Stockport: Hillgate Tabernacle (Independent), 1801–36 (420).

Bishop Samuel Wilberforce Papers, Bodleian Library.

Bright Papers, British Library Add. MSS. 43383–92.

Brougham Papers, University College London.

Broughton Papers, British Library Add. MSS. 36467–72.

Bunting Letters, Methodist Church Archives, London.

Cairns Papers, Public Record Office, 30/51.

Chalmers Papers, New College, Edinburgh.

Churton Papers, Pusey House, Oxford.

Clarendon Papers, Bodleian Library.

Clerk of Penicuik Papers, Scottish Record Office, Edinburgh, GD 18.

Cobden Papers, British Library Add. MSS. 43647–78.

Dalhousie Papers, Scottish Record Office, GD 45/14.

Derby Papers, Knowsley, Merseyside.

Disraeli Papers, Hughenden Manor, Buckinghamshire (National Trust).

Ellice Papers, National Library of Scotland, Edinburgh.

Fitzwilliam Papers, City Library, Sheffield.

George Hadfield: MS. 'Personal narrative', 1860, Central Library, Manchester (Archives Dept.).

George Melly Papers, Liverpool Local History Library.

Gladstone Papers, British Library Add. MSS. 44086–835.

Goulburn Papers, Surrey County Record Office, Kingston-upon-Thames.

Graham Papers, on microfilm at Bodleian Library, MS. Films 107–50.
Gresley Papers, Pusey House.
Grey of Howick Papers, Durham University.
Hatherton Papers, Staffordshire Record Office.
Henry Richard Papers, National Library of Wales, Aberystwyth, MSS. 5503–5B.
Holland House Papers, British Library Add. MSS. 51520–957 (nos. provisional)
J. B. Smith Papers, Central Library, Manchester (Archives Dept.).
Keble Papers, Keble College, Oxford.
Keble–Newman Letters, Pusey House.
Liddon Papers, Keble College.
Lists of Members of Fish Street Independent Chapel, Hull (Local History Library, Hull, Nos. 14 and 15).
Matthews Papers, National Library of Wales, MSS. 8321–6E.
Minto Papers, National Library of Scotland.
Minutes of Liberation Society (executive committee), Greater London Record Office, County Hall, London.
Minutes of Dundee Town Council, District Council Offices, Dundee.
Minutes of Church of Scotland Presbytery of Dundee, Scottish Record Office, CH2/103.
Minutes of United Presbyterian Presbytery of Dundee, S.R.O., CH3/91.
Minutes of Church of Scotland Presbytery of Edinburgh, S.R.O., CH2/121.
Minutes of Free Church of Scotland Presbytery of Edinburgh, S.R.O., CH3/111.
Minutes of United Presbyterian Presbytery of Edinburgh, S.R.O., CH3/111.
Minutes of Church of Scotland Presbytery of Glasgow, S.R.O., CH2/171.
Minutes of Free Church of Scotland Presbytery of Glasgow, S.R.O., CH3/146.
Minutes of United Presbyterian Presbytery of Glasgow, S.R.O., CH3/146.
Minutes of Protestant Dissenting Deputies, Guildhall, London.
Parliamentary Election Documents (miscellaneous), National Library of Wales.
Peel Papers, British Library Add. MSS. 40181–617.
Pusey Papers, Pusey House.
Records of Consistory Court, Diocese of St. David's, National Library of Wales, SD/CCCm/539–42.
Russell Papers, Public Record Office, 30/22.
Rutherfurd Papers, National Library of Scotland.
Salisbury Papers, Christ Church, Oxford.
Selborne Papers, Lambeth Palace, London.
Thomas Gee Papers, National Library of Wales MSS. 8305–19E.
Wharncliffe Papers, City Library, Sheffield.
Wiseman Papers, Archbishop's House, Westminster.

II NEWSPAPERS AND PERIODICALS

Anti-Patronage Reporter (originally *Church Patronage Reporter*; Scottish)
Blackwood's Edinburgh Magazine
British Critic
British Quarterly Review
Bulwark, or Reformation Journal

Caledonian Mercury
Catholic Institute Magazine (Liverpool)
Catholic Vindicator.
Chronicle of Convocation of Canterbury
Church Institution Circular
Church Patronage Reporter, 1829–32 (later *Anti-Patronage Reporter*, 1833–4;
    Scottish)
Congregational Magazine
Contemporary Review
Daily Scotsman
Dissenter (Perth)
Dundee Courier
Dundee, Perth and Cupar Advertiser
Eclectic Review
Edinburgh Evening Courant
Edinburgh Review
Guardian
Jewish Chronicle and Hebrew Observer
Journal of Convocation
Leeds Mercury
Liverpool Courier
Liverpool Mercury
Manchester Guardian
Monthly Repository
Nonconformist
Nonconformist Elector (1847)
North British Review
Northern Star
Patriot
Penny Protestant Operative
Primitive Methodist Magazine
Protestant Elector (1847)
Protestant Magazine
Protestant Sentinel (Liverpool, 1841–2)
Quarterly Review
Record
Saturday Review
Scotsman
Scottish Protestant
Tablet
The Times
United Methodist Free Churches Magazine
United Presbyterian Magazine
Voluntary Church Magazine (Glasgow)
Watchman
Weekly Scotsman
Witness

III PARLIAMENTARY DEBATES AND PAPERS

Hansard's *Parliamentary Debates*, 3rd Ser., vols. xiv–cxciii.

Mirror of Parliament, 1831–41.

Report of Select Committee of House of Commons on the Law of Church Patronage in Scotland; 1834 (512), v. 1.

Report of Select Committee of House of Commons on Orange Institutions in Great Britain and the Colonies; 1835 (605), xvii. 1.

Report of Select Committee of House of Commons on Church Rates; 1851 (541), ix. 1.

Report of Select Committee of House of Commons on the Annuity Tax (Edinburgh); 1851 (617), vii. 1.

Report of Religious Census of 1851 for England and Wales, ed. H. Mann; 1852–3 (1969), lxxxix. 1.

Report of Her Majesty's Commissioners on Maynooth College:
Part I. Report and Appendix, 1854–5 (1896), xxii. 1;
Part II. Minutes of Evidence, 1854–5 (1896–I), xxii. 355.

Report of Select Committee of House of Lords on Church Rates; 1859 (179. Sess. 2), v. 15.

Report of Select Committee of House of Lords on Church Rates; 1860 (154), xxii. 159.

Report of Select Committee of House of Commons on Jewish Relief Act; 1859 (205. Sess. 1), iii. 35.

Report of Select Committee of House of Commons on the Edinburgh Annuity Tax Abolition Act (1860) and Canongate Annuity Tax Act; 1866 (379), viii.1.

IV REFERENCE WORKS

Annual Register.

Baptist Hand-Book.

BOASE, F., *Modern English Biography* (6 vols., London, 1965).

Cartoons from 'Punch' (4 vols., London, 1906).

Congregational Year Book.

Crockford's Clerical Directory.

DAWSON, J. H. (ed.), *Abridged Statistical History of Scotland* (2nd edn., Edinburgh, 1857).

Dictionary of National Biography.

Fasti Ecclesiae Scoticanae.

Journals of the House of Commons, vols. lxxxvii–cxxiii.

McCalmont's Parliamentary Poll-Book, 1832–1918, ed. J. Vincent and M. Stenton (Brighton, 1971).

MULHALL, M. G., *The Dictionary of Statistics* (4th edn., London, 1899).

OLLARD, S. L., CROSSE, G., and BOND, M. F. (eds.), *A Dictionary of English Church History* (3rd edn., London, 1948).

SMALL, R. (ed.), *History of the Congregations of the United Presbyterian Church, 1733–1900* (2 vols., Edinburgh, 1904).

STOCKS, J. E., *A Chronological List of reports of Committees of both Houses of the Convocation of Canterbury, 1847–1921* (1921).

The New Statistical Account of Scotland (15 vols., Edinburgh, 1845).
The Oxford Dictionary of the Christian Church (2nd edn.), ed. F. L. Cross and E. A. Livingstone (London, 1974).
WILKIE, T., *The Representation of Scotland* (Paisley, 1895).
WILLIAMS, W. R., *Parliamentary History of Wales, 1541–1895* (Brecknock, 1895).

V. CONTEMPORARY BOOKS, PAMPHLETS AND POLL-BOOKS
(Place of publication is London unless otherwise stated; anonymous
pamphlets are listed under titles)

A Churchman's Notes on Lord John Russell's Reply to the Bishops (1847).
Acts of the General Assembly of the Church of Scotland, 1638–1842 (Edinburgh, 1843).
Address of the Scottish Reformation Society to the Electors of Scotland (Edinburgh, 1852).
Address to the Protestants of the Empire, issued by National Club, 12 Mar. 1851 (1851).
A Dialogue between a Voluntary and a Churchman (Dundee, 1836).
A full Report of the Speeches against Patronage in the Church of Scotland, delivered at the public meetings held in Glasgow and Edinburgh, 14 Nov. and 2 Dec. 1833 (Glasgow, 1833).
ALEXANDER, W. L., *Memoirs of the Life and Writings of Ralph Wardlaw, D.D.* (Edinburgh, 1856).
A Protest for Protestant Electors, by Esse Quam Videri ('A Protestant Churchman') (1868).
A Report of the Proceedings and Speeches at the Voluntary Church meeting held at Jedburgh on 27 May 1835 (Jedburgh, 1835).
ARNOLD, M., *Culture and Anarchy*, ed. R. H. Super (Ann Arbor, 1965).
ARNOLD, T., *Principles of Church Reform* (1833), ed. M. J. Jackson and J. Rogan (1962).
Authentic Report of the Great Protestant Meeting at Liverpool, 29 Oct. 1835 (Liverpool, 1835).

BAINES, E., jun., *The Social, Educational and Religious State of the Manufacturing Districts* (1843).
——*Letters to the Rt. Hon. Lord John Russell ... on State Education* (1846).
—— *Education best promoted by Perfect Freedom* (Leeds, 1854).
—— *The Life of Edward Baines* (2nd edn., 1859).
BALLANTYNE, J., *A Comparison of Established and Dissenting Churches* (Edinburgh, 1824).
BENNETT, W. J. E., *The Parish Priest and the Prime Minister* (1851).
—— *Why Church Rates should be abolished* (1861).
BIBER, G. E., *Bishop Blomfield and his Times* (1857).
BINNEY, T., *The Ultimate Object of Evangelical Dissenters avowed and advocated* (1834).
—— *Dissent not Schism* (1835).
—— *The Dissenters and the Papacy* (1850).

BLACKBURN, J., *The Three Conferences held by the Opponents of the Maynooth Endowment Bill* (1845).

BLOMFIELD, A., *A Memoir of C. J. Blomfield, Bishop of London* (2 vols., 1863).

BOWYER, Sir G., *The Private History of the Creation of the Catholic Hierarchy* (1868).

BRAITHWAITE, J. B., *Memoirs of Joseph John Gurney* (2 vols., Norwich, 1854).

BRICKNELL, W. S., *The Judgement of the Bishops upon Tractarian Theology* (Oxford, 1845).

BRIDGES, J., *An Appeal to all Classes on the subject of Church Patronage in Scotland* (Glasgow, 1824).

BRODRICK, G. C. and FREMANTLE, W. H., *A Collection of the Judgements of the Judicial Committee of the Privy Council in Ecclesiastical Cases* (1865).

BROWN, C. J., *Church Establishments defended, with special reference to the Church of Scotland* (Glasgow, 1833).

BROWN, T. KENWORTHY, *The Madeira Chaplaincy treated of . . . in a letter addressed to the Rev. R. T. Lowe* (1848).

BRYCE, J., *Ten Years of the Church of Scotland* (2 vols., Edinburgh, 1850).

BUCHANAN, R., *The Ten Years' Conflict* (2 vols., Glasgow, 1849).

BURKE, EDMUND, *Works and Correspondence* (8 vols., 1852).

BURNET, JOHN, *The Church of England and the Church of Christ* (1840).

BURTON, E., *Thoughts on the Separation of Church and State* (1834).

CAMPDEN, VISCOUNT, *The British Chaplaincy in Madeira* (1847).

CARLILE, R., *Church Reform : the only means to that end, stated in a letter to Sir Robert Peel* (1835).

Catholic Young Men's Society of G.B., *Report of Second General Conference, in Catholic Club, Liverpool, 13 Oct. 1861* (Liverpool, 1862).

CHADWICK, E., *Report on the Sanitary Condition of the Labouring Population, 1842,* ed. M. W. Flinn (Edinburgh, 1965).

CHALMERS, T., *Lectures on the Establishment and Extension of National Churches* (Glasgow, 1838).

CHURTON, E., *Memoir of Joshua Watson* (2 vols., 1863).

CLIFFORD, J. B., *The Dissenters, the Liberation Society and the Church of England* (Bristol Church Defence Association Tracts, n.d.).

COBBETT, W., *Legacy to Parsons* (1947; original edn., 1835).

COCKBURN, HENRY, LORD, *Memorials of his Time* (Edinburgh, 1856).

—— *Journal,* ed. T. Cleghorn (2 vols., Edinburgh, 1874).

COLERIDGE, S. T., *On the Constitution of Church and State according to the Idea of Each,* ed. J. Barrell (1972); original edn., 1830.

COLQUHOUN, J. C., *On the Objects and Uses of Protestant Associations* (1839).

—— *The Uses of the Established Church to the Protestantism and Civilization of Ireland* (Protestant Association Publications, No. 3; 2nd edn., 1839).

—— *Hints on the question now affecting the Church of Scotland . . . with a letter to Viscount Sandon* (Glasgow, 1840).

Committee of Laymen of Church of England, Tract No. 9, 'Church Rates' (1858); Tract No. 13, 'Church Rates' (1859).

CONDER, E. R., *Josiah Conder : A Memoir* (1857).

CONYBEARE, W. J., *Essays Ecclesiastical and Social* (1855).

COPLESTON, W. J., *Memoir of Edward Copleston, Bishop of Llandaff* (1851).

Correspondence between the Lord Bishop of London, the Chaplain and the Congregation of the British Church Establishment in Madeira (1846).

CROLY, G., *England the Fortress of Christianity* (Protestant Association Publications, No. 8, 1839).

DALE, R. W. (ed.), *The Life and Letters of John Angell James* (1861).

DENISON, G. A., *The Public Sin of the Divorce Act : a sermon* (1857).

—— *The Churches of England and Ireland, One Church by identity of Divine Trust* (1868).

DISRAELI, B., *The Life of Lord George Bentinck* (1852).

—— *Coningsby, or the New Generation* (1927); original edn., 1844.

—— *Tancred* (1927); original edn., 1847.

DODSWORTH, W., *A Letter to the Rev. E. B. Pusey on the position which he has taken in the present crisis* (1850).

D'OYLY, G., *A Letter to the Rt. Hon. Earl Grey, on the subject of Church Rates* (1834).

DRUMMOND, H., *Remarks on Dr. Wiseman's Sermon on the Gorham Case* (1850).

DUNCOMBE, T. H. (ed.), *The Life and Correspondence of T. S. Duncombe* (2 vols., 1868).

DUNLOP, ALEXANDER MURRAY, *An Answer to the Dean of Faculty's Letter to the Lord Chancellor* (Edinburgh, 1839).

DYER, W. H., *Papal Policy and the English Nonconformists* (1851).

ELLENBOROUGH, Earl of, *Political Diary, 1828–30*, ed. Lord Colchester (2 vols., 1881).

ESDAILE, JAMES, *The Spirit, Principle and Reasoning of Voluntaryism exposed* (Perth, 1834).

—— *The Voluntary Church Scheme without foundation in Scripture, Reason or Common Sense* (Perth, 1834).

Essays and Reviews, by F. Temple, R. Williams, B. Powell, H. B. Wilson, C. W. Goodwin, M. Pattison, and B. Jowett; ed. J. Parker (1860).

First Blast of the Trumpet against the Monstrous Usurpations of Church Patrons in Scotland, by 'John Knox the Younger' (Edinburgh, 1833).

Friendly Address to the Dissenters of Scotland, by Robert Candlish, 24 Dec. 1840 (Edinburgh, 1840).

Friendly Reply to the Friendly Address . . . , by Hugh Heugh, 7 Jan. 1841 (Edinburgh 1841).

Second Friendly Address to the Dissenters of Scotland, by Robert Candlish? (Edinburgh, 1841).

Friendly Reply to a second Friendly Address, by Hugh Heugh (Edinburgh, 1841).

FROUDE, R. H., *Remains*, ed. J. Keble and J. H. Newman (4 vols., London and Derby, 1838–9).

GIRDLESTONE, C., *Church Rates lawful, but not always expedient* (1833).

GLADSTONE, W. E., *The State in its Relations with the Church* (1838; also 4th ed., revised and enlarged, 2 vols., 1841).

—— *Church Principles considered in their Results* (1840).

—— *Remarks on the Royal Supremacy: a letter to the Bishop of London* (1850).

GLEIG, G. R., *A Letter to the Bishop of London on Church Reform* (1833).

GORDON, J. E., *On the Admission of Roman Catholics to Parliament, and their Violation of their Oath* (Protestant Association publications, No. 9, 3rd edn., 1839).

GRANT, BREWIN, *The Irish Church, an English Dissenter's view of it, or Mr. Gladstone's Missing Link* (1868).

GRESLEY, J. M., *The Real Occasion of the 'Papal Aggression'*: No. 1 of *Plain Sermons on Present Events* (1850).

HALL, C. NEWMAN, *Dissent and the Papal Bull—No Intolerance: a response to the cry of 'No Popery'* (1850).

HANNA, W., *Memoirs of the Life and Writings of Thomas Chalmers* (4 vols., Edinburgh, 1850–2).

—— (ed.), *A Selection from the Correspondence of the late Thomas Chalmers* (Edinburgh, 1853).

HARE, J. C., *A Few Words on the rejection of the episcopal bill to amend the Ecclesiastical Court of Appeal* (1850).

HARE, W. H., *The Designs and Constitution of the Society for the Liberation of Religion from State Patronage and Control* (1861).

HENLEY, Lord, *A Plan of Church Reform* (6th edn., 1832).

Hereford Protestant Association, *Report of Second Annual Meeting* (Cheltenham, 1837).

Hints for the Considerate . . . or, how should the members and adherents of the Free Church conduct themselves towards the Establishment . . .? (Perth, 1844).

HOOK, W. F., *On the means of rendering more efficient the Education of the People* (1846).

HOPE, J., *A Letter to the Lord Chancellor on the Claims of the Church of Scotland* (1839).

HUSENBETH, F. C., *The Life of Monsignor Weedall* (1860).

INDGE, J., *Anti-Popery and all its inroads* (1850).

Is Papal Supremacy recognized by the law of England? or, is the papal hierarchy legal? by a member of the Middle Temple (1851).

JOHNES, A. J., *An Essay on the Causes which have produced Dissent from the Established Church in the Principality of Wales* (1831, reprinted 1870).

—— *A Letter to Lord John Russell on the operation of the Established Church Bill, with reference to the interests of the Principality of Wales* (1836).

KEBLE, J., *The Christian Year: Thoughts in Verse for the Sundays and Holydays throughout the Year* (one-vol. edn., Oxford, 1827).

—— *National Apostasy considered* (Oxford, 1833).

—— *Church Matters in 1850* (Oxford, 1850).

—— *A Letter to Sir Brook W. Brydges, Bt., M.P.* (1852).

—— *A Very Few Plain Thoughts on the proposed admission of Dissenters to the University of Oxford* (Oxford, 1854).

LEWIS, G. C., *Addresses and Speeches relative to the Election for the County of Hereford in 1852* (1857).

Liverpool Working Men's Protestant Reformation Society, *First Annual Report, 1853–4* (Liverpool, 1854).

LORD, JAMES, *An Appeal to Protestants on the subject of the approaching Election* (1846).

—— *A Lecture on the encroachments of Popery and the duties of Protestants* (1847).

—— *Popery at the Hustings* (1852).

—— *Digest of the Maynooth Commission Report* (1855).

—— *Suggestions for settling the Maynooth College question* (1858).

LOVAINE, LORD (ed.), *Speeches in Parliament and some miscellaneous pamphlets of the late Henry Drummond* (2 vols., 1860).

LOWE, R. T., *Protest against the ministrations in Madeira of the Rev. T. K. Brown, in opposition to episcopal authority and in violation of the laws and conditions of the Church of England* (Funchal, 1848).

MACGILL, H. M., *The Life of Hugh Heugh* (2nd edn., Edinburgh, 1852).

M'KERROW, J., *History of the Secession Church* (2 vols., Glasgow, 1841).

MCLAREN, D., *The Corn Laws condemned . . . by upwards of five hundred Ministers of different Denominations resident in Scotland* (Edinburgh, 1842).

—— *History of the Resistance to the Annuity Tax* (4th edn., Edinburgh, 1851).

MCNEILE, H., *Speech in defence of Established Church, at Second Annual Meeting of Protestant Association, 10 May 1837* (3rd edn., London, 1839).

—— *Anti-Slavery and Anti-Popery* (1838).

—— *Lectures on the Church of England* (1840).

—— *England's Caesar: speech to Liverpool Protestant Operative Association, Dec. 1843* (Liverpool, 1844).

—— *Civil Rule an Ordinance of God, urged in opposition to the Supremacy of the Pope: speech to Liverpool Protestant and Reformation Society, 1 June 1846* (Liverpool, 1846).

—— *The Royal Supremacy discussed* (1850).

—— et al., *Addresses by H. Cairns, T. R. Birks and H. McNeile on the identity of the Churches of England and Ireland*, at the Irish Church Missions' Anniversary Breakfast (1864).

MAHON, LORD and CARDWELL, E. (eds.), *Memoirs by the Rt. Hon. Sir Robert Peel* (2 vols., 1856–7).

MANNING, H. E., *The Principle of the Ecclesiastical Commission examined, in a letter to the Rt. Rev. the Lord Bishop of Chichester* (1838).

MARSDEN, J. B., *Memoirs of the Life and Labours of the Rev. Hugh Stowell* (1868).

MARSHALL, A., *Ecclesiastical Establishments considered* (Glasgow, 1829).
—— *Ecclesiastical Establishments further considered* (Glasgow, 1831).
MASHEDER, R., *Dissent and Democracy—their mutual relations and common objects; a historical review* (1864).
MAURICE, F. D., *On Right and Wrong Methods of supporting Protestantism—a letter to Lord Ashley* (1843).
Meeting of the Church Institution, Northampton, 15 Nov. 1862 (Northampton, n.d.; pamphlet in British Library).
MEREWETHER, F., *Popery a New Religion, compared with that of Christ and His Apostles* (Ashby-de-la-Zouch, 1835).
—— *A Pastoral Address to the inhabitants of Whitwick, Leics., on the opening of a monastery within the limits of that parish* (Ashby-de-la-Zouch, 1845).
—— *A Letter to C. W. Packe, M.P., on the desirableness and necessity of a Church Association in Parliament* (1849).
—— *A Letter to Benjamin Disraeli, suggesting an adequate mode of repelling the late Papal Aggression* (1851).
—— *A Reply to Lord Stanley's Pamphlet on Church Rates* (1853).
—— *A Letter on Church Rates* (1855).
—— *A Respectful Appeal to the laity of the County of Leicester* (Leicester, 1858).
—— *Establishment or non-Establishment?* (1862).
MIALL, E., *The Nonconformist's Sketch-Book—a series of views of a State Church and its attendant evils* (1845).
—— *The British Churches in relation to the British People* (1849).
—— *The Fixed and the Voluntary Principles—eight letters to the Earl of Shaftesbury* (1859).
MOUNT EDGECUMBE, EARL OF, *Considerations on the Policy of a State endowment for the Roman Catholic Church of Ireland* (Bath, 1847).
NEWCASTLE, FOURTH DUKE OF, *Thoughts in Times Past tested by subsequent events* (1837).
NEWMAN, J. H., *Lectures on the present position of Catholics in England* (1851).
—— *Apologia pro Vita sua*, ed. M. J. Svaglic (Oxford, 1967).
NIHILL, D., *Suggestions on the revival of Ecclesiastical Assemblies in the Church of England* (1834).
NOEL, BAPTIST, *The Case of the Free Church of Scotland* (1844).
NORTHCOTE, Sir S. H., BT., *A Statement of Facts connected with the Election of the Rt. Hon. W. E. Gladstone as member for the University of Oxford in 1847, and with his re-elections in 1852 and 1853* (Oxford and London, 1853).

OFFOR, G., *The Triumph of Henry VIII over the Usurpations of the Church* (1846).
On the Educational Clauses of Sir James Graham's Factory Bill: a letter to the Hon. J. Stuart Wortley, by the Leeds Wesleyan Deputation (Leeds, 1843).

PAUL, W., *A History of the Origin and Progress of Operative Conservative Societies* (3rd edn., Durham, n.d. [1838]).
PEEL, Sir R., *Letter to the Electors for the Borough of Tamworth* (2nd edn., 1847).
PERCEVAL, D. M., *Maynooth and the Jew Bill* (1845).

PHILLIPPS, Lisle, *A Letter to the Earl of Shrewsbury on the re-establishment of the Hierarchy* (1850).

PHILLPOTTS, H., *Reply to the Addresses of the Clergy of the Archdeaconry of Exeter on the recent Romish Aggression* (1850).

Poll-books:

    Edinburgh, 1852 Election (Edinburgh, 1854; copy in Guildhall Library, London).

    Kingston-upon-Hull, 30 June 1841, 29 July 1847, 8 July 1852, 28 Mar. 1857, and 1868 (Hull, 1841, 1847, 1852, 1857, 1868; kept in Local History Library, Hull).

    Manchester: 1832 Election and 1839 by-election (Archives Dept., Central Library, Manchester).

    Stockport: 1859 Election (in J. B. Smith Papers, S. 332; Archives Dept., Central Library, Manchester).

PRIDEAUX, C. G., *A Practical Guide to the Duties of Churchwardens* (3rd edn., 1845; 7th edn., 1855; 12th edn., 1871).

Proceedings (and Debates) of the General Assembly of the Free Church of Scotland, 1843–73 (Edinburgh, 1843–73).

Proposed Evangelical Alliance: an address on behalf of the London branch of the provisional committee (1845).

Proposed Evangelical Alliance: report of the speeches delivered at . . . Liverpool, 16 Dec. 1845 (Liverpool, 1845).

Protestant Alliance:

    The Maynooth Endowment Act, Protestant Alliance Tract, No. 1 (1852).

    First Annual Report, 1852.

    Second Annual Report, 1853.

    Correspondence between the 'Protestant Alliance' and the Examiners in Law and Modern History (Oxford, 1858).

Protestant Aggression: remarks on the Bishop of Durham's letter to the Archdeacon of Lindisfarne, by a Catholic clergyman (1850).

Protestant Association:

    Publications, vol. i (including *Statement of Views and Objects*, and first, second, and third annual reports; 1839).

    A Few Facts to awaken Protestants (Publications, No. 11, 1839).

    Address to the Electors of Great Britain and Ireland (Bath, 1841).

    Fifth Annual Report (1841).

    Sixteenth Annual Report (1852).

    Foreign or Domestic Legislation: an address to the electors, by the Protestant Association (1852).

PUGIN, A. W. N., *Church and State, or Christian Liberty—an earnest address on the establishment of the hierarchy*, ed. E. W. Pugin (1875).

PUSEY, E. B., *The Royal Supremacy not an Arbitrary Authority but limited by the Laws of the Church, of which Kings are Members* (Oxford, 1850).

Reasons for Reviving the Action of Convocation (printed for the Chester and Manchester Church Union, 1850).

Regulations of the Church Defence and Anti-Patronage Electoral Association (Edinburgh, 1840).

Report and Addresses of Bristol Church Defence Association (London and Bristol, 1866).

Report of the Speeches delivered in the North United Secession Church, Perth, at the formation of the Perthshire Voluntary Church Association (Dundee, 1833).

Report of the Speeches at a meeting in Edinburgh, 23 Dec. 1835, to form a Protestant Association (Edinburgh, 1835).

Report of the Speeches on the Church question, at a Blairgowrie public meeting, 24 Feb. 1836 (Perth, 1836).

Report of the Speeches at a great meeting of Scottish Dissenters, Edinburgh, 2 July 1845 (Edinburgh, 1845).

Report presented at the First Annual Meeting of the Religious Freedom Society (1840).

RICHARD, H., *Memoirs of Joseph Sturge* (1864).

—— *Letters on the Social and Political Condition of the Principality of Wales* (1866).

ROBERTSON, G. H., *Remarks on the Society lately established for improving the system of Church Patronage in Scotland* (2nd edn., Edinburgh, 1825).

ROGERS, REV. J. GUINNESS, *The Ritualistic Movement in the Church of England, a Reason for Disestablishment* (1869).

SCHOLEFIELD, J., *An Argument for a Church Establishment* (Cambridge, 1833).

Scottish Central Board for Extending the Voluntary Principle:
    First Annual Report (Edinburgh, 1835).
    Fourth Annual Report (Edinburgh, 1838).

SINCLAIR, SIR G., BT. (ed.), *Selections from the Correspondence carried on during certain recent negotiations for the adjustment of the Scottish Church question* (Edinburgh, 1842).

—— *A Letter addressed to the non-established Presbyterian Communions of Scotland* (Edinburgh, 1854).

Society for improving the system of Church Patronage (in Scotland):
    Prospectus of Society . . . May 1823 (Edinburgh?).
    Account of Proceedings of First Annual Meeting (Edinburgh, 1825).
    Account of the Proceedings of the third annual meeting of the Aberdeen Auxiliary Society for improving the system of Church Patronage in Scotland, held at Aberdeen, 2 May 1828 (Aberdeen, 1828).
    Account of Proceedings of third annual meeting (Edinburgh, 1829).
    Account of Proceedings at fourth annual meeting, held in Dundee, 11 Nov. 1829 (Dundee, 1829).
    Annual Report of the Directors of the Church Patronage Society for 1830 (n.p.).

Speeches at a Glasgow Public Meeting, 31 Jan. and 1 Feb. 1833 (Glasgow, 1833).

SPOONER, R., *Maynooth Morals* (1852).

STANLEY, A. P., *The Life and Correspondence of Thomas Arnold* (6th edn., 1846).

—— *Essays chiefly on questions of Church and State, from 1850 to 1870* (new edn., 1884).

STANLEY, LORD, *The Church Rate Question Considered* (1853).

STANMORE, LORD (ed.), *Selections from the Correspondence of the Earl of Aberdeen* (11 vols., privately printed 1854–88, in British Library; one vol. consists entirely of correspondence on the Church of Scotland, 1838–43; the vol. for 1845–8 was published at Colombo).

STRUTHERS, G., *History of the Rise, Progress and Principles of the Relief Church* (Glasgow, 1843).

Suggestions for a Practical Use of the Papal Aggression: a letter to the Lord Bishop of Manchester, by one of his clergy (1851).

TAYLOR, E., *An Account of Orangeism—a key to the late religious riots and to the frantic opposition to the Irish Church disestablishment* (1868).

TAYLOR, J., *National Establishments of Religion* (1839).

The Case of the Dissenters, in a letter addressed to the Lord Chancellor (1833).

The Catholic Question: report of the great town's meeting held in the Town Hall, Birmingham, 11 Dec. 1850 (Birmingham, 1850).

The Church and the Wesleyans: their differences shown to be essential (Oxford, 1843).

The Earl of Aberdeen's Correspondence with the Rev. Dr. Chalmers, etc., 14 Jan–27 May 1840 (Edinburgh, 1840).

The Government of Lord Aberdeen and the Government of Lord Derby, by an Irish Catholic (Dublin, 1853).

The Hampden Controversy (1847).

The Irish Church question considered in a letter addressed to the Rt. Hon. B. Disraeli, by 'a Winchester Churchman' (n.d.).

The Maynooth Endowment Act (Protestant Alliance Trace No. 1, 1852).

The Position of Popery in Great Britain, and the means in Scotland for resisting it; being the report of operations of the Scottish Reformation Society for 1862 (Edinburgh, 1863).

The Principles and Objects of the Church Defence Institution (n.d. [1871]).

The Royal Supremacy discussed in a correspondence between Archdeacon [Robert] Wilberforce and the Rev. Hugh McNeile (1850).

THELWALL, A. S., *Proceedings of the Anti-Maynooth Conference* (1845).

—— *Tractarianism Dishonest* (Brighton Protestant Tracts, Brighton, 1851).

Tracts for the Times, 1833–40:

No. 36, *An Account of Religious Sects at present existing in England* (1834).

No. 57, *Sermons on Saints' Days*, 3 (1835).

No. 59, *The Position of the Church of Christ in England, relatively to the State and the Nation* (1835).

TRELAWNY, SIR J. S., BT., *An Epitome of the Evidence given before the Select Committee of the House of Commons on Church Rates* (1852).

TURNER, A., *The Scottish Secession of 1843* (Edinburgh, 1859).

Ubi Lapsus? British encouragement to Papal Aggression, by a Layman (1851).

VAUGHAN R., *Religious Parties in England: their Principles, History and Present Duty* (2nd edn., 1838).

—— *Popular Education in England, with a reply to Mr. Baines* (1846).

Voluntaryism and the Anti-Papal Agitation (printed for private circulation, Edinburgh, 1850).

Vox Populi, or patrons paid off, by their successors in office, the Church Patronage
   Society (Edinburgh, 1825).

WADE, J., *The Extraordinary Black Book—an exposition of abuses in Church and
   State* . . . (new edn., 1832).
WARDLAW, R., *National Church Establishments examined* (1839).
What will the Bishops do? (1847).
WISEMAN, N., *An Appeal to the Reason and Good Feeling of the English People on
   the subject of the Catholic Hierarchy* (1850).
WOODWARD, G. H., *Claims of the Protestant Association on public support* (Pro-
   testant Association, Publications, No. 1, 1839).

VI. LATER BOOKS AND ARTICLES

(The place of publication of books is London unless otherwise stated)

ABRAHAMS, L., 'Sir I. L. Goldsmid and the admission of the Jews of England to
   Parliament', *Transactions of the Jewish Historical Society of England,* iv (1899–
   1901), 116–76.
AKENSON, D. H., *The Church of Ireland: Reform and Revolution, 1800–85* (New
   Haven, 1971).
ALLCHIN, A. M., *The Silent Rebellion: Anglican Religious Communities, 1845–1900*
   (1958).
ALTHOLZ, J. L., *The Liberal Catholic Movement in England* (1962).
——— 'The Political Behavior of the English Catholics, 1850–67', *Journal of British
   Studies,* iii (1964), 89–103.
ALTHOLZ, J. L., MCELRATH, D., and HOLLAND, J. C. (eds.), *The Correspond-
   ence of Lord Acton and Richard Simpson* (3 vols., Cambridge, 1971–5).
ANDERSON, OLIVE, *A Liberal State at War—English Politics and Economics during
   the Crimean War* (1967).
——— 'Gladstone's Abolition of Church Rates: a minor political Myth and its
   historiographical Career', *JEH* xxv (1974), 185–98.
'The Incidence of Civil Marriage in Victorian England and Wales', *Past and
   Present,* 69 (Nov. 1975), 50–87.
ANSON, P. F., *Underground Catholicism in Scotland, 1622–1878* (Montrose,
   1970).
APPLEMAN, P. *et al.* (eds.), *1859—Entering an Age of Crisis* (Bloomington (Indi-
   ana), 1959).
ARGYLL, EIGHTH DUKE OF, *Autobiography and Memoirs,* ed. Dowager Duchess of
   Argyll (2 vols., 1906).
ARNSTEIN, W. L. 'The Murphy Riots: a Victorian Dilemma', *Victorian Studies,*
   xix.1 (1975–6), 51–71.
ASHLEY, E., *The Life of H. J. Temple, Viscount Palmerston, 1845–65* (2 vols.,
   1876).
ASHWELL, A. R. and WILBERFORCE, R. G., *Life of the Rt. Rev. Samuel Wilberforce*
   (3 Vols., 1880–2).
ASPINALL, A. (ed.), *Three Early Nineteenth Century Diaries* (1952).

AWDRY, F., *A Country Gentleman of the Nineteenth Century—a short memoir of Sir William Heathcote, Bt.* (Winchester, 1906).
AYERST, D. (ed.), *The Guardian Omnibus, 1821–1971* (1973).

BAGENAL, P. H., *The Life of Ralph Bernal Osborne, M.P.* (1884).
BAIRD, J. G. A. (ed.), *Private Letters of the tenth Marquess of Dalhousie* (1911).
BALFOUR, LADY FRANCES, *The Life of George, fourth Earl of Aberdeen* (2 vols., 1922).
BALLEINE, G. R., *A History of the Evangelical Party in the Church of England* (3rd edn., 1951).
BARKER, T. C. and HARRIS, J. R., *A Merseyside Town in the Industrial Revolution —St. Helens, 1750–1900* (Liverpool, 1954).
BATTISCOMBE, GEORGINA, *John Keble—a study in limitations* (1963).
—— *Shaftesbury* (1974).
BEALES, D., *From Castlereagh to Gladstone, 1815–85* (1969).
BEBBINGTON, D. W., 'The Life of Baptist Noel: its Setting and Significance', *Baptist Quarterly*, N.S. xxiv (1971–2), 389–411.
BECK, G. A. (ed.), *The English Catholics, 1850–1950* (1950).
BECKERLEGGE, O. A., *The United Methodist Free Churches—a study in freedom* (1957).
BELL, P. M. H., *Disestablishment in Ireland and Wales* (1969).
BELLESHEIM, A., *History of the Catholic Church of Scotland*, vol. IV (Edinburgh, 1890).
BENNETT, F., *The Story of W. J. E. Bennett* (1909).
BENSON, A. C. and ESHER, VISCOUNT (eds.), *The Letters of Queen Victoria, 1837–61* (3 vols., 1907).
BEST, G. F. A., *Temporal Pillars—Queen Anne's Bounty, the Ecclesiastical Commissioners and the Church of England* (Cambridge, 1964).
—— *Shaftesbury* (1964).
—— *Mid-Victorian Britain, 1851–75* (1971).
—— 'The Religious Difficulties of National Education in England, 1800–70', *Cambridge Hist. Jl.* xii (1956), 155–73.
—— 'The Protestant Constitution and its Supporters, 1800–1829', *Trans. Royal Hist. Soc.* 5th Ser. viii (1958), 105–27.
—— 'The Evangelicals and the Established Church in the early Nineteenth Century', *Journal of Theological Studies*, new Ser., ix (1958), 63–78.
—— 'The Constitutional Revolution, 1828–32', *Theology*, lxii (1959), 226–34.
—— 'The Whigs and the Church Establishment in the Age of Grey and Holland', *History*, xlv (1960), 103–18.
—— 'The Road to Hiram's Hospital', *Victorian Studies*, v (1961–2), 135–50.
BINFIELD, J. C. G., 'The Thread of Disruption—some nineteenth century churches in eastern England', *Transactions of the Congregational Historical Society*, xx (1965–70), 156–65.
BIRRELL, C. M., *The Life of William Brock, D.D.* (1878).
BLAKE, R., *Disraeli* (1966).
BOLAM, C. G., GORING, J., SHORT, H. L., and THOMAS, R., *The English Presbyterians* (1968).

BOSSY, J., *The English Catholic Community, 1570–1850* (1975).

BOWEN, D., *The Idea of the Victorian Church* (Montreal, 1968).

BOWMER, J. C., *Pastor and People—a study of Church and Ministry in Wesleyan Methodism, 1791–1858* (1975).

BRADFIELD, B. T., 'Sir Richard Vyvyan and the Country Gentlemen, 1830–4', *EHR* lxxxiii (1968), 729–43.

BRADY, W. M., *Annals of the Catholic Hierarchy in England and Wales, 1585–1876* (1883).

BRASH, J. I. (ed.), *Papers on Scottish Electoral Politics, 1832–54* (Scottish History Society Publications, 4th Ser., vol. 11, Edinburgh, 1974).

BRENDON, P., *Hurrell Froude and the Oxford Movement* (1974).

BRIGGS, A., *1851* (Historical Association Publication, 1951).

—— *The Age of Improvement* (1959).

—— (ed.), *Chartist Studies* (1959).

BRIGGS, J. and SELLERS, I. (eds.), *Victorian Nonconformity* (1974).

BRILIOTH, Y., *The Anglican Revival—studies in the Oxford Movement* (1925).

—— *Three Lectures on Evangelicalism and the Oxford Movement* (1934).

BROCK, M., *The Great Reform Act* (1973).

BRODERICK, J. F., *The Holy See and the Irish movement for the Repeal of the Union with England, 1829–47* (Rome, 1951).

BROSE, OLIVE, *Church and Parliament: the reshaping of the Church of England, 1828–60* (1959).

BROWN, T. (ed.), *Annals of the Disruption* (Edinburgh, 1893).

BUCKLE, G. E. (ed.), *The Letters of Queen Victoria, 2nd Ser., 1862–78* (2 vols., 1926).

BUNTING, T. P. and STRINGER ROWE, G., *The Life of Rev. Dr. Jabez Bunting* (2 vols.: vol. i 1859, vol. ii 1887).

BURGESS, H. J., *Enterprise in Education—the Story of the Work of the Established Church in the Education of the People prior to 1870* (1958).

BURGON, J. W., *Lives of Twelve Good Men* (2 vols., 1889).

BURKE, T., *A Catholic History of Liverpool* (Liverpool, 1910).

BURLEIGH, J. H. S., *A Church History of Scotland* (Edinburgh, 1960).

BUTLER, C., *The Life and Times of Bishop Ullathorne* (2 vols., 1926).

CAHILL, G., 'The Protestant Association and the Anti-Maynooth Agitation of 1845', *Catholic Historical Review*, xliii (1957) 273–308.

—— 'Irish Catholicism and English Toryism', *Review of Politics*, xix (1957), 62–76.

CARPENTER, S. C., *Church and People, 1789–1889* (1933).

CASS, A. N., *Methodism in Dundee, 1759–1959* (Dundee, n.d.).

CECIL, LADY GWENDOLEN, *Life of Robert, Marquess of Salisbury* (4 vols., 1921–32).

CHADWICK, O., *The Mind of the Oxford Movement* (1960).

—— *The Victorian Church* (pts. I and II, 1966–70).

—— *The Secularization of the European Mind in the Nineteenth Century* (1976).

CHARLES, CONRAD, 'The Origins of the Parish Mission in England and the early Passionate Apostolate, 1840–50', *JEH* xv (1964), 60–75.

CHEW, R., *James Everett, a Biography* (1875).
—— *William Griffith—Memorials and Letters* (1885).
CHURCH, R. A., *Economic and Social Change in a Midland Town—Victorian Nottingham* (1966).
CHURCH, R. W., *The Oxford Movement, 1833–45*, ed. G. Best (Chicago and London, 1970).
CLARK, G. KITSON, *Peel and the Conservative Party, 1832–41* (2nd edn., 1964).
—— *The Making of Victorian England* (1965).
—— *Churchmen and the Condition of England, 1832–85* (1973).
COCKSHUT, A. O. J., *Anglican Attitudes—a study of Victorian religious controversies* (1959).
—— *Truth to Life—the Art of Biography in the Nineteenth Century* (1974).
COLEMAN, D. C., *Courtaulds—an economic and social history* (2 vols., Oxford, 1969).
COLERIDGE, J. T., *A Memoir of the Rev. John Keble* (3rd edn., 2 vols., 1870).
CONACHER, J. B., *The Aberdeen Coalition, 1852–5* (Cambridge, 1968).
—— *The Peelites and the Party System, 1846–52* (Newton Abbot, 1972).
—— 'Peel and the Peelites, 1846–50', *EHR* lxxiii (1958), 431–52.
—— 'The Politics of the "Papal Aggression" Crisis, 1850–1', *Canadian Catholic Historical Association Report* (1959), 13–27.
CONDON, MARY D., 'The Irish Church and the Reform Ministries', *Journal of British Studies*, iii (1964), 120–42.
COOK, T. G. (ed.), *Local Studies and the History of Education* (1972).
CORISH, P. J. (ed.), *A History of Irish Catholicism*, vol. vi (Dublin, 1968).
COWAN, C., *Reminiscences* (privately printed, 1878).
COWHERD, R. G., *The Politics of English Dissent, 1815–48* (1959).
COWLING, M., *1867—Disraeli, Gladstone and Revolution* (Cambridge, 1967).
CROWTHER, MARGARET A., *Church Embattled—religious controversy in mid-Victorian England* (Newton Abbot, 1970).
CULLEN, M. J., 'The Making of the Civil Registration Act of 1836', *JEH* xxv (1974), 39–59.
CUNNINGHAM, J., *The Church History of Scotland* (2nd edn., 2 vols., Edinburgh, 1882).
CUNNINGHAM, V., *Everywhere Spoken Against—Dissent in the Victorian Novel* (Oxford, 1975).
CURRIE, R., *Methodism Divided* (1968).

DAVIDSON, R. T. and BENHAM, W., *The Life of Archibald Campbell Tait, Archbishop of Canterbury* (3rd edn., 2 vols., 1891).
DAVIES, E. T., *Religion in the Industrial Revolution in South Wales* (Cardiff, 1965).
DAVIES, G. C. B., *Henry Phillpotts, Bishop of Exeter* (1954).
DAVIES, R. E. and RUPP, G. (eds.), *History of thr Methodist Church in Great Britain* (vol. I, 1965).
DAVIS, R. W., *Dissent in Politics, 1780–1830: the Political Life of William Smith, M.P.* (1971).
—— *Political Change and Continuity, 1760–1885: a Buckinghamshire study* (Newton Abbot, 1972).

DELL, R. S., 'Social and Economic Theories and Pastoral Concerns of a Victorian Archbishop [J. B. Sumner],' *JEH*, xvi (1965), 196–208.

DENISON, G. A., *Notes of My Life* (2nd edn., Oxford, 1878).

DENISON, LOUISA E. (ed.), *Fifty Years at East Brent—the letters of G. A. Denison* (1902).

DESSAIN, C. S., and GORNALL, T. (eds.), *The Letters and Diaries of John Henry Newman*, vols. XI–XXII (1961–72), XXIII–IV (Oxford, 1973).

DISRAELI, R. (ed.), *Lord Beaconsfield's Letters, 1830–52* (1887).

DREYER, F. A., 'The Whigs and the Political Crisis of 1845', *EHR* lxxx (1965), 514–37.

DRIVER, C., *Tory Radical—the Life of Richard Oastler* (New York, 1946).

DRUMMOND, A. L. and BULLOCH, J., *The Scottish Church, 1688–1843* (Edinburgh, 1973).

—— *The Church in Victorian Scotland, 1843–74* (Edinburgh, 1975).

DRUMMOND, J. and UPTON, C. B., *The Life and Letters of James Martineau* (2 vols., 1902).

EDWARDS, D. L., *Leaders of the Church of England, 1828–1944* (1971).

EDWARDS, MALDWYN, *After Wesley—a Study of the Social and Political Influence of Methodism, 1791–1849* (1935).

ELLIOTT, A. R. D., *Life of G. J. Goschen, first Viscount Goschen, 1831–1907* (2 vols., 1911).

ERICKSON, A. B., *The Public Career of Sir James Graham* (Oxford, 1952).

ESCOTT, H., *A History of Scottish Congregationalism* (Glasgow, 1960).

EVANS, D., *The Life and Work of William Williams, M.P.* (Llandyssul, 1940).

EVANS, E. J., 'Some reasons for the growth of English rural anti-clericalism, c. 1750–1830', *Past and Present*, 66 (Feb. 1975), 84–109.

EVANS, T., *The Background of Modern Welsh Politics, 1789–1846* (Cardiff, 1936).

EVERITT, A., *The Pattern of Rural Dissent: the Nineteenth Century* (University of Leicester, Dept. of English Local History Occasional Papers, 2nd. Ser. No. 4; Leicester, 1972).

Extracts from the Records of the Burgh of Glasgow, vol. XI (1823–33), ed. R. Renwick (Glasgow, 1906).

FAULKNER, H. U., *Chartism and the Churches* (New York, 1916).

FERGUSON, W., *Scotland, 1689 to the Present* (Edinburgh, 1968).

FEUCHTWANGER, E. J., *Gladstone* (1975).

FIGGIS, J. N., *Churches in the modern State* (1913).

FINESTEIN, I. 'Anglo-Jewish Opinion during the Struggle for Emancipation, 1828–58', *Transactions of the Jewish Historical Society of England*, xx (1959–61), 113–43.

FINLAYSON, G. B. A. M., 'The Politics of Municipal Reform, 1835', *EHR* lxxxi (1966), 673–92.

FLEMING, J. R., *A History of the Church in Scotland, 1843–74* (Edinburgh, 1927).

FOOT, M. R. D. and MATTHEW, H. C. G. (eds.), *The Gladstone Diaries*, vols. I–IV (Oxford, 1968–74).

FORBES, D., *The Liberal Anglican Idea of History* (Cambridge, 1952).

FOSTER, J., *Class Struggle and the Industrial Revolution* (1974).
FOTHERGILL, B., *Nicholas Wiseman* (1963).
FURNEAUX, R., *William Wilberforce* (1974).

GARNETT, R. and E., *The Life of William Johnson Fox* (1909).
GASH, N., *Politics in the Age of Peel* (1953).
—— *Mr. Secretary Peel* (1961).
—— *Reaction and Reconstruction in English Politics, 1832–52* (Oxford, 1965).
—— *Sir Robert Peel* (1972).
GATHORNE-HARDY, A. E., *Gathorne Hardy, first Earl of Cranbrook, a Memoir* (2 vols., 1910).
GAY, J. D., *The Geography of Religion in England* (1971).
GILBERT, A. D., *Religion and Society in Industrial England, 1740–1914* (1976).
GILL, F. C., *The Romantic Movement and Methodism* (1937).
GILLEY, S., 'The Roman Catholic Mission to the Irish in London', *Recusant History*, x (1969–70), 123–41.
—— 'Protestant London, No-Popery and the Irish Poor, 1830–60', pt. I, *Recusant History*, x (1969–70), 210–30; pt. II, *Recusant History*, xi (1971–2), 21–46.
—— 'The Garibaldi Riots of 1862', *Hist. Jl.* xvi (1973), 697–732.
GLADSTONE, W. E., *Gleanings of Past Years, 1843–78* (7 vols., 1879).
GOOCH, G. P. (ed.), *The Later Correspondence of Lord John Russell, 1840–78* (2 vols., 1925).
GORDON, Sir A., *The Earl of Aberdeen* (1893).
GOWLAND, D. A., 'Political Opinion in Manchester Wesleyanism, 1832–57', *Proceedings of the Wesley Historical Society*, xxxvi (1967–8), 93–104.
GRANT, J., *Memoirs of Sir George Sinclair* (1870).
GRAY, W. F., 'Chalmers and Gladstone: an unrecorded Episode', *Records of the Scottish Church History Society*, x (1950), 8–17.
GREAVES, R. W., *The Corporation of Leicester, 1689–1836* (Oxford, 1939).
—— 'The Jerusalem Bishopric, 1841', *EHR* lxiv (1949), 328–52.
GREGORY, B., *Sidelights on the Conflicts of Methodism, 1827–52* (1899).
GUEDALLA, P. (ed.), *Gladstone and Palmerston, being their Correspondence, 1851–65* (1928).
GUTTSMAN, W. L., 'The General Election of 1859 in the Cities of Yorkshire', *International Review of Social History*, ii (1957), 231–58.
GWYNN, D. R., *The Second Spring, 1818–52—a study of the Catholic revival in England* (1942).
—— *Lord Shrewsbury, Pugin and the Catholic Revival* (1946).
—— *Father Dominic Barberi* (1947).
—— *Cardinal Wiseman* (Dublin, 1950).
—— *Father Luigi Gentili and his Mission, 1801–48* (Dublin, 1951).

HAILE, M. and BONNEY, E., *Life and Letters of John Lingard, 1771–1851* (1911).
HALES, E. E. Y., *Revolution and Papacy, 1769–1846* (Notre Dame, Indiana, 1966).
HALÉVY, É., *A History of the English People in the Nineteenth Century* (vols. I–IV, 1949–51).

HALL, C. NEWMAN, *Autobiography* (1898).

HAMPDEN, HENRIETTA (ed.), *Some Memorials of R. D. Hampden, Bishop of Hereford* (1871).

HANDLEY, J. E., *The Irish in Scotland* (one-vol. edn., Glasgow, 1964).

HANHAM, H. J., *Elections and Party Management : Politics in the time of Disraeli and Gladstone* (1959).

—— *Scottish Nationalism* (1969).

HANKINSON, F., 'Dissenters' Chapels Act, 1844', *Transactions of the Unitarian Historical Society*, viii (1943–6), 52–7.

HÄRDELIN, A., *The Tractarian Understanding of the Eucharist* (Uppsala, 1965).

HARRISON, B., *Drink and the Victorians, 1815–72* (1971).

—— 'The Sunday Trading Riots of 1855', *Hist. Jl.* viii (1965), 219–45.

HARRISON, J. F. C., *The Early Victorians, 1832–51* (1971).

HART, A. TINDAL, *The Curate's Lot* (1970).

HARWOOD, W. H. (ed.), *Henry Allon, the story of his Ministry* (1894).

HENDERSON, G. D., *The Claims of the Church of Scotland* (1951).

HENNOCK, E. P., *Fit and Proper Persons—ideal and reality in nineteenth-century urban government* (1973).

HENRIQUES, URSULA, *Religious Toleration in England, 1787–1833* (1961).

—— 'The Jewish Emancipation Controversy in Nineteenth Century Britain', *Past and Present*, 40 (Aug. 1968), 126–46.

HILL, Sir F., *Victorian Lincoln* (Cambridge, 1974).

HILL, R. L., *Toryism and the People, 1832–46* (1929).

HOBHOUSE, S., *Joseph Sturge, his Life and Work* (1919).

HOBSBAWM, E. J. and RUDÉ, G., *Captain Swing* (1969).

HODDER, E., *The Life and Work of the Seventh Earl of Shaftesbury* (3 vols.,1880–2).

—— *The Life of Samuel Morley* (2nd edn., 1887).

HOLLIS, PATRICIA (ed.), *Pressure from Without in early Victorian England* (1974).

HOLT, T. G., 'A Note on some Eighteenth Century Statistics', *Recusant History*, x (1969–70), 3–9.

HOLYOAKE, G. J., *The Life of Joseph Rayner Stephens* (1881).

—— *Sixty years of an Agitator's Life* (2 vols., 1892).

HOOD, E. PAXTON, *Thomas Binney, his Mind, Life and Opinions* (1874).

HOPPEN, K. T., 'Tories, Catholics and the General Election of 1859', *Hist. Jl.* xiii (1970), 48–67.

HUGHES, E., 'The Bishops and Reform, 1831–3: some fresh Correspondence', *EHR* lvi (1941), 459–90.

HUNTER, W. W., *A Life of the Earl of Mayo* (2nd edn., 2 vols., 1876).

HYAMSON, A. M., *David Salomons* (1939).

INGLIS, K. S., *Churches and the Working Classes in Victorian England* (1964).

—— 'Patterns of Religious Worship in 1851', *JEH* xi (1960), 74–86.

ISICHEI, ELIZABETH, *Victorian Quakers* (1970).

JACKSON, J. A., *The Irish in Britain* (1963).

JAMIE, D., *John Hope, Philanthropist and Reformer* (Edinburgh, 1900).

JENNINGS, L. J. (ed.), *The Correspondence and Diaries of the late Rt. Hon. John Wilson Croker* (2nd edn., 3 vols., 1885).

JOHNSON, D. W. J., 'Sir James Graham and the "Derby Dilly"', *University of Birmingham Historical Journal*, iv (1953–4), 66–80.

JOHNSON, L. G., *General T. Perronet Thompson, 1783–1869* (1957).

JONES, E. R., *Life and Speeches of Joseph Cowen, M.P.* (1885).

JONES, I. G., 'The Liberation Society and Welsh Politics, 1844–1868', *Welsh HR* i. 2 (1961), 193–224.

—— 'The Election of 1868 in Merthyr Tydfil', *Journal of Modern History*, xxxiii (1961), 270–86.

—— 'Dr. Thomas Price and the Merthyr Tydfil Election of 1868: a Study in Nonconformist Politics', pts. I and II, *Welsh HR* ii. 2 and 3 (1964–5), 147–72, 251–70.

—— 'Cardiganshire Politics in the Mid-Nineteenth-Century—a study of the elections of 1865 and 1868', *Ceredigion*, v (1964), 14–41.

—— 'Merioneth Politics in Mid-Nineteenth Century—the politics of a rural economy', *Journal of the Merioneth Historical and Record Society*, v (1965–8), 273–326.

JONES, J. R., 'The Conservatives and Gladstone in 1855', *EHR* lxxvii (1962), 95–8.

JONES, O. W. and WALKER, D. (eds.), *Links with the Past—Swansea and Brecon historical essays* (Llandybie, Cards., 1974).

JONES, R. T., *Congregationalism in England, 1662–1962* (1962).

JONES, W. D., *Lord Derby and Victorian Conservatism* (Oxford, 1956).

KEBBEL, T. E. (ed.), *Selected Speeches of the Earl of Beaconsfield* (2 vols., 1882).

KEMP, BETTY, 'The General Election of 1841', *History*, xxxvii (1952), 146–57.

KENT, J., *Jabez Bunting, the last Wesleyan* (1955).

—— *The Age of Disunity* (1966).

KIERNAN, V., 'Evangelicalism and the French Revolution', *Past and Present*, 1 (Feb. 1952), 44–56.

KIRK-SMITH, H., *William Thomson, Archbishop of York, 1819–90* (1958).

KRIEGEL, A. D., 'The Irish Policy of Lord Grey's Government', *EHR* lxxxvi (1971), 22–45.

LAMBERT, R. S., *The Cobbett of the West—a study of Thomas Latimer and the struggle between pulpit and press at Exeter* (1939).

—— *The Railway King, 1800–71* (1964 (reprint)).

LANDELS, T. D., *William Landels, D. D., a Memoir* (1900).

LANG, A., *Life, Letters and Diaries of Sir Stafford Northcote* (Edinburgh, 1891).

LATHBURY, D. C. (ed.), *Correspondence on Church and Religion of W. E. Gladstone* (2 vols., 1910).

LEADER, R. E., *The Life and Letters of J. A. Roebuck* (1897).

LEECH, H. J. (ed.), *The Public Letters of John Bright* (1885).

LEETHAM, C., *Luigi Gentili, a Sower for the Second Spring* (1965).

LEISHMAN, J. F., *Matthew Leishman of Govan and the Middle Party of 1843* (Paisley, 1924).

LEWIS, REV. SIR G. F. (ed.), *Letters of Sir George C. Lewis to various friends* (1870).

LIDDON, H. P., *The Life of Edward Bouverie Pusey*, ed. J. O. Johnston and R. J. Wilson (4 vols., 1893–7).

LINCOLN, A., *Some Political and Social Ideas of English Dissent, 1763–1800* (New York, 1971).

LOCHHEAD, MARION, *Episcopal Scotland in the Nineteenth Century* (1966).

LOWE, J. C., 'The Tory Triumph of 1868 in Blackburn and in Lancashire', *Hist. Jl.* xvi (1973), 733–48.

LUCAS, E., *The Life of Frederick Lucas, M.P.* (2 vols., 1886).

LYNCH, M. J.: 'Was Gladstone a Tractarian? W. E. Gladstone and the Oxford Movement, 1833–45', *Journal of Religious History*, viii (1975), 364–89.

MACAULAY, T. B., *Works—Essays and Biographies*, vol. iii (1907).

McCLATCHEY, DIANA, *Oxfordshire Clergy, 1777–1869* (Oxford, 1960).

McCLELLAND, V. A., *Cardinal Manning, his Public Life and Influence, 1865–92* (Oxford, 1962).

—— *English Roman Catholics and Higher Education, 1830–1903* (1972).

—— 'The Irish Clergy and Archbishop Manning's visitation of the Western District of Scotland, 1867', pts. 1 and 2, *Catholic Historical Review*, liii (1967–8), 1–27, 229–50.

McCORD, N., *The Anti-Corn Law League, 1838–46* (1958).

McDOWELL, R. B., *Public Opinion and Government Policy in Ireland, 1801–46* (1952).

MacEWEN, A. R., *The Life and Letters of John Cairns* (1895).

MACHIN, G. I. T., *The Catholic Question in English Politics, 1820 to 1830* (Oxford, 1964).

—— 'The Maynooth Grant, the Dissenters and Disestablishment, 1845–7', *EHR* lxxxii (1967), 61–85.

—— 'The Disruption and British Politics, 1834–43', *Scottish Historical Review*, li (1972), 20–51.

—— 'A Welsh Church Rate Fracas, Aberystwyth 1832–1833', *Welsh HR* vi. 2 (1973), 462–8.

—— 'Lord John Russell and the Prelude to the Ecclesiastical Titles Bill, 1846–51', *JEH* xxv (1974), 277–95.

—— 'Gladstone and Nonconformity in the 1860s: the Formation of an Alliance', *Hist. Jl.* xvii (1974), 347–64.

MACINTYRE, A., *The Liberator: Daniel O'Connell and the Irish Party, 1830–47* (1965).

MACKIE, J. B., *The Life and Work of Duncan McLaren* (2 vols., 1888).

MACKINTOSH, W. H., *Disestablishment and Liberation* (1972).

MACLAREN, A. A., *Religion and Social Class—the Disruption years in Aberdeen* (1974).

MACLEOD, D., *Memoir of Norman Macleod, D.D.* (2 vols., 1876).

MacSUIBHNE, P., *Paul Cullen and his Contemporaries, with their letters from 1820 to 1902* (3 vols., Naas, Co. Kildare, 1961–5).

MAGNUS, Sir P., *Gladstone* (1954).

MALTBY, S. E., *Manchester and the Movement for National Elementary Education, 1800–70* (Manchester, 1918).

MANNING, B. L., *The Protestant Dissenting Deputies* (Cambridge, 1952).

MARSH, P. T., *The Victorian Church in Decline—Archbishop Tait and the Church of England, 1868–82* (1969).

MARTINEAU, JANE, *Life of Henry, fifth Duke of Newcastle* (1908).

MARWICK, W. H., 'Quakers in Victorian Scotland', *Journal of the Friends' Historical Society*, lii (1969), 66–77.

MATHIESON, W. L., *Church and Reform in Scotland, 1797–1843* (Glasgow, 1916).

—— *English Church Reform, 1815–40* (1923).

MAXWELL, SIR H., *Life and Letters of George William Frederick, fourth Earl of Clarendon* (2 vols., 1913).

MAYOR, S., 'R. W. Dale and Nineteenth Century Thought', *Transactions of the Congregational Historical Society*, xx (1965–70), 4–18.

MEACHAM, S., *Lord Bishop: the Life of Samuel Wilberforce* (Cambridge, Mass., 1970).

MIALL, A., *The Life of Edward Miall* (1884).

MIALL, C. S., *Henry Richard, M.P.* (1889).

MOLESWORTH, SIR G. L., *The Life of J. E. N. Molesworth, an eminent divine of the nineteenth century* (1915).

MONTGOMERY, R. M., 'The Significance of the Dissenters' Chapels Act of 1844', *Transactions of the Unitarian Historical Society*, viii (1943–6), 45–51.

MONYPENNY, W. F. and BUCKLE, G. E., *The Life of Benjamin Disraeli, Earl of Beaconsfield* (6 vols., 1910–20).

MOODY, T. W., 'The Irish University Question in the Nineteenth Century', *History*, xliii (1958), 89–109.

MOORE, D. C., 'The Other Face of Reform', *Victorian Studies*, v (1961–2), 7–34.

MOORE, R., *Pit-men, Preachers and Politics: the effects of Methodism in a Durham mining community* (1974).

MORAN, P. F. (ed.), *The Pastoral Letters and other writings of Cardinal Cullen* (3 vols., Dublin, 1882).

MORGAN, JANE, 'Denbighshire's *Annus Mirabilis*: the Borough and County Elections of 1868', *Welsh HR* vii. 1 (1974), 63–87.

MORGAN, KENNETH O., *Wales in British Politics, 1868–1922* (2nd edn., Cardiff, 1970).

MORGAN, W. T., 'Disciplinary Cases against Churchwardens in the Consistory Courts of St. David's', *Journal of the Historical Society of the Church in Wales*, x (1960), 17 ff.

—— 'Disputes concerning seats in church before the Consistory Courts of St. David's', *Journal of the Historical Society of the Church in Wales*, xi (1961), 65–89.

MORLEY, J., *The Life of Richard Cobden* (1906); original edn., 2 vols., 1879.

—— *The Life of William Ewart Gladstone* (3 vols., 1903).

MORRISH, P. S. 'The Manchester Clause', *Church Quarterly*, i. 4 (April 1969), 319–26.

MOZLEY, ANNE (ed.), *Letters and Correspondence of John Henry Newman during his Life in the English Church* (2 vols., 1891).

MOZLEY, T., *Reminiscences chiefly of Oriel College and the Oxford Movement* (2nd edn., 2 vols., 1882).

MUIRHEAD, I. A., 'Catholic Emancipation in Scotland—the debate and the after-math', *Innes Review*, xxiv. 2 (1973), 103–20.

MURPHY, J., *The Religious Problem in English Education—the crucial experiment* (Liverpool, 1959).

MURSELL, A., *James Phillippo Mursell, his Life and Work* (1886).

NEALE, J. MASON, *Letters*, ed. by his daughter (1910).

NEW, C. W., *Lord Durham* (Oxford, 1929).

New Cambridge Modern History, ix (1793–1830) (Cambridge, 1965); x (1830–70) (Cambridge, 1960).

NEWSOME, D., *The Parting of Friends: A Study of the Wilberforces and Henry Manning* (1966).

NIAS, J. C. S., *Gorham and the Bishop of Exeter* (1951).

NICHOLLS, D. (ed.), *Church and State in Britain since 1820* (1967).

NICOLSON, A. (ed.), *Memoirs of Adam Black* (2nd edn., Edinburgh, 1885).

NORMAN, E. R., *The Catholic Church and Ireland in the Age of Rebellion, 1859–73* (1965).

—— *Anti-Catholicism in Victorian England* (1968).

—— *Church and Society in England, 1770–1970* (Oxford, 1976).

NOSSITER, T. J., *Influence, Opinion and Political Idioms in Reformed England—case studies from the North-East, 1832–74* (Brighton, 1975).

NOWLAN, K. B., *The Politics of Repeal: a Study in the Relations between Great Britain and Ireland, 1841–50* (1965).

OLLARD, S. L., *A Short History of the Oxford Movement* ed. A. M. Allchin (1963).

OLNEY, R. J., *Lincolnshire Politics, 1832–85* (1973).

O'MEARA, KATHLEEN ('Grace Ramsay'). *Thomas Grant, first Bishop of Southwark* (2nd edn., 1886).

OMOND, G. W. T., *The Lord Advocates of Scotland*, 2nd Ser., 1834–80 (1914).

O'REILLY, B., *John MacHale, Archbishop of Tuam—his Life, Times and Correspondence* (2 vols., New York, 1890).

ORNSBY, R., *Memoir of James Robert Hope-Scott* (2 vols., 1884).

ORR, J. E., *The second Evangelical Awakening* (1949).

OVERTON, J. H. and WORDSWORTH, ELIZABETH, *Christopher Wordsworth, Bishop of Lincoln, 1807–85* (1888).

PALMER, R., EARL OF SELBORNE, *Memorials*, pt. I: *Family and Personal, 1766–1865* (2 vols., 1896).

—— *Memorials*, pt. II: *Personal and Political, 1865–95* (2 vols., 1898).

PALMER, W. P., *A Narrative of Events connected with the Publication of the Tracts for the Times* (1883).

PARKER, C. S. (ed.), *Sir Robert Peel, from his Private Correspondence* (3 vols., 1899).

—— (ed.), *Life and Letters of Sir James Graham, Bt.* (2 vols., 1907).

PATTERSON, A. T., *Radical Leicester, 1780–1850* (Leicester, 1954).

—— *The Beginnings of modern Southampton, 1836–67* (Southampton, 1971).

PECK, W. G., *The Social Implications of the Oxford Movement* (1933).

PEEL, A. (ed.), *Letters to a Victorian Editor* (1929).
—— *These Hundred Years—a history of the Congregational Union of England and Wales, 1831–1931* (1931).
PELLING, H., *Social Geography of British Elections, 1885–1910* (1967).
PERKIN, H., *The Origins of Modern English Society, 1780–1880* (1969).
PERRY, W., *The Oxford Movement in Scotland* (Cambridge, 1933).
—— *Alexander Penrose Forbes, Bishop of Brechin* (1939).
PICKERING, W. S. F., 'The 1851 Religious Census—a useless experiment?', *British Journal of Sociology*, xviii (1967), 382–407.
PICTON, J. A., *Memorials of Liverpool* (2 vols., Liverpool, 1903).
PINNEY, T. (ed.), *Letters of Lord Macaulay* (vols. i–iv, 1974-7).
PINTO-DUSCHINSKY, M., *The Political Thought of Lord Salisbury, 1854–68* (1967).
PREST, J., *Lord John Russell* (1972).
PUGH, R. K. and MASON, J. F. A. (eds.), *The Letter-Books of Samuel Wilberforce, 1843–68*, Oxfordshire Record Society, xlvii (1969) (Oxford, 1970).
PURCELL, E. S., *Life of Cardinal Manning* (2nd edn., 2 vols., 1896).
—— *Life and Letters of Ambrose Phillipps de Lisle* (2 vols., 1900).

RAINES, F. R., *The Vicars of Rochdale* (Chetham Society Publications, N.S. ii, pt. 2, Manchester, 1883).
RALLS, W., 'The Papal Aggression of 1850: a study in Victorian anti-Catholicism', *Church History*, xliii (1974), 242–56.
RAMM, AGATHA (ed.), *Political Correspondence of Mr. Gladstone and Lord Granville, 1868–76* (Camden Society Publications, 3rd Ser. lxxxi-ii, 1952).
RANSOME, MARY (ed.), *Wiltshire Returns to the Bishop's Visitation Queries, 1783*, Wiltshire Record Society, xvii (Devizes, 1972).
READ, D., *The English Provinces, c. 1760–1960—a study in influence* (1964).
REARDON, B. M. G., *From Coleridge to Gore—a century of religious thought in Britain* (1971).
REID, S. J., *Life and Letters of the first Earl of Durham, 1792–1840* (2 vols., 1906).
REID, T. WEMYSS, *The Life, Letters and Friendships of Richard Monckton Milnes, first Lord Houghton* (2 vols., 1891).
REYNOLDS, J. S., *Evangelicals at Oxford, 1735–1871* (Oxford, 1953).
RIGG, J. H., *Oxford High Anglicanism* (2nd edn., 1899).
ROBERTSON, W., *The Life and Times of the Rt. Hon. John Bright* (3 vols., 1883).
ROBSON, R. (ed.), *Ideas and Institutions of Victorian Britain: essays in honour of G. Kitson Clark* (1967).
ROE, W. G., *Lamennais and England* (1966).
ROGERS, J. GUINESS, *An Autobiography* (1903).
ROSE, E., 'The Stone Table in the Round Church and the Crisis of the Cambridge Camden Society', *Victorian Studies*, x (1966-7), 119–44.
ROTH, C., *History of the Jews in England* (1941).
ROYLE, E., *Victorian Infidels—the origins of the British secularist movement, 1791–1866* (Manchester, 1974).
RUSSELL, Earl, *Recollections and Suggestions, 1813–73* (1875).
RUSSELL, R. (ed.), *Early Correspondence of Lord John Russell, 1805–40* (2 vols., 1913).

St. John-Stevas (ed.), *Bagehot's Historical Essays* (1971).

Salter, F. R., 'Political Dissent in the 1830s', *Trans. Royal Hist. Soc.* 5th Ser. iii (1953), 125–43.

—— 'Congregationalism and the Hungry Forties', *Transactions of the Congregational Historical Society*, xvii. 4 (1955), 107–16.

—— 'Dissenters and Public Affairs in mid-Victorian England', 21st lecture to the Friends of Dr. Williams' Library (1967).

Sanders, C. R., *Coleridge and the Broad Church Movement* (Durham, North Carolina, 1942).

Sanders, L. C. (ed.), *Lord Melbourne's Papers* (2nd edn., 1890).

Schreuder, D. M., 'Gladstone and Italian Unification, 1848–70: the Making of a Liberal?', *EHR* lxxxv (1970), 475–501.

Searby, P., 'Gladstone in West Derby Hundred: the Liberal Campaign in South-West Lancashire in 1868', *Transactions of the Historic Society of Lancashire and Cheshire*, cxi (1960), 139–66.

Selborne, Earl of: see Palmer, R.

Sellers, I. A., 'Nonconformist Attitudes in later nineteenth century Liverpool', *Transactions of Historic Society of Lancashire and Cheshire*, cxiv (1963), 215–39.

Semmel, B., *The Methodist Revolution* (1974).

Senior, H., *Orangeism in Ireland and Britain, 1795–1836* (1966).

Seymour, C., *Electoral Reform in England and Wales, 1832–85* (new edn., Newton Abbot, 1970).

Short, K. R. M., 'Benjamin Evans, D.D., and the radical Press', *Baptist Quarterly*, N.S. xix (1961–2), 243–52.

—— 'English Baptists and the Corn Laws', *Baptist Quarterly*, N.S. xxi (1965–6), 309–20.

—— 'The English Regium Donum', *EHR* lxxxiv (1969), 59–78.

—— 'London's General Body of Protestant Ministers: its disruption in 1836', *JEH* xxiv (1973), 377–93.

Simpson, P. C., *The Life of Principal Rainy* (2 vols., 1909).

Skeats, H. S., and Miall, C. S., *History of the Free Churches in England, 1688–1891* (1891).

Smith, F., *The Life and Work of Sir James Kay-Shuttleworth* (1923).

Smith, F. B., *The Making of the Second Reform Bill* (Cambridge, 1966).

Smith, P. (ed.), *Lord Salisbury on Politics: a selection from his articles in the Quarterly Review, 1860–83* (Cambridge, 1972).

Smith, T., *Memoirs of James Begg, D.D.* (2 vols., Edinburgh, 1885–8).

Smyth, C., 'The Evangelical Movement in Perspective', *Cambridge Historical Journal*, vii (1941–3), 160–74.

Soloway, R. A., *Prelates and People: ecclesiastical social thought in England, 1783–1852* (1969).

Southgate, D., *The Passing of the Whigs, 1832–86* (1962).

—— (ed.), *The Conservative Leadership, 1832–1932* (1974).

Sprigge, S. S., *The Life and Times of Thomas Wakley* (1899).

Spring, D., 'The Clapham Sect: some Social and Political Aspects', *Victorian Studies*, v (1961–2), 35–48.

Stanmore, Lord, *Sidney Herbert, a Memoir* (2 vols., 1906).

STEPHEN, M. D., 'Gladstone and the composition of the Final Court in Ecclesiastical Causes, 1850–73', *Hist. Jl.* ix (1966), 191–200.

STEPHENS, W. R. W., *The Life and Letters of the Very Rev. W. F. Hook* (2 vols., 1878).

—— *Memoir of the Rt. Hon. W. Page Wood, Baron Hatherley* (2 vols., 1883).

STEPHENSON, A. M. G., *The First Lambeth Conference, 1867* (1967).

STEWART, R., *The Politics of Protection, 1841–52* (Cambridge, 1971).

STRACHEY, L. and FULFORD, R. (eds.), *The Greville Memoirs, 1814–60* (8 vols., 1938).

STUART, C. H., 'The Formation of the Coalition Cabinet of 1852', *Trans. Royal Hist. Soc.* 5th Ser. iv (1954), 45–68.

SUMNER, G. H., *Life of C. R. Sumner, Bishop of Winchester* (1876).

SWARTZ, HELEN M. and M. (eds.), *Disraeli's Reminiscences* (1975).

SWEET, J. B., *A Memoir of the late Henry Hoare . . . with a narrative of the Church movements with which he was connected from 1848 to 1865* (1869).

SYKES, N., *Church and State in England in the Eighteenth Century* (Cambridge, 1934).

SYMONDSON, A. (ed.), *The Victorian Crisis of Faith* (1970).

TAYLOR, A. J. P., *The Italian Problem in European Diplomacy, 1847–9* (Manchester, 1934).

TAYLOR, E. R., *Methodism and Politics, 1791–1851* (Cambridge, 1935).

TAYLOR, GERTRUDE W., *John Wesley and the Anglo-Catholic Revival* (1905).

TAYLOR, H. A., 'Politics in Famine-Stricken Preston, 1861–5', *Transactions of the Historic Society of Lancashire and Cheshire*, cvii (1955), 121–39.

THOMIS, M. I., *Politics and Society in Nottingham, 1785–1835* (1969).

THOMPSON, A. F., 'Gladstone's Whips and the General Election of 1868', *EHR* lxiii (1948), 189–200.

THOMPSON, D. M. (ed.), *Nonconformity in the Nineteenth Century* (1972).

—— 'The 1851 Religious Census—problems and possibilities', *Victorian Studies*, xi (1967–8), 87–97.

THOMPSON, E. P., *The Making of the English Working Class* (Harmondsworth, 1968).

THOMPSON, F. M. L., 'Whigs and Liberals in the West Riding, 1830–60', *EHR* lxxiv (1959), 214–39.

THOMPSON, K. A., *Bureaucracy and Church Reform—the organisational response of the Church of England to social change, 1800–1965* (Oxford, 1970).

Threads from the Life of John Mills, Banker, by his wife (Manchester, 1899).

TORRENS, W. M., *Memoirs of Lord Melbourne* (2 vols., 1878).

TREBLE, J. H., 'The Attitude of the Roman Catholic Church towards Trade Unionism in the North of England, 1833–42', *Northern History*, v (1970), 93–113.

TREVELYAN, SIR G. O., *The Life and Letters of Lord Macaulay* (1908).

TREVOR, MERIOL, *Newman—the Pillar of the Cloud* (1962).

—— *Newman—Light in Winter* (1962).

ULLATHORNE, W. B., *History of the Restoration of the Catholic Hierarchy in England* (1871).

—— *Letters*, ed. Anon. (1892).
—— *From Cabin-Boy to Archbishop—the autobiography of Archbishop Ullathorne* (1941).

VIDLER, A., *The Orb and the Cross—a normative study in the relations of Church and State with reference to Gladstone's early writings* (1945).
—— *The Church in an Age of Revolution—1780 to the present day* (Harmondsworth, 1961).
VINCENT, J., *The Formation of the Liberal Party, 1857–68* (1966).
—— *Poll-Books: How Victorians Voted* (Cambridge, 1967).
—— 'The Effect of the Second Reform Act in Lancashire', *Hist. Jl.* xi (1968), 84–94.

WADDINGTON, J., *Congregational History—continuation to 1850* (1878).
WALKER, R. B., 'Religious Changes in Cheshire, 1750–1850', *JEH* xvii (1966), 77–94.
—— 'Religious Changes in Liverpool in the Nineteenth Century', *JEH*, xix (1968), 195–211.
—— 'The Growth of Wesleyan Methodism in Victorian England and Wales', *JEH*, xxiv (1973), 267–84.
WALKER, W. M., 'Irish Immigrants in Scotland—their priests, politics and parochial life', *Hist. Jl.* xv (1972), 649–67.
WALLING, R. A. J. (ed.), *The Diaries of John Bright* (1930).
WALPOLE, S. H., *The Life of Lord John Russell* (2 vols., 1889).
WALSH, W., *Progress of the Church in London during the last fifty Years* (1887).
WARD, B., *The Sequel to Catholic Emancipation, 1830–50* (2 vols., 1915).
WARD, J. T., *The Factory Movement, 1830–55* (1962).
—— *Sir James Graham* (1967).
—— and Treble, J. H., 'Religion and Education in 1843: Reaction to the Factory Education Bill', *JEH* xx (1969), 79–110.
WARD, WILFRID, *William George Ward and the Oxford Movement* (1889).
—— *W. G. Ward and the Catholic Revival* (1893).
—— *The Life and Times of Cardinal Wiseman* (2 vols., 1897).
—— *The Life of John Henry, Cardinal Newman* (2 vols., 1912).
WARD, W. R., *Victorian Oxford* (1965).
—— *Religion and Society in England, 1790–1850* (1972).
—— (ed.), *Early Victorian Methodism—the Correspondence of Jabez Bunting, 1830–58* (Oxford, 1976).
WATT, H., *Thomas Chalmers and the Disruption* (Edinburgh, 1943).
WEARMOUTH, R. F., *Methodism and the Working-Class Movements of England, 1800–50* (1947).
WEBSTER, A. B., *Joshua Watson, the Story of a Layman, 1771–1855* (1954).
WELCH, P. J., 'Contemporary Views on the Proposals for the Alienation of Capitular Property in England, 1832–40', *JEH* v (1954), 184–95.
—— 'Anglican Churchmen and the establishment of the Jerusalem Bishopric', *JEH* viii (1957), 193–204.

—— 'The Revival of an active Convocation of Canterbury, 1852–5', *JEH* x (1959), 188–97.

—— 'Blomfield and Peel—a study in co-operation between Church and State, 1841–6', *JEH* xii (1961), 71–84.

WHIBLEY, C., *Lord John Manners and his Friends* (2 vols., Edinburgh and London, 1925).

WHYTE, J. F., *The Cambridge Movement* (Cambridge, 1962).

WHYTE, J. H., *The Independent Irish Party, 1850–9* (Oxford, 1958).

WICKHAM, E. R., *Church and People in an Industrial City* [Sheffield] (1958).

WILLIAMS, D., 'The Pembrokeshire Elections of 1831', *Welsh HR* i.1 (1960), 37–64.

—— 'The Census of Religious Worship of 1851 in Cardiganshire', *Ceredigion*, iv (1961), 113–27.

WILLIAMS, GLANMOR (ed.), *Merthyr Politics—the making of a working-class tradition* (Cardiff, 1966).

WILLIAMS, GWYN A., 'The Making of Radical Merthyr, 1800–1836', *Welsh HR* i.2 (1961), 161–87.

WILLIAMS, W. E., *The Rise of Gladstone to the Leadership of the Liberal Party, 1859–68* (Cambridge, 1934).

WILLS, W. D., 'The Established Church in the Diocese of Llandaff, 1850–70—a study of the evangelical movement in the South Wales coalfield', *Welsh HR* iv.3 (1969), 235–67.

WILSON, A., *The Chartist Movement in Scotland* (Manchester, 1970).

WILSON, E. C., *An Island Bishop, 1762–1838: Memorials of William Ward, D.D., Bishop of Sodor and Mann, 1828–38* (1931).

WILSON, W., *Memorials of R. S. Candlish* (Edinburgh, 1880).

WITHRINGTON, D. J., 'The Free Church Educational Scheme, 1843–50', *Records of the Scottish Church History Society*, xv (1963–5), 103–15.

WOLF, L., *Sir Moses Montefiore* (1884).

WOOLLEY, S. F., 'The Personnel of the Parliament of 1833', *EHR* liii (1938), 240–62.

WRIGHT, L. C., *Scottish Chartism* (Edinburgh, 1953).

YOUNG, G. M. and HANDCOCK, W. D. (eds.), *English Historical Documents*, xii.1, 1833–74 (1956).

YOUNG, URBAN, *The Life and Letters of the Ven. Dominic Barberi* (1926).

VII. UNPUBLISHED THESES

ANDREWS, JULIA H., 'Political Issues in the County of Kent, 1820–1846', (London M.Phil. 1967).

BEST, G. F. A., 'Church and State in English Politics, 1800–33' (Cambridge Ph.D. 1955).

BINFIELD, J. C. G., 'Nonconformity in the Eastern Counties, 1840–85, with reference to its social background' (Cambridge Ph.D. 1965).

BOWMER, J. C., 'Church and Ministry in Wesleyan Methodism from the death of John Wesley to the death of Jabez Bunting, 1791–1858' (Leeds Ph.D. 1967).

BRADFIELD, B. T., 'Sir Richard Vyvyan and Tory Politics, 1825–46' (London Ph.D. 1965).

BURROWS, B. E., 'The Maynooth Agitation and its effect on Liverpool Politics, 1845–7' (Dundee M.A. Hons. 1969).

CAMERON, J. R., 'The Disruption in Lochaber' (Dundee M.A. Hons. 1970).

CAMERON, K. J., 'Anti-Corn Law Agitations in Scotland, with particular reference to the Anti-Corn Law League' (Edinburgh Ph.D. 1971).

CLOSE, D. H., 'The General Elections of 1835 and 1837 in England and Wales' (Oxford D.Phil. 1966).

CRAW, ALISON, 'The Scottish Disruption and its effect on Politics, with special reference to Edinburgh' (Dundee M.A. Hons 1969).

DAVID, I. W. R., 'Political and Electioneering Activity in South East Wales, 1820–52' (Wales M.A. 1959).

DREYER, F. A., 'The Administration of Lord John Russell, 1846–52' (St. Andrews Ph.D. 1962).

FOSKETT, CANON R., 'John Kaye and the Diocese of Lincoln' (Nottingham Ph.D., 1957).

FRASER, D., 'Politics in Leeds, 1830–52' (Leeds Ph.D. 1969).

GOWLAND, D. A., 'Methodist Secessions and Social Conflict in South Lancashire, 1830–57' (Manchester Ph.D. 1966).

GREENFIELD, R. H., 'The Attitude of the Tractarians to the Roman Catholic Church, 1833–50' (Oxford D.Phil. 1956).

GUIRRON, D. F., 'The Ecclesiastical Titles Crisis: its effect on Liverpool, including the election of 1852' (St. Andrews M.A. Hons. 1969).

HANHAM, H. J., 'The General Election of 1868: a study in the bases of mid-Victorian politics' (Cambridge Ph.D. 1954).

HARDMAN, B. E. 'The Evangelical Party in the Church of England, 1855–65' (Cambridge Ph.D. 1964).

KITCHING, J., 'Roman Catholic Education from 1700 to 1870' (Leeds Ph.D. 1967).

LEA, J. H., 'Baptists in Lancashire, 1837–85' (Liverpool Ph.D. 1970).

LOWERSON, J. R., 'The Political Career of Sir Edward Baines, 1800–90' (Leeds M.A. 1965).

MARSHALL, B. R., 'The Theology of Church and State in relation to the Concern for Popular Education in England, 1800–1870' (Oxford D.Phil. 1956).

MARTIN, H. R., 'The Politics of the Congregationalists, 1830–56 (Durham Ph.D. 1971).

MASON, B. J., 'The Rise of Combative Dissent, 1832–59' (Southampton M.A. 1958).

MONTGOMERY, A. B., 'The Voluntary Controversy in the Church of Scotland, 1829–1843' (Edinburgh Ph.D. 1953).

MORGAN, W. T., 'The Consistory Courts of the Diocese of St. David's, 1660–1858' (Wales M.A. 1962).

NEWTON, J. S., 'The Political Career of Edward Miall' (Durham Ph.D. 1975).

NOSSITER, T. J., 'Elections and Political Behaviour in Co. Durham and Newcastle, 1832–74' (Oxford D.Phil. 1968).

PARRY, O., 'The Parliamentary Representation of Wales and Monmouthshire during the Nineteenth Century, but mainly until 1870' (Wales M.A. 1924).

RAM, R. W., 'The Political Activities of Dissenters in the East and West Ridings of Yorkshire, 1815–1850' (Hull M.A. 1964).

ROBERTSON, G. B., 'Spiritual Awakening in the North-East of Scotland and the Disruption of the Church in 1843' (Aberdeen Ph.D. 1971).

SALBSTEIN, M. C. N., 'The Emancipation of the Jews in Britain, with particular reference to the debate concerning the admission of the Jews to Parliament, 1828–60' (London Ph.D. 1974).

SCHIEFEN, R. J., 'The Organization and Administration of Roman Catholic Dioceses in England and Wales in the Mid-Nineteenth Century' (London Ph.D. 1970).

SCULLY, F. M., 'Relations between Church and State in England between 1829 and 1839' (Oxford B.Litt. 1935).

SELLERS, I., 'Liverpool Nonconformity, 1786–1914' (Keele Ph.D. 1969).

THOMPSON, D. M., 'The Churches and Society in Leicestershire, 1851–81' (Cambridge Ph.D. 1969).

TODD, A., 'The Effect of the Disruption on the Educational Schemes of the Church of Scotland and the Free Church, 1843–50' (Dundee M.A. Hons. 1972).

WHITAKER, P., 'The Growth of Liberal Organisation in Manchester from the Eighteen Sixties to 1903' (Manchester Ph.D. 1956).

WHITTAKER, M.B., 'The Revival of Dissent, 1800–1835' (Cambridge M.Litt. 1959).

WRIGHT, D. G., 'Politics and Opinion in Nineteenth Century Bradford, 1832–80' (Leeds Ph.D. 1966).

ADDENDA

BROOKE, J. and GANDY, JULIA (eds.), *Wellington: Political Correspondence*, I, 1833–Nov. 1834 (1975).

EVANS, E. J., *The Contentious Tithe: the tithe problem and English agriculture, 1750–1850* (1976).

FRASER, D., *Urban Politics in Victorian England* (Leicester, 1976).

HEMPTON, D. N., 'Methodism and Anti-Catholic Politics, 1800–46' (St. Andrews Ph.D. 1977).

JONES, W. D. and ERICKSON, A. B., *The Peelites, 1846–57* (Ohio, 1972).

KRIEGEL, A. D. (ed.), *The Holland House Diaries, 1831–40* (1977).

OBELKEVICH, J., *Religion and Rural Society: South Lindsey, 1825–75* (Oxford, 1976).

SALBSTEIN, M. C. N., *The Emancipation of the Jews in Britain: an essay on the preconditions* (privately published, 1977).

HAMER, D. A., *The Politics of Electoral Pressure: a study in the history of Victorian reform agitations* (Brighton, 1977).

BINFIELD, C., *So Down to Prayers: studies in English Nonconformity* (1977).

Index